# XVA: Credit, Funding and Capital Valuation Adjustments

*For other titles in the Wiley Finance series
please see www.wiley.com/finance*

# XVA: Credit, Funding and Capital Valuation Adjustments

ANDREW GREEN

WILEY

*Library of Congress Cataloging-in-Publication Data*

Green, Andrew,
   XVA : credit, funding and capital valuation adjustments / Andrew Green.
     pages cm. — (The wiley finance series)
   Includes bibliographical references and index.
   ISBN 978-1-118-55678-8 (hardback) — ISBN 978-1-118-55675-7 (ebk) —
ISBN 978-1-118-55676-4 (ebk) — ISBN 978-1-119-16123-3 (ebk)   1. Finance.
2. Derivative securities.   I. Title.
   HG173.G744 2015
   332.64'57–dc23

                                        2015019353

A catalogue record for this book is available from the British Library.

ISBN 978-1-118-55678-8 (hardback)   ISBN 978-1-118-55675-7 (ebk)
ISBN 978-1-118-55676-4 (ebk)      ISBN 978-1-119-16123-3 (obk)

Cover Design: Wiley
Cover Image: ©iStock/Tuomas Kujansuu

Set in 10/12pt Times by Aptara Inc., New Delhi, India
Printed in Great Britain by TJ International Ltd, Padstow, Cornwall, UK

*For Simone*

# Contents

## CHAPTER 5

### Analytic Models for CVA and DVA  **83**

## CHAPTER 6

### Modelling Credit Mitigants  **91**

## CHAPTER 7

### Wrong-way and Right-way Risk for CVA  **109**

## CHAPTER 11
### The Funding Curve    187

## PART THREE
### KVA: Capital Valuation Adjustment and Regulation

## CHAPTER 12
### Regulation: the Basel II and Basel III Frameworks    195

## PART FIVE
### Managing XVA

### CHAPTER 21
### Calculating XVA Sensitivities 425

### CHAPTER 22
### Managing XVA 447

# List of Tables

# List of Figures

# Acknowledgements

I would like to thank both Dr Chris Dennis and Dr Chris Kenyon for kindly agreeing to review this book prior to publication and for their work on a number of research topics that are contained within this book. Any errors or omissions are my own, however.

I would also like to thank the many colleagues and peers from both market and academia with whom I have had useful discussions on quantitative finance over many years. This includes colleagues from my current and past employers but also includes a great many others.

I owe a debt of gratitude to my many teachers over a number of years, but perhaps most of all to my DPhil supervisor, Professor James Binney, whose own publications inspired me ultimately to write my own book.

Finally I would like to thank friends and family for putting up with my absence during the writing process.

## CHAPTER 1

# Introduction: The Valuation of Derivative Portfolios

*Price is what you pay. Value is what you get.*

—Warren Buffett
*American business magnate, investor and philanthropist (1930–)*

## 1.1 WHAT THIS BOOK IS ABOUT

This book is about *XVA* or *Valuation Adjustments*, the valuation of the credit, funding and regulatory capital requirements embedded in derivative contracts. It introduces *Credit Valuation Adjustment (CVA)* and *Debit Valuation Adjustment (DVA)* to account for credit risk, *Funding Valuation Adjustment (FVA)* for the impact of funding costs including *Margin Valuation Adjustment (MVA)* for the funding cost associated with initial margin, *Capital Valuation Adjustment (KVA)* for the impact of Regulatory Capital and *Tax Valuation Adjustment (TVA)* for the impact of taxation on profits and losses. The book provides detailed descriptions of models to calculate the valuation adjustments and the technical infrastructure required to calculate them efficiently. However, more fundamentally this book is about the valuation and pricing of derivative contracts. The reality is that credit, funding and capital concerns are very far from minor adjustments to the value of a single derivative contract or portfolio of derivatives. The treatment of CVA, DVA, FVA, MVA, KVA and TVA as adjustments reflects the historical development of derivative models and typical bank organisational design rather than the economic reality that places credit, funding and capital costs at the centre of accurate pricing and valuation of derivatives.

Since the seminal papers by Fischer Black and Myron Scholes and Robert C. Merton published in 1973, derivative pricing and valuation has been centred in the Black-Scholes-Merton framework complete with its simplifying assumptions:

- Arbitrage opportunities do not exist.
- Any amount of money can be borrowed or lent at the risk-free rate which is constant and accrues continuously in time.
- Any amount of stock can be bought or sold including short selling with no restrictions.

- There are no transaction taxes or margin requirements.
- The underlying asset pays no dividend.
- The asset price is a continuous function with no jumps.
- The underlying asset has a constant volatility.
- Neither counterparty to the transaction is at risk of default.
- The market is complete, that is there are no unhedgeable risks.

It could also be argued that there are additional implicit assumptions underlying the Black-Scholes-Merton framework:

- No capital requirement or costs associated with regulatory requirements such as liquidity buffers
- No price impact of trading
- The Modigliani-Millar theorem on the separation of funding and investment decisions applies to derivatives (Modigliani and Miller, 1958).

However, even in the mid-1970s it was clear that these assumptions were there to simplify the problem of option pricing and were not a reflection of reality. Subsequently, a number of authors sought to relax these assumptions:

- Constant interest rates – Merton (1973)
- No dividends – Merton (1973)
- No transaction costs – Ingersoll (1976)
- Jumps – Merton (1976), Cox and Ross (1976).

Subsequently, the original formulation of Black-Scholes in terms of partial differential equations has been replaced by measure-theoretic probability through the work of Harrison and Kreps (1979), Harrison and Pliska (1983) and Geman, Karoui and Rochet (1995). The Black-Scholes model itself has been steadily adapted to match market prices such as through the use of market implied volatilities that display a *skew* or *smile* relative to the single flat volatility assumption of Black-Scholes, implicitly indicating that the stock price distribution has fatter tails than those implied by the log-normal distribution. Nevertheless, the essential framework of risk-neutral valuation through replication has remained largely unchanged even though the mathematical machinery used by quantitative analysts has been enhanced significantly and the computational power available to derivatives businesses has grown exponentially.

The survival of the model is best illustrated through belief in the *law of one price*. The law of one price can be stated as follows:

*The same asset must trade at the same price on all markets (or there is an arbitrage opportunity).*

This simple statement seems very persuasive at first glance. If an asset is quoted at price $x$ on market X and at price $y$ on market Y and $x < y$ then asset buyers acting rationally should

1. buy assets from market X if they need to consume the asset
2. buy assets from market X and sell on market Y to make a riskless profit of $(y - x)$,

that is, this market permits arbitrage.[1] However, in the context of derivatives it is not clear that the law of one price always applies:

- Over-the-counter (OTC) derivatives trade under bilateral agreements brokered under ISDA rules. The considerable variations in the terms of these legal rules mean that each ISDA (possibly coupled with a CSA) is effectively unique and hence so are the derivatives contracts traded between the two parties to the ISDA agreement.
- Counterparty risk is always present in practice because even under the strongest CSA terms there will still be delays between movements in portfolio mark-to-market valuations and calls/returns on collateral. Counterparty risk makes each derivative with a different counterparty unique with a distinct valuation. The traditional understanding of the law of one price no longer applies, as there are multiple derivatives with the same basic parameters with different prices. However, the law of one price could be preserved if we consider each pair of counterparties to be a different "market", although this reduces the "law" to irrelevance. If both counterparties to a trade use a unilateral model of CVA, where only the risk of the counterparty defaulting is considered, neither party will agree on the value of the transaction so the value is asymmetric between the two counterparties. The introduction of bilateral models for counterparty risk and DVA allows symmetry of valuation to be restored,[2] but FVA models have again broken the symmetry. The introduction of KVA and the realisation that different institutions have different capital regimes has broken the symmetry irrevocably.
- Counterparties clearly have asymmetric access to markets.
- Many derivatives, particularly for large corporates, are transacted on an auction basis. This means that there is one agreed price with the derivative provider that the corporate ultimately selects. However, individual derivative dealers will have different values for the same underlying transaction.
- Once transacted many corporate derivatives are essentially illiquid. Novations of trades to third parties do occur, but infrequently. If the derivative dealer were to instigate a novation this might threaten the banking relationship. Smaller counterparties will typically have a limited number of banking relationships or perhaps only one banking relationship. Novations would likely prove impossible to do in such cases as with no established banking relationship it is unlikely other derivative providers would have sufficient information on the small counterparty to be able to provide the required credit limits. The deal could only be torn up by agreement with the relationship bank.
- Counterparties will often transact a derivative under completely different accounting regimes. For example, a corporate may hold a derivative under IRS 39 hedge accounting rules, while the bank counterparty may include the derivative in a trading book under mark-to-market accounting rules.

The only case where the law of one price might be said to hold is in the case of very liquid exchange-traded derivatives such as futures or exchange-traded options (ETOs). In such cases, given the derivative is entirely commoditised and that margin arrangements are equal for

---

[1]Of course in reality there may be reasons why it is not possible to actually execute the trade, such as lack of access to both markets, regulatory prohibitions and so on.
[2]See section 3.3.3.

all market participants then the price can be said to be that of the last transaction that took place on the exchange. However, the law of one price has remained persistent in the world of quantitative finance.

The reality of the derivatives market in the aftermath of the default of Lehman brothers is very different from the idealised one encapsulated in the assumptions underlying the Black-Scholes model and risk-neutral valuation:

  ▪ Apparent arbitrage opportunities sometimes persist in the market. For example the *Repurchase Overnight Index Average Rate* (RONIA) is frequently higher than the *Sterling Overnight Index Average Rate* (SONIA) despite the fact RONIA relates to a secured lending market while SONIA relates to unsecured lending. In reality this reflects an inability to close the apparent arbitrage and market segmentation. The repo and OIS swap markets are separate, while constructing a trade which would close the apparent arbitrage is difficult because of the large notional of the offsetting positions that would be required.
  ▪ Banks cannot borrow money unsecured at a hypothetical "risk-free rate" and bank funding costs are significantly higher than any rate considered to be risk free such as an overnight index swap (OIS) rate.
  ▪ Banks cannot borrow money in any quantity. At various points following the collapse of Lehman Brothers, European banks found it difficult to fund themselves in US dollars, prompting central banks to set up large cross-currency swap positions (Lanman and Black, 2011).
  ▪ Short selling regulations (European Parliament and the Council of the European Union, 2012a) have made short selling more difficult to do in practice.
  ▪ The cost of trading derivatives is significant, particularly if KVA is considered.

The assumptions underlying risk neutral valuation are very clearly at variance with market conditions after the default of Lehman Brothers.[3]

This book, therefore, comprises two things. Firstly it is a practical guide to CVA, DVA, FVA and KVA, including both the mathematical models and the implementation of systems to perform the calculations. Secondly, it is a guide to the future of derivative valuation but one that is as yet incomplete as the transition away from risk-neutral valuation to a more realistic valuation framework is not yet complete. This chapter presents a picture of how derivative pricing and valuation has changed since the *credit crisis* and as such provides an introduction to the book as a whole but one that is naturally coupled with the last chapter on the future of derivatives.

## 1.2  PRICES AND VALUES

### 1.2.1  Before the Fall...

In 1996 when I first entered the derivatives market, the standard work on derivative pricing was John Hull's seminal *Options, Futures, and Other Derivatives*, then in its third edition (1997) and now in its eight edition (2011). For vanilla fixed income derivatives such as interest

---

[3]In my view it is precisely this break with the past that has led to such a vigorous debate around funding valuation adjustment, a subject that is discussed in section 1.4.1.

rate swaps the standard reference was Miron and Swanell's *Pricing and Hedging Swaps* (1991). The modelling approach for the valuation of interest rate swaps in 1996 involved the discounting of the future fixed cash flows using a discount function and the floating leg could be readily replicated with two notional cash flows at the start and end of the swap, if there was no margin on the floating leg, or equivalently by discounting the projected forward rate cash flows of the floating leg. There was a single discounting and projection curve for each currency. The yield curve (sometimes known as the swap curve to distinguish it from bond curves) was constructed using a simple bootstrap approach starting with cash deposits, followed by interest rate futures contracts and completed by interest rate swaps. Once the zero-coupon bond prices for different tenor points had been obtained the discount function was obtained on any date through log-linear interpolation.

Valuing interest rate swaps was straightforward and the discounting curve was driven by xIBOR rates. Cross-currency swaps were more involved and a spread or basis between currencies was required to revalue cross-currency swaps to par. Nevertheless single currency derivative books were typically valued using the single currency discount curve so that cross-currency and single currency books were valued inconsistently. Tenor basis existed in the sense that anyone who wanted to swap a 3M xIBOR rate for a 6M xIBOR rate was charged a spread but these spreads were small and reflected operational costs of the transaction. Tenor basis was essentially ignored for valuation purposes.

In 1996 CVA was not calculated and funding costs were not explicitly considered. Counterparty credit risk was managed through traditional credit limits set by the credit risk function within a bank. The Basel I framework had already been introduced but capital management was considered a back office function.

By the time the credit crisis began in 2007, many banks used a multi-currency discounting framework where USD was usually considered the primary curve with no currency basis and all other currencies had separate projection and discounting curves constructed in such a way as to reprice to par all of the single currency instruments used to construct the curve and the cross-currency swaps. CVA was commonly calculated and charged by tier one banks, with some institutions using unilateral models and some bilateral models. FAS 157 (2006) introduced a CVA(DVA) reporting requirement with wording that implies a bilateral model should be used.

## 1.2.2 The Post-Crisis World...

As the crisis hit, the market reacted rapidly and tenor basis spreads and the spread between three-month LIBOR and OIS widened rapidly. The USD three-month LIBOR and OIS reached a peak of 365bp just after the collapse of Lehman Brothers in 2008, having averaged 10bp prior to August 2007 (Sengupta and Tam, 2008). This prompted banks to switch to using multiple projection curves for rates with different tenors (see for example Kenyon and Stamm, 2012). It was also realised that the discount curve, normally believed to be based on three-month rates was not the appropriate choice for discounting trades transacted under CSA agreements. CSAs typically pay a rate of interest on posted collateral equal to the overnight rate in the collateral currency and hence it rapidly became market practice to use OIS-based curves to discount collateralised cash flows (Piterbarg, 2010; Piterbarg, 2012).

While CVA had been marked by many tier one banks prior to the crisis, a number of banks switched from the use of unilateral to bilateral models during the crisis. Bank CDS spreads widened significantly leading to dramatic increases in DVA accounting benefit where it was

**TABLE 1.1**    Components of derivative prices before and after the financial crisis of 2007–2009.

| Pre-Crisis | Post-Crisis |
|---|---|
| Risk-neutral price (LIBOR discounting) | Risk-neutral price (OIS discounting) |
| Hedging costs | Hedging costs |
| CVA | CVA (DVA?) |
| Profit | Profit |
| | FVA (including cost of liquidity buffers) |
| | KVA (lifetime cost of capital) |
| | MVA/CCP costs |
| | TVA (tax on profits/losses) |

marked. Competitive pressure on pricing also pushed banks to include DVA in derivative pricing as many corporate customers had CDS spreads that were significantly tighter than the bank counterparties they were trading with. Accounting standards moved to recommend bilateral CVA models because of the symmetrical valuation. Some banks chose to actively manage DVA, while others chose to warehouse some or all of the risk.

Unsecured funding costs became a focus as bank funding spreads widened significantly as their CDS spreads did and a number of models were produced (see for example Burgard and Kjaer, 2011b; Burgard and Kjaer, 2011a; Morini and Prampolini, 2011; Pallavicini, Perini and Brigo, 2012)). FVA remains controversial as will be discussed in detail in section 1.4; however, most practitioners accept that it must be included in pricing and accounting practice with most major banks now taking FVA reserves.

Post-Crisis, regulatory capital is a scarce and expensive resource that must be carefully managed by banks. Capital management is no longer a back office function and now resides firmly in the front office as a core activity for tier one banks. The cost of regulatory capital has to be priced into every new transaction to determine if a trade is expected to be profitable. Capital modelling is now based in the much more complex Basel II.5 and Basel III regimes (and their implementation by regional regulatory bodies).

In 2015 pricing a "vanilla" interest rate swap involves multiple projection and discount curves for the baseline valuation and a large-scale Monte Carlo simulation at counterparty level to calculate CVA, FVA and KVA; it is a long way from the single yield curve discount models of the mid-1990s (see Table 1.1). Indeed, as will become apparent in this book, single trades can no longer be valued in isolation and trade valuation is an exercise in allocation of portfolio level numbers down to individual trades.

## 1.3    TRADE ECONOMICS IN DERIVATIVE PRICING

### 1.3.1    The Components of a Price

Table 1.1 illustrates the components of pricing before and after the financial crisis of 2007–2009. Not all of these components apply to all trades and to understand the terms under which a derivative is transacted it is useful to divide counterparties into three types: unsecured, CSA and CCP. Of course, in reality the range of counterparty arrangements is a continuum between unsecured and an idealised CSA with full instantaneous transfer of collateral but it is useful to separate them for the purpose of this discussion. Each of these three cases will have different pricing components.

## Unsecured Pricing

- Risk-neutral valuation
- Hedging/management costs
- CVA
- FVA
- KVA
- Profit (Tax/TVA).

For trades that are unsecured the components of the price begin with the baseline risk-neutral valuation, although there remains industry debate about the appropriate choice of discount curve for this, with both OIS and xIBOR-based discount curves used in the market. Hedging and trading desk management costs should be charged and this includes effects such as bid-offer, lifetime re-hedging costs and cost of supporting infrastructure such as system maintenance and staff. A profit margin will also typically be charged. Given there is no collateral to mitigate the exposure to the counterparty, CVA will be calculated based on the full expected exposure profile. If a bilateral CVA model is used there will also be a DVA benefit term. The same expected exposure will give rise to FVA. The lifetime cost of maintaining regulatory capital, KVA, will also be included, although this might be a *hurdle rate* or minimum return level rather than a cash amount.

## CSA Pricing

- Risk-neutral valuation: CSA-based (OIS) discounting
- Hedging/Management costs
- Residual CVA (including impact of collateralisation)
- Residual FVA (including impact of collateralisation)
- COLVA/Collateral effects
- KVA
- Bilateral Initial Margin MVA
- Profit.

For trades covered by a CSA the baseline risk-neutral valuation will be discounted using a curve appropriate to the terms of the CSA. Given that the CSA is imperfect in the sense that the collateral transferred to support the mark-to-market of the trade is done on a discrete periodic basis rather than a continuous basis, a residual counterparty exposure will remain. This residual exposure leads to *residual CVA* and *residual FVA*. There may also be a COLVA adjustment to account for collateral effects in pricing that cannot be captured by a discounting approach such as collateral optionality. Capital must be held against collateralised portfolios and this gives rise to KVA, although the presence of collateral significantly reduces the amount of capital that must be held through the counterparty credit risk and CVA capital terms. The *leverage ratio* comes into importance here, however, as while collateral reduces the CCR and CVA terms, it has a restricted impact on the leverage ratio. Market risk capital will be held unless there are other market risk offsetting trades. Hedging and trading desk management costs should again be charged as should the profit margin. Under BCBS 226 (2012e) and BCBS 242 (2013e), trades supported by CSA agreements will also require bilateral initial margin to be held in a similar way to the way that CCP initial margin requirements operate.

## CCP Pricing

- Risk-neutral valuation: CCP methodology including CCP discount curves
- Hedging/Management costs
- Residual CVA (including impact of variation margin)
- Residual FVA (including impact of variation margin)
- COLVA/Collateral effects
- KVA
- Initial margin
- Liquidity buffers
- Default fund
- Profit.

For trades cleared through a CCP the components of a price include similar components to those of a trade supported by a CSA agreement. Residual exposure above the collateral provided as variation margin gives rise to CVA and FVA as with CSA pricing. Hedging and trading management costs are the same as is the addition of a profit margin. The lifetime cost of capital is also present although the risk-weight applied to qualifying CCPs is the relatively low value of 2% (BCBS, 2012c). As with CSA pricing a COLVA adjustment may be needed. In addition to variation margin, three other payments are often made to CCPS: *initial margin*, *liquidity buffers* and *default fund* contributions. The initial margin is designed to cover exposure that might arise due to market movements during a close-out period and hence prevent loss should a counterparty subsequently default. Liquidity buffers can also be applied if the risk position of a CCP member is large. All CCP clearing members are required to post default fund contributions which are designed to be used in the event of the default of a CCP member.

## 1.3.2    Risk-Neutral Valuation

In all three of the cases studied in section 1.3.1 a baseline risk-neutral valuation model is still used. The risk-neutral valuation is the value as seen by the derivative trader and is the value this trader is tasked with hedging. Normally this trader will be an asset-class specialist with experience of hedging in the markets underlying the derivative and so this is where the majority of the market risk on the trade is managed. The risk-neutral trade level valuation makes the usual assumptions of no credit or funding risk so in effect this valuation assumes that a perfect CSA agreement is in place. However, in general the choice of discounting curve varies depending on the arrangements under which the derivative has been traded.

**Unsecured**    The choice of discount curve is still a matter of debate in the industry and depends on internal factors. Many banks have left the baseline valuation of unsecured trades using xIBOR-based discounting models (Solum Financial Partners, 2014). In many cases this will be exactly the same multi-currency discounting model that was prevalent before the credit crisis, typically where all other currencies had cross-currency basis quoted against the US

**TABLE 1.2** The possible choices of discounting for the baseline risk-neutral valuation of unsecured derivative trades.

| Discounting | Motivation |
| --- | --- |
| xIBOR | ▪ Matches pre-crisis discounting (e.g. if this was USD based and included cross-currency basis)<br>▪ Close-out reference value may be assumed to still be xIBOR based for unsecured trades |
| Single OIS curve | ▪ Central FVA management function<br>▪ Single OIS curve discounting assumed to be reference close-out value (e.g. EONIA for European bank) |
| Multiple OIS curves | ▪ Central FVA management function<br>▪ Single currency trading desks do not want cross-currency exposure<br>▪ Multiple OIS curve discounting assumed to be reference close-out value |
| Funding discounting | ▪ Asset-class trading desks manage own funding costs<br>▪ Discounting model of FVA adopted |

dollar interest rates. Other choices are also possible including OIS discounting. The choice may be made to use a single currency discount curve for all unsecured trades, say for example Fed Funds. A further alternative might be to allow single currency derivatives to be discounted using the appropriate OIS curve for that currency and treat multi-currency trades differently. This has the advantage that single currency trading books would not be exposed to any cross-currency effects. If the bank elects to use funding discounting models for unsecured trades, then the discount rate will be the bank's internal cost of funds curve. The possible choices and motivating factors are listed in Table 1.2.

The choice of discounting depends on three key factors: organisational design, internal bank modelling of funding costs and the expected reference close-out in the event of default. Note that this reflects the practical reality of what happens in banks rather than theoretical correctness of any models used.

**Organisation design** Organisational design[4] determines which trading desks manage which risks. Broadly there are two main choices; either each individual trading desk manages their own funding (*distributed model*) or there is a central management desk for funding (*centralised model*). In the distributed model each trading desk will need to know the funding impact of all unsecured trades on their book. This would most likely be done using a funding discounting approach, although other models could be used. In the centralised model the asset-class trading desks will either wish to measure the funding risk and lay it off with the central desk or not be exposed to it at all. If the asset-class desks hedge out funding risks with the central desk then they will measure the funding cost and hedge it out through funding basis swaps, otherwise the asset-class desk would value all their unsecured trades either at xIBOR or OIS and be oblivious to funding considerations, with the central funding desk calculating and managing FVA directly.

---

[4]See Chapter 22 for a broader discussion of organisational design.

**Bank models of funding costs**   The bank model of funding costs also plays a role in determining the choice of discounting for unsecured trades. As will be discussed at length in Chapter 9 there are broadly two types of model for FVA, discounting approaches and exposure-based approaches. Discounting approaches simply adjust the discount curve, while exposure-based approaches use models similar to those used for CVA. Discounting-based approaches simply adjust the risk-neutral valuation by using the cost of funds as the discount rate and hence the risk-neutral valuation. Exposure-based approaches apply FVA as an adjustment to the portfolio valuation in the same way as CVA so the underlying risk-neutral valuation remains unchanged.

**Reference close-out**   The reference close-out value is the final factor in determining the choice of unsecured discounting model. To be consistent with the CVA model the unsecured reference valuation should match that used in the CVA model so that in the event of default the risk-neutral valuation matches the claim value made against the administrators of the defaulted counterparty and the CVA becomes the realised loss on the trade once the actual recovery rate is known. Note that the use of funding discounting models implies that the CVA model *has to be changed to be consistent with this choice of FVA model.*[5]

**CSA**   CSA and OIS discounting will be discussed in detail in Chapter 8; however, it should be noted here that the implications of Piterbarg (2010) and Piterbarg (2012) are that the appropriate discount rate for fully collateralised counterparties is the rate of interest received on the posted collateral. Hence the discount curve depends on the terms of the CSA agreement. In the simplest case where collateral can only be posted in cash in a single currency then the rate of interest received on posted collateral is normally the overnight rate in that currency. Hence the appropriate discount curve is the OIS curve in the same currency as this curve represents the market expected overnight rate extended out to longer maturities. In the case where cash in multiple currencies can be posted the appropriate discount curve is a blended curve which represents the rate earned on the cheapest-to-deliver currency.[6] Many CSAs allow a variety of securities to be posted as collateral and in this case the choice of appropriate discount curve becomes more complex.

**CCP**   The discount curve used by CCPs to determine the value for the purposes of margin calls is determined by the internal models of the CCP. For single currency interest rate swaps cleared through LCH.Clearnet SwapClear this is currently a single currency OIS discounting methodology, having switched over from a LIBOR methodology during 2010 (LCH, 2010a). This can be viewed as the risk-neutral valuation of the interest rate swap, but there is no guarantee that a clearing member's own risk-neutral valuation will match that of SwapClear and this could become problematic because of the privileged position held by CCPs (Kenyon and Green, 2013c).

---

[5]See Chapter 8.

[6]Chapter 8 discusses the construction of OIS discounting curves in more detail. It should be noted that collateral substitution where one piece of collateral is exchanged for another depends on the local legal framework and that collateral can be viewed as "sticky" in some jurisdictions. The pricing of the embedded cheapest-to-deliver option is not straightforward, therefore.

### 1.3.3 Hedging and Management Costs

The bid-offer spread quoted by trading desks has always been included in prices and reflects the trading desk cost of managing the trade. This is normally considered to include the cost of hedging the market risk on the trade at inception and any future re-hedging costs due to market movements and embedded nonlinear risk. There are however other elements that should be considered:

■ *Staff costs* are a very significant fraction of the cost base of any bank. This includes trading and sales staff with primary responsibility for managing market risk and interacting with the customer. However, there are many other support functions involved including quantitative analysts, finance professionals and business controllers, risk managers, audit and operations staff.

■ *Legal and other professional fees* are also a cost. Over-the-counter (OTC) derivatives are traded under the legal framework provided by ISDA (1992; 2002), which requires set-up and maintenance costs. Some transactions require external ratings, which means engagement with rating agencies and the payment of fees.

■ *IT and other infrastructure costs* are also a significant part of the cost base of a bank. This covers everything from buildings, lighting and air conditioning through to the cost of IT system development, maintenance and hardware. For complex derivative products, even the cost of running the valuation and risk on a daily basis can be expensive due to hardware and the energy required to both power and cool it. Of course it is not just trading systems themselves, there are huge numbers of other risk systems for CVA, PFE, VaR etc that also consume resources.

### 1.3.4 Credit Risk: CVA/DVA

Part I of this book discusses CVA and DVA in detail, including models for unsecured and secured portfolios. Here I examine the CVA impact on pricing in each of the three cases.

**Unsecured**    Unsecured portfolios represent the standard case for CVA as both counterparties are fully exposed to each other. In most cases, close-out netting will apply meaning that the exposure on default will be to the netted value of the portfolio. If unilateral models are used then the CVA is only calculated on the exposure to the counterparty. In theory this would give rise to asymmetry in the price obtained by both counterparties as each would only charge for the credit risk of the other and take no account of their own risk of default. It is this theoretical asymmetry that has been one of the key drivers behind the introduction of bilateral CVA models and DVA. If bilateral models are used then both counterparties can agree on the credit valuation adjustment as the two terms in the calculation, CVA and DVA, are mirror images of each other. Counterparty A calculates $CVA_A$ and $DVA_A$, while B calculates $CVA_B$ and $DVA_B$ with the following symmetry holding:

$$CVA_A = DVA_B$$
$$DVA_A = CVA_B.$$

Of course in practice this symmetry would certainly not hold as both counterparties would operate different CVA models and may be operating under different accounting regimes. For example, one could be a bank with the derivative held in its trading book using mark-to-market accounting while the other might be a corporate using IAS 39 hedge accounting rules (IASB, 2004). There are also a number of other issues to be addressed when pricing unsecured derivatives such as including the impact of right-way or wrong-way risk and dealing with illiquid counterparties. Counterparties that deal on an unsecured basis are more likely to be smaller names with no traded CDS contracts, although some will be larger corporates or governmental entities.

**CSA** In the case of perfect collateralisation, where any change in mark-to-market is instantaneously covered by a transfer of collateral to support it, there is no credit exposure and hence no CVA or DVA. In practice, of course, even the strongest of bilateral CSA agreements do not display this behaviour and have a daily collateral call. In general all CSAs have a minimum transfer amount (MTA) and many have non-zero thresholds. Many CSAs will also have asymmetric thresholds giving *one-way CSAs*. Some CSAs have credit-rating dependent features such as thresholds that reduce on downgrade, volatility buffers or a requirement to novate the trade if the derivative issuer falls below a certain rating. CSAs can have a much lower call frequency such as weekly or monthly and this is particularly true of non-bank counterparties who do not have the operational capacity to manage collateral on a daily basis. In general, a default is not recognised immediately and often there is a recognised *cure* or *grace* period where a counterparty that has failed to make a collateral payment is allowed time to make the payment. In general, a *margin period of risk* is included when modelling collateral to allow an estimate of the realistic expected exposure. In the Basel III regulatory framework this is set at ten days unless the counterparty is a significant financial institution in which case the margin period is increased to twenty days.[7] During the margin period of risk no collateral is assumed to be transferred by the counterparty but often it is assumed that the bank must continue to make collateral payments, even if the counterparty has previously failed to make a collateral payment. Collateral disputes can also give rise to exposure and to the regulatory margin period of risk if more than two disputes occur in the previous two quarters (European Parliament and the Council of the European Union, 2013a; European Parliament and the Council of the European Union, 2013b).

CSAs are imperfect and give rise to residual exposure and hence there is credit risk and so CVA can be calculated and charged. However, not all banks mark CVA on collateralised names, particularly those with low or zero thresholds and a daily call frequency.

**CCP** CCP *variation margin* arrangements are very similar to a strong CSA with a daily call frequency and in some circumstances collateral can be called intraday. Given the presence of initial margin the residual expected exposure to the derivative trades themselves will be very small or zero.[8] However, there remains the possibility of exposure to the CCP itself through the initial margin and the default fund. If the initial margin is bankruptcy remote then the exposure generated by posted initial margin can be excluded from CVA. However, this is not the case for the default fund contributions which are designed to be used in the event of the default of a member. The default fund certainly generates exposure and hence credit risk.

---

[7]Except for repo transactions where the margin period of risk is set at five days.
[8]Of course with sufficiently large market moves, almost any initial margin can be exceeded as is clear from the removal of the CHF-EUR peg by the Swiss National Bank on 15 January 2015.

## 1.3.5 FVA

FVA was initially controversial in the quantitative finance community as is clear from the series of papers by John Hull and Alan White (2012b; 2012c; 2014b) and the responses to them by Castagna (2012), Laughton and Vaisbrot (2012), Morini (2012) and Kenyon and Green (2014c). The debate around FVA is discussed in section 1.4.1 and FVA models are presented in Part II; however, it is clear that most market practitioners believe a pricing adjustment should be made for the cost of funding unsecured derivative transactions. In this context FVA represents the costs and benefits from managing the collateral on hedges used to eliminate market risk from the unsecured transactions. FVA and CVA together can be viewed as the cost of not trading under a perfect CSA agreement. The accounting status of FVA is now in transition with increasing numbers of banks taking reserves.

**Unsecured**  As with CVA, unsecured trades are the standard case for FVA as both counterparties are fully exposed to each other. Symmetric models with both funding cost and benefits as well as asymmetric models with only funding costs have been proposed with a key determining factor being the potential overlap with DVA benefit. Broadly speaking, methodologies for FVA are either based on discounting, as noted earlier, or on exposure-based models that are extensions of CVA.

**CSA**  The discussion on residual exposure from CVA also applies in the context of FVA so that deviations from a perfect CSA could give rise to *residual FVA*. If we view FVA as the cost of providing an effective loan or the benefit of an effective deposit through a derivative then the residual exposure just gives rise to a residual funding cost or benefit. However, as will be discussed later, if we view the FVA as the cost of maintaining collateral on a hedge trade then the argument for residual FVA on CSA trades is much weaker, although funding costs and benefits will still arise from mismatches in collateral requirements due to differing CSA terms. What is clear is that FVA does not apply to the secured portion of the exposure unless the assets provided as collateral cannot be rehypothecated. Lack of rehypothecation may be due to legal terms within the CSA or because the asset provided as collateral may be ineligible under other CSAs.

**CCP – Variation Margin**  Given the degree of overcollateralisation for trades cleared through CCPs any residual exposure is likely to be small to zero. With this in mind the FVA component due to a mismatch between valuation and variation margin is likely to be close to zero.

**Other Sources of FVA**  Central counterparties also require that initial margin be posted in addition to variation margin. Large net risk positions can give risk to volatility buffers and all members of the CCP are required to contribute to a default fund that will be used to cover any losses in the event of the default of a member. All of this additional collateral needs to be funded through unsecured borrowing and hence gives rise to *Margin Valuation Adjustment (MVA)*. Modelling the exposure at future times arising from these collateral buffers is complex. Initial margin is generally calculated using VaR models which means estimating expected future VaR. The volatility buffers use risk multipliers based on estimates of market depth so that large risk positions that cannot be quickly closed are penalised. The default fund, in the case of LCH, is based on all positions of all clearing members and so is very difficult to estimate as the positions of other members are unknown. In addition the methodology used by central counterparties is not always public, making models difficult to build.

The Basel Committee proposal on bilateral margin for financial counterparties BCBS 226 (2012h) and BCBS 242 (2013e) would similarly give rise to a funding requirement to maintain the initial margin collateral buffer.

Regulatory liquidity frameworks including FSA047/048 as applied in the UK (Financial Conduct Authority, 2014, section 12) and the liquidity framework under Basel III (BCBS, 2013b) also require the maintenance of an internal liquidity buffer to protect an institution from outflow in the event of a credit downgrade. This *liquidity buffer* has to be held in liquid assets by the bank against a two-notch downgrade of long-term rating by credit rating agencies. Many CSAs and ISDAs contain provisions for additional collateral in the event one or more rating agencies downgrade the counterparty below certain certain rating levels. In addition non-derivative products such as deposits may contain provisions to allow the counterparty to withdraw the deposit if the bank's credit rating falls below a certain level. The liquidity buffer must be funded through unsecured borrowing and hence is a type of FVA. Trades with counterparties that have embedded *downgrade triggers* in their documentation should include the cost of funding any additional liquidity buffer in the price of a new transaction.

### 1.3.6   Regulatory Capital and KVA

Under the Basel III framework (BCBS, 2011b) there are three key contributors to regulatory capital requirements:

- Market risk
- Counterparty Credit Risk (CCR)
- Regulatory CVA.

In addition some transactions will be subject to other capital provisions through *Specific Risk*, *Incremental Risk Charge (IRC)* and *Wrong-way Risk*. The incremental cost of capital due to a new trade is significant and has to be included in the price of a new derivative. This is not a funding cost, however, as there is no requirement to hold collateral or an asset return, rather there is a requirement to hold shareholders' capital against the risk of loss on the derivative portfolio. This capital is not free and shareholders require a return on this capital. Often bank management will state a target return on capital or direct staff within the bank to accept transactions that exceed a minimum return on capital. The Basel framework requires an amount of capital to be held based on the application of the capital rules to the current portfolio, giving a *spot capital requirement*.[9] However, the spot capital requirement is not necessarily a good measure of the expected capital requirement throughout the life of a transaction. An interest rate swap, for example, will be entered at close to zero value but will then diverge away from it, given additional CCR and CVA capital requirements during its lifetime. Hence the cost that

---

[9]Note that sometimes this spot capital requirement is referred to in terms of *RWA* or *Risk-Weighted Assets* as this is the regulatory asset value against which the capital must be held. In reality the Basel framework is written partially in terms of RWA and partly in terms of direct capital requirements but RWA is frequently used in finance as a shorthand way of describing all capital requirements.

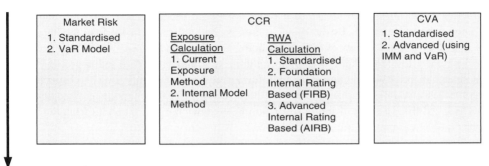

Increasing Complexity

**FIGURE 1.1**   The different calculation methodologies available for market risk, counterparty credit risk and CVA under the Basel III framework. The more complex methodologies requiring regulatory approval are lower down the figure.

needs to be priced into to new derivatives is the *lifetime cost of capital* which measures the cost of all future capital requirements. Part III discusses approaches to how this lifetime cost of capital can be estimated.

Once we have a measure of the lifetime cost of capital, KVA, then new transactions can be priced in such a way as to achieve the desired minimum profit to achieve the desired return for shareholders. However, this will not remain constant as market moves can lead to higher or lower capital requirements. Both the CCR and CVA terms are driven by the portfolio mark-to-market and so the lifetime cost of capital will have market risk sensitivities in a similar way to CVA and FVA. This leads to the question as to whether or not capital can be managed in a manner similar to CVA and FVA. It certainly can be managed passively through managing the back book of trades through novation and trade cancellation. Counterparties with large trade portfolios between them may find that capital as well as operational costs and risks can be reduced through compression trades that seek to replace a large portfolio with a smaller number of trades with the same risk profile. Active management of the CVA and CCR terms is embedded into Basel III through the capital mitigation that is available from the use of single name and index CDS trades to hedge counterparty risk. In theory trades could be used to hedge the market risk sensitivities of the lifetime cost of capital. Such trades would be in place to generate retained profits at exactly the time additional capital would be needed. In reality, however, these transactions would likely attract additional capital themselves making hedging involve iteration/optimisation rather than simply constructing a trade to offset the risk directly.

One further point to note here is that the amount of capital required depends on the regulatory approvals that the institution has in place. For each of three main contributors to regulatory capital listed above, the calculation method depends on status, with more advanced institutions allowed to use internal modelling subject to appropriate approvals and oversight. The different approaches are illustrated in Figure 1.1.

It should be immediately clear that regulatory capital will not be the same for all market participants because the methodology in use in each institution is different. The cost of capital of each institution will also be different as each will set individual target returns. Even in the absence of book-specific effects, such as netting, the cost of capital embedded in the derivative price can be significantly different between different banks.

Regulatory uncertainty and regulatory divergence are also major issues. Further regulatory proposals have been made by the Basel Committee and more will be made in the future. For example, under the " review of the trading book" fundamental (2012g; 2013c) major changes will be made to the market risk capital framework, with the standardised approach revised and changes to IMM including a switch to *expected shortfall* from VaR. The two non-IMM approaches to counterparty credit risk will be replaced in 2017 with the *standardised approach* (BCBS, 2014b). The cost of future regulation is unknown but it will certainly apply to long-dated derivatives that are transacted today.

## 1.4   POST-CRISIS DERIVATIVE VALUATION OR HOW I LEARNED TO STOP WORRYING AND LOVE FVA

### 1.4.1   The FVA Debate and the Assault on Black-Scholes-Merton

As noted earlier, bank CDS spreads were very narrow prior to the start of the credit crisis in 2007. AA or better rated banks were able to fund themselves at the rate implied by the LIBOR discounting curve or in some cases below. FVA adjustments were not made as they were not needed. After the default of Lehman brothers as credit spreads widened sharply so did funding costs. The spread between overnight rates and rates of longer tenors widened significantly with the US Dollar OIS-3M LIBOR spread reaching 365bp just after the collapse of Lehman Brothers in September 2008 (Sengupta and Tam, 2008). Unsecured funding costs became very significant for the first time in the history of derivative markets.

Initially unsecured funding was seen in the context of multiple yield curve models. These models were introduced to account for *tenor basis* or the large discrepancies observed between instruments with different payment frequencies, observable through the prices of basis swaps. *Cross-currency basis* was already well established in yield curve frameworks and pre-crisis yield curve models were already contructed in such a fashion as to reprice both single currency and cross-currency swaps. These cross-currency models implicitly used 3M US Dollar LIBOR as the primary discount curve and all other currencies were marked with currency basis with respect to US Dollars. The main justification for the use of US Dollar discounting was its role as global reserve currency. A number of papers were published on multiple curve discount models including Henrard (2007); Henrard (2009), Ameritrano and Bianchetti (2009), Chibane and Sheldon (2009), Fujii, Shimada and Takahashi (2010b) and Bianchetti (2010). A number of authors then extended the multiple curve frameworks into models designed to value exotic interest rate derivative products while accounting for both tenor and cross-currency basis and models of this type were presented by Mercurio (2010b), Fujii, Shimada and Takahashi (2009) and by Kenyon (2010) in the short rate modelling framework.

A parallel development to this was the realisation that the use of 3M xIBOR curves as the primary discounting curve was incorrect for derivative portfolios secured by collateral under CSA agreements. Market practitioners realised that the correct discount curve was in fact the OIS curve, at least for CSAs which accepted collateral in a single currency and paid the overnight unsecured rate of interest on posted collateral on a daily basis. This was driven by a realisation that the OIS curve was considered risk free while the rapidly increased divergence between the OIS rate and 3M xIBOR rates clearly demonstrated that xIBOR was perceived as far from risk free by market participants (see for example Hull and White, 2013). Piterbarg clearly demonstrated that the interest rate paid on collateral was the correct discount rate under a perfect single currency CSA agreement (Piterbarg, 2010) and subsequently in the multi-currency case (Piterbarg, 2012).[10]

Unsecured derivatives were seen as just another discount curve, with valuations either remaining at 3M xIBOR discounted values or moved to a discount curve equivalent to the bank cost of funds if this was higher than 3M xIBOR. It quickly became apparent that such models led to *double counting* of benefit from DVA and funding for those institutions that used bilateral CVA models. The primary driver for both funding and DVA was the market perception of credit worthiness; in the context of funding this was seen through the yield on bank funding instruments and their spread over instruments considered risk free such as high quality government bonds and through the bank CDS curve in the case of DVA. This led Burgard and Kjaer (2011b) and Burgard and Kjaer (2011a) to produce a self-consistent framework the included CVA, DVA and FVA through a similar PDE approach to that used by Piterbarg in the context of collateralisation. Morini and Prampolini (2011) also developed a model including both DVA and FVA from a probabilistic approach. Kenyon and Stamm (2012) developed a portfolio level model for FVA, while Pallavicini, Perini and Brigo (2012) produced a portfolio level model that incorporates cash flows from collateral as well as individual trades using a probabilistic approach.

In the 25th anniversary edition of *Risk Magazine*, John Hull and Alan White (2012b) wrote an article arguing that FVA should not be applied to derivatives. The response from market practitioners was an immediate vigorous counterargument that funding costs should be priced into derivatives, beginning with Laughton and Vaisbrot (2012) in the next issue of *Risk Magazine* and followed by Castagna (2012) and Morini (2012). Hull and White published a further two papers as the debate continued (2012c; 2014b). Kenyon and Green (2014c) and Kenyon and Green (2014b) continued the debate with Hull and White (2014c) in the context of the implications of regulatory associated costs.

Hull and White (2012b) based their argument on eight key points:

1. Discounting at the risk-free rate is a consequence of risk-neutral valuation.
2. Hedging involves buying and selling zero cost instruments and so hedging does not affect valuations.
3. The *Fischer-Hirshleifer Separation Principle* (Hirshleifer, 1958)/*Modigliani-Millar Theorem* (Modigliani and Miller, 1958) imply that pricing and funding should be kept separate.
4. Banks invest in Treasury instruments and other low-yielding securities without charging funding costs.
5. FVA is equal to the change in DVA from the fair value option on the bank's own issued debt.
6. FVA is a form of anti-economic valuation adjustment.
7. Proponents of FVA do not require the derivatives desk to earn a bank's weighted average cost of capital.
8. The FVA adjusted price is a *Private Valuation*.

Laughton and Vaisbrot (2012) countered that Hull and White's arguments were based on complete markets where all risks can be hedged, while in practice markets are incomplete

---

[10]OIS discounting models are discussed in Chapter 9.

and this introduces subjectivity into valuations; hence the *law of one price* no longer holds. Furthermore, Laughton and Vaisbrot argue that the Black-Scholes-Merton model relies upon both no arbitrage and the ability to borrow and lend at the risk-free rate in unlimited size, while in reality there is no deep liquid two-way market in borrowing and lending cash and that apparent arbitrage opportunities are visible in the market because of the practical difficulties in conducting arbitrage. Furthermore Laughton and Vaisbrot suggest that models should be practically useful to traders and that as a result the cost of borrowing is an exogenous factor that is unaffected by a single trade and that no value should be attributed to profit or loss on own default through DVA as it is impossible to monetise.

Antonio Castagna (2012) argued against points 1, 2, 3, 4 and 5 in the list above. Discounting using the risk-free rate may not be appropriate, argues Castagna, as it does not cover the cost of the replication strategy. Hedging does not always involve buying and selling zero cost instruments as the funding rate has to be paid if money is borrowed to purchase an asset. Castagna argues that the Modigliani-Millar theorem does not apply to derivatives. The argument proposed by Hull and White (2012b) that banks invest in low yielding instruments is simply false as these assets are mostly funded through the repo market. Finally, Castagna suggests that FVA cannot be offset by gains or losses through DVA from the fair value of own debt option as any such gains cannot be realised in the event of default.

Massimo Morini (2012) argues that it makes sense for a lender to charge funding costs as it will be left with a carry loss in the event it does not default itself, even if it does not make sense for the borrower. Morini suggests that FVA might be a benefit for shareholders on the basis that the shareholders of a limited liability company are effectively holding a call option on the value of the company. Like Castagna, Morini argues against the use of the Modigliani-Millar theorem but on the basis that Hull and White assume that the market response to the choice of projects undertaken by the company is linear as expressed through funding costs. Morini demonstrates that even in the case of a simple Black-Cox model the market response is nonlinear. Finally, Morini agrees with Hull and White's assertion that risk-free discounting is appropriate in derivative pricing.

What does this debate actually mean in practice? The answer to at least some degree is that quants protest too much when theoretical arguments are challenged by the market. Ultimately mathematics is a tool used in finance to, for example, value products, risk manage them, produce economic models, etc. All models have assumptions and if the market changes and the assumption is no longer valid the models have to change to remain useful. This is not the first time that models have "failed" to some degree. Skew and smile on vanilla options have long been present showing deviations from the Black-Scholes model. This demonstrates that the market believes the distribution of the underlying asset is not log-normal as assumed by the Black-Scholes model. During the credit crisis the Gaussian Copula models used to value CDOs were unable to match market prices. However, it is clear that FVA presents a broader challenge to quantitative finance than previous issues such as volatility smile. The fundamental assumptions underlying much of quantitative finance theory since Black-Scholes are challenged by FVA. Valuation is undergoing a paradigm shift away from these standard assumptions towards models that encompass more realism and away from the simplifying assumptions of the Black-Scholes framework.

Kenyon and Green (2014c) and Kenyon and Green (2014b) demonstrated that in the presence of holding costs the assumptions underlying the Modigliani-Miller theorem are violated. Regulatory costs, through capital requirements, act as holding costs leading to the direct consequence that Modigliani-Miller does not apply to derivatives and hence to FVA.

Furthermore it is clear that there is no single risk-neutral measure that spans the market and that no two market participants will agree on price. Hull and White (2012b) maintain that FVA should not be charged; however, the market as a whole has reached the opposite conclusion with numerous banks taking reserves for FVA, including a headline-grabbing figure of $1.5bn by J.P. Morgan in January 2014 (Levine, 2014).

### 1.4.2  Different Values for Different Purposes

The so-called *law of one price* argues that the same asset must trade at the same price on all markets or there is an arbitrage opportunity. For example, if gold trades at $X$ on market A and at $Y$ on market B and $X < Y$, in the absence of transport and other cost differentials all trades will take place on market A. The question is whether or not this argument applies to OTC unsecured derivatives markets.

Superficially it would appear that the law of one price should apply to unsecured derivatives if the term sheet for the transaction is the same across multiple banks. However, the terms under which those trades actually take place, that is the ISDA agreement, are frequently different so even in legal terms the trades are different. Add in the counterparty risk of dealing with the banks on an unsecured basis and it should be clear that each deal done with a different bank is different. If two banks offer the same derivative an arbitrager will find it very difficult to arbitrage them by taking opposite positions because of counterparty risk and capital considerations. Most unsecured derivatives are actually traded with corporate customers who use them to hedge balance sheet risks. Often the corporate will use hedge accounting rules and be focused on cash flows while the bank will use mark-to-market accounting. Many of these derivatives will be transacted one way round as corporates use the derivatives as a hedge on a natural risk. For example, many corporate fixed rate loans are structured as a floating rate loan with an interest rate swap in which the corporate receives the floating rate and pays the fixed rate. Derivatives transacted with corporates will also be frequently difficult to novate to a third party, particularly for trades with smaller corporates as they may have few banking relationships or indeed may have only one banking relationship. Other banks, particularly those from outside of the geographical region, may be reluctant to perform the credit analysis and *know your client* checks necessary to establish a relationship. The law of one price simply does not apply in such circumstances.

A useful analogy to consider when thinking about derivatives is that of the manufacturing industry. Consider manufacturing cars; all cars are designed to carry passengers and luggage but we clearly do not expect them all to cost the same. Cars have different designs and features and these feed into the price. The value of the car will depreciate at different rates after the purchase. The cost of the car is driven by a wide variety of factors including the cost of components, labour costs, transport costs, etc. In general the price will be determined by

$$\text{Price} = \text{Production Cost} + \text{Profit Margin.}$$

Why should derivatives be any different?

**What is a Derivative Price?**  The price of a derivative is just the price at which the transaction is dealt. For unsecured derivatives the price achieved is the end result of a negotiation process, which lies in sharp contrast to exchange traded derivatives where prices are determined by supply and demand in a very liquid market. As a negotiation both parties will try

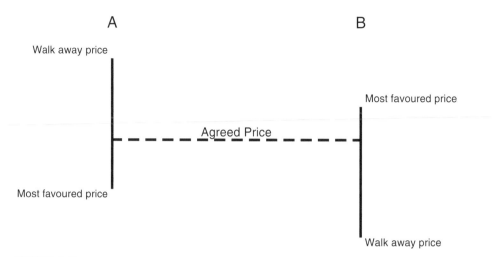

**FIGURE 1.2**    A diagram of a price negotiation between two parties A and B. Both parties have a *most favoured price* that they would ideally like to transact at and a *walk way price* below which they will not trade. The agreed price must lie between the most favoured price and walk away price of both parties. If these ranges do not overlap then no agreement is possible.

to reach an agreed price that satisfies the needs and expectations of both parties. Figure 1.2 illustrates the negotiation process.

It should be clear that:

$$Price \neq Value$$

**What is a Derivative Valuation?**    A valuation is a numerical measure of the worth of a contract. The *law of one price* suggests that there is just one valuation for a derivative; in reality this is not the case and different agents have different measures of worth in different contexts. Here I consider three valuations, but the list is not exhaustive:

- Accounting valuation
- Trading valuation
- Regulatory valuation.

There is nothing new here and bond traders, for example, have used the concept of relative value for many years. Before the crisis these different valuations generally coincided for unsecured derivatives as bank credit spreads were narrow and funding costs were negligible. The credit crisis drove the valuations apart and it is unlikely they will ever coincide again for unsecured derivatives. Valuation, even of simple products, has become a challenge.

**Accounting valuations**    Accounting valuations aim to provide an objective measure of the value of assets and liabilities on the balance sheet. Accounting valuation methodology is driven by

- Accounting standards (FSB, IFRS)
- Accounting principles (e.g. GAAP)
- Company law.

Sometimes these can be in conflict when market practice changes and it can take some time for these to be reflected back into accounting standards.

**Trading valuations**   These provide a valuation measure that reflects all of the risk factors that the derivative is currently understood to be subject to. The valuation, and more importantly, the associated sensitivities, provide the means by which the trader can make appropriate risk management decisions in order to maintain the value of a book of derivative transactions exposed to market volatility. The trader is charged with risk management to fulfil a duty to shareholders and other stakeholders. There is no requirement for objectivity in valuation as the risk factors can be a function of the institution itself.

**Regulatory valuations**   Regulatory valuations are those used by the regulator to define capital requirements. Regulatory valuations are increasingly becoming distinct from accounting valuations. For example, the regulator has disallowed DVA as a contributor to capital (BCBS, 2011a) and while this does not directly impact the valuation of individual trades it has affected the effective book valuation. The forthcoming *Prudent Valuation* regime (EBA, 2012; EBA, 2013a; EBA, 2014c) will require banks to calculate *Additional Valuation Adjustments (AVA)* to adjust the value of a trade down to that based on a the 90% confidence level, given market price uncertainty. The adjusted value will be that used for regulatory capital purposes.

### 1.4.3   Summary: The *Valuation Paradigm Shift*

Different agents have different perspectives and drivers and the valuations they use will reflect this. Derivative pricing reflects manufacturing costs and these costs include CVA, FVA, MVA, KVA and TVA. Representatives of companies, including banks, are required to operate on a going concern basis and to factor in the management of all visible risk factors into valuations. *Realism* is an important element of trading valuations that have to reflect the actual cost of manufacturing derivatives. Derivative valuation theory is not invalid but has been shown to be out of date and hence needs to be updated to reflect market reality. This book aims to provide the required update.

## 1.5   READING THIS BOOK

This book can be read in two ways. Firstly it can be read as a *manifesto* for the change in derivative valuation and the move away from the pure Black-Scholes-Merton framework. This is a controversial topic and will no doubt remain so for some time. The book can also be read as a practical guide to the calculation of valuation adjustments and it is therefore up to the reader what model elements are selected from those discussed.

The book is organised into five main parts. Part I discusses models for counterparty credit risk and CVA, while Part II discusses FVA models as an extension to CVA model. The regulatory capital framework and KVA model are introduced in Part III. The implementation of XVA models is discussed in part IV and this section of the book is aimed to be a practical guide for those who are building bespoke internal models as well as those who may be buying third-party systems. Finally Part V discusses the management of XVA principally through active hedging programmes.

# CVA and DVA: Counterparty Credit Risk and Credit Valuation Adjustment

## CHAPTER 2

# Introducing Counterparty Risk

*Take calculated risks. That is quite different from being rash.*

—George S. Patton
*US general (1885–1945)*

## 2.1 DEFINING COUNTERPARTY RISK

Counterparty credit risk, sometimes known simply as *credit risk* or *default risk*, can be defined as the risk that a counterparty will fail to make payments that are due to another party. Consider a simple fixed rate loan in which the borrower makes annual fixed payments to the lender for five years before repaying the loan principal. The borrower defaults if they fail to pay any of the interest payments or the loan principal. The same is true for bonds and other securities, except the default will occur on payment to the securities holder. Derivatives also expose counterparties to credit risk. Some derivatives such as interest rate swaps involve bidirectional payments throughout their life which implies that both counterparties have default risk to each other, and that the direction of the risk changes during the life of the transaction.

Counterparty credit risk is only present when one counterparty has an *exposure* to the other. The *exposure at default* (EAD)[1] is the total amount owed by the defaulting party to the non-defaulting party,

$$EAD = \max(V, 0), \tag{2.1}$$

where $V$ is the total value. There is no exposure if the non-defaulting party owes the defaulting party money and this gives the max function in equation (2.1). If the exposure is positive and the defaulting party owes the non-defaulting party money, this value will form the basis of the claim the creditor will make against the defaulter through bankruptcy proceedings. The *expected positive exposure*[2] (EPE) is the expected exposure of party A to their counterparty

---

[1]The *regulatory EAD* is a separate but related quantity that I will discuss later in Chapter 12.
[2]Or sometimes simply *expected exposure* (EE), although this can be confused with the forward value $V_t$ which is sometimes also known as expected exposure.

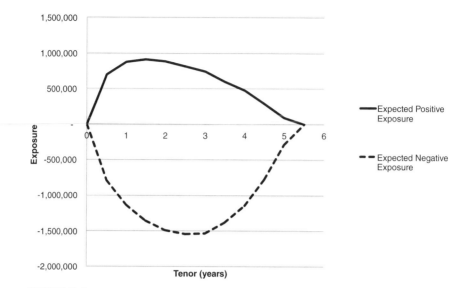

**FIGURE 2.1** The expected positive and expected negative exposure profiles for a five-year interest rate swap with a notional of £100m at trade inception.

B at some future date with the expectation or average taken over all possible future outcomes on the date of interest as defined in equation (2.2).[3]

$$EPE(t) = \mathbb{E}_t \left[ \max(V, 0) | \mathcal{F}_t \right]. \tag{2.2}$$

The *expected exposure profile* is simply the expected exposure as a function of time. These exposure measures play a crucial role in the calculation of CVA. The *expected negative exposure* is the expected exposure that party B has to party A as seen from the perspective of A:

$$ENE(t) = \mathbb{E}_t \left[ \max(-V, 0) | \mathcal{F}_t \right]. \tag{2.3}$$

The expected negative exposure enters the calculation of debit and funding valuation adjustments (DVA and FVA). The expected positive and negative exposure profiles for a five-year receivers interest rate swap are illustrated in Figure 2.1.

Given the exposure at the time default occurs, the amount recovered is usually expressed as a percentage, $R$, the *recovery rate*.[4] Hence the recovered amount is given by

$$R \times \max(V, 0). \tag{2.4}$$

---

[3] $\mathcal{F}_t$ is the *filtration* to time $t$. This is a technical element of stochastic calculus and the filtration simply represents all information such as asset prices up to time $t$. Where necessary I will include technical elements like this but they will be left out where appropriate and when it simplifies the presentation.
[4] The specification of the recovery as a percentage of price is the most common approach but other specifications are possible, see Schönbucher (2003).

The recovery rate is commonly used in the credit derivatives market. The *loss-given-default* or LGD is often used in traditional credit risk and is simply one minus the recovery rate,

$$LGD = (1 - R). \qquad (2.5)$$

### 2.1.1 Wrong-way and Right-way Risk

*Wrong-way risk* is an important element of understanding credit exposure, although it is defined in a number of different ways. One traditional definition originating in credit risk modelling defines wrong-way risk as the risk that the exposure at default is larger than the exposure immediately prior to default. ISDA[5] defines wrong-way risk in a much broader sense as occurring whenever the exposure to a counterparty is adversely correlated to the risk of the default of that counterparty (D'Hulster, 2001). This definition is the one most commonly applied in CVA modelling circles and is the one I use here. ISDA goes on to define *specific* wrong-way risk as associated with a particular transaction that has been poorly structured such as a repo agreement collateralised with the borrower's own bonds, and *general* or *conjectural* wrong-way risk as when credit quality and counterparty exposure are adversely linked through macro-economic factors. A simple example of this latter condition can be seen in the interest rate swaps market. A typical lending arrangement between a bank and a corporate counterparty involves a floating rate loan coupled with an interest rate swap in which the corporate pays fixed and receives a floating rate. The effective structure is then a fixed rate loan. In an economic recession interest rates typically fall at the same time that corporates experience a deterioration in their credit quality. The interest rate swap must be marked-to-market by the bank and as interest rates fall the value of the receiver swap increases, increasing the derivative exposure to the corporate. Hence this is an example of general wrong-way risk.

*Right-way risk* is the inverse of wrong-way risk and occurs whenever exposure and credit quality are favourably correlated. A classic example of this is a trade with a gold producer in which the exposure is linked to the gold price. As the gold price increases the exposure increases; however, the value of gold reserves also increases and hence the credit worthiness of the gold miner also increases. A deeper investigation of the gold miner case study is revealing. If the gold miner has sold forward all the remaining reserves at a low price, the increasing gold price would have no impact on the credit worthiness of the gold miner. The transactions may be off balance sheet and not readily visible to external analysis. In practice assessing wrong-way and right-way risk is a complex process and the co-dependence between counterparty and macro-economic factors difficult to estimate.

## 2.2 CVA AND DVA: CREDIT VALUATION ADJUSTMENT AND DEBIT VALUATION ADJUSTMENT DEFINED

*Credit Valuation Adjustment* or *CVA* is the market price of credit risk on a financial instrument that is marked-to-market, typically an OTC derivative contract. Hence CVA is defined as the

---

[5]International Swaps and Derivatives Association.

difference between the price of the instrument including credit risk and price where both counterparties to the transaction are considered free of credit risk,

$$\boxed{\text{CVA} = V(\text{default free}) - V(\text{credit risky}).}$$ (2.6)

Note that as defined in equation (2.6) CVA will always be positive if we consider only the credit risk of the counterparty. This sign convention is the one often used by CVA management functions; however, note that the accounting impact of the same number is negative as in this case the credit risk reduces the value of the derivative so that

$$V(\text{credit risky}) < V(\text{default free}).$$

There are a variety of different models for CVA and the market uses models in which only the credit riskiness of the counterparty is considered (unilateral), and models in which the credit worthiness of both counterparties is considered (bilateral).

Bilateral CVA models add an additional term, *Debit Valuation Adjustment* or *DVA* that arises from the credit risk of the reporting institution. As the credit worthiness of the institution declines, usually marked through widening CDS spreads, the institution books an accounting gain on its derivative portfolio, with the gain reflecting the fact that should the reporting institution default it will not fully repay all its obligations. DVA is a very controversial topic as it acts to increase the accounting value of a portfolio of derivatives at the same time that the credit worthiness of the institution is declining. There is also considerable debate around whether DVA can be effectively hedged or monetised.

There are in fact two types of DVA appearing in accounts, *derivative DVA*, as described above and *debt DVA* that arises when an institution opts to fair value its own issued debt. In this case the institution books an accounting gain when their debt declines in value. In theory the institution could buy back the debt thus crystallising the gain, although in practice this does not often happen. The institution is unlikely to have funds available to buy back debt in such a scenario.

CVA was introduced as a financial reporting requirement under FAS 157 issued in September 2006 by the *Financial Accounting Standards Board* (FASB) and coming into force for all entities with fiscal years beginning after 15 November 2007. The requirement to consider credit risk was also introduced by the *International Accounting Standards Board* through IFRS 39 (IASB, 2004) that was endorsed by the European Commission in 2005. IAS 39, unlike FAS 157, did not explicitly state that own credit risk should be taken into account (McCarroll and Khatri, 2011). This was subsequently changed in IFRS 13 (IASB, 2012) and IFRS 9 (IASB, 2014).

## 2.3  THE DEFAULT PROCESS

While in simple terms default occurs when the counterparty fails to make a payment, in reality the process is a complex legal one that varies between legal jurisdictions. The case of the default of sovereigns and supranational entities is more complex still as it enters the domain of international law. The legal process can be a long one, lasting many years, particularly in the case of large multinational entities; Enron filed for bankruptcy protection on 2 December

2001 (BBC, 2002), however, the company did not emerge from bankruptcy until 14 July 2004 (Hays, 2004). This then poses two important questions; what types of default are there and when do we consider default to have occurred?

The Credit default swaps market has defined a number of different *Credit Events* that trigger the payout on CDS contracts on the defaulted entity. The *2003 ISDA Credit Derivatives Definitions* (ISDA, 2003; Parker and Brown, 2003) sets out six different credit events:

- Bankruptcy
- Failure to pay
- Obligation acceleration
- Obligation default
- Repudiation/moratorium
- Restructuring.

The exact definitions of these conditions are not important here, it is sufficient to recognise that there are a variety of credit events that can be considered to constitute a default. However, even these definitions are specific to the CDS market and do not necessarily reflect the practicalities of the default of a derivative counterparty and hence the impact on CVA calculation and the operation of a CVA desk. For a major international corporate or financial with traded CDS contracts it is likely that the CDS contract definition and trigger event will coincide with the failure of the derivative contract and this was certainly the case with the collapse of Lehman Brothers. However, for smaller entities the default process may be less clear cut. If there are no CDS contracts the CDS definitions are irrelevant. The event of default may be due to the restructuring of a counterparty portfolio in response to difficulties faced by the counterparty. The restructuring may be enacted by a group of creditors if there is more than one or the single bank counterparty if the defaulted entity only had a single banking relationship. In such cases it is not even clear if a credit event on one part of the portfolio automatically means that a default has occurred on all of the portfolio of transactions. So for example, an impairment may be taken on a loan by the lending bank but not on derivatives with the same counterparty. The key point to take away is that what constitutes a default is not always certain and that a CVA desk faces a range of different counterparties with a range of different possible credit events.

A second key question is when does default occur? Again this can vary, depending on the circumstances of the default. A failure to pay, for example, can be accompanied by a *grace period* which can vary from a few days up to a month. This is intended to ensure that issues such as IT system failure do not cause a technical default. Nevertheless, default cannot be confirmed until the grace period has passed. A counterparty could be placed in a workout process by its bank or bankers before impairments are taken. Restructuring may be inevitable but no actual credit event has occurred. From a CVA perspective the time that default is recognised depends on both external factors and internal management processes. For large counterparties with liquid CDS contracts, recognition of the default will tally closely with external market action and the close-out process for CDS contracts. For smaller illiquid counterparties the process will be governed by internal management process and will link with the internal impairment and workout process. Nevertheless, a CVA management function will typically be forced to recognise the loss and make good the derivatives trading desk long before any workout process has been concluded.

### 2.3.1   Example Default: The Collapse of Lehman Brothers

The most significant default in recent years was the collapse of the investment bank Lehman Brothers in 2008, at the height of the credit crisis. The collapse of the US subprime mortgage market led to significant losses on transactions linked to pools of mortgages, including mortgage and asset-backed securities and credit derivatives such as CDOs. This had already led to the collapse of Bear Stearns and its subsequent rescue by J.P. Morgan (Winnett and Arlidge, 2008). The problems of Lehman Brothers became visible with the publication of a second quarter loss of $2.8bn, coupled with $17bn of write downs on assets including mortgage and asset-backed securities, commercial mortgages and leveraged loans in June 2008 (Quinn, 2008d). On 9 September, negotiations around the sale of a stake in the bank to Korean Development Bank collapsed, prompting a 30% fall in the share price on a single day (Onaran, 2008). On 11 September the Lehman share price fell as much as 46%, while Lehman Brothers began exploring the possibility of selling itself to Bank of America (Quinn, 2008b). On 13 September Barclays Bank engaged in takeover talks, but subsequently pulled out on 14 September (Quinn, 2008c). With no rescue options left, Lehman Brothers filed for bankruptcy on the morning of 15 September 2008 (Quinn, 2008a).

When Lehman Brothers Holding Incorporated filed for bankruptcy, the court appointed PricewaterhouseCoopers (PWC) as administrators of the four main legal entities that comprised Lehman Brothers: Lehman Brothers Limited, Lehman Brothers Holdings plc, Lehman Brothers International (Europe) and LB UK RE Holdings Ltd (PWC, 2011). Clearing houses such as LCH.Clearnet acted swiftly to close out Lehman Brothers exchange-traded instrument positions in the weeks following the default (LCH, 2012d). Significant parts of the Lehman Brothers business were sold off rapidly after the bankruptcy with Barclays purchasing the New York investment banking and capital markets business on 16 September 2008 (Teather, Clark and Treanor, 2008) and Nomura purchasing Lehman Brother's European and Middle East businesses on 22 September 2008 (Telegraph Staff, 2008). The CDS market auction process to determine the payout on Lehman Brothers took place on 10 October 2008 and set a recovery rate of 8.625% (Barr, 2008), a relatively low figure in historical terms. The final recovery rate is now expected to be around 18% (Carmiel, 2012). A year after the bankruptcy, Tony Lomas of PWC suggested the administration process could take 10–20 years to complete (Ebrahimi, 2009), because of the complexity of the business. Nevertheless, unsecured creditors have now started to receive payments (Rushton, 2014).

## 2.4   CREDIT RISK MITIGANTS

There are a number of ways of reducing counterparty credit risk and these can be placed into six categories; netting, collateral/security, clearing, capital, break clauses and purchasing credit protection.

### 2.4.1   Netting

A *close-out netting agreement* provides the legal framework for assets and liabilities to be netted together when closing out a portfolio of derivatives in the event of a default of one of the counterparties. Close-out netting significantly reduces credit exposure, with research by ISDA suggesting a reduction of 85% (Mengle, 2010). To see how this works consider the following

|  | | **Netting** | **No Netting** | |
|---|---|---|---|---|
| Trade 1 | £ 1,000,000 | | =40% x £1,000,000 | |
| Trade 2 | -£ 500,000 | | -£ 500,000 | |
| Net | £ 500,000 | =40% x £500,000 | | |
| Recovery | | £ 200,000.0 | -£ 100,000.0 | |
| A's Loss | | -£ 300,000.0 | -£ 600,000.0 | |

**FIGURE 2.2** The impact of close-out netting reducing overall credit exposure.

example where A and B have two derivatives transactions between them, one with a value of £1m and the second with a value of −£0.5m as seen by A. B then defaults and A recovers 40% of the claim value. If the two derivatives net then the credit exposure at default is £0.5m and A will recover £0.2m, a net loss of £0.3m. However, if the trades do not net each trade will be treated separately with A recovering £0.4m on the trade with a value of £1m but having to pay £0.5m back to the administrators of B on the second transaction with a negative value. A's net position is −£0.1m with no netting, a net loss of £0.6m. This is illustrated in Figure 2.2.

Netting is enshrined in the *ISDA Master Agreement* which is the bilateral agreement between counterparties that provides the legal framework for OTC derivative trading. Netting is enshrined in English law but in some other jurisdictions separate legislation has been needed to allow close-out netting to be implemented. The legal enforceability of netting remains a concern for market participants and the use of netting has faced challenges in the aftermath of the 2008 financial crisis (Mengle, 2010).

## 2.4.2 Collateral/Security

Credit risk can be mitigated or eliminated entirely if the counterparty provides some form of security to cover the value of the liability which will be returned when the liability is repaid. Examples of this type of secured transaction are repos and reverse repos. A *repo* or *repurchase agreement* is a trade in which one counterparty sells bonds to another counterparty and agrees to repurchase them at a fixed price at an agreed date in the future.[6] Repo transactions are a type of secured lending. If the bonds decline in value during the period of the repo additional collateral must be supplied, either more of the same bond, a higher quality bond, or cash.

Derivative transactions can also be collateralised in a similar way to repos through a *CSA* or *Credit Support Annex* agreement. CSAs provide the terms of a bilateral agreement between two counterparties that allows for collateral to be posted between them to secure the derivative. The CSA is an annex to the ISDA Master Agreement between the two parties. Standard ISDA and CSA agreements are provided by the International Swaps and Derivatives Association Inc., although in practice all ISDAs and CSAs contain some variation in terms and conditions and this has recently prompted ISDA to propose a standard CSA agreement (ISDA, 2011). There are two main versions of the ISDA master agreements, known by their publication dates in 1992 and 2002, respectively, and these will be discussed in more detail in Chapter 3. The settlement conditions embodied in these documents do have an impact on recovery rates.

---

[6]A *reverse repo* is the opposite transaction where one counterparty buys bonds and agrees to sell them again at a fixed price at an agreed date in the future (see Figure 2.3). Hence each repo transaction is paired with a reverse repo for the counterparty.

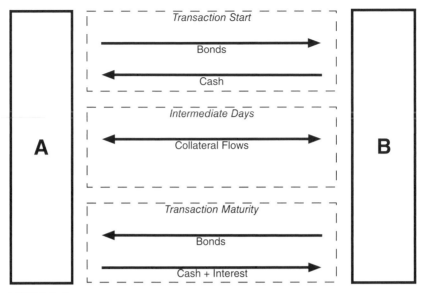

**FIGURE 2.3**    The repo/reverse repo transaction flows.

Derivatives can have both positive and negative mark-to-market values. Hence, most CSA agreements provide support for both counterparties to post collateral, if required, during the lifetime of the transaction or portfolio of transactions if a netting agreement is in place. There are a number of key parameters associated with CSA agreements that control the amount and timing of collateral postings and these are described in Table 2.1. CSA agreements significantly reduce counterparty credit risk but do not eliminate it entirely. The risk is reduced, however, to the discrepancy between the value of the derivatives and the value of the collateral at the time default is recognised. In practice there will be a period between the date on which the last collateral is received and the date when the position is closed, even if the call frequency is daily. Both derivative and collateral value could vary in this period. Care must also be taken if there is a relationship between the counterparty and the collateral that is posted. If there is an adverse relationship this could lead to significant wrong-way risk in which the counterparty defaults and the value of the collateral declines sharply. One significant feature of most CSA agreements is that the collateral can be *rehypothecated* or reused by passing on to other parties in support of other CSA agreements.[7]

In some transaction types such as those linked to commercial real estate or project finance the derivatives form part of a financing package that includes loans and other facilities. Frequently these transactions are secured on an asset such as, for example, a building or railway rolling stock in the case of train leasing transactions. In these cases, should the counterparty default then the derivative originator will be able to claim the assets used to secure the financing. Security thus acts in a similar fashion to financial collateral under a CSA, although it is not rehypothecable in most cases. Unlike a CSA, however, no further margin call can be made so a risk of loss will occur if the value of the financing package exceeds that of the security.

---

[7]This is significant in the context of funding valuation adjustment which will be discussed in Chapter 9.

**TABLE 2.1**   Key CSA parameters.

| | |
|---|---|
| **Base Currency** | The base currency is the reference currency in which the portfolio value and exposure are calculated. It is also the currency in which the parameters of the CSA are defined. |
| **Eligible Currency** | Eligible currencies are the set of currencies in which cash collateral can be posted. |
| **Threshold** | Each counterparty has a threshold of exposure below which no collateral is posted. Typically for CSAs between banks, these are set at zero and collateral is always posted in support of derivative transactions and the portfolio is fully collateralised. The thresholds can be non-zero and this reduces the need to exchange collateral when exposure is low, giving a lower operational overhead. If the threshold is finite for one counterparty and infinite for the other then the arrangement is known as a *one-way CSA*. In this case only one counterparty is ever required to post collateral. Thresholds can be rating-dependent and reduce as credit ratings decline and this is one type of *downgrade trigger*. |
| **Minimum Transfer Amount** | The minimum transfer amount is the minimum amount of collateral than can be exchanged between two parties. This value is usually non-zero and is set to reduce the operational overhead associated with moving collateral so that minor movements in the mark-to-market value do not result in the need to post or return small amounts of collateral. |
| **Independent Amount** | An independent amount is collateral that must be posted irrespective of the mark-to-market of the portfolio of transactions. An independent amount can also be triggered by a downgrade. |
| **Eligible Credit Support** | Eligible credit support is the list of acceptable types of collateral. This normally includes cash in an eligible currency and may include other types of financial security like government bonds. The CSA will also specify a valuation percentage or haircut amount to apply to the credit support instrument. The haircuts will normally vary with type of collateral, its maturity and be relative to the collateral market price. |
| **Rounding** | The rounding is simply the amount that the collateral transfer is rounded to; again this is to facilitate operational convenience. |
| **Call Frequency** | The call frequency specifies how frequently a margin call can be made for collateral. For CSAs between banks this is commonly daily but for other institutions it can be less frequent to reduce the operational burden. Of course, a lower call frequency means larger credit exposure because of mismatches between the mark-to-market and the collateral value. |
| **Other Downgrade Triggers** | CSAs and ISDAs can contain other collateral provisions that are typically triggered by a downgrade to the credit rating of one of the counterparties below a specified level. The downgrade trigger provisions vary but normally specify that the position be over-collateralised in some way; for example, the posted collateral may have to be 1.25 times the portfolio mark-to-market. |
| **Replacement Rights** | The ability for a counterparty to change the collateral composition at will. |

The security itself may also vary in value, so commercial real estate may lose value in an economic recession. For example, consider a shopping mall provided as security against a loan. If the shopping mall performs well then all of the shops will be rented and the shopping mall owner will have no difficulties paying off the loan. If, however, the shopping mall performs badly with many unrented shops and worse than expected income the shopping mall owner may face difficulty making payment on the loan. If the shopping mall owner defaults then the bank will receive an asset which is already under performing.

The asset may secure more than one set of financing transactions or the package itself may be syndicated among a number of banks leading to additional complexity.

### 2.4.3 Central Clearing and Margin

*Central Counterparties* or *CCPs* have been seen by regulators as a means of reducing counterparty credit risk in the aftermath of the 2008 credit crisis.[8] In reality CCPs have been a feature of the market for many years in the guise of clearing houses associated with exchanges. The *London Clearing House*,[9] for example, was formed in 1888 to clear commodities contracts and started clearing financial futures for *London International Financial Futures Exchange* (LIFFE) in 1982. CCPs now provide clearing for standardised derivative contracts such as interest rate swaps and credit default swaps and in 2009 the G20 leaders mandated that all standardised OTC derivative contracts be cleared by the end of 2012 (Financial Stability Board, 2010). While regulators and world leaders have seen CCPs as critical to reducing system market risks (G20, 2009), others have suggested that CCPs themselves lead to systemic risks (Duffie and Zhu, 2011; Kenyon and Green, 2013c).

Central clearing operates in much the same way as a bilateral CSA contract in that collateral must be supplied to support the movements in the mark-to-market of the portfolio of derivatives. This collateral is known as *variation margin* in the context of clearing. The frequency of calls for variation margin is typically daily. The rules of individual CCPs vary but considering LCH.Clearnet SwapClear as an example, three additional elements of margining are present: *initial margin*, *liquidity multipliers* and *default fund*. The initial margin is similar to initial margin in CSA agreements in that it must be supplied independently of the current mark-to-market of the counterparties' derivative portfolio. However, LCH.Clearnet Swapclear specifies the initial margin as a dynamic quantity with its *PAIRS* methodology (LCH, 2012e) using a historical Value-at-Risk measurement. Significant intraday market moves can trigger margin calls for additional initial margin (LCH, 2012b). For positions with large net risk, LCH.Clearnet SwapClear specifies a series of liquidity multipliers to increase the margin position to reflect the limits of market liquidity should the position be required to be closed out completely (LCH, 2010b). Finally a default fund has been created from contributions from all large clearing members to allow the clearing house to survive one or more defaults by clearing members (LCH, 2012a).

---

[8]Note that it is important to distinguish CCPs from exchanges. An exchange is a venue for the trading of commoditised derivative contracts that are in general liquid. Exchange-traded derivatives are supported by variation and initial margin and make use of clearing houses. A CCP is a venue for clearing standard derivatives that would otherwise have been traded bilaterally. They are not multiparty trading venues in the same sense as an exchange.

[9]Now called *LCH.Clearnet* following the merger of the London Clearing House with the French Clearnet in 2003 (LCH, 2012c).

Only standardised OTC derivative contracts can be cleared through CCPs. In response to a desire that all transactions between significant financial institutions be margined, the *Basel Committee on Banking Supervision* has issued a consultation document that will enforce similar rules on OTC derivatives traded between financial institutions (BCBS, 2012h). Most of these contracts are currently traded under CSA agreements and hence are already subject to collateral support. However, the proposal will add the requirement for both counterparties to post initial margin, although there will be no additional posting requirements such as for CCP default funds.

### 2.4.4  Capital

Collateral can be viewed as a means of ensuring that the defaulter pays in the event of a default. Capital, in contrast, is a way of holding sufficient reserves to enable the non-defaulting entity to manage the loss arising from the default. Capital therefore is a mechanism in which the non-defaulting party 'pays' for the default. *Regulatory capital* is the amount of capital that a financial institution must hold in order to satisfy its regulator. The *Basel Accords* are a series of regulatory frameworks that provide a methodology for calculating the amount of capital required to support banking businesses that have been proposed by the international body the *Basel Committee on Banking Supervision* within the *Bank for International Settlements* (BCBS, 2012a). There have been four major developments of the regulatory capital framework, known as Basel I introduced in 1988, Basel II introduced in 2006, Basel II.5 introduced in the immediate aftermath of the 2008 financial crisis and Basel III introduced in 2010 for implementation on 1 January 2013 (BCBS, 2012d). Implementation of the Basel framework is at varying stages globally with the European Union being one of the most advanced through *Capital Requirements Directive 4* or *CRDIV*. The impact of capital on pricing derivatives is discussed in Chapter 12.

### 2.4.5  Break Clauses

Many OTC derivative contracts contain one or more *break clauses* that provide for the early termination of a derivative contract. There are two types of break clause, *mandatory* and *optional*. A mandatory break clause terminates the trade prior to the natural maturity date, with the remaining value of the derivative settled by a cash payment. So, for example, a twenty-year interest rate swap with a mandatory break clause after five years will terminate five years after the start of the transaction with the mark-to-market value of the remaining fifteen years of the transaction paid in cash on the appropriate settlement date immediately after the mandatory break date. Ignoring credit risk, funding costs and capital considerations, the value of the two trades with and without the break clause will be the same. However, the expected exposure of the trade with a mandatory break is terminated after five years and hence the credit risk and CVA are much lower. In practice, trades with mandatory break clauses reduce the initial cost of the derivative for the counterparty and the trades are often restructured just prior to the break date. Figure 2.4 illustrates a swap with a break clause half way through the underlying term.

Optional break clauses give the option to one or both counterparties to terminate the derivative on one or more dates prior to the natural maturity of the trade. Settlement then proceeds in the same way as a mandatory break clause, with a cash settlement of the mark-to-market of the remaining trade. In practice, optional break clauses have been rarely, if

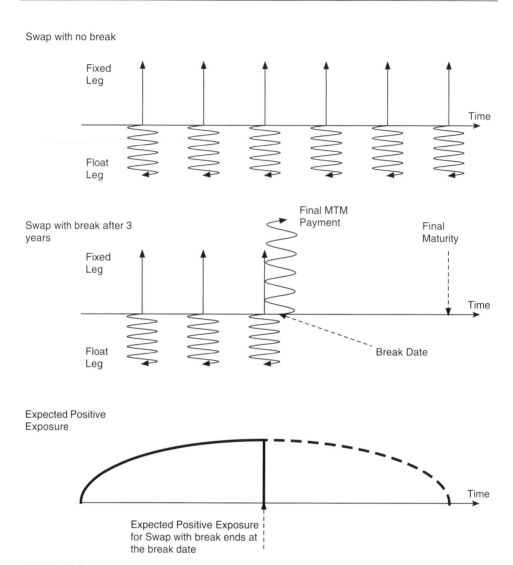

**FIGURE 2.4** A swap with and without a break clause and the associated expected positive exposure profile. For the swap with the break clause, the CVA is lower.

ever, exercised irrespective of any considerations of optimal exercise. The argument has been that exercising the break clause would ruin the relationship with the client. Internally within banks the right to exercise the credit break has often sat with client relationship management who have had few incentives to use the breaks.[10] However, many derivative dealers are now arguing that optional break clauses should now be exercised and actively used as a credit mitigant (Cameron, 2012).

---

[10]Optional breaks are often colloquially referred to as *mutual breaks* because of the bilateral nature of the option to break in most cases.

## 2.4.6 Buying Protection

The idea of buying "insurance" or "protection" against counterparty default is quite an old one. *Bond insurance* or *financial guaranty insurance* was introduced by *American Municipal Bond Assurance Corp* or *AMBAC* in 1971 (Milwaukee Sentinal, 1971). Municipal bond insurance is a type of insurance in which the bond insurer guarantees the interest and principal payments on a municipal bond. A number of bond insurance companies were created and they became known as *monolines* as they did not have other lines of insurance business. Bond insurance was a generally successful business but after the development of structured credit derivative products many bond insurers entered the credit derivatives market leading to significant losses. Ambac filed for protection from creditors under chapter 11 on 8 November 2010 (Ambac, 2010).

Credit default swaps offer the main means by which credit protection can be bought and sold, and as such are the primary mechanism for CVA trading desks to hedge out credit risks. Physically settled single name CDS contracts pay out the notional amount in exchange for a defaulted bond, although cash settled variants that pay

$$(1 - Recovery) \times Notional$$

on default are also available. Hence, single name CDS provide a means of directly protecting a notional amount against the default of a specific counterparty. There are some complications in that the CDS is triggered by a number of specific default conditions and that some, like voluntary restructuring, are typically excluded. This means that the CDS does not always pay out when losses are taken. The Greek sovereign restructuring provides an example of this where the initial voluntary debt exchange did not trigger the sovereign CDS, only the later use of a 'collective action clause' triggered the CDS as it involved an element of coercion (Oakley, 2012).

CDS trade only a limited number of reference names and so in many cases buying single name CDS to hedge CVA is not possible. CDS indices such as the *iTraxx* and *CDSIndex Company* series can provide an alternative. These are liquidly traded indices which include a basket of underlying CDS contracts. They respond to changes in underlying perceptions of creditworthiness in the underlying basket of names and hence can be used to hedge general sensitivity to CDS spreads. Usually the members of a CDS index are also traded through the single name CDS market. CDS and CDS indices are discussed in Chapter 4 and active management of CVA in Chapter 22.

## CHAPTER 3

# CVA and DVA: Credit and Debit Valuation Adjustment Models

*The only certainty is that nothing is certain.*

—Pliny the Elder
*Natural Philosopher (AD 23–79)*

## 3.1 INTRODUCTION

Recall the definition of CVA, given in equation (2.6). Re-arranging this formula gives

$$V(\text{credit risky}) = V(\text{default free}) - \text{CVA} \tag{3.1}$$

$$\hat{V} = V + U, \tag{3.2}$$

where in the second line I have introduced the notation,

$V$ = Unadjusted value, i.e. Black-Scholes-Merton

$\hat{V}$ = Economic value including CVA (and later XVA)

$U$ = Valuation adjustments, i.e. CVA (and later XVA).

This formula highlights that CVA is the adjustment to the underlying price of the derivative. In reality the full value of the derivative should include the impact of credit risk but CVA is treated separately for a number of reasons:

- CVA is normally calculated at a counterparty level and not at trade level. This follows from the existence of netting rules which mean that the value of a portfolio is typically netted together when calculating its value in the event of a default. If each individual trade were treated on an individual basis and the netting rules ignored then the CVA would be overestimated if a unilateral model is used (it could be over or underestimated in the case of a bilateral model but it will certainly be incorrect). Trade level CVA is possible but this requires a special technique and this is discussed in section 3.6.

- CVA is usually managed separately from the underlying derivative. CVA trade management is a very different activity from risk management of the underlying derivatives and requires different skills and experience. In addition derivative trading activities are normally aligned by asset class whereas CVA is counterparty aligned and crosses all asset classes.

- CVA is often accounted for separately in published accounts. This leads to a separation of internal financial reporting activity as well as book management.

As noted earlier, there are essentially two types of models for CVA: unilateral models that only consider the credit risk of the counterparty and bilateral models that consider the credit risk of both counterparty and self. Equation (3.1) is the definition of CVA in both cases. Funding costs add further complexity but these will be introduced later in Chapter 9. In the case of bilateral models it is useful to write

$$U = \text{CVA} + \text{DVA} \tag{3.3}$$

where CVA is a cost and DVA is a benefit. Bilateral CVA models naturally provide two terms, a term that reduces accounting value due to counterparty risk and a term that increases accounting value due to risk of own default, with the first term an integral over the expected positive exposure and the second an integral over the expected negative exposure, weighted by default probabilities. These two terms are frequently called CVA and DVA respectively, which can lead to confusion over the definition of CVA. Furthermore in certain institutions DVA is seen as the difference between a unilateral CVA model and a bilateral one, that is as the benefit from own credit risk. As we have already noted DVA is also used to refer to the accounting benefit from using the fair value accounting option on own issued debt. To avoid confusion on this last point DVA from issued debt will be called *DVA2* in line with the convention adopted by John Hull and Alan White (2012b).

### 3.1.1   Close-out and CVA

When a default occurs the non-defaulting party must lodge a claim of money owed with the bankruptcy court as part of bankruptcy proceedings. If the derivative portfolio has been traded under an ISDA agreement then the value of the claim is governed by the legal language enshrined in the version of the ISDA master agreement that has been signed, either 1992 (ISDA, 1992) or 2002 (ISDA, 2002), or the more recent ISDA close-out protocol (ISDA, 2009c). These different ISDA documents use different language to describe what can be taken into consideration when calculating the close-out value and the mechanics by which the calculation is done. Several leading quantitative analysts have highlighted issues with potential ambiguity of language in these documents leading to calls for further clarification from ISDA (Brigo and Morini, 2011; Carver, 2011).

The precise nature of the close-out value has a significant impact on the exposure at default and hence on the CVA itself. The following possible variations of close-out have been identified:

- **Risk-free close out**. The close-out value is the portfolio value assuming no counterparty credit risk at all. This is the simplest case as it corresponds to the sum of the underlying derivative values netted according to the netting agreements in place between the two parties. One could argue this case is the one likely to be implemented in practice, given the simplicity.
- **Risky close out**. The close-out value of the portfolio is its value immediately prior to default including all valuation adjustments. The valuation adjustments made could include the CVA, DVA and FVA, immediately prior to default, depending on which type of adjustments and models are used by the non-defaulting party. Risky close-out is chosen as an example by Burgard and Kjaer (2011b); Burgard and Kjaer (2011a); Burgard and Kjaer (2013) in their papers on FVA, while Wei (2011) has examined the impact of risky-close out on a standard interest rate swap. If the total valuation adjustment was negative on the value of the portfolio of trades with the defaulted counterparty, risky close-out would lower the claim value and the ultimate recovery amount. Hence it is not clear whether the non-defaulting party would seek to include a negative adjustment on a rational basis. Nevertheless, anecdotal evidence suggests that dealers are keen on using a risky close-out assumption.
- **Replacement cost: DVA-only**. If a bilateral CVA model is used the one possible close-out would ignore the CVA prior to default but include the DVA term. This would be done on the basis that any replacement trade would naturally include the non-defaulting party's DVA as the counterparty replacing the transaction would inevitably charge for their CVA which would always equal this DVA. Brigo and Morini (2011) and Gregory and German (2012) examine the impact of this close-out condition. Gregory and German highlight that this potentially removes some of the difficulties surrounding the use of DVA at the expense of additional complexity in the CVA calculation, while Brigo and Morini point to the lower overall recovery if replacement cost is used. The actual wording of the 2009 ISDA close-out protocol is "quotations (either firm or indicative) for replacement transactions supplied by one or more third parties that may take into account the creditworthiness of the Determining Party at the time of the quotation" (ISDA, 2009c). This suggests that the correct procedure would be to include DVA. Given that DVA would increase the book value of the trade this would also be entirely rational as it would increase the claim value and hence the potential recovery value, In practice whether this would be successful is not clear. It is also worth noting that any actual replacement trade used by the non-defaulting party to close out the market risk position would be transacted with interbank counterparties under a CSA. If the original trade was unsecured then the CVA and DVA of this actual replacement trade would be much smaller than that of the original trade and the close-out provision would not necessarily represent the actual replacement cost of the original trade.
- **Replacement cost: Funding costs**. The ISDA close-out protocol also includes the statement that "the Determining Party may include costs of funding, to the extent costs of funding are not and would not be a component of the other information being utilised" (ISDA, 2009c). Hence another possible adjustment would be to include funding costs, possibly alongside DVA, depending on the type of model used.

For the purposes of this chapter, I will consider only risk-free close-out as the other options add considerably to the complexity of the CVA (and FVA) calculation. However, I will return to the topic of close-out when considering models of FVA in Chapter 9.

## 3.2   UNILATERAL CVA MODEL

In this section I introduce the unilateral CVA model that assumes only the counterparty can default. Two different approaches are taken to derive the CVA, an expectation-led approach and a replication-based approach. In the context of pure CVA it could be argued that the expectation approach is simpler; however, I will use replication repeatedly throughout the book and so it is useful to also present this method of derivation.

### 3.2.1   Unilateral CVA by Expectation

Consider a portfolio of trades between a bank B and a counterparty C traded on an unsecured basis. The portfolio of trades generates a series of cash flows, $C(t, T)$, between time $t$ and the maturity time $T$ in the absence of a default. The cash flows described by $C(t, T)$ may be contingent in the sense that they may depend on option exercises but are not dependent on the default of the counterparty in any way. I assume that only the counterparty can default and that this occurs at time $\tau$. Under these conditions the fair value of the portfolio is given by

$$\hat{V}_t = V(t < \tau) + V_{Recovery}(t \geq \tau) \tag{3.4}$$

The value of the cash flows prior to the default time is given by

$$V(t < \tau) = \mathbb{E}[C(t, \tau)\mathbb{1}_{\tau < T} + C(t, T)\mathbb{1}_{\tau \geq T}|\mathcal{F}_t], \tag{3.5}$$

where $\mathbb{1}_{condition}$ is an indicator function for *condition* and $\mathcal{F}_t$ is the filtration up to time $t$. The value of the cash flow prior to default is split into two parts, conditioned on whether or not default occurs prior to the maturity $T$. The recovery value at the time of default is given by

$$V_{Recovery}(\tau) = R(V_\tau)^+ + (V_\tau)^-, \tag{3.6}$$

where $(V_\tau)^+$ and $(V_\tau)^-$ are the positive and negative parts of the portfolio value respectively and $R$ is the recovery rate or fraction. Note that the portfolio value at close-out, $V_\tau$, is the risk-free close-out discussed above. Hence, using equations (3.5), (3.4) and (3.6), we obtain an expression for the portfolio value at time $t$ when the counterparty is subject to default risk,

$$\hat{V}_t = \mathbb{E}[C(t, \tau)\mathbb{1}_{\tau < T} + C(t, T)\mathbb{1}_{\tau \geq T} + \mathbb{E}[\{R(V_\tau)^+ + (V_\tau)^-\mathbb{1}_{\tau < T}\}|\mathcal{F}_t]|\mathcal{F}_t]. \tag{3.7}$$

Using the linearity of expectations and the tower property this reduces to

$$\hat{V}_t = \mathbb{E}[C(t, \tau)\mathbb{1}_{\tau < T}|\mathcal{F}_t] + \mathbb{E}[C(t, T)\mathbb{1}_{\tau \geq T}|\mathcal{F}_t] + \mathbb{E}[\{R(V_\tau)^+ + (V_\tau)^-\mathbb{1}_{\tau < T}\}|\mathcal{F}_t]. \tag{3.8}$$

This expression can be simplified by using the fact that $V_t = (V_t)^+ + (V_t)^-$, giving

$$\hat{V}_t = \mathbb{E}[C(t, \tau)\mathbb{1}_{\tau < T}|\mathcal{F}_t] + \mathbb{E}[C(t, T)\mathbb{1}_{\tau \geq T}|\mathcal{F}_t] - \mathbb{E}[(1 - R)(V_\tau)^+\mathbb{1}_{\tau < T}|\mathcal{F}_t] \tag{3.9}$$
$$+ \mathbb{E}[\hat{\Pi}_\tau\mathbb{1}_{\tau < T}|\mathcal{F}_t].$$

Using the fact that $V_t = \mathbb{E}[C(t,T)|\mathcal{F}_t]$, the tower property of expectations and with some rearrangement we obtain

$$\hat{V}_t = \mathbb{E}[C(t,T)|\mathcal{F}_t] - \mathbb{E}[(1-R)(V_\tau)^+ \mathbb{1}_{\tau<T}|\mathcal{F}_t]. \tag{3.10}$$

Hence by the definition in equation (3.1), the unilateral CVA is given by

$$\text{CVA}(t) = \mathbb{E}[(1-R)(V_\tau)^+|\mathcal{F}_t]. \tag{3.11}$$

Up to this point I have made no assumptions about the behaviour of the underlying state variables. To proceed further and obtain the standard CVA formula we need to assume that the credit risk is independent of any market risk factors.[1] Once this is done the expectation in equation (3.11) can be represented as an integral over time,

$$\text{CVA}(t) = \int_{s=t}^{T} \lambda_C(s)e^{-\int_{u=0}^{s}\lambda_C(u)du}\mathbb{E}\left[e^{-\int_{u=0}^{s}r(u)du}(1-R)(V_s)^+|\mathcal{G}_t\right]ds, \tag{3.12}$$

where $\lambda_C(s)$ is the counterparty hazard rate, $r$ is the short rate, $\mathcal{G}_t$ is the filtration to time $t$ containing only market state variable information and the inner expectation is made in the risk-neutral measure with the money market account as numeraire. Introducing a time partition $t = t_0 < t_i < \ldots < t_n = T$ allows the integral to be approximated using a summation,

$$\text{CVA}(t) = (1-R)\sum_{i=0}^{n-1}[\Phi(\tau > t_i) - \Phi(\tau > t_{i+1})]\mathbb{E}\left[\exp^{-\int_{u=0}^{t_i}r(u)du}(V_{t_i})^+|\mathcal{G}_t\right], \tag{3.13}$$

where $\Phi(\tau > t)$ is the survival probability up to time $t$ of the counterparty and I have assumed that the recovery rate is deterministic. Equation (3.13) is the standard expression for CVA and is very similar to the form used by the Basel Committee in Basel III (2011).[2] An example unilateral CVA calculation can be found in Table 3.1.

### 3.2.2 Unilateral CVA by Replication

The same CVA formula can also be derived using replication in the same way as the Black-Scholes model. To obtain an expression for unilateral CVA, the risk of counterparty default must be considered alongside the Brownian motion driving the stock price. A summary of the notation used in this section and in the equivalent bilateral CVA replication model can be found in Table 3.2.

---

[1]Technically this allows the filtration $\mathcal{F}_t$ to be factored into two components $\mathcal{H}_t$ associated with default risk and $\mathcal{G}_t$ corresponding to market state variables so that $\mathcal{F}_t = \mathcal{H}_t \vee \mathcal{G}_t$. This assumption is standard in CVA approaches but will be relaxed in Chapter 7.
[2]The integral in equation (3.12) could be approximated numerically in other ways such as via the trapezium rule.

**TABLE 3.1**   An example unilateral CVA calculation for a five-year GBP interest rate swap. The counterparty CDS spread is set at 300 basis points for all maturities and the counterparty recovery is 40%.

| Tenor (years) | Expected Positive Exposure | Counterparty Survival Probability | Counterparty Interval Default Probability | Unilateral CVA Contribution |
|---|---|---|---|---|
| 0 | 0 | 100.000% | | |
| 0.5 | 701,997 | 97.530% | 2.470% | 10,403.60 |
| 1.0 | 877,137 | 95.046% | 2.484% | 13,072.85 |
| 1.5 | 914,128 | 92.713% | 2.333% | 12,795.96 |
| 2.0 | 880,804 | 90.362% | 2.351% | 12,424.62 |
| 2.5 | 816,664 | 88.108% | 2.254% | 11,044.56 |
| 3.0 | 739,458 | 85.910% | 2.198% | 9,751.97 |
| 3.5 | 603,905 | 83.768% | 2.142% | 7,761.39 |
| 4.0 | 473,606 | 81.657% | 2.111% | 5,998.69 |
| 4.5 | 290,466 | 79.633% | 2.024% | 3,527.42 |
| 5.0 | 93,556 | 77.628% | 2.005% | 1,125.48 |
| 5.5 | 0 | 75.701% | 1.927% | 0 |
| | | | **Total** | 87,906.54 |

Consider a derivative portfolio between a bank B and a counterparty C, with an economic value $\hat{V}$ including CVA adjustment where the same portfolio has value $V$ in the absence of counterparty credit risk. Hence

$$\hat{V} = V + U, \tag{3.14}$$

where $U$ is the valuation adjustment.

The stock price is assumed to follow geometric Brownian motion,

$$dS = \mu_S S dt + \sigma_S S dW. \tag{3.15}$$

The risk-free bonds obey the expected relation,

$$dP = rPdt, \tag{3.16}$$

while the zero-coupon zero-recovery counterparty bonds have the dynamics,

$$dP_C = r_C P_C dt - P_C dJ_C. \tag{3.17}$$

Given these dynamics, Itô's lemma can be applied to the economic value $\hat{V}$,

$$d\hat{V} = \frac{\partial \hat{V}}{\partial t} dt + \frac{1}{2}\sigma_S^2 S^2 \frac{\partial^2 \hat{V}}{\partial S^2} dt + \frac{\partial \hat{V}}{\partial S} dS + \Delta \hat{V}_C dJ_C. \tag{3.18}$$

**TABLE 3.2** Notation used in unilateral and bilateral CVA replication models. The same notation, with some additions, will also be used in the FVA model described in Chapter 9 and also in the KVA model discussed in Chapter 13.

| Parameter | Description |
|---|---|
| $\hat{V}(t,S)$ | The value of the derivative or derivative portfolio (including valuation adjustments) |
| $V$ | The risk-free value of the derivative or derivative portfolio (excluding valuation adjustments) |
| $U$ | The valuation adjustment |
| $X$ | Collateral |
| $\Pi$ | Replicating portfolio |
| $S$ | Underlying stock |
| $P_C$ | Counterparty bond (zero recovery) |
| $P_B$ | Bank bond (zero recovery) |
| $P$ | Credit risk-free bond with yield $r$ |
| $\beta_S$ | Cash account associated with stock |
| $\beta_C$ | Cash account associated with counterparty bond |
| $\beta_X$ | Cash account associated with collateral |
| $\beta_B$ | Cash account associated with bank bond |
| $r$ | risk-free rate |
| $r_C$ | Yield on counterparty bond |
| $r_X$ | Yield on collateral position |
| $M_B$ | Close-out value on bank default |
| $M_C$ | Close-out value on counterparty bonds |
| $\alpha_C$ | Holding of counterparty bonds |
| $\alpha$ | Holding of credit risk-free bonds |
| $\alpha_B$ | Holding of bank bonds |
| $\delta$ | Stock position |
| $\gamma_S$ | Stock dividend yield |
| $q_S$ | Stock repo rate |
| $q_C$ | Counterparty bond repo rate |
| $q_B$ | Bank bond repo rate |
| $J_C$ | Default indicator for counterparty |
| $J_B$ | Default indicator for bank |
| $\lambda_C$ | Effective financing rate of counterparty bond $\lambda_C = r_C - q_C$ |
| $\lambda_B$ | Instantaneous probability of bank default (hazard rate) |
| $s_F$ | Funding spread in the case where there is one issuer bond, $s_F = r_F - r$ |
| $s_X$ | Spread on collateral, $s_X = r_X - r$ |
| $\Delta\hat{V}_C$ | Change in the value of the derivative on counterparty default |
| $\Delta\hat{V}_B$ | Change in the value of the derivative on bank default |

On the default of the counterparty the economic value of the portfolio is given by the close-out condition,

$$\hat{V}(t,S,1) = g_C(M_C,X).$$  (3.19)

Under standard close-out conditions, $g_C$ is given by,

$$g_C = R_C(V - X)^+ + (V - X)^- + X.$$  (3.20)

The funding equation will take on a great deal of significance later when discussing FVA and KVA. Here, however, it is trivial and shows that the difference between the economic value of the portfolio and the collateral can be funded at the risk-free rate,

$$\hat{V} - X + \alpha P = 0. \tag{3.21}$$

The next task it to build a replicating portfolio, $\Pi$, consisting of a position in stock, counterparty bond and risk-free bond. There are cash accounts associated with the stock, collateral and counterparty bond and the change in each cash account, prior to rebalancing, is given by the following expressions,

$$d\bar{\beta}_S = \delta(\gamma_S - q_S)S dt \tag{3.22}$$
$$d\bar{\beta}_X = -r_X X dt \tag{3.23}$$
$$d\bar{\beta}_C = -\alpha_C q_C P_C dt. \tag{3.24}$$

Hence the change in the replicating portfolio is given by

$$d\Pi = \delta dS + \delta(\gamma_S - q_S)S dt + \alpha dP + \alpha_C dP_C + \alpha_C q_C P_C dt - r_X X dt. \tag{3.25}$$

Adding the replicating portfolio to the derivative gives,

$$
\begin{aligned}
d\hat{V} + d\Pi = {} & \left[ \frac{\partial \hat{V}}{\partial t} + \frac{1}{2}\sigma^2 S^2 \frac{\partial^2 \hat{V}}{\partial S^2} + \delta(\gamma - q)S + \alpha_C(r_C - q_C)P_C - r_X X + \alpha r P \right] dt \\
& + \left[ \delta + \frac{\partial \hat{V}}{\partial S} \right] dS \\
& + \left[ \Delta \hat{V}_C + \alpha_C P_C \right] dJ_C.
\end{aligned}
\tag{3.26}
$$

Assuming replication of the derivative by the hedging portfolio,

$$d\hat{V} + d\Pi = 0 \tag{3.27}$$

Eliminating the sources of risk from equation (3.26) requires that

$$\delta = -\frac{\partial \hat{V}}{\partial S} \tag{3.28}$$
$$\alpha_C P_C = g_C - \hat{V}. \tag{3.29}$$

Hence the first term in equation (3.26) gives a PDE for $\hat{V}$:

$$\frac{\partial \hat{V}}{\partial t} + \frac{1}{2}\sigma^2 S^2 \frac{\partial^2 \hat{V}}{\partial S^2} - \frac{\partial \hat{V}}{\partial S}(\gamma_S - q_S) + \alpha r P + (r_C - q_C)(g_C - \hat{V}) - r_X X = 0 \tag{3.30}$$

$$\hat{V}(T, S) = H(S).$$

The operator $\mathcal{A}_t$ is now defined to simplify the presentation as

$$\mathcal{A}_t := \frac{1}{2}\sigma^2 S^2 \frac{\partial^2}{\partial S^2} - (\gamma - q)S \frac{\partial}{\partial S}. \tag{3.31}$$

The hazard rate in the risk-neutral measure is $\lambda_C$ and I make the assumption that this is given by

$$\lambda_C = r_C - q_C, \tag{3.32}$$

that is the difference between the bond yield and repo rate. Using equations (3.21) and (3.31) allows the PDE to be written as

$$\frac{\partial \hat{V}}{\partial t} + \mathcal{A}_t \hat{V} - r\hat{V} + \lambda_C(g_C - \hat{V}) - s_X X = 0. \tag{3.33}$$

Using equation (3.14) in the PDE and noting that $V$ satisfies the Black-Scholes-Merton PDE, that is

$$\frac{\partial V}{\partial t} + \mathcal{A}_t V - rV = 0, \tag{3.34}$$

gives a PDE for the valuation adjustment $U$,

$$\frac{\partial U}{\partial t} + \mathcal{A}_t U - (r + \lambda_C)U = -\lambda_C(g_C - V) + s_X X \tag{3.35}$$

$$U(T, S) = 0.$$

Applying the Feynman-Kac theorem gives an integral expression for $U$,

$$U = \text{CVA} + \text{COLVA}, \tag{3.36}$$

where

$$\text{CVA}(t) = -\int_t^T \lambda_C(u)e^{-\int_t^s (r(u)+\lambda_C(u))du} \mathbb{E}\left[V(s) - g_C(V(s), X(s))\right] ds \tag{3.37}$$

$$\text{COLVA}(t) = -\int_t^T e^{-\int_t^s r(u)+\lambda_C(u)du} \mathbb{E}\left[s_X(s)X(s)\right] ds. \tag{3.38}$$

Using the standard close-out condition as described by equation (3.20) leads to the standard expression for CVA, and essentially identical with equation (3.12),

$$\text{CVA}(t) = -(1 - R)\int_t^T \lambda_C(u)e^{-\int_t^s (r(u)+\lambda_C(u))du} \mathbb{E}\left[(V(s) - X(s))^+\right] ds \tag{3.39}$$

$$\text{COLVA}(t) = -\int_t^T e^{-\int_t^s r(u)+\lambda_C(u)du} \mathbb{E}\left[s_X(s)X(s)\right] ds. \tag{3.40}$$

Of course a second term is present, COLVA, that represents any difference from the risk-free rate in the return paid/earned on posted collateral. This term will reappear later in discussion of funding costs but if $s_X = 0$ or $X = 0$ then COLVA $= 0$.

## 3.3  BILATERAL CVA MODEL: CVA AND DVA

### 3.3.1  Bilateral CVA by Expectation

If we now allow that the bank, B, can also default as well as the counterparty, C, we will obtain a bilateral CVA model containing two terms, a CVA cost term relating to the counterparty and a DVA benefit term relating to the bank. The value of the portfolio at time $t$ in the presence of credit risk is represented by

$$
\begin{aligned}
\hat{V}_t &= \mathbb{E}[C(t, \min(\tau_B, \tau_C)) \mathbb{1}_{\min(\tau_B, \tau_C) < T}] + \mathbb{E}[C(t, T) \mathbb{1}_{\min(\tau_B, \tau_C) > T}] \\
&\quad + \mathbb{E}[\{R_C(V_{\min(\tau_B, \tau_C)})^+ + (V_{\min(\tau_B, \tau_C)})^-\} \mathbb{1}_{\tau_C < \tau_B < T}] \\
&\quad + \mathbb{E}[\{R_B(V_{\min(\tau_B, \tau_C)})^- + V_{\min(\tau_B, \tau_C)})^+\} \mathbb{1}_{\tau_B < \tau_C < T}]
\end{aligned}
\tag{3.41}
$$

where the filtration, $\mathcal{F}_t$, has been dropped for clarity. The first two terms represent the value of cash flows occurring before the time the first counterparty defaults $\min(\tau_B, \tau_C)$ or $T$ if both counterparties default after maturity. The second term represents the value of the remaining cash flows on the default of C, conditioned on this occurring before the default of B and the third term represents the value of the remaining cash flows on the default of B, conditioned on this occurring before the default of C. It should be immediately apparent that this is a first-to-default problem and hence involves conditional probability. The third term in equation (3.41) can be expanded out using the same approach adopted above to eliminate the negative part of the portfolio value,

$$
\begin{aligned}
\mathbb{E}[\{R_C(V_{\min(\tau_B, \tau_C)})^+ &+ (V_{\min(\tau_B, \tau_C)})^-\} \mathbb{1}_{\tau_C < \tau_B < T}] = \\
&\mathbb{E}[(R_C - 1)(V_{\min(\tau_B, \tau_C)})^+ \mathbb{1}_{\tau_C < \tau_B < T}] + \mathbb{E}[V_{\min(\tau_B, \tau_C)} \mathbb{1}_{\tau_C < \tau_B < T}].
\end{aligned}
\tag{3.42}
$$

Hence equation (3.41) becomes

$$
\begin{aligned}
\hat{V}_t &= \mathbb{E}[C(t, \min(\tau_B, \tau_C)) \mathbb{1}_{\min(\tau_B, \tau_C) < \tau}] + \mathbb{E}[C(t, T) \mathbb{1}_{\min(\tau_B, \tau_C) > T}] \tag{3.43} \\
&\quad + \mathbb{E}[(R_C - 1)(V_{\min(\tau_B, \tau_C)})^+ \mathbb{1}_{\tau_C < \tau_B < T}] \\
&\quad + \mathbb{E}[(R_B - 1)(V_{\min(\tau_B, \tau_C)})^- \mathbb{1}_{\tau_B < \tau_C < T}] \\
&\quad + \mathbb{E}[V_{\min(\tau_B, \tau_C)} \mathbb{1}_{\min(\tau_B, \tau_C) < T}] \\
&= \mathbb{E}[C(t, T)] - \mathbb{E}[(1 - R_C)(V_{\min(\tau_B, \tau_C)})^+ \mathbb{1}_{\tau_C < \tau_B < T}] \\
&\quad - \mathbb{E}[(1 - R_B)(V_{\min(\tau_B, \tau_C)})^- \mathbb{1}_{\tau_B < \tau_C < T}],
\end{aligned}
$$

where I have used the result that $\mathbb{1}_{\min(\tau_B,\tau_C)<T} = \mathbb{1}_{\tau_C<\tau_B<T} + \mathbb{1}_{\tau_B<\tau_C<T}$. Hence the bilateral CVA is given by

$$\text{BCVA}(t) = \mathbb{E}[(1 - R_C)(V_{\min(\tau_B,\tau_C)})^+ \mathbb{1}_{\tau_C<\tau_B<T}] + \mathbb{E}[(1 - R_B)(V_{\min(\tau_B,\tau_C)})^- \mathbb{1}_{\tau_B<\tau_C<T}].$$

(3.44)

The two terms in equation (3.44) are known as CVA and DVA respectively. It should be noted that the second term is always negative because the negative part of the portfolio is taken through the $()^-$ operator.[3] In terms of accounting impact the CVA term is a cost while the DVA term is a benefit. Note also that the above derivation implicitly assumes that simultaneous defaults cannot occur, which in practice is a fair assumption in the context of CVA.

Again making the assumption that market and credit state variables are independent of each other allows the two expectation terms to be represented in integral form,

$$\text{BCVA}(t) = \int_{s=t}^{T} \lambda_C(s) e^{-\int_{u=t}^{s}(\lambda_C(u)+\lambda_B(u))du} \mathbb{E}^r\left[ e^{-\int_{u=t}^{s} r(u)du}(1-R_C)(V_s)^+|\mathcal{G}_t \right] ds$$

$$+ \int_{s=t}^{T} \lambda_B(s) e^{-\int_{u=t}^{s}(\lambda_C(u)+\lambda_B(u))du} \mathbb{E}^r\left[ e^{-\int_{u=t}^{s} r(u)du}(1-R_B)(V_s)^-|\mathcal{G}_t \right] ds.$$

(3.45)

where $\lambda_C$ and $\lambda_B$ are the hazard rates for the counterparty and bank respectively. Partitioning the time interval $t = t_0 < t_i < \ldots < t_n = T$ gives

$$\text{BCVA}(t) = (1 - R_C) \sum_{i=0}^{n-1} [\Phi((t_i < \tau_C < t_{i+1}) \cap (\tau_B > t_{i+1}))]$$

(3.46)

$$\times \mathbb{E}^r\left[ \exp\left( -\int_{u=0}^{t_{i+1}} r(u)du \right)(V_{t_{i+1}})^+|\mathcal{G}_t \right]$$

$$+ (1 - R_B) \sum_{i=0}^{n-1} [\Phi((t_i < \tau_B < t_{i+1}) \cap (\tau_C > t_{i+1}))]$$

$$\times \mathbb{E}^r\left[ \exp\left( -\int_{u=0}^{t_{i+1}} r(u)du \right)(V_{t_{i+1}})^-|\mathcal{G}_t \right].$$

To proceed any further the dependence between the default times $\tau_B$ and $\tau_C$ needs to be specified. The standard assumption for bilateral CVA models is that these are independent and

---

[3]That is the negative operator does not take the absolute value of the negative part but retains its sign.

this allows equation (3.46) to be written as

$$
\begin{aligned}
\mathrm{BCVA}(t) = (1 - R_C) \sum_{i=0}^{n-1} [\Phi(\tau_C > t_{i+1}) - \Phi(\tau_C > t_i)]\Phi(\tau_B > t_{i+1}) \\
\times \mathbb{E}^r \left[ \exp\left(-\int_{u=0}^{t_{i+1}} r(u)du\right)(V_{t_{i+1}})^+ | \mathcal{G}_t \right] \\
+ (1 - R_B) \sum_{i=0}^{n-1} [\Phi(\tau_B > t_{i+1}) - \Phi(\tau_B > t_i)]\Phi(\tau_C > t_{i+1}) \\
\times \mathbb{E}^r \left[ \exp\left(-\int_{u=0}^{t_{i+1}} r(u)du\right)(V_{t_{i+1}})^- | \mathcal{G}_t \right],
\end{aligned}
\tag{3.47}
$$

where the first term is the CVA and the second term is the DVA. In the independent case the conditional probability has reduced to a multiplication yet both terms remain dependent on the survival probabilities of both bank and counterparty. The DVA is not simply the opposite of the unilateral CVA described above. The bilateral CVA can be positive or negative overall depending on the relative sign of the two terms, in turn driven by the credit spreads of bank and counterparty and the relative sizes of the expected positive and expected negative exposures. As the bank credit spread widens the DVA gives an accounting gain. An example bilateral CVA calculation is given in Table 3.3.

## 3.3.2  Bilateral CVA by Replication

As in section 3.2.2 it is possible to derive the same formula for bilateral CVA by replication. The derivation follows that given earlier with the addition of the risk that the bank B can now default. The notional for this case is also given in Table 3.2.

The dynamics are again given by equations (3.15) and (3.17), with the addition of dynamics for $P_B$, a zero-recovery, zero-coupon bond issued by the bank,

$$
dP_B = r_B P_B dt - P_B dJ_B.
\tag{3.48}
$$

Itô's lemma now gives the following for the economic value $\hat{V}$,

$$
d\hat{V} = \frac{\partial \hat{V}}{\partial t}dt + \frac{1}{2}\sigma_S^2 S^2 \frac{\partial^2 \hat{V}}{\partial S^2}dt + \frac{\partial \hat{V}}{\partial S}dS + \Delta\hat{V}_C dJ_C + \Delta\hat{V}_B dJ_B.
\tag{3.49}
$$

The close-out conditions on the default of the counterparty and the bank are given by

$$
\hat{V}(t, S, 1, 0) = g_C(M_C, X)
\tag{3.50}
$$

$$
\hat{V}(t, S, 0, 1) = g_B(M_B, X)
\tag{3.51}
$$

respectively, where under standard close-out conditions, $g_C$ and $g_B$ are given by,

$$
g_C = R_C(V - X)^+ + (V - X)^- + X
\tag{3.52}
$$

$$
g_B = (V - X)^+ + R_B(V - X)^- + X.
\tag{3.53}
$$

**TABLE 3.3** An example bilateral CVA calculation for a five-year GBP interest rate swap. The counterparty CDS spread is set at 300 basis points for all maturities, while the bank CDS spread is 100 basis points. Both counterparty and bank recovery are 40%.

| Tenor (years) | Expected Positive Exposure | Expected Negative Exposure | Bank Survival Probability | Bank Interval Default Probability | Counterparty Survival Probability | Counterparty Interval Default Probability | Bilateral CVA Contribution | Bilateral DVA Contribution |
|---|---|---|---|---|---|---|---|---|
| 0 | | | 100.000% | | 100.000% | | | |
| 0.5 | 701,997 | −790,189 | 99.170% | 0.830% | 97.530% | 2.470% | 10,317.25 | −3,837.94 |
| 1.0 | 877,137 | −1,138,387 | 98.320% | 0.850% | 95.046% | 2.484% | 12,853.23 | −5518.16 |
| 1.5 | 914,128 | −1,358,724 | 97.509% | 0.811% | 92.713% | 2.333% | 12,477.22 | −6,129.77 |
| 2.0 | 880,804 | −1,485,909 | 96.678% | 0.831% | 90.362% | 2.351% | 12,011.88 | −6,694.69 |
| 2.5 | 816,664 | −1,542,157 | 95.868% | 0.810% | 88.108% | 2.254% | 10,588.20 | −6,603.59 |
| 3.0 | 739,458 | −1,533,924 | 95.064% | 0.804% | 85.910% | 2.198% | 9,270.61 | −6,357.04 |
| 3.5 | 603,905 | −1,378,604 | 94.267% | 0.797% | 83.768% | 2.142% | 7,316.43 | −5,522.39 |
| 4.0 | 473,606 | −1,146,750 | 93.469% | 0.798% | 81.657% | 2.111% | 5,606.92 | −4,483.49 |
| 4.5 | 290,466 | −768,355 | 92.690% | 0.779% | 79.633% | 2.024% | 3,269.56 | −2,859.85 |
| 5.0 | 93,556 | −286,472 | 91.905% | 0.785% | 77.628% | 2.005% | 1,034.37 | −1,047.42 |
| 5.5 | | | 91.140% | 0.765% | 75.701% | 1.927% | 0 | 0 |
| | | | | | | Total | 84,745.66 | −49,054.34 |
| | | | | | | BCVA | 35,691.32 | |

The funding equation remains unchanged as we assume that the bank continues to fund itself at the risk-free rate, despite the fact that it is now credit risky. This assumption is of course inconsistent and will be changed in the context of funding as discussed in Chapter 9. The bank will hold a position in its own bonds to hedge own default and hence there will be an additional cash account associated with this position,

$$d\bar{\beta}_B = -\alpha_B q_B P_B dt. \tag{3.54}$$

Hence the change in the replicating portfolio is now given by

$$d\Pi = \delta dS + \delta(\gamma_S - q_S)S dt + \alpha dP + \alpha_C dP_C - \alpha_C q_C P_C dt$$
$$+ \alpha_B dP_B - \alpha_B q_B P_B dt - r_X X dt. \tag{3.55}$$

Adding equation (3.55) to equation (3.49) gives

$$d\hat{V} + d\Pi = \left[ \frac{\partial \hat{V}}{\partial t} + \frac{1}{2}\sigma^2 S^2 \frac{\partial^2 \hat{V}}{\partial S^2} + \delta(\gamma - q)S + \alpha_C(r_C - q_C)P_C \right.$$

$$\left. + \alpha_B(r_B - q_B)P_B - r_X X + \alpha r P \right] dt$$

$$+ \left[ \delta + \frac{\partial \hat{V}}{\partial S} \right] dS$$

$$+ \left[ \Delta \hat{V}_C + \alpha_C P_C \right] dJ_C$$

$$+ \left[ \Delta \hat{V}_B + \alpha_B P_B \right] dJ_B. \tag{3.56}$$

Assuming replication of the derivative by the hedging portfolio gives

$$d\hat{V} + d\Pi = 0. \tag{3.57}$$

Eliminating the sources of risk from equation (3.56) requires that

$$\delta = -\frac{\partial \hat{V}}{\partial S} \tag{3.58}$$

$$\alpha_C P_C = g_C - \hat{V} \tag{3.59}$$

$$\alpha_B P_B = g_B - \hat{V}. \tag{3.60}$$

Hence the first term in equation (3.56) gives a PDE for $\hat{V}$:

$$\frac{\partial \hat{V}}{\partial t} + \frac{1}{2}\sigma^2 S^2 \frac{\partial^2 \hat{V}}{\partial S^2} - \frac{\partial \hat{V}}{\partial S}(\gamma_S - q_S) + \alpha r P \tag{3.61}$$

$$+ (r_C - q_C)(g_C - \hat{V}) + (r_B - q_B)(g_B - \hat{V}) - r_X X = 0$$

$$\hat{V}(T, S) = H(S).$$

Using the operator $\mathcal{A}_t$ and noting that the hazard rates in the risk-neutral measure are $\lambda_C$ and $\lambda_B$ given by

$$\lambda_C = r_C - q_C \tag{3.62}$$
$$\lambda_B = r_B - q_B. \tag{3.63}$$

allows the PDE to be written as

$$\frac{\partial \hat{V}}{\partial t} + \mathcal{A}_t \hat{V} - r\hat{V} + \lambda_C(g_C - \hat{V}) + \lambda_B(g_B - \hat{V}) - s_X X = 0. \tag{3.64}$$

Using the Ansatz $\hat{V} = V + U$ in the PDE and noting that $V$ satisfies the Black-Scholes-Merton PDE again gives a PDE for the valuation adjustment $U$,

$$\frac{\partial U}{\partial t} + \mathcal{A}_t U - (r + \lambda_C + \lambda_B)U = -\lambda_C(g_C - V) - \lambda_B(g_B - V) + s_X X \tag{3.65}$$
$$U(T, S) = 0.$$

Applying the Feynman-Kac theorem gives an integral expression for $U$,

$$U = \text{CVA} + \text{DVA} + \text{COLVA}, \tag{3.66}$$

where

$$\text{CVA} = -\int_t^T \lambda_C(s)e^{-\int_t^s (r(u)+\lambda_C(u)+\lambda_B(u))du}\mathbb{E}\left[V(s) - g_C(V(s), X(s))\right] ds \tag{3.67}$$

$$\text{DVA} = -\int_t^T \lambda_B(s)e^{-\int_t^s (r(u)+\lambda_C(u)+\lambda_B(u))du}\mathbb{E}\left[V(s) - g_B(V(s), X(s))\right] ds \tag{3.68}$$

$$\text{COLVA} = -\int_t^T e^{-\int_t^s (r(u)+\lambda_C(u)+\lambda_B(u))du}\mathbb{E}\left[s_X(s)X(s)\right] ds. \tag{3.69}$$

Using the standard close-out conditions leads to the standard expression for bilateral CVA,

$$\text{CVA} = -(1 - R_C)\int_t^T \lambda_C(s)e^{-\int_t^s (r(u)+\lambda_C(u)+\lambda_B(u))du}\mathbb{E}\left[(V(s) - X(s))^+\right] ds \tag{3.70}$$

$$\text{DVA} = -(1 - R_B)\int_t^T \lambda_B(s)e^{-\int_t^s (r(u)+\lambda_C(u)+\lambda_B(u))du}\mathbb{E}\left[(V(s) - X(s))^-\right] ds \tag{3.71}$$

$$\text{COLVA} = -\int_t^T e^{-\int_t^s (r(u)+\lambda_C(u)+\lambda_B(u))du}\mathbb{E}\left[s_X(s)X(s)\right] ds. \tag{3.72}$$

### 3.3.3 DVA and Controversy

One of the key drivers for the introduction of bilateral models of CVA was the fact that it reintroduced symmetry of valuation as the CVA term of one party is, at least in principle, the DVA of the other. The *law of one price*, as was discussed earlier in Chapter 1, could at least be said to hold for unsecured derivative transactions between two parties. This principle has proved attractive for accountancy firms and accounting standards boards with both the Financial Accounting Standards Board and the International Accounting Standards Board now including provision for bilateral CVA in FAS 157 (FASB, 2006) and IFRS 13 respectively (IASB, 2012). In practice the symmetry almost invariably breaks down as there is no common standard for models across the two parties to the transaction. Differences in methodology on the calculation of expected exposure profiles, the assignment of recovery rates and the calibration of default probabilities will yield different CVA and DVA values. Nevertheless, this approach allows both parties to agree a price in theory, while if both used unilateral CVA models in theory the valuation of the deal would never cross. Bilateral CVA models were used by some banks from the inception of CVA models, while others switched during the height of the financial crisis of 2007–9, either on the basis of changing accounting standards or competitive pressures. During the financial crisis bank spreads jumped from a small number of basis points to several hundred points and it was difficult in such market conditions to ask clients to compensate for CVA on a unilateral basis when the bank CDS spread was often much larger than that of the client.

One major counterargument to the use of DVA is whether it can be hedged or monetized in any way. In general market practice has been to derive the default probabilities from CDS spreads.[4] However, an entity cannot trade in its own CDS and so the exposure to an entity's own CDS spread cannot be directly hedged. Selling protection on yourself is meaningless as it would only pay out the recovery value should you default. A name could in principle buy CDS on itself but this would only benefit the bondholder recovery in the event of default and not the shareholders to whom the company's staff have a fiduciary duty.[5] An alternative to the CDS would be to trade in the entity's own issued debt and this has been suggested by Burgard and Kjaer (2011b); Burgard and Kjaer (2011a); Burgard and Kjaer (2013). However, whether this is feasible in practice when managing a CVA trading desk is questionable as there are restrictions and practical limitations on the trading and issuance of own debt. Another possible argument that can be pursued is that the portfolio of underlying trades coupled with protection bought by both counterparties on each other constitutes a fully hedged portfolio even if both counterparties are unable to hedge the sensitivity to their own CDS spread. Own credit spread sensitivities could be hedged by proxies such as the *iTraxx Financial* credit default swap index or a basket of the CDS of similar names. Using a proxy curve opens the possibility of tracking errors if the company's own CDS spread diverges from the basket or if a name within the basket diverges significantly or defaults. The lack of available hedges has been a major reason given for opposition to the use of DVA (Carver, 2010; Carver, 2012b).

As noted earlier, the term DVA is used to refer to derivative DVA as described here (DVA1) and the fair value accounting option for own issued debt (DVA2). Opposition to the use of both types of DVA is frequently encountered in the press and in analyst commentary (Carver, 2012a). The opposition comes from the seeming paradox of an accounting gain while the reporting entity is under stress with credit spreads widening. DVA is also frequently cited as contravening the principle of accounting on a *going concern* basis (see ASB, 2000). Under

---

[4]See Chapter 4 for details of how credit curves are constructed.
[5]In theory the name could buy enough CDS to ensure bondholder recovery was 100% and that there was residual value for shareholders. Of course it would be impossible to buy such an amount of CDS in practice.

Basel III, DVA is not considered as part of the additional CVA capital charge (BCBS, 2011b). Subsequently the Basel Committee have made their opposition to derivative DVA clear by excluding it from consideration as part of tier one capital (BCBS, 2011a).

In the context of funding, the expected exposure gives rise to funding benefits, which are tangible and can be managed, unlike DVA. Hence as will become clear, many dealers favour a model which gives rise to funding benefit, FBA, rather than DVA. This will be discussed in more detail in Chapter 9.

## 3.4 MODELLING DEPENDENCE BETWEEN COUNTERPARTIES

In equation (3.47) I assume that the default time of the bank B and counterparty C were independent of each other. While this is a typical assumption made with bilateral CVA models, the dependence between names can be modelled using Copula techniques. Base correlation implied from the prices of the tranches of CDOs suggest typical correlation values of between 30% and 100%, with default times being positive correlated and the degree of co-dependence determined by factors such as industry sector and geographical location.

### 3.4.1 Gaussian Copula Model

The Gaussian Copula model became the industry standard approach for modelling default time dependence for *Collateralised Debt Obligations* (CDO) and similar products prior to the 2007–2009 credit crisis. The model, originally proposed by David X. Li (2000), became popular because of its tractability. CDOs are basket credit products that depend on the defaults of many underlying reference names. Default time correlations for each pair of underlying credits are impossible to observe so as a simplifying assumption these models used a one-factor approach where the credits were assumed to have a single systemic risk factor coupled with idiosyncratic independent (Gaussian) risk factors (see for example Hull and White, 2004). In reality the model was used in a similar way to Black-Scholes in the pricing of European options, with the correlation parameter being determined from the prices of CDO tranches rather than exogenously specified. As a single correlation did not match the prices of all the tranches in a CDO this led to the concept of a *correlation smile* (Cifuentes and Katsaros, 2007; O'Kane and Livesey, 2004). A number of other problems with the model were apparent prior to the crisis. It was well known, for example, that as the risk of default of a name increased it became independent of the default risk of other names and simultaneous defaults have zero probability (see for example Schönbucher, 2003). Hence under the Gaussian Copula model the tail risk of multiple defaults and credits contagion events was underpriced. The Gaussian Copula model has received significant negative press in the aftermath of the 2007–2009 credit crisis and has been seen as one of its causal factors (Salmon, 2009).

The Gaussian Copula model is not a viable model of credit correlation because of these defects; however, it remains useful as an introduction to Copula techniques. Hence I present it as a simple introduction to how dependence between default times can be added to the bilateral CVA model. *I do not recommend it as a suitable model for bilateral CVA.*

A Gaussian Copula model can be used in the context of a bilateral CVA model. No simplification is required as there are only two names involved so a single correlation can be used to define the co-dependence of the default times. Copula models take two or more marginal distributions and join them to produce a multivariate probability distribution. *Sklar's theorem*[6] provides the main result: if $H$ is an n-dimensional cumulative distribution function with marginal distributions $F_1, F_2, \ldots, F_n$ then there exists an n-copula $C$ such that for all x in $\mathbb{R}^n$,

$$H(x_1, \ldots, x_2) = C(F_1(x_1), \ldots, F_n(x_n)). \tag{3.73}$$

The Gaussian Copula uses the multivariate normal distribution, $\Psi^n$,

$$C_{N(R)}(u_1, \ldots, u_n) = \Psi^n[\Psi^{-1}(u_1), \ldots, \Psi^{-1}(u_n)], \tag{3.74}$$

which in two dimensions has the form

$$C_{N(R)}(u, v) = \int_{-\infty}^{\Psi^{-1}(u)} \int_{-\infty}^{\Psi^{-1}(v)} \frac{1}{2\pi(1-\rho^2)^{1/2}} \exp\left\{-\frac{s^2 - 2\rho st + t^2}{2(1-\rho^2)}\right\} ds\, dt. \tag{3.75}$$

The dependence between the default times in equation (3.46) can be written as follows:

$$\Phi((t_i < \tau_B < t_{i+1}) \cap (\tau_C > t_i + 1)) = \Phi[\tau_B > t_i, \tau_C > t_{i+1}] - \Phi[\tau_B > t_{i+1}, \tau_C > t_{i+1}]. \tag{3.76}$$

This allows the default times to be joined through the use of the survival copula, which in two dimensions is given by

$$\hat{C}(u, v) = u + v - 1 + C(1 - u, 1 - v), \tag{3.77}$$

with $C(u, v)$ given by equation (3.75). Note that the survival copula is related to the joint survival function, $\bar{C}$, through (Nelson, 2006),

$$\bar{C}(u, v) = \Phi[U > u, V > v] = 1 - u - v + C(u, v) = \hat{C}(1 - u, 1 - v). \tag{3.78}$$

Using the survival copula allows the marginal survival probabilities of $B$ and $C$ to be joined with a single correlation parameter, $\rho$ providing the co-dependence.

### 3.4.2 Other Copula Models

The Marshall-Olkin bivariate exponential distribution was designed to be used in the context of two component systems to examine failure (Nelson, 2006; Marshall and Olkin, 1967). Three types of failure are possible under this distribution; each component can fail independently and both can fail together. The three shocks are driven by three independent Poisson processes and we can assume that the intensities of these processes are $\lambda_1$, $\lambda_2$ and $\lambda_3$. The survival function is given by

$$\Phi[X > x, Y > y] = \bar{H}(x, y) = \Phi[Z_1 > x]\Phi[Z_2 > y]\Phi[Z_{12} > max(x, y)] \tag{3.79}$$

$$= \exp[-\lambda_1 x - \lambda_2 y - \lambda_{12} \max(x, y)].$$

---

[6]A full description of copulas can be found in Nelson (2006).

The marginal survival functions for the two components are given by

$$F(x) = \exp\left[-(\lambda_1 + \lambda_{12})x\right] \tag{3.80}$$

$$G(y) = \exp\left[-(\lambda_2 + \lambda_{12})y\right], \tag{3.81}$$

thus allowing the individual marginals to be calibrated, once the combined intensity is known. This can be used to define the Marshall-Olkin family of copula functions, which gives much stronger dependence in stressed scenarios and the possibility of simultaneous default.

There are a large number of different copula functions to draw on and sources like Nelson (2006) provide a full description. Many of the copula functions have been applied in the context of CDO pricing in an attempt to improve on the Gaussian Copula model with its known deficiencies. However, the fundamental issue of the applicability of DVA remains, now potentially compounded by one or more dependence parameters such as the Gaussian correlation. While it may be possible to extract implied correlations between the bank B and counterparty C from CDO tranches and other sources, it is almost certainly impossible to hedge the dependence. Given this it could be argued that modelling the dependence between counterparties in the context of bilateral CVA models is of questionable benefit.

## 3.5 COMPONENTS OF A CVA CALCULATION ENGINE

The formulas for unilateral and bilateral CVA allow the logical components of a CVA calculation engine to be identified. Figure 3.1 illustrates the four main logical components: the Monte Carlo simulation, trade valuation, expected exposure calculation and credit integration.

### 3.5.1 Monte Carlo Simulation

The expected exposure is calculated using Monte Carlo simulation because of the need for a generic calculation method that will work across all netting sets irrespective of its constituents, the underlying assets and the implied dimensionality of the calculation. A Monte Carlo simulation is used to generate multiple *states-of-the-world* and in each state the portfolio is valued. The unilateral and bilateral CVA calculations as defined by equations (3.13) and (3.47) respectively are not obviously path-dependent calculations as the summation is taken over a series of expected exposures at different discrete time points. However, in practice each of these expectations is path-dependent as last cash flows depend implicitly on the values obtained earlier along a given path. Hence it is optimal to run a *multi-step* Monte Carlo simulation which is used to generate the full expected exposure profile. The Monte Carlo model must be calibrated so this module logically contains mode calibration components. Calibration could be historical or risk neutral, although in general risk neutral is market standard practice. Monte Carlo simulation for CVA is discussed in Chapter 16.

### 3.5.2 Trade Valuation and Approximations

The portfolio must be valued in each state generated by the Monte Carlo simulation so each trade must be valued on each path and on every simulation stopping date until trade maturity. With many thousand simulation paths and potentially hundreds of Monte Carlo simulation

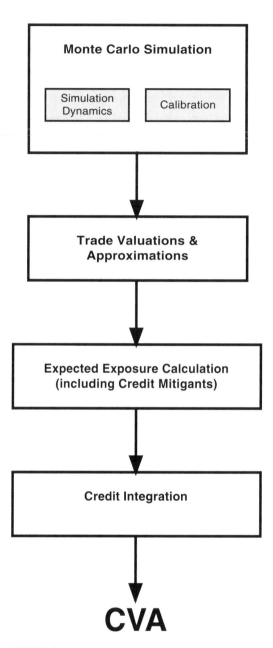

**FIGURE 3.1** The components of a CVA calculation engine.

stopping dates, strict performance constraints must be applied to the trade valuation routines that are used. Only trade valuations that are sufficiently fast can be used and typically these are analytic or semi-analytic models. Models involving computationally intensive approaches are not practical to be called inside a Monte Carlo simulation; it would make little sense to value trades using Monte Carlo methods inside a second Monte Carlo simulation. Whenever trade valuation routines are too slow, an approximation must be used. Trade valuation and approximation techniques for use in a CVA calculation are described in Chapter 19.

Note that option trades lead to the XVA calculation being implicit as the optimal exercise decision should be based on the difference in economic value for the portfolio with and without exercise. Given that the economic value includes XVA an exercise decision leads implicitly to a requirement to know the XVA at future times. Most XVA models ignore this issue, however.

### 3.5.3 Expected Exposure Calculation

In the cases presented above the expected exposure calculation is simply a matter of taking the positive or negative part of the netted portfolio value. However, in the case where collateral is posted or security is held against the exposure, the calculation is more complex. The modelling of credit mitigants is discussed in Chapter 6.

### 3.5.4 Credit Integration

The final step of the model is integration over the expected exposure profile with the survival probability functions for counterparty and self, depending on whether unilateral or bilateral models have been chosen. In the case of independence this is a simple numerical integral. However, if wrong-way or right-way risk is to be considered the calculation becomes more difficult. The survival probability function is normally obtained from CDS spreads and this process is described in chapter 4. Right-way and wrong-way risk models are discussed in Chapter 7.

## 3.6 COUNTERPARTY LEVEL CVA VS. TRADE LEVEL CVA

In the presence of netting the CVA of individual trades does not sum to the CVA of the netting set. In unilateral models netting is always beneficial so that

$$V_{UCVA} < \sum_{i=1}^{n} V_{UCVA}^{i}.$$

However, in bilateral models netting can be a benefit or a penalty depending on whether the bilateral CVA is positive or negative. If the DVA term dominates then netting will penalise as it acts to reduce both EPE and ENE. Netting implies that CVA has to be calculated at counterparty level and this is also the natural unit of management as the credit sensitivities will also be managed by buying and selling CDS on an individual counterparty basis when such CDS contracts exist and are liquid.

However, there are many reasons why a trade level CVA calculation is desired:

- *Incremental CVA* – For new or amended trades the CVA will need to be calculated on an incremental basis so the impact of the change in CVA is understood. This will normally be part of a charge made to the client as part of the new transaction.

■ *Allocated CVA* – CVA may need to be allocated to trade level for management information purposes. Management structures within banks are normally arranged by asset class and hence CVA may need to be reported in the same way.

### 3.6.1  Incremental CVA

Incremental CVA can only be calculated on a differential basis, that is through two calculations, one with the original portfolio and one with the new portfolio. This gives two separate sets of expected exposure profiles to which the relevant CVA formula is applied with the difference giving the incremental CVA. The key issue is to maximise the performance of the calculation. The Monte Carlo simulation used to generate the exposure profiles can be run only once, rather than twice, by including all the trades from both original and new portfolios. The simulation then needs to keep track of the value of both portfolios by applying appropriate filters on trade valuations along each Monte Carlo path. Note that this has the added benefit that exactly the same simulation paths will be used to generate both old and new expected exposure profiles, which gives a more accurate result in the same way that common random numbers enhance the accuracy of sensitivities calculated by finite difference approximation.[7]

Further performance enhancement can be gained by using the results of a previous calculation. Say, for example, that a new trade was added to the portfolio during the current trading day. The old portfolio will have been calculated during the overnight batch calculation of the CVA for P & L purposes. If the CVA on the new portfolio can be calculated using the same set of Monte Carlo paths as the old portfolio then if the paths and path-wise values for all trades were stored as part of the overnight batch process, they could be re-used intraday for pricing and risk management purposes. The simulation would be re-run but only valuing the new trade and with re-aggregation of results on each path at each stopping date. The re-use criteria would depend precisely on the organisation of the Monte Carlo simulation. If a fixed set of random numbers is used for each stochastic factor the task is relatively simple to achieve as the same set of random numbers is always used for the same stochastic factor.[8] If the random numbers are allocated dynamically this means the compatibility criterion is that the simulation stopping dates remain the same and that no new asset classes are added that alter the allocation of random numbers. This fact incremental pricing technique also relies on the ability to store down the trade value for each path and each stopping date as part of an overnight batch process, a data intensive operation requiring large amounts of storage. Of course if the paths are re-used from the previous batch calculation no changes in market data will be captured so the price will not be based on current market conditions but rather those when the Monte Carlo simulation was last calibrated.

### 3.6.2  Allocated CVA

CVA can be allocated to trade level as demonstrated by Gregory (2012), Pykhtin and Rosen (2010) and Kenyon and Green (2014a). Following from the Euler allocation process that has

---

[7]The benefits of common random numbers when sensitivities are calculated by finite difference are described by Boyle, Broadie and Glasserman (1997).

[8]Note that this arrangement is not always optimal and I refer the reader to Chapter 16 for more information on the organisation of the Monte Carlo simulation.

previously been applied in credit risk contexts (Avanitis and Gregory, 2001), Value-at-Risk (Jorion, 2000) and to capital allocation (Tasche, 2008), it is possible to allocate CVA (and indeed any XVA metric that uses expected exposures). The aim of this exercise is to provide allocated CVA such that

$$CVA = \sum_{i=1}^{n} CVA^i_{attributed},$$ (3.82)

so that additivity is recovered for the trade level CVA. In general the expected exposure is not additive because of netting rules so that

$$EPE \neq \sum_{i=1}^{n} EPE^i_{trade}.$$ (3.83)

To progress define the allocated expected positive exposure,

$$EPE = \sum_{i=1}^{n} EPE^i_{allocated}.$$ (3.84)

Recall the definition of expected exposure for a portfolio of netted trades,

$$EPE = \mathbb{E}\left[\max\left(\sum_{i=1}^{n} V_i, 0\right)\right],$$ (3.85)

where the $V_i$ are the trade values. The value can be re-written with a multiplicative factor $\alpha_i$, which is deterministic and by writing $x_i = V_i/\alpha_i$, equation (3.85) becomes,

$$EPE = \mathbb{E}\left[\max\left(\sum_{i=1}^{n} \alpha_i x_i, 0\right)\right] = f(\alpha).$$ (3.86)

$f(\alpha)$ is a *homogeneous function of order one* and using *Euler's homogeneous function theorem*[9] this can be written

$$EPE = \sum_{i=1}^{n} \frac{\partial}{\partial \alpha_i} f(\alpha),$$ (3.87)

and the allocated expected positive exposure is

$$EPE_{allocated} = \frac{\partial}{\partial \alpha_i} f(\alpha).$$ (3.88)

---

[9] A homogeneous function of order $m$ can be written $mg(\mathbf{x}) = \sum_{i=1}^{n} x_i \frac{\partial g}{\partial x_i}$

The expression for unilateral CVA, equation (3.13), can now be written in terms of the allocated expected positive exposure,

$$CVA = (1 - R) \sum_{j=0}^{m-1} [\Phi(\tau > t_j) - \Phi(\tau > t_{j+1})] \sum_{j=1}^{n} \frac{\partial}{\partial \alpha_i} f(\alpha). \tag{3.89}$$

Changing the order of the summations gives the final result,

$$CVA = \sum_{i=1}^{n} \sum_{j=0}^{m-1} (1 - R)[\Phi(\tau > t_j) - \Phi(\tau > t_{j+1})] \frac{\partial}{\partial \alpha_i} f(\alpha)$$

$$= \sum_{i=1}^{n} CVA_{allocated}^{i}.$$

Clearly the same result can be applied in the case of bilateral CVA,

$$BCVA = (1 - R_C) \sum_{j=0}^{m-1} [\Phi(\tau_C > t_{j+1}) - \Phi(\tau_B > t_j)]\Phi(\tau_B > T) \times \sum_{i=1}^{n} \frac{\partial}{\partial \alpha_i} f(\alpha) \tag{3.90}$$

$$+ (1 - R_B) \sum_{j=0}^{m-1} [\Phi(\tau_B > t_{j+1}) - \Phi(\tau_B > t_j)]\Phi(\tau_C > T) \times \sum_{i=1}^{n} \frac{\partial}{\partial \alpha_i} g(\alpha)$$

$$= \sum_{i=1}^{n} CVA_{allocated}^{i} + \sum_{i=1}^{n} DVA_{allocated}^{i},$$

where $g(\alpha) \equiv \mathbb{E}^r \left[ \exp \left( - \int_{u=0}^{t} r(s)ds \right) (\sum_{i=1}^{n} \alpha_i x_i)^- \right]$.

**Calculating CVA Allocation**   Calculating the CVA allocation in practice requires that the sensitivities of the expected positive (and negative) exposure profiles be calculated. This can be readily done by finite difference approximation. To do this a series of pre-multipliers, $\alpha_i$, are introduced and the expected positive exposure calculation becomes

$$EPE(t_j) = \mathbb{E} \left[ \max \left( \sum_{i=1}^{n} \alpha_i V_i(t_j), 0 \right) \right] \tag{3.91}$$

$$= \frac{1}{M} \sum_{k=1}^{M} \max \left( \sum_{i=1}^{n} \alpha_i V_{ik}(t_j), 0 \right),$$

where $M$ is the number of Monte Carlo paths. In the baseline CVA calculation, $\alpha_i = 1$ so the usual CVA result is obtained. Subsequently a small shift, $\Delta$, is applied to each trade in the portfolio in turn giving

$$EPE_{shift(j)} = \frac{1}{M} \sum_{k=1}^{M} \max \left( \sum_{i=1}^{n} \alpha_i V_{ik}(t_j), 0 \right), \tag{3.92}$$

where

$$\alpha_i = 1 + \Delta \quad \text{for} \quad i = j$$
$$\alpha_i = 1 \quad \text{for} \quad i \neq j.$$

Hence the sensitivies are given by

$$\frac{\partial}{\partial \alpha_i} EPE(\alpha) \approx \frac{EPE_{shift(j)} - EPE}{\Delta}. \tag{3.93}$$

This does not require multiple simulations to achieve this result and the baseline expected exposure calculations and all shifts can be calculated simultaneously in a single Monte Carlo run. When there are $m$ trades in the portfolio this calculation requires $m + 1$ running summations to be kept rather than the single one for a standard CVA calculation. This imposes additional memory overhead in the calculation but limited impact on computational performance as it only requires $m$ additional multiply operations.

## 3.7 RECOVERY RATE/LOSS-GIVEN-DEFAULT ASSUMPTIONS

The recovery rate, $R$, appears in the formula for unilateral and bilateral CVA. This recovery rate has been assumed to be deterministic and that $(1 - R)$ is a multiplicative factor determining the loss on an exposure. As will be discussed in Chapter 4 the recovery rate is an assumption used when obtaining the survival probability function from a strip of CDS spreads. A key question is whether or not these two recovery rates take the same value.

A physically settled single name CDS written against senior unsecured debt allows one or more of these senior debt instruments to be used to settle the CDS contract in the event of default. The protection buyer hands over *notional* amount of defaulted bonds and receives *notional* in cash from the protection seller, less any adjustments for accrual on the CDS contract. In the context of CVA, if the counterparty has a liquid CDS contract traded in the market and the derivative exposures rank *pari passu* with the senior unsecured debt of the counterparty then there seems little doubt that the CDS recovery rate should also be used in the context of CVA. If the derivative portfolio ranks higher (or lower) than the unsecured debt then an adjustment to the recovery rate may be appropriate as less (or more) notional of CDS would need to be purchased by the bank's CVA trading desk to appropriately hedge the exposure.

In the context of illiquid counterparties with no CDS contracts the choice of recovery rate is much more difficult to justify. A CVA trading function can only hedge the CDS spread risk and cannot hedge the loss on default through the CDS market. Further discussion of the management of spread and default risk including risk warehousing can be found in Chapter 22.

Some derivative portfolios will be secured by one or more assets. These are not collateral arrangements in the sense of a CSA agreement as typically no additional security is provided should the total exposure exceed value of the assets. In such circumstances the recovery rate is driven by the asset value so it is questionable whether a recovery *rate* is a suitable way to estimate the expected loss and hence the CVA. Alternative models for such situations are discussed in Chapter 6.

# CDS and Default Probabilities

*If scientific reasoning were limited to the logical processes of arithmetic, we should not get very far in our understanding of the physical world. One might as well attempt to grasp the game of poker entirely by the use of the mathematics of probability.*

—Vannevar Bush
*American Engineer and Administrator of the Manhattan Project (1890–1974)*

## 4.1 SURVIVAL PROBABILITIES AND CVA

As is clear from Chapter 3, the survival probability function is central to the calculation of CVA and this chapter presents a description of how this function can be obtained. In general, for CVA calculations the survival probability function is obtained from credit default swap spreads and this is the focus of the chapter. Historical survival probabilities have been used in the past and thus remains an option and the merits of historical and market implied survival probabilities are discussed in section 4.2. Pricing models for CDS are well known in the market but are included here for completeness in section 4.3. The approach of bootstrapping the survival probability function from CDS is similarly well known but there are complexities unique to CVA that do not present themselves in the CDS market and so these are discussed in section 4.4. With the introduction of Basel III, CDS can be used to hedge regulatory CVA (see Chapter 12). This means that the hazard rate implied from CDS spreads also contains an element related to the benefit gained from capital relief. A model which considers the impact of this capital relief is presented in section 4.5. The chapter concludes with an evaluation of the different approaches to linking counterparties to liquid CDS contracts in section 4.6.

The standard reduced form model for the default process is as the first jump of a Poisson process with a deterministic *hazard rate* $\lambda(t)$. Hence under this model the survival probability is given by

$$P(\tau > T) = \exp\left(-\int_t^T \lambda(s)ds\right), \tag{4.1}$$

and the default probability is given by

$$P(\tau \leq T) = 1 - \exp\left(-\int_t^T \lambda(s)ds\right). \tag{4.2}$$

## 4.2 HISTORICAL VERSUS IMPLIED SURVIVAL PROBABILITIES

Credit risk assessment has long made use of survival probability models for individual coun-terparties. Such *PD* models are a feature of both internal economic capital models and the Basel framework for regulatory capital. Banks that have been granted permission to use the *foundation internal ratings based* approach (FIRB) can use their own internal PD models in the assessment of counterparty credit risk capital under Basel II (BCBS, 2006b).[1] These PD models are based on historical default rates experienced by the institution. Internal ratings are often simply a ranking of internal PD on an discrete scale. External ratings provided by rating agencies are also based on PD models derived from historical default rates and other factors.

Some institutions have adopted historical default probabilities for marking CVA positions and some quantitative analysts have advocated that CVA should be treated as a banking book item and managed on an actuarial basis (Artaud and Berger, 2011). However, the use of historical probabilities for CVA is the exception to the rule and market standard practice is to mark CVA using risk-neutral default probabilities derived from CDS spreads or sometimes CDS indices. The drivers behind this approach are as follows:

- CVA is a valuation adjustment made to account for the credit risk on a portfolio of derivatives that are themselves subject to risk-neutral valuation. CVA should therefore be marked using the same risk-neutral valuation principle to be consistent.
- While CVA is now an element of accounting valuations and the regulatory capital frame-work, its origins lie in a desire by banks to actively manage their derivative counterparty risk. When marked to risk-neutral default probabilities, the CVA credit spread sensitivity and loss on default risk can be hedged by buying the same CDS contracts.
- The Basel III regulatory framework uses CDS spreads to generate the CVA regulatory capital for banks that have *internal model method* (IMM) approval for their credit exposure engine. Capital mitigation is available for banks that hedge their CVA risk.

While it is clear that the use of risk-neutral implied survival probabilities to calculate CVA is the industry standard approach for accounting purposes, there remain challenges to this view. Firstly I note that the CDS price contains some element related to capital relief gained from hedging regulatory CVA as discussed in section 4.5 below. Secondly the reality is that most CVA cannot be directly hedged. Most counterparties do not have a liquid CDS contract associated with them leading to the mapping process described in section 4.6. Given that the default risk cannot be hedged in such cases, risk warehousing is inevitable and this leads directly

---

[1] Banks granted *advanced internal ratings based* approach (AIRB) can also use their internal LGD values for capital purposes.

to incomplete markets and the physical measure. The consequences of risk warehousing on XVA are discussed in Chapter 22.

## 4.3    CREDIT DEFAULT SWAP VALUATION

### 4.3.1    Credit Default Swaps

Credit default swaps are insurance-like derivatives that are designed to offer protection against the default of a reference obligation. They allow the owner of a bond to buy default protection so that in the event of a default by the bond issuer they are compensated by the protection seller. Of course the CDS just protects the bond owner against the default of the bond issuer, interest rate risks remain. The CDS consist of two legs, a premium leg and a default leg. The premium leg consists of a stream of payments from the protection buyer to the protection seller until the default of the reference obligation or maturity. The protection (or default) leg consists of a compensating payment from the protection seller to the protection buyer on the default of the reference obligation. These flows are illustrated in Figure 4.1.

There are a number of variations on the basic product that are frequently traded. In most cases an accrued fee for the period from the last payment to the time of default must be paid by the protection buyer to the protection seller, reducing the default payment slightly. Settlement can be either physical through bonds or in cash. Physical settlement involves the protection buyer handing over *notional* amount of defaulted bonds and return for *notional* in cash. The delivery of the bond means that where multiple bonds can be delivered into the contract there is a *cheapest-to-deliver* option, although this is infrequently priced into the deal. Cash settlement involves the payment of $(1 - Recovery\ Rate) \times notional$ by the protection seller to the protection buyer. The recovery rate is usually set through an auction process administered by ISDA. Digital CDS contracts involving the payment of a fixed amount on the default of the reference name are also possible but trade only infrequently. CDS contracts are most often denominated in US dollars but prices are also quoted in other currencies. Where the currency of the CDS and the reference obligation are different, this is known as a *Quanto CDS*. The sovereign CDS market has normally been a Quanto CDS market as protection

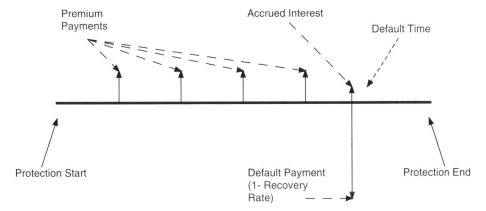

**FIGURE 4.1**    The cash flows of a credit default swap.

buyers frequently do not want to take the additional currency risk associated with sovereign default, so for example CDS quoted on European sovereigns were most often quoted in US dollars. The quanto effect must be included within the CDS pricing model.

The market standard convention for CDS is to use a relatively fixed date schedule where the protection associated with the CDS contract always ends on the 20th of the quarterly IMM month, whether or not this is a good business day.[2] So a one-year CDS run until the 20th of the IMM month that follows the end of the one-year period, so all CDS contracts run for slightly longer that the tenor would suggest unless traded just before the 20th of the IMM month. The 20th of the IMM month is known as the CDS roll date as CDS traded after this date run three months longer. On the CDS roll date both old and new contracts can trade simultaneously. The CDS roll date does add some complexity to carry behaviour in the CDS market, and this can disproportionately impact CVA desks so this is discussed in section 4.4.2. Protection payments usually occur on the next good business day after the CDS roll date. The CDS market thus behaves in a different manner to the interest rate swap market, where the tenor and date schedules change daily.

**Restructuring ("Doc") Clauses**   The documentation clause in a CDS contract provides the list of qualifying credit events that will trigger the CDS. These include the list of ISDA credit events discussed in section 2.3 with variations around what types of restructuring qualify. Under the 2003 ISDA Credit Definitions four types of restructuring clause are defined:

**Old restucturing**   Where restructuring of the underlying debt obligation by, for example, changing the coupon or extending the maturity, is considered a credit event.

**Modified restructuring**   Where restructuring is considered a credit event but only debt with a maturity of less than 30 months can be delivered into the CDS contract.

**Modified modified restructuring**   Where restructuring is considered a credit event but only debt with a maturity of less than 60 months can be delivered into the CDS contract.

**No restructuring**   Where restructuring does not trigger the CDS contract.

Revised ISDA Credit Definitions came into force on 2 October 2014 (ISDA, 2014a) which modified the details of the restructuring clauses although the four classes remain in place. The reader is referred to the 2003 or 2014 Credit Definitions as appropriate for full details.

In general the *Modified Restructuring* clause is the most common in the North American investment grade CDS market, while high yield CDS generally trade with the *No Restructuring* clause. In Europe the *Modified Modified Restructuring* clause is the most common restructuring clause.

**ISDA Big Bang and Small Bang Protocols**   In 2009 ISDA introduced two sets of changes to standard CDS market conventions, known as the *big bang protocol* (ISDA, 2009a; Markit, 2009b) and the *small bang protocol* (ISDA, 2009b; Markit, 2009a). Both protocols introduced a number of changes intended to streamline the CDS market and make central clearing easier.

---

[2]The *International Money Market* date occurs on the third Wednesday of the month and is the date of maturity for exchange-traded futures and options. The quarterly dates are associated with the maturity of three-month futures and these occur in March, June, September and December.

The big bang protocol introduced three changes into Global CDS contracts:

- Hardwiring of CDS auction process following a credit event to eliminate the need for CDS market participants to sign up to each auction separately
- The formation of Determination Committees to make binding decisions on whether a credit event has occurred
- The effective date of the CDS contract to be changed to the current day less 60 days for credit events and 90 days for succession events. This eliminates any issues around the start date of protection which was previously T+1.

In addition the big bang protocol introduced fixed coupons into the North American single name CDS market, with coupons fixed at either 100bp or 500bp and value adjustments made through upfront payments.

The small bang protocol extended the use of auctions to restructuring events and expanded the use of fixed coupons in CDS trades to European markets, with fixed spreads of 25bp, 100bp, 500bp and 1000bp.

## 4.3.2 Premium Leg

The valuation of the legs of a CDS contract follows a similar methodology to that used to calculate CVA. The approach to valuation adopted here is similar to that of Hull and White (2000) and Schönbucher (2003). The *premium* or *fee* leg is simply the value of the fee conditioned on the survival of the reference entity to the payment date of the fee,

$$V_{premium}^i(t_0) = \mathbb{E}\left[\exp\left(-\int_{s=t_0}^{t_i} r(s)ds\right) C_i \alpha_i \mathbb{1}_{\{\tau > t_i\}} | \mathcal{F}_t\right], \tag{4.3}$$

where $C_i$ is the premium paid at time $t_i$ and $\alpha_i$ is the day-count fraction (normally 30/360). I make the market standard assumption of independence between rates and credit. In practice interest rates only impact CDS through discounting and introducing a dependence would have little impact. In models with stochastic process for hazard rates and interest rates this approximation is also used to simplify calibration (see for example Brigo and Mercurio, 2006). This means that the above expression reduces to

$$V_{premium}^i(t_0) = C_i \alpha_i B(t_0, t_i) P(\tau > t_i), \tag{4.4}$$

where $B(t, T_l)$ is the value of the discount bond maturity at time $t_i$. Hence, the value of the premium leg excluding accrued premium is given by

$$V_{premium}(t_0) = \sum_{i=1}^{n} C_i \alpha_i B(t_0, t_i) P(\tau > t_i). \tag{4.5}$$

If the accrued premium must be paid at the time of default the value of this component must be added to the premium leg. The premium $C_i$ accrues over the period $t_{i-1}$ to $t_i$ and default could occur at any point in the interval. To proceed I introduce a fine time partition on the interval $[t_{i-1}, t_i]$ given by

$$t_{i-1} = s_0 \leq \ldots \leq s_j \leq \ldots \leq s_m = t_i.$$

This will simplify the calculation and lead to an expression for the accrued coupon that is a straightforward summation. I further assume that the hazard rate $\lambda_j$ and interest rate $r_j$ are constant over a small subinterval $[s_{j-1}, s_j]$. The value of the accrued premium paid on default is given by

$$V^i_{accrued}(t_0) = \mathbb{E}\left[\exp\left(-\int_{u=t_0}^{\tau} r(u)du\right) C_i \alpha_i \frac{(\tau - t_{i+1})}{(t_i - t_{i-1})} \mathbb{1}_{\{t_{i-1} \leq \tau \leq t_i\}}\right] \tag{4.6}$$

$$= \frac{C_i \alpha_i}{t_i - t_{i-1}} \int_{t_{i-1}}^{t_i} (u - t_{i-1})\lambda(u) \exp\left(-\int_{t_0}^{u} (r(v) + \lambda(v))dv\right) du,$$

where I have used the fact that the density function for the Poisson process is given by $\lambda(t) \exp\left(-\int_0^t \lambda_s ds\right)$. Partitioning allows the integral to be expressed as a sum of integrals over the sub intervals $[s_{j-1}, s_j]$, over which the short and hazard rates are constant,

$$V^i_{accrued}(t_0) = \frac{C_i \alpha_i}{t_i - t_{i-1}} \sum_{j=1}^{m} \int_{s_{i-1}}^{s_i} (u - t_{i-1})\lambda_j \exp\left(-\int_{s_{i-1}}^{u} (r_j + \lambda_j)dv\right) du. \tag{4.7}$$

The inner integral can be split around the lower limit of the sum and this allows the expression to be re-written as

$$V^i_{accrued}(t_0) = \frac{C_i \alpha_i}{t_i - t_{i-1}} \sum_{j=1}^{m} B(t, t_{j-1})P(\tau > t_{j-1}) \tag{4.8}$$

$$\times \int_{s_{i-1}}^{s_i} (u - t_{i-1})\lambda_j \exp\left[-(r_j + \lambda_j)(u - s_{j-1})\right] du.$$

$$= \frac{C_i \alpha_i}{t_i - t_{i-1}} \sum_{j=0}^{n-1} B(t, t_{j-1})P(\tau > t_{j-1})$$

$$\times \left[-\left(\frac{(u - s_{j-1})\lambda_j}{r_j + \lambda_j} + \frac{\lambda_j}{(r_j + \lambda_j)^2}\right) \exp\left[-(r_j + \lambda_j)(u - s_{j-1})\right]\right]_{s_{j-1}}^{s_j},$$

where integration by parts has been used. Expanding and using

$$B(t_0, T) = \exp\left(-\int_{t_0}^{T} r(s)ds\right)$$

$$P(\tau > T) = \exp\left(-\int_{t_0}^{T} \lambda(s)ds\right),$$

gives

$$
V^i_{accrued}(t_0) = \frac{C_i \alpha_i}{(t_i - t_{i-1})} \sum_{j=1}^{m} \lambda_j \left[ \frac{B(t, s_{j-1})P(\tau > s_{j-1}) - B(t, s_j)P(\tau > s_j)}{(r_{j-1} + \lambda_{j-1})^2} \right. \tag{4.9}
$$
$$
\left. + \frac{(s_{j-1} - t_i)B(t, s_{j-1})P(\tau > s_{j-1}) - (s_j - t_i)B(t, s_j)P(\tau > s_j)}{(r_j + \lambda_j)} \right].
$$

The value of the accrued premium is given by summing equation (4.9) over all premium coupons,

$$
V_{accrued}(t_0) = \sum_{i=1}^{n} \frac{C_i \alpha_i}{(t_i - t_{i-1})} \sum_{j=1}^{m} \lambda_j \left[ \frac{B(t, s_{j-1})P(\tau > s_{j-1}) - B(t, s_j)P(\tau > s_j)}{(r_{j-1} + \lambda_{j-1})^2} \right.
$$
$$
\left. + \frac{(s_{j-1} - t_i)B(t, s_{j-1})P(\tau > s_{j-1}) - (s_j - t_i)B(t, s_j)P(\tau > s_j)}{(r_j + \lambda_j)} \right]. \tag{4.10}
$$

### 4.3.3  Protection Leg

The *protection* or *default* leg pays $(1 - R)$ on the default of the reference name so the value is given by

$$
V_{prot}(t_0) = \mathbb{E} \left[ \exp \left( -\int_{t_0}^{\tau} r(s)ds \right) (1 - R) \mathbb{1}_{\{\tau < T\}} \right]. \tag{4.11}
$$

This expectation is very similar in form to that found in the accrued calculation in equation (4.6). I resolve the expectation to an integral over the instantaneous probability of default,

$$
V_{prot}(t_0) = (1 - R) \int_{t_0}^{T} \lambda(s) \exp \left( -\int_{t_0}^{s} (\lambda(v) + r(v))dv \right) ds, \tag{4.12}
$$

where I have assumed that the recovery rate, $R$, is constant. To evaluate the expectation I adopt the same approach as used above where the interval $[t, T]$ is partitioned into small segments such that $t = u_0 \leq u_1 \leq \ldots \leq u_k \leq \ldots \leq u_p = T$, giving

$$
V_{prot}(t_0) = (1 - R) \sum_{k=1}^{p} \int_{u_{k-1}}^{u_k} \lambda(s) \exp \left( -\int_{t_0}^{s} (\lambda(v) + r(v))dv \right) ds. \tag{4.13}
$$

As earlier the short and hazard rates are assumed to be constant over each time partition segment and this allows equation (4.13) to be simplified to a sum:

$$
\begin{aligned}
V_{prot}(t_0) &= (1 - R) \sum_{k=1}^{p} B(t_0, u_k) P(\tau > u_k) \lambda_k \left[ -\frac{\exp\left(-(\lambda_k + r_k)(v - u_k)\right)}{(\lambda_k + r_k)} \right]_{u_{k-1}}^{u_k} \\
&= (1 - R) \sum_{k=1}^{p} \frac{\lambda_k}{\lambda_k + r_k} \left[ B(t_0, u_{k-1}) P(\tau > u_{k-1}) - B(t_0, u_k) P(\tau > u_k) \right].
\end{aligned}
\tag{4.14}
$$

### 4.3.4   CDS Value and Breakeven Spread

Hence the value of a credit default swap from the perspective of the protection buyer is given by

$$
V_{CDS} = V_{premium} + V_{accrued} - V_{prot},
\tag{4.15}
$$

and the breakeven spread where the value of the CDS is zero is given by

$$
S = \frac{(1 - R) \sum_{k=1}^{p} \frac{\lambda_k}{\lambda_k + r_k} \left[ B_{u_{k-1}} P_{u_{k-1}} - B_{u_k} P_{u_k} \right]}{\sum_{i=1}^{n} \alpha_i \left\{ B_{t_i} P_{t_i} + \frac{\alpha_i}{(t_i - t_{i-1})} \sum_{j=1}^{m} \lambda_j \left[ \frac{B_{s_{j-1}} P_{s_{j-1}} - B_{s_j} P_{s_j}}{(r_{j-1} + \lambda_{j-1})^2} + \frac{(s_{j-1} - t_i) B_{s_{j-1}} P_{s_{j-1}} - (s_j - t_i) B_{s_j} P_{s_j}}{(r_j + \lambda_j)} \right] \right\}},
\tag{4.16}
$$

where $B_T \equiv B(t, T)$ and $P_T \equiv P(\tau > T)$.

## 4.4   BOOTSTRAPPING THE SURVIVAL PROBABILITY FUNCTION

Having obtained an expression for the value of a credit default swap in terms of the survival probability function, $P(\tau > t)$, it is possible to use this to bootstrap this function from a set of CDS spreads. Typically CDS spreads will be available with maturities at $6M, 1Y, 2Y, 3Y, 5Y, 7Y, 10Y, 20Y, 30Y$, although liquidity is frequently very limited in longer maturity CDS contracts. Once the form of the survival probability function is chosen it can be calibrated using equation (4.15).

Given the standard form of the survival probability function,

$$
P(\tau > T) = \exp\left(-\int_{s=0}^{T} \lambda(s) ds\right),
\tag{4.17}
$$

parametrisation depends on the choice of functional form for the hazard rate $\lambda(t)$. Three choices of parametrisation present themselves:

- Piecewise constant
- Piecewise linear
- Cubic spline.

The standard model most frequently used in the CDS market is the piecewise constant hazard rate model. This approach has been adopted for a number of reasons:

- Piecewise constant hazard rates have been found to be numerically stable and behave better than alternatives such as piecewise linear.
- There is no information on the hazard rate between CDS maturities. Piecewise constant hazard rates provide the simplest possible assumption on behaviour between market observations.
- As can be seen from the conventions of the CDS market, the knot points of any credit curve calibrated to CDS spreads will always lie on the 20th of the IMM months. The cash flows associated with premium payments will always occur shortly after the 20th IMM depending on the local calendar. Hence the CDS market is really not very sensitive to dates away from the 20th IMM month and is relatively insensitive to the behaviour of the instantaneous probability of default on arbitrary dates. The choice of piecewise constant hazard rates is a suitable choice when modelling the credit curve.

The segments of the hazard rate function are chosen to match the maturity dates of the CDS spreads in the curve, so for the maturities listed above the segments would be, $0-6M$, $6M-1Y$, $1Y-2Y$, $2Y-3Y$, $3Y-5Y$, $5Y-7Y$, $7Y-10Y$, $10Y-20Y$, $20Y-30Y$. Each segment can be fitted using successive CDS spreads, with the hazard rate segment chosen to ensure the CDS has zero value. A simple Newton-Raphson type root finder is sufficient to calibrate the model. An example of a piecewise constant hazard rate curve is given in Figure 4.2. The CDS spreads are given in Table 4.1.

**TABLE 4.1** The CDS spreads used to generate the hazard rates in Figure 4.2

| Tenor (Years) | CDS spreads (in BPS) |
|---|---|
| 6M | 46 |
| 1Y | 52 |
| 2Y | 71 |
| 3Y | 94 |
| 4Y | 116 |
| 5Y | 137 |
| 7Y | 158 |
| 10Y | 173 |
| 15Y | 176 |
| 20Y | 179 |
| 30Y | 178 |

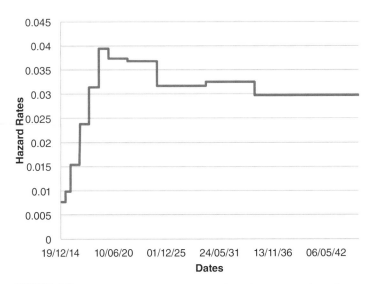

**FIGURE 4.2**    The hazard rate values for a piecewise constant hazard rate model of a credit curve.

The piecewise linear hazard rate model has the advantage that the hazard rate is a continuous function. The calibration process follows the same pattern as for the piecewise constant model, with successive CDS spreads used to calibrate segments of the hazard rate. While this model has been discussed in academic literature (Brigo and Alfonsi, 2005), in practice the piecewise constant model is used. Piecewise linear hazard rates are numerically unstable and can lead to arbitrage where the implied hazard rate and hence probability becomes negative (O'Kane, 2008).

Alternatives such as cubic splines have not in general been used in the construction of credit curves, unlike in the construction of yield curves where such models have become widely used. The advantage of a cubic spline would be that the hazard rate, which is also the instantaneous probability of default, is continuous and smooth. The disadvantage is the same as that experienced when it is used in the construction of yield curves, that is the need for a global fit and consequential non-locality of risk. A twenty-year swap rate shift will impact the entire curve fit and the risk can appear non-intuitive. More advanced types of spline fitting can mitigate this behaviour, however. The primary reason why spline curves have not been applied to credit curves is related to the structure of the CDS market as discussed earlier, that is CDS traders are not really exposed to the hazard rate between CDS maturities.

### 4.4.1    Upfront Payments

Before the introduction of the ISDA big bang and small bag CDS protocols (see section 4.3.1) most credit default swaps were entered at par, that is a market value of zero, paralleling interest rate swap market conventions. This meant that CDS market quotes assumed an initial mark-to-market value of 0 and hence, during the bootstrap process, equation (4.15) was used with $V_{CDS} = 0$. As names became distressed and market perception of the risk of a credit event increased dealers often quoted CDS with an upfront payment and a running fixed coupon of say 500bp. If a CDS is quoted upfront then the bootstrap can still be used but $V_{CDS}$ is no longer zero. Frequently, however, spreads are quoted on the basis of a zero mark-to-market, even if the actual traded contract has non-zero value. The CDS valuation model can be used to convert between upfront and par conventions.

As discussed earlier, the ISDA big bang and small bang CDS protocols introduced CDS contracts with fixed coupon sizes of 100 and 500bp in North America and 25, 100, 500 and 1000bp in Europe.

### 4.4.2 Choice of Hazard Rate Function and CVA: CVA Carry

CVA is sensitive to a series of cash flows occurring on a set of arbitrary dates, corresponding to the cash flows of the underlying instruments in the portfolio between bank and counterparty. CVA is therefore much more sensitive to the form of the instantaneous hazard rate and this impacts CVA through the carry on the portfolio. Suppose a piecewise constant credit curve were used and also that the spreads were fixed. Consider the contribution to the CVA of a single fixed cash flow at time $T$. As the hazard rates remain constant between roll dates, the daily carry on the cash flow will be small and smooth as the cash flow gets steadily closer to being paid and no default occurs. The piecewise constant hazard rate will ensure that the value of the cash flow increases at a constant rate as the instantaneous probability of default is constant. However, when the CDS roll occurs, the hazard rate segments are redefined and can change significantly. The cash flow carry will still be continuous but will now occur at a different rate than before the CDS roll. This discontinuous nature to the carry on the CVA position can lead to P&L volatility. This effect is illustrated in Figure 4.3.

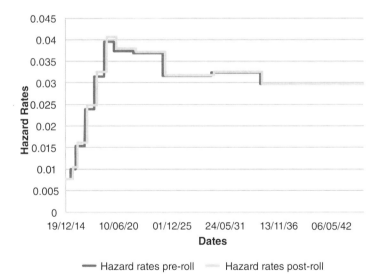

Hazard rates pre-roll     Hazard rates post-roll

**FIGURE 4.3** The hazard rate values for a piecewise constant hazard rate model of a credit curve just prior to the CDS roll date and on the next business date after the roll. The CDS spreads were held constant at the values given in Table 4.1. The shift in the hazard rates and the date segments over which they are defined can be seen in the differences between the two curves.

### 4.4.3  Calibration Problems

The piecewise constant hazard rate model of credit curves may be standard but it is not without problems. One issue surrounds the calibration of the survival probability function as it is relatively straightforward to specify a set of CDS spreads that imply a hazard rate segment is negative. This situation can occur frequently with relatively high spreads, where the longer maturity hazard rate segments become particularly sensitive to the spread level. Longer maturity CDS spreads are also often quite illiquid so it is common for long maturity CDS spread quotes to become stale and cause the credit curve to fail during construction. The most basic solution is to adjust the spreads until the curve builds, however, when bootstrapping a credit curve from CDS spreads it is possible to estimate the acceptable range of CDS spreads for the next segment of the curve and hence check that the quoted CDS spread will still allow the curve to be constructed.

Assume that there are $n$ CDS spreads in the curve and that $n-1$ have already been successfully used to construct the survival probability function to the maturity of the $(n-1)th$ CDS at time $t_{n-1}$. For the piecewise constant hazard rate function the survival probability to time $T$ where $t_{k-1} \leq T < t_k$ is given by

$$P(\tau > T) = \exp\left(-\int_{t_0}^{T} \lambda(s)ds\right) \tag{4.18}$$

$$= \exp\left(-\lambda_k(T - t_{k-1})\right) P(\tau > t_{k-1}).$$

Hence, given that we know all of the $\lambda_i$ are positive and finite for hazard rate segments 1 through $n-1$, it is possible to use the fact that

$$0 \leq \lambda_n,$$

to set limits on acceptable values of $s_n$, the $n$th CDS spread.

To simplify the proof, assume that no accrued interest is payable on the CDS contracts and so the value of the $n$th CDS spread is given by

$$0 = V^n_{CDS}(t_0) = V^n_{prem}(t_0) - V^n_{prot}(t_0). \tag{4.19}$$

The protection leg can be written as

$$V^n_{prot}(t_0) = (1 - R) \sum_{a=1}^{A} \frac{\lambda_a}{\lambda_a + r_a} \left[B(t_0, u_{a-1})P(\tau > u_a) - B(t_0, u_a)P(\tau > u_a)\right]$$

$$= V^{n-1}_{prot}(t_0)$$

$$+ (1 - R) \sum_{a=\hat{A}}^{A} \frac{\lambda_a}{\lambda_a + r_a} \left[B(t_0, u_{a-1})P(\tau > u_{a-1}) - B(t_0, u_a)P(\tau > u_a)\right], \tag{4.20}$$

where $t_0 = u_0 < \ldots < u_a < \ldots < u_{\hat{A}} = t_{n-1} < \ldots < u_A = t_n$ is the time partition over which the protection leg is calculated. Similarly the premium leg can be written

$$V^n_{prem}(t_0) = s_n \sum_{b=1}^{B} \alpha_i B(t_0, t_b) P(\tau > t_b)$$

$$= s_n \sum_{b=1}^{\hat{B}} \alpha_i B(t_0, v_b) P(\tau > v_b) + s_n \sum_{b=\hat{B}}^{B} \alpha_i B(t_0, v_b) P(\tau > v_b) \quad (4.21)$$

$$= \frac{s_n}{s_{n-1}} V^{n-1}_{prem}(t_0) + s_n \sum_{b=\hat{B}}^{B} \alpha_i B(t_0, v_b) P(\tau > v_b),$$

where $t_0 = v_0 < \ldots < v_b < \ldots < v_{\hat{B}} = t_{n-1} < \ldots < v_B = t_n$ is the time partition defined by the premium accrual periods/payment dates.

Using equations (4.21), (4.20) and (4.19) gives an expression for the nth CDS spread

$$s_n = \frac{V^{n-1}_{prot}(t_0) + (1-R) \sum_{a=\hat{A}}^{A} \frac{\lambda_a}{\lambda_a + r_a} \left[ B(t_0, u_{a-1}) P(\tau > u_{a-1}) - B(t_0, u_a) P(\tau > u_a) \right]}{\frac{1}{s_{n-1}} V^{n-1}_{prem}(t_0) + \sum_{b=\hat{B}}^{B} \alpha_i B(t_0, v_b) P(\tau > v_b)}. \quad (4.22)$$

To identify the limits of $s_n$ we need to evaluate this expression in the limit $\lambda_n \to 0$.[3] Taking limits, to ensure positive hazard rates

$$\boxed{s_n > s_{min} = \frac{V^{n-1}_{prot}}{\frac{1}{s_{n-1}} V^{n-1}_{prem} + P(\tau > t_{n-1}) \sum_{b=\hat{B}}^{B} \alpha_i B(t_0, v_b)}.} \quad (4.23)$$

It is a straightforward exercise to extend this approach to include the accrued fee leg.

## 4.5 CDS AND CAPITAL RELIEF

As will be discussed in detail in Chapter 12, under Basel III (BCBS, 2011b) hedging of CVA using single name and index CDS contracts provides capital relief. The CDS provides capital relief through the hedge prior to default and hence the CDS contract not only provides a payout on default of the reference name, but also provides an effective cash flow stream prior to default, offsetting cost of capital the CVA hedging bank would otherwise face. This effect implies that the market implied default probability should be adjusted to take account of this effect.

---

[3]The other limit $\lambda_n \to \infty$ implies instantaneous default after $t_{n-1}$ and so is not terribly useful.

The difficulty is that not all CDS are used to hedge CVA, so not all market participants gain this benefit. Furthermore, even for CVA hedging activity the amount of any capital relief depends on regulatory status with banks using internal models receiving different benefits from those using the standardised approach. The corporate exemption under CRDIV means that for EU domiciled corporates there is no requirement to hold CVA capital so CDS on such names should show no capital benefit, although the exemption itself remains under discussion and hence some market expectation that capital relief may be available in the future may still be present. In theory then the existence of different capital reliefs for different market participants could lead to differential pricing for OTC CDS, but to date this has not been seen.

The presence of capital relief suggests that the economic value of CDS should be modified to reflect it by adding a capital protection leg to the CDS pricing model. This revised model allows estimates of how much of the CDS price reflects CVA hedging by banks. Furthermore it provides a means of generating market implied hazard rates including the effect of capital relief and therefore provides an alternative interpretation of market CDS spreads.

The relief leg would have the value

$$V_{relief}(t_0) = \int_{t_0}^{T} \mathbb{E}\left[D_{cap}(t_0, s)H(K_{relief}(t), t)\mathbb{1}_{\tau \geq s}\right] ds, \qquad (4.24)$$

where $D_{cap}(t_a, t_b)$ is a stochastic capital discount factor from time $t_a$ to time $t_b$, $H$ is the instantaneous cost of capital and $K_{relief}(t)$ is the capital relief from unit notional of CDS protection at time $t$. Kenyon and Green (2013b) use the above expression to assess the degree of capital relief present in CDS prices and conclude that it lies in the range 20–50%.[4]

## 4.6 LIQUID AND ILLIQUID COUNTERPARTIES

Counterparties for which there are liquid CDS contracts are relatively easy to handle in a risk-neutral modelling framework. In the usual case where the derivatives rank *pari passu* with senior unsecured debt then the CVA should be marked using the CDS spreads for the counterparty. Hedging the expected exposure fully with these CDS contracts will allow the credit spread sensitivity and the instantaneous loss on default to be hedged, at least in theory.

Unfortunately there are only around 3000 counterparties worldwide for which CDS spreads are quoted and even then there are significant questions around how liquid some CDS contracts really are. Hence the majority of all derivatives counterparties that banks face will have no quoted CDS contracts. Unless an alternative source of market credit risk information is available such as liquid corporate bonds, the requirement to mark CVA using implied survival probabilities can therefore only be met by linking each counterparty with a representative CDS curve through a mapping process. This mapping process will mean that any CDS hedges used to hedge the associated spread risk will not be effective on the actual default of the counterparty and that as a result some of the risk is "warehoused". The implications of risk warehousing are considered in Chapter 22 and in Kenyon and Green (2015c).

The nature of the mapping process is largely within the control of each bank, subject to appropriate oversight from bank auditors. However, under Basel III (BCBS, 2011b), the CDS

---

[4]See Kenyon and Green (2013b) for further details.

mapping process for the CVA capital charge where a bank has IMM approval is required to be based on three factors: industry sector, rating and geography. These three factors are in reality the only pieces of information available to a bank on which to base the CDS map so the Basel III regulations reflect industry practice. However, even these three factors can be problematic. The number of CDS contracts available in the US market is much larger than in other regions, making it much easier to construct a map for US entities that those in other regions of the world. Outside the US it can prove difficult to find sufficient liquid CDS in all industry sectors and ratings in order to construct an appropriate mapping. If geography is ignored, however, then it is likely that banks would inevitably be forced to map to large numbers of counterparties to US CDS. One could therefore question how appropriate such a map would be.

### 4.6.1 Mapping to Representative CDS

Illiquid names can be mapped directly to the single name CDS of a different company. Usually the chosen company is similar in profile to the illiquid entity, ideally having a similar creditworthiness, sector and being based in the same region, although this may not be possible. The advantage of such an approach to mapping is that the liquid CDS contract can be readily traded and, if a good choice has been made, then the liquid CDS contract will be representative of the credit risk in the illiquid name and will respond to the same systemic and sector-specific risk drivers.

To hedge the illiquid name, CDS contracts on the mapped name would be traded, with the nature of the map allowing the entire CDS spread sensitivity to be hedged. From a P&L perspective the credit risk of the CVA could be potentially entirely eliminated. However, this would still hide significant basis risk between the illiquid name and the name it was mapped to. If the mapped name was subject to idiosyncratic risk factors then it could cease to be representative of the risk of the illiquid name. If the idiosyncratic risk drove the CDS spread wider this would drive the CVA on the illiquid name higher to inappropriately high levels or to inappropriately low levels if the reverse was true. If CVA hedging was in place this would still track the marked CVA.

If the mapped name defaulted while the illiquid name did not the CDS contracts would pay out, resulting in a windfall gain for the CVA desk. However, the CVA would need to be marked to another CDS contract and re-hedged appropriately. If the illiquid name defaulted but the mapped name did not then the CDS contract would not trigger and hence not provide any compensation for the defaulted name. The CVA desk would therefore face a loss, although the hedging CDS contracts could be sold and this might provide partial compensation, particularly if the CDS widened either in response to systemic factors prior to the default or after the default in response to negative market sentiment following the default.[5]

Overall, mapping to representative single name CDS contracts has advantages from an accounting perspective but does so at the expense of considerable basis risk that is not immediately visible. A stress testing approach, where the impact of idiosyncratic risk is assessed could mitigate some of the basis risk or at least allow it to be assessed.[6]

---

[5]See Chapter 22.

[6]In advance of Chapter 12 it is worth noting that a mapping to representative CDS may offer significant capital advantages, especially under IMM if allowed by the local regulator.

## 4.6.2  Mapping to Baskets and Indices

Another alternative is to map illiquid names directly to CDS indices provided by *Markit* and the *CDS Index Company*, although the latter is now also owned by Markit. These consist of a number of regional benchmark indices in broad categories of creditworthiness and for Europe a number of sector indices for certain specific industrial sectors. The CDS Index Company *CDX* series cover North America, while Markit *iTraxx* cover the rest of the world with most focus on Europe.

If the mapping process is designed to map directly to traded indices then hedging the CVA CV01 sensitivities will be relatively straightforward and just a matter of trading the indices. Theoretically if counterparties were mapped directly to single indices or weighted combinations of them, the error could be eliminated in the absence of defaults in the index. However, such a map would still be artificial and have implicit basis risk. Indices or combinations of indices will never accurately reflect the risk of a specific illiquid counterparty.

If the counterparty defaults the hedge will again not pay out leading to potentially significant losses. If defaults occur in the basket this will lead to gains to the index buyer but will potentially lead to tracking errors that accumulate over time. An approach purely based on mapping to traded indices may, therefore, lead to a sense of false security where P&L volatility remains low until a crisis strikes and the defaults of illiquid names lead to losses by the CVA trading desk, even though supposedly fully hedged.[7]

Markit currently provide a service that produces average curves for a series of market sectors and ratings and this could provide another means of marking illiquid names. Rating/sector combination curves are available for all "whole" rating categories (AAA, AA, A, BBB, BB, B, CCC) and for twelve sectors that have been constructed by Markit partners using baskets of single name CDS. At present there is no geographical breakdown. The major advantage of this service is that is provides a far richer set of "index" curves to mark to than any other source. However, there are a number of disadvantages in that the rating and sectors categories are broader than most banks would normally use for their own internal processes. This means that some form of map between internal ratings and sector information and the Markit rating and sector categories is still required. For rating information this could involve some sort of interpolation to a finer set of ratings as most internal scales will already have attachment points onto the major external rating systems. For sector information this will involve the institution designing a bespoke map between internal information in whatever form it is held and the Markit sectors. The Markit sector information is also provided next day which may make it unsuitable for use in marking CVA at the close of business.

The Markit provided data set is of course not exclusive and a bespoke set of non-traded average CDS curves could be created on a proprietary basis from single name CDS curves. Such a set of average CDS curves could be made as granular as desired, although with the limitation that the amount of available curve data for some combinations of sector, rating and geography may be insufficient to create a suitable curve.

Hedging a map based on non-traded average CDS curve is more complex than one based on traded indices. In theory a hedge could be constructed from the components of each average curve. However, the exact curve constituents may not always be provided by external data vendors if a third-party data set has been selected. Even if the curve constituents are known,

---

[7]As noted above in the context of a representative CDS map, a pure index map would theoretically offer capital advantages. This is further discussed in Chapter 12.

in practice it likely to prove too expensive and inefficient to hedge using the underlying components of each curve. In practice then it is likely that hedging will involve the use of proxies and this will naturally lead to tracking errors. Of course any such hedge will still not pay out when the default of an illiquid name occurs.

### 4.6.3 Cross-sectional Maps

One alternative to the above mapping processes of proxy CDS curves, based on intersection approaches, is one based on a *cross-section* approach. In a recent ISDA paper (ISDA, 2012), the following model was proposed, itself based on the work of Chourdakis et al. (2013) and McEwen, Kyriakos and Jeannin (2012). The proxy spread for a given counterparty is defined by *n* factors and so the proxy spread can be written

$$S^i_{proxy} = \prod_{j=1}^{n} m_j. \tag{4.25}$$

ISDA give five factors:

1. Global factor
2. Industry sector
3. Regional factor
4. Rating factor
5. Seniority factor

although there is no reason why there could not be more or fewer factors. The central three factors, sector, region and rating, are those enshrined in Basel III (BCBS, 2011b) for use in calculating CVA capital with IMM approval. Each weighting factor $m_j$ will take a different value depending on the range of values the underlying factor can take. So for example if ratings were divided into the full S&P-style scheme there would be nineteen ratings from AAA to CCC- and $m_{rating}$ could take nineteen different values.

To calibrate the cross-section model, Chourdakis et al. (2013) propose a linear regression approach. They note that equation (4.25) can be written as follows if the log of both sides is taken:

$$y^i = \log S^i_{proxy} = \sum_{j=1}^{m} A_{ij} \log m_j, \tag{4.26}$$

where the sum over *j* is now taken over all values of all factors and the matrix $A_{ij}$ consists of indicator values with 1 where the proxy matches a particular value of the factor and 0 otherwise. So if the counterparty has rating AA then matrix $A_{ij}$ would have 1 in the column associated with rating AA and 0 in all the other rating columns and this is illustrated in Table 4.2. Calibration can then be achieved through least-squares regression. A series of liquid curves have their factor values identified and then the weights chosen to minimise the difference between the generated proxy spreads and the actual CDS spreads. Once calibrated the factors can be used to generate proxy curves for illiquid names based on the sector, region, rating and seniority.

**TABLE 4.2**  An example factor matrix for the cross-sectional mapping method.

| Name | Ratings | | | | Sectors | | | Regions | | | Seniority | |
|---|---|---|---|---|---|---|---|---|---|---|---|---|
| | | | | | Financials | Telecoms | | North America | Europe | | Senior | Subordinated |
| | AAA | AA+ | AA | ... | | | ... | | | ... | | |
| ctpy 1 | 0 | 1 | 0 | | 0 | 1 | | 1 | 0 | | 1 | 0 |
| ctpy 2 | 0 | 0 | 1 | | 1 | 0 | | 0 | 1 | | 1 | 0 |

The advantage of this cross-sectional approach and the calibration process outlined above is that the amount of data available for calibration is much higher than other approaches. For example the rating factor is calibrated using all of the rating information across all sectors, geographies and seniorities. The alternatives outlined above rely on having a sufficient number of curves within a given combination of factors to be able to generate a meaningful average curve. This model is also far less susceptible to rating transitions in the calibrating data set. Intersectional approaches, where a small number of curves contribute to the proxy curve, can be adversely affected when the composition of the basket changes, typically when a rating changes and a contributor moves into or out of the basket (see ISDA, 2012: 13–17).

As presented the CDS spreads would be calibrated for each tenor separately and then combined to give a proxy CDS curve that could then be bootstrapped in the usual way to generate the survival probability function. However, it should be noted that if the CDS spreads are calibrated separately for each tenor there is no guarantee the curve will build. If this were to be the case then the minimum spread level, given by equation (4.23), could be used to allow the curve to be constructed.

The linear regression method is not the only possible way this model could be calibrated. There is some evidence to suggest that models of this type have been used where the calibration of regional factors has been done directly to sovereign CDS spreads rather than single name CDS in specific regions. If this is done then all proxy spreads from a given region then have some dependence on the sovereign CDS spreads. The advantage of an approach like this is that a fraction of the risk could be hedged with the relatively liquid sovereign CDS market.[8] However, this automatically leads CVA hedging desks to buy sovereign CDS which in turn may have driven sovereign CDS spreads themselves wider and been part of the so-called sovereign *doom loop* (Hume, 2010; Murphy, 2012; Pollack, 2011). There are, of course, other explanations for the sovereign doom loop. CVA desks may have been buying sovereign CDS contracts to hedge direct exposures or as a proxy hedge irrespective of what type of mapping was used. Nevertheless it is worth noting that the choice of mapping does drive CVA hedging behaviour and, given the size of CVA desk positions, could have consequences for the market as a whole.

---

[8]Note that the short selling regulations introduced on 1 November 2012 in Europe appear to have had a significant impact on the liquidity of the sovereign CDS market at the time of writing.

## CHAPTER 5

# Analytic Models for CVA and DVA

*The primary factor in a successful attack is speed.*
—Lord Mountbatten, 1st Earl Mountbatten of Burma
*British Admiral and Statesman (1900–1979)*

## 5.1 ANALYTIC CVA FORMULAE

As discussed earlier the standard approach to calculating CVA involves the use of a Monte Carlo simulation to calculate the expected exposure as this is the most general solution and allows the impact of close-out netting to be fully included. Nevertheless there is a place for analytic models, although they are limited compared to the general solution provided by Monte Carlo models. A limited number of analytic solutions are available for the CVA of single derivatives and these are derived in this chapter, covering interest rate swaps, interest rate caps and floors and FX forwards. The main advantage of analytic formulae over Monte Carlo is speed, with computational performance several orders of magnitude greater than that of a Monte Carlo simulation. As most of these formulae are for trades on a standalone basis, the CVA calculation will not be correct for more than one transaction in a given netting set. In the case of unilateral CVA models the CVA calculated on a standalone basis will also be conservative compared to a netted portfolio. However, if bilateral CVA models are used there is no guarantee that the standalone CVA value will be conservative. Analytic CVA formulae are frequently used as a point of comparison for Monte Carlo models and sometimes used in pricing where performance is critical.

## 5.2  INTEREST RATE SWAPS

### 5.2.1  Unilateral CVA

Recall equation (3.13),

$$
\text{CVA}(t_0) = (1 - R) \sum_{i=0}^{n-1} [\Phi(\tau > t_i) - \Phi(\tau > t_{i+1})] \mathbb{E} \left[ \exp \left( - \int_{u=t_0}^{t_i} r(u) du \right) (V_{t_i})^+ | \mathcal{G}_t \right],
$$

where the recovery rate is assumed to be constant and the expectation uses the risk-neutral measure with the rolled-up money market account, $\exp \left( \int_{u=t_0}^{t} r(u) du \right)$ as numeraire. We can write the value of the interest rate swap as

$$
V_{swap}(t_0) = \sum_{j=1}^{m} (S - K) \alpha_j B(t_0, t_j), \tag{5.1}
$$

where

- $\alpha_j$ is the day-count fraction over which the coupon accrues.
- $B(t_0, t_j)$ is the value (at $t_0$) of a discount factor maturing at time $t_j$.
- $K$ is the fixed rate of the swap.
- The fixed and floating leg frequencies and day count bases are assumed to be the same for simplicity.
- $S$ is the par swap rate where

$$
S = \frac{\sum_{k=1}^{n} \left[ f_{(k-1)k} \alpha_k B(t_0, t_k) \right]}{\sum_{k=1}^{n} \alpha_j B(t_0, t_k)} \tag{5.2}
$$

and

$$
f_{(k-1)k} = \frac{1}{\alpha_k} \left[ \frac{B'(t_0, t_{k-1})}{B'(t_0, t_k)} - 1 \right]. \tag{5.3}
$$

- $B'(t_0, t_k)$ is the value (at $t_0$) of the discount factor maturing at time $t_j$ that is associated with the appropriate rate projection curve. This could be xIBOR or some other rate projection curve.

At some future time $t$ the value of the remaining cash flows of the swap is given by

$$
V_{swap}(t) = \sum_{j=p}^{m} (S - K) \alpha_j B(t_0, t_j), \tag{5.4}
$$

where the summation now occurs over all cash flows after time $t$, from index $j = p$ to $j = m$. Hence for an interest rate swap where the bank pays fixed and receives floating the CVA is given by substituting equation (5.4) into equation (3.13),

$$\text{CVA}^{swap}(t_0) = (1 - R) \sum_{i=0}^{n-1} [\Phi(\tau > t_i) - \Phi(\tau > t_{i+1})] \tag{5.5}$$

$$\times \mathbb{E}\left[\exp\left(-\int_{u=t_0}^{t_i} r(u)du\right)(\sum_{j=p}^{m}(S - K)\alpha_j B(t_0, t_j))^+|\mathcal{G}_t\right]. \tag{5.6}$$

The expectation is just the value of a physically settled European swaption,

$$V_{PS}(t_0, t_i, K) = \mathbb{E}\left[\exp\left(-\int_{u=t_0}^{t_i} r(u)du\right)(\sum_{j=p}^{m}(S - K)\alpha_j B(t_0, t_j))^+|\mathcal{G}_t\right]. \tag{5.7}$$

Hence the unilateral CVA becomes

$$\text{CVA}^{swap}(t_0) = (1 - R) \sum_{i=0}^{n-1} [\Phi(\tau > t_i) - \Phi(\tau > t_{i+1})] V_{PS}(t_0, t_i, K). \tag{5.8}$$

If the swap is one in which the bank receives fixed and pays floating the formula becomes

$$\text{CVA}^{swap}(t_0)(1 - R) \sum_{i=0}^{n-1} [\Phi(\tau > t_i) - \Phi(\tau > t_{i+1})] V_{RS}(t_0, t_i, K), \tag{5.9}$$

where $V_{RS}(t_0, t_i, K)$ is the value of a receiver's European swaption.

Hence the CVA on an interest rate swap can be represented as a weighted sum over the values of coterminal European swaptions with exercise dates corresponding to the cash flows of the swap. Note that no specification of the model has been made so any choice can be made. The standard models would be Black's model (Black, 1976) with the appropriate choice of implied volatility from a strike-dependent surface, SABR (Hagan et al., 2002; Obłój, 2008) or a variant of it such as ZABR (Andreasen and Huge, 2011). Typically these models are used as a parametric way of maintaining an accurate implied volatility surface rather than implying term structure consistent dynamics. In general it is much more challenging to build a term structure model fully consistent with the smile and skew in the implied volatility surface than it is to use models such as SABR for vanilla interest rate option pricing. Chapter 16 will discuss this in much more detail but it is worth noting the following here:

■ The analytic model for CVA on interest rate swaps can be made consistent with smile and skew in interest rate implied volatility if the appropriate strike and forward-rate dependent volatility is used.
■ Considerable differences in CVA can be seen between this analytic approach and a term structure interest rate model used to drive a Monte Carlo simulation unless the dynamics

are identical. So for example to test a CVA Monte Carlo model using HJM dynamics, the HJM model should also be used to determine the price of the European swaptions in the above formula.

## 5.2.2  Bilateral CVA

It is relatively straightforward to extend the unilateral model to the case of bilateral CVA. Equation (3.47) gives the expression for bilateral CVA. Using equation (5.4) for the residual swap value, the positive part of this value is given by

$$(V(t_i))^+ = \left( \sum_{j=p}^{m} (S - K)\alpha_j B(t_i, t_j) \right)^+ \tag{5.10}$$

and the negative part by

$$(V(t_i))^- = \left( \sum_{j=p}^{m} (S - K)\alpha_j B(t_i, t_j) \right)^- \tag{5.11}$$

$$= - \left( \sum_{j=p}^{m} (K - S)\alpha_j B(t_i, t_j) \right)^+.$$

Inputting these expressions into equation (3.47) gives a formula written in terms of the value of payers, $V_{PS}$, and receivers, $V_{RS}$, European swaptions:

$$\boxed{\begin{aligned}
\text{BCVA}^{swap} &= (1 - R_C) \sum_{i=0}^{n-1} [\Phi(\tau_C > t_{i+1}) - \Phi(\tau_C > t_i)]\Phi(\tau_B > t_i)V_{PS}(t_0, t_i, K) \\
&+ (1 - R_B) \sum_{i=0}^{n-1} [\Phi(\tau_B > t_{i+1}) - \Phi(\tau_B > t_i)]\Phi(\tau_C > t_i)V_{RS}(t_0, t_i, K).
\end{aligned}} \tag{5.12}$$

This expression assumes the default times of B and C are independent of each other, but the copula techniques described in section 3.4.1 could also be applied here.

## 5.3  OPTIONS: INTEREST RATE CAPLETS AND FLOORLETS

The credit risk-free value of an interest rate caplet is given by

$$V_{t_0}^{caplet}(T, K) = \mathbb{E}^r \left[ \exp \left\{ - \int_{t_0}^{T} r(s)ds \right\} (f(t_s, T) - K)^+ \Big| \mathcal{G}_{t_0} \right], \tag{5.13}$$

where $t_s$ is the date of rate fixing, $T$ is the payment date, $f(t_s, T)$ is the forward rate and the expectation has been taken in the risk-neutral measure with the rolled-up money market account as numeraire. Substituting this expression into the unilateral CVA formula, equation

(3.13) gives

$$
\mathrm{CVA}^{caplet}(t_0) = (1 - R) \sum_{i=0}^{n-1} [\Phi(\tau > t_i) - \Phi(\tau > t_{i+1})]
$$

$$
\times \mathbb{E}\left[ e^{-\int_{t_0}^{t_i} r(s)ds} \left( \mathbb{E}\left[ e^{-\int_{t_0}^{T} r(u)du} (f(t_s, T) - K)^+ \Big| \mathcal{G}_{t_i} \right] \right)^+ \Big| \mathcal{G}_{t_0} \right]. \quad (5.14)
$$

The max function can be eliminated as the caplet value is always zero or greater and then using the tower property of expectations allows the inner expectation to be eliminated:

$$
= \mathbb{E}\left[ e^{-\int_{t_0}^{t_i} r(s)ds} \mathbb{E}\left[ e^{-\int_{t_i}^{T} r(u)du} (f(t_s, T) - K)^+ \Big| \mathcal{G}_{t_i} \right] \Big| \mathcal{G}_{t_0} \right]
$$

$$
= \mathbb{E}\left[ e^{-\int_{t_0}^{T} r(s)ds} (f(t_s, T) - K)^+ \Big| \mathcal{G}_{t_0} \right]
$$

$$
= V_{t_0}^{caplet}(T, K), \quad (5.15)
$$

and replaced with the value of an interest rate cap. Given this has no dependence on the partition equation (5.14) reduces to

$$
\boxed{\mathrm{CVA}^{caplet}(t_0) = (1 - R) \left[ \Phi(t_0) - \Phi(T) \right] V_{t_0}^{caplet}(T, K),} \quad (5.16)
$$

that is the value of the interest rate cap weighted by the loss-given-default and the probability of default before the cash flow associated with the cap is paid. The result also holds for the unilateral CVA on an interest rate floorlet. In general similar formulae can be derived for all European-style options that resolve to a single cash flow. Of course in general groups of caplets and floorlets are sold in one transaction as caps and floors and this is much more complex to calculate because all the caplets or floorlets will net together and in this case a full term structure model must be used to derive the CVA. However, this simple approach would give an upper bound on the unilateral CVA if all the caplets/floorlets were treated as non-netted.

The CVA of the interest rate caplet under a bilateral CVA model is given by substituting equation (5.13) into equation (3.47), giving

$$
\mathrm{BCVA}^{caplet} = (1 - R_C) \sum_{i=0}^{n-1} [\Phi(\tau_C > t_{i+1}) - \Phi(\tau_C > t_i)]\Phi(\tau_B > t_i)
$$

$$
\times \mathbb{E}\left[ e^{-\int_{t_0}^{t_i} r(s)ds} \left( \mathbb{E}\left[ e^{-\int_{t_i}^{T} r(u)du} (f(t_s, T) - K)^+ \Big| \mathcal{G}_{t_i} \right] \right)^+ \Big| \mathcal{G}_{t_0} \right]
$$

$$
+ (1 - R_B) \sum_{i=0}^{n-1} [\Phi(\tau_B > t_{i+1}) - \Phi(\tau_B > t_i)]\Phi(\tau_C > t_i)
$$

$$
\times \mathbb{E}\left[ e^{-\int_{t_0}^{t_i} r(s)ds} \left( \mathbb{E}\left[ e^{-\int_{t_i}^{T} r(u)du} (f(t_s, T) - K)^+ \Big| \mathcal{G}_{t_i} \right] \right)^- \Big| \mathcal{G}_{t_0} \right]. \quad (5.17)
$$

The second term is zero as it contains the negative part of an expression which is always positive. This simply reflects that only the option buyer has exposure to the option seller after the premium has been paid. Eliminating the second max function and using the tower property of expectations gives

$$\text{BCVA}^{caplet} = (1 - R_C)V_{t_0}^{caplet}(T, K) \sum_{i=0}^{n-1} [\Phi(\tau_C > t_{i+1}) - \Phi(\tau_C > t_i)]\Phi(\tau_B > t_i). \qquad (5.18)$$

Unfortunately the summation does not simplify in this case because of the conditional probability. The only the difference in this case is the extra conditioning on the survival of the bank, B.

## 5.4  FX FORWARDS

The value of an FX forward with strike $K$ is given by

$$V^{FXFwd}(t) = B_d(t, T)[F(T) - K] \qquad (5.19)$$

where $F(T)$ is the value of the FX spot rate at maturity of the forward contract and $B_d$ is the domestic currency discount factor maturing at T. Following the same procedure as for the interest rate swaps and caps gives the unilateral CVA for the FX forward as

$$\text{CVA}^{FXFwd}(t_0) = (1 - R) \sum_{i=0}^{n-1} [\Phi(\tau > t_i) - \Phi(\tau > t_{i+1})]$$
$$\times \mathbb{E}^d \left[ e^{-\int_{t_0}^T r_d(s)ds} (F(T) - K)^+ \Big| \mathcal{G}_{t_0} \right], \qquad (5.20)$$

where the expectation is taken in the domestic risk-neutral measure with the domestic rolled-up money market account as numeraire. The expectation term is the value of an FX call option with strike $K$, maturing at time $T$ and hence the CVA on an FX forward is simply given by the value of the FX option maturing at the same time with the same strike level and weighted by the loss-given-default and the probability of counterparty default before the maturity date of the FX forward,

$$\text{CVA}^{FXFwd}(t_0) = (1 - R)[\Phi(\tau > t_0) - \Phi(\tau > T)]V^{FXCall}(t_0, T, K). \qquad (5.21)$$

The bilateral result is obtained from equation (3.47), which gives

$$\text{BCVA}^{FXFwd} = (1 - R_C) \sum_{i=0}^{n-1} [\Phi(\tau_C > t_{i+1}) - \Phi(\tau_C > t_i)]\Phi(\tau_B > t_i)$$
$$\times \mathbb{E}^d \left[ e^{-\int_{t_0}^{t_i} r_d(s)ds} (F(T) - K)^+ \Big| \mathcal{G}_{t_0} \right]$$

$$+ (1 - R_B) \sum_{i=0}^{n-1} [\Phi(\tau_B > t_{i+1}) - \Phi(\tau_B > t_i)] \Phi(\tau_C > t_i)$$

$$\times \mathbb{E}^d \left[ e^{-\int_{t_0}^{t_i} r_d(s)ds} (F(T) - K)^- \Big| \mathcal{G}_{t_0} \right]. \tag{5.22}$$

The first term in this expression is a function of the value of an FX call option with strike $K$, as in the unilateral case, equation (5.21). Using $(F(T) - K)^- = (K - F(T))^+$, we see that the second term is a function of the value of an FX put option with strike $K$. Hence the final result is given by

$$\boxed{\begin{aligned} \text{BCVA}^{FXFwd} &= (1 - R_C) \sum_{i=0}^{n-1} [\Phi(\tau_C > t_{i+1}) - \Phi(\tau_C > t_i)] \Phi(\tau_B > t_i) V^{FXCall}(t_0, T, K) \\ &+ (1 - R_B) \sum_{i=0}^{n-1} [\Phi(\tau_B > t_{i+1}) - \Phi(\tau_B > t_i)] \Phi(\tau_C > t_i) V^{FXPut}(t_0, T, K). \end{aligned}} \tag{5.23}$$

## CHAPTER 6

# Modelling Credit Mitigants

*I am prepared for the worst, but hope for the best.*

—Benjamin Disraeli
*British Prime Minister 1868, 1874–1880*

## 6.1 CREDIT MITIGANTS

Credit mitigants were introduced in section 2.4. This chapter discusses how these can be incorporated into CVA models. There are four types of credit mitigant considered here: close-out netting, break clauses, financial collateral usually provided under the terms of a CSA agreement, and non-financial security, typically real estate.

## 6.2 CLOSE-OUT NETTING

Close-out netting is simultaneously the most important and simplest of all credit mitigants. Section 2.4.1 described netting and gave a simple example of its use in an example close-out situation. Setting aside the legal risks associated with the applicability of close-out netting and the potential for *cherry picking* of contracts on terms favourable to the defaulted entity, incorporating netting into CVA and DVA models is straightforward.

Recall the formula for unilateral CVA,

$$\text{CVA}(t) = \mathbb{E}[(1 - R)(V(\tau))^+|\mathcal{F}_t], \tag{6.1}$$

where $\tau$ is the default time. In this expression, $V(t)$, is the reference close-out value of the portfolio of trades at time $t$. In the case of a fully netted portfolio of $n$ trades this is given by,

$$V(t) = \sum_{i=1}^{n} V_i(t),$$

where the $V^i(t)$ are the values of the underlying trades assuming no credit risk and hence the CVA of a netted portfolio is given by[1]

$$\text{CVA}^{\text{netted}}(t) = \mathbb{E}\left[(1-R)\max\left(\sum_{i=1}^{n} V^i(\tau), 0\right)|\mathcal{F}_t\right]. \tag{6.2}$$

If none of the trades net then the max function must be applied to each trade individually giving a non-netted CVA of

$$\text{CVA}^{\text{non-netted}}(t) = \mathbb{E}\left[(1-R)\sum_{i=1}^{n}\max\left(V^i(\tau), 0\right)|\mathcal{F}_t\right]. \tag{6.3}$$

In reality trade portfolios can be subject to multiple netting agreements where multiple groups of trades net together in close-out but these groups do not net with each other. Each group of trades that net is called a *netting set*. If the trades are grouped into $j = 1 \dots m$ netting sets, each containing $n_j$ trades, then the unilateral CVA is given by

$$\text{CVA}^{\text{netting set}}(t) = \mathbb{E}\left[(1-R)\sum_{j=1}^{m}\max(\sum_{i=1}^{n_j} V^{ij}(\tau), 0)|\mathcal{F}_t\right], \tag{6.4}$$

where $V^{ij}(t)$ is the value of the $i$th trade in netting set $j$. Under unilateral CVA models netting *always* reduces CVA.

The extension to bilateral CVA models is trivial:

$$\text{BCVA}^{\text{netted}}(t) = \mathbb{E}\left[(1-R_C)\max\left(\sum_{i=1}^{n} V^i_{\min(\tau_B,\tau_C)}, 0\right)\mathbb{1}_{\tau_C<\tau_B<T}\right]$$

$$+ \mathbb{E}\left[(1-R_B)\max\left(-\sum_{i=1}^{n} V^i_{\min(\tau_B,\tau_C)}, 0\right)\mathbb{1}_{\tau_B<\tau_C<T}\right] \tag{6.5}$$

$$\text{BCVA}^{\text{non-netted}}(t) = \mathbb{E}\left[(1-R_C)\sum_{i=1}^{n}\max\left(V^i_{\min(\tau_B,\tau_C)}, 0\right)\mathbb{1}_{\tau_C<\tau_B<T}\right]$$

$$+ \mathbb{E}\left[(1-R_B)\sum_{i=1}^{n}\max\left(-V^i_{\min(\tau_B,\tau_C)}, 0\right)\mathbb{1}_{\tau_B<\tau_C<T}\right] \tag{6.6}$$

$$\text{BCVA}^{\text{netting set}}(t) = \mathbb{E}\left[(1-R_C)\sum_{j=1}^{m}\max\left(\sum_{i=1}^{n_j} V^{ij}_{\min(\tau_B,\tau_C)}, 0\right)\mathbb{1}_{\tau_C<\tau_B<T}\right]$$

$$+ \mathbb{E}\left[(1-R_B)\sum_{j=1}^{m}\max\left(-\sum_{i=1}^{n_j} V^{ij}_{\min(\tau_B,\tau_C)}, 0\right)\mathbb{1}_{\tau_B<\tau_C<T}\right]. \tag{6.7}$$

---

[1]Note that the max function is used explicitly here for clarity rather than the $()^+$ operator.

The key point to note in the case of bilateral CVA models is that netting does not always act as a credit mitigant. Consider the case where the DVA term is larger than the CVA term and hence the bilateral CVA for a particular counterparty increases the value of the derivative book. In such circumstances the introduction of close-out netting reduces the absolute close-out value of the portfolio and hence the absolute expected positive and expected negative exposures. However, as the bilateral CVA is value additive this effect is reduced and hence introducing netting has a negative impact on P&L.

## 6.3 BREAK CLAUSES

Section 2.4.5 introduced the two types of break clauses, *mandatory* and *optional*, that can be included as a credit mitigant in trade documentation. In this section I describe how these can be included in CVA models.

### 6.3.1 Mandatory Break Clauses

Mandatory break clauses result in the termination of a trade prior to the natural maturity with a cash flow equal to the mark-to-market value[2] of the trade at the mandatory break date to compensate for the early termination. After the break date the trade has ceased to exist, has zero mark-to-market and hence gives rise to no exposure. In trading systems, however, often no distinction is made between trades with and without mandatory break clauses and they have the same mark-to-market value in the absence of CVA, FVA and regulatory capital considerations.

In a CVA calculation mandatory breaks can be handled by simply setting the trade mark-to-market to zero after the break date. The cash flow occurring on the break date will be equal to the credit risk-free mark-to-market on that date and so up to and including the break date valuing the underlying trade as if it has no break will give the correct CVA. Ideally the break date and day after the break should be included in any Monte Carlo simulation schedule in order to capture the fall in the expected exposure and hence calculate CVA accurately. The impact of breaks on FVA calculations will be discussed in Chapter 9.

### 6.3.2 Optional Break Clauses

Optional break clauses give the right to one or both parties to terminate the derivative on a date or dates prior to the natural maturity with a cash flow equal to the trade mark-to-market settling the trade. As noted earlier, historically few optional break clauses have actually been exercised because of the potential detrimental effect on a client relationship. However, post crisis there is an expectation that optional break clauses will be exercised more frequently than in the past. The key question for each institution is whether or not to include optional break clauses in the CVA calculation and if the choice is made how to approach modelling them.

**Simple Treatments**   The simplest treatment of optional break clauses and the least conservative is to assume they will be always be exercised. For mutual breaks, as discussed in

---

[2]That is the credit risk-free value.

the next section, there is some justification for this approach. If this is adopted then optional break clauses are modelled as mandatory break clauses. However, the institution may feel this is too aggressive and choose to reduce the impact of the break clauses in some way. One option is to recognise some breaks but not others to reflect which are likely to be exercised. So, for example, a bank may choose to recognise breaks on trades with expert clients such as significant financial institutions but not recognise breaks on trades with other counterparties. To a degree the choice will reflect bank accounting policy as dictated by the bank finance department and external auditors, and the internal organisational design of the bank and who holds the right to exercise break clauses. If breaks are fully recognised then the CVA desk must either have the right to exercise the break or be compensated should optimal exercise not occur.

The typical modelling requirement arising from a simple treatment of optional breaks is the ability to selectively exercise break clauses and see the impact on expected exposure profiles and CVA. A fine grained capability would allow exercise of individual breaks on individual trades. However, in many cases the break clauses on different trades with the same counterparty are aligned to the same date. Hence in practice it may be sufficient to have the ability to exercise the first break on all trades with a given counterparty.

**Optimal Exercise**   The optional nature of the break clauses immediately raises the question of optimal exercise. There are two cases to consider, mutual breaks and one-sided breaks.

**Mutual breaks**   These give both parties the right to terminate the contract on the break date. As is shown by Giada and Nordio (2013), under a bilateral CVA model a mutual break clause will always be exercised and the same is also true under a unilateral CVA model. If a contract has multiple breaks, as is frequently the case with long maturity trades, then only the first break is relevant.

Consider the value of a single derivative between counterparties $A$ and $B$ under a bilateral CVA model. The value of the trade as seen by $A$ at the break date $\hat{t}$ is given by

$$V^A(\hat{t}) = V^0(\hat{t}) + V^A_{CVA}(\hat{t}) + V^A_{DVA}(\hat{t}) \qquad (6.8)$$

and by $B$ as

$$V^B(\hat{t}) = -V^0(\hat{t}) + V^B_{CVA}(\hat{t}) + V^B_{DVA}(\hat{t}), \qquad (6.9)$$

where

$$V^A = -V^B$$
$$V^A_{CVA} = -V^B_{DVA}$$
$$V^A_{DVA} = -V^B_{CVA}.$$

$A$ and $B$ will exercise the break clause under the following conditions:

$$V^A(\hat{t}) < V^0(\hat{t}) \qquad (6.10)$$
$$V^B(\hat{t}) < -V^0(\hat{t}), \qquad (6.11)$$

which must always be true for either $A$ or $B$ since we have a symmetric valuation where $V^A = -V^B$. This must also be true if this derivative is part of a portfolio of trades between the two counterparties.

In the unilateral case both counterparties will have different valuations of the derivative contract where each includes the CVA of the counterparty only so:

$$V^A(\hat{t}) = V^0(\hat{t}) + V^A_{CVA}(\hat{t}) \tag{6.12}$$

$$V^B(\hat{t}) = -V^0(\hat{t}) + V^B_{CVA}(\hat{t}), \tag{6.13}$$

where in both cases the CVA will reduce the overall value of the derivative, although both agree on the risk-neutral value, $V^0(\hat{t})$. Given that this is the case the condition for exercise of the break in equations (6.10) and (6.11) is always satisfied by both parties and so the break will always be exercised.

The impact of FVA (Chapter 9) and KVA (Chapter 13) on breaks is to complicate the picture significantly. It is very unlikely that the counterparties will agree on the value of the derivative as their funding and capital costs are different and fundamentally asymmetric in a similar way to unilateral CVA models. In these circumstances full optimal exercise modelling will be required in the same manner as for unilateral breaks, discussed below.

**One-sided breaks**  One-sided breaks give one party the right to terminate the contract and I will assume this is party $A$. Here a unilateral CVA model is the easiest case to consider and I will examine this first.

The value of the derivative contract as seen by $A$ on the break date $\hat{t}$ is

$$V^A(\hat{t}) = V^0(\hat{t}) + V^A_{CVA}(\hat{t}). \tag{6.14}$$

As with the mutual case, the CVA always reduces the value of the contract below its risk-neutral value so that

$$V^A(\hat{t}) < V^0(\hat{t}), \tag{6.15}$$

and exercise will therefore always occur at the first break date. Again here the impact of FVA and KVA would be to add complexity to the picture. In this case only the funding and capital costs of the counterparty with the option to break are relevant. Ignoring KVA, if a bilateral FVA model were used with the unilateral CVA model then the value of the derivative at the break date is given by

$$V^A(\hat{t}) = V^0(\hat{t}) + V^A_{CVA}(\hat{t}) + V^A_{FVA}(\hat{t}), \tag{6.16}$$

where $V^A_{FVA}(\hat{t})$ can be positive or negative. Clearly it will not always be the case that $V^A(\hat{t}) < V^0(\hat{t})$ and so the model must be extended to consider the option exercise.

With a bilateral CVA model or any kind of CVA model combined with FVA and/or KVA considerations exercise of the optional break is not always optimal and so the model must be extended to value the optionality correctly. Consider the case of a bilateral CVA model with a unilateral break held by counterparty $A$. The value of the derivative at the exercise date is given by

$$V^A(\hat{t}) = V^0(\hat{t}) + V^A_{CVA}(\hat{t}) + V^A_{DVA}(\hat{t}),$$  (6.17)

and so $A$ will exercise the break clause if $V^0(\hat{t}) > V^A(\hat{t})$ as $A$ will then receive $V^0(\hat{t})$ in cash at the break clause settlement date as determined by the ISDA agreement.[3] So $A$ will exercise if the valuation adjustment is net negative,

$$V_{DVA}(\hat{t}) < -V_{CVA}(\hat{t}).$$  (6.18)

The value of the derivative at $\hat{t}$ can be written using the bilateral CVA formula given by equation (3.44),

$$V^A(\hat{t}) = V^0(\hat{t}) + \mathbb{E}\left[(1-R_B)(V_{\min(\tau_A,\tau_B)})^+ \mathbb{1}_{\{\tau_B<\tau_A<T\}}\right]$$
$$+ \mathbb{E}\left[(1-R_A)(V_{\min(\tau_A,\tau_B)})^- \mathbb{1}_{\{\tau_A<\tau_B<T\}}\right],$$  (6.19)

and so at $t_0 < \hat{t}$ the value becomes

$$V^A(t_0) = V^0(t_0) + \mathbb{E}\left[(1-R_B)(V_{\min(\tau_A,\tau_B)})^+ \mathbb{1}_{\{\tau_B<\tau_A<T\}} \mathbb{1}_{\{\tau_B<\hat{t}\}}\right]$$
$$+ \mathbb{E}\left[(1-R_A)(V_{\min(\tau_A,\tau_B)})^- \mathbb{1}_{\{\tau_A<\tau_B<T\}} \mathbb{1}_{\{\tau_A<\hat{t}\}}\right]$$
$$+ \mathbb{E}\left[\mathbb{1}_{\{\min(\tau_A,\tau_B)>\hat{t}\}}(V_{CVA}(t) + V_{DVA}(t))^+\right].$$  (6.20)

This expression for a single break can readily be extended for the case of multiple break clauses. Giada and Nordio (2013) derive an expression for an analytic formula for an equity forward but in all practical cases with complex instruments or netted portfolios a numerical solution is needed. The key issue is that the CVA and DVA are required at future times in order to determine optimal exercise. As we will see later this type of implicit CVA formula will also appear when FVA is considered under certain assumptions. In the case of a single asset such a portfolio of products in a single currency a tree model might be a viable means of solving equation (6.20) but as most CVA calculations will have high numbers of dimensions the *Longstaff-Schwartz* regression technique (Longstaff and Schwartz, 2001), discussed in Chapter 19, is the only practical solution method.

---

[3]Clearly there is also a second order credit effect here as the exercise of the break clause might itself cause counterparty $B$ to default. The break would mandate $B$ to make a cash payment equal to the value of the derivative immediately and $B$ may not have sufficient liquidity to make the payment. If $B$ did default then $A$ would only receive $R_B V^0(\hat{t})$. There is an element of wrong-way risk here as the more distressed $B$ is the more likely exercise of the break clause and the more likely $B$ will default if the break is exercised. This is not factored into the above calculation.

## 6.4   VARIATION MARGIN AND CSA AGREEMENTS

The Credit Support Annex agreement was introduced in section 2.4.2 and Table 2.1 provides a description of all the key parameters that appear within them. This section provides three approaches to including financial collateral supplied as variation margin in CVA models: a simple payout modification, direct modelling of collateral and the look-back method. Financial collateral can be cash in an eligible currency or eligible securities where the eligibility is specified in the CSA agreement. Later in the section the impact of collateral on trade level attribution of CVA, discussed in section 3.6.2, is examined and how downgrade triggers, a feature of some CSAs, can be modelled.

Under collateralisation the CVA formulae must be modified to take account of the reduced exposure due to the value of the collateral. Assuming that at time $t$ collateral amount $X(t)$ has been posted or received then the expression for unilateral CVA becomes

$$\mathrm{CVA}(t) = \mathbb{E}\left[(1 - R_C)(V_\tau - X_\tau)^+\right], \tag{6.21}$$

and for bilateral CVA,

$$
\begin{aligned}
\mathrm{BCVA}(t) = {} & \mathbb{E}\left[(1 - R_C)(V_{\min(\tau_B,\tau_C)} - X_{\min(\tau_B,\tau_C)})^+ \mathbb{1}_{\tau_C < \tau_B < T}\right] \\
& + \mathbb{E}\left[(1 - R_B)(V_{\min(\tau_B,\tau_C)} - X_{\min(\tau_B,\tau_C)})^- \mathbb{1}_{\tau_B < \tau_C < T}\right].
\end{aligned}
\tag{6.22}
$$

### 6.4.1   Simple Model: Modifying the Payout Function

The simplest assumption to make in regard to modelling collateral is to assume that collateral is always posted instantaneously to fulfil the collateral requirement. So under a CSA with zero threshold and zero minimum transfer amount there would be no CVA since in equations (6.21) and (6.22) $V(t) = X(t)$ and there would be no exposure.

If the CSA defines threshold levels $H_B$ and $H_C$ for counterparties $B$ and $C$ respectively and the currency of the CSA is the same as the currency in which the portfolio is valued then making the same assumption leads to zero exposure above the threshold level. The collateral value is given by $X(t) = max(V(t) - H, 0)$. Hence under a unilateral model the CVA is given by

$$\mathrm{CVA}(t) = \mathbb{E}\left[(1 - R_C)\min(\max(V_\tau, 0), H_C)\right], \tag{6.23}$$

where the max function has been included explicitly. The payout function now has the character of a call spread. Bilateral CVA becomes

$$
\begin{aligned}
\mathrm{BCVA}(t) = {} & \mathbb{E}\left[(1 - R_C)\min(\max(V_{\min(\tau_B,\tau_C)}, 0), H_C)\mathbb{1}_{\tau_C < \tau_B < T}\right] \\
& + \mathbb{E}\left[(1 - R_B)\min(\max(-V_{\min(\tau_B,\tau_C)}, 0), H_B)\mathbb{1}_{\tau_B < \tau_C < T}\right].
\end{aligned}
\tag{6.24}
$$

This analysis ignores the *minimum transfer amount*, $M$, which is small in most CSAs but not all. To be conservative the minimum transfer amount could be added to the counterparty exposure so that the threshold in equation (6.23) is adjusted:

$$\bar{H}_C = H_C + M_C.$$

In the bilateral case, the self-exposure threshold could also be modified giving

$$\bar{H}_B = H_B + M_B$$

and retaining symmetry between B and C in the bilateral model. However, this is not conservative as the increase in threshold increases the self-exposure and hence the DVA benefit that is taken. A counterparty may therefore choose to only modify the counterparty term in the bilateral CVA model, giving a conservative but asymmetric treatment.

Of course the currency in which the portfolio value is measured may differ from the currency of the CSA agreement so, for example, a UK bank would likely value their derivative portfolio in GBP but when dealing with a US bank may have the terms of the CSA written in USD. If this is the case the threshold has to be adjusted by the FX rate, $Y_t$, inside the expectation operator. Hence unilateral and bilateral CVA are given by

$$\text{CVA}(t) = \mathbb{E}\left[(1 - R_C) \min(\max(V_\tau, 0), Y_\tau H_C)\right] \tag{6.25}$$

$$\text{BCVA}(t) = \mathbb{E}\left[(1 - R_C) \min(\max(V_{\min(\tau_B, \tau_C)}, 0), Y_{\min(\tau_B, \tau_C)} H_C) \mathbb{1}_{\tau_C < \tau_B < T}\right]$$
$$+ \mathbb{E}\left[(1 - R_B) \min(\max(-V_{\min(\tau_B, \tau_C)}, 0), Y_{\min(\tau_B, \tau_C)} H_B) \mathbb{1}_{\tau_B < \tau_C < T}\right]. \tag{6.26}$$

Some CSAs require an independent amount to be posted, irrespective of the market value of the underlying derivative portfolio. The independent amount is normally fixed in size, although it may be rating-dependent. Often independent amounts are one-way in that only one of the counterparties is required to post the independent amount. Assume C is required to post $I_C$ to B. In the simple model, given that the independent amount will almost always be accompanied by a full requirement to supply variation margin collateral, C's exposure to B will be overcollateralised and hence the unilateral CVA and the first term in the bilateral CVA model will be zero. However, this independent amount, unless it is held under conditions that are bankruptcy remote from B, adds to C's exposure to B. Hence bilateral CVA would become:

$$\text{BCVA}(t) = \mathbb{E}\left[(1 - R_B)(\min(\max(-V_{\min(\tau_B, \tau_C)}, 0), Y_{\min(\tau_B, \tau_C)} H_B) - I_C) \mathbb{1}_{\tau_B < \tau_C < T}\right]. \tag{6.27}$$

These simplistic approaches do allow collateral to be included in the CVA calculation but the collateral is not modelled at all, nor is the time delay between a missed payment and default actually occurring. Hence this model will underestimate the exposure to the counterparty and hence underestimate CVA in a unilateral model. Under a bilateral model the exposure of both counterparties will be underestimated and so the bilateral CVA can be under or over estimated.

## 6.4.2 Modelling Collateral Directly

The collateral account can be modelled directly within a Monte Carlo simulation used to estimate the expected exposure. The collateral is modelled on each collateral call date by applying the rules in the CSA to calculate the movement of collateral in response to changes in the value of the associated derivative portfolio. Consider first the simplest case of a CSA with no thresholds in which cash collateral is posted or received in a single currency in support of a portfolio that is valued in the same currency. Let $t_i$ be the current collateral call date and $t_{i-1}$ be the previous collateral call date. Assume that when collateral is called it is received immediately. The portfolio value at time $t$ is given by $V_t$ and the collateral account value by $X_t$. A minimum transfer amount of $M$ is in operation. I assume, without loss of generality, that the portfolio value, $V_t$, is positive throughout this section. The amount of collateral posted or received at time $t_i$ is given by

$$A^C(t_i) = (V(t_i) - X(t_i)) \quad \text{if} \quad |V(t_i) - X(t_i)| \geq M \tag{6.28}$$
$$A^C(t_i) = 0 \quad \text{if} \quad |V(t_i) - X(t_i)| < M. \tag{6.29}$$

If a threshold $H$ is in place if $V_t$ is positive then the required collateral amount is adjusted by subtracting threshold from the value of the portfolio so,

$$A^C(t_i) = (V(t_i) - H - X(t_i)) \quad \text{if} \quad |V(t_i) - H - X(t_i)| \geq M \quad \text{and if} \quad V(t_i) \geq H \tag{6.30}$$
$$A^C(t_i) = 0 \quad \text{if} \quad |V(t_i) - H - X(t_i)| < M \quad \text{and if} \quad V(t_i) \geq H \tag{6.31}$$
$$A^C(t_i) = X(t_i) \quad \text{if} \quad V(t_i) < H \quad \text{collateral is returned.} \tag{6.32}$$

Rounding is typically a feature of CSA agreements and can be included when collateral is modelled directly. If rounding is applied the collateral transfer amount $A^C$ should be rounded appropriately. In general, however, the rounding levels are small and have little impact on counterparty credit exposure and hence on CVA or FVA.

If the portfolio is valued in a different currency to the terms in which the CSA is written then an FX conversion must be introduced, so for example equations (6.28) and (6.29) would become

$$A^X(t_i) = (Y(t_i)V(t_i) - X(t_i)) \quad \text{if} \quad |V(t_i) - X(t_i)| \geq M \tag{6.33}$$
$$A^C(t_i) = 0 \quad \text{if} \quad |Y(t_i)V(t_i) - X(t_i)| < M \tag{6.34}$$

where $Y(t_i)$ is the FX rate.

In reality the situation may be far more complex as the CSA may allow the posting of collateral in multiple currencies and also allow assets such as bonds to be posted, sometimes with haircuts. If this is the case then modelling collateral directly requires:

- Each pool of collateral used to support the CSA must be modelled separately and then the total value of the collateral calculated in the currency of the CSA. Hence the total value of the collateral at time $t$, $X_t$, is given by the sum over the $n$ individual pools,

$$X(t) = \sum_{j=1}^{n} Y_j(t)c_j(t), \tag{6.35}$$

where the $Y_j$ are the FX rates required to convert from the currency of collateral pool $j$ to the currency of the CSA and the $c_j$ are the values of the individual collateral pools. In practice this means that all assets must also be valued inside the model. For cash this is straightforward but adding such as government or corporate bonds and asset-backed securities that are sometimes allowable under CSA agreements can be complex. The modelling of asset values within a Monte Carlo simulation is considered in Part IV.

▪ When considering what collateral is actually posted, there is a *cheapest-to-deliver* calculation required to optimise what is posted or called back. This calculation also requires an understanding of whether collateral substitution is allowed in the jurisdiction that the CSA operates under. Some jurisdictions allow free right of substitution meaning that the collateral poster has the right to call back all existing posted collateral and replace it with something else. Where the right of substitution applies then the posted collateral will always be the cheapest to deliver on the collateral call date.[4] If the right of substitution is not present then the collateral is "sticky" but additional posted or recalled collateral will still represent the optimal choice. The calculation of the cheapest-to-deliver collateral on any given date is generally straightforward and this is simply a process of ranking the relative cost of funding the collateral versus the interest received on the posted collateral.

An independent amount is straightforward to model directly as it just represents a fixed element in the collateral account, that is we can write $X(t) = X_{\text{variable}}(t) + I$ where I is the independent amount. The independent amount will likely be subject to the same cheapest-to-deliver considerations unless constraints are imposed on how it is posted in the CSA. $X(t)$ has been calculated (typically on each path in a Monte Carlo simulation) then the expected exposure and CVA is given by equation (6.21) or (6.22). However, this assumes two things, firstly that the collateral transfer is instantaneous and secondly that default is recognised immediately, while in reality neither of these assumptions is true. Interbank collateral transfers will most often be same day but this may not be the case for smaller counterparties who may have some time to respond to the collateral call for operational reasons. A delay in the collateral transfer can be modelled simply by not updating the collateral account value, $X(t)$, with the transfer amount, $A^C(t)$, immediately so that

$$X(t) = \sum_{j=1}^{n} Y_j(t)c_j(t) + A^C(t - \text{call delay}). \tag{6.36}$$

Default is often not recognised immediately, frequently because there is a grace period while the distressed counterparty is allowed time to post the collateral without having the failure to pay constitute a default. Also once default has occurred it may not be possible to close out the position immediately. Hence, typically exposure models embed the *cure period* or *margin period of risk* of a certain number of working days where collateral is assumed to have not been posted. The impact of the cure period can be included by using the value of the collateral account on the date 'cure period' days before the exposure measurement, so

---

[4]Although this does not mean that the collateral will actually prove to be the optimal asset to have been posted as the rate earned on the posted collateral may change due to market events between collateral call dates.

equations (6.21) or (6.22) would become

$$\text{CVA}(t) = \mathbb{E}\left[(1 - R_C)(V(\tau) - X(\tau - \Delta t_{cure}))^+\right] \tag{6.37}$$

$$\text{BCVA}(t) = \mathbb{E}\left[(1 - R_C)(V(\min(\tau_B, \tau_C)) - X(\min(\tau_B, \tau_C) - \Delta t_{cure}))^+ \mathbb{1}_{\tau_C < \tau_B < T}\right]$$

$$+ \mathbb{E}\left[(1 - R_B)(V(\min(\tau_B, \tau_C)) - X(\min(\tau_B, \tau_C) - \Delta t_{cure}))^- \mathbb{1}_{\tau_B < \tau_C < T}\right], \tag{6.38}$$

where $\Delta t_{cure}$ is the cure period.

Modelling collateral directly is the most accurate way of capturing all of the effect that impact exposure has under collateralisation. It can, for example, capture the spike in exposure that follows a large payment, such as the exchange of notional at the end of a cross-currency swap that may not be balanced by a collateral transfer until the next working day. This disadvantage is the computational cost of performing the calculation. If collateral calls occur daily then the collateral should be modelled daily and this would naturally lead to a Monte Carlo simulation with a one-business-day time step, which over the 30–40 years that some trades run would be very expensive.[5] Credit exposure systems for credit limit checking might well be interested in exposure spikes such as the one described, particularly over the near term. However, from a CVA perspective such a spike would only be weighted by one day of probability that the counterparty would default. In general this will be a small contributor to the overall CVA figure and it is questionable, therefore, whether directly modelling the collateral account is absolutely necessary for CVA calculations.[6] With this in mind the *lookback method* offers a compromise of accuracy against computational performance.

### 6.4.3 Lookback Method

The two principal drivers of exposure under CSA agreements are non-zero thresholds and volatility over the cure period due to changes in portfolio and collateral value. Given that the thresholds are fixed,[7] the primary requirement is to model the behaviour of the derivative portfolio and any supporting collateral over the cure period. Consider measuring the expected exposure on $t_E$, using the assumption that the portfolio is fully collateralised as per the CSA at the start of the cure period, that is

$$X(t_{CS}) = \max(V(t_{CS}) - H, 0) \tag{6.39}$$

where

$$t_{CS} = t - \Delta t_{cure}$$

where I have again assumed that P(t) is positive, the behaviour of the collateral can be modelled over the cure period. In practice this means that for each date on which the expected exposure is required, one additional date needs to be considered $\Delta t_{cure}$ days before. In terms of a Monte

---

[5]Although the computational performance available using GPUs could make this feasible. See Chapter 20 for details.

[6]Note, however, that a large payment may itself prompt the counterparty to default.

[7]Unless there is a downgrade trigger and this is considered in section 6.4.4.

Carlo simulation this approach would simply double the number of time steps required rather than introducing a very large number as under the direct modelling approach.

When adopting this approach what is left unknown is the precise composition of the collateral portfolio at the start of the cure period; all that is known is its value. To model the behaviour the composition of the collateral portfolio has to be assumed and three different possibilities suggest themselves when collateral is received from a counterparty:

1. Assume the optimal composition of collateral based on the market state at time $t_{CS}$.
2. Assume at time $t$ that the worst performing eligible assets were chosen.
3. Assume at time $t$ that the best performing eligible assets were chosen.

The last two choices use a variant of perfect foresight to set upper and lower bounds on the exposure at time $t$ while the first choice will give more realistic exposures. Note however that all three choices assume that collateral is not "sticky". For choice 1, the approach simply applies a collateral optimisation based on the eligible currencies and assets under the CSA. Choices 2 and 3 calculate the difference in value between time $t - \Delta t_{cure}$ and time $t$ for eligible currencies and assets, with choice 2 choosing the worst performer and choice 3 the best. Consider an example with the CSA which allows cash collateral to be posted in GBP, USD and EUR with the currency of CVA measurement being GBP. The collateral value assuming the worst performing currency will be given by

$$X(t) = \min \left( 1, \frac{Y_{USDGBP}(t)}{Y_{USDGBP}(t_{CS})}, \frac{Y_{EURGBP}(t)}{Y_{EURGBP}(t_{CS})} \right) \max(V(t_{CS}) - H, 0), \qquad (6.40)$$

while the best performing currency will be given by

$$X(t) = \max \left( 1, \frac{Y_{USDGBP}(t)}{Y_{USDGBP}(t_{CS})}, \frac{Y_{EURGBP}(t)}{Y_{EURGBP}(t_{CS})} \right) \max(V(t_{CS}) - H, 0). \qquad (6.41)$$

When collateral is posted to a counterparty the same three assumptions are available. This will affect the DVA term under bilateral CVA models. Assuming perfect foresight and the choice of the best performing asset would reduce the exposure to the posting counterparty while the worst would maximise it. Given that the DVA term acts as a benefit, choosing to minimise the exposure is conservative so the most conservative choice would be to assume that the counterparty posts the worst performing asset to you while assuming that you post the best performing asset to the counterparty. This will, however, break the symmetry of the bilateral CVA model.

### 6.4.4 Modelling Downgrade Triggers in CSA Agreements

CSA agreements sometimes contain rating-dependent features often known as *downgrade triggers*. Parameters such as the threshold can be made dependent on the external ratings of the company and should these ratings fall below a certain threshold the parameter will change in value. So for example the threshold above which collateral must be posted may start at a high value for an AAA rated entity but fall steadily towards zero as the credit rating declines. In theory any of the CSA parameters can be made rating-dependent but variable thresholds are the most common feature and it is also possible that a counterparty may be forced to post an initial amount if their rating falls below a certain level. Break clauses can also be rating-dependent and, for example, come into effect if a rating falls below a certain level. In some cases a counterparty may be forced to replace itself if its rating falls below a threshold, and this is a common feature of swaps provided to SPVs.

CSAs and ISDA agreements may also contain provisions for *volatility buffers* to provide overcollateralisation of derivatives if the rating falls below a threshold. Generally CSAs use volatility buffer methodology defined by rating agencies. Each rating agency publishes their own volatility buffer methodology and they can be quite complex. Standard and Poor's, for example (Standard and Poor's, 2012), use a volatility buffer that is dependent on the notional, weighted average life, derivative type and currency. The rating agency models have also developed over time and a CSA or ISDA may make specific reference to the methodology at the time the agreement was signed. Such overcollateralisation requirements can be incorporated into the collateral methodology described above but are not discussed here.

Downgrade triggers potentially have significant impact on expected exposures and hence on CVA. A reduced threshold would reduce exposure at a time the derivative counterparty is at increased risk of default; however, the overcollateralisation from volatility buffers can create an exposure where there was none before as the excess collateral posted to a counterparty can be lost in the event that they default. Here a *weighted expected exposure* model is defined and an outline of how a full stochastic treatment of rating transitions could be developed.

**Weighted Expected Exposure Model**   Recall equations (3.13) and (3.47), the inner expectation of the unilateral model and the CVA term of the bilateral model is known as the expected positive exposure or EPE, while the inner expectation of the DVA term is the expected negative exposure or ENE. So at some time $t_i$ in the discrete time partition we have

$$\text{EPE}(t_i) = \mathbb{E}\left[\exp\left(-\int_{u=0}^{t_i} r(u)du\right)(V(t_i) - X(t_i))^+\right] \tag{6.42}$$

$$\text{ENE}(t_i) = \mathbb{E}\left[\exp\left(-\int_{u=0}^{t_i} r(u)du\right)(V(t_i) - X(t_i))^-\right]. \tag{6.43}$$

Both weighted expected exposure models rely on the calculation of the EPE and ENE profiles (that is at each discrete $t_i$) for each rating-dependent state $j$ (for the counterparty) and $k$ (for the bank) so we have

$$\text{EPE}_j(t_i) \quad \text{for} \quad 0 < \ldots < t_i < \ldots < T, \quad 1 < \ldots < j < \ldots < m$$

for the unilateral model and

$$\text{EPE}_{jk}(t_i), \text{ENE}_{jk}(t_i) \quad \text{for} \quad 0 < \ldots < t_i < \ldots < T,$$
$$1 < \ldots < j < \ldots < m, \quad 1 < \ldots < k < \ldots < q$$

for the bilateral case.

Assume that the current rating for counterparty $B$ is $k_B$ and for counterparty $C$ is $j_C$, and that there are rating transition probabilities available for $B$ and $C$. These probabilities are also assumed to remain constant for the lifetime of the portfolio so we have two vectors of probabilities $p^B_{k_B k}$ and $p^C_{j_C j}$ representing the probability of transition from the current state to any other rating state. This also encompasses the probability that the rating will not change, that is $p^B_{k_B k_B}$ and $p^C_{j_C j_C}$.[8] We know that

$$\sum_{k=1}^{q} p^B_{k_B k} = \sum_{j=1}^{m} p^C_{j_C j} = 1.$$

We can write the unilateral CVA as a weighted sum over the expected exposures in each state:

$$\text{CVA}(t) = (1 - R) \sum_{i=0}^{n-1} [\Phi(\tau > t_i) - \Phi(\tau > t_{i+1})] \sum_{j=1}^{m} p^C_{j_C j} \text{EPE}_j(t_{i+1}) \qquad (6.44)$$

and for the bilateral as a weighted sum over the two rating states

$$\text{BCVA}(t) = (1 - R_C) \sum_{i=0}^{n-1} [\Phi(\tau_C > t_{i+1}) - \Phi(\tau_C > t_i)] \Phi(\tau_B > T)$$

$$\times \sum_{j=1}^{m} \sum_{k=1}^{q} p^C_{j_C j} p^B_{k_{Bk}} \text{EPE}_{jk}(t_{i+1}).$$

$$(1 - R_C) \sum_{i=0}^{n-1} [\Phi(\tau_B > t_{i+1}) - \Phi(\tau_B > t_i)] \Phi(\tau_C > T)$$

$$\times \sum_{j=1}^{m} \sum_{k=1}^{q} p^C_{j_C j} p^B_{k_{Bk}} \text{ENE}_{jk}(t_{i+1}). \qquad (6.45)$$

It is clear that the model simply weights the expected exposure generated in each rating state with the probability of being in that state. This model has implicitly made two assumptions. The first assumption is that the transition probabilities are independent of the default probability, that is that default is equally likely from each rating category. In reality this is not the case and the default probability will change depending on the rating, with transition to default much more likely from lower credit ratings. This can be corrected relatively easily by conditioning the default probability on the credit rating, which gives the following expression for unilateral CVA:

$$\text{CVA}(t) = (1 - R) \sum_{i=0}^{n-1} \sum_{j=1}^{m} p^C_{j_C j} [\Phi(\tau > t_i | j) - \Phi(\tau > t_{i+1} | j)] \text{EPE}_j(t_{i+1}), \qquad (6.46)$$

and the bilateral model follows trivially from this. However, this may add complexity to the calibration of the probabilities, a point I will return to later in this section. The second assumption is that the transition to each rating is independent of time and this ignores the

---

[8] The transition probabilities could be provided by an external vendor provided data set or from the bank's own historical transition probability data.

more realistic behaviour of a counterparty either steadily declining or increasing in rating with movements of 1–2 notches up or down at a time.

**Markov Chain** We can view the rating transition as a *Markov Chain* where each rating is a possible state in the chain and we have a transition probability matrix between each rating state which, in the case of unilateral CVA, consists just of the counterparty rating states and in the bilateral CVA case consists of pairs of self and counterparty ratings. There are two possible ways of treating default:

1. Default can be kept independent of the rating transitions as in the first version of the model described above.
2. Default can be made an absorbing state within the Markov chain itself.

**Case 1** Use the Markov Chain to generate an effective expected exposure profile. For each $t_i$ in the time partition the approach described above generates a set of EPE and ENE values for each credit rating and hence state in the Markov Chain. The rating transition probabilities are then generated for each time step in the partition, $\Delta t_i = t_i - t_{i-1}$, giving $p_j^C(\Delta t_i)$ for the unilateral model. The effective exposure is generated using a Monte Carlo simulation, which is described in algorithm 1. Once the algorithm has completed the expected exposure profile can be inserted into equation (3.13) as before. The model can be trivially extended to the bilateral case. Of course this model suffers from the problem discussed earlier in that rating transition is assumed independent of default probability.

---

**Algorithm 1** Monte Carlo simulation for rating-dependent expected exposures

---

 **for** $i = 1 \rightarrow n$ **do**
  SumEPE$_i \leftarrow 0$
 **end for**
 $a \leftarrow 0$
 **for** $a = 1 \rightarrow paths$ **do**
  $i \leftarrow 0$
  $j \leftarrow j_C$
  **for** $i = 1 \rightarrow n$ **do**
   randno = UniformRand()
   j = GetNextRatingState(randno)
   SumEPE$_i \leftarrow$ SumEPE$_i + EPE_j(t_i)$
  **end for**
 **end for**
 **for** $i = 1 \rightarrow n$ **do**
  EPE$(t_i) \leftarrow$ SumEPE$_i/paths$
 **end for**

---

**Case 2** Use a Markov Chain to directly generate the CVA by only counting the expected exposure when a transition to the default state is made. The expected exposure can continue to be used here as the market state and probability of default remain independent. Algorithm 2 describes the process. Given the jump to default implicit in this model a large number of Monte Carlo paths will be needed to achieve convergence.

---

**Algorithm 2** Monte Carlo simulation for rating-dependent expected exposures

---

$\text{SumCVA}_i \leftarrow 0$

$a \leftarrow 0$

**for** $a = 1 \rightarrow paths$ **do**

    $i \leftarrow 0$

    $j \leftarrow j_C$

    **for** $i = 1 \rightarrow n$ **do**

        randno = UniformRand()

        j = GetNextRatingState(randno)

        **if** $j = default$ **then** $\text{SumCVA} = (1 - R)EPE_{j-1}(t_i)$

        **end if**

    **end for**

**end for**

$CVA \leftarrow \text{SumCVA}/paths$

---

The key question with the models described in this section is how to obtain the transition probabilities. Market standard practice is to use implied default probabilities to calculate CVA. Currently there are no traded instruments that provide a payout on rating transition and so there are no market implied probabilities available. However, historical transition probabilities are often available from a bank's own internal data and Moody's have provided transition probabilities from their own rating analysis of bonds for many years. The models that keep the default probability separate from the transition probability could use these historical rating transition probabilities directly and still retain the market implied nature of the calculation by continuing to use market implied probabilities for default.[9] This justifies the assumption made earlier even if it is clearly incorrect. The second alternative is to take the transition probability matrix and rescale it so that the transition probability to default matches the market implied figure. A rescaling model of this type is described by Jarrow, Lando and Turnbull (1997).

**Full Stochastic Treatment of Rating Transitions**    The ideal model to treat rating transitions would be one with both stochastic credit spreads and stochastic rating transitions. There are many conceivable ways of achieving this but it is important to note that market behaviour is such that credit spread movements often occur before changes in ratings. Studies have shown that CDS spreads have predictive power in relation to changes in credit ratings (Kou and Varotto, 2005). As we will see later in Part IV, stochastic credit spreads will be implemented by imposing dynamics on the hazard rate, $\lambda$. Ratings changes could be introduced by simply assuming that the rating changes when the hazard rate or equivalently the CDS spread passes through some threshold. A more sophisticated model might use some kind of regime switching to model rating changes or use a jump process. However, as is clear from the above discussion, calibration of the model is already very difficult because of the paucity of available data and so a more sophisticated approach may simply not be viable.

---

[9]Note that the probabilities would likely have to be rescaled to eliminate the default itself as most such transitions also include the transition to default not just ratings above default.

## 6.5  NON-FINANCIAL SECURITY AND THE DEFAULT WATERFALL

Many derivatives with corporate customers are transacted as a package with other financial products such as loans or bonds. For example, floating rate loans are often packaged with an interest rate swap to effectively create a fixed rate loan. Loan packages are often transacted against a package of non-financial security with a typical example being commercial real estate and the loan package secured by the property. These security arrangements do not work in the same way as a CSA and there will rarely be any kind of "collateral call" should the value of the loan package exceed the value of the security. Nevertheless in such cases the derivative is secured rather than the standard assumption for CVA that the derivative ranks *pari passu* with other senior unsecured claims. The derivative might therefore be expected to recover better than a senior unsecured claim with the same counterparty. Other variations are possible, for example derivatives which rank senior to other claims such as senior bond issuance. In general then there are cases to consider where non-financial security and the derivative ranking in the default waterfall need to be considered.

The justification for adjusting the effective recovery away from the market standard recovery assumption can also be made on hedging grounds. If the derivative is expected to recover better or worse than a senior unsecured bondholder then any CDS hedge also needs to be adjusted as it will either be an under hedge or over hedge in the event of counterparty default.

When the default waterfall is considered there is no general formula to use and each case must be considered separately as the waterfall will depend entirely on the ranking and available security which will differ in each case. The general principle is to modify the CVA payout function to reflect the correct expected loss. To illustrate this I consider two simple examples of a loan package consisting of a floating rate loan with principal $L$ and an interest swap with value $P(t)$ and a security with value $S$. In the first example the derivative ranks junior to the loan; in the second example the derivative ranks *pari passu* with the loan. For simplicity I assume that in the event of default the claim value for the loan is equal to the loan principal and that this does not amortise. The two cases are illustrated in Figure 6.1.

Consider first case 1. If at the time of default the value of the loan plus that of the derivative exceeds the value of the security a loss occurs, that is if

$$V(\tau) + L > S(\tau)$$

then a loss occurs and all of that loss falls on the derivative. If the value of the security is less than that of the loan then the loan experiences a loss and the derivative has a 100% loss. To include this in the CVA calculation we must change the familiar formula to take the LGD factor, $(1 - R_C)$, inside the expectation operator and consider the loss directly. Hence the expression for CVA in case 1 becomes:

$$\mathrm{CVA}(t) = \sum_{i=0}^{n-1} [\Phi(\tau > t_i) - \Phi(\tau > t_{i+1})]\mathbb{E}\left[(V(t_{i+1}) - (S(t_{i+1}) - L)^+)^+\right]. \qquad (6.47)$$

Case 2 is slightly more complex because of the *pari passu* ranking. Again a loss occurs if the value of the derivative plus that of the loan exceeds the value of the security. This time,

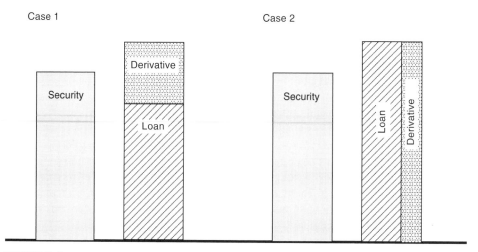

**FIGURE 6.1**  Two example loan packages with security. In case 1 the derivative ranks lower than the loan and in case 2 it ranks *pari passu* with the loan.

however, the loss is experienced in equal proportion by both the loan and the derivative and a total loss on the derivative is only experienced if the security value falls to zero. Hence the expression for unilateral CVA becomes

$$\text{CVA}(t) = \sum_{i=0}^{n-1} [\Phi(\tau > t_i) - \Phi(\tau > t_{i+1})] \mathbb{E} \left[ \left( \frac{V(t_{i+1})(L + V(t_{i+1})) - S(t_{i+1})}{(L + V(t_{i+1}))} \right)^+ \right]. \quad (6.48)$$

Dealing with bilateral CVA models depends on the treatment of loan and derivative in the event of self-default. In such cases it is very unlikely that any security would be provided by the bank to the corporate customer and hence the DVA term can simply be treated as normal with the payout modification occurring only in the CVA term.

Cases 1 and 2 provide very simple examples and in reality there can be a high degree of complexity in the waterfall. The loss is assumed to be total above the security value which may not in fact be the case as there may be other assets available to settle claims against the defaulted entity. The loan and/or the derivative may be syndicated to other parties so there may be a need to include the impact of multiple parties in the default waterfall model. There may be multiple groups of loans and derivatives with different rankings and it is not that unusual to see one class of derivatives ranking senior to another. Furthermore the security value itself must be carefully considered and there is likely to be some element of wrong-way risk. If the asset was commercial real estate, for example, then the risk of default is likely to be high precisely when the asset value is under pressure. This could be dealt with in a number of different ways, the simplest being a suitable haircut on the present value of the security through to a full stochastic model of its value.

## CHAPTER 7

# Wrong-way and Right-way Risk for CVA

*If there is a wrong way to do something, then someone will do it.*
—Edward A. Murphy Jr.
*American aerospace engineer (1918–1990)*

## 7.1 INTRODUCTION: WRONG-WAY AND RIGHT-WAY RISKS

Wrong-way and right-way risks were defined in section 2.1.1 and in this chapter I introduce a number of different modelling approaches. Because of the negative implications of wrong-way risks these have received more attention from practioners and the research community but the same frameworks are equally applicable to right-way situations. Wrong-way risk is a popular topic at CVA conferences but it is fair to say that the literature contains relatively few contributions and this is a reflection of the difficult and sometimes intractable nature of the problem.

In the context of CVA, wrong-way risk and right-way risk can be defined thus:

> Wrong-way risk occurs whenever there is an adverse co-dependence between the exposure to a counterparty and the risk that the counterparty will default, while right-way risk occurs whenever the is a favourable co-dependence.

The key difference between wrong-way/right-way risk in CVA and when considering broader counterparty risk measures is that the mark-to-market nature of CVA means that wrong-way/right-way risk feeds directly into P&L. Co-dependence between the credit spread and exposure is therefore important in CVA while the exposure itself is more of a consideration in more traditional approaches to credit risk. CVA is clearly affected by such co-dependence and under a unilateral CVA model the intuitive behaviour will, in general, be observed, in the sense that wrong-way risk will increase CVA, while right-way risk will decrease CVA. In bilateral CVA models and models where FVA is included the behaviour can be far more complex, in part due to the more complex dependency structure with two counterparties and/or funding considerations involved and this will be discussed later in sections 7.5 and 9.8. Fundamentally wrong-way and right-way risk remove the assumption of independence between the expected exposure and the survival probability. Hence the simple model of an integral over a separately calculated expected exposure cannot be used.

The stochastic process driving credit in CVA should be thought of as a doubly stochastic process even if it is not modelled in this way with the hazard rate and the jump to default as the two stochastic elements. With this in mind there are three elements to consider in the context of wrong-way/right-way risk:

1. The movement of the hazard rate/CDS spread
2. The joint distribution of default and exposure
3. The recovery rate and other variables.

Each factor applies in a different way dependent on the context. So for example for a counterparty with a liquid CDS contract that is used for hedging will have a lower concern for the realised recovery in the event of default as the CDS will pay out the realised recovery in the auction. However, for an illiquid counterparty any credit spread hedging will be done via proxy credit curves and exposure to the realised recovery still remains and so any co-dependence between recovery rate and default risk are critically important.

The remainder of the chapter tackles the question of how to model the dependence between the key elements, in particular that between the hazard rate and the exposure. There are broadly two possible approaches, distribution models that impose a relationship between the probability of default and exposure either through the use of copula techniques or similar frameworks, and stochastic credit models with diffusive correlation dependencies with other assets and potentially dependent jump processes; these two approaches are covered in sections 7.2 and 7.4 respectively.

### 7.1.1 Modelling Wrong-way Risk and CVA

Recall the expression for unilateral CVA,

$$\text{CVA}(t) = \mathbb{E}\left[\exp\left(-\int_{s=t}^{\tau} r(s)ds\right)(1-R)(V(\tau))^+\right], \tag{7.1}$$

which becomes in the case where credit and market state variables are independent,

$$\text{CVA}(t) = (1-R)\int_{t}^{T}\exp\left(-\int_{s=t}^{u} r(s)ds\right)\mathbb{E}\left[(V(u))^+\right]d\Phi(t,u), \tag{7.2}$$

where this is an integral over all possible default times. Implicitly, however, we have set

$$\mathbb{E}\left[(V(u))^+\right] = \mathbb{E}\left[(V(u))^+|u=\tau\right] \tag{7.3}$$

that is the exposure conditioned on default. Hence we can define the wrong-way (right-way) unilateral CVA formula using

$$\mathrm{CVA}^{WW}(t) = (1 - R) \int_t^T \exp\left(- \int_{s=t}^u r(s)ds\right) \mathbb{E}\left[(V(u))^+ | u = \tau\right] d\Phi(t, u), \qquad (7.4)$$

which in discrete form becomes

$$\mathrm{CVA}^{WW}(t) = (1 - R) \sum_{i=0}^n \sum_{j=1}^m \exp\left(- \int_{s=t}^u r(s)ds\right) v_j^+$$

$$\times \Phi(V^+ = v_j^+ | t_i < \tau < t_{i+1})\Phi(t_i < \tau < t_{i+1}). \qquad (7.5)$$

Equation (7.5) makes it clear that the key issue is modelling the dependency between the exposure and the survival probability.

## 7.2 DISTRIBUTIONAL MODELS OF WRONG-WAY/ RIGHT-WAY RISK

### 7.2.1 Simple Model: Increased Exposure

The simplest possible model of wrong-way risk is to increase the exposure relative to the expected exposure profile. The expected exposure could be readily replaced with one of the percentiles of the value distribution, say the 95th percentile. The justification for this approach lies where the wrong-way risk is manifested by the exposure conditioned on default being higher that the expected exposure. The advantage of this approach lies in its simplicity which simply replaces the EPE with an appropriate percentile. It can be made as conservative as necessary and it could be hedged in exactly the same way as the standard CVA model, which would lead to an effective over-hedge of the exposure. The first problem with the model, common with most wrong-way risk models, lies in the difficulty of calibration. Here the choice is limited to the selection of percentile but there is no guidance on what is appropriate beyond a risk assessment of the relationship between the expected exposure and the exposure conditional on default.

As an example consider the unilateral CVA on a 30-year interest rate swap using a credit curve with a flat CDS spread at 2%. Figure 7.1 illustrates the EPE and percentiles at 75%, 90%, 95% and 99% and Table 7.1 gives the CVA using each profile. As is clear the CVA increases rapidly for the higher percentile profiles.

### 7.2.2 Copula Models

In principle what wrong-way and right-way risk models do is to join the exposure distribution with a distribution for the probability of default in a way other than assuming that the two are independent of each other. We can impose an analytic form on the distribution of the probability of default relatively easily and hence we have the marginal distribution for this. In general, however, we do not have a analytic form for the distribution of exposure values

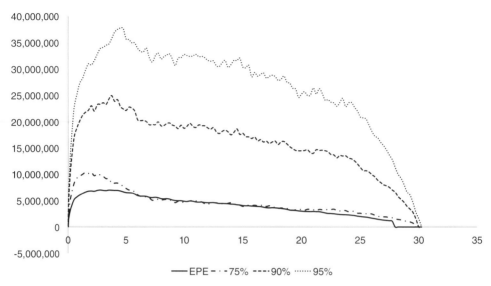

**FIGURE 7.1**    The EPE and percentile profiles of a 30-year interest rate swap.

$\max(P(t), 0)$. The distribution of exposures is normally only known empirically from the Monte Carlo method unless it is derived from one of the small number of cases which are analytically tractable as discussed in Chapter 5. The obvious choice is to join these marginal distributions using a copula and this is the approach suggested by Rosen (2011); Rosen and Saunders (2012).

Recall the Gaussian Copula model discussed in the context of bilateral CVA models in section 3.4.1. In that case the copula was used to join the marginal distributions of default time between the two counterparties. Each distribution was continuous in that case but there is no objection to using a copula where one of the distributions is discrete as long as it can be inverted. The distribution of portfolio mark-to-market, $P(t)$ is only known empirical on a set of discrete time points $t_i$ and on a set of discrete Monte Carlo paths $k = 1, \ldots, N_{paths}$. In a standard Monte Carlo model each path is equally likely and hence has a probability $1/N_{paths}$ and so at each time point $t_i$, the empirical distribution of portfolio values can be obtained by ranking the portfolio values such that

$$P_{k=0}(t_i) < \ldots < P_{k=m}(t_i) < \ldots < P_{k=N_{paths}(t_i)}.$$

**TABLE 7.1**    The unilateral CVA of a 30-year interest rate swap using the EPE and percentile profiles.

| Profile | CVA |
| --- | --- |
| EPE | 2,200,291 |
| 75% | 2,590,677 |
| 90% | 8,404,413 |
| 95% | 13,593,052 |
| 99% | 29,557,431 |

The cumulative probability function up to path $m$ is then simply,[1]

$$CDF_{value}(P_k(t_i)) = \sum_{k=1}^{m} \frac{1}{N_{paths}} = \frac{m}{N_{paths}}. \tag{7.6}$$

The survival probability function directly provides the cumulative probability function so that we have

$$CDF_{survival} = P(\tau > t_i) = \exp\left(-\int_{t_0}^{t_i} \lambda(s)ds\right), \tag{7.7}$$

where $\lambda(t)$ is the hazard rate. Given equations (7.6) and (7.7) we can readily invert these into standard normal variables using the normal inverse CDF function and so obtain two standard normal variables, $X$ and $Y$, that can be combined using a bivariate Gaussian Copula as defined by the bivariate normal cumulative distribution function in equation (3.75).

Equation (7.5) demonstrated that to calculate wrong-way risk we need to obtain

$$\Phi(P^+ = p_j^+ | t_i < \tau < t_{i+1})\Phi(t_i < \tau < t_{i+1})$$

or equivalently

$$\Phi(P = p_j | t_i < \tau < t_{i+1})\Phi(t_i < \tau < t_{i+1}). \tag{7.8}$$

The probability of a given exposure conditioned on default occurring in the time interval $t_i$ to $t_{i+1}$ can be written in terms of the univariate and bivariate Gaussian CDFs, $C(u)$ and $C_2(u, v, \rho)$ respectively,[2]

$$\begin{aligned}\Phi(P = p_j | t_i < \tau < t_{i+1})\Phi(t_i < \tau < t_{i+1}) &= C_2(C^{-1}(P = p_j), C^{-1}(\Phi(t_{i+1})), \rho)\\ &\quad - C_2(C^{-1}(P = p_{j-1}), C^{-1}(\Phi(t_{i+1})), \rho)\\ &\quad - C_2(C^{-1}(P = p_j), C^{-1}(\Phi(t_i)), \rho)\\ &\quad + C_2(C^{-1}(P = p_{j-1}), C^{-1}(\Phi(t_i)), \rho).\end{aligned} \tag{7.9}$$

Hence we can use this probability *weight* directly in equation (7.5) to calculate the unilateral CVA under the Gaussian Copula model.

As an example, consider the unilateral CVA under the Gaussian Copula model using the same 30-year GBP interest rate swap used above. Equation (7.9) amounts to a simple exercise

---

[1] Note it is better to actually shift the cumulative probability function by $-1/2(N_{paths})$ so that the first and last point do not correspond to a cumulative probability of 0 or 1.

[2]

$$C(u) = \int_{-\infty}^{u} \frac{1}{\sqrt{2\pi}} \exp\left\{-\frac{v^2}{2}\right\}$$

$$C_2(u, v, \rho) = \int_{-\infty}^{u} \int_{-\infty}^{v} \frac{1}{2\pi\sqrt{1-\rho^2}} \exp\left\{-\frac{s^2 + t^2 - 2\rho st}{2(1-\rho^2)}\right\}$$

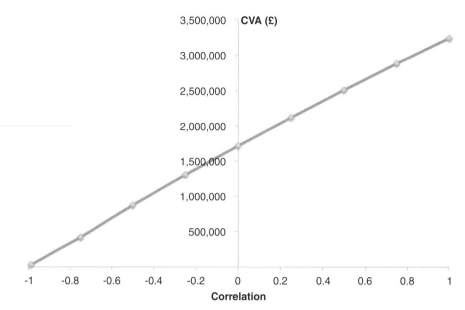

**FIGURE 7.2** The unilateral CVA for a 30-year GBP interest rate swap using the bivariate Gaussian Copula model.

in re-weighting the steps along each path, replacing the original unconditional probability of default with this expression and as such is straightforward to implement. Computationally this is more expensive than the simple CVA integration models as it requires repeated calls to the bivariate Gaussian CDF and the inverse univariate CDF. In practice this is still unlikely to be a big overhead compared to the overall Monte Carlo simulation. The results from the 30-year interest rate swap are illustrated in Figure 7.2.

Ultimately this approach leads to a parametric form where the copula parameters, the correlation in the case of the Gaussian Copula, govern the extent of wrong-way or right-way behaviour. As can be seen from Figure 7.2, the correlation gives a wide range of CVA values with the a relatively linear response to the correlation as it runs between −1 and 1. The key issue is then how to choose the parameters of the copula. It is not immediately clear how this should be done and there seems to be no formal mechanism for calibration to historical data or otherwise. The correlation provides a simple mechanism for changing the co-dependence and so is useful as a *stress parameter* but the model does not readily admit a price of wrong-way or right-way risk.

### 7.2.3 Linear Models and Discrete Models

John Hull and Alan White (2012a) have proposed an alternative approach to wrong-way/right-way risk by modelling the hazard rate as a function of a state variable associated with the expected exposure. So, for example, this could be an appropriate swap rate for a portfolio of interest rate swaps or, as Hull and White themselves suggest, the gold price for a gold producer that has not conducted any hedging. Hull and White then explore an example in which the state variable is the portfolio value $P(t)$ and so the hazard rate is given by

$$\lambda(t) = \exp\left[a(t) + b(t)P(t)\right], \qquad (7.10)$$

where $b(t)$ determines the degree of dependence on the portfolio value and $a(t)$ is used to normalise the model such that the marginal distribution matches that implied by the CDS market.

In practice this model operates on a discrete set of Monte Carlo paths in a very similar way to the Gaussian Copula model. Equation (7.12) gives a series of probability weights that can be applied to each Monte Carlo path, that is for each time step we have a probability weight given by

$$w_j(t_i) = \frac{\exp\left\{-\exp\left[a_i + b_i P_{ij}\right]\right\}}{(\Phi(\tau > t_i) - \Phi(\tau > t_{i-1}))}, \qquad (7.11)$$

where $a(t_i)$ is chosen such that $\sum_{j=1}^{N_{paths}} w_j(t_i) = 1$. The only difference, therefore, between this method and the copula method is the form of the weighting function.

As an example of this approach consider the following variant on the Hull-White model with a functional form that depends on the positive exposure, $\max(P(t), 0)$ rather than the portfolio value. This means that the paths which lead to zero exposure will all have the same weight while those with positive exposure have a strong dependence between the hazard rate (and hence probability of default) and exposure. In this case the hazard rate is given by

$$\lambda(t) = \exp\left[a(t) + b(t)\max(P(t), 0)\right], \qquad (7.12)$$

and the probability weights by

$$w_j(t_i) = \frac{\exp\left\{-\exp\left[a_i + b_i \frac{EPE_{ij}}{EPE(t_i)_{95\%}}\right]\right\}}{(\Phi(\tau > t_i) - \Phi(\tau > t_{i-1}))}, \qquad (7.13)$$

where the exposure has been normalised by the 95th percentile for convenience that allows the function $b$ to represent the dependence as a fraction. Figure 7.3 illustrates the results for the same 30-year GBP interest rate swap. It is immediately clear that this model gives a similar dependence structure to the Gaussian Copula.

This type of model is very straightforward and introduces a dependence between a state variable and the hazard rate in an intuitive way. The problem of calibration remains, however, and it is not clear how to set the $b$ parameter that governs the dependence. Broadly, both the Hull-White type models and the copula models rely on a re-weighting of the Monte Carlo paths generated for the standard CVA calculation without dependence. As such they can be thought of as based on a *change of measure* argument. Both sets of models fit within the framework described by Glasserman and Yang (2013) in the context of examining the maximum CVA due to wrong-way risk.

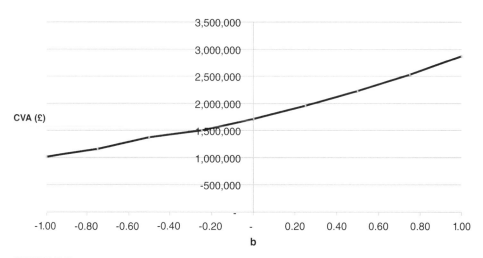

**FIGURE 7.3**    The unilateral CVA for a 30-year GBP interest rate swap using the Hull-White variant wrong-way risk model.

## 7.3   A GENERALISED DISCRETE APPROACH TO WRONG-WAY RISK

Glasserman and Yang (2013) consider a discrete linear programming approach to bounding wrong-way risk in CVA. In reality this approach is actually a very general approach to modelling the dependence between market state and default time as will now be demonstrated.

In CVA models we have two components, a "market" model which generates the value of the exposures at discrete simulation times, that is

$$X = (V_1, \ldots, V_T),$$ (7.14)

and a credit model that generates paths of default time indicators,

$$Y = (\mathbb{1}_{\{\tau=1\}}, \ldots, \mathbb{1}_{\{\tau=T\}}).$$ (7.15)

Glasserman and Yang (2013) seek to find the largest possible value of

$$\mathbb{E}\left[\sum_{i=1}^{T} X_i Y_i\right] = \mathbb{E}\left[\sum_{i=1}^{T} V_i \mathbb{1}_{\{\tau=i\}}\right] = \mathbb{E}\left[V_\tau \mathbb{1}_{\{\tau \le T\}}\right]$$ (7.16)

while holding the marginal distributions described by equations (7.14) and (7.15) constant.

For the unilateral CVA calculation we construct $N$ Monte Carlo paths each with $M$ time steps, that is we build a matrix of exposures such that,

$$C_{ij} = \begin{pmatrix} V_{11} & \cdots & V_{1T} \\ V_{21} & \cdots & V_{2T} \\ \vdots & \ddots & \vdots \\ V_{N1} & \cdots & V_{NT} \end{pmatrix}$$ (7.17)

For each time step and path we also construct a matrix of default probabilities, representing the probability that the counterparty will default in the time interval between time $t_i$ and time $t_{i+1}$,

$$
P_{ij} = \begin{pmatrix} q^1_{\{\tau=1\}} & \cdots & q^1_{\{\tau=T\}} \\ q^2_{\{\tau=1\}} & \cdots & q^2_{\{\tau=T\}} \\ \vdots & \ddots & \vdots \\ q^N_{\{\tau=1\}} & \cdots & q^N_{\{\tau=T\}} \end{pmatrix} \tag{7.18}
$$

In the standard unilateral CVA model all the $q^i_{\{\tau=1\}}$ are identical for all paths so that

$$
\begin{aligned}
q^1_{\{\tau=1\}} &= q^2_{\{\tau=1\}} = \ldots = q^N_{\{\tau=1\}} = q_{\{\tau=1\}}/N \\
q^1_{\{\tau=2\}} &= q^2_{\{\tau=2\}} = \ldots = q^N_{\{\tau=2\}} = q_{\{\tau=2\}}/N \\
&\vdots \\
q^1_{\{\tau=T\}} &= q^2_{\{\tau=T\}} = \ldots = q^N_{\{\tau=T\}} = q_{\{\tau=T\}}/N.
\end{aligned}
$$

In models which consider right-way or wrong-way risk these expressions no longer hold. All that is required is that equations (7.6) and (7.7) are satisfied or in this matrix notation

$$
\sum_i P_{ij} = q_{\{\tau=i\}} \tag{7.19}
$$

$$
\sum_j P_{ij} = 1/N \tag{7.20}
$$

$$
P_{ij} \geq 0. \tag{7.21}
$$

Glasserman and Yang (2013) aim to find the worst case wrong-way risk, that is they define the linear programming problem that

$$
\text{CVA}_{\max} = \max_P \sum_{ij} P_{ij} C_{ij} \tag{7.22}
$$

subject to equations (7.19) through (7.21). This is a relatively straightforward constrained optimisation problem.

The key point to make is that *any* unilateral CVA Monte Carlo model must satisfy equations (7.19) through (7.21) and that the problem of defining a wrong-way/right-way risk model reduces to specifying how the pathwise default probabilities are generated.

This approach can readily be extended to the bilateral CVA model, which has two sets of expected exposures and two sets of marginal default probabilities. As will be seen in later chapters all XVAs have a similar form in that they are expressed as an integral over time, over an expected exposure profile of some sort. Hence this formalism can readily be extended to other XVA metrics.

## 7.4 STOCHASTIC CREDIT MODELS OF WRONG-WAY/RIGHT-WAY RISK

Stochastic credit models are discussed in more detail in Chapter 16 in the context of implementing CVA for credit derivatives and for wrong-way risk so it is sufficient to provide an overview here. The standard approach is to assume some dynamics for the hazard rate; an example would be an Ornstein-Uhlenbeck process with jumps,

$$d\lambda(t) = (\psi(t) - b(t)\lambda(t))dt + \sigma_\lambda(t)dW_t + c(t)dJ_t. \tag{7.23}$$

This allows a diffusive type correlation between Brownian motions to be used to express a dependence between credit and other asset classes. The jump process can also be used to specify a direct dependence on another asset class or on an event. So for example in a scenario with multiple names a jump in the hazard rate may be driven by the default of a related entity, thus allowing default contagion effects to be modelled. However, jumps are often added to hazard rate processes in order to ensure a high enough spread volatility, which in turn causes problems. Firstly the compensating adjustment to the diffusive drift may mean the dynamics become unrealistic and secondly the jumps reduce the impact of the diffusive correlation dependence.

It is best to avoid simulating the jump to default directly if at all possible as the digital nature of the problem will lead to a very significant increase in the number of Monte Carlo paths required to achieve satisfactory convergence. Hence the best practical approach is to use the stochastic hazard rate in a similar way to the methods discussed above and use it to generate a series of probability weights for each Monte Carlo path. Hence the integrated hazard rate is used to generate the survival probability function,

$$P(\tau > T) = \exp\left(-\int_{t=0}^{T} \lambda(t)dt\right) \tag{7.24}$$

and hence along each path $j$ the weight is given by

$$w_j(t_i) = \exp\left(-\int_{t=0}^{t_i}(\psi(t) - b(t)\lambda(t))dt - \int_{t=0}^{t_i}\sigma_\lambda(t)dW_t - \int_{t=0}^{t_i}c(t)dJ_t\right)$$
$$- \exp\left(-\int_{t=0}^{t_{i-1}}(\psi(t) - b(t)\lambda(t))dt - \int_{t=0}^{t_{i-1}}\sigma_\lambda(t)dW_t - \int_{t=0}^{t_{i-1}}c(t)dJ_t\right). \tag{7.25}$$

Seen this way, even a stochastic credit process can fit into the generalised framework for wrong-way risk of Glasserman and Yang (2013).

The advantages of using a stochastic process for credit in right-way/wrong-way risk models are considerable. Firstly it is a dynamical model for a process that is clearly dynamic as credit spreads are very volatile. The doubly stochastic nature of the credit process is therefore fully captured. Secondly it is more intuitive as the credit process is directly linked to other assets through diffusive correlations and jump relationships. A Gaussian correlation could be selected using historic correlations in the first instance or treated as a stress parameter. Calibration is still problematic as the volatility of the credit process must be chosen. CDS swaptions would be the natural choice of calibrating instrument as this would give a market implied volatility. In reality, however, CD swaptions rarely trade and so an alternative must be selected. Historical spread volatility is certainly an option and would still give very high volatilities.

### 7.4.1 Sovereign Wrong-way Risk

Sovereign wrong-way risk was once a topic restricted to modelling credit risk in emerging markets. Clearly the default of Greece in 2012 (Bases and James, 2012) has changed this and sovereign risk is an important element of CVA calculation. In particular the relationship between sovereign default and FX movements cannot be ignored. One way to model this is with a shared jump process, the jump to default of the sovereign simultaneously triggering a devaluation. This behaviour is a classic example of wrong-way risk on a fully collateralised portfolio. Consider the case where the counterparty is a bank located in sovereign country S and that bank supplies collateral under a CSA to you in its native currency $X_S$. On the default of the sovereign it is very likely that the bank will also default, while at the same time the currency jumps down in a devaluation reducing the value of the collateral.

While it is easy to visualise how such models could work the problem of calibration remains. The key question in the sovereign example is how big would the devaluation be in such circumstances? The number of sovereign defaults is tiny in the modern era so there is little or no historical evidence. FX traders may be able to provide some intuitive insight and the FX option market may contain some information embedded in the volatility skew but overall there is very little information to base pricing decisions on.

## 7.5 WRONG-WAY/RIGHT-WAY RISK AND DVA

Bilateral CVA models introduce an additional layer of complexity into wrong-way/right-way risk models as now the dependence structure must be extended to cover both counterparty and self-default probability. The Glasserman and Yang (2013) wrong-way risk framework can be extended to the bilateral case by simply adding an extra dimension to the probability weights. A more general stochastic treatment of wrong-way risk would involve the introduction of two stochastic hazard rates with at least a diffusive correlation dependence between them.

# FVA: Funding Valuation Adjustment

## CHAPTER 8

# The Discount Curve

*Nothing in life and nothing that we do is risk-free.*

—Ken Salazar
*US Politician 1955–*

## 8.1 INTRODUCTION

Discounting is intimately related to funding and hence funding valuation adjustment and so this chapter presents an overview of the construction of the discount curve. The chapter is presented in order of the chronological development of discounting methodology, beginning with the original single curve discount models that were current in the mid-1990s. Modelling moved on rapidly to include cross-currency and the tenor basis in the pre- and post-millenium period before CSA discounting became important in the aftermath of the 2007–2009 crisis. The latest topic of debate is the valuation of the collateral option embedded in most CSA agreements. This chapter is not meant to be comprehensive and there are many more detailed treatments of the subject available such as that of Kenyon and Stamm (2012).

## 8.2 A SINGLE CURVE WORLD

One of the very first lessons in modern finance I experienced when joining the finance industry and the derivatives market was about the time value of money. The yield curve or discount curve provided the means to value future cash flows. In the mid-1990s, single currency derivatives were typically valued using a single discount curve. Fixed cash flows were valued by simply multiplying by the discount factor on the payment date and floating flows were valued by replicating the LIBOR payment with two equal and opposite flows equal to the notional. Hence the floating leg of a swap could be valued by replacing the leg with two notional flows at the start of the swap and at its maturity.

The discount curve itself consisted of a table of discount factors $P(0, t_i)$ for a set of discrete dates $t_i$ and an interpolation scheme. A number of different interpolation schemes were used in such models with one of the most popular being log-linear interpolation (see for example Hagan and West, 2008), that is to obtain a discount factor at time $t_i < t < t_{i+1}$,

$$P(0, t) = \exp\left( \log_e(P(0, t_{i+1})) \frac{(t - t_i)}{(t_{i+1} - t_i)} + \log_e(P(0, t_i)) \frac{(t_{i+1} - t)}{(t_{i+1} - t_i)} \right). \tag{8.1}$$

Log-linear interpolation is clearly based on linear interpolation of the continuously compounded rate between the two discrete tenor points. Other forms of interpolation which were sometimes used including smooth methods such as cubic splines. However, log-linear interpolation meant that risk did not spread along the curve.

The discount factor table itself was built using a bootstrap approach, similar to that described in section 4.4 in the context of the credit curve. Three sets of instruments were typically used: deposits, interest rate futures and interest rate swaps. The deposits were the easiest to include as they simply defined the discount factor at their own maturity,

$$P(0, t) = \frac{1}{1 + r(0, t)\alpha(0, t)}, \tag{8.2}$$

where $r(0, t)$ is the deposit rate and $\alpha(0, t)$ is the day-count fraction for the deposit period.[1] In some markets there is a settlement delay meaning the deposit rate does not start immediately but in, say, two business days. If this is the case the *overnight* and *tom-next* rates can be used to bootstrap the curve out to the start of the deposit strip proper (see for example Kenyon and Stamm, 2012). The deposit rate maturity structure that is typically encountered is

$$O/N, T/N, 1W, 2W, 1M, 2M, 3M, 6M, 12M.$$

The number of money market rates used depended on the individual market. Markets with interest rate futures would typically use money market rates to the start of the first future, while those without would use them through to the first interest rate swap point.

Par interest rate forwards can be expressed in terms of discount factors using

$$f(t_1, t_2) = \frac{1}{\alpha(t_1, t_2)} \left( \frac{P(0, t_1)}{P(0, t_1)} - 1 \right), \tag{8.3}$$

where again $\alpha(t_1, t_2)$ is the day count basis and $t_2 > t_1$. If the discount factor is known at $t_1$ then this formula can be inverted to bootstrap to $t_2$,

$$P(0, t_2) = \frac{P(0, t_1)}{1 + \alpha(t_1, t_2)f(t_1, t_2)}. \tag{8.4}$$

In practice the futures contracts are far more liquid than interest rate forwards and so these are used instead. Interest rate futures are typically of three months' duration with maturities on the third Wednesday of the IMM months, that is March, June, September and December, the future covering the three-month period following the maturity date. Futures are well known

---

[1] Most currencies use an *actual-360* day count basis for money markets, although the sterling market uses *actual-365*.

to require a convexity adjustment relative to the forward rate, because of the daily margining requirement; they also settle at the beginning of the period. Models expressing the convexity adjustment in terms of interest rate volatility have been developed (see for example Vaillant, 1995), but in general these models are not actually used in yield curve construction and the convexity adjustment is marked directly in basis points by the interest rate trader. The futures prices are quoted on an inverse basis as $100 - F$ where $F$ is the futures rate. The number of futures included in a curve depends on the number of futures quoted in a particular market and their liquidity. The futures then allow the discount table to be bootstrapped out where successive futures extend the curve using the discount factor generated but the previous future or deposit. Note, however, that the dates may not always align so that futures may overlap each other slightly or even be non-overlapping by a few business days. Overlapping futures require interpolation to generate the base discount bond price, while the non-overlapping case will require the discount function to be extrapolated to the start of the next instrument.

Par swap rates, $S(0, t_n)$, are given by the equation

$$S(0, t_n)N \sum_{i=1}^{n} P(0, t_i)\alpha_F(t_{i-1}, t_i) - N \sum_{j=1}^{m} f(t_{j-1}, t_j)\alpha_L(t_{j-1}, t_j)P(0, t_j) = 0, \qquad (8.5)$$

where $N$ is the notional and the $\alpha_F$ and $\alpha_L$ are the day-count fractions for the fixed and floating legs respectively. Using the knowledge that there is only a single curve allows the floating leg to be replaced by an exchange of notional,

$$S(0, t_n)N \sum_{i=1}^{n} P(0, t_i)\alpha_F(t_{i-1}, t_i) - N + NP(0, t_n) = 0. \qquad (8.6)$$

In most currencies the frequency of payments on the two legs is more frequent than the maturities of standard swap rate quotes. So for example, a GBP interest rate swap of greater than one year would normally be quoted with semi-annual payments on both fixed and floating legs. However the market will only quote swap rates at annual points for shorter maturities with quotes only at five or ten-year frequency for maturities longer than 20 years. A typical set of swap rates quotes might be at

$$1Y, 2Y, 3Y, 5Y, 7Y, 10Y, 12Y, 15Y, 20Y, 25Y, 30Y.$$

This means that the bootstrap process requires some additional information to fill in the intermediate discount factors between swap maturities. Essentially there are only two options, either assume a functional form for the behaviour of the discount function at intermediate dates in the same manner as was done in the context of credit curves or interpolate the input swap rates to the intermediate dates. The former approach gives much more control over the form of the rate at the intermediate point but, historically, often the latter approach was used. Swap rates were often interpolated linearly from the quoted tenor points to the intermediate dates. This may have followed market practice for quoting swap rates between tenors but often gave rise to strange effects in the forward rates derived from the associated discount function.

The single curve was bootstrapped to the longest maturity swap and then used to generate discount factors at all intermediate points. The approach is simple and could easily be implemented, even on a spreadsheet. The single curve was able to explain the prices of single currency derivatives with one floating leg. Basis swaps were not explained by the curve model which would price both legs of a basis swap equal irrespective of the payment frequency. However, pre-crisis basis swaps spreads were typically small and reflected the price of the operational costs of doing a trade rather than any perceptions that tenor basis was a major risk factor.

Cross-currency swaps were also not explained by the single curve model. A cross-currency basis swap is normally structured as two floating legs in two different currencies with an exchange of notional at the start and end of the swap. Under the single curve model it is easy to see that both legs combined with the notional flows should value to zero at inception. However in the market cross-currency basis swaps were quoted at a spread. The demands of the cross-currency basis swaps and the desire to have a single framework that could consistently value single and multi-currency derivatives led to the first step towards a multi-curve discounting framework.

## 8.3 CURVE INTERPOLATION AND SMOOTH CURVES

Curve interpolation methods have progressed considerably since the use of log-linear interpolation was standard in the mid-1990s. Log-linear interpolation guarantees that all instantaneous forward rates are positive and that the behaviour of the curve is local; however, it also suffers from the deficiency that the instantaneous forward rate is undefined at knot points $t_i$ and the function is discontinuous at these points (Hagan and West, 2008). Various experiments with *splines* were conducted, using quadratic, cubic (Adams, 2001; McCulloch, Huston and Kochin, 2000) and quartic splines (Adams, 2001). These approaches share a common problem with oscillatory behaviour in the forward rates to varying degrees.

Hagan and West (2008) propose a series of properties that must be satisfied by the interpolation method used in the curve:

1. Instantaneous forward rates must be positive, to avoid arbitrage, and continuous. Continuity is required as many interest rate derivatives are sensitive to the stability of forward rates.
2. The interpolation method must be *local* in character so that if an input is changed it only affects the local region and not the whole discount function.
3. The forward rates must be stable so that a change in an input rate of $x$ basis points does not lead to a change in the forward rates that is much greater than $x$.
4. The hedges implied by the curve should be local so that delta risk at a tenor point gives hedges in the same region and not leaking materially across the curve.
5. Input instruments should be exactly reproduced by the bootstrap process.

In a review of existing methods Hagan and West found very few methods that satisfied these requirements.

Two curve interpolation methods that have been found to produce discount curves with desirable properties are *Monotone Convex* methods and those based on *tension splines*. Hagan and West (2006); Hagan and West (2008) propose the use of Monotone Convex methods which interpolate in the domain of the instaneous forward rates rather than the discount bond prices themselves. This allows them to place constraints on the positivity and continuity of the forward rates directly. Andersen (2007) proposes the use of generalised tension B-splines (GB splines) as a means of controlling the oscillatory behaviour found with ordinary splines. These approaches represent the current standard for discount curve construction where "smoothness" has been a very important element.

## 8.4  CROSS-CURRENCY BASIS

With the introduction of cross-currency basis, a single curve per currency is insufficient to match the prices of both single currency and multi-currency products. To cater for this in each currency save a base currency, two curves must be used, one for projection of forward floating rates and another to discount with. The base currency is usually chosen to be USD, as the cross-currency basis is always quoted against USD. In the base currency there remains a single curve for both projection and discounting.

The first stage of the curve construction process is to build the base currency curve in the same way as described above in section 8.2. The next step is to build the discount curve in the foreign currency (see Fujii, Shimada and Takahashi, 2010a). The par rate of a cross-currency basis swap is given by

$$
N_f \left\{ -P_d^f(0, t_0) + \sum_{j=1}^{m} (f^f(t_{j-1}, t_j) + b_m) \alpha_L^f(t_{j-1}, t_j) P_d^f(0, t_j) + P_d^f(0, t_m) \right\}
$$
$$
= X(0) N_d \left\{ -P_d^d(0, t_0) + \sum_{j=1}^{m} f^d(t_{j-1}, t_j) \alpha_L^d(t_{j-1}, t_j) P_d^d(0, t_j) + P_d^d(0, t_m) \right\}, \quad (8.7)
$$

where $b_m$ is the basis for tenor $t_m$, $X(0)$ is the FX rate at $t = 0$, the superscripts $f$ and $d$ indicate *foreign* and *domestic* currencies respectively and the subscript $d$ has been introduced to indicate that bond prices are from the discount curve. The right hand side of this expression is zero as there is only a single curve in the domestic currency and hence equation (8.6) holds. For the foreign leg the swap rate relationship given by equation (8.5) still holds,

$$
S^f(0, t_n) N \sum_{i=1}^{n} P_d^f(0, t_i) \alpha_F(t_{i-1}, t_i) - N \sum_{j=1}^{m} f^f(t_{j-1}, t_j) \alpha_L(t_{j-1}, t_j) P_d^f(0, t_j) = 0. \quad (8.8)
$$

Assuming for simplicity that the frequencies of fixed and floating leg are the same, this equation can be used to eliminate terms in the foreign forward rate to give

$$
\sum_{j=1}^{m} \left\{ S^f(0, t_m) \alpha_F(t_{j-1}, t_j) + b_m \alpha_L^f(t_{j-1}, t_j) \right\} P_d^f(0, t_j) = P_d^f(0, t_0) - P_d^f(0, t_m). \quad (8.9)
$$

This expression can be used with the basis to bootstrap the foreign discount curve. Once the discount function has been obtained it can be substituted into equation (8.8) and used to derive the foreign forward rate curve from the perspective of the domestic investor.

The forward rate curve itself can be specified in terms of foreign projection discount bonds, $P_p^f(0, t)$, using

$$f(t_1, t_2) = \frac{1}{\alpha(t_1, t_2)} \left( \frac{P_p^f(0, t_1)}{P_p^f(0, t_2)} - 1 \right). \tag{8.10}$$

The usual relationships between bonds of different maturities still hold so we have

$$P_d^f(t, t_2) = P_d^f(t, t_1) P_d^f(t_1, t_2) \tag{8.11}$$

$$P_p^f(t, t_2) = P_p^f(t, t_1) P_p^f(t_1, t_2), \tag{8.12}$$

but there is no longer a simple relationship between the forward rate and the discount curve bonds. If we define a *discounting* forward rate, $f_d$, (see Bianchetti, 2010) using

$$f_d(t_1, t_2) = \frac{1}{\alpha(t_1, t_2)} \left( \frac{P_d(0, t_1)}{P_d(0, t_2)} - 1 \right), \tag{8.13}$$

it is possible to define an additive forward cross-currency basis curve $b^X$ such that

$$P_p(0, t, T) = \frac{1}{1 + [f_d(t, T) + b^X(t, T)]\alpha(t, T)}. \tag{8.14}$$

A straightforward rearrangement of the above expressions shows that the basis curve is given by

$$b^X(t, T) = f_p(t, T) - f_d(t, T) \tag{8.15}$$

$$= \frac{1}{\alpha(t, T)} \left( \frac{P_p(0, t)}{P_p(0, T)} - \frac{P_d(0, t)}{P_d(0, T)} \right). \tag{8.16}$$

This description is simplified as there was no discussion of the other curve instruments. Money market deposits relate purely to the discount function, while futures clearly depend on the forward rates and hence on the projection curve. Further information is also available through FX forwards. The FX forwards effectively consist of the exchange of two notional flows at some date in the future. As such they depend only on the discount function of the two currencies and the spot FX rate. Combining all the available information will allow the discount and projection curves in each foreign currency to be constructed.

## 8.5 MULTI-CURVE AND TENOR BASIS

During the 2007–2009 crisis period tenor basis became a major issue. Tenor basis swap spreads widened dramatically as investors expressed a strong preference for shorter tenors over longer tenors because of market perception of default risk amongst banks. With tenor basis now significant, a single curve could no longer be used to project all of the rates for a given currency and a separate basis curve was required for each tenor of projection, with curves typically required for floating rates of maturities,

$$OIS, 1M, 3M, 6M, 12M.$$

To cater for these additional projection curves while maintaining consistency with cross-currency basis the procedure described above can be modified in a straightforward way. In the domestic currency, one tenor will also be chosen to be the discount curve, with the three-month curve being a common choice initially, although OIS replaced this in the context of collateralised trades (see section 8.6 below). This curve will then be bootstrapped in the same way as described in section 8.2 except with the restriction that only instruments that reference the discount curve or three-month rates will be included. The discount bond prices give discount factors directly, while three-month futures are appropriate as they reference three-month rates. Beyond the futures strip, interest rate swaps with a quarterly floating leg frequency will be used to extend the discount/three-month projection curve out as far as required in maturity. Once the discount curve is available then the remaining projection curves can be constructed. The value of a basis swap is given by

$$\sum_{j=1}^{m_y}(f^y(t_{j-1},t_j) + b_m^y)\alpha_L^f(t_{j-1},t_j)P_d(0,t_j) = \sum_{i=1}^{m_x}f^x(t_{i-1},t_i)\alpha_L^d(t_{i-1},t_i)P_d(0,t_i), \quad (8.17)$$

where the superscripts $x$ and $y$ indicate that the projection periods for the forward rates are different and correspond to the two time partitions described by $t_i$ and $t_j$ respectively. If the forwards $f^x$ have the same "frequency" as the discount curve, then equation (8.17) can be used to bootstrap the projection forwards $f^y$ given a strip of basis swap spreads $b_m^y$.

In the foreign currency the discount curve does not correspond to any projection curve. However, once the discount curve and one of the projection curves have been obtained as described in section 8.4 then equation (8.17) can be used to obtain the remaining projection curves from tenor basis swap prices, from the perspective of the domestic investor.

## 8.6  OIS AND CSA DISCOUNTING

### 8.6.1  OIS as the Risk-free Rate

During the financial crisis period of 2007–2009 the spread between xIBOR rates and overnight index swap (OIS) rates increased massively. Figure 8.1 illustrates the spread between the three-month EURIBOR fixing rate and the three-month EONIA swap rate between the beginning of 2007 and the end of 2009. The spread increased sharply from 6bp at the start of 2007 to a peak of 180bp just after the collapse of Lehman Brothers, before falling back to below 30bp at year end 2009. Similar increases in xIBOR-OIS spreads were seen in USD and GBP and the xIBOR-OIS spread became regarded as a benchmark of market stress (Sengupta and Tam, 2008). xIBOR rates represent the average rate that the banks on the rate setting panel can borrow unsecured in the market, while OIS rates represent the average fixed rate that a panel of banks will pay or receive against the compounded overnight rate. As discussed earlier in this

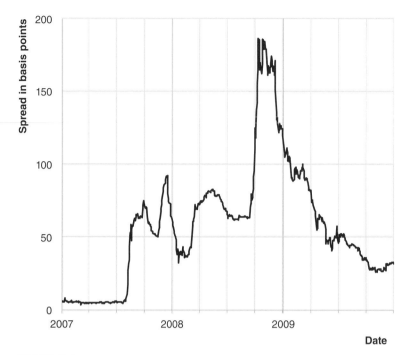

**FIGURE 8.1**   The spread between 3-month EURIBOR and 3-month EONIA swap rate during the financial crisis period of 2007–2009. The spread started the period at only 6 basis points before peaking around 180 basis points and then falling below 30 basis points at the end of 2009. (Source: European Banking Federation)

chapter, banks had typically discounted derivatives using curves based on three-month xIBOR, whether secured or unsecured, so the drastic increase in xIBOR-OIS spread had significant implications for the way banks priced and valued derivatives.

The key question is why banks used xIBOR discounting in the first place.[2] There are two possible explanations for this, firstly that the xIBOR discount curve was used as a proxy for the risk-free rate and secondly that the xIBOR curve represented the bank's own cost of funding for derivatives. The xIBOR curve pre-crisis was usually taken to represent the risk of a AA rated bank and certainly the xIBOR panel contributors were in general rated at AA or above. While this was not free of counterparty risk, it was very close to the rates implied by the bonds of highly rated governments and hence close to a curve that could be regarded as risk free, while still being associated with a highly liquid market that could be used for risk management. The second explanation, that xIBOR represented the banks' cost of funds is also plausible as xIBOR rates referenced the unsecured borrowing rate of banks. The choice of the three-month xIBOR rate for discounting would therefore represent an expectation that banks

---

[2]Here *xIBOR* is the generic term used for interest rate benchmarks such as ICE LIBOR (formerly BBA LIBOR), EURIBOR and TIBOR.

were using an average three-month duration for funding transactions. In reality it is not clear what duration banks were using for funding transactions pre-crisis.

In the crisis period both explanations of the use of xIBOR discounting were severely challenged. The idea that the xIBOR curve represented anything like a risk-free rate was demolished absolutely as the spread between xIBOR and OIS swaps blew out to very high levels. The notion that xIBOR represented the cost of funding on unsecured derivatives was also challenged by pressure to extend the term of funding and reduce liquidity risk from regulators. If banks were funding at terms longer than three months then the actual cost of funding should be included in the derivative price and this led to the introduction of Funding Valuation Adjustment models.

The market rapidly bifurcated into two separate cases, discounting for derivatives traded under CSA agreements and those that remained unsecured. For derivatives traded under CSAs there was a realisation that the discount curve should be tied to the rate earned on collateral posted in support of the derivative (Hull and White, 2014b; Piterbarg, 2010). This led to the broad topic of *OIS discounting* explored further in section 8.6.2. For trades that had no CSA and were traded unsecured, basic valuations have tended to remain at xIBOR discounted values but with a Funding Valuation Adjustment as described in Chapter 9, although the picture is mixed. The recent survey by Solum Financial Partners (2014) indicates that 85% of respondents discounted unsecured derivatives using a LIBOR curve either in the currency of the trade or in the currency in which the bank funded itself. Whether this is in fact the correct approach is open to question. As will be seen in Chapter 9, FVA models clearly involve discounted expectations where the discounting is done using the risk-free rate, which is not xIBOR. The key factor in such models is that the funding spread is defined relative to the discounting curve, whether that is xIBOR or OIS-based.

There remains a question over what is the closest proxy to the risk-free rate? Hull and White (2014b) argue that OIS rates represent the closest available benchmark rate to a risk-free rate. The overnight rate itself is clearly not risk free as it is the rate for borrowing money unsecured overnight. Repo rates could be argued to be closer to the risk-free rate as they are based on collateralised lending transactions (Longstaff, 2000). Nevertheless as Hull and White (2014b) point out, there is considerable variation in repo rates depending on the collateral posted and the approach adopted to determining collateral haircuts. Furthermore, the repo-market index rate RONIA can be above or below the equivalent unsecured rate as referenced by OIS (Kaminska, 2012). In practice the OIS rate has been generally accepted to be the closest proxy to the risk-free rate. OIS swap rates therefore provide a means of building a OIS-based curve out into the future as they reference the compounded overnight rate. The OIS swaps themselves have limited counterparty credit risk as they are usually traded between interbank market participants under CSAs or are cleared through CCPs.

## 8.6.2 OIS and CSA Discounting

To demonstrate that the discount rate on derivatives traded under a CSA should be the same as the rate earned or paid on the associated collateral pool I follow the argument presented by Piterbarg (2010; 2012) as this is closely related to the semi-replication model of Burgard and Kjaer (2013) which will be discussed at length in Chapter 9.

Consider a derivative contract $V(t, S)$ that is dependent on the asset $S$. Assume that the derivative contract is supported by a collateral account with value $X(t)$ and that the rate of interest paid on collateral balances is $r_X(t)$. The unsecured funding rate for the bank is $r_F(t)$ and the funding spread is defined by

$$s_F(t) = r_F(t) - r_X(t). \tag{8.18}$$

Both counterparties are assumed to be free of default risk. Stock positions can be funded through the repo market with rate $q(t)$ and the stock itself pays dividends at a rate $\gamma(t)$. The dynamics of the stock price in the $\mathbb{P}$ measure are given by

$$\frac{dS(t)}{S(t)} = \mu(t)dt + \sigma_S(t)dW_S(t). \tag{8.19}$$

The rate on the collateral account is stochastic and the dynamics are parametrised through collateral discount bond prices $P_X(t, T)$,

$$\frac{dP_X(t, T)}{P_X(t, T)} = r_X(t)dt - \sigma_X(t, T)dW_X(t). \tag{8.20}$$

Using Itô's lemma the change in the derivative value is given by

$$dV(t) = \left[\frac{\partial V}{\partial t} + \frac{1}{2}\sigma_S(t)^2 S^2 \frac{\partial^2 V}{\partial S^2}\right] dt + \frac{\partial V}{\partial S} dS. \tag{8.21}$$

The replicating portfolio consists of a position, $\delta$, in the stock, $S(t)$, and a cash account. The change in the cash account prior to rebalancing comes from three sources: the return on collateral position, $X$, the funding of the difference between the derivative value and the collateral position and the return on the stock position. This gives three terms:

$$d\bar{\beta}_X = -r_X(t)X(t)dt \tag{8.22}$$
$$d\bar{\beta}_F = -r_F(t)(V(t) - X(t))dt \tag{8.23}$$
$$d\bar{\beta}_S = -(\gamma(t) - q(t))\delta(t)S(t)dt. \tag{8.24}$$

Hence, the total change in the value of the replicating portfolio is given by

$$d\Pi(t) = \delta(t)dS(t) - r_X(t)X(t)dt - r_F(t)(V(t) - X(t))dt - (\gamma(t) - q(t))\delta(t)S(t)dt. \tag{8.25}$$

The value of the replicating portfolio must be equal and opposite to that of the derivative so that $\Pi + V = 0$. This implies that the change in the combined portfolio must also be zero so that

$$
\begin{aligned}
d\Pi + dV &= 0 \\
&= \left[\frac{\partial V}{\partial t} + \frac{1}{2}\sigma_S(t)^2 S^2 \frac{\partial^2 V}{\partial S^2}\right. \\
&\quad \left. - r_X(t)X(t) - r_F(t)(V(t) - X(t)) - (\gamma(t) - q(t))\delta(t)S(t)\right] dt \\
&\quad + \left[\delta(t) + \frac{\partial V}{\partial S}\right] dS.
\end{aligned}
\tag{8.26}
$$

As with the standard Black-Scholes derivation the stochastic source of risk is eliminated by choosing the stock holding to make the term in $dS$ zero,

$$\delta(t) = -\frac{\partial V}{\partial S}. \tag{8.27}$$

This gives a PDE for the value of the derivative,

$$\frac{\partial V}{\partial t} + \frac{1}{2}\sigma_S(t)^2 S^2 \frac{\partial^2 V}{\partial S^2} + (q(t) - \gamma(t))S(t)\frac{\partial V}{\partial S} - r_X(t)X(t) - r_F(t)(V(t) - X(t)) = 0. \tag{8.28}$$

This expression can be rearranged to give a Black-Scholes type PDE on the left-hand side with a collateral term on the right,

$$\frac{\partial V}{\partial t} + \frac{1}{2}\sigma_S(t)^2 S^2 \frac{\partial^2 V}{\partial S^2} + (q(t) - \gamma(t))S(t)\frac{\partial V}{\partial S} - r_F(t)V(t) = X(t)(r_X(t) - r_F(t)). \tag{8.29}$$

Using the Feynman-Kac theorem gives the value of the derivative:

$$V_{\text{NO\_CSA}}(t) = \mathbb{E}_t\left[e^{\int_t^T r_F(s)ds}V(T)\right]$$
$$+ \mathbb{E}_t\left[\int_t^T e^{-\int_t^s r_F(u)du}(r_F(s) - r_X(s))X(s)ds\right]. \tag{8.30}$$

If there is no collateral posting, $X(t) = 0$ the equation (8.30) shows that the appropriate discount rate is the funding rate, $r_F$, so that

$$V(t) = \mathbb{E}_t\left[e^{\int_t^T r_F(s)ds}V(T)\right]. \tag{8.31}$$

It is important to note that this result was derived in the absence of counterparty credit risk and I will revisit this in Chapter 9.

Equation (8.29) can be written in terms of the funding spread, $s_F(t)$, defined by equation (8.18),

$$\frac{\partial V}{\partial t} + \frac{1}{2}\sigma_S(t)^2 S^2 \frac{\partial^2 V}{\partial S^2} + (q(t) - \gamma(t))S(t)\frac{\partial V}{\partial S} - r_X(t)V(t) = s_F(t)(V(t) - X(t)). \tag{8.32}$$

Using the Feynman-Kac theorem on this PDE gives the result

$$V(t) = \mathbb{E}_t\left[e^{\int_t^T r_X(s)ds}V(T)\right]$$
$$- \mathbb{E}_t\left[\int_t^T e^{-\int_t^s r_X(u)du}s_F(t)(V(t) - X(t))ds\right]. \tag{8.33}$$

In the case of perfect collateralisation $X(t) = V(t)$ and the second term disappears leaving the final result,

$$V_{\text{CSA}}(t) = \mathbb{E}_t \left[ e^{\int_t^T r_X(s)ds} V(T) \right]. \qquad (8.34)$$

With full collateralisation the appropriate discount rate is the rate paid on the collateral account. The risk-free rate does not appear.

Most CSAs involve the payment of interest on positive collateral balances to the poster of collateral and in general the rate of interest is the overnight rate in the collateral currency. With this in mind the discount curve must be constructed from OIS swaps as described above.

### 8.6.3 Multi-currency Collateral and the Collateral Option

The CSAs in place with central counterparties for clearing single currency interest rate swaps are single currency while the new standard ISDA CSA agreement proposes to collateralise derivatives in 17 different currency categories with single currency collateralisation for each category (Cameron, 2014a). However, legacy CSA agreements which cover the bulk of bilateral trading arrangements allow the posting of multiple types of collateral asset in multiple currencies. So, for example, a CSA may allow the posting of cash in EUR, USD and GBP and government securities issued by the USA, UK and Germany with haircuts applied to the government bonds depending on maturity. In practice banks engage in *collateral optimisation* across all of their collateral positions and aim to post the *cheapest-to-deliver* collateral under each CSA, subject to collateral availability and to the legal rules and regulatory regime in each geographical region. This implies that there is embedded optionality in the CSA in much the same way that bond futures and CDS contracts have an embedded option associated with the fact that multiple bonds can be delivered under the terms of the contract.

The embedded collateral option is in fact very complex to value. If, however, we consider just cash collateral in multiple currencies then the problem is simplified considerably. Consider a CSA with two eligible currencies, domestic $d$ which is the currency of the trade in question and foreign $f$ which is the other possible collateral currency. The collateral rates in the domestic and foreign currency are $c_d(t)$ and $c_f(t)$ respectively. Intuitively to construct a cheapest-to-deliver discount curve based on the collateral rates in each currency, foreign currency collateral rates must be adjusted to take account of the basis in the cross-currency market. This adjustment rate can be labelled $r_{d,f}(t)$. Then the collateral option in the simple two currency case is defined as the maximum of the two collateral rates as seen in the domestic currency, giving

$$\max(c_d(t), c_f(t) + r_{d,f}(t)) = c_d(t) + \max(c_f(t) + r_{d,f}(t) - c_d(t), 0)$$
$$= c_d(t) + q_{d,f}(t). \qquad (8.35)$$

If the collateral rates and adjustment rate are assumed to be deterministic, the cheapest-to-deliver discount curve is given by

$$P_{\text{ctd}}(t, T) = \exp\left\{ -\int_t^T \left( c_d(t) + \max(c_f(t) + r_{d,f}(t) - c_d(t), 0) \right) ds \right\}, \quad (8.36)$$

which can obviously be extended to more than two currencies.

To justify this approach theoretically I will use the multi-currency collateral framework developed by Piterbarg (2010; 2012). In this framework we have the two collateral rates already mentioned, the FX rate, $X(t)$, expressed in units of domestic currency per unit of foreign currency, and four zero-coupon bonds,

$$P_{d,d}(t, T)$$
$$P_{f,f}(t, T)$$
$$P_{d,f}(t, T)$$
$$P_{f,d}(t, T),$$

where the first subscript indicates the currency of denomination and the second subscript the currency of collateralisation.

Consider first the domestic zero-coupon bond collateralised in the domestic currency. Party A buys the zero-coupon bond from party B at time $t$ and the cash flows occur as follows:

1. A purchases the bond and pays $P_{d,d}(t, T)$ to B at time $t$.
2. B then gives collateral to the value $P_{d,d}(t, T)$ to A.
3. An instant later at time $t + dt$ A returns the collateral, $P_{d,d}(t, T)$, back to B.
4. A then pays B the interest due on the collateral of $c_d(t)P_{d,d}(t, T)dt$.
5. B then gives collateral $P_{d,d}(t + dt, T)$ to A and so on until the maturity of the bond at time $T$.

The net cash flow at time $t$ is zero and that at time $t + dt$ is given by

$$- P_{d,d}(t, T) - c_d(t)P_{d,d}(t, T)dt + P_{d,d}(t + dt, T) = dP_{d,d}(t, T) - c_d(t)P_{d,d}(t, T)dt. \ (8.37)$$

The foreign zero-coupon bond collateralised in the foreign currency follows an identical pattern, but the foreign bond collateralised in domestic currency requires FX translation. The cash flows occur as follows:

1. A purchases the bond at time $t$ and pays B $P_{f,d}(t)$ in foreign currency.
2. B then gives collateral to cover the mark-to-market of the bond in domestic currency, $P_{f,d}(t)X(t)$.
3. At time $t + dt$ A returns the collateral, $P_{f,d}(t, T)X(t)$ to B.
4. A then pays interest to B on the collateral, $c_d(t)P_{f,d}(t)X(t)dt$.
5. B then gives collateral $P_{f,d}(t + dt)X(t + dt)$ to A and so on until maturity $T$.

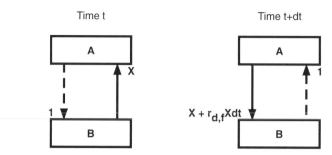

**FIGURE 8.2**  Cash flows for an instantaneous FX swap.
The solid lines are cash flows in the domestic currency and
the dash lines are in the foreign currency.

The net cash flow at time $t + dt$ is given by

$$d(P_{f,d}(t, T)X(t)) - c_d(t)P_{f,d}(t, T)X(t)dt. \tag{8.38}$$

To determine the drift of the FX rate, consider an instantaneous FX swap where A gives B one unit of foreign currency and receives $X(t)$ units of domestic currency at time $t$. An instant later B pays back the one unit of foreign currency and receives $X(t) + r_{d,f}(t)X(t)dt$ from A. The cash flows are illustrated in Figure 8.2. In fact this "swap" is nothing more than a loan arrangement where a domestic loan is collateralised by foreign currency. Hence $r_{d,f}$ is the instantaneous rate on this loan arrangement and the cash flow at $t + dt$ is given by

$$dX(t) - r_{d,f}(t)X(t)dt. \tag{8.39}$$

These relationships allow the dynamics to be specified with the domestic zero-coupon bond collateralised in the domestic currency as numeraire. In this measure, $Q^d$,

$$\frac{dX(t)}{X(t)} = r_{d,f}(t)dt + \sigma_X(t)dW_X^d(t) \tag{8.40}$$

$$\frac{dP_{d,d}(t, T)}{P_{d,d}(t, T)} = c_d(t)dt + \sigma_{d,d}(t, T)dW_{d,d}^d(t) \tag{8.41}$$

$$\frac{d(P_{f,d}(t, T)X(t))}{(P_{f,d}(t, T)X(t))} = c_d(t)dt + \sigma_{f,d}(t, T)dW_{f,d}^d(t). \tag{8.42}$$

Hence the value of the domestic bond is given by

$$P_{d,d}(t, T) = \mathbb{E}_t^d\left[e^{-\int_t^T c_d(s)ds}\right]. \tag{8.43}$$

In the foreign measure, $Q^d$, the same argument also gives the dynamics and with the foreign zero-coupon bond collateralised in foreign currency as numeraire, the dynamics are given by

$$\frac{d(1/X(t))}{(1/X(t))} = -r_{d,f}(t)dt + \sigma_{1/X}(t)dW_X^f(t) \tag{8.44}$$

$$\frac{dP_{f,f}(t,T)}{P_{f,f}(t,T)} = c_f(t)dt + \sigma_{f,f}(t,T)dW_{f,f}^f(t) \tag{8.45}$$

$$\frac{d(P_{d,f}(t,T)/X(t))}{(P_{d,f}(t,T)/X(t))} = c_f(t)dt + \sigma_{d,f}(t,T)dW_{d,f}^f(t). \tag{8.46}$$

The value of the domestic bond collateralised in the foreign currency is given by

$$P_{d,f}(t,T) = X(t)\mathbb{E}_t^f\left[e^{-\int_t^T c_f(s)ds}\frac{1}{X(T)}\right]. \tag{8.47}$$

The change of measure between $Q^f$ and $Q^d$ is given by

$$\left.\frac{dQ^f}{dQ^d}\right|_{F_t} = e^{-\int_t^T r_{d,f}(s)ds}\frac{X(t)}{X(0)}, \tag{8.48}$$

and hence the value of the domestic bond under foreign collateralisation in the $Q^d$ measure is given by

$$P_{d,f}(t,T) = \mathbb{E}_t^d\left[e^{-\int_t^T (c_f(s)+r_{d,f}(s))ds}\right]. \tag{8.49}$$

This then proves the assertion made earlier on the choice of collateral rate given in equation (8.35).

Of course there is a element of optionality involved and to value that option involves the calculation of terms like

$$P_{d,d}(0,T)\mathbb{E}_T^d\left[e^{-\int_0^T \max(q_{d,f}(s),0)ds}V(T)\right], \tag{8.50}$$

when valuing a derivative with payout $V(T)$. Piterbarg (2010) proposes the approximation,

$$\mathbb{E}_T^d\left[e^{-\int_0^T \max(q_{d,f}(s),0)ds}\right] \approx e^{-\int_0^T \mathbb{E}^{d,T}[\max(q_{d,f}(s),0)]ds}, \tag{8.51}$$

using Jensen's inequality. The right-hand side of this expression can be calculated in closed form. Antonov and Piterbarg (2014) propose a number of approximations for the solution of the collateral option problem.

**Sticky Collateral and the General Collateral Option**    The above derivation for collateral choice in the two currency case assumes that the collateral posted to the counterparty can be changed at any time. In some jurisdictions this is the case but in some the counterparty posting the collateral does not have the right of substitution. Where this is the case a change can only be made when additional collateral is required. The collateral is therefore *sticky* and this needs to be factored in to the model. In practice collateral switching can occur over a relatively short period of time by using market volatility. Any new collateral requests would be fulfilled only in the cheapest-to-deliver asset, while any remaining suboptimal collateral would be recalled whenever there was excess collateral. Piterbarg (2013) proposes a model which considers the optimal posting of collateral under the stickiness constraint.

Of course many CSAs contain provisions for the posting of many different types of asset not just cash collateral. Non-cash assets will typically also involve the use of haircuts on the asset value, depending on its maturity. Hence the valuation of the optimality condition for collateral and hence finding the appropriate choice of discount curve for a particular CSA is very complex. At the time of writing, how to value this option for a realistic computational cost remains an open area of research.

## 8.7 CONCLUSIONS: DISCOUNTING

The CSA discount curve can be seen as complimentary to FVA as it provides a mechanism to deal with the funding of collateralised trades while FVA deals with funding on unsecured trades. Hence, FVA is the subject of the next chapter.

## CHAPTER 9

# Funding Costs: Funding Valuation Adjustment (FVA)

*President Merkin Muffley: [Calling the Soviet Premier] ... Now then, Dmitri, you know how we've always talked about the possibility of something going wrong with the Bomb... The \*Bomb\*, Dmitri... The \*hydrogen\* bomb!... Well now, what happened is... ahm... one of our base commanders, he had a sort of... well, he went a little funny in the head...*

—Stanley Kubrick
*Dr. Strangelove or: How I Learned to Stop Worrying and Love the Bomb (1964)*

## 9.1 EXPLAINING FUNDING COSTS

In sections 1.3.5 and 1.4 I introduced *Funding Valuation Adjustment (FVA)* and the controversy that surrounds it following the papers on the subject by John Hull and Alan White (2012b); Hull and White (2012c, 2014b). In this chapter I provide a more detailed discussion of FVA in its primary context, that of unsecured derivative transactions. There are other sources of funding costs such as initial margin but these are covered in Chapter 10. The primary purpose here is to motivate the existence of FVA intuitively and to provide a model for FVA that is consistent with CVA. It is important to note that FVA is the quantity that has finally made clear the separation of valuation types as discussed in section 1.4.2. We must therefore first ask what type of valuation is the FVA model appropriate for? In practice the models do make a distinction between different types of valuation so in practice they can be considered as *trading valuation* models. The accounting and regulatory impact of FVA and how the trading models discussed here can be applied to calculate FVA in these contexts will be discussed in Chapter 11.

### 9.1.1 What is FVA?

There are four basic ways to explain the existence of FVA:

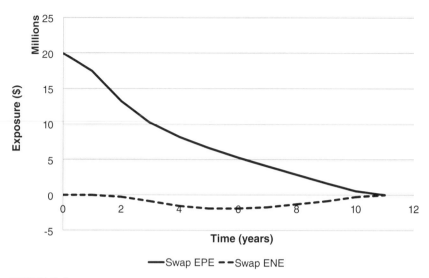

**FIGURE 9.1**   The exposure profile of an in-the-money interest rate swap.

**1. Effective Loans and Deposits**   *FVA is the cost (benefit) of the effective loan (deposit) created by an unsecured derivative*

The easiest way to understand funding for derivatives is to look at the funding costs on loans and funding benefits from deposits. Banks making loans have long used *loan transfer pricing* to establish a pricing mechanism. A loan price, that is the spread that is charged to the client, is based on two things, the cost to the bank of funding the loan and a credit spread to account for the counterparty credit risk. The cost of funding the loan represents the cost to the bank of obtaining the loan principal to pay to the borrower. This can come from multiple sources such as other bank deposits or from the bank itself borrowing funds in the wholesale markets. A deposit made to the bank can therefore be seen as a funding benefit as it provides the bank with cash that can be lent out as loans. The bank of course pays interest to the depositor.

Figures 9.1 and 9.3 illustrate the expected positive and negative exposure profiles for two interest rate swaps, one in the money and one out of the money. Both swaps are US Dollar swaps where the bank receives the fixed rate on a $100m notional with the in-the-money example having a high coupon (5%) and the out-of-the-money example having a low coupon (1%). Figures 9.2 and 9.4 also illustrates the exposure profile of a loan and a deposit with the notional scaled to give the same mark-to-market as the two interest rate swaps. It is easy to see that the off-market swaps generate substantial exposures, with the in-the-money swap having a loan-like profile and the out-of-the-money swap having a deposit-like profile. Hence there is a strong argument for suggesting that derivatives, like loans, should charge derivative counterparties for funding costs and compensate counterparties for funding benefits. Of course many derivatives have both expected positive and expected negative exposures so unlike the loans and deposits a single derivative can attract both funding charges and benefits.

**2. Cost (Benefit) of Collateral on Market Risk Hedges**   Consider a hypothetical case where a bank trades a derivative on a back-to-back basis with a corporate counterparty, that is,

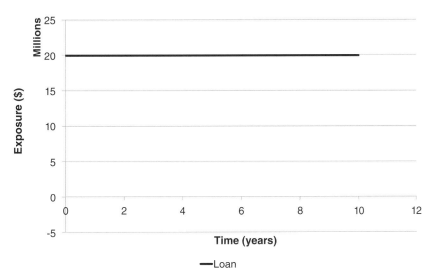

**FIGURE 9.2** The exposure profile of a loan with notional scaled to give the same MTM as the swap above.

it trades the identical but opposite trade with the interbank OTC derivatives market. If there was no counterpart credit risk, funding costs or capital requirements then this action would eliminate the risk from the counterpart transaction by hedging it exactly in the market. There are two cases to consider, one where the bank trades with the corporate under a CSA and one where it does not.

Figure 9.5 illustrates case 1, where the bank trades with the corporate under a CSA. For simplicity assume that the terms of the CSA between corporate and bank and between bank

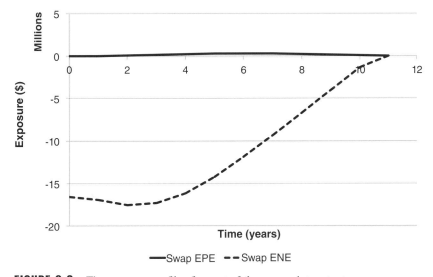

**FIGURE 9.3** The exposure profile of an out-of-the-money interest rate swap.

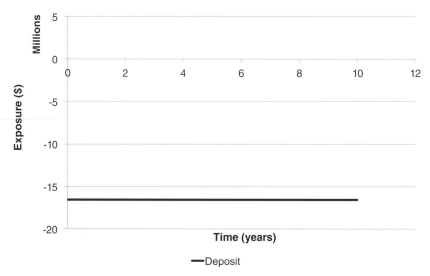

**FIGURE 9.4**   The exposure profile of a deposit with notional scaled to give the same MTM as the swap above.

and interbank market have the same terms and conditions. We can also assume that these CSAs are idealised so that all collateral transfers occur instantaneously and that there is no threshold and that the minimum transfer amount is zero. If the corporate transaction has a positive mark-to-market to the bank then the corporate will post an amount of collateral equal to the value to the bank. The mark-to-market of the hedge trade will be equal and opposite to that

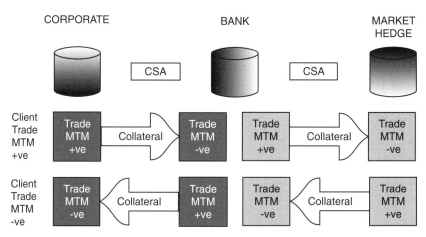

**FIGURE 9.5**   The collateral flows associated with a client trade fully secured using a CSA and hedged in the market under an identical CSA. When the client trade has a positive mark-to-market to the bank it receives collateral from the client and immediately posts this to the hedge counterparty. When the client trade has a negative mark-to-market to the bank it posts collateral to the client but receives collateral from the hedge counterparty. Assuming both CSAs allow rehypothecation of collateral there is no additional funding requirement.

of the corporate trade and hence the bank will need to post collateral to the interbank market counterparty. As rehypothcation is allowed the bank simply gives the collateral it received from the corporate to the market counterparty. If the corporate trade has a negative mark-to-market then the collateral flow reverses with the interbank market counterparty posting collateral to the bank which then rehypothecates this to the corporate. In both cases the bank faces no collateral shortfall and hence there are no funding costs. Given both trades are fully collateralised there is no counterparty credit risk either.

Case 2, where than bank trades with the corporate under an ISDA with no CSA, is illustrated in Figure 9.6. Now if the corporate trade has a positive mark-to-market the corporate is not required to post collateral to the bank. However, the bank hedge trade will have a negative mark-to-market and the bank will be required to post collateral under its CSA to the interbank market counterparty. Given there is no collateral available for rehypothecation the bank will

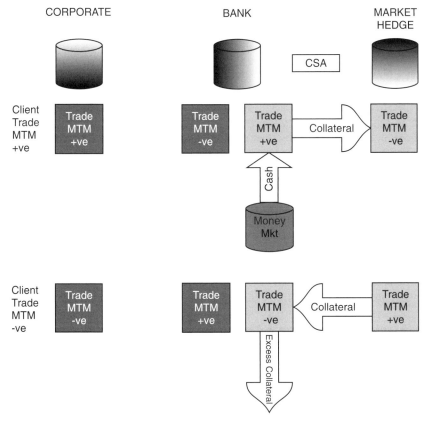

**FIGURE 9.6** The collateral flows associated with an unsecured client trade that is hedged in the market under a CSA. When the client trade has a positive mark-to-market to the bank, the hedge trade has a negative mark-to-market and requires collateral. As there is no collateral available from the client, the bank borrows unsecured in the money markets. When the client trade has a negative mark-to-market to the bank it is not required to post collateral to the client but receives collateral from the hedge counterparty. The bank now has excess collateral that could be rehpothecated elsewhere.

have to borrow funds unsecured to fulfil the collateral requirement. This unsecured funding will have a cost associated with it. Now if the reverse is true and the corporate trade has a negative mark-to-market to the bank then it is not required to post collateral to the corporate. Nevertheless the interbank market hedge will have a positive mark-to-market and the interbank counterparty will post collateral to the bank. The bank now has excess collateral and if the market counterpart CSA allows rehypothecation the collateral can be reused elsewhere in the bank's portfolio. The collateral excess has a funding benefit associated with it.

Hence we can see that the funding mismatch caused by the collateral requirements/pledges on the hedge trade leads to funding costs and funding benefits. This is a very real effect that the bank has to manage. It should also be clear that there is a new risk factor introduced by the funding rate. The funding rate is not necessarily constant and as was clear in the 2007–2009 credit crisis and during the subsequent eurozone crisis unsecured funding spreads can widen sharply in a crisis situation. Banks therefore not only face funding costs from collateral mismatches but funding risks and these risks need to be managed. Finally, it is also clear that the ability to rehypothecate collateral is critical as without this the funding costs would magnify enormously as each collateral shortfall would need to be funded through unsecured borrowing.

**3. No Repo Market for Derivatives**    When a bank buys a security such as a government bond it must fund the purchase. In practice it does so by repoing the bond out through the securities financing market. Similarly if a bank needs to borrow a bond for some purpose such as to use as collateral the bank will perform a reverse-repo transaction. The bond repo is a secured loan in which the bond is "sold" temporarily in return for cash with an agreement to buy back the bond later at a pre-agreed price. In this way the bank can buy the bond and then lend it out again to fund the bond's purchase. It is precisely this mechanism that allows banks to purchase securities that appear to have a much lower yield than their own cost of funds.[1]

The derivative market has no such supporting repo finance available to it. When a bank buys a derivative it cannot fund it by repoing it to another counterparty. As will be shown later in this chapter in section 9.4.1, if such a repo market did exist it would eliminate the need for FVA on derivatives. While this may seem like an ideal mechanism to deal with FVA there is no likelihood of a fully fledged repo market developing for derivatives. Bonds are easy to repo precisely because they are standardised liquid assets which is not the case for derivatives.

**4. Cost (Benefit) of Not Having a CSA**    As should be clear from the discussion of CSA collateral in (2) above, the presence of a CSA which allows rehypothecation eliminates FVA. Hence we can view FVA on unsecured derivatives as the cost of not having a CSA. This is a reasonable argument to make as CSAs reduce funding cost and counterparty risk for banks. CSAs do have operational overheads associated with them and many corporate counterparties

---

[1]This is one question that was raised by John Hull and Alan White (Hull and White 2012b) and used as a argument against the existence of FVA for derivatives. However, the argument is incorrect as in general banks will not buy securities outright that yield less than their own cost of funds as to do so would lead to a loss being made. The only circumstances in which a bank would invest in low yielding securities without repoing them is if is has no other choice. Such circumstances arise from regulations such as the requirement to hold liquid assets against the possibility of cash outflow on a credit downgrade of the bank.

do not have the scale, technical expertise and ready sources of liquidity to engage in CSAs. Hence FVA can be viewed as the cost of doing business on a basis that suits the counterparty that is not willing or able to pledge collateral under a CSA.

### 9.1.2 General Principle of Funding Costs

We can now state a general principle of where funding costs occur:

1. Funding costs occur whenever there is a collateral shortfall due to the lack of a natural source of rehypothecable collateral.
2. Funding costs occur when an asset buffer of cash or securities must be maintained where the buffer cannot be funded through the repo markets.

## 9.2 FIRST GENERATION FVA: DISCOUNT MODELS

During the credit crisis of 2007–2009 it was quickly realised by some institutions that the practice of discounting all derivatives by discount curves derived from three-month xIBOR rates was incorrect. As has already been discussed in Chapter 8, one impact of this debate was to move the discounting of secured derivatives to use discount curves that are based on the rate of interest received on collateral posting under the associated CSAs. In general collateral receives the overnight rate and hence secured derivatives are now discounted using curves derived from OIS swap rates. The three-month xIBOR curve was nominally associated with a AA credit rating but during the crisis many of the submitting banks had rating downgrades that placed them well below AA. Many banks also faced funding costs well in excess of the three-month xIBOR rate. The tenor used for derivative funding has also increased significantly and well beyond three months. Funding tenors have been increased due to regulatory change and a recognition that using only short-term funding sources for derivative portfolios could lead to a dangerous market situation and the possibility of default should market liquidity become unavailable.

This challenge to the use of three-month xIBOR discount curves led to early discounting models of funding costs where the discount rate was shifted from three-month xIBOR to a funded adjusted rate. Typically this was done by introducing a funding spread to the discount curve, that is

$$B(t, T) = \exp\left(-\int_t^T (r_{3M}(s) + s_F(s))ds\right). \tag{9.1}$$

There are several problems apparent with this approach. For purely unsecured derivatives the model appears supportable at least without detailed analysis. However, it is clear that there are many different states between unsecured and fully secured. A CSA may have non-zero thresholds or large minimum transfer amounts and it is not clear how to adjust the model in these cases. In some cases CSAs can have asymmetric thresholds between counterparties and in the case of a *one-way CSA* only one counterparty is required to post collateral. The discounting model clearly cannot cater with any form of asymmetry.

A second problem is that there is no engagement at all with credit risk in the discount approach. Yet it is immediately clear that the primary cause of widening bank funding costs during the crisis was perceptions of bank creditworthiness. This leads on to the discussion of potential *double counting* of funding and credit benefits which is discussed in the next section.

## 9.3 DOUBLE COUNTING AND DVA

It is relatively easy to show that discount models of FVA lead to double counting of DVA benefit, if a bilateral CVA model is used. The arguments in this section are based on those in Morini and Prampolini (2011); however, for simplicity I have restricted the argument to the case where either the borrower or the lender is free of credit risk.

Consider a risky borrower, B, taking a loan provided by credit risk-free lender, L. The lender pays the loan premium $P$ to the borrower today and receives a cash flow, $K$, at the maturity of the loan, time $T$. The borrower receives a DVA benefit from the risk it may default between now and time $T$, while the lender has a CVA cost associated with the risk of counterparty default. The discount rate is assumed to be deterministic and comprise the risk-free rate $r$ and the funding spread $s_B = \gamma_B + \lambda_B$, where $\lambda_B$ is the default intensity for B and $\gamma_B$ is the bond-CDS basis. For simplicity we assume that the recovery rate for B is zero.

The value of the transaction from the perspective of L is

$$
\begin{aligned}
V_L &= \mathbb{E}\left[e^{-rT}K\mathbb{1}_{\{\tau_B > T\}}\right] - P \\
&= e^{-rT}Ke^{-\lambda_B T} - P,
\end{aligned}
\tag{9.2}
$$

where $\tau_B$ is the default time of B and $\mathbb{1}$ is an indicator function. Note that L discounts the cash flow at the risk-free rate. The value without credit risk is

$$
V'_L = e^{-rT}K - P,
\tag{9.3}
$$

and hence the CVA is given by

$$
V_L^{CVA} = e^{-rT}K(1 - e^{-\lambda_B T}).
\tag{9.4}
$$

The value from the perspective of B is

$$
\begin{aligned}
V_B &= -\left(\mathbb{E}\left[e^{-(r+s_B)T}K\mathbb{1}_{\{\tau_B > T\}}\right] - P\right) \\
&= -e^{-rT}Ke^{-s_B T}e^{-\lambda_B T} + P \\
&= -e^{-rT}Ke^{-2\lambda_B T}e^{-\gamma_B T} + P.
\end{aligned}
\tag{9.5}
$$

The unadjusted value would be

$$
V'_B = -e^{-rT}K + P,
\tag{9.6}
$$

so the price adjustment (XVA) is therefore given by

$$
V_B^{XVA} = -e^{-rT}K(1 - e^{-2\lambda_B T}e^{-\gamma_B T}).
\tag{9.7}
$$

If funding costs had been ignored then we would have obtained the DVA

$$V_B^{\text{DVA}} = -e^{-rT} K (1 - e^{-\lambda_B T}),$$ (9.8)

and B's DVA would be equal and opposite to L's CVA

$$V_B^{\text{DVA}} = -V_L^{\text{CVA}}$$ (9.9)

thus ensuring that the valuation was symmetric between B and L. Now it is very clear that the valuation is asymmetric between B and L; this is not a problem in itself and the impact on asymmetry on valuation will be explored in section 9.6. What is disturbing is the fact that equation (9.7) contains a factor of 2 times the default intensity, $\lambda_B$, and has seemingly got twice the discounting benefit. This could be potentially corrected by ignoring the credit spread element of the funding cost and just using $s_B = \gamma_B$.

Consider the opposite case where the borrower is risk free and the lender can default. The value of the loan from the perspective of borrower and lender is given by

$$V_L = e^{-(r+\lambda_L+\gamma_L)T} K - PV_B = -e^{-rT} K + P.$$ (9.10)

In this case B has no CVA as he has no exposure to the lender and L has no DVA as the borrower has no exposure to it. The adjustment is therefore pure FVA in this case and the valuation is again asymmetric. Here though the transaction would never actually happen as L cannot lend economically at less than its funding spread, while B being credit risk free can borrow from other credit risk free counterparties at the risk-free rate $r$.

It should be clear from this argument that there is an overlap between FVA benefits and DVA. A simple discounting model fails to capture this interaction between funding and credit risk.

## 9.4  SECOND GENERATION FVA: EXPOSURE MODELS

Given that simple discount models do not work in cases other than simple unsecured derivatives and lead to double counting with bilateral CVA models suggests an alternative must be found that allows these effects to be incorporated. The alternative is exposure-based models that derive directly from CVA models. These allow funding costs to be included into counterparty level calculations but do not directly link FVA across all derivative transactions in a portfolio.[2]

Second generation models can be divided broadly into two classes of model, those based on an expectation approach and those based on replication. There are advantages and disadvantages to both approaches and ultimately they can be linked through the Feynman-Kac theorem. The expectation-driven models do not need to directly specify the dynamics that are used in the model until a numerical implementation is attempted. However, it is not intuitive to build a model in this way and guarantee that all the required elements are included. There

---

[2]Even so exposure-based FVA models that use a symmetric funding model with funding benefits and funding costs will have effective netting of these benefits and costs across all portfolios as long as collateral can be rehypothecated.

are a number of such models in the literature of this type including those developed by Morini and Prampolini (2011), and Pallavicini, Perini and Brigo (2012). Replication approaches are in general more intuitive as they allow the relationships between cash positions to be described explictly. However, PDE models do require the dynamics of each asset to be specified before a PDE can be constructed. While the PDE obtained from this can be solved directly using a PDE solver, this is not really that useful in practice. The PDE approaches can be linked to expectations through the Feynman-Kac theorem and hence can be used to give a general formula for XVA terms. Even if the assumptions used include deterministic rates, for example, once the Feynman-Kac theorem has been applied it is relatively straightforward to generalise the resulting formulae. PDE models of this type were introduced by Burgard and Kjaer in a series of papers, (2011a; 2011b; 2013). Antonov, Bianchetti and Mihai (2013) have also developed a model of this type, while Stephane Crépey (2015a; 2015b) has developed a BSDE framework that incorporates both approaches.

Section 9.4.1 presents a derivation of the Burgard-Kjaer semi-replication model and a full exploration of the options available within the modelling framework and their consequences. This model also forms the basis of the later KVA models described in Chapter 13. The notation used in the derivation in summarised in Table 9.1.

## 9.4.1 The Burgard-Kjaer Semi-Replication Model

Consider a derivative contract between a bank B and a counterparty C, with an economic value $\hat{V}$ including XVA adjustments for credit risk and funding costs and a value $V$ that assumes no credit risk or funding costs. The total XVA adjustment is given by

$$\hat{V} = V + U, \tag{9.11}$$

where $U$ is the total XVA adjustment. The Burgard-Kjaer model derives an expression for $U$ under the assumption of full replication except, possibly, on the default of the bank, B, hence this is a semi-replication model.

The hedging portfolio consists of the underlying stock, $S$, counterparty bonds $P_C$ which can default with zero recovery, and two bonds issued by the bank, $P_1$ and $P_2$, with different seniorities and recovery rates, $R_1$ and $R_2$ respectively. Only a single stock is used for simplicity but the model can be extended to multiple assets. The dynamics of the instruments are given by the SDEs:

$$dS = \mu S dt + \sigma S dW \tag{9.12}$$

$$dP_C = r_C P_C^- dt - P_C^- dJ_C \tag{9.13}$$

$$dP_1 = r_1 P_1^- dt - (1 - R_1) P_1^- dJ_B \tag{9.14}$$

$$dP_2 = r_2 P_2^- dt - (1 - R_2) P_2^- dJ_B, \tag{9.15}$$

where $J_C$ and $J_B$ are the jump to default of C and B respectively, and the superscript $-$ sign indicates the pre-default price of the bond. If there is no bond-CDS basis in the bank bonds then,

$$r_1 - r = (1 - R_1)\lambda_B \tag{9.16}$$

$$r_2 - r = (1 - R_2)\lambda_B, \tag{9.17}$$

**TABLE 9.1** Notation used in the Burgard-Kjaer semi-replication model and also in the KVA model discussed in Chapter 13. This notional was also used in the replication models discussed in sections 3.2.2 and 3.3.2.

| Parameter | Description |
| --- | --- |
| $\hat{V}(t, S)$ | The value of the derivative or derivative portfolio (including valuation adjustments) |
| $V$ | The risk-free value of the derivative or derivative portfolio (excluding valuation adjustments) |
| $U$ | The valuation adjustment |
| $X$ | Collateral |
| $\Pi$ | Replicating portfolio |
| $S$ | Underlying stock |
| $P_C$ | Counterparty bond (zero recovery) |
| $P_i$ | Issuer bond with recovery $R_i$ |
| $d\bar{\beta}_S$ | Change in cash account associated with stock (prior to rebalancing) |
| $d\bar{\beta}_C$ | Change in cash account associated with counterparty bond (prior to rebalancing) |
| $d\bar{\beta}_X$ | Change in cash cash account associated with collateral (prior to rebalancing) |
| $r$ | Risk-free rate |
| $r_C$ | Yield on counterparty bond |
| $r_i$ | Yield on issuer bond $i$ |
| $r_X$ | Yield on collateral position |
| $r_F$ | Yield on issues bond (one-bond case) |
| $M_B$ | Close-out value on issuer default |
| $M_C$ | Close-out value on counterparty bonds |
| $\alpha_C$ | Holding of counterparty-bonds |
| $\alpha_i$ | Holding of issuer bond $i$ |
| $\delta$ | Stock position |
| $\gamma_S$ | Stock dividend yield |
| $q_S$ | Stock repo rate |
| $q_C$ | Counterparty bond repo rate |
| $J_C$ | Default indicator for counterparty |
| $J_B$ | Default indicator for issuer |
| $\lambda_C$ | Effective financing rate of counterparty bond $\lambda_C = r_C - r$ |
| $\lambda_B$ | Spread of a zero-recovery zero-coupon issuer bond (such that for all $i$, $(1 - R_i)\lambda_B = r_i - r$) |
| $s_F$ | Funding spread in the case where there is one issuer bond, $s_F = r_F - r$ |
| $s_X$ | Spread on collateral, $s_X = r_X - r$ |
| $\Delta\hat{V}_C$ | Change in the value of the derivative on counterparty default |
| $\Delta\hat{V}_B$ | Change in the value of the derivative on issuer default |
| $\epsilon_h$ | Hedging error on default of the issuer |
| $P$ | Value of issuer bond portfolio prior to issuer default $P = \sum_i \alpha_i P_i$ |
| $P_D$ | Value of issuer bond portfolio in default $P_D = \sum_i R_i \alpha_i P_i$ |

where $\lambda_B$ is the hazard rate for bank B's default. In a similar fashion we write that the hazard rate for C, $\lambda_C$, is given by

$$\lambda_C = r_C - q_C, \tag{9.18}$$

where $q_C$ is the repo rate for the counterparty bonds. The trade can be collateralised according to a CSA agreement and the total collateral posted in support of the transaction is given by $X$.

If $\hat{V}(t, S, J_B, J_C)$ is the value of the derivative at time t, then the value of the derivative when B defaults first or C defaults first is given by

$$\hat{V}(t, S, 1, 0) = g_B(M_B, X) \tag{9.19}$$

$$\hat{V}(t, S, 0, 1) = g_C(M_C, X), \tag{9.20}$$

where $M_B$ and $M_C$ are the close-out values of the derivative on the default of B and C respectively. The model can take a number of different assumptions around close-out but the usual one is that

$$M_B = M_C = V. \tag{9.21}$$

When this is the case the close-out functions become

$$g_B = (V - X)^+ + R_B(V - X)^- + X \tag{9.22}$$

$$g_C = R_C(V - X)^+ + (V - X)^- + X, \tag{9.23}$$

when the collateral is zero these equations take a form familiar from Chapter 3:

$$g_B = V^+ + R_B V^- \tag{9.24}$$

$$g_C = R_C V^+ + V^-. \tag{9.25}$$

To proceed it is necessary to find the change in the value of the derivative so using Itô's lemma gives

$$d\hat{V} = \frac{\partial \hat{V}}{\partial t} dt + \frac{1}{2}\sigma^2 S^2 \frac{\partial^2 \hat{V}}{\partial S^2} dt + \frac{\partial \hat{V}}{\partial S} dS + \Delta \hat{V}_B dJ_B + \Delta \hat{V}_C dJ_C. \tag{9.26}$$

The (semi-)replicating portfolio, $\Pi(t)$, consists of positions in the stock, the bonds, collateral and a cash position. Hence the change in the portfolio is given by (gains equation)

$$d\Pi(t) = \delta(t)dS(t) + \alpha_1(t)dP_1(t) + \alpha_2(t)dP_2(t) + \alpha_C(t)dP_C(t) + d\bar{\beta}_S(t) + d\bar{\beta}_C(t) - r_X X dt, \tag{9.27}$$

where $r_X$ is the rate of interest received or paid on the collateral balance, $X$. $d\bar{\beta}_S(t)$ and $d\bar{\beta}_C(t)$ are the funding equations for the stock and counterparty bond, prior to rebalancing[3]

$$d\bar{\beta}_S(t) = \delta(t)(\gamma - q)S dt \tag{9.28}$$

$$d\bar{\beta}_C(t) = -\alpha_C q_C P_C dt. \tag{9.29}$$

---

[3]For further discussion on this point the reader is referred to Brigo et al. (2012); Burgard and Kjaer (2012b); Kenyon and Green (2015a).

The bank bonds are used to fund or invest any excess cash not funded by collateral and hence there is a funding constraint equation that must be obeyed:

$$\hat{V} - X + \alpha_1 P_1 + \alpha_2 P_2 = 0. \tag{9.30}$$

To ensure semi-replication the replicating portfolio must be equal and opposite to the value of the derivative, except possibly at the default of the bank, that is $\Pi + \hat{V} = 0$. Adding the replicating portfolio to the derivative gives

$$
\begin{aligned}
d\hat{V} + d\Pi = & \left[ \frac{\partial \hat{V}}{\partial t} + \frac{1}{2}\sigma^2 S^2 \frac{\partial^2 \hat{V}}{\partial S^2} + \delta(t)(\gamma - q)S - \alpha_C q_C P_C - r_X X \right. \\
& \left. + \alpha_1 r_1 P_1 + \alpha_2 r_2 P_2 \right] dt \\
& + \left[ \delta + \frac{\partial \hat{V}}{\partial S} \right] dS \\
& + \left[ \Delta \hat{V}_C + \alpha_C P_C \right] dJ_C \\
& + \epsilon_h dJ_B,
\end{aligned}
\tag{9.31}
$$

where $\epsilon_h$ is the hedge error on the default of B and is given by

$$\epsilon_h = \left[ \Delta \hat{V}_B - (1 - R_1)P_1 - (1 - R_2)P_2 \right]. \tag{9.32}$$

Setting

$$\delta = -\frac{\partial \hat{V}}{\partial S} \tag{9.33}$$

$$\alpha_C = -\frac{\Delta \hat{V}_C}{P_C}, \tag{9.34}$$

eliminates sources of risk from the stock $S$ and the default of counterparty bonds.

The operator $\mathcal{A}_t$ defined in equation (3.31) can again be used to simplify the presentation. An expression for the position in counterpart bonds is also needed to eliminate terms in $\alpha_1$ and $\alpha_2$. Starting with the funding constraint equation (9.30) and multiplying this by the risk-free rate gives

$$(\alpha_1 P_1 + \alpha_2 P_2)r = rX - r\hat{V}. \tag{9.35}$$

Subtracting $\alpha_1 P_1 r_1 + \alpha_2 P_2 r_2$ from both sides gives

$$\alpha_1 P_1 (r - r_1) + \alpha_2 P_2 (r - r_2) = rX - r\hat{V} - \alpha_1 P_1 r_1 + \alpha_2 P_2 r_2. \tag{9.36}$$

Using equations (9.16) and (9.17) and the expression for the hedging error, equation (9.32), gives

$$\alpha_1 r_1 P_1 + \alpha_2 r_2 P_2 = rX - (r + \lambda_B)\hat{V} - \lambda_B(\epsilon_h - g_B). \tag{9.37}$$

Using this expression allows a PDE for $\hat{V}$ that is satisfied everywhere apart from on the default of the bank:

$$\frac{\partial \hat{V}}{\partial t} + \mathcal{A}_t \hat{V} - (r + \lambda_B + \lambda_C)\hat{V} = s_X X - \lambda_C g_C - \lambda_B g_B + \lambda_B \epsilon_h, \tag{9.38}$$

which is subject to the terminal boundary condition

$$\hat{V}(T, S) = H(S), \tag{9.39}$$

where $H(S)$ is the derivative payout and $s_X \equiv r_X - r$ is the spread over the risk-free rate paid on the collateral account.

Using the definition of $U$ in equation (9.11) and noting that $V$ must satisfy the Black-Scholes PDE,

$$\frac{\partial V}{\partial t} + \mathcal{A}_t V - rV = 0, \tag{9.40}$$

allows a PDE for $U$ to be formed,

$$\frac{\partial U}{\partial t} + \mathcal{A}_t U - (r + \lambda_B + \lambda_C)U = s_X X - \lambda_C(g_C - V) - \lambda_B(g_B - V) + \lambda_B \epsilon_h, \tag{9.41}$$

where the terminal boundary condition is given by the fact that the XVA adjustment must vanish at maturity,

$$U(T, S) = 0. \tag{9.42}$$

Applying the Feynman-Kac theorem to equation (9.41) gives an expression for the total XVA adjustment as a summation of terms,

$$U = \text{CVA} + \text{DVA} + \text{FCA} + \text{COLVA}, \tag{9.43}$$

where

$$\text{CVA} = -\int_t^T \lambda_C(s) e^{-\int_t^s r(u) + \lambda_B(u) + \lambda_C(u) du} \mathbb{E}\left[V(s) - g_C(V(s), X(s))\right] ds \tag{9.44}$$

$$\text{DVA} = -\int_t^T \lambda_B(s) e^{-\int_t^s r(u) + \lambda_B(u) + \lambda_C(u) du} \mathbb{E}\left[V(s) - g_B(V(s), X(s))\right] ds \tag{9.45}$$

$$\text{FCA} = -\int_t^T \lambda_B(s) e^{-\int_t^s r(u) + \lambda_B(u) + \lambda_C(u) du} \mathbb{E}\left[\epsilon_h(s)\right] ds \tag{9.46}$$

$$\text{COLVA} = -\int_t^T s_X(s) e^{-\int_t^s r(u) + \lambda_B(u) + \lambda_C(u) du} \mathbb{E}\left[X(s)\right] ds. \tag{9.47}$$

Here the PDE has yielded four terms, the familiar CVA and DVA along with two new terms, FCA or *Funding Cost Adjustment* and COLVA or *Collateral Valuation Adjustment*.

For the remainder of the discussion on the Burgard-Kjaer model I will assume that $X = 0$ so that the trade is entirely unsecured as this makes the presentation clearer. It is relatively easy to add the collateral back into the expressions if needed and indeed this is done in the KVA presentation in Chapter 13. If $X = 0$ the COLVA term is zero and will not be included.

**Standard Close-out: $M_B = M_C = V$** Assume the standard close-out with no collateral means that $g_B$ and $g_C$ take the form given in equation (9.24) and (9.25). When these expressions are substituted into the CVA and DVA terms in equations (9.44) and (9.45) these expressions resolve to the same form encountered earlier in Chapter 3,

$$\text{CVA} = -(1 - R_C) \int_t^T \lambda_C(s) e^{-\int_t^s r(u) + \lambda_B(u) + \lambda_C(u) du} \mathbb{E}\left[V(s)^+\right] ds \tag{9.48}$$

$$\text{DVA} = -(1 - R_B) \int_t^T \lambda_B(s) e^{-\int_t^s r(u) + \lambda_B(u) + \lambda_C(u) du} \mathbb{E}\left[V(s)^-\right] ds. \tag{9.49}$$

The form of the FCA term depends on the hedging error and hence on the choice of hedging strategy.

**Perfect replication** In this case the hedging error is zero so $\epsilon_h = 0$ and the FCA term is zero. With no collateral this simply resolves to the bilateral CVA formula with CVA and DVA given by the expressions above. The hedge ratios that allow perfect replication are

$$\alpha_1 = \frac{R_2 \hat{V} - g_B}{(R_1 - R_2) P_1} \tag{9.50}$$

$$\alpha_2 = \frac{R_1 \hat{V} - g_B}{(R_2 - R_1) P_2}. \tag{9.51}$$

By taking a long position in one of the two bonds and a short position in the other the bank is able to hedge is funding costs exactly. This is a form of balance sheet management exercise and in theory can eliminate funding costs. The bank is effectively taking a spread position in bonds with different seniorities in the waterfall. There is also an implicit assumption in the model that the derivative hedging activity has no impact on the overall bank balance sheet. In practice it is unlikely a bank would be able to hedge in this way.

**Semi-replication with no shortfall on default** This strategy uses two bonds but does not aim to explicitly monetise the potential windfall of own default. The strategy retains the possibility of generating a windfall on default but ensures there will be no shortfall. The strategy assumes there are two bonds, one with zero recovery, $P_1$ and one with recovery, $P_2$, where $R_2 = R_B$. The strategy is defined by the holdings of the two bonds,

$$\alpha_1 P_1 = -(\hat{V} - V) = -U \tag{9.52}$$

$$\alpha_2 P_2 = -\alpha_1 P_1 - \hat{V} = -V \tag{9.53}$$

where the holding of $P_1$ bonds is equal to the XVA value $U$ and $P_2$ is then given by the funding constraint equation. So the risk-free value $V$ is funded by bonds with recovery $R_B$ and the XVA adjustment is funded by zero-recovery bonds. Given the structure of the hedging portfolio this is probably more feasible that the perfect replication case.

In the case of standard bilateral close-out conditions the hedging error is given by

$$\epsilon_h = (1 - R_B)V^+, \tag{9.54}$$

so that this strategy leads to a windfall to the bondholders of the issuer of $\max(V, 0)$ on the default of the issuer.

Using this approach gives the following formulae for the XVA terms:

$$\text{CVA} = -(1 - R_C) \int_t^T \lambda_C(s) e^{-\int_t^s r(u) + \lambda_B(u) + \lambda_C(u) du} \mathbb{E}\left[V(s)^+\right] ds \tag{9.55}$$

$$\text{DVA} = -(1 - R_B) \int_t^T \lambda_B(s) e^{-\int_t^s r(u) + \lambda_B(u) + \lambda_C(u) du} \mathbb{E}[V(s)^-] ds \tag{9.56}$$

$$\text{FCA} = -(1 - R_B) \int_t^T \lambda_B(s) e^{-\int_t^s r(u) + \lambda_B(u) + \lambda_C(u) du} \mathbb{E}\left[V(s)^+\right] ds. \tag{9.57}$$

The expressions can be interpreted in two separate ways; we can see this as adding a funding cost term to the existing bilateral CVA model or we can see DVA as a *funding benefit* term. We can in fact combine the last two terms as a symmetric FVA adjustment,

$$\text{FVA} = \text{DVA} + \text{FCA} \tag{9.58}$$

$$= -(1 - R_B) \int_t^T \lambda_B(s) e^{-\int_t^s r(u) + \lambda_B(u) + \lambda_C(u) du} \mathbb{E}[V(s)] ds. \tag{9.59}$$

This understanding of DVA as a funding adjustment is perfectly justified, particularly if the hazard rate $\lambda_B$ is derived from issued bonds rather than calibrated to own CDS prices.

**Semi-replication with one bond** In this case the bank issues a single bond with one recovery rate $R_F$ so that the hedge ratios are given by,

$$\alpha_1 P_1 = 0 \tag{9.60}$$
$$\alpha_2 P_2 = -\hat{V} = V + U. \tag{9.61}$$

The remaining bond is relabelled $P_F$ with a yield given by $r_F = r + s_F$. In this case the hedge ratio is determined entirely by the funding equation and the bank cannot hedge its own default. This situation is much closer to reality where banks operate on a going concern basis where funding is sought for operational reasons and little consideration is given to what happens after the bank has defaulted. Furthermore banks have limited ability to issue bonds of different seniorities. The hedge error is therefore given by

$$\epsilon_h = g_B + P_D, \tag{9.62}$$

where $P_D$ is the post-default bond portfolio value,

$$P_D = -R_F \hat{V}. \tag{9.63}$$

To avoid recursive terms this is inserted into the original PDE for $\hat{V}$, equation (9.38), to give

$$\frac{\partial \hat{V}}{\partial t} + \mathcal{A}_t \hat{V} - (r_F + \lambda_C)\hat{V} = -\lambda_C g_C, \tag{9.64}$$

where the fact that $(r_F - r) = (1 - R_F)\lambda_B$ has been used. $g_B$ does not appear in this equation at all and this reflects the fact that no attempt is made to hedge own default. If there is no counterparty default risk this just reduces to funding adjusted discounting as described in Piterbarg (2010) and discussed in Chapter 8.

The PDE for the XVA adjustment becomes

$$\frac{\partial U}{\partial t} + \mathcal{A}_t U - (r_F + \lambda_C)U = -\lambda_C(g_C - V) + s_F V, \tag{9.65}$$

where $s_F = r_F - r$. This gives the following XVA terms under Feynman-Kac when standard close-out conditions are used:

$$\mathrm{CVA} = -(1 - R_C) \int_t^T \lambda_C(s) e^{-\int_t^s r_F(u) + \lambda_C(u) du} \mathbb{E}\left[V(s)^+\right] ds \tag{9.66}$$

$$\mathrm{FVA} = -\int_t^T s_F(s) e^{-\int_t^s r_F(u) + \lambda_C(u) du} \mathbb{E}\left[V(s)\right] ds. \tag{9.67}$$

The hazard rate for bank default has dropped out of these expressions and only the funding spread remains. It is important to note that the CVA term now includes a cost of funding adjustment in the discounting term. The FVA term is symmetric and corresponds to the integral over the expected valuation profile with the funding spread. This FVA term can be split into two to correspond to funding benefit and funding cost:

$$\mathrm{FVA} = \mathrm{FVA}_{\mathrm{benefit}} + \mathrm{FVA}_{\mathrm{cost}} \tag{9.68}$$

$$= -\int_t^T s_F(s) e^{-\int_t^s r_F(u) + \lambda_C(u) du} \mathbb{E}\left[V(s)^-\right] ds \tag{9.69}$$

$$= -\int_t^T s_F(s) e^{-\int_t^s r_F(u) + \lambda_C(u) du} \mathbb{E}\left[V(s)^+\right] ds. \tag{9.70}$$

The expressions obtained using this strategy are identical to those that would be obtained by ignoring the default risk of the bank entirely but assuming that the derivative portfolio must be funded at the funding rate $r_F$. In this case the dynamics of the derivative $\hat{V}$ become

$$d\hat{V} = \frac{\partial \hat{V}}{\partial t} dt + \frac{1}{2}\sigma^2 S^2 \frac{\partial^2 \hat{V}}{\partial S^2} dt + \frac{\partial \hat{V}}{\partial S} dS + \Delta \hat{V}_C dJ_C. \tag{9.71}$$

The expression for the portfolio becomes

$$d\Pi(t) = \delta(t)dS(t) + \alpha_C(t)dP_C(t) + d\beta_S(t) + d\beta_C(t) + d\beta_F(t), \tag{9.72}$$

where additionally,

$$d\beta_F(t) = r_F(t)\hat{V}(t)dt. \tag{9.73}$$

The derivative and portfolio combined gives

$$d\hat{V} + d\Pi = \left[\frac{\partial \hat{V}}{\partial t} + \frac{1}{2}\sigma^2 S^2 \frac{\partial^2 \hat{V}}{\partial S^2} + \delta(t)(\gamma - q)S - \alpha_C q_C P_C - s_F \hat{V}\right] dt$$
$$+ \left[\delta + \frac{\partial \hat{V}}{\partial S}\right] dS$$
$$+ \left[\Delta \hat{V}_C + \alpha_C P_C\right] dJ_C. \tag{9.74}$$

Again setting

$$\delta = -\frac{\partial \hat{V}}{\partial S}$$

$$\alpha_C = -\frac{\Delta \hat{V}_C}{P_C},$$

eliminates all sources of risk and leaves the PDE which must be satisfied,

$$\frac{\partial \hat{V}}{\partial t} + \mathcal{A}_t \hat{V} - (r + s_F + \lambda_C)\hat{V} = -\lambda_C g_C. \tag{9.75}$$

Hence the PDE for the XVA adjustment is given by

$$\frac{\partial U}{\partial t} + \mathcal{A}_t U - (r_F + \lambda_C)U = -\lambda_C(g_C - V) + s_F V, \tag{9.76}$$

which is of course identical to equation (9.65) and yields the same XVA terms through the application of the Feynman-Kac theorem.

This form of CVA with symmetric FVA is popular with practitioners as the DVA, commonly believed to be unhedgeable, is removed and the trading desk is left managing funding cost and funding benefits which are much more tangible. The CVA term is unilateral but with a funding discounting adjustment such that future exposures are discounted at the banks, funding rate.

**Non-standard Close-out Conditions**    The standard close-out assumption that $M_B = M_C = V$ is the most commonly encountered, partly because it is also the simplest to implement. However, as was noted earlier in section 3.1.1 there is debate around the actual close-out that occurs in practice under the 1992 and 2002 ISDA agreements (ISDA, 1992, 2002) and the 2009 ISDA close-out protocol (ISDA, 2009c). The impact of close-out conditions on XVA has been discussed by Burgard and Kjaer (2011b); Burgard and Kjaer (2011a); Burgard and Kjaer (2012a); Burgard and Kjaer (2012c), Brigo and Morini (2011) and Gregory and German (2012). There are three cases to consider:

- Full risky close-out where $M_B = M_C = \hat{V}^-$, that is the value of the derivative immediately prior to default including XVA
- Survivor funding close-out where $M_B = V_{FB}$ and $M_C = V_{FC}$
- Bank funding close-out where $M_B = M_C = V_{FB}$.

**Risky close-out: $M_B = M_C = \hat{V}^-$** Consider a risky close-out in the single-bond hedging/symmetric funding case with no collateral. The close-out condition for the counterparty is then given by

$$g_C = R_C \hat{V}^+ + \hat{V}^-, \tag{9.77}$$

and hence the PDE for $\hat{V}$ is given by

$$\frac{\partial \hat{V}}{\partial t} + \mathcal{A}_t \hat{V} - (r + s_F)\hat{V} = (1 - R_C)\lambda_C \hat{V}^+. \tag{9.78}$$

Writing a revised split formula for $\hat{V}$,

$$\hat{V} = \bar{V} + \bar{U}, \tag{9.79}$$

where $\bar{V}$ is a solution of the funding-discounting PDE

$$\frac{\partial \bar{V}}{\partial t} + \mathcal{A}_t \bar{V} - (r + s_F)\bar{V} = 0. \tag{9.80}$$

The XVA adjustment PDE becomes

$$\frac{\partial \bar{U}}{\partial t} + \mathcal{A}_t \bar{U} - (r + s_F)\bar{U} = (1 - R_C)\lambda_C \bar{U}^+, \tag{9.81}$$

giving a unilateral CVA formula via the Feynman-Kac theorem,

$$\text{CVA} = -(1 - R_C) \int_t^T \lambda_C(s) e^{-\int_t^s r(u)s_F(u) + \lambda_C(u)du} \mathbb{E}\left[(\bar{V} + \bar{U})^+\right] ds. \tag{9.82}$$

The approach allows the recovery of simple funding discounting for the underlying valuation model, reducing the XVA adjustment to a unilateral CVA formula. However, the formula so obtained is implicit in the XVA term as $\bar{U}$ appears inside the integral. This is much more difficult to solve and will require regression approaches that give an approximate formula for $\bar{U}$ that can be used inside the exposure simulation coupled with some form of iterative procedure.

**Survivor funding close-out: $M_B = V_{FB}$ and $M_C = V_{FC}$**   If only the survivor's funding costs are considered and the counterparty risk is ignored then the value of the derivatives must satisfy the PDEs (Burgard and Kjaer, 2012c),

$$\frac{\partial V_{FB}}{\partial t} + \mathcal{A}_t V_{FB} - r_{FB} V_{FB} = 0$$
$$V_{FB}(T, S) = H(S) \tag{9.83}$$

$$\frac{\partial V_{FC}}{\partial t} + \mathcal{A}_t V_{FC} - r_{FC} V_{FC} = 0$$
$$V_{FC}(T, S) = H(S). \tag{9.84}$$

Here counterparty risk is no longer considered so the value of the derivative just satisfies a funding adjusted PDE as per Piterbarg (2010).

For the strategy of the semi-replication with no shortfall, the bond hedge ratios are modified such that

$$\alpha_1 P_1 = -(\hat{V} - M_B)\alpha_2 P_2 = -M_B = -V_{FC}, \tag{9.85}$$

that is that the own bond portfolio is aimed to match the close-out value when the bank defaults, $M_B$. In this case the hedging error is given by

$$\epsilon_h = (1 - R_B)V_{FC}^+, \tag{9.86}$$

while the close-out values become

$$g_B = V_{FC}^+ + R_B V_{FC}^- \tag{9.87}$$
$$g_C = R_C V_{FB}^+ + V_{FB}^-. \tag{9.88}$$

With these conditions the PDE for XVA becomes

$$\frac{\partial U}{\partial t} + \mathcal{A}_t U - (r + \lambda_B + \lambda_C)U = (1 - R_C)\lambda_C V_{FB}^+ + (1 - R_B)\lambda_b V_{FC}^-$$
$$+ \lambda_C(V - V_{FB}) + \lambda_B(V - V_{FC})$$
$$+ \lambda_B(1 - R_B)V_{FC}^+. \tag{9.89}$$

Using Feynman-Kac the following is obtained for XVA:

$$U(t, S) = -(1 - R)_C \int_t^T \lambda_C(s)e^{-\int_t^s (r(u)+\lambda_B(u)+\lambda_C(u))du} \mathbb{E}[V_{FB}^+(s)]ds$$

$$- (1 - R)_B \int_t^T \lambda_B(s)e^{-\int_t^s (r(u)+\lambda_B(u)+\lambda_C(u))du} \mathbb{E}[V_{FC}^-(s)]ds$$

$$+ \int_t^T \lambda_C(s)e^{-\int_t^s (r(u)+\lambda_B(u)+\lambda_C(u))du} \mathbb{E}[V_{FB}(s) - V(s)]ds$$

$$+ \int_t^T \lambda_B(s)e^{-\int_t^s (r(u)+\lambda_B(u)+\lambda_C(u))du} \mathbb{E}[V_{FC}(s) - V(s)]ds$$

$$- \int_t^T s_{FB}(s) e^{- \int_t^s (r(u) + \lambda_B(u) + \lambda_C(u)) du} \mathbb{E}[V_{FC}^+(s)] ds, \tag{9.90}$$

where $s_{FB} = (1 - R_B)\lambda_B$. The expression contains three familiar terms, with the first and second terms corresponding to CVA and DVA and the last term corresponding to FCA. The exposures are adjusted to reflect the funding adjusted close-out. The third and fourth terms are adjustment terms to the CVA and DVA to reflect the difference between the close-out value and the Black-Scholes value $V$. Although these expressions may seem complex, they are much more straightforward to implement than those found in the risky close-out section. The two adjusted close-out values, $V_{FB}$ and $V_{FC}$, rely only on simple discounting-style adjustments to the trade valuation. This adjustment could be readily applied inside a Monte Carlo simulation if the funding spreads are deterministic as trade valuation would be modified by a discounting spread.

For the one-bond strategy/exclusion of bank default risk the PDE for $\hat{V}$ is still given by equation (9.38). Replacing $g_C$ is this equation gives the PDE,

$$\frac{\partial \hat{V}}{\partial t} + \mathcal{A}_t \hat{V} - (r + s_F + \lambda_C)\hat{V} = -\lambda_C(V_{FB}^- + R_C V_{FB}^+). \tag{9.91}$$

Splitting $\hat{V}$ into $V_{FB}$ that satisfies equation (9.83) and an XVA adjustment $U_{FB}$ gives the PDE,

$$\frac{\partial U}{\partial t} + \mathcal{A}_t U - (r_F + \lambda_C)U = - - \lambda_C(1 - R_C)V_{FB}^+, \tag{9.92}$$

and hence there is a single CVA term given by

$$U_{FB}(t, S) = -(1 - R_C) \int_t^T \lambda_C(s) e^{- \int_t^s (r_F(u) + \lambda_C(u)) du} \mathbb{E}[V_{FB}^+(s)] ds. \tag{9.93}$$

$V_{FB}$ is already funding adjusted so in this model the FVA and CVA terms are completely separable with FVA $= V_{FB} - V$. Furthermore the funding adjustment is of the simple discount type.

**Bank funding close-out: $M_B = M_C = V_{FB}$**  When the close-out occurs at the bank's cost of funds irrespective of who defaults then the one-bond strategy results remain unchanged as $M_C$ does not appear in the equations. For the two-bond semi-replication strategy the PDE for $\hat{V}$ becomes

$$\begin{aligned}
\frac{\partial \hat{V}}{\partial t} + \mathcal{A}_t \hat{V} - (r + \lambda_B + \lambda_C)\hat{V} &= -\lambda_C(R_C V_{FB}^+ + V_{FB}^-) \\
&\quad - \lambda_B(V_{FB}^+ + R_B V_{FB}^-) \\
&\quad + \lambda_B(1 - R_B)V_{FB}^+ \\
&= -\lambda_C(R_C V_{FB}^+ + V_{FB}^-) \\
&\quad - \lambda_B R_B V_{FB}^-. \tag{9.94}
\end{aligned}$$

Using the same split between $V_{FB}$ and $U_{FB}$ gives the following PDE for $U_{FB}$,

$$
\frac{\partial U_{FB}}{\partial t} + \mathcal{A}_t U_{FB} - (r + \lambda_B + \lambda_C) U_{FB} = -\lambda_C (R_C V_{FB}^+ + V_{FB}^-)
$$
$$
- \lambda_B R_B V_{FB} - r_B V_{FB}
$$
$$
+ (r + \lambda_B + \lambda_C) V_{FB}
$$
$$
= -\lambda_C (R_C V_{FB}^+ + V_{FB}^-)
$$
$$
= -(1 - R_C)\lambda_C V_{FB}^+. \tag{9.95}
$$

Which gives just a CVA term as all the terms on the right-hand side containing $\lambda_B$ have cancelled out,

$$
U_{FB} = -(1 - R_C) \int_t^T \lambda_C(s) e^{-\int_t^s (r(u)+\lambda_B(u)+\lambda_C(u))du} \mathbb{E}[V(s)_{FB}^+] ds. \tag{9.96}
$$

So in this case again it is possible to split funding costs from CVA entirely.

## 9.5   RESIDUAL FVA AND CSAs

In the above discussion I quickly dropped the inclusion of collateral, $X$, to simplify the presentation. Without $X$ included the above expressions hold for fully unsecured derivatives. It should also be clear that if $X = V$ then the XVA terms disappear and the value is given simply by the Black-Scholes PDE. In reality though, even with a strong CSA with daily collateral calls, the collateral position will never exactly equal the value of the derivative portfolio. This gives the potential for a lack of rehypothecable collateral and hence funding costs because of a collateral shortfall.

For CSAs with daily collateral calls, zero thresholds and small minimum transfer amounts it is questionable whether or not a separate FVA charge should be made. Note that here a CSA with these properties is referred to as a *strong* CSA, while others are referred to as *weak* CSAs. The operational issues around collateral mean there will be small shortfalls and small overcollateralised positions across the portfolio from these CSAs so at portfolio level it could be argued to cancel out. Furthermore there is also an argument that the market will price in the effective FVA on these deals through the discounting models for highly collateralised portfolios.

For CSAs with lower frequency collateral calls such as weekly or monthly, non-zero thresholds or large minimum transfer amounts, there is a high probability that $X < V$. If this is the case then an FVA adjustment should be made. This reflects the fact that the hedge trade for the market risk on the portfolio will itself probably be collateralised under a strong CSA and hence any weak CSA will lead to a collateral shortfall and thus funding costs.

There is also the case for $X > V$, that is overcollateralisation. This can arise through a variety of different provisions in CSAs and ISDAs but this will be covered in Chapter 10 alongside FVA on initial margin which is the primary source of overcollateralisation.

## 9.6 ASYMMETRY

All of the above funding models derived using the Burgard-Kjaer semi-replication framework share one property and that is that all of them give valuations that are asymmetric between the two parties. That is the two parties will never agree on the *value* of the transaction, even at trade inception. As was discussed in Chapter 1, both parties do not need to agree on a value to trade, they only need to agree on a *price*. As is illustrated in Figure 1.2 as long as both parties believe that the value to them is greater than the price of the transaction then they will trade. In fact it is precisely this asymmetry that allows trading to happen. Nevertheless the asymmetry in FVA models has proved one of the more vexing elements, particularly in the context of accounting for FVA. One paper, *FVA – Putting funding into the equation* (Sommer et al., 2013), by accounting firm *KPMG* explicitly modified the CVA term to retain symmetry once funding has been included. However, in general, it is not necessary that XVA models produce symmetric valuations between counterparties. As will be demonstrated in the following two case studies, asymmetry is a fact of life for economic valuations at least.

### 9.6.1 Case 1: Corporate vs. Bank Asymmetry

Table 9.2 lists the differences in the trade economics between a bank and a corporate that have executed a derivative transaction. It should be immediately clear that the corporate and bank are in completely different positions and hence that the value both parties see for the transaction should be different. The corporate uses the derivative to manage a balance sheet exposure and as such is more interested in how the derivative affects the balance sheet through cash flows than the actual mark-to-market. The corporate also uses hedge accounting to avoid the impact of mark-to-market volatility. The bank in contrast has traded a large number of such derivatives with many counterparties and manages the mark-to-market of the book of trades, hence the mark-to-market and sensitivies are the metrics of primary interest to the bank. Banks do make use of IAS 39 hedge accounting in some circumstances but mostly for their own balance sheet management not corporate trades. The bank and the corporate are in

**TABLE 9.2**   Asymmetries between a bank and a corporate counterparty.

|  | **Corporate** | **Bank** |
|---|---|---|
| Portfolio | Use the derivative to hedge balance sheet exposures and provide cash flow control | The derivative is part of a large derivative portfolio with many counterparties |
| MTM | Interested in cash flow management not MTM | Manage the trade MTM |
| Accounting | Uses IAS-39 hedge accounting (IASB, 2004) | Uses IFRS 13 (IASB, 2012) |
| Capital | Does not have to place regulatory capital against the position | Must have appropriate regulatory capital in place |
| Funding | Funding costs are derived from market borrowing costs and cost of cash raised through normal business activities, e.g. product sales | Funding costs derived from treasury activities including wholesale funding market activities, retail deposits, etc. |

**TABLE 9.3**   Asymmetries between two banks.

|  | Bank A | Bank B |
| --- | --- | --- |
| Business Model | Large International Bank (Broker-Dealer) | European Regional Bank |
| Regulatory Approvals | Has IMM approval for market and counterparty credit risk | Has IMM approval for market risk but uses CEM and AIRB for counterparty credit risk |
| SVaR | SVaR window corresponds to the 2008–2009 post-Lehman crisis | SVaR window corresponds to 2010–2011 eurozone crisis |
| Funding | Funding costs are derived largely from wholesale market borrowing costs | Funding costs derived from treasury activities including wholesale funding market activities, retail deposits, etc. |

completely different regulatory regimes, and the bank must hold regulatory capital while the corporate does not need to. Finally the sources of funding costs are also different with the corporate to at least some degree relying on their business as a source of cash, while the bank relies upon the traditional sources of retail deposits and wholesale funding.

### 9.6.2   Case 2: Bank vs. Bank Asymmetry

Table 9.3 lists the differences between the economics of two banks, one a large international bank and the second a European regional bank. Even with two banks the trade economics of the derivative between them are different. The regulatory capital framework will be described in more detail in Chapter 12 but it is sufficient here to note that the way that regulatory capital is calculated is different between the two banks and they will each have to hold different amounts of capital. The funding costs of the two institutions are also different. The European bank relies to some degree on retail deposits, while the large international bank does not have a large depositor base to draw on and so largely uses wholesale market funding.

## 9.7   RISK NEUTRALITY, CAPITAL AND THE MODIGLIANI-MILLER THEOREM

Asymmetry has major implications for derivative valuation theory. Asymmetry leads to trading businesses having different holding costs for the same positions and this in turn leads directly to the conclusion that there is no single market wide risk-neutral measure. Risk-neutral measures remain but only idiosyncratic ones, private to each individual trading institution. Hence valuations are not universal but specific to the institution. This can be demonstrated using the following argument from Kenyon and Green (2014b).

### 9.7.1   No Market-wide Risk-neutral Measure

Two steps are required to demonstrate that this is the case. The first step is to demonstrate that there is no common risk-neutral measure if market participants face different holding costs. The second step is to demonstrate that this is in fact the case in current derivative markets.

**No Common Risk-neutral Measure**  **Definition.**  (Shreve, 2004) Let $\mathbb{P}$ be the physical measure, then a probability measure $\mathbb{Q}$ is said to be risk-neutral if:

1. $\mathbb{Q}$ and $\mathbb{P}$ are equivalent;
2. under $\mathbb{Q}$ discounted stock prices are martingales.

**Theorem 9.1.** If there are market participants with different idiosyncratic continuous dividends when holding the same stock then there is no common risk-neutral measure for all participants.

**Proof.** Let the stock price from the perspective of market participant A be the following in the $\mathbb{P}$ measure,

$$dS_A(t) = (\mu_A + \gamma_A)S_A(t)dt + \sigma_A(t)dW^{\mathbb{P}_A}(t),$$

where $\gamma_A$ is the objective dividend received by $A$ and $\mu_A$ is the $\mathbb{P}$-measure drift observed by $A$. Hence in the idiosyncratic risk-neutral measure of $A$, the stock price follows the dynamic,

$$dS_A(t) = (r + \gamma_A)S_A(t)dt + \sigma_A(t)dW^{\mathbb{Q}_A}(t), \qquad (9.97)$$

where $r$ is the risk-free rate. The dividends are idiosyncratic and hence the rates of return for different participants are different and there is no common risk-neutral measure. $\square$

The existence of different dividends for different participants through different holding costs ensures that each has an idiosyncratic risk-neutral measure.

**Market Participants have Idiosyncratic Holding Costs**  To demonstrate this is the case, it must be shown that different market participants have different funding and capital requirements for the same derivative and that capital and funding represent non-zero costs. Consider two different scenarios.

**Scenario 1: Two banks with the same trades**  Consider the case illustrated in Figure 9.7. Banks $A$ and $B$ have two back-to-back interest rate swaps, one with a client on an uncollateralised basis and the second hedge trade with the clearing house and collateralised. It should be clear from Table 9.3 that both banks could easily face different regulatory capital requirements if they have different regulatory status. The funding requirement for both banks will be the same if only the pair of trades is considered. The trade with the clearing house will be subject to collateralisation under the CCP's own rules and be subject to a requirement to provide a default fund contribution. If only these trades are considered these requirements will be the same.

**Scenario 2: Bank B has two clients**  In the second case, as illustrated in Figure 9.8, the setup is identical to the first scenario for bank $A$, but banks $B$ has a second client with an identical but opposite interest rate swap to the first. This second trade has also been hedged out with a trade cleared through the CCP. This second cleared trade offsets the first trade. The funding requirements for both banks will be different because:

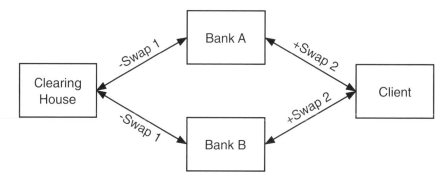

**FIGURE 9.7**   Holding costs scenario 1. Two banks *A* and *B* have exactly the same trades with the same two counterparties, a clearing house and a client. The trades with the clearing house are fully collateralised, while the client trades are uncollateralised. The swap trades 1 and 2 are identical apart from the sign and the fixed rate and represent a client trade that has been hedged with a cleared trade.

- The initial margin will be significantly lower for bank B than bank A.
- If the two CCP trades for bank B offset then the variation margin will be zero.
- The default fund contributions will also likely be different as these are often weighted by the initial margin requirement.

In addition the capital requirements will differ because of the following, irrespective of any differences in regulatory status,

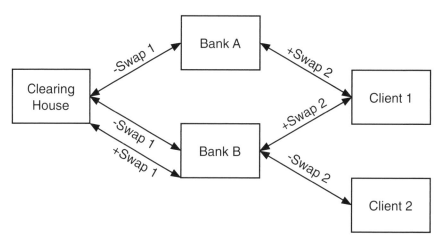

**FIGURE 9.8**   Holding costs scenario 2. Like scenario 1, two banks *A* and *B* have exactly the same trades with the same two counterparties, a clearing house and a client. However, here bank *B* has a second client with an identical but opposite trade to the first client. To hedge this second transaction a second trade is cleared through the CCP, which offsets the first. As before, the trades with the clearing house are fully collateralised, while the client trades are uncollateralised.

- Bank *B* has two pairs of offsetting trades which will mean low or zero market risk and hence smaller market risk capital requirements than *A*.
- Capital requirements for facing the CCP will likely differ as the default fund contributions will also differ between *A* and *B*.

**Capital and Funding Costs are Not Zero as Trading Businesses are Risky** Trading businesses are clearly risky as they have unavoidable losses due to business costs. For example a trading business faces costs from:

- Institutional costs such as salaries and facilities
- Trading costs due to bid-ask spreads
- Regulatory requirements to hold funding buffers, in case of rating downgrade for example.

In addition there are clear business risks from the following:

- Hedging is not continuous nor are markets. Gap events do occur and hedging cannot be perfect in practice.
- Derivatives like CDS and Barrier options contain digital features that are difficult to hedge perfectly.
- Market incompleteness and unhedgable risk.
- Uncertain future regulation.

Hence trading businesses are risky and investors will charge these businesses for funding and capital as a result.

### 9.7.2 Consequences

The primary consequence is that the economic value of derivatives is idiosyncratic but this should come as no surprise, given the discussion in Chapter 1. All banks have different business strategies and different competitive advantages and the economic valuations of the products simply reflect that.

### 9.7.3 The Modigliani-Miller Theorem

The Modigliani-Miller theorem (1958) states that in perfect markets the capital structure of a company, that is the mix of equity and debt investors, does not affect the weighted-average cost of capital. As was seen earlier, the Modigliani-Miller theorem was used by Hull and White (2012b) in their argument against the introduction of FVA. However, the theorem relies on the assumption that investors do not change the project's cash flows. This is clearly not the case with derivatives as the regulatory status of the firm does change the cash flows. Furthermore when new projects are undertaken the capital requirements also change. Hence, the presence of holding costs invalidates the application of Modigliani-Miller to derivative markets as its assumptions have been shown not to hold.

## 9.8   WRONG-WAY/RIGHT-WAY RISK AND FVA

As with CVA and DVA, FVA may also have wrong-way and right-way risk. In the context of funding a wrong-way risk position would see funding costs rising at the same time that the requirement for funding rises, while right-way risk would see the opposite. Of course wrong-way type behaviour was clearly experienced by some banks during the 2007–2009 crisis period with bank funding spreads widening sharply at the same time as their net collateral requirement increased, with the latter being driven by the sharp fall in interest rates.

Wrong-way/right-way risk can be included in FVA calculations in broadly the same way as with CVA and DVA models. The dependence between the funding spread, $s_F(t)$ and the underlying assets needs to modelled. The obvious choice would be to make the funding spread stochastic and then model the dependence through Gaussian correlation. This is relatively straightforward and amounts to a model similar to a multi-currency interest rate model. A second approach would seek to model the defence through copula models or the approach of Glasserman and Yang (2013) as described in Chapter 7.

## CHAPTER 10

# Other Sources of Funding Costs: CCPs and MVA

*Will Emerson: You know, the feeling that people experience when they stand on the edge like this isn't the fear of falling – it's the fear that they might jump.*

—J.C. Chandor
*Margin Call (2011)*

## 10.1 OTHER SOURCES OF FUNDING COSTS

The primary source of FVA discussed to date is on unsecured derivatives. However, the *general principle of funding costs* in section 9.1.2 suggests that any situation in which there is a collateral shortfall leads to additional funding costs. There are four cases to consider: central counterparty funding costs, bilateral initial margin introduced in BCBS 226 and 261 (BCBS, 2012h; BCBS, 2013d), volatility buffers and other overcollateralisation mechanisms and liquidity buffers held against rating downgrade. As I will describe, each of these cases leads to additional FVA. The most complex case to model is that of fudging costs on VaR-based Initial Margin or *Margin Valuation Adjustment* (MVA) and this is discussed in section 10.3 in detail. The theoretical justification for FVA on overcollateralised positions is provided in section 10.2.

### 10.1.1 Central Counterparty Funding Costs

Central counterparties (CCPs) typically require three different types of margin collateral to be posted to them (or to a bankruptcy remote third-party custodian account) and also a contribution to the default fund.

**Variation Margin** The most basic type of collateralisation required by CCPs is variation margin. This is collateral posted in support of the change of mark-to-market on the derivative portfolio. This operates in exactly the same way as a CSA does and hence can be modelled in exactly the same way as the collateral described in Chapter 9. The only potential difference is that with CCPs the unit of collateralisation may be much more restricted than under a typical CSA with, for example, single currency interest rate swaps segregated into separate collateralisation units. Overall this will lead to higher funding costs because of the lack of netting but will not change the way FVA will be modelled.

**Initial Margin**    Central counterparties also require initial margin to be posted to them to support any trades that are cleared. The initial margin is required to cover movements in the mark-to-market of the trade portfolio during any potential close-out situation such as a default by the clearing member. High margin requirements are a feature of CCPs as they have very limited capital and hence limited ability to absorb losses. The methodology used to generate the initial margin requirement varies from one exchange to another but a popular choice is the historical Monte Carlo simulation approach to calculating Value-at-Risk (VaR) or variants of it such as Conditional Value-at-Risk (CVaR). For example, LCH.Clearnet SwapClear uses a proprietary model called PAIRS that is based on CVaR (LCH, 2013). The parameters used for the historical simulation vary with differences in the length of the lookback period, close-out period over which market changes are calculated and in the confidence limit (Cameron, 2011; Rennison, 2013).

To see how funding costs arise when initial margin is required, consider the following examples. Recall that in section 9.1.1 two cases were examined to motivate FVA on unsecured derivatives, one with a corporate trade under a CSA hedged with a market counterparty also under a CSA and one where the corporate trade was unsecured but hedged with a market counterpart under a CSA. Consider again the case where both trade and hedge are transacted under identical CSAs with both allowing rehypothecation as illustrated in Figure 9.5. This case ended with no FVA as there was no collateral shortfall, with the collateral simply rehypothecated by the bank from one counterparty to the other. Now consider a similar situation where the bank now clears the trade with the market counterpart through a CCP. For simplicity assume that the variation margin demanded by the CCP is equal to that posted under the CSA. The CCP, however, also requires initial margin to be posted irrespective of the sign of the trade mark-to-market. This example is illustrated in Figure 10.1. In the case with clearing, the variation margin is again provided by rehypothecation with the direction of collateral flow determined by the sign of the value of the corporate trade. However, as the initial margin must always be provided there is no ready source of rehypothecable collateral and therefore the bank must borrow unsecured unless it has spare unused assets on the balance sheet. Hence the initial margin gives rise to a funding cost and hence a funding valuation adjustment on the corporate trade. Of course if the corporate did not have a CSA in place then the variation margin would also lead to FVA.

**Volatility Buffers**    CCPs can also add additional margin requirements in the form of volatility buffers. These are additional margin requirements when risk positions exceed available market depth measures, which suggest that in the event of close-out the CCP would take longer than anticipated to close out the position and hence face the risk of further loss from adverse market movements. Clearly, like initial margin, the volatility buffer is an additional margin requirement that is not naturally supported by rehypothecation. Hence volatility buffers also give rise to FVA. The exact methodology is determined by the CCP, although in at least one case this is implemented as a multiplier on the initial margin.

**Default Fund**    The *Default Fund* consists of a series of fees paid by clearing members to provide a pool of assets to cover losses in the event of a default by one or more members. As

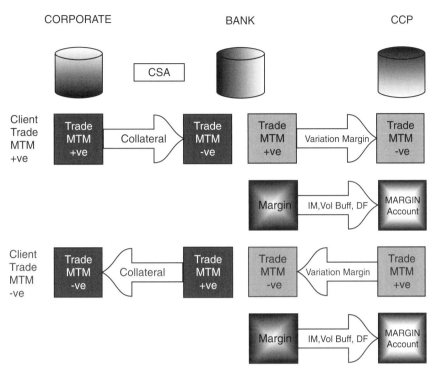

**FIGURE 10.1** The collateral flows associated with a trade between a bank and a corporate and the associated hedge cleared through a CCP. The variation margin is met with rehypothecation of collateral; however, the initial margin, volatility buffer and default fund contributions must be posted irrespective of the mark-to-market of the trade. Given there is no rehypothecable source of collateral, the bank must borrow unsecured to fund the initial margin and this unsecured borrowing gives rise to FVA.

noted earlier, CCPs are typically lightly capitalised entities and so the default fund is another form of self-defence mechanism to prevent the CCP itself collapsing when faced with losses. While initial margin seems to cover all losses arising from close-out, in practice this may not be the case, particularly in a systemic crisis where multiple clearing members default. The details of how the default fund operates is up to each individual CCP but the two key properties from a modelling perspective are:

1. The size of each member's contribution is a function of their own position and that of all other clearing members.
2. The default fund may need to be recharged if losses are experienced.

The problem is that it may be impossible to accurately predict what the default fund will be in a particular set of circumstances as only the default fund contribution of the clearing member will be known. Those of other members will not necessarily be public knowledge. This lack of information makes modelling difficult if not impossible without simplifying assumptions. The fact that the default fund may need to be recharged will also be difficult to model.

### 10.1.2 Bilateral Initial Margin

The Basel Committee on Banking Supervision has proposed that all financial firms and systemically important non-financial entities should post initial margin bilaterally to support OTC derivatives trading (BCBS, 2012h; BCBS, 2013d). The motivations for this move are partly to disincentivise OTC derivative trading in favour of central clearing and partly to move to a *defaulter pays* model of default management rather than the current system where non-defaulters suffer losses on default of their counterparties and are forced to hold reserves and capital against such an eventuality. The exact methodology is yet to be determined with the Basel Committee initially proposing that bank approved market risk VaR models be used for the purpose of calculating initial margin (BCBS, 2012h). The proposals have now been revised to allow more flexibility and the derivatives industry, under the auspices of ISDA, has proposed a market standard initial margin calculator, SIMM (ISDA, 2013). At the time of writing the methodology to be used for this initial margin calculator is unknown but the proposal, if adopted, would see the calculation process given over to a third party. The principles behind bilateral initial margin and CCP initial margin are the same and so are the consequences for FVA.

### 10.1.3 Rating Agency Volatility Buffers and Overcollateralisation

Initial margin is just a form of overcollateralisation but there are a number of other forms overcollateralisation can take. The simplest is the *initial amount* which is a provision that can be included in CSAs for a fixed amount of collateral to be posted up front before any derivative trading takes place. Given that the initial amount is fixed, the cost of the associated FVA is straightforward in all FVA models as the expected overcollateralisation profile is flat.

More complex are the *rating agency volatility buffers* discussed previously in Chapter 6. Each rating agency provide models for the overcollateralisation of derivative portfolios when the rating of a counterparty falls below a certain threshold. This language can be included in ISDA agreements but is frequently included in CSAs. Often the provisions from multiple agencies will be included in the legal documentation with the aim of the transaction counterparty posting the largest collateral amount given by multiple different volatility buffer methodologies. The approach to calculating the buffers differs between agencies and has changed through time as agencies have updated their models. A CSA though will typically reference a specific version of the calculation. As an example consider the approach provided by Standard & Poor's in their 2012 publication *Counterparty Risk Framework Methodology and Assumptions* (Standard and Poor's, 2012). The volatility buffer for swap products is given as a fixed percentage of trade notional, depending on the weighted-average life of the remaining deal, the credit rating and the type of swap. Here the overcollateralisation profile must be modelled directly and in the case of the Standard & Poor's methodology will be deterministic but a function of time. The FVA can then be calculated by integrating over the profile, depending on which FVA model has been selected.

### 10.1.4 Liquidity Buffers

After the financial crisis of 2007–2009 where it became apparent that liquidity drain following rating downgrade was a significant factor in the default and near-default of financial entities, regulators mandated that banks should hold asset pools against the prospect of liquidity loss on downgrade. For example, it is clear from testimony to the *Financial Crisis Inquiry Commission* (FCIC, 2010) that the rating downgrade of AIG and subsequent collateral call for an additional $8.2bn was a significant factor behind its move into conservatorship in September 2008. Liquid outflow after rating downgrade can take a wide variety of different forms. In the context of derivatives the primary example of this is through rating triggers built into ISDA agreements and CSAs. A CSA can, for example, contain thresholds that tighten as an entity is downgraded or introduce volatility buffers such as those described in section 10.1.3. Away from derivatives, downgrades can lead to loss of bank deposits, particularly if bank depositors impose rating conditions. Regulators ask banks to hold a liquidity buffer equal to the cash outflow that would be experienced on a rating downgrade (Financial Conduct Authority, 2014).

The liquidity buffer must be held in liquid assets such as government bonds. However, these assets must be retained by the bank and cannot be funded through the repo market. The liquidity buffer, therefore, leads to an additional FVA for any derivative portfolios which have downgrade triggers associated with them.[1] Liquidity buffers can be expensive to maintain and in some cases it may be preferable for a bank to renegotiate a CSA to post collateral immediately rather than hold a liquidity buffer.

## 10.2 MVA: MARGIN VALUATION ADJUSTMENT BY REPLICATION

The semi-replication model used to derive FVA in Chapter 9 and also to derive unilateral and bilateral CVA models in Chapter 3 can also be applied to derive an expression for MVA (Green and Kenyon, 2015). The model follows the same conventions as used previously and uses the notation given in Table 9.1 with the additions given in Table 10.1. The model includes initial margin posted to the counterparty, $I$, and received from the counterparty $\tilde{I}$. All initial margin is assumed to be held in a segregated account and therefore to be bankruptcy remote. Note also that while the term initial margin is used throughout this section, the model can be applied generally to any overcollateralisation, although if such collateral is not bankruptcy remote then the close-out conditions would need to be modified accordingly. The collateral $X$ therefore equates to the variation margin and therefore can be both positive and negative and is also assumed to rehypothecable. The two initial margin pools have a fixed sign and cannot be rehypothecated.

As before the dynamics of the underlying assets are given by

$$dS = \mu S dt + \sigma S dW \tag{10.1}$$

$$dP_C = r_C P_C dt - P_C dJ_C \tag{10.2}$$

$$dP_i = r_i P_i dt - (1 - R_i)P_i dJ_B \quad \text{for} \quad i \in 1, 2, \tag{10.3}$$

---

[1] In general the downgrade trigger impact is itself rating-dependent. So, for example, thresholds may steadily decrease with rating, meaning the size of the liquidity buffer is itself rating-dependent. To price this correctly would therefore require a full risk-neutral rating transition model.

**TABLE 10.1**    Additional notation use in the semi-replication model of MVA.

| Parameter | Description |
| --- | --- |
| $I$ | Initial margin posted to counterparty (assumed to be held in a segregated account) |
| $\tilde{I}$ | Initial margin received from counterparty (assumed to be held in a segregated account). Note that if the counterparty is a CCP then $\tilde{I} = 0$ |
| $d\bar{\beta}_I$ | Change in cash cash account associated with initial margin (prior to rebalancing) |
| $r_I$ | Yield on posted initial margin |
| $r_{\tilde{I}}$ | Yield on received initial margin |
| $s_I$ | Spread on posted initial margin |

with the economic value on default given by,

$$\hat{V}(t, S, 1, 0) = g_B(M_B, X, I) \tag{10.4}$$
$$\hat{V}(t, S, 0, 1) = g_C(M_C, X, \tilde{I}), \tag{10.5}$$

which now includes the impact of initial margin. Under standard close-out conditions the two $g$ functions are given by

$$g_B = (V - X + I)^+ + R_B(V - X + I)^- + X - I \tag{10.6}$$
$$g_C = R_C(V - X - \tilde{I})^+ + (V - X - \tilde{I})^- + X + \tilde{I}. \tag{10.7}$$

Here the initial margin is used to further reduce loss in the event of default and a loss only occurs in the event that the close-out derivative value exceeds both $X$ and the appropriate pool of initial margin.

The derivative funding constraint equation now becomes

$$\hat{V} - X + I + \alpha_1 P_1 + \alpha_2 P_2 = 0. \tag{10.8}$$

This equation now includes the posted initial margin which must be funded through the issuance of bonds. The sign of $I$ is constant unlike $X$ and the initial margin must be posted irrespective of the sign of the derivative economic value $\hat{V}$. There is no corresponding term in the received initial margin as this margin cannot be rehypothecated. In the case of a CCP then no initial margin would be posted to $B$ in any case.

The growth in the cash accounts, prior to rebalancing is

$$d\bar{\beta}_S(t) = \delta(t)(\gamma - q)Sdt \tag{10.9}$$
$$d\bar{\beta}_C(t) = -\alpha_C q_C P_C dt \tag{10.10}$$
$$d\bar{\beta}_X(t) = -r_X X dt \tag{10.11}$$
$$d\bar{\beta}_I = r_I I dt - r_{\tilde{I}} \tilde{I} dt, \tag{10.12}$$

where there is now a cash account for the return received on initial margin posted to the counterparty and the return paid on any initial margin received from the counterparty.

Using Itô's lemma on the economic value gives the same result as previously:

$$d\hat{V} = \frac{\partial \hat{V}}{\partial t}dt + \frac{1}{2}\sigma^2 S^2 \frac{\partial^2 \hat{V}}{\partial S^2}dt + \frac{\partial \hat{V}}{\partial S}dS + \Delta\hat{V}_B dJ_B + \Delta\hat{V}_C dJ_C. \tag{10.13}$$

Assuming the portfolio, $\Pi$, is self-financing, the change in its value is given by

$$dΠ = \delta dS(t) + \delta(\gamma - q)Sdt + \alpha_1 dP_1 + \alpha_2 dP_2$$
$$+ \alpha_C dP_C - \alpha_C q_C P_C dt - r_X X dt + r_I I dt - r_{\tilde{I}} \tilde{I} dt. \tag{10.14}$$

Adding the change in the derivative and replicating portfolio together gives

$$d\hat{V} + dΠ = \left[ \frac{\partial \hat{V}}{\partial t} + \frac{1}{2}\sigma^2 S^2 \frac{\partial^2 \hat{V}}{\partial S^2} + \delta(t)(\gamma - q)S - \alpha_C q_C P_C - r_X X \right.$$

$$\left. + \alpha_1 r_1 P_1 + \alpha_2 r_2 P_2 + r_I I - r_{\tilde{I}} \tilde{I} \right] dt$$

$$+ \left[ \delta + \frac{\partial \hat{V}}{\partial S} \right] dS + \left[ \Delta\hat{V}_C + \alpha_C P_C \right] dJ_C + \epsilon_h dJ_B, \tag{10.15}$$

where as above $\epsilon_h = \left[ \Delta\hat{V}_B - (P - P_D) \right]$ is the hedging error on issuer default. The portfolio replicates the derivative except on the default of the issuer so that $d\hat{V} + dΠ = 0$. For this to hold the usual assumptions are made to eliminate the sources of risk:

$$\delta = -\frac{\partial \hat{V}}{\partial S} \tag{10.16}$$

$$\alpha_C P_C = g_C - \hat{V}. \tag{10.17}$$

Finally a PDE is obtained for $\hat{V}$, which is identical to that in equation (9.38) aside from the addition of terms relating to initial margin,

$$\frac{\partial \hat{V}}{\partial t} + \mathcal{A}_t \hat{V} - (r + \lambda_B + \lambda_C)\hat{V} = s_X X - \lambda_C g_C - \lambda_B g_B + \lambda_B \epsilon_h - r_I I + r_{\tilde{I}} \tilde{I}$$

$$\hat{V}(T, S) = 0, \tag{10.18}$$

where $\mathcal{A}_t$ is defined by equation (3.31) and the bond funding equation has again been used to derive an expression that is used to eliminate the terms in $\alpha_1$ and $\alpha_2$,

$$\alpha_1 r_1 P_1 + \alpha_2 r_2 P_2 = rX - rI - (r + \lambda_B)\hat{V} - \lambda_B(\epsilon_h - g_B). \tag{10.19}$$

Using the same Ansatz with $\hat{V} = V + U$, where $V$ satisfies the Black-Scholes equation, gives a PDE for the valuation adjustment:

$$\frac{\partial U}{\partial t} + \mathcal{A}_t U - (r + \lambda_B + \lambda_C)U = s_X X - \lambda_C(g_C - V) - \lambda_B(g_B - V)$$

$$+ \lambda_B \epsilon_h - s_I I + r_{\tilde{I}} \tilde{I}$$
$$U(T, S) = 0. \tag{10.20}$$

Applying the Feynman-Kac theorem gives an integral representation for the valuation adjustment,

$$U = \text{CVA} + \text{DVA} + \text{FCA} + \text{COLVA}, \tag{10.21}$$

where

$$
\begin{aligned}
\text{CVA} &= -\int_t^T \lambda_C(s) e^{-\int_t^s r(u) + \lambda_B(u) + \lambda_C(u) du} \\
&\quad \times \mathbb{E}\left[V(s) - g_C(V(s), X(s), \tilde{I}(s))\right] ds \tag{10.22} \\
\text{DVA} &= -\int_t^T \lambda_B(s) e^{-\int_t^s r(u) + \lambda_B(u) + \lambda_C(u) du} \\
&\quad \times \mathbb{E}\left[V(s) - g_B(V(s), X(s), I(s))\right] ds \tag{10.23} \\
\text{FCA} &= -\int_t^T \lambda_B(s) e^{-\int_t^s r(u) + \lambda_B(u) + \lambda_C(u) du} \mathbb{E}\left[\epsilon_h(s)\right] ds \tag{10.24} \\
\text{COLVA} &= -\int_t^T s_X(s) e^{-\int_t^s r(u) + \lambda_B(u) + \lambda_C(u) du} \mathbb{E}\left[X(s)\right] ds \\
&\quad + \int_t^T s_I(s) e^{-\int_t^s r(u) + \lambda_B(u) + \lambda_C(u) du} \mathbb{E}\left[I(s)\right] ds \\
&\quad - \int_t^T r_{\tilde{I}}(s) e^{-\int_t^s r(u) + \lambda_B(u) + \lambda_C(u) du} \mathbb{E}\left[\tilde{I}(s)\right] ds. \tag{10.25}
\end{aligned}
$$

The only apparent difference between these expressions and those in Chapter 9 is the appearance of additional integrals in COLVA. The COLVA term now contains an adjustment for the return on the posted initial margin for the difference between this return, $r_I$ and the risk-free rate $r$. The second additional integral represents any return, $r_{\tilde{I}}$ which must be paid on received initial margin. As the initial margin cannot be rehypothecated, there is no way to fund this payment and hence the full return appears rather than a spread over the risk-free rate. There is no apparent MVA term, relating to the funding cost of the posted initial margin. In fact this lies with the FCA terms and to see this the funding strategy has to be specified explicitly.

## 10.2.1   Semi-replication with no Shortfall on Default

Consider first the funding strategy of semi-replication with no shortfall on default of the issuer (see section 9.4.1 and Burgard and Kjaer, 2013). This strategy uses two issuer bonds, a zero recovery bond, $P_1$, which funds the valuation adjustment and a bond with recovery $R_2 = R_B$, which is determined using the funding equation (10.8):

$$\alpha_1 P_1 = -U \tag{10.26}$$
$$\alpha_2 P_2 = -(V - X + I). \tag{10.27}$$

With these hedge ratios, the hedge error becomes with standard close-out:

$$\epsilon_h = (1 - R_B)[V - X + I]^+ . \tag{10.28}$$

Using these expressions in the PDE for $U$, equation (10.20) gives

$$\frac{\partial U}{\partial t} + \mathcal{A}_t U - (r + \lambda_B + \lambda_C)U = s_X X - \lambda_C (1 - R_C) [V - X - \tilde{I}]^+$$
$$+ \lambda_B (1 - R_B)[V - X + I] - s_I I + r_{\tilde{I}} \tilde{I}$$
$$U(T, S) = 0. \tag{10.29}$$

Hence the application of the Feynman-Kac theorem gives

$$U = \text{CVA} + \text{FVA} + \text{COLVA} + \text{MVA} \tag{10.30}$$

where

$$\text{CVA} = -(1 - R_C) \int_t^T \lambda_C(s) e^{-\int_t^s r(u) + \lambda_B(u) + \lambda_C(u) du}$$
$$\times \mathbb{E} \left[ (V(s) - X(s) - \tilde{I}(s))^+ \right] ds \tag{10.31}$$

$$\text{FVA} = -(1 - R_B) \int_t^T \lambda_B(s) e^{-\int_t^s r(u) + \lambda_B(u) + \lambda_C(u) du} \mathbb{E}[V(s) - X(s)] ds \tag{10.32}$$

$$\text{COLVA} = -\int_t^T s_X(s) e^{-\int_t^s r(u) + \lambda_B(u) + \lambda_C(u) du} \mathbb{E}[X(s)] ds$$
$$- \int_t^T r_{\tilde{I}}(s) e^{-\int_t^s r(u) + \lambda_B(u) + \lambda_C(u) du} \mathbb{E}[\tilde{I}(s)] ds \tag{10.33}$$

$$\text{MVA} = -\int_t^T \left[ (1 - R_B)\lambda_B(s) - s_I(s) \right] e^{-\int_t^s r(u) + \lambda_B(u) + \lambda_C(u) du} \mathbb{E}[I(s)] ds. \tag{10.34}$$

The MVA forms an integral over the expected initial margin profile with a cost term equal to the issuer funding spread $s_F(t) = (1 - R_B)\lambda_B(t)$, reduced by the return over the risk-free rate provided on the posted initial margin, $s_I$. The term in $s_I$ has been integrated into the MVA integral for clarity and was originally part of COLVA. An equivalent approach will yield an expression for MVA under other funding strategies.

## 10.3   CALCULATING MVA EFFICIENTLY

### 10.3.1   Sizing the Problem

As is clear from equation (10.34), MVA involves an integral over the expected initial margin profile. Typically the IM is calculated using VaR or CVaR through historical simulation. and essentially this means a Monte Carlo inside Monte Carlo, which would be computationally intensive to calculate.

To see just how computationally intensive, consider first how many trade valuations are required to estimate the expected positive exposure on a portfolio of interest rate swaps that might be cleared,

$$
\begin{aligned}
\text{Valuations} &= 10^4 \quad \text{(Number of swaps)} \\
&\times 10^3 \quad \text{(Number of paths)} \\
&\times 10^2 \quad \text{(Number of time steps)} \\
&= 10^9.
\end{aligned}
$$

Assuming that each valuation takes $1\mu s$, then this exposure profile would take $1000s$ or just under 17 minutes to evaluate on a single processing core. Now to calculate the VaR or CVaR using brute force historical simulation inside the main Monte Carlo loop will give

$$
\begin{aligned}
\text{Valuations} &= 10^4 \quad \text{(Number of swaps)} \\
&\times 10^3 \quad \text{(Number of paths)} \\
&\times 10^2 \quad \text{(Number of time steps)} \\
&\times 10^3 \quad \text{(Number of scenarios)} \\
&= 10^{12}.
\end{aligned}
$$

This would take $10^6$ seconds to calculate or around 277 hours on a single processing core if the VaR methodology relied on direct revaluation in each state. If the VaR model relied on delta-gamma approximations then this cost might be lower but at the cost of the requirement to estimate the sensitivities of the portfolio in each Monte Carlo state.

Clearly brute force calculations of the expected IM profile are prohibitively expensive. An alternative technique to accelerate the calculation must be found. Parallelising the calculation is of course perfectly possible and indeed each path is independent and can be calculated on a separate core if required; however, this is unnecessary. The following algorithm by Green and Kenyon (2015) provides a highly efficient alternative. Before discussing the algorithm the Longstaff-Schwartz approach (2001) to derivative valuation must be introduced and its use in the generation of expected exposure.

## 10.3.2   Aside: Longstaff-Schwartz for Valuations and Expected Exposures

The Longstaff-Schwartz algorithm for valuing American or Bermudan-style options was introduced in 2001 and represents the most successful and widely used form of "American Monte Carlo". A detailed explanation of the algorithm and its practical implementation in the context of valuation can be found in a number of publications including Piterbarg (2003a). The method as used for valuation is outlined here and then its extension for use in expected exposure calculations. The Longstaff-Schwartz approach for expected exposure is widely used by practitioners (see for example Cesari et al., 2009).

To explore the basic idea behind the algorithm consider the problem of valuing a Bermudan swaption. The Bermudan swaption is an option with multiple opportunities to enter an interest rate swap with a fixed maturity. At the last exercise date the option is identical to a European swaption, providing the opportunity to enter an interest rate swap at the given fixed rate $K$.

Earlier options provide the option holder with the opportunity of exercising into the interest rate swap or retaining the future unexercised options. A Monte Carlo model cannot be used to value this product without modification as at each exercise date a decision must be made while the Monte Carlo path only provides one future realised state. The Monte Carlo would still allow the underlying swap to be valued as this only requires the realised yield curve on the given path at that time step. So the unmodified Monte Carlo can provide the *exercise value*. If at each stopping date the Monte Carlo could be enhanced to provide a *continuation value* then the decision about whether to exercise the option could be made. The Longstaff-Schwartz algorithm is a linear regression-based method of identifying the continuation value. It provides an analytic function depending on market state variables that gives an approximate continuation value at each time step in the Monte Carlo simulation. As such it is often described as providing the *exercise boundary* as it gives a function which determines the zone of exercise.

When Longstaff-Schwartz is used for trade valuation, the primary purpose of the regression function is to determine where exercise occurs. When an exercise decision is actually made the exercise value itself is normally used as the value on that specific path. However, for some more exotic products where the product being exercised into itself has optionality, regression functions can be used for both continuation and exercise value.

The key feature of the Longstaff-Schwartz for exposure modelling is that it provides a functional approximation to the continuation value and in fact can be used to provide an approximate value for a derivative. Once this function has been obtained it can be used inside a Monte Carlo simulation to value the associated transaction. At each time step and path in the simulation the required state variables are calculated and inserted into the formula to give the trade value in that Monte Carlo state. This is immensely powerful, although great care must be taken to ensure that the regression function provides a good approximation to the value of the derivative across the full range of states generated by the Monte Carlo simulation at a given time step. The use of the Longstaff-Schwartz approach is also highly performant as it requires only the evaluation of a simple analytic function to value the trade. Of course there is computational cost associated with the regression "calibration" process. I will return to the use of Longstaff-Schwartz for valuations later in Chapter 19, but the primary focus here is its use in the estimation of initial margin.

To proceed to estimate a regression function for the value of a derivative, the following algorithm is used:

1. Choose a series of *explanatory variables*

$$O_1(\omega, t_k), \ldots, O_{n_O}(\omega, t_k) \tag{10.35}$$

upon which the value, cash flows and exercise state of the derivative depend. These explanatory variables should be quantities that are physically relevant to the derivative. So for example, in the context of a Bermudan swaption an appropriate choice would be the swap rate for the residual underlying swap rate and the value of the first forward rate. Empirically the choice of explanatory variables makes a significant difference to the quality of the regression and hence the accuracy of the overall result so they must be selected carefully. In general it is appropriate to evaluate several alternative choices before making a final decision.

**2.** Choose a set of *basis functions*

$$f_1(O_i(\omega, t_k)), \ldots, f_{n_f}(O_i(\omega, t_k)) \tag{10.36}$$

These basis functions in the chosen state variables form a basis for the least-squares regression. The choice of basis functions and the number of functions to use has been a matter of some debate. Piterbarg (2003a), in the context of pricing, argues in favour of low-order polynomials such as polynomials of degree two on the basis that the regression functions need to work near the exercise boundary so functions that will be influenced by outlying values should be avoided. Moreno and Navas (2003) examined five different series of polynomial, *Power*, *Legendre*, *Laguerre*, *Hermite A* and *Hermite B*, and find that the method is not strongly influenced by the choice of polynomial. Glasserman and Yu (2004) examine how the number of polynomials relates to the number of paths in the simulation and conclude that the required number of paths grows at least exponentially in the degree of the approximating polynomials. It is important to note that in the context of expected exposure the regression functions must perform well into the wings of the distribution not just close to an exercise barrier (if indeed there is an exercise barrier for the product under consideration). In the context of VaR calculations the region of interest extends further still and the state space needs to be expanded to cater for this problem.[2]

**3.** Run the *calibration* Monte Carlo simulation. Generate a set of Monte Carlo paths in the risk-neutral measure using an appropriate choice of dynamics. The Monte Carlo should place time steps on all important dates for the trade or trades in question such as cash flow dates and exercise dates. When Longstaff-Schwartz is used in a pricing context the normal process would place Monte Carlo time steps on all the exercise and cash flow dates of the trade. As each trade is valued independently this makes perfect sense. However, in the context of an expected exposure calculation the choice of time steps is driven by other considerations and always operates at the level of the portfolio. Hence in this case time steps on dates other than the exercise dates will be required. This first Monte Carlo can be thought of as a *calibration* as it is used to regress for the valuation function.

**4.** Perform regression algorithm. Working backwards from the maturity of the derivative at $t_K = T$:

   **(a)** At observation date $t_k$, calculate the value of the derivative as a discounted sum of cash flows $C(\omega, t_j)$ for times $t_j > t_k$ including all future exercise decisions on each path $\omega$,

$$F(\omega, t_k) = \sum_{j=k+1}^{K} e^{-\int_{t_k}^{t_j} r(\omega, s) ds} C(\omega, t_j). \tag{10.37}$$

   **(b)** At each observation date use least-squares regression of all the continuation values against the basis functions, $f_m(O_i(\omega, t_k)$ in order to calibrate the coefficients, $\alpha_m$. That

---

[2]See Green and Kenyon (2014a ) or the discussion in 10.3.3 below.

is the algorithm seeks to find

$$\min\left(\sum_{\omega}\left\|\sum_{m=1}^{n_f}\alpha_m f_m(O_i(\omega,t_k)) - F(\omega,t_k)\right\|^2, \alpha_m \in \mathcal{R}\right). \qquad (10.38)$$

5. The regression functions $\bar{F}$ defined by

$$\bar{F}(\alpha_m, O_i(\omega,t_k), t_k) = \sum_{m=1}^{n^f}\alpha_m f_m(O_i(\omega,t_k)) \qquad (10.39)$$

provide a valuation of the derivative at time $t_k$, given the state variables $O_i$ calculated on path $\omega$.
6. Run a second independent Monte Carlo simulation. This simulation should use independent random numbers to avoid biasing the result. In practice for expected exposure calculations this will be the main Monte Carlo simulation used for this purpose. Trade valuations are replaced by the regression functions $\bar{F}$. Note also that this second simulation will have a configuration determined by the expected exposure calculation. It is not necessary for the calibration and exposure simulations to have the same configuration. For example, consider a multi-currency portfolio containing interest rate swaps in USD and GBP but a single USD Bermudan swaption. The exposure generation process has been chosen to place a time step every three months until portfolio maturity. The interest rate swaps will be valued using cash flow discounting but the Bermudan swaption will use Longstaff-Schwartz. Hence inside the exposure simulation regression functions will be needed on the 3M tenor points but these will not coincide with the cash flows or option exercise opportunities of the Bermudan swaption. To obtain the regression functions it is necessary to use a union of the event dates of the Bermudan swaption and the quarterly simulation schedule of the exposure simulation. However, the calibration will only need USD interest rates so the calibration simulation can be configured as a single currency simulation.

### 10.3.3   Calculating VaR *inside* a Monte Carlo

The initial margin requirement, $I(t)$, is frequently determined using a VaR or CVaR type model using historical simulation. To calculate the *Expected Initial Margin Profile*, $\mathbb{E}[I(t)]$, would require a Monte Carlo simulation to calculate the expectation and a second historical Monte Carlo simulation nested inside the first at each time step and on each path to estimate the initial margin in that Monte Carlo state. As noted above, the computational cost of such a calculation is prohibitive, save for small portfolios. Hence an efficient approximation is required.

**VaR and the Risk-neutral Measure**   Given that VaR is most commonly calculated using a historical simulation approach then technically this is a physical measure calculation. However, the expectation over the initial margin in equation (10.34) lies in the risk-neutral measure. In the approach described below the assumption is made that the VaR shocks are exogenously specified and do not change during the lifetime of the portfolio. This assumption avoids the need to have a physical measure residing with a risk-neutral model and is equivalent to assuming a fixed SVaR-style window. It is tempting to consider ageing the shocks inside the risk-neutral simulation, with new shocks being generated along each path from the realised Monte Carlo states. Unfortunately this is incorrect as the distribution used to generate these shocks is the risk-neutral one, not the physical measure.

**The State Space in VaR models**    Before proceeding to discuss the algorithm, it is important to assess the size of the required state space as this will have an impact on the choice of model. CCPs often use long historical periods which typically include periods of market stress within them. VaR and CVaR are normally applied with very high percentiles such as the 99% one-sided confidence limits used in Basel III (BCBS, 2011b) and 97.5% figure used in the proposed fundamental review of the trading book, BCBS-265 (2013c). Hence the shifts derived from such a scheme should be expected to be large because of the combination of high percentiles and market stress. The relative shocks for USD yield curves were in the range −30% to +35% over the calibration period.

The large range of such shocks mean that the state space generated by a standard Monte Carlo model will be insufficient to allow Longstaff-Schwartz to generate reasonable regression functions. In general the confidence limits will be sampled poorly by a Monte Carlo and the region required by the VaR shifts will not covered at all. Hence the approximation method must be appropriate for the large changes not covered by the standard simulation. This is what is provided by the *Longstaff-Schwartz Augmented Compression* algorithm.

**The VaR calculation**    In outline, VaR under historical simulation consists of the following approach:

1. Obtain a time series of historical data of the appropriate length.
2. Generate shifts by differencing the data over the specified time horizon (e.g. 10 business days). A variety of different approaches are used for this process. The shifts can be absolute or relative and sometimes a local volatility scaling is applied.
3. Apply each shift to the current market state and estimate the value of the trade or portfolio. The valuation can be generated by fully valuing the trade or portfolio using the shifted market data inside a valuation model; this is known a *full revaluation*. Given the computational expense the valuations can sometimes be generated using a Taylor series approximation on the trade sensitivities, an approach sometimes known as *delta-gamma* or *delta-gamma-vega* approximation. However, the issues around the size of the shifts occurring suggest strongly that only a full revaluation approach would yield accurate VaR estimates. LSAC is geared around the use of full revaluation approaches.
4. Form a mark-to-market vector with the valuation from each scenario.
5. Sort the vector.
6. For VaR read off the value at the desired percentile; for CVaR take the average of values outside the desired percentile.

**Longstaff-Schwartz Augmented Compression (LSAC)**    The revaluation of the portfolio must be computationally efficient if the VaR or SVaR calculation is to be efficient and hence for the MVA calculation as a whole to be efficient. The Longstaff-Schwartz regression functions provide such an efficient valuation mechanism as each is simply a polynomial in the explanatory variables. The value of the portfolio in the base state on each path and at each observation is simply given by the regression function $\bar{F}$. To obtain the value of the portfolio in each VaR scenario on the path $\omega$ at time step $t_k$, simply apply the VaR shocks to the state variables generated by the Monte Carlo to give a series of shocked state variables, $\hat{O}_i^j(\omega, t_k)$ and then use the regression function to value the portfolio in each VaR scenario, $j$,

$$V^j(\omega, t_k) \approx \bar{F}(\alpha_m, O_i^j(\omega, t_k), t_k). \tag{10.40}$$

The values $V^j$ can then be used to calculate the VaR or CVaR on Monte Carlo path $\omega$ at time step $t_k$ using the method described above.

Regression functions are used universally for valuation, irrespective of the type of underlying trade, even where analytic formulae exist. Secondly, the regression function has been used to replace a portfolio valuation and hence is providing portfolio compression. The use of *Longstaff-Schwartz Augmented Compression* in this way provides a means of valuing a portfolio that is largely independent of portfolio size. Clearly there are set-up costs involved in the calibration of the regression functions, which is itself dependent on the number of cash flows associated with the portfolio. Nevertheless, as is shown below in section 10.3.4, the performance is constant and independent of the number of trades in the portfolio.

As was noted above, the state space from the Monte Carlo on its own is inadequate to allow the Longstaff-Schwartz technique to be applied to VaR and CVaR calculations and requires augmentation. There are two issues apparent immediately:

1. At time $t = 0$ the regression cannot be performed as there is only one point. Hence we cannot use the regression approach to calculate the VaR at this point. However, this is unlikely to be a limitation as the cost of performing the VaR with brute force is less given that there is only a single point to compute rather than the thousands required inside the Monte Carlo simulation.[3]
2. At times $t > 0$ the state region given by the Monte Carlo is smaller than that required by VaR calculations with the kind of extreme moves observed during periods of stress. If this is not corrected there is no guarantee that the regression functions will give sufficiently accurate results in the region covered by VaR.

There are two possible methods to augment the state space, *shocked-state augmentation* and starting the Monte Carlo simulation early.

**Early start Monte Carlo**  Starting the simulation earlier than time $t = 0$ will give a wider distribution of paths at later times that would be obtained if the simulation started at time $t = 0$ and a sufficiently early start will ensure that the paths span the required state space required by VaR at all times $t \geq 0$.

An early start simulation was suggested by Wang and Caflisch (2010) in their *Modified Least Squares Monte Carlo* that used the early start to obtain the regression function at time $t = 0$ so that sensitivities of the derivative could be calculated. The early start criterion here is different in that the requirement is driven by the need to ensure the state space covered by the simulation is sufficiently large. This approach is also suitable where path continuity is needed such as with American and Bermudan-style options. For such products the continuation value

---

[3]This can, however, be done using the early start technique given here.

must be compared with the exercise value as was discussed in section 10.3.2, and this requires that the distribution between time steps be respected.

**Shocked-state augmentation**    If the portfolio only contains instruments without American or Bermudan exercise features then a simpler approach to augmenting the state space can be used. At present this is certainly the case for central counterparties, which only clear vanilla products. This approach is known as *shocked-state augmentation*. Given that there is no backward induction step needed then the regressions at each time step are independent of each other and can therefore be computed in parallel.

The key aim of shocked-state augmentation is to generate a big enough state space so that the resulting regression is derived using states that exceed all those that would be obtained from the VaR shocks. This will ensure that the regression function is essentially used to "interpolate" rather than "extrapolate".

The dimensionality of the state space for VaR is determined by the dimensionality of the VaR shock and this in turn is determined by the characteristics of the asset class in question. If the asset class is FX then the VaR state space may contain a single dimension, while if it is a yield curve then there will be as many dimensions as yield curve instruments. In general, the state space of the VaR model will be larger than the dimension of the Monte Carlo model.

The augmentation process proceeds by adding exactly one VaR shock to each path at each stopping date. This requires there to be more Monte Carlo paths than VaR shocks and given this is the case some VaR shocks will be used more than once at each stopping date. The shocks are simply drawn from a list in sequence and applied to the Monte Carlo states. The portfolio is then valued as the sum of the component trades at each augmented path and stopping date. A regression is then performed for the portfolio value against appropriate state variables. A least-squares fit is used to penalise large fitting errors as these are more likely under extreme scenarios.

This approach does not require any additional Monte Carlo paths and is complete at $t = 0$, as even though there is a single portfolio value shared by all paths, the strategy of adding one shock per path is guaranteed to fill the space required for VaR by construction. Hence VaR should be exact at $t = 0$ given sufficient basis functions.

Once the regression functions for the portfolio value have been obtained at each time step, a second Monte Carlo simulation is performed to estimate the expected margin profile. At each stopping date and on each path in this simulation the regression function is used to obtain the portfolio value under each VaR shock. The portfolio values are then ranked and the VaR obtained from the appropriate percentile. The VaR from each path is then averaged to give the expected initial margin.

### 10.3.4    Case Study: Swap Portfolios

As an example of the LSAC technique consider applying the approach to the calculation of MVA on a variable size portfolio of interest rate swaps. The Basel Committee paper on Bilateral Initial Margin (BCBS, 2013d) gives the following specification for the VaR model to be used to calculate initial margin:

- 99% one-sided VaR.
- 10-day shifts to generate the scenarios (overlapping).

■ 5-year window to generate the shifts that must include a period of significant stress. In the tests the period begins just prior to the onset of the credit crisis in January 2007.
■ The 5-year window means there are 1294 shocks.

The VaR shocks were defined as a change to the zero yield curve. The yield curve had 18 instruments and hence the VaR shocks were defined at 18 maturities:

$$0, 0.5, 1, 2, 3, 4, 5, 6, 7, 8, 9, 10, 11, 12, 15, 20, 25, 30 \quad \text{years.}$$

The shocks were applied as relative changes to zero yields so given a zero yield at maturity $T$ to $r$, the shocked discount factor was $e^{-rT(1+s)}$. Linear interpolation was used between maturities.

To test the calculation technique a means of generating a suitable portfolio of interest rate swaps needs to be found. The algorithm used for this purpose needs to generate comparable portfolios with varying numbers of interest rate swaps that have an exposure profile that is "off-market". The following approach was used to generate test portfolios with $n$ USD interest rate swaps with standard market conventions:

■ $n$ swaps, each with maturity $i \times \frac{30}{n}$ in years for $i = 1, \ldots, n$.
■ Each swap has a notional of $\$100m \times (0.5 + \epsilon)$ where $\epsilon \sim U(0, 1)$.
■ Each swap has a strike $K = \$2.5\% \times (y + x)$ where $x \sim U(0, 1)$ and $y = 1$ (except for the special case of a balanced portfolio where $y = 1.455$).
■ Gearing is equal to $(0.5 + z)$ where $z \sim U(0, 1)$.
■ Pay/receive fraction $P$ given by $90\%, 50\%, 10\%$, depending on the choice of portfolio composition.

The basis functions for the regression in the case of swap portfolios were unsurprisingly chosen to be $m$ swaps, $m$ annuities and a constant with the basis functions having lengths $\frac{1}{m} \times 30$, as these provide a good explanation of the behaviour of the swap portfolios. Portfolios with different types of instruments would need basis functions to be chosen appropriately. The LSAC approach demonstrated good accuracy in the VaR calculation with errors of a few basis points when compared to a brute force calculation.

For a portfolio with 10,000 swaps the LSAC approach is around 100 times faster than brute force calculation.[4] The performance is also independent of portfolio size as expected. This approach makes the computation of MVA feasible for most portfolios.

The MVA cost is illustrated in Table 10.2. The off market portfolios show that the MVA is around 40% of the cost of FVA on an identical portfolio that was unsecured, while the on market portfolio shows a cost of 2 basis points. These figures show that even for well balanced portfolios MVA is a significant issue when one considers that pre-crisis the bid-offer spread on interest rate swaps was around 0.25 basis points. For the off market portfolios with significant market risk positions the initial margin is costly. For many banks hedging corporate unsecured transactions through into the interbank market with trades cleared through CCPs this is exactly the position they will be faced with: limit market risk across the whole portfolio but two offsetting risk positions on corporate and hedge portfolios. MVA adds a significant cost overhead on these portfolios, on top of the existing FVA. Central clearing does offer

---

[4]All computations were performed using an NVIDIA K40 GPU card and implemented in CUDA C.

**TABLE 10.2**   Table of MVA costs for the three separate portfolios. For the two off market portfolios it is clear that the MVA is around 40% of the unsecured FVA, making it a significant contributor to overall P%L. Even with the well matched portfolio MVA adds two basis points to costs in a market that pre-crisis quoted bid-offer spreads around 0.25 basis point.

| Portfolio Payer % | Exposure as % Notional | FVA bps of Notional | MVA bps of Notional |
|---|---|---|---|
| 90% | 26.4 | 115 | 53 |
| 50% | 2.6 | 0 | 2 |
| 10% | 8.9 | −113 | 56 |

benefits in terms of capital reductions as will be seen in Part III, but at the cost of additional funding requirements.

### 10.3.5   Adapting LSAC to VaR under Delta-Gamma Approximation

VaR can also be calculated using the so-called *delta-gamma* or *delta-gamma-vega* which is of course a Taylor series approximation to the full revaluation method. The principal driver for this approach is performance, as typically the Taylor series approximation will be computationally cheaper to use than full revaluation and the sensitivities will often be calculated anyway for trading book risk management. Differences will be found between full revaluation and a Taylor series approximation as the Taylor series will be truncated after a few terms and the sensitivities themselves may only be accurate locally to the current market state with errors appearing under the large shifts often seen in VaR/SVaR calculations. The LSAC approach can be adapted to match the behaviour of the Taylor series approximation. The key issue is that to estimate VaR in each Monte Carlo state the sensitivities of the portfolio will be needed. These can be obtained analytically by differentiating the valuation function $\bar{F}$ with respect to the state variables $O_i(\omega, t_k)$ in a similar way to that described by Wang and Caflisch (2010). These analytic sensitivities can then be used with the VaR scenario shifts to generate the Taylor series approximation to the portfolio values and hence the VaR or CVaR. I will return to the use of Longstaff-Schwartz regression in the context of sensitivity calculations in Chapter 21.

## 10.4   CONCLUSIONS ON MVA

Margin Valuation Adjustment or the FVA associated with initial margin and related overcollateralisation processes is a growing issue in the market. Regulators have pushed hard for as many derivatives as possible to be cleared through CCPs and for those between financial firms that are not cleared, bilateral initial margin will be introduced by 2019 (BCBS, 2013d). Margin reduces counterparty credit risk and hence reduces CCR and CVA capital, however, it does so by introducing additional funding costs in the form of MVA. As will be seen in Chapter 15, derivatives trading activity is increasingly an exercise in XVA optimisation where the different XVA terms are played off against each other to minimise overall costs and maximise returns.

A further point to make is that by introducing margin requirements regulations have effectively transformed credit risk into liquidity risk.[5] Of course the default of Lehman Brothers and the transfer of AIG into conservatorship were both the result of a lack of liquidity not counterparty credit risk losses themselves. Central clearing may have significantly reduced the risk of contagion events where the default of one entity leads to another as inter-market transactions will all now be heavily overcollateralised. However, the additional liquidity requirement may make individual defaults more likely.

---

[5]More detail on this transformation process can be found in Gregory (2012); Kenyon and Green (2013a).

## CHAPTER 11

# The Funding Curve

*We are to admit no more causes of natural things than such as are both true and sufficient to explain their appearances. Therefore, to the same natural effects we must, so far as possible, assign the same causes.*

—Sir Issac Newton
*Physicist and Mathematician (1643–1727)*

## 11.1 SOURCES FOR THE FUNDING CURVE

The FVA models discussed in Chapters 9 and 10 presupposed the existence of either a bank funding curve,

$$r_F(t) = r(t) + s_F(t) \tag{11.1}$$

or risky bank bonds where

$$r_B(t) - r(t) = (1 - R_B)\lambda_B(t). \tag{11.2}$$

The models assumed that the funding spread $s_F(t)$ or hazard rate $\lambda_B(t)$ were deterministic rates but no mention was made about where these rates came from. The role of this chapter, therefore, is to explore this question in more detail.

With the move towards including FVA in bank accounting statements there are two identifiable cases that need to be considered, *internal economic valuations* and *external accounting valuations*. This division recognises that for the purposes of accounting any funding curve is likely to be based on an externally visible source of information. Internal economic valuations are not constrained by this and can be based on purely internal funding cost measures. The possible options for both cases are presented in sections 11.2 and 11.3.

A further point to note is that in the models presented above the funding curve is assumed to be in a single currency, normally the currency of the bank's issued debt. In practice of course a bank may issue debt in multiple currencies and the funding requirement associated with the posting of collateral will be multi-currency and multi-asset. This issue is discussed in section 11.4.

Finally the *term* of the funding is central to the choice of funding curve. Broadly speaking there are two approaches, *term funding* in which the term of the funding is chosen to match the term of the funding requirement and *rolling funding* where the term of the funding is shorter than that of the funding requirement and there is then a need to roll the funding.

### 11.1.1   Term Funding

One argument in favour of term funding is that this approach is more consistent with risk neutrality. As the funding matches the term of the funding requirement then the risk associated with the funding curve has been eliminated. In particular the risk associated with rolling any funding has been removed as the model effectively prices the forward funding cost into the funding curve. Of course the funding curve remains deterministic and so any FVA wrong-way or right-way risk is ignored.

There are a number of problems with the use of a term funding assumption. A term funding curve implicitly assumes that it is possible to obtain forward funding, that is funding that starts at some time $t_S$ and matures at some later time $t_M$. Equivalently this can be done by borrowing at $t = 0$ for maturity $t_M$ and lending the funds until time $t_S$. In practice bank funding markets simply do not provide this capability. Even if derivative funding is obtained from the bank treasury internally it is not always clear that a matched term funding profile can be generated. Furthermore, derivatives are frequently contingent on future events which may change the future funding requirement. Derivatives are also frequently restructured in some way prior to contractual maturity, which in itself will change the future funding requirement. A traditional bank treasury function is focused on providing funding for loans which require a block of term funding and so bank treasury functions are not always well equipped to deal with more volatile products such as derivatives.

### 11.1.2   Rolling Funding

Banking has historically been based on the idea of maturity transformation, lending funds for term but funding these loans with shorter term deposits. This maturity transformation is central to the *fractional reserve banking system* where a bank holds a fraction of deposits to cover short-term depositor requirements but lends the remainder out. These loans may themselves be deposited elsewhere with the same principle applying and so fractional reserve banking leads to a credit multiplier effect (see for example Friedman, 1992). Given this is the case, even for loan books then there is a strong argument that the funding term for a derivative portfolio is shorter than contract maturity and then the funding curve should reflect this. The key question then becomes what is the appropriate term to use for the funding? I will return to this when discussing *funding strategies* below in section 11.2.5.

## 11.2   INTERNAL FUNDING CURVES

### 11.2.1   Bank CDS Spread

The use of $\lambda_B$ in the derivation of FVA under the Burgard-Kjaer semi-replication model (Burgard and Kjaer, 2013) described in Chapter 9 and the relationship of this to the funding spread,

$$s_F(t) = (1 - R_B)\lambda_B(t), \tag{11.3}$$

suggests that the funding spread can be linked directly to the hazard rate, which in turn can be calibrated to the bank's own CDS prices. Burgard and Kjaer explicitly link $\lambda_B$ to the two bank zero-coupon bonds, $P_1$ and $P_2$, which suggests that their own intention is to link the hazard rate to bonds rather than CDS. Nevertheless, DVA has typically been marked using bank own CDS prices to calibrate a piecewise constant hazard rate function. If this were to be used for the funding spread in the semi-replication model then the FCA term would simply appear as an additional cost term with the same input parameters as the existing DVA.

This approach shares the problems introduced by DVA itself and discussed in Chapter 3, namely that the bank cannot trade in their own CDS. If the bank insists on retaining the DVA using the older bilateral model marked to the CDS spread then the use of the same spread for the funding cost term would lead to a significant reduction in the overall sensitivity to the bank CDS spread as the FCA would offset DVA to some degree, depending on the relative size and shape of the overall EPE and ENE. The other point to note with the approach is that it is effectively marking the funding at term.

## 11.2.2 Bank Bond Spread

As noted above, Burgard and Kjaer link the hazard rate, $\lambda_B$, and hence the funding spread, $s_F$, to bank bonds. The bank bond curve provides a natural calibration point as it is ultimately a source of wholesale funding for the bank. The bank bond yield provides a measure of both bank creditworthiness and bank funding liquidity. Again the use of the bank bond curve implies effectively marking the funding at term.

## 11.2.3 Bank Bond-CDS Basis

Some models such as that of Morini and Prampolini (2011) and studies of the funding such as that by Sommer et al. (2013) conclude at least in theory that there are two components to a funding spread, one associated with the default risk of the issuer and then a liquidity spread, $\gamma_B$,

$$s_F(t) = (1 - R_B)\lambda_B(t) + \gamma_B(t). \tag{11.4}$$

The liquidity spread, $\gamma_B$, would be expected to be positive at all times. It is tempting to identify this liquidity premium with the bond-CDS basis.

CDS prices historically have been thought to be a relatively pure measure of market implied default probability as was implicit in the discussion of credit curves in Chapter 4. Bond yields also contain market views on the creditworthiness of the issuer but in addition contain liquidity information, partly because the bond itself will typically be funded through the repo market. Hence if a hazard rate is extracted from CDS prices and one is also bootstrapped from bond prices, they will not be the same and there will be a basis between then. There are a number of different measures of the bond-CDS basis, the most popular of which is to compare the CDS spread with the *Z spread* of the corresponding bond. The Z spread is defined by (see Neftci, 2008)

$$P(t_0) = \sum_{i=1}^{n} \frac{C(t_i)}{1 + \alpha_i(s(t_i) + z))^i} \tag{11.5}$$

where $s(t_i)$ is the zero rate, $C(t_i)$ are the cash flows of the bond and $z$ is a constant that is adjusted to set the price, $P(t_0)$, equal to the dirty price of the bond. This is not as precise a measure as say looking at the equivalent CDS spreads generated from the hazard rate curve derived from a bond curve (sometimes called the PECDS spread) but is more commonly used in the market.

The bond-CDS basis is therefore defined as

$$\text{basis} = \text{CDS spread} - \text{Z spread}, \tag{11.6}$$

and we could reasonably expect the basis to be negative. In reality the bond-CDS basis can be positive or negative and highly volatile as innumerable studies of the basis before, during and after the crisis have shown. The key point is that the bond-CDS basis is a long way from being a pure measure of liquidity costs and is not really suitable for use in this way. Furthermore recent work has also demonstrated that the introduction of CVA capital in Basel III can have a significant effect on CDS prices themselves. Hedging CVA capital using single name and index CDS gives benefits beyond those normally associated with CDS hedging, namely default protection. Kenyon and Green (2013b) show that this effect may account for up to half the price of the CDS. Hence CDS prices themselves can no longer really be viewed as pure measures of market implied default probability.

### 11.2.4 Bank Treasury Transfer Price

The bank treasury function will typically produce a two-way transfer price curve for loans and term deposits. This is the base price of the loan or interest rate for the deposit as a function of maturity. Loans will also have a credit charge applied on top. Different currencies may have different rates applied to them and there will also typically be a bid-offer spread. These curves represent the *transfer price* applied by the bank treasury.

The transfer price curve is principally a tool for use in lending at spot for term and for taking term deposits. It is not necessarily a curve that can be used to imply forward lending rates and may in fact not generate sensible forward rates. It is of course a term funding curve and so would represent term funding in a derivative context. Often bank treasury transfer curves will also be adjusted to reflect the *axe* or desire of the institution to borrow or lend at particular terms. So for example the bank may have lent substantial amounts at a particular tenor and then adjusts the price at that tenor to discourage further lending. Despite the apparent similarity of the funding loans and derivatives, the transfer price curve may not be appropriate for derivatives.

### 11.2.5 Funding Strategy Approaches

The reality of almost all banking activity is that banks borrow for shorter maturities than the full maturity term of the funding requirement. Given that this is the case and that yield curves are typically upward sloping why do banks not simply borrow at the overnight rate and roll the funding daily? To do so would be an enormous risk as if the interbank lending markets were to close for any reason then any bank with a funding shortfall would default. The fact that liquidity risk of this nature contributed to the collapse of Bear Stearns and Lehman Brothers and was a major factor behind the move of AIG into conservatorship. Indeed RBS is thought to have required direct central bank funding in order to survive in the aftermath of the default of Lehman Brothers (Elliott and Treanor, 2009). It is precisely this liquidity risk that prompted the Basel Committee to introduce rules on liquidity. Under the *liquidity coverage ratio* banks are required to hold liquid assets equal to 100% of their 30-day cash outflow under a liquidity stress scenario (BCBS, 2013b).

Bank regulation therefore places a lower bound on the funding term but banks themselves may have policies which reflect a minimum term exceeding 30 days. Another approach to funding then is to seek an optimal strategy that minimises the cost of funding subject to internal and external constraints on the appropriate term. Kenyon and Green (2014d) develop theoretically optimal funding strategies for the physical ($\mathcal{P}$) and risk-neutral ($\mathcal{Q}$) measures and then demonstrate the approach in USD, JPY, EUR and GBP. The resulting strategies achieve 44% to 71% efficiency when compared to perfect information. Such approaches allow a funding curve to be developed based on the optimal funding strategy which is shorter than term but long enough to satisfy constraints such as regulations. This is of course a rolling funding approach and will usually be lower cost than a term strategy simply because most yield curves are upward sloping. This of course comes at the risk that funding may be more expensive when rolled.

## 11.3 EXTERNAL FUNDING CURVES AND ACCOUNTING

With a number of banks moving to include FVA within their accounting statements, there has been an increasing debate within the industry about how this should be done. The accounting standards for both the US and Europe make no explicit mention of FVA in their current standards documents (IASB, 2012; FASB, 2006) and so bank finance departments must rely on general accounting principles rather than explicit guidance. If FVA becomes a standard element of bank accounting statements then I would anticipate that accounting standards bodies will issue specific guidance at some point in the future.

Asymmetry has produced some debate amongst accountants, as was noted in section 9.6. However, symmetry does not appear to be an explicit requirement for accounting statements. Hence, both symmetric and asymmetric FVA models could potentially be used.

One issue that has been raised is whether or not the funding curve should be externally visible. Bank internal funding curves such as the transfer price curves or any funding costs derived from a funding strategy are clearly not visible outside the bank. The bank could of course publish its own funding curve but even then there would be a desire to use a curve that was based on independently obtained benchmark rates. CDS prices and bond yield curves do satisfy this requirement as the closing prices are available to all market participants. However, these curves remain idiosyncratic.

One fundamental measure of value frequently encountered in accounting contexts is the concept of the *exit price*. That is the price that a derivative would clear in the market should it become necessary to novate it to another party. In practice one could question how many unsecured derivatives could be considered liquid enough for such a clearing price to exist but the basic principle is clear. In some cases exit prices may be visible, particularly for larger banks with many derivative transactions. Novation activity may be sufficiently visible for a market funding curve to be visible. Indeed the fact that such information was visible is one of the reasons stated by J.P. Morgan as motivating their decision to take a charge for FVA in January 2014 (Whittall, 2014). What this means is that for accounting purposes the funding curve should be universal across all banks and not be idiosyncratic. The obvious choice, therefore, would be a market consensus pricing service. Markit, the financial information service provider, introduced a pricing survey that included FVA in late 2013 thus providing a benchmark for the funding curve (Cameron, 2014b).

## 11.4  MULTI-CURRENCY/MULTI-ASSET FUNDING

The funding requirement can be in multiple currencies and indeed multiple assets if the optimal collateral posting requirement is in the form of securities and not cash. Clearly the cost of obtaining cash in different currencies will differ as will the net cost of obtaining a specific security (through unsecured borrowing and a reverse repo transaction to obtain the security). The key question then is how to obtain a single funding curve. The simplest way would be to generate a weighted funding curve based on the current net collateral requirement. Of course this ignores the fact that the collateral posting requirement is itself a function of market state.

# KVA: Capital Valuation Adjustment and Regulation

# Regulation: the Basel II and Basel III Frameworks

*Rules are not necessarily sacred, principles are.*

—Franklin D. Roosevelt
*32nd President of the United States (1882–1945)*

## 12.1 INTRODUCING THE REGULATORY CAPITAL FRAMEWORK

Regulatory capital has become a major focus of regulators and banks alike in the aftermath of the 2007–2009 post-Lehman crisis and the subsequent eurozone crisis in 2010–2012. A number of problems were identified with the regulatory capital framework including the need for significant increases in capital held by banks. Historically, regulatory capital and bank return on capital was rarely a major consideration for front office staff in trading and sales functions, rather it was either a finance or risk function to compile regulatory returns. Capital did not often figure directly into derivatives pricing, although it was more often a consideration for banking book trades such as loans. With the large increase in capital requirements and a post-crisis focus on the risks associated with investing in banks, regulatory capital was transformed into a major issue for derivative trading businesses. Since the crisis many banks have created front office capital management functions whose task is to manage the capital of the bank deployed in support of trading activities. Frequently capital management has been combined directly with other *resource management* functions such as CVA and FVA management and collateral management.

Part III of this book is dedicated to the impact of regulatory capital on derivative pricing and management. It is not intended as a general introduction to the Basel regulatory capital framework or indeed post-crisis regulation in general, much of which has no direct impact on pricing at all. For detailed information on the Basel framework, the reader is referred to the framework documents themselves which are provided on the website of the Basel Committee on Banking Supervision (http://www.bis.org/bcbs/). Of course these documents themselves refer only to the global regulatory proposals which are implemented by local regulators. In Europe regulation is implemented under the tripartite legislature of the European Union, that is the European Parliament, the European Commission and the Council of Ministers with individual nation states implementing the framework through national regulators. The European Union implementation of Basel III (BCBS, 2011b) is known as CRD IV (European Parliament and the Council of the European Union, 2013b; European Parliament and the Council of the European Union, 2013a). There are some important differences between the original Basel Committee proposals and what is actually included in CRD IV.

This chapter provides an outline description of current and future regulation with pricing impact. The focus is on the Basel framework but some of the differences to be found in CRD IV are indicated. This choice is based on simple practicality – personally being located in Europe means European regulation is much more familiar. Chapter 13 gives a description of the KVA capital pricing model which is an extension of the Burgard-Kjaer model framework discussed in Chapter 9, while Chapter 14 discusses CVA risk warehouse and the capital and tax implications of such an approach. Finally Chapter 15 adds together counterparty credit risk, funding and capital at a bank-wide portfolio level.

### 12.1.1  Economic Capital

Before the advent of the regulatory capital framework banks as a matter of course still held capital against risks. To determine how much capital should be held *economic capital* models were constructed and these allowed the bank to identify the amount of capital that should be held in order to remain solvent over a given time horizon with a specified level of confidence. Economic capital models are internal models that are not based on any specific regulatory requirement and are designed to allow the bank to plan and risk manage their books. They are also frequently used to assess relative performance between businesses. In many cases the economic capital model is driven by the needs of the banking book rather than the trading book as the latter traditionally involves an active risk management strategy, while banking book assets were traditionally managed using a portfolio approach. Economic capital modelling has a long established literature with a focus on counterparty credit risk. A review of economic capital modelling in the banking sector was conducted by the Basel Committee on Banking Supervision (BCBS, 2009c).

### 12.1.2  The Development of the Basel Framework

*The Basel Committee on Banking Supervision* was established in the aftermath of the collapse of the Bretton Woods exchange rate system in 1973, which led to the collapse of the West German bank Bankhaus Herstatt in June 1974 and the Franklin National Bank of New York in October 1974 (BCBS, 2013a). The G10 established the committee to ensure that no bank would be outside of supervision and to provide minimum standards for supervision and ensure consistency across members. These principles were laid out in the *Concordat* issued in 1975 (BCBS, 1975) and later revised in 1983 (BCBS, 1983) in *Principle for the supervision of banks' foreign establishments*. Further updates to the Concordat were made in 1990 to improve cross-border supervision (BCBS, 1990), while in 1992 the principles were reformulated as minimum standards (BCBS, 1992). Supervisors from outside the G10 were included in the working group that led to a report on *The supervision of cross-border banking* (BCBS, 1996c) and were also included in the formulation of the *Core principles for effective banking supervision* in 1997 (BCBS, 1997). This paper set out 25 principles for effective banking supervision that were later revised in 2006 (BCBS, 2006a). The principles were subsequently reformulated in 2012 (BCBS, 2012f).

**Basel I**   Following the oil price shocks in the 1970s, Latin American countries began to run large current account deficits, while oil exporting countries ran large current account surpluses (Sims and Romero, 2013). US Banks began to act as intermediaries between the two groups and Latin American debt rose rapidly from \$29bn to \$327bn by 1982 (Sims and Romero, 2013). In the same year the Latin American debt held by the nine largest US banks amounted to 176% of capital (Sims and Romero, 2013). In the late 1970s and early 1980s major western economies raised interest rates sharply to deal with the inflation sparked by the oil crisis leading to a major global recession. The Latin American Debt crisis began in June 1982 when Mexico announced that it would not service its debt and other Latin American countries made similar announcements shortly afterwards (Sims and Romero, 2013). The Basel Committee became concerned that the capital ratios of the major international banks were deteriorating as a result of the crisis and began to develop a standard approach to capital adequacy (BCBS, 2013a). A consultative paper was issued by the Basel Committee in December 1987 (BCBS, 1987) which led directly to the 1988 *Basel Capital Accord* (BCBS, 1988). The accord set a minimum capital ratio of 8% (capital to risk-weighted assets) (BCBS, 2013a). The accord was steadily adopted by virtually all countries, not just the members of the G10.

The Basel Accord set out not only the minimum capital ratio but a standard way of calculating both constituents, *regulatory capital* and *risk-weighted assets*. For regulatory capital the document specifies what elements can be counted towards total capital. A series of risk-weights are specified for different categories of assets.

A number of updates were made to the Basel I framework over time. In 1991 the Basel Accord was amended to allow the inclusion of general provisions for losses on loans to be included in tier two capital, subject to certain conditions (BCBS, 1991). Netting agreements have already been identified as a major credit risk mitigant in section 2.4.1. The Basel Accord was extended to recognise netting on derivative exposures in 1995 (BCBS, 1995) along with an extension of the matrix of add-on factors to equities, precious metals and commodities, alongside modifications to the maturity treatment. Further modifications related to multilateral netting arrangements for foreign exchange contract were introduced in 1996 (BCBS, 1996b).

Only credit risk was considered initially in the Basel Accord. In 1996 the according was extended to cover Market Risk (BCBS, 1996a). The market risk capital framework offered two options, a *standardised approach* and *internal model method*. The standardised approach assessed market risk through a series of tables of risk-weights for different asset classes. The internal model method allowed banks, subject to the agreement of supervisory bodies, to produce their own model to assess market risk. This model would produce a *Value-at-Risk* for each element of market risk at the 99% confidence level using a 10-day holding period.

**Basel II**   In 2004 the Basel Committee published the *Revised Capital Framework* (BCBS, 2004), which followed a long period of consultation beginning in 1999 (BCBS, 1999). The regulatory framework was re-orientated around three key *pillars*:

- ▪ Pillar 1: Minimum Capital Requirement
- ▪ Pillar 2: Supervisory Review
- ▪ Pillar 3: Market Discipline.

Following the publication of the revised capital framework in 2004, which targeted the banking book, the Basel Committee published *The Application of Basel II to Trading Activities and the Treatment of Double Default Effects*, which focused on the trading book. A comprehensive version of Basel II was subsequently released in 2006 (BCBS, 2006b).

Pillar 1 is focussed on the minimum capital requirement and hence has implications for the pricing of derivatives. The aim of Pillar 1 is to ensure that banks have sufficient capital resources to cover the three main source of risk, *credit risk*, *operational risk* and *market risk*. Pillar 2 had two key aims, firstly for banks to assess their capital and risks holistically and add capital above the minimum capital requirement where appropriate to do so. For example, risks not captured in Pillar 1 such as interest rate risk on the banking book (Bundesbank, 2007), would be required to add capital under Pillar 2. The second aim was to provide supervisors with appropriate tools to assess overall risks in banks and allow them to adjust overall capital requirements as appropriate. The third pillar is focused on the use of disclosure as a means of encouraging best practice in banking (BCBS, 2013a).

**Basel II.5**  During the crisis period of 2007–2009 the Basel Committee issued two intermediate provisions as a means of strengthening the Basel II framework before a full revision could be undertaken. The first of these was *Principles for sound liquidity risk management and supervision* (BCBS, 2008) introduced in September 2008. This document provides guidance on the identification and measurement of liquidity risk, establishing liquidity risk tolerance, the maintenance of adequate liquidity levels and a number of other liquidity-related issues. The paper was issued in direct response to liquidity problems experienced during the early phase of the credit crisis. In July 2009 the Basel Committee issued *Enhancements to the Basel II framework* (BCBS, 2009a). The paper provided a series of enhancements to Basel II, with specific focus on securitised and re-securitised products. Changes were made to all three pillars of the Basel framework including increased capital requirements for securitisations, reflecting that the root cause of the financial crisis lay in CDOs and related products. Colloquially these enhancements became known as Basel II.5.

**Basel III**  In December 2010 the Basel Committee proposed a complete overhaul of the Basel framework to reflect the lessons of the crisis period in *Basel III: A global regulatory framework for more resilient banks and banking systems* (BCBS, 2011b).[1] Basel made significant changes to all three Basel pillars as well as revising and extending liquidity measures and introducing the category of *systemically important financial institutions* or *SIFIs*.

Under Pillar 1 both capital and risk measurement were altered. The minimum capital requirement for common equity was raised from 2% to 4.5% of risk-weighted assets with an additional 2.5% capital conservation buffer, giving a total common equity of 7% of RWAs. The common equity tier 1 capital requirement, including common equity, was raised from 4% to 6%. If the capital of the institution fell below the capital conservation buffer threshold, restrictions on dividend payments by the bank would be imposed. The bank would also be required to present a plan to the regulator to bring the capital above the buffer. The capital conservation buffer comes into effect between 1 January 2016 and 1 January 2019. Contractual terms of capital instruments were modified to allow conversion to common shares in the event the issuing bank became non-viable in the opinion of regulators. An additional countercyclical

---

[1]The document was later revised in June 2011.

**TABLE 12.1**  Basel III revised capital requirements as a percentage of risk-weighted assets (BCBS, 2011b).

| | Common Equity Tier 1 | Tier 1 Capital | Total Capital |
|---|---|---|---|
| Minimum | 4.5% | 6.0% | 8.0% |
| Conservation Buffer | 2.5% | | |
| Minimum plus Conservation Buffer | 7% | 8.5% | 10.5% |
| Countercyclical Buffer | 0–2.5% | | |

buffer of common equity in the range 0–2.5% was also introduced to allow supervisors to increase capital requirements when they judged that systemic risk was increasing. A decision to raise the countercyclical buffer would be pre-announced by up to 12 months. In addition SIFIs faced an additional common equity tier 1 (CET1) capital requirement of 1–2.5% depending on the systemic importance of the institution. The capital requirement under Basel III is summarised in Table 12.1, while the transitional arrangements are given in Table 12.2.

The measurement of risk-weighted assets was also changed in Basel III. The counterparty credit risk framework was strengthened along with a new capital requirement for CVA VaR on derivatives, following the observation by the Basel Committee that losses due to CVA impact on mark-to-market were greater during the crisis than losses due to defaults. Basel III also provided incentives to clear derivatives through central counterparties with CCPs receiving a favourable risk-weight of 2%. The capital treatment of securitisations was strengthened with a requirement for banks to conduct more rigorous analysis of externally rated securitisation exposures.[2] The treatment of market risk was changed with the introduction of a requirement for SVaR or Value-at-Risk using a period of market stress. The incremental risk charge was also introduced to capture the default and credit migration risks associated with unsecuritised credit products.

The final change to Pillar 1 was the introduction of the *leverage ratio*. The leverage ratio provides a limit on the leverage that banks can run and also provides a holistic counterpart to the traditional capital ratio.

Pillar 2 was also changed in a number of ways. The capture of off-balance sheet risks and securitisation exposures featured highly alongside several governance-related measures. Banks were incentivised to better manage risks and returns over the long term alongside bank compensation practices. Valuation and accounting standards were also covered as well as stress testing.

Additional disclosure requirements were added to Pillar 3. More disclosure of exposure to securitisations and off-balance sheet vehicles were introduced alongside a requirement to publish more information on how regulatory capital ratios were calculated.

In addition to the three pillars, further requirements were introduced for liquidity management. Basel III introduced the *liquidity coverage ratio* or *LCR* that requires banks to have enough high quality liquid assets available to withstand a 30-day period of funding stress. The *Net stable funding ratio* or *NSFR* was also introduced as a measure of liquidity mismatches over the longer term and to incentivise banks to use stable long-term sources of funding rather

---

[2]Under Dodd-Frank references to external ratings are prohibited for securitisations.

**TABLE 12.2** The timetable for phasing in new capital requirements under Basel III (after BCBS, 2011b).

| | 2011 | 2012 | 2013 | 2014 | 2015 | 2016 | 2017 | 2018 | As of 1 Jan 2019 |
|---|---|---|---|---|---|---|---|---|---|
| Leverage Ratio | Supervisory monitoring | | Parallel run 1 Jan 2013 - 1 Jan 2017 Disclosure starts 1 Jan 2015 | | | | | Migration to Pillar 1 | |
| Minimum common equity capital ratio | | | 3.5% | 4% | 4.5% | 4.5% | 4.5% | 4.5% | 4.5% |
| Capital conservation buffer | | | | | | 0.625% | 1.25% | 1.875% | 2.5% |
| Minimum common equity plus capital conservation buffer | | | 3.5% | 4.0% | 4.5% | 5.125% | 5.75% | 6.375% | 7.0% |
| Phase-in of deductions from CET1 (including amounts exceeding the limit for DTAs, MSRs and financials ) | | | | 20% | 40% | 60% | 80% | 100% | 100% |
| Minimum Tier 1 Capital | | | 4.5% | 5.5% | 6% | 6% | 6% | 6% | 6% |
| Minimum Total Capital | | | 8% | 8% | 8% | 8% | 8% | 8% | 8% |
| Minimum Total Capital plus conservation buffer | | | 8% | 8% | 8% | 8.625% | 9.25% | 9.875% | 10.5% |
| Capital instruments that no longer qualify as non-core Tier 1 capital or Tier 2 capital | | | Phased out over 10-year horizon beginning 2013 | | | | | | |
| Liquidity coverage ratio | Observation period starts | | | | Introduce minimum standard | | | | |
| Net stable funding ratio | Observation period starts | | | | | | | Introduce minimum standard | |

**TABLE 12.3** The different approaches to market risk, counterparty credit risk and CVA capital calculations, depending on regulatory status (after Green, Kenyon and Dennis, 2014).

| Classification | Alternatives | Calculation Type |
|---|---|---|
| Counterparty Credit Risk | *EAD Calculation* | |
| | CEM | Function of Netting Set Value |
| | Standardised | Function of Netting Set Value |
| | Internal Model Method | Exposure Profile |
| | *Weight Calculation* | |
| | Standardised | External Ratings |
| | FIRB | Internal & External Ratings |
| | AIRB | Internal & External Ratings, Internal LGDs |
| CVA Capital | Standardised | Function of EAD |
| | Advanced | VaR/SVaR on Regulatory CVA or CS01 |
| Market Risk | Standardised | Deterministic Formulae |
| | Internal Model Method | VaR + SVaR |

than short-term wholesale funding. Finally a set of reporting requirements were introduced to allow an assessment of bank and market-wide liquidity.

### 12.1.3 Pillar I: Capital Types and Choices

The primary elements of the regulatory framework with pricing impact are those associated with the capital ratio in Pillar 1. Central for derivatives are the three main sources of capital requirement: *Market Risk*, *Counterparty Credit Risk* and *Credit Valuation Adjustment*. For each of these sources of risk-weighted assets or capital requirements there is a variety of different approaches available to banks, depending on their regulatory status. These are discussed in more detail below but are summarised in Table 12.3. It is also useful to introduce some regulatory capital terminology and this is listed in Table 12.4.

**TABLE 12.4** Common regulatory acronyms.

| Term | Description |
|---|---|
| EAD | Exposure-at-default |
| CEM | Current Exposure Method |
| CCR | Counterparty Credit Risk |
| VaR | Value-at-Risk |
| SVaR | Stressed Value-at-Risk |
| IRC | Incremental Risk Charge |
| IMM | Internal Model Method |
| FIRB | Foundation Internal Ratings-Based |
| AIRB | Advanced Internal Ratings-Based |
| PD | Probability of Default (usually over 1 year) |
| LGD | Loss-given-default |

## 12.2  MARKET RISK

Market risk capital is the capital required to offset potential losses on market risk on traded products. As noted earlier this was introduced in the Basel II framework (BCBS, 2006b) and enhanced with the addition of measures to cater for periods of market stress in Basel III (BCBS, 2011b). In the Basel III implementation of market risk capital there are two possible approaches, *standardised* and *internal model method* for those banks with appropriate supervisory authorisation. The rules for market risk capital will change again as a result of the forthcoming *fundamental review of the trading book* (BCBS, 2013c), discussed in section 12.6.1. Market risk capital is calculated on a net basis across the portfolio, whether standardised or internal model method approaches are used.

### 12.2.1  Trading Book and Banking Book

Market risk capital applies to the trading book and not the banking book. Under Basel II/III the trading book is defined as the set of positions that are held for one of the following purposes:

1. Held for resale or with the intention of benefitting from short-term movements in market prices
2. Arising from matched principal broking
3. To hedge other positions in the trading book.

The banking book consists of positions which are not in the trading book. The *fundamental review of the trading book* will change the boundary definition and the ability to move from one designation to the other (see section 12.6.1).

### 12.2.2  Standardised Method

The standardised method for market risk uses a series of formulae to generate the capital requirement, with different approaches used for four different categories of market risk: interest rate, equity, foreign exchange and commodities. A number of choices are available to the implementing bank for each category of risk and the reader is referred directly to the documentation in Basel II for details (BCBS, 2006b) or to BIPRU (Financial Conduct Authority, 2014) where a good description of the practical implementation of the standardised approach is given. Here I will summarise the approach for an interest rate swap as these are used as examples in Chapter 13 on KVA.

It is important to note that the market risk capital under the standardised approach is formulaic and does not depend on market conditions, rather it depends simply on trade properties. The scheme itself has been calibrated by the Basel Committee to give the capital levels they required.

Interest rate swaps are split into their two constituent legs for the purposes of market risk capital. The floating leg is treated as a notional position in a government floating rate security with a maturity equal to the next fixing date, while the fixed leg is treated as a notional position in a government fixed rate security with maturity equal to the residual maturity of the swap. Consider an interest rate swap with a residual maturity of 10 years, where the bank

**TABLE 12.5**   Risk-weights used in the interest rate maturity method under Basel II (table after Financial Conduct Authority, 2014).

| | Maturity band | | |
|---|---|---|---|
| **Zone** | **Coupon > 3%** | **Coupon < 3%** | **Postion risk adjustment** |
| One | $0 \leq 1$ month | $0 \leq 1$ month | 0.00% |
| | $> 1 \leq 3$ months | $> 1 \leq 3$ months | 0.20% |
| | $> 3 \leq 6$ months | $> 3 \leq 6$ months | 0.4% |
| | $> 6 \leq 12$ months | $> 6 \leq 12$ months | 0.7% |
| Two | $> 1 \leq 2$ years | $> 1.0 \leq 1.9$ years | 1.25% |
| | $> 2 \leq 3$ years | $> 1.9 \leq 2.8$ years | 1.75% |
| | $> 3 \leq 4$ years | $> 2.8 \leq 3.6$ years | 2.25% |
| Three | $> 4 \leq 5$ years | $> 3.6 \leq 4.3$ years | 2.75% |
| | $> 5 \leq 7$ years | $> 4.3 \leq 5.7$ years | 3.25% |
| | $> 7 \leq 10$ years | $> 5.7 \leq 7.3$ years | 3.75% |
| | $> 10 \leq 15$ years | $> 7.3 \leq 9.3$ years | 4.5% |
| | $> 15 \leq 20$ years | $> 9.3 \leq 10.6$ years | 5.25% |
| | $> 20$ years | $> 10.6 \leq 12.0$ years | 6.00% |
| | | $> 12.0 \leq 20.0$ years | 8.00% |
| | | $> 20$ years | 12.50% |

receives three-month GBP LIBOR and pays a fixed rate of 2.7%. The fixed leg pays annually and the floating leg every three months. For simplicity I assume that at the time the capital is calculated, there is exactly three months to the next floating leg fixing.

Assuming the use of the *interest rate maturity method*, the two legs have risk-weights assigned to them using Table 12.5. The floating leg will have a risk falling into the 3–6 month time band and hence have a risk-weight of 0.4% assigned to it, irrespective of the fixing rate. The fixed leg will fall into the 9.3–10.6-year time band for instruments with a coupon of less than 3% and hence it will have a risk-weight of 5.25%. All the legs for the portfolio will have risk-weights assigned in this fashion, with the long and short positions in each band summed to give a weighted long and weighted short position per band. The long and short positions are then matched at three different levels, per time band, per time zone and between zones 1 and 2 and zones 2 and 3 and then finally between zones 1 and 3. The total interest rate market risk capital requirement is then given the sum of (see Financial Conduct Authority, (2014):

- 10% of the total amount matched in each time band
- 40% of the amount matched within zone 1
- 30% of the amount matched in zone 2 and zone 3
- 40% of the amount matched between zones 1 and 2, and between zones 2 and 3
- 150% of the amount matched between zones 1 and 3
- 100% of the unmatched positions.

This process is illustrated in Table 12.6 using the interest rate swap as an example here with a notional of £100.

**TABLE 12.6**   The standardised market risk calculation using the maturity method for a 10-year GBP interest rate swap with a fixed rate of 2.7% (adapted from Financial Conduct Authority, 2014, §7.2.61).

| Zone | Totals | | Postion risk adjustment | Weighted longs | Weighted shorts |
| | longs | shorts | | | |
|---|---|---|---|---|---|
| One | | | 0.00% | | |
| | | | 0.20% | | |
| | 100 | | 0.4% | 0.4 | |
| | | | 0.7% | | |
| Two | | | 1.25% | | |
| | | | 1.75% | | |
| | | | 2.25% | | |
| Three | | | 2.75% | | |
| | | | 3.25% | | |
| | | | 3.75% | | |
| | | | 4.5% | | |
| | | 100 | 5.25% | | 5.25 |
| | | | 6.00% | | |
| | | | 8.00% | | |
| | | | 12.50% | | |

| same band | | same zone | | different zone | |
| Long | Short | Long | Short | Long | Short |
|---|---|---|---|---|---|
| | | | | 0.4 | 0 |
| 0.4 | | 0.4 | | | |
| | | | | 0 | 0 |
| | | | | 0 | 5.25 |
| | 5.25 | | 5.25 | | |
| **0 matched** | | **0 matched** | | **0.4 matched** | |

| | | | | | | |
|---|---|---|---|---|---|---|
| Matched within bands | 0 | @ | 10% | = | 0 |
| Matched within zone 1 | 0 | @ | 40% | = | 0 |
| Matched within zones 2 & 3 | 0 | @ | 30% | = | 0 |
| Matched between zones 1 & 2 and 2 & 3 | 0 | @ | 40% | = | 0 |
| Matched between zones 1 & 3 | 0.4 | @ | 150% | = | 0.6 |
| Unmatched | 4.85 | @ | 100% | = | 4.85 |
| | | | | total = | £5.45 |

## 12.2.3   Internal Model Method (IMM)

If a bank receives supervisory authorisation to use IMM for market risk then they can implement their own model for market risk capital. The general principles behind all such models are the same and are based on Value-at-Risk using a one-sided 99% confidence limit using price shocks generated over 10-day intervals. The time series of data used for VaR must be at least one year. A continuous period of one year containing a period of significant market stress that is relevant for the bank in question must also be used to generate SVaR.

The market risk capital requirement is then the sum of the VaR and SVaR contributions where the VaR and SVaR contributions are given by the maximum of the current VaR (SVaR) and the average of the last 60 business days multiplied by the *multiplication factor* as defined by the regulator but with a minimum value of three.

A variety of different approaches can be used to calculate Value-at-Risk including variance-covariance approximations, historical simulation and Monte Carlo methods. Historical simulation is the most common type. Value-at-Risk models can use either *delta-gamma-vega*[3] or full revaluation of the product in each scenario. The scenarios themselves are generated by applying the shocks to the current market state but this can also be done in several ways such as applying additive shocks or relative shocks. Volatility weighting can also sometimes be applied. It is worth noting that different methodologies can produce widely different VaR and SVaR figures for the same portfolio and that in all cases VaR is very sensitive to the input market data time series. Market data must undergo some form of *cleaning* to ensure that spurious values are corrected. For more information on the problems that can be encountered with VaR models see Kenyon and Green (2014e).

## 12.3 COUNTERPARTY CREDIT RISK

The counterparty credit risk capital for each counterparty is given by

$$RWA = w \times 12.5 \times EAD, \tag{12.1}$$

where $w$ is the weight and the EAD is the exposure-at-default of the counterparty. Recall Table 12.3 – this shows that the calculation methodology is divided into two parts with a range of approaches available for the weight calculation and for the estimation of the EAD.

### 12.3.1 Weight Calculation

There are two possible ways the weight can be calculated, either using the *standardised* approach or using the *internal ratings-based approach* which itself is divided into *foundation* and *advanced* methodologies.

**Standardised Method**   For those banks without supervisory authorisation to use FIRB or AIRB approaches, they must use the standardised approach. This simply assigns a risk-weight to the counterparty based on its external rating and the sector within which it operates. Counterparties without an external rating have the risk-weight of 100% assigned to them. Table 12.7 provides risk-weights for institutions for which a qualifying credit assessment is available.

---

[3]That is a Taylor series approximation.

**TABLE 12.7** Standardised risk-weights for credit quality steps for corporates and the mapping to credit ratings from major rating agencies (after Prudential Regulation Authority, 2006).

| Credit quality step | Corp. Risk-weight | S&P | Moody's | Fitch | DBRS |
|---|---|---|---|---|---|
| 1 | 20% | AAA to AA- | Aaa to Aa3 | AAA to AA- | AAA to AAL |
| 2 | 50% | A+ to A- | A1 to A3 | A+ to A- | AH to AL |
| 3 | 50% | BBB+ to BBB- | Baa1 to Baa3 | BBB+ to BBB- | BBBH to BBBL |
| 4 | 100% | BB+ to BB- | Ba1 to Ba3 | BB+ to BB- | BBH to BBL |
| 5 | 100% | B+ to B- | B1 to B3 | B+ to B- | BH to BL |
| 6 | 150% | CCC+ and below | Caa1 and below | CCC+ and below | CCC |

**Internal Ratings-based Approach**    The two key inputs to the weight calculation for those banks that have permission to use the internal ratings-based approach are the *probability-of-default (PD)* and *loss-given-default (LGD)*. Banks with permission to use FIRB supply the PD, while the LGD is provided using supervisory estimates. For corporates the supervisory LGD is 45%. Banks with AIRB status also supply the LGD based on their own LGD models. The PD is the minimum of 0.03% and the bank's estimated probability of default over one year. The weight (for derivatives) is then calculated according to

$$w = LGD\left(\Phi\left(\frac{\Phi^{-1}(PD)}{\sqrt{1-\rho}} + \Phi^{-1}(0.999)\sqrt{\frac{\rho}{1-\rho}}\right) - PD\right) \times \frac{1+(M-2.5)b}{1-1.5b} \quad (12.2)$$

where

$$\rho = 0.12\frac{1-e^{-50 \times PD}}{1-e^{-50}} + 0.24\frac{1-(1-e^{-50 \times PD})}{1-e^{-50}} \quad (12.3)$$

$$b = (0.11852 - 0.05478\log(PD))^2 \quad (12.4)$$

$$M = \min\left(5.0, \max\left(1.0, \frac{\sum_{i=1}^{N_{\text{trades}}} m_i N_i}{\sum_{i=1}^{N_{\text{trades}}} N_i}\right)\right), \quad (12.5)$$

and $m_i$ and $N_i$ are the residual trade maturity and notional.[4]

## 12.3.2 EAD Calculation

There are three possible ways of calculating the regulatory exposure-at-default for a counterparty. For those banks with regulatory approval to use the internal models method for counterparty exposures, the bank's own expected exposure model can be used as described in section 12.3.3. For those without approval to use the IMM approach either the Current Exposure Method (CEM) or standardised approach must be selected. The CEM and standardised

---

[4]Note that the maturity calculation differs under IMM.

**TABLE 12.8**  Add-ons for the CEM calculation.

| | Interest Rates | FX and Gold | Equities | Precious Metals Except Gold | Other Commodities |
|---|---|---|---|---|---|
| One year or less | 0.00% | 1.00% | 6.00% | 7.00% | 10.00% |
| Over one year to five years | 0.50% | 5.00% | 8.00% | 7.00% | 12.00% |
| Over five years | 1.50% | 7.50% | 10.00% | 8.00% | 15.00% |

approaches are due to be replaced by the revised standardised approach, which is discussed in section 12.6.2.

**CEM**  Under the current exposure method, the EAD is given by the accounting value of the trade plus an *add-on* that aims to capture the exposure of the transaction over its remaining life.

$$EAD = V_i + A(m_i, N_i, \text{asset class}) \tag{12.6}$$

The add-on is a percentage of the trade notional that is determined by the residual maturity and asset class of the trade. The add-ons are given by Table 12.8.

Bilateral netting is supported through the net-to-gross ratio adjustment for add-ons which create a net add-on value for the portfolio,

$$A_{\text{Net}} = 0.4 A_{\text{Gross}} + 0.6 N_{GR} A_{\text{Gross}}, \tag{12.7}$$

where $N_{GR}$ is the net-to-gross ratio of replacement costs that is given by

$$N_{GR} = \frac{\left( \sum_{i=1}^{N_{\text{trades}}} V_i \right)^+}{\sum_{i=1}^{N_{\text{trades}}} (V_i)^+}. \tag{12.8}$$

The net-to-gross ratio will vary between 0 and 1 and will equal 1 when there is no netting and 0 when the sum of the mark-to-markets is less than or equal to zero.

**Standardised**  For the standardised approach, the EAD is given by

$$EAD = \beta \max \left( \sum_i V_i^{\text{trade}} - \sum_l V_l^{\text{collateral}}, \right.$$

$$\left. \sum_j \left\{ \left| \sum_i R_{ij}^{\text{trade}} - \sum_l R_{lj}^{\text{collateral}} \right| CCF_j \right\} \right), \tag{12.9}$$

where $V_i^{\text{trade}}$ is the value of trade $i$, $V_l^{\text{collateral}}$ is the value of collateral $l$, $R_{ij}^{\text{trade}}$ is the risk from trade $i$ in hedging set $j$, $R_{lj}^{\text{collateral}}$ is the risk associated with collateral $l$ in hedging set $j$, $\beta$ is the multiplier and is set equal to 1.4 and $CCF_j$ is the supervisory credit conversion factor

**TABLE 12.9**  Summary of risk factor calculations (BCBS, 2006b; Financial Conduct Authority, 2014). Here FX is the FX rate to convert to the trades' native currency, $N_{\text{eff}}$ is the effective notional value of the underlying instrument, $D_{\text{mod}}$ is the modified duration, and $\delta_{\text{equivalent}}$ is the delta equivalent notional value of the underlying.

| Type | Calculation Method |
|---|---|
| Linear risk profile (not debt instrument) | $FX \times N_{\text{eff}}$ |
| Debt instruments & payment legs | $FX \times N_{\text{eff}} \times D_{\text{mod}}$ |
| OTC derivative with nonlinear risk (not debt instrument) | $\Delta_{\text{equivalent}}$ |
| OTC derivative (underlying debt instrument) | $\Delta_{\text{equivalent}} \times D_{\text{mod}}$ |
| Collaterals | Assume collateral received is claim on counterparty today, posted collateral is obligation due today |

for hedging set $j$. The supervisory credit conversion factors can be found in BIPRU section 13.5.22 (Financial Conduct Authority, 2014).[5] The risk factors are determined from the risk type and underlying instrument and these are summarised in Table 12.9.

### 12.3.3  Internal Model Method (IMM)

Under the internal model method approach the EAD is given by an effective maximum EPE over the next year, where the expected exposure is calculated using the bank's internal approved exposure model. The EAD is given by

$$EAD = \alpha \times \text{Effective EPE}, \qquad (12.10)$$

where the Effective EPE is the sum over the average effective expected exposure profile,

$$\text{Effective EPE} = \sum_{k=1}^{\min(maturity, 1year)} \text{Effective EE}(t_k) \times \Delta t_k. \qquad (12.11)$$

The effective expected exposure is given by the maximum expected exposure reached up to that point in time, that is, the effective expected exposure profile only increases in size but this is limited to the first year of the exposure, hence,

$$\text{Effective EE}(t_k) = \max \left[ \text{Effective EE}(t_{k-1}), \text{Effective EE}(t_{k-1}) \right]. \qquad (12.12)$$

The multiplier $\alpha$ has the default value of 1.4, although with supervisory approval a bank can estimate its own value subject to a floor of 1.2.

Basel III (BCBS, 2011b) introduced the requirement that the capital charge be the higher of that calculated using the current parameter calibration and that based on a stressed parameter calibration.

---

[5]BIPRU is a convenient source for much of the underlying Basel regulation as in many areas it has a clearer presentation that the original Basel or CRD IV documentation.

## 12.4 CVA CAPITAL

Basel III (BCBS, 2011b) introduced CVA capital requirements to counter potential losses due to credit valuation adjustment. There are two possible calculation methods for the capital requirement, *standardised* and *advanced*. To obtain approval to use the advanced internal model method a bank must both have approval for exposure calculations, that is the CCR calculation, and approval for market-risk IMM for the specific interest-rate risk of bonds using VaR/SVaR. Both standardised and advanced methodologies make provision for the reduction in the capital requirement for CVA hedging under certain conditions.

Although CVA capital is a key new component of capital, the European implementation excludes a number of counterparty types from CVA capital (European Parliament and the Council of the European Union, 2013b; European Parliament and the Council of the European Union, 2012b):

- Transactions cleared through a CCP
- Transactions with non-financial counterparties established within the EU or transactions with non-financial counterparties established anywhere that fall below the EMIR clearing threshold
- Intragroup transactions
- Transactions with pension scheme arrangements
- Members of the European System of Central Banks and other bodies that manage public debt, the Bank for International Settlements, multilateral development banks, public sector bodies either owned by central governments or guaranteed by central governments explicitly, the European Financial Stability Facility and the European Stability Mechanism.

### 12.4.1 Standardised

The standardised CVA capital charge is given by the formula

$$
K_{\text{CVA}} = 2.33\sqrt{h}\left\{ \left( \sum_i 0.5w_i\left(M_i\text{EAD}_i^{\text{total}} - M_i^{\text{hedge}}B_i\right) - \sum_{\text{ind}} w_{\text{ind}}M_{\text{ind}}B_{\text{ind}}\right)^2 \right. \tag{12.13}
$$

$$
\left. + \sum_i 0.75w_i^2\left(M_i\text{EAD}_i^{\text{total}} - M_i^{\text{hedge}}B_i\right)^2 \right\}^{\frac{1}{2}},
$$

where the notation is defined in Table 12.10.

The formula is designed to give 75% capital benefit for single name hedges and 25% capital benefit for index hedges, with the reduction reflecting the lower correlation between an index hedge and a single exposure. However, if an index contains the single name associated with the exposure then the single name can be subtracted from the index notional and treated as a single name hedge. CDS hedges for CVA must be specifically designated as such and not be maintained as part of a broader inventory in order to provide capital relief.

Examination of the formula shows that it is based on a weighted sum over EADs multiplied by the effective maturity of the netting set. As such it can be seen as a relatively crude CVA-like formula, although the probability is determined by the weight table and not by the prices of CDS contracts. Mitigation is given for CDS hedging although the nature of the formula is a

**TABLE 12.10**   Notation used in the CVA capital formula for the standardised approach.

| Notation | Description |
|---|---|
| $h(= 1)$ | Risk horizon (1 year in units of years) |
| $w_i$ | Risk-weight of ith counterparty |
| $EAD_i^{total}$ | Exposure at default of counterparty i. This is discounted at a nominal rate of 5% ($\frac{1-e^{-0.05M_i}}{0.05M_i}$) for non-IMM banks (IMM banks have this included in $M_i$) |
| $B_i$ | Single name CDS hedge notional |
| $B_{ind}$ | Index CDS hedge notional |
| $w_{ind}$ | Risk-weight of index hedge where the weight is given by mapping the index to the weight table using the average spread (see Table 12.11). |
| $M_i$ | Effective maturity of the portfolio with counterparty i. For non-IMM banks this is the (uncapped) notional weighted average maturity. |
| $M_i^{hedge}$ | Maturity of hedge instrument i. |
| $M_{ind}$ | Maturity of index hedge. |

**TABLE 12.11**   The weight table (using rating terminology from Standard and Poor's).

| Rating | Weight $w_i$ |
|---|---|
| AAA | 0.7% |
| AA | 0.7% |
| A | 0.8% |
| BBB | 1.0% |
| BB | 2.0% |
| B | 3.0% |
| CCC | 10.0% |

considerable distance from the CVA models discussed in Part I. Hence an optimal CDS hedge from the perspective of the bank's economic/accounting CVA may not be optimal for capital and vice versa.

The formula is also clearly global, spanning all counterparties as the first term contains a sum over all counterparties that is subsequently squared. This means that to calculate the incremental impact of a single new trade will require the whole formula to be recalculated. However, if there is no single name or index CDS hedging and there are a large number of counterparties, the capital formula can be approximated by[6]

$$K_{CVA} \approx \sum_i \frac{2.33}{2} \sqrt{h} w_i M_i EAD_i^{total}. \tag{12.14}$$

---

[6]To see this consider equation (12.13) in the absence of hedging,

$$K_{CVA} = 2.33\sqrt{h} \left\{ \left( \sum_i 0.5 w_i M_i EAD_i^{total} \right)^2 + \sum_i 0.75 w_i^2 \left( M_i EAD_i^{total} \right)^2 \right\}^{\frac{1}{2}},$$

In the limit of a large number of counterparties, the first term in the expression will be much larger than the second as it is the square of a sum, while the second is the sum of a square. Hence the first term will

**TABLE 12.12**  Notation used in IMM CVA formulae.

| Notation | Description |
|---|---|
| $\text{LGD}_{\text{MKT}}$ | The loss-given-default of the counterparty based on a market instrument of the counterparty or on a proxy spread if an instrument of the counterparty is not available, where the proxy is based on the rating, industry sector and geographical location. |
| $s_i$ | The spread for tenor maturity at time $t_i$. |
| $\text{EE}_i$ | Expected exposure at tenor $i$ as calculated by the bank's internal exposure engine. |
| $D_i$ | Discount factor for tenor $i$. |

## 12.4.2  Advanced

If a bank has regulatory approval to use the advanced CVA approach then it must use a VaR approach alongside a regulatory CVA formula similar to the unilateral CVA models described in Chapter 3. For banks that use a full revaluation approach to VaR the CVA is given by calculating the CVA using the following formula in each VaR scenario:

$$\text{CVA} = \text{LGD}_{\text{MKT}} \sum_{i=1}^{T} \max \left( 0, \exp \left( -\frac{s_{i-1} t_{i-1}}{\text{LGD}_{\text{MKT}}} \right) - \exp \left( -\frac{s_i t_i}{\text{LGD}_{\text{MKT}}} \right) \right) \quad (12.15)$$
$$\times \left( \frac{\text{EE}_{i-1} D_{i-1} + \text{EE}_i D_i}{2} \right),$$

where the notation is summarised in Table 12.12. Note that only the credit spread sensitivity is considered so that the expected exposures remain constant in all scenarios. If the bank uses a VaR model based on sensitivities then it must calculate the regulatory CS01's using

$$\text{CS01}_i = 0.0001 t_i \exp \left( -\frac{s_i t_i}{\text{LGD}_{\text{MKT}}} \right) \left( \frac{\text{EE}_{i-1} D_{i-1} + \text{EE}_{i+1} D_i + 1}{2} \right). \quad (12.16)$$

To calculate the capital requirement the bank must apply both VaR and SVaR. For SVaR the calibration of the exposure engine should be done under stressed conditions. This in fact highlights another probable difference between CVA capital and economic CVA as the bank must use its approved exposure engine for this calculation. The IMM approved exposure engine will almost certainly use a historical calibration, rather than the risk-neutral one used by the economic CVA calculation. This is because the usage requirements for IMM exposure engines mean that they must also be used by the bank for credit risk management, normally though the use of PFE to set credit limits. To gain IMM approval the engine must also satisfy backtesting requirements which are also more appropriate in the context of historical calibration. Hence,

---

dominate giving,

$$K_{\text{CVA}} \approx 2.33 \sqrt{h} \left\{ \left( \sum_i 0.5 w_i M_i \text{EAD}_i^{\text{total}} \right)^2 \right\}^{\frac{1}{2}}$$
$$= \sum_i \frac{2.33}{2} \sqrt{h} w_i M_i \text{EAD}_i^{\text{total}}.$$

while the CVA formula is at least superficially similar to a unilateral CVA formula, there are in practice considerable differences. Nevertheless the formula does suggest that a hedge use for economic purposes for unilateral CVA will also prove to be a reasonable capital hedge. One final point to make is that the IMM CVA formulae use CDS spreads directly rather than use a model to infer the survival probability function, $P(\tau > t)$.[7]

**Proxy Spreads**  Under Basel III (BCBS, 2011b) banks with IMM approval for CVA must use the counterparty spread where it is available and a proxy spread based on the counterparty's rating, industry sector and geographical location. Under CRD IV (European Parliament and the Council of the European Union, 2013b; European Parliament and the Council of the European Union, 2013a), the mechanism by which proxy spreads should be assigned to illiquid counterparties was delegated to the European Banking Authority who published draft technical standards in December 2013 (EBA, 2013b).

The technical standards provide a series of requirements relating to how the mapping from the counterparty to the CDS market should be made. The rating, sector and region are subject to the following minimum standards:

- Rating – the rating must be set by using a predetermined hierarchy of internal and external sources. The rating must be mapped to a set of credit quality steps in accordance with Article 384(2) of CRD IV (Regulation) (2013).
- Sector – there must be at least the three sectors considered: public sector, financials and others.
- Geography – the following four regions must be considered at a minimum:
  - Europe
  - North America
  - Asia
  - Rest of World.
- The proxy spread must reflect available credit default swap spreads and spreads of other liquid traded credit risk instruments.
- The appropriateness of a spread should be determined by its volatility not level.

In addition the technical standards specify that additional attributes can be considered when setting the proxy spread as long as the attributes reflect characteristics of positions in the CVA portfolio and that they satisfy data quality requirements. The technical standards also specify that the sovereign rating may be used for regional government entities if there is a strong relationship with the sovereign and that either the regional government has the same rating as the sovereign or is unrated. The standards also make clear that $LGD_{MKT}$ must be that used by market participants to extract the survival probabilities from CDS spreads.

Proxy spreads have already been extensively discussed in section 4.6 including a number of possible approaches. It should be noted that the cross-section mapping approach (Chourdakis

---

[7] Kenyon and Green (2013b) demonstrated that regulatory capital can account for up to 40% of the spread of a CDS contract. If the CVA capital is hedged with CDS then the capital portion of the CDS spread effectively cancels out. If, however, the CVA capital is not hedged then there is effectively a double impact. The CDS spread is wider *because* other market participants are using the CDS to hedge its CVA capital and so increasing the demand. The institution not hedging its CVA capital has to mark the capital requirement using the full CDS spread and so sees a "double impact".

et al., 2013) emerged during a regulatory consultation exercise. The EBA technical standards do not significantly change the approaches available for mapping CDS. However, even the minimum standards do present a challenge to create a map into a CDS market which still has relatively few available CDS contracts for non-US names.

## 12.5 OTHER SOURCES OF REGULATORY CAPITAL

### 12.5.1 Incremental Risk Charge (IRC)

The incremental risk charge was introduced as part of the Basel II framework with guidelines on its calculation published in July 2009 (BCBS, 2009b). The charge was introduced to cater for credit-risk related products in trading books whose risk was not properly incorporated into VaR. Such products may experience sharp losses less than twice a year and hence fall outside VaR. The incremental risk charge is based upon an estimate of the default and migration risk of the credit product at a confidence level of 99.9% over a one-year period. The Basel document lays down a series of principles that a bank's IRC methodology must follow rather than a specific methodology. The liquidity of positions must be incorporated into the model and a liquidity horizon estimated, based on an estimate of the time it would take to liquidate or fully hedge the position under stressed market conditions. The scope of IRC is all positions that lead to capital for specific interest rate risk, although securitisations are explicitly excluded. In practice IRC falls mainly on traded debt as it is intended to capture the risk of default or downgrade and the associated *gap* risk.[8]

### 12.5.2 Leverage Ratio

Basel III (BCBS, 2011b) also introduced the *leverage ratio*. The Basel Committee found that during the financial crisis many banks were in highly levered positions even though they showed strong capital ratios. The excess leverage then contributed to the severity of the crisis as banks were forced to deleverage their balance sheets at a time of crisis that put further downward pressure on asset prises due to the need to sell assets quickly. Hence the Basel Committee concluded that measures should be introduced to control leverage and to provide a "backstop" measure that was not risk based to sit alongside the existing risk-based capital framework. Such a non-risk based approach would be common across institutions and hence provide an independent measure with no internal modelling involved.

The leverage ratio is given by

$$\text{Leverage Ratio} = \frac{\text{Capital Measure}}{\text{Exposure Measure}}, \qquad (12.17)$$

where the monthly leverage ratio is averaged over each quarter for reporting purposes. The leverage ratio under Basel III should be constained to be 3% or greater.

The *Capital Measure* is given by the Tier 1 equity capital measure (CET1) as defined under Basel III. The capital and exposure measures should be consistent so items deducted from capital should also be excluded from exposure. Furthermore threshold deductions including

---

[8]A default or downgrade may lead to a sharp change or gap in the price of the bond.

significant investments in unconsolidated financial institutions should be applied consistently between capital and exposure measures so that the assets of these entities appear only in the proportion that the capital associated with them does.

The *Exposure Measure* is calculated according to a set of general measurement principles with specific rules for the treatment of securities financing transactions, derivatives and off-balance sheet items. For non-derivative on-balance sheet items such as loans the exposure measure should be taken after specific provisions and valuation adjustments have been made. Non-cash collateral cannot be included to offset exposure and loans and deposits cannot be netted. Securities financing transactions exposures should be included by using the accounting exposure and netting rules as per the Basel II framework. Derivatives should be included by using the accounting exposures plus an add-on calculated using the current exposure method described in section 13.3.2. Derivative netting should be calculated using the regulatory netting framework of Basel II. Off-balance sheet items should be included using a 100% Credit Conversion Factor while for those commitments that are unconditionally cancellable at any time a CCF of 10% should be used.

This covers the basic Basel III requirement. However, both the EU and US implementations of the leverage ratio have been modified. Under CRD IV the EBA were delegated the authority to provide technical standards for the calculation of the leverage ratio (EBA, 2014a; EBA, 2014b). US regulatory authorities have also implemented their own version of the Basel III requirement with even higher leverage ratio requirements than proposed by the Basel Committee (Office of the Comptroller of the Currency, Treasury; the Board of Governors of the Federal Reserve System; and the Federal Deposit Insurance Corporation, 2014a). Hence leverage ratio requirements vary significantly between different regulatory regimes.

## 12.6 FORTHCOMING REGULATION WITH PRICING IMPACT

Following the introduction of the Basel III framework, the Basel Committee began a process of further revising elements of the regulatory capital framework as well as introducing regulation intended to further the goal of clearing as many derivative products as possible. In addition, in Europe, the EBA, acting under authority delegated to them by CRD IV, introduced the concept of Prudent Valuation to allow for uncertainties in the valuation process for derivative products.[9] While EMIR introduced mandatory clearing of derivative products between certain classes of institution. This does not constitute the full list of forthcoming regulation but this section is intended to cover the main elements with impact on pricing.

### 12.6.1 Fundamental Review of the Trading Book

The Basel Committee introduced a proposal for a review of the market risk capital framework in 2012 (BCBS, 2012g) and then later revised these proposals in a second (BCBS, 2013c) and third (BCBS, 2014a) consultative document. The proposals follow a decision by the Basel Committee to address the perceived shortcomings of the market risk capital framework experienced during the financial crisis, and to further strengthen it following the introduction of Basel II.5 in 2009 (BCBS, 2009a).

---

[9]Note also that the concept of prudential valuation has been written out of accounting standards.

**The Trading Book/Banking Book Boundary** Derivative products are usually held in the Trading Book, accounted for using mark-to-market accounting and actively risk managed. However, it is entirely possible to use derivatives in a Banking Book context, for example, hedging strategic interest rate risk implicit in fixed-rate loans. Trading Book and Banking Book get different capital treatments under the Basel framework. The Basel Committee felt that the rules surrounding the boundary between Banking Book and Trading Book were a problem in the current regime:

> *A key determinant of the existing boundary has been banks' effectively self-determined intent to trade, an inherently subjective criterion that has proved difficult to police and insufficiently restrictive from a prudent perspective in some jurisdictions. (BCBS, 2013c)*

The concerns stated by the Basel Committee include objectivity in the definition, opportunities for capital arbitrage, the permeability of the boundary, alignment with risk management practice and ease of use. The Basel Committee opted to retain the trading evidence-based approach that was used under Basel II but with significant additional restrictions. A pure valuation-based approach was rejected. The supervisor has also now been given clear authority to redesignate instruments as appropriate.

The major changes in the definition are:

- **Definition of the Trading Book** – instruments must be included in the trading book if they meet certain specific criteria. For example, if an instrument is managed on a trading desk (see contents below) then it must be in the trading book. Net short equity positions must also be in the trading book.
- **Contents of the Trading Book** (examples – not an exhaustive list)
  - Asset or liability designated as "held for trading" under IFRS or US GAAP
  - Instruments arising from market-marking or underwriting activity
  - Listed equities or investments in equity funds
  - Naked short positions, all shorts of cash instruments
  - Options.
- **Contents of the Banking Book** – the banking book is still defined as anything which is not in the trading book. For example:
  - Unlisted equity
  - Real estate holdings
  - Equity investments in illiquid funds or derivatives written on such funds.[10]
- **Permeability** – in general redesignation of an instrument after the initial designation as trading or banking book is not allowed. The supervisor must explicitly approve any redesignation and this can only occur in exceptional circumstances, of which market conditions are not an acceptable reason.
- **Reducing Capital Arbitrage** – should redesignation be allowed then no capital benefit can be gained. The different in capital is held as a fixed capital requirement and then amortised as authorised by the supervisor.

---

[10]Where illiquidity is considered to be defined as where the bank faces difficulty to liquidate or mark-to-market an instrument.

- **Supervisor redesgnation** – the supervisor has the authority to redesignate if an instrument has, in their view, been incorrectly designated.
- **Valuation** – trading book instruments should be valued daily.
- **Reporting** – banks must report on how boundary is determined including inventory agent, daily limits, intraday limits and market liquidity.

With these restrictions in place assets that would previously have been marked as banking book may now forced to be held in the trading book and vice versa. The likelihood is that at least to some degree, positions were held in the most favourable way that reduced the overall capital requirement, or at least that this was a major concern for the Basel Committee. Hence it is likely that the changes in the banking book/trading book boundary will increase overall capital requirements.

**Credit Risk**    Given that credit products were a major source of losses during the financial crisis, their treatment under market risk capital has come in for extra scrutiny. The committee has proposed different treatments for securitised and non-securitised credit exposures.

**Securitised**    Securitised products such as CDOs and CLOs were a major source of loss during the financial crisis and as a result the Basel Committee has stipulated that all such products be treated under the revised standardised approach and hence IMM is not allowed for securitised products.

**Non-securitised**    Non-securitised credit exposures can continue to be included in IMM models; however, the Basel Committee will introduce an additional Incremental Default Risk (IDR) charge for non-securitised credit products in the trading book. Banks must have a separate internal model for the default risk on trading book positions. The model will be based on VaR at the 99.9% level using a one-year time horizon.

**Expected Shortfall (ES)**    The Basel Committee found that during the crisis period VaR models did not give an accurate measure of tail risks. Hence the committee have proposed replacing VaR with Expected Shortfall, sometimes known as Conditional Value-at-Risk (CVaR). Expected shortfall takes an expectation of all of the points outside the chosen percentile. The Basel Committee has proposed a confidence level of 97.5%. As such it is sensitive to all the tail events in the sample of scenarios. This sensitivity can itself cause problems as it makes the model far more sensitive to bad data as is illustrated by Kenyon and Green (2014e). Furthermore the averaging of the points makes the model non-elicitable, a technical issue, but one that makes backtesting with expected shortfall impossible (Emmer, Kratz and Tasche, 2013; Ziegel, 2014). Hence backtesting will remain based on VaR, while the actual calculation will move to expected shortfall.

The use of expected shortfall should be expected to increase capital requirements overall as all tail events are used in the calculation.

**Market Illiquidity**    During the financial crisis there was a very significant drain on liquidity across many different markets. Under such circumstances the assumption made in the Basel II framework for market risk that a position could be exited in 10 working days proved to be invalid. As a result the market shifts used to calculate capital under IMM will now change

**TABLE 12.13**   Market liquidity horizons under the fundamental review of the trading book (BCBS, 2013c). These form the time horizon over which the market shifts used in the internal model method Value-at-Risk calculation.

| Liquidity Horizon (days) | Risk Factor Category |
| --- | --- |
| 10 | Equity Price (large cap) |
| 20 | Interest Rate, Sovereign Credit Spread (IG), Equity Price (small cap), Equity ATM Volatility (large cap), FX Rate, Energy Price, Precious Metal Price |
| 60 | Interest Rate ATM Volatility, Interest Rate (other), Sovereign Credit Spread (HY), Corporate Credit Spread (IG), FX ATM Volatility, FX(other), Other Commodities Price, Energy Price ATM Volatility, Precious Metal ATM Volatility |
| 120 | Corporate Credit Spread (HY), Equity Price ATM Volatility (small cap), Equity (other), Other Commodities Price ATM Volatility, Commodity (other) |
| 250 | Credit Spread Structured (Cash and Synthetic), Credit (other) |

to better reflect the liquidity horizons of different markets under stressed conditions. The proposed liquidity horizons are listed in Table 12.13.

Intuitively the longer liquidity horizons should give larger overall shifts and hence a higher expected shortfall value than shorter ones. It is certainly true that a directional move over a longer horizon would give a larger move over 20 days than 10 days. However, if the underlying asset shows mean-reverting behaviour this is not necessarily true. If a jump in the price were to occur then if the liquidity horizon was 10 days then 10 market shifts will contain the jump. However, if the liquidity horizon was 20 days then 20 market shifts would contain the jump. This would move the distribution of market shifts but may still not affect the tail. Overall the impact should be expected to give higher capital requirements but a detailed analysis of individual asset time series would be required to give anything more than a qualitative impact assessment.

**Diversification**   The Basel Committee stated that they believe that under the existing capital regime IMM approaches overstate the potential benefit from diversification, while the standardised method understated them. In particular the committee was concerned that portfolio correlation estimates were not stable under crisis conditions and that diversification benefits may not be realised as a result. To cater for this the committee has proposed to constrain the diversification benefit by simply requiring the total expected shortfall to be a simple sum of the expected shortfall of each broad risk category. This reduction in diversification benefit is likely to result in increased capital requirements for IMM banks.

**Relationship between IMM and Standardised Approach to Market Risk**   Under BCBS 265 all IMM banks must also calculate the standardised approach to market risk capital and must publish this at trading desk level. This aim is to provide a means by which investors and others can judge the level of risk being taken by a bank on a directly comparable basis with other institutions. The Basel Committee also raised the prospect of using the standardised approach as either a floor on capital or as a surcharge and a final decision has yet to be reached on this point. The pricing impact of this will largely be dictated by the final decision on how to apply the floor/surcharge. Nevertheless the fact that the standardised market risk capital is to be published may make this the de facto standard for banks, pushing them to use this level of capital irrespective of what internal modelling using ES would suggest.

**Revised IMM Rules**    The review also proposes a much more granular approach to IMM where individual trading desks are approved to use IMM.[11] Each trading desk will be required to satisfy both a P&L attribution process requirement where the desk demonstrates that their risk management process accurately captures the risk factors that drive their business. Secondly each desk will also be required to satisfy a backtesting requirement where predicted losses are reconciled with actual losses. Should a desk fail either requirement they would be required to use the standardised approach. The advantage of this approach is that the hurdle for the use of the IMM approach for an institution is much lower and a bank can move to IMM in steps. However, with higher testing requirements it seems likely that some institutions on IMM today may find that individual trading desks may be required to revert back to the standardised approach.

**Revised Standardised Approach to Market Risk**    The fundamental review of the trading book also presents a substantial revision of the standardised approach to market risk. The methodology remains formula based for each asset class and hence is similar to the previous approach. Full details can be found in BCBS (2013c).

### 12.6.2  Revised Standardised Approach to Credit Risk

During 2013 the Basel Committee began consulting on a revised approach to credit risk for banks which did not have IMM status. This consultation would lead to the two available methodologies for credit risk under the Basel II framework, CEM and standardised, being replaced with a single framework, initially known as the non-Internal Model Method (NIMM) (BCBS, 2013f). These proposals were subsequently finalised as the *Revised standardised approach for measuring counterparty credit risk exposures* (BCBS, 2014b).

The two earlier methods, CEM and standardised, both received criticism (BCBS, 2014b). CEM is simple to implement but lacks risk sensitivity, is unable to differentiate between margined and un-margined transactions, has a simplistic netting implementation and was observed to have failed to capture the level of volatility seen during the financial crisis through the PFE add-on. The standardised method is recognised as being more risk sensitive but also complex to implement. It was also seen by the Basel Committee as failing to differentiate between margined and un-margined transactions and failing to capture the volatility seen during the financial crisis.

The revised standardised approach can be seen as partially a hybrid of the two earlier approaches. The EAD is given by

$$EAD_{SA} = \alpha \times (RC + PFE),   \tag{12.18}$$

where RC is the replacement cost and PFE is an add-on value to capture the exposure element. $\alpha = 1.4$ is the supervisor multiplier found previously in the IMM approach.

---

[11] In practice what will constitute a trading desk for the purposes of this definition is not yet clear.

The replacement cost for un-margined transactions is given by the usual formula,

$$RC = \max(V - C, 0),\qquad(12.19)$$

where $V$ is the value of the transactions in the netting set and $C$ is the value of the collateral held after haircuts where the collateral is not variation margin. For margined trades the formula is modified,

$$RC = \max(V - C, TH + MTA - NICA),\qquad(12.20)$$

where TH is the threshold, MTA is the minimum transfer amount and NICA is the *net independent collateral amount*. NICA is the amount of collateral available to the bank to offset losses in the event of the default of the counterparty. Hence NICA is given by the total of any collateral posted by the counterparty to the bank, whether segregated or not, minus any collateral posted by the bank to the counterparty that is held in an unsegregated account and hence would be lost on the default of the counterparty. The term, $TH + MTA - NICA$ is the largest exposure that would not trigger a call for variation margin.

The PFE add-on has the form

$$PFE = m(V, C, AddOn^{agg}) \times AddOn^{agg}\qquad(12.21)$$

The multiplier $m$ is given by the formula

$$m(V, C, AddOn^{agg}) = \min \left\{ 1, f + (1-f)\exp\left(\frac{V-C}{2(1-f)AddOn^{agg}}\right) \right\},\qquad(12.22)$$

where $f$ is the *floor* which is set at 5%. The aim of the multiplier is to give benefits for trades which are out of the money and for overcollateralisation as in both cases the multiplier will be less than 1.

The add-ons are an aggregate across the five asset classes; interest rates, FX, equity, credit and commodity:

$$AddOn^{agg} = \sum_{a=1}^{5} AddOn^{a}.\qquad(12.23)$$

Derivative trades are categorised according to the primary risk driver with hybrids being categorised according to risk sensitivities.

The calculation of the add-on factors is specific to each asset class. All add-ons are based on four key factors:

1. *Adjusted Notional* – actual notional adjusted, in the case of interest rate and credit products, for the supervisory duration. The adjusted notional is given by the trade notional converted to the domestic current and multiplied by the supervisory duration, given by (BCBS, 2014b),

$$SD_i = \frac{\exp(-0.05 \times S_i) - \exp(-0.05 \times E_i)}{0.05},\qquad(12.24)$$

where $S_i$ and $E_i$ are the start and end dates of the period referenced by the derivative floored by 10 business days. Once the derivative has started $S_i = 0$.

2. *Maturity Factor* – $MF_i^{(type)}$ – the time horizon for the type of transaction calculated at trade level. The maturity factors also depend on whether the trade is margined or un-margined.

3. *Supervisory Delta* – an adjustment made to reflect whether then trade is long or short and whether it is an option, CDO tranche or a linear product.

4. *Supervisory Factor* – an adjustment to the notional to reflect volatility.

Trades with each counterparty are first separated into hedging sets for each asset class and aggregated, then the hedging sets are aggregated to asset-class level before equation (12.23) is applied.

The formulae for the add-ons themselves vary per asset class and full details of the calculations can be found in BCBS (2014b). The approach can be seen to give an approximate PFE for each asset class and hence provide a measure of future exposure to the counterparty. While it is not risk sensitive in the sense of an internal model, it does provide more realism than the earlier approaches. It also remains formula based, which is an important consideration in the context of *KVA*. There is also considerable emphasis on benefits for margined transactions which, given that cleared trades are margined, is in keeping with the general thrust by regulatory bodies to clear as many transactions as possible.

### 12.6.3  Bilateral Initial Margin

As noted earlier in the context of MVA in Chapter 10 the Basel Committee has proposed the introduction of bilateral initial margin for uncleared derivatives between financial institutions (BCBS, 2012h; BCBS, 2013d; BCBS, 2015). The current timetable for the introduction of bilateral IM will see a rolling introduction based on the size of positions between 2016 and 2020. The initial proposal suggested that banks' approved VaR models would be used for this purpose, however, the finance industry lobbied for the introduction of a single standardised IM calculation approach to ensure a level playing field for all market participants and to avoid diversity of collateral requirements for the two parties to a portfolio of derivatives. A proposal for a standardised initial margin method (SIMM) is currently under development by ISDA (ISDA, 2013).

### 12.6.4  Prudent Valuation

*Prudent Valuation* was introduced as a regulatory requirement in Europe in CRD IV (European Parliament and the Council of the European Union, 2013b), which required the EBA to develop technical standards for a prudent valuation framework. Originally the accounting regime was focussed on prudent valuation but this has now been removed from accounting standards in favour of "fair value".[12]

Article 105 of CRD IV (Regulation) describes a number of categories of valuation adjustments, known as additional valuation adjustments or AVAs, that should be used to achieve a prudent valuation. The article also implies that the prudent valuation methodology should be

---

[12]Where fair value is normally considered to be an estimate of the exit price that would be obtained under normal market conditions.

applied to all trading book positions. Article 34 of CRD IV (Regulation) requires institutions to deduct the aggregate AVA for all fair value assets and liabilities from CET1, suggesting that the prudent valuation framework applies to all fair valued positions irrespective of whether they are held in trading or banking book. The EBA published final draft technical standards on prudent valuation in March 2014 (EBA, 2014c) with implementation scheduled for 20 days after final publication in the *Official Journal of the European Union*.

Prudent valuation adjustment has a direct impact on regulatory capital as it is subtracted from CET1. Hence it will impact pricing as new trades will effectively consume more capital due to the AVA adjustments.

The EBA technical standards offer two different approaches for the calculation of prudent valuation adjustment, *simplified* and *core*. The simplified approach can be used if the sum of the absolute value of fair valued assets and liabilities is less that €15bn. If the total exceeds this level the core approach must be used. If an institution starts below the threshold but subsequently exceeds it, the EBA allows six months to switch from simplified to core method.

At present prudent valuation is only a requirement for EU institutions as it forms part of CRD IV and not the broader Basel framework. However, there is a possibility that prudent valuation will be proposed to the Basel Committee for wider application.

**Simplified**  The simplified prudent valuation method uses a straightforward 0.1% fraction of the sum of the absolute value of contributing values:

$$\text{AVA} = 0.001 \sum_i ||V_i||. \tag{12.25}$$

Exactly offsetting positions are excluded and fair value assets and liabilities for which a change in the accounting value only has a partial impact on CET1 should only be included in the same proportion as their impact.

**Core**  The core approach to prudent valuation is substantially more complex than the simplified approach and involves calculating AVAs in nine different categories. These AVAs are then summed to obtain the total CET1 deduction.

The AVAs must be calculated either using the rules for each category or the fallback method if this is not possible. The fallback method calculated the AVA as the sum of the following three terms:

1. 100% of the net unrealised profit
2. 10% notional value for derivatives
3. 25% of the absolute difference between the fair value and the unrealised profit.

As with the simplified approach, fair value assets and liabilities for which a change in the accounting value only has a partial impact on CET1 should only be included in the same proportion as their impact. Should an institution already have a prudent valuation adjustment methodology in place, then only the excess AVA above this should be subtracted from CET1, subject to supervisory approval.

**1. Market price uncertainty**  The *market price uncertainty* AVA is designed to capture the uncertainty in market price inputs to the value. The AVA can be set to zero if the institution can provide firm evidence of a liquid two-way market and no material uncertainty in valuation.

The market price input could be a single piece of data such as the price of the instrument or it could be a matrix of inputs as is typical with derivative products. If there is a matrix of inputs then the AVA should be assessed with respect to each one. All valuation inputs should be mapped to market tradable instruments. The institution is allowed to reduce the number of inputs in the matrix if the valuation exposure from the reduced input is the same as that from the unreduced input, the reduced parameter matrix can be mapped to market tradable inputs and if,

$$0.1 < \frac{\sigma_{100\,\text{days}}(V_{\text{reduced}} - V_{\text{unreduced}})}{\sigma_{100\,\text{days}}(V_{\text{reduced}})}. \tag{12.26}$$

Once the matrix of inputs has been identified then if there is sufficient data to construct a plausible range of input values these should be used to estimate the 90% confidence limit on the value of the product.[13] If this is not possible the institution must notify the regulator and use expert judgement to make the confidence limit estimate.

Once the AVAs have been obtained the total category level AVA is calculated using either of the following two approaches,

Method 1:

$$\text{APVA}_i = 0.5(V_i^{\text{fair}} - V_i^{\text{prudent}}) \tag{12.27}$$
$$\text{AVA} = \sum_i \text{APVA}_i,$$

Method 2:

$$\text{APVA}_i = \max(0, V_i^{\text{fair}} - 0.5(V_i^{\text{expected}} + V_i^{\text{prudent}})) \tag{12.28}$$
$$\text{AVA} = \sum_i \text{APVA}_i.$$

**2. Close-out costs**   The AVA for close-out costs is meant to capture the uncertainty in the value the transaction could be sold for if the institution had to close out the position. If the market price AVA was assessed using an exit price then there is no additional close-out AVA. In addition if the institution can demonstrate that there is 90% confidence of closing out at the mid price then the close-out AVA can be set to zero. If this is not the case then the close-out AVA calculation follows the same approach of identification of a price input matrix and parameter reduction as used for the market price AVA. Once done the institution is required to calculate a 90% confidence interval using bid-offer spread data on the price inputs. If this is not possible expert judgement can be used but the supervisor must be notified. Aggregation is performed using either equation (12.27) or (12.28).

**3. Model risk**   Model risk is covered by an AVA. The preferred calculation methodology is to generate a range of possible values using alternative models and/or alternative calibrations,

---

[13]The Prudent Valuation regime has adopted a 90% confidence level as the standard measure of prudence across all of the AVAs. Where possible the confidence limited is estimated statistically. In cases where expert judgement is used the confidence limit has to be estimated.

and then to use this range to estimate a 90% confidence limit. This will be challenging for some products as the number of possible alternative models and calibration approaches is small, even ignoring the cost and difficulty of building multiple valuation models for all products. The alternative is to use expert judgement but this is designed to be used in a small number of cases. Even where expert judgement is used it must also be applied to a material sample of transactions where multiple models are available, in order to provide a measure of the accuracy of the expert judgement process. Model risk AVAs are also aggregated using either equation (12.27) or (12.28).

**4. Unearned credit spreads**   The AVA due to *unearned credit spreads* is broadly speaking the uncertainty in CVA accounting models. The requirements of this AVA are in fact to assess the uncertainty in CVA due to market risk, close-out and model risk under this categories.

**5. Investing and funding costs**   Although FVA has hitherto received little regulatory attention, it is included in prudent valuation through the *investing and funding costs* AVA. Like the unearned credit spreads AVA, this AVA requires institutions to assess uncertainty in investing or funding costs due to market risk, close-out and model risk.

**6. Concentrated positions**   The *concentrated positions* AVA is designed to provide a valuation adjustment for positions that are sufficiently large when compared to market liquidity and the institution's ability to trade that market, that a prudent close-out will take longer than ten days. If a market price exists for the size of the position in question then no AVA is required. If an AVA is required then the institution must estimate an AVA based on the volatility of valuation input, the volatility of the bid offer and the impact that the exit strategy would have on market prices. The aggregated AVA is simply the sum of the concentrated position AVA for individual positions.

**7. Future administrative costs**   If the market risk and close-out AVAs imply that the institution will be able to fully exit a position then a no *future administrative costs* AVA will be required. If this not the case then an AVA should be made including administrative and hedging costs of the expected life of the transaction.

**8. Early termination**   An adjustment for costs associated with non-contractual *early termination* of trades should be made by considering the fraction of trades that have terminated early on a historical basis and the losses that were associated with them.

**9. Operational risk**   The *operational risk* AVA does not apply to those institutions who use the *Advanced Measurement Approach for Operation Risk* (BCBS, 2011d; BCBS, 2011c) as long as they can demonstrate that it accounts fully for operational risk. For other institutions the AVA is given by

$$\text{AVA}_{\text{op. risk}} = 0.1 \times (\text{AVA}_{\text{market risk}} + \text{AVA}_{\text{close-out}}). \tag{12.29}$$

**TABLE 12.14** The clearing thresholds under EMIR (European Parliament and the Council of the European Union, 2012b; King, 2013).

| Asset Class | Threshold |
| --- | --- |
| Credit Derivatives | €1bn |
| Equity Derivatives | €1bn |
| Interest Rate Derivatives | €3bn |
| FX | €3bn |
| Commodities and others (combined) | €3bn |

## 12.6.5 EMIR and Frontloading

The *European Market Infrastructure Regulations* (EMIR) (European Parliament and the Council of the European Union, 2012b; King, 2013) introduce a number of requirements for EU banks that are aimed to satisfy the G20 statement made in the aftermath of the crisis:

> *All standardised OTC derivative contracts should be traded on exchanges or electronic trading platforms, where appropriate, and cleared through central counter parties by end-2012 at the latest.*
>
> *OTC derivative contracts should be reported to trade repositories.*
> *Non-centrally cleared contracts should be subject to higher capital requirements.*
>
> G20, Pittsburgh 2012 *(King, 2013)*

EMIR came into force on 16 August 2012, with technical standards and the requirements they impose in force on 15 March 2013. The requirement for higher capital for non-centrally cleared derivatives has already been covered earlier in this chapter. What has not been discussed so far is the impact of the mandatory clearing requirement that EMIR imposes on qualifying institutions.

All standardised derivatives between any institution that is either a financial counterpart or a non-financial counterpart that is above the clearing threshold (known as *NFC+*) are subject to mandatory clearing. As a European regulation this primarily applies where one or both institutions are within the EU. The clearing thresholds are given in Table 12.14. Once the threshold has been breached the clearing obligation applies to all trades not just those that breach the threshold. However, transactions designed to reduce risk to commercial activity or which are part of treasury activities do not count toward the threshold.

The *European Securities and Markets Authority* (ESMA) determines whether or not a product for which clearing is available should be subject to the mandatory clearing requirement. Once a product has been determined as requiring mandatory clearing it is listed in the public register published by ESMA (ESMA, 2014). Once a CCP has been authorised to clear a type of derivative by ESMA *frontloading* of those derivatives by clearing them through the CCP becomes mandatory. However, once the CCP has been authorised, ESMA has up to six months to consult and draw up technical standards for the cleared product (ISDA, 2014b). Once this has been done the European Commission has three months to endorse the standard before passing them on to the European Parliament and the Council of the European Union who then have two months to accept the rules if unmodified by the European Commission and up to six months if they have been modified (ISDA, 2014b). Once accepted by all three parts of the European Union legislature the rules will be published in the *Official Journal of the European Union* and come into force 20 days later. Hence the period between a CCP being authorised and when clearing becomes mandatory varies between 9 and 16 months.

Trades that are cleared are subject to IM, VM, volatility buffers and default fund contributions if a clearing member and similar margin requirements if proceeding through client clearing. As was made clear in Chapter 10 this leads to a need to price in MVA. The problem is that the EMIR frontloading requirement leads to uncertainty during the period when the rules are being put in place by the various European legislative bodies. It is not clear exactly what trades will fall under the clearing requirement and when clearing will begin. Hence the margin requirements and so the MVA is uncertain and this has added to concerns in the market about how such trades should be priced (ISDA, 2014b).

## CHAPTER 13

# KVA: Capital Valuation Adjustment

*Most men would rather deny a hard truth than face it.*

—Tyrion Lannister

G. R. R. Martin's *A Game of Thrones*

## 13.1  INTRODUCTION: CAPITAL COSTS IN PRICING

Chapter 12 introduced the elements of the regulatory capital framework that have pricing impact. Some banks have been using proprietary models to include capital costs in derivative pricing for some time and this has become increasingly common in the aftermath of the financial crisis with the increase in regulatory capital requirements. This chapter, based on Green, Kenyon and Dennis (2014), formalises the inclusion of the cost of capital by extending the Burgard-Kjaer semi-replication model (Burgard and Kjaer, 2013), discussed in Chapter 9 in the context of FVA. The analysis will result in a new valuation adjustment term, KVA or *Capital Valuation Adjustment*.[1]

The Burgard-Kjaer semi-replication model was chosen as the basis of this work primarily because of its simplicity and transparency. The use of a replication approach makes it easy to see how cash flows are treated, something that is not always that straightforward in an expectation-theoretic approach. The resulting PDE makes clear the inter-relationships between funding, capital and counterparty credit risk. An expectation-theoretic approach is possible, where capital calculations are included alongside all other cash flows related to the transaction. Such an approach would be an extension of the C&FVA model presented by Pallavicini, Perini and Brigo (2012). The reader is referred to Elouerkhaoui (2014) for a model of this type.

### 13.1.1  Capital, Funding and Default

Two fundamental questions need to be answered before proceeding to develop the model:

1. What actually *is* capital?

---

[1]"K" is used here as "C" has already been taken by credit valuation adjustment.

**2.** How is capital *used* or *allocated* (by derivative trading operations within banks)?

Measurement of capital was discussed in Chapter 12 and it is clear from the discussion that capital is mainly constituted by shareholders equity capital, that is funds that are raised by selling shares to shareholders. Hence it is similar to the discussion around the source of the funding curve in Chapter 11; however, the funding curve discussion is centred on the use of debt rather than equity. Capital can be therefore be seen as a form of funding. However, a bank cannot sell equity as readily as it can issue debt instruments. Selling shares in an existing company is normally done through a *rights issue* and is a major undertaking. Equity does not therefore provide a practical means for banks to fund themselves except on a strategic basis, either because they have a shortfall in capital or because the bank wishes to make an acquisition funded through equity. Capital can come through other sources such as retained earnings but this does not change the approach to charging for capital or the level of the charge.

Given that capital is a type of funding, how can it be used by a derivatives trading desk? There are two possible answers to this:

- The capital is simply *rented* by the trading desk from shareholders for the purpose of fulfilling regulatory capital requirements. The desk pays shareholders a fee of $\gamma_K(t)$ per unit of capital. No capital is used up in this process and the desk simply borrows and returns the capital as required by the regulatory framework.
- The capital is rented by the trading desk and used to fulfil part of the overall funding requirement.

To allow for the possible use of (equity) capital as funding in the KVA model, a parameter will be introduced, $\phi$, to represent the fraction of capital $K$ that can be used by the desk as part of funding. The extent to which capital can be used for funding will depend on the bank's internal policy. The base case with $\phi = 0$ may best reflect market practice.[2]

## 13.2   EXTENDING SEMI-REPLICATION TO INCLUDE CAPITAL

To include the cost of regulatory capital in pricing or economic valuation the Burgard-Kjaer semi-replication model (Burgard and Kjaer, 2013) can be extended. In the derivation that follows the notation is summarised in Tables 9.1 and 13.1. Given that this is a direct extension of the Burgard-Kjaer model, all of the consequences discussed above in Chapter 9 also follow here.

The derivation is identical to that described in section 9.4, with the addition of another term to account for the change in the cash account associated with regulatory capital,

$$d\bar{\beta}_K = -\gamma_K(t)Kdt. \tag{13.1}$$

This term reflects the treatment of capital as being borrowed from shareholders to support the derivative trading business and in return paying a cash fee in the form of the cost of capital

---

[2]Of course capital as funding may require a realignment of bank practice as otherwise the trading desk could end up overcharging for capital.

**TABLE 13.1** Notation used in the KVA model (in addition to that listed in Table 9.1).

| Parameter | Description |
|---|---|
| $K$ | Capital requirement |
| $d\bar{\beta}_K$ | Change in cash account associated with capital |
| $\gamma_K(t)$ | The cost of capital (the assets comprising the capital may themselves have a dividend yield and this can be incorporated into $\gamma_K(t)$) |
| $\phi$ | Fraction of capital available for derivative funding |

$\gamma_K(t)$. There is no term in $dJ_B$, so there is no impact on the default of the issuer. It can be argued that the same capital could also be used to compensate creditors in the event of issuer default and this could be modelled by adding a further jump term. However, this model assumes that this is already factored into the recovery rates on issuer bonds, $R_i$.[3]

The bond funding equation also needs to be modified to account for the potential use of capital as a source of derivative funding,

$$\hat{V} - X + \alpha_1 P_1 + \alpha_2 P_2 - \phi K = 0. \tag{13.2}$$

The change in the value of the derivative portfolio has the same form as earlier,

$$d\hat{V} = \frac{\partial \hat{V}}{\partial t} dt + \frac{1}{2}\sigma^2 S^2 \frac{\partial^2 \hat{V}}{\partial S^2} dt + \frac{\partial \hat{V}}{\partial S} dS + \Delta \hat{V}_B dJ_B + \Delta \hat{V}_C dJ_C. \tag{13.3}$$

The change in the value of the replicating portfolio, $\Pi$ is now given by

$$d\Pi(t) = \delta(t)dS(t) + \alpha_1(t)dP_1(t) + \alpha_2(t)dP_2(t) + \alpha_C(t)dP_C(t) \tag{13.4}$$
$$\delta(t)(\gamma - q)Sdt - \alpha_C q_C P_C dt - \gamma_K(t)Kdt.$$

Adding the derivative and replicating portfolio together gives

$$d\hat{V} + d\Pi = \left[ \frac{\partial \hat{V}}{\partial t} + \frac{1}{2}\sigma^2 S^2 \frac{\partial^2 \hat{V}}{\partial S^2} + \delta(\gamma_S - q_S) + \alpha_1 r_1 P_1 + \alpha_2 r_2 P_2 \right. \tag{13.5}$$

$$\left. + \alpha_C r_C P_C - \alpha_C q_C P_C - r_X X - \gamma_K K \right] dt$$

$$+ \epsilon_h dJ_B \tag{13.6}$$

$$\left[ \delta + \frac{\partial \hat{V}}{\partial S} \right] dS \tag{13.7}$$

$$\left[ g_C - \hat{V} - \alpha_C P_C \right] dJ_C. \tag{13.8}$$

---

[3]There is also no term in $dJ_C$ in this expression. Consideration was given to the possibility that capital could be used to offset losses in the event of counterparty default. This was rejected, however, as any such losses directly impact the balance sheet in any case. The trading desk could not use the capital to offset their own losses.

where

$$\epsilon_h = \left[ \Delta \hat{V}_B - (P - P_D) \right] \tag{13.9}$$
$$= g_B - X + P_D - \phi K$$
$$= \epsilon_{h_0} + \epsilon_{h_K}$$

is the hedging error on the default of the counterparty. The hedging error has been split into two parts, $\epsilon_{h_0}$ which does not depend on capital, and $\epsilon_{h_K}$ which does. Note that $\epsilon_{h_K} \neq -\phi K$ as the bond portfolio contains a dependence on capital through the derivative funding equation, and hence $P_D$ contains capital terms.

Assuming replication of the derivative by the hedging portfolio, except possibly at the default of the issuer, gives

$$d\hat{V} + d\Pi = 0 \tag{13.10}$$

The usual assumptions to eliminate other sources of risk give

$$\delta = -\frac{\partial \hat{V}}{\partial S} \tag{13.11}$$

$$\alpha_C P_C = g_C - \hat{V}. \tag{13.12}$$

Hence the first term in equation (13.5) gives a PDE for $\hat{V}$:

$$\frac{\partial \hat{V}}{\partial t} + \frac{1}{2}\sigma^2 S^2 \frac{\partial^2 \hat{V}}{\partial S^2} + \delta(\gamma_S - q_S) + \alpha_1 r_1 P_1 + \alpha_2 r_2 P_2 \tag{13.13}$$
$$+ \alpha_C r_C P_C - \alpha_C q_C P_C - r_X X - \gamma_K K = 0$$
$$\hat{V}(T, S) = H(S).$$

Using the bond funding equation (13.2) and with the yield of the issuer bonds, $r_i = r + (1 - R_i)\lambda_B$, and the definition of $\epsilon_h$ in equation (13.9) it is possible to derive the following expression,

$$\alpha_1 r_1 P_1 + \alpha_2 r_2 P_2 = rX - (r + \lambda_B)\hat{V} - \lambda_B(\epsilon_h - g_B) - r\phi K. \tag{13.14}$$

Substituting this into equation (13.13) gives

$$\frac{\partial \hat{V}}{\partial t} + \mathcal{A}_t \hat{V} - (r + \lambda_B + \lambda_C)\hat{V} \tag{13.15}$$
$$+ (g_c + \psi K)\lambda_C + g_B \lambda_B - \epsilon_h \lambda_B - s_X X - \gamma_K K + r\phi K = 0,$$

where the operator $\mathcal{A}_t$ defined as

$$\mathcal{A}_t := \frac{1}{2}\sigma^2 S^2 \frac{\partial^2}{\partial S^2} - (\gamma - q)S\frac{\partial}{\partial S}. \tag{13.16}$$

has been used.

Using the same approach as discussed earlier the value of the derivative can be written as

$$\hat{V} = V + U, \tag{13.17}$$

where $V$ satisfies the Black-Scholes PDE,

$$\frac{\partial V}{\partial t} + \mathcal{A}_t V - rV = 0. \tag{13.18}$$

This allows a PDE for $U$ to be identified,

$$\frac{\partial U}{\partial t} + \mathcal{A}_t U - (r + \lambda_B + \lambda_C)U = \tag{13.19}$$
$$-(g_c - V)\lambda_C - (g_B - V)\lambda_B + \epsilon_h \lambda_B + s_X X + \gamma_K K - r\phi K$$
$$U(T, S) = 0.$$

Applying the Feynman-Kac theorem gives

$$U = \text{CVA} + \text{DVA} + \text{FCA} + \text{COLVA} + \text{KVA}, \tag{13.20}$$

where

$$\text{CVA} = -\int_t^T \lambda_C(s)e^{-\int_t^s r(u)+\lambda_B(u)+\lambda_C(u)du} \mathbb{E}\left[V(s) - g_C(V(s), X(s))\right] ds \tag{13.21}$$

$$\text{DVA} = -\int_t^T \lambda_B(s)e^{-\int_t^s r(u)+\lambda_B(u)+\lambda_C(u)du} \mathbb{E}\left[V(s) - g_B(V(s), X(s))\right] ds \tag{13.22}$$

$$\text{FCA} = -\int_t^T \lambda_B(s)e^{-\int_t^s r(u)+\lambda_B(u)+\lambda_C(u)du} \mathbb{E}\left[\epsilon_h(s)\right] ds \tag{13.23}$$

$$\text{COLVA} = -\int_t^T s_X(s)e^{-\int_t^s r(u)+\lambda_B(u)+\lambda_C(u)du} \mathbb{E}\left[X(s)\right] ds \tag{13.24}$$

$$\text{KVA} = -\int_t^T (\gamma_K(s) - \phi r(s))e^{-\int_t^s r(u)+\lambda_B(u)+\lambda_C(u)du} \mathbb{E}\left[K(s)\right] ds \tag{13.25}$$

Here we see that the new KVA term takes the form of an integral over the expected capital requirement. The cost of capital is given by $(\gamma_K(t) - \phi r(t))$ where we see that the cost of capital is reduced if $\phi$ is non-zero. The expressions could have been written in a different form to reflect the use of capital as funding giving modified FCA and KVA terms,

$$\text{FCA}' = -\int_t^T (\lambda_B(s)\mathbb{E}\left[\epsilon_h(s)\right] - r(s)\phi\mathbb{E}_t\left[K(s)\right])e^{-\int_t^s r(u)+\lambda_B(u)+\lambda_C(u)du} ds \tag{13.26}$$

$$\text{KVA}' = -\int_t^T \gamma_K(u)e^{-\int_t^s r(u)+\lambda_B(u)+\lambda_C(u)du} \mathbb{E}\left[K(s)\right] ds. \tag{13.27}$$

Of course here we have derived KVA in the general context. It could equally have been specialised to any of the semi-replication approaches noted by Burgard and Kjaer and discussed in Chapter 9. It is straightforward to derive the corresponding KVA term in each case.

## 13.3  THE COST OF CAPITAL

The cost of capital is represented by $\gamma_K(t)$ and clearly it and the expected capital requirement profile are the major drivers of KVA. The question then is what value should this parameter take? In many ways this resembles the discussion of how to obtain the funding curve, as discussed in Chapter 11.

The cost of capital is the return that must be paid to shareholders for the use of their capital to support business activities. The shareholders, represented by the board of directors whom they appoint, choose to invest their capital in the derivatives business in order to achieve the required return. If the return is not achieved then the board of directors, acting on behalf of shareholders, may decide to invest their capital in other business lines. This means that the cost of capital depends on the choices made by the board in consultation with the shareholders and what the target return on capital is set at. Hence the cost of capital, like the cost of funding, is idiosyncratic. It is only externally visible to the extent that the board makes a statement about the return on capital; even then any such return target may not be exactly the target applied to a specific business within the firm as the cost of capital for different business lines may vary. A reasonable proxy for the return on capital is the return on equity target. A recent review of banks by Reboul et al. (2014) suggests a typical bank target of 10%, although this may vary through time and depend on the returns available on other assets.

As was noted earlier, the return on capital target may be modified if capital by the bank is held in liquid assets such as treasury bonds. Such assets will produce a yield themselves and this reduces the effective cost of capital.

## 13.4  KVA FOR MARKET RISK, COUNTERPARTY CREDIT RISK AND CVA REGULATORY CAPITAL

The critical element in calculating KVA from a modelling perspective is the generation of the expected capital profile, $\mathbb{E}_t[K(t)]$. $K$ is, with one notable exception that is discussed below, a function of state. Hence to calculate the expected capital profile requires a Monte Carlo simulation and a similar process to the way the other exposure profiles are calculated for other XVA terms.

$K$ was discussed extensively in Chapter 12 with a full review of the different metrologies to be used for market risk, CCR and CVA capital terms. The calculation of the expected capital profile using a Monte Carlo simulation is best divided between standardised and IMM approaches.

### 13.4.1  Standardised Approaches

**Market Risk**    The standardised approach to market risk capital depends primarily on the properties of the underlying trade and has very little state dependence. Considering the interest rate case presented in section 12.2.2, it is clear that the only state dependence of the capital on an interest rate swap will come from the floating coupon which, of course, varies in size. However, given that the floating coupon typically has a maturity of less than one year and that the weight values in Table 12.5 are the same irrespective of the coupon size in this case, then the table can be seen to be independent of market state. $K_{MR}$ remains time-dependent as the fixed leg maturity will roll down through the table at later observation points in the integral. Given the state independence, in the case of a standard interest rate swap *no Monte Carlo is needed to perform the calculation* and a time-dependent profile for $\mathbb{E}_t[K_{MR}(t)]$ can be determined directly.

**CCR and CVA**    Both current methodologies that are used to determine the EAD input to both CCR and CVA capital requirement calculations, CEM and standardised, use state-dependent formulas. The replacement methodology, the revised standardised approach, has the same property. Hence to calculate the expected cost of capital requires a Monte Carlo simulation in which the EAD and then the capital requirement is calculated using the appropriate formula in each Monte Carlo state on each simulation time step. Given that in all cases the EAD is a function of the trade valuation in each state and the properties of the residual trade at that point in time, this can be calculated using the same Monte Carlo simulation as was used to calculate the expected exposure profiles. In practice this resolves to a slightly more complex *payout* formula applied at each step of the XVA Monte Carlo. Given that the formulae for capital remain relatively straightforward this will not add significantly to the computational cost of an XVA calculation.

### 13.4.2  IMM Approaches

**Market Risk**    The internal model method for market risk capital currently uses VaR/SVaR and will move to the closely related expected shortfall measure under the *fundamental review of the trading book* (BCBS, 2013c). As such the calculation of the expected capital profile presents the same problem as was identified in the context of MVA in Chapter 10. Hence the same approach, using the *Longstaff-Schwartz Augmented Compression*, can be applied here.

**CCR and CVA**    Both CCR and CVA under the internal model method rely on the calculation of an expected exposure profile using the institution's approved exposure engine, itself a Monte Carlo model and typically calibrated historically. Hence to calculate CCR and CVA KVA terms under IMM using brute force would require Monte Carlo within Monte Carlo. The solution to this particular problem is not straightforward but an approach where Longstaff-Schwartz is used to estimate future CCR and CVA capital requirements would appear viable. The Longstaff-Schwartz approach has been long used to estimate XVA and is used by market practioners in similar contexts.

## 13.5  THE SIZE OF KVA

How big is KVA compared to the other XVA terms? Choosing the case of semi-replication with no shortfall at own default, as described in Chapter 9, the first issuer bond is chosen to have zero recovery and used to hedge the difference between $\hat{V}$ and $V$. The second issuer bond, $P_2$ has recovery $R_2 = R_B$ and the hedge position is determined by the bond funding equation

(13.2). Hence we have

$$\alpha_1 P_1 = -U \tag{13.28}$$

$$\alpha_2 P_2 = -(V - \phi K). \tag{13.29}$$

The value of the issuer bond portfolio in default is then given by

$$P_D = -R_B(V - \phi K) \tag{13.30}$$

and hence the hedge error is given by

$$\epsilon_h = (1 - R_B)[V^+ - \phi K]. \tag{13.31}$$

For regular bilateral close-out conditions with $g_B$ and $g_C$ taking the form

$$g_B = (V - X)^+ + R_B(V - X)^- + X \tag{13.32}$$

$$g_C = R_C(V - X)^+ + (V - X)^- + X, \tag{13.33}$$

and assuming that the trade is uncollateralised so that $X = 0$ gives the following XVA integrals,

$$\text{CVA} = -(1 - R_C) \int_t^T \lambda_C(s) e^{-\int_t^s \lambda_B(u) + \lambda_C(u) du} \mathbb{E}\left[ e^{-\int_t^s r(u) du} (V(u))^+ \right] ds \tag{13.34}$$

$$\text{DVA} = -(1 - R_B) \int_t^T \lambda_B(s) e^{-\int_t^s \lambda_B(u) + \lambda_C(u) du} \mathbb{E}\left[ e^{-\int_t^s r(u) du} (V(u))^- \right] ds \tag{13.35}$$

$$\text{FCA} = -(1 - R_B) \int_t^T \lambda_B(s) e^{-\int_t^s \lambda_B(u) + \lambda_C(u) du} \mathbb{E}\left[ e^{-\int_t^s r(u) du} (V(u))^+ \right] ds \tag{13.36}$$

$$\text{KVA} = -\int_t^T \gamma_K(s) e^{-\int_t^s \lambda_B(u) + \lambda_C(u) du} \mathbb{E}\left[ e^{-\int_t^s r(u) du} K(s) - r_B(u)\phi \right] ds, \tag{13.37}$$

where the integral over the short rate has been moved inside the expectation as interest rates are now stochastic. While the XVA terms have not been explicitly derived in the presence of stochastic interest rates, intuitively it should be clear that this is the form that the expressions will take as the CVA and DVA terms are identical with those derived using an expectation-led approach in Chapter 3. It is possible to derive this explicitly if one makes interest rates stochastic and chooses a dynamic for those rates. The nature of the Feynman-Kac theorem means that any diffusive processes will lead, via Itô's lemma, to the same form of PDE and hence the same form of XVA. Indeed the Feynman-Kac theorem can itself be generalised to multi-dimensional stochastic processes and jump-diffusion, although in the latter case a PIDE is the equivalent form not a PDE.

Consider the XVA on a 10-year GBP interest rate swap with semi-annual payment schedules and a fixed rate of 2.7%. The issuer spread is assumed to be 100bp for all maturities and the issuer recovery rate is 40%. The XVA is calculated for four different counterparties, with ratings and spreads given by Table 13.2. The counterparty recovery rate is also assumed to be 40% in all cases.

**TABLE 13.2** Counterparty data for the four example counterparties.

| Rating | Spread (bp) | Standardised Risk-Weight | CVA Risk-Weight $w_i$ |
|--------|-------------|--------------------------|----------------------|
| AAA | 30 | 20% | 0.7% |
| A | 75 | 50% | 0.8% |
| BB | 250 | 100% | 2% |
| CCC | 750 | 150% | 10% |

The examples are calculated assuming that the issuer calculates market risk capital using the standardised approach and uses CEM to estimate the EAD. The CCR is then calculated using the standardised approach with external ratings, while the CVA capital is calculated using the standardised approach with the large number of counterparties approximation as given by equation (12.14). The issuer is assumed to hold the minimum capital ratio requirement of 8% and that the issuer cost of capital is 10%.

The results of the XVA calculations are given in Table 13.3. The results immediately show that the KVA term is similar in size to the other XVA terms. The CCR and CVA terms increase as the counterparty credit rating worsens, as expected. The market risk component is larger than the other terms but this reflects the fact that the trade is completely unhedged (see the discussion on CVA risk warehousing in section 14.4). In practice a bank would be unlikely to run a position like this unhedged and so the market risk capital is artificially large. The decline in the market risk component as the counterparty credit risk increases reflects the extra "discounting" effect given by the term $e^{-\int_t^s \lambda_B(u)+\lambda_C(u)du}$ as the counterparty hazard rate increases. The cases with $\phi = 1$ show a reduced KVA by around 25%.

**TABLE 13.3** XVA results for a single interest rate swap. The results are quoted in bp of the trade notional.

| $\phi$ | Swap | Rating | CVA | DVA | FCA | KVA MR | KVA CCR | KVA CVA | Total | IR01 |
|--------|------|--------|-----|-----|-----|----|-----|-----|-------|------|
| 0 | Pay | AAA | −4 | 39 | −14 | −262 | −3 | −9 | −253 | 9.50 |
| 0 | Pay | A | −10 | 38 | −14 | −256 | −8 | −10 | −259 | 9.62 |
| 0 | Pay | BB | −31 | 33 | −12 | −234 | −14 | −22 | −279 | 10.03 |
| 0 | Pay | CCC | −68 | 24 | −9 | −185 | −16 | −87 | −341 | 11.29 |
| 1 | Pay | AAA | −4 | 39 | −14 | −184 | −2 | −6 | −170 | 9.47 |
| 1 | Pay | A | −10 | 38 | −14 | −180 | −4 | −7 | −176 | 9.56 |
| 1 | Pay | BB | −31 | 33 | −12 | −166 | −7 | −16 | −198 | 9.91 |
| 1 | Pay | CCC | −68 | 24 | −9 | −134 | −8 | −63 | −260 | 10.97 |
| 0 | Rec | AAA | −12 | 14 | −39 | −262 | −7 | −18 | −325 | −9.61 |
| 0 | Rec | A | −29 | 14 | −38 | −256 | −18 | −20 | −347 | −9.80 |
| 0 | Rec | BB | −84 | 12 | −33 | −234 | −31 | −46 | −416 | −10.47 |
| 0 | Rec | CCC | −177 | 9 | −24 | −185 | −34 | −174 | −587 | −12.37 |
| 1 | Rec | AAA | −12 | 14 | −39 | −184 | −4 | −12 | −237 | −9.55 |
| 1 | Rec | A | −29 | 14 | −38 | −180 | −9 | −14 | −256 | −9.70 |
| 1 | Rec | BB | −84 | 12 | −33 | −166 | −16 | −32 | −318 | −10.28 |
| 1 | Rec | CCC | −177 | 9 | −24 | −134 | −18 | −123 | −467 | −11.88 |

**TABLE 13.4** XVA results for an interest rate swap which has been hedged with a back-to-back swap under a perfect CSA.

| $\phi$ | Swap | Rating | CVA | DVA | FCA | MR | KVA CCR | CVA | Total | IR01 |
|---|---|---|---|---|---|---|---|---|---|---|
| 0 | Pay | AAA | −4 | 39 | −14 | 0 | −3 | −9 | 9 | 0.61 |
| 0 | Pay | A | −10 | 38 | −14 | 0 | −8 | −10 | −3 | 0.72 |
| 0 | Pay | BB | −31 | 33 | −12 | 0 | −14 | −22 | −45 | 1.13 |
| 0 | Pay | CCC | −68 | 24 | −9 | 0 | −16 | −87 | −156 | 2.39 |
| 1 | Pay | AAA | −4 | 39 | −14 | 0 | −2 | −6 | 13 | 0.57 |
| 1 | Pay | A | −10 | 38 | −14 | 0 | −4 | −7 | 3 | 0.66 |
| 1 | Pay | BB | −31 | 33 | −12 | 0 | −7 | −16 | −32 | 1.01 |
| 1 | Pay | CCC | −68 | 24 | −9 | 0 | −8 | −63 | −125 | 2.07 |
| 0 | Rec | AAA | −12 | 14 | −39 | 0 | −7 | −18 | −63 | −0.71 |
| 0 | Rec | A | −29 | 14 | −38 | 0 | −18 | −20 | −91 | −0.90 |
| 0 | Rec | BB | −84 | 12 | −33 | 0 | −31 | −46 | −182 | −1.57 |
| 0 | Rec | CCC | −177 | 9 | −24 | 0 | −34 | −176 | −402 | −3.47 |
| 1 | Rec | AAA | −12 | 14 | −39 | 0 | −4 | −12 | −53 | −0.65 |
| 1 | Rec | A | −29 | 14 | −38 | 0 | −9 | −14 | −76 | −0.80 |
| 1 | Rec | BB | −84 | 12 | −33 | 0 | −16 | −32 | −153 | −1.38 |
| 1 | Rec | CCC | −177 | 9 | −24 | 0 | −18 | −123 | −333 | −2.98 |

The second example introduces a back-to-back market risk hedge for the interest rate swap only. The second opposite interest rate swap offsets the original trade perfectly and is traded with a separate counterparty under a perfect CSA agreement. Such a perfect CSA agreement has instantaneous transfer of collateral, no threshold and no minimum transfer amount and hence there is no CVA, DVA or FCA for this additional trade. However, the trade does give rise to additional capital requirements for the CCR and CVA terms under the standardised approaches. The market risk capital of the whole portfolio is now zero as both trades can be explicitly removed from market risk capital when traded back-to-back in this way. The results of this second example are given in Table 13.4. In this table a further column has been added for the net portfolio IR01,[4] which is *not zero*. The XVA terms for the portfolio themselves have interest rate risk, even if, for the purposes of the capital calculation, the combined portfolio has no risk. The optimal market risk (capital) hedge leaves an open risk position.

The final example uses the same approach as the last case with a back-to-back hedging swap, except this time the notional of the hedge swap has been adjusted to reduce the net portfolio IR01 to zero at trade inception. The portfolio including all XVA terms is fully hedged. However, because the trade and hedge are not identical and opposite they will generate a small amount of market risk capital. The results can be found in Table 13.5.

---

[4]The IR01 is the absolute change in value for a one basis point move in the yield curve.

**TABLE 13.5** XVA results for an interest rate swap which has been hedged with a back-to-back swap under a perfect CSA and the size of the swap is adjusted to give zero IR01 at trade inception.

| $\phi$ | Swap | Rating | CVA | DVA | FCA | KVA MR | KVA CCR | KVA CVA | Total | IR01 |
|---|---|---|---|---|---|---|---|---|---|---|
| 0 | Pay | AAA | −4 | 39 | −14 | −17 | −4 | −12 | −13 | 0 |
| 0 | Pay | A | −10 | 38 | −14 | −20 | −11 | −13 | −30 | 0 |
| 0 | Pay | BB | −31 | 33 | −12 | −28 | −20 | −31 | −88 | 0 |
| 0 | Pay | CCC | −68 | 24 | −9 | −45 | −22 | −127 | −249 | 0 |
| 1 | Pay | AAA | −4 | 39 | −14 | −12 | −3 | −8 | −1 | 0 |
| 1 | Pay | A | −10 | 38 | −14 | −13 | −5 | −9 | −14 | 0 |
| 1 | Pay | BB | −31 | 33 | −12 | −18 | −9 | −23 | −59 | 0 |
| 1 | Pay | CCC | −68 | 24 | −9 | −29 | −12 | −92 | −187 | 0 |
| 0 | Rec | AAA | −12 | 14 | −39 | −20 | −8 | −21 | −87 | 0 |
| 0 | Rec | A | −29 | 14 | −38 | −25 | −20 | −23 | −122 | 0 |
| 0 | Rec | BB | −84 | 12 | −33 | −40 | −36 | −54 | −234 | 0 |
| 0 | Rec | CCC | −177 | 9 | −24 | −67 | −41 | −213 | −512 | 0 |
| 1 | Rec | AAA | −12 | 14 | −39 | −13 | −4 | −14 | −69 | 0 |
| 1 | Rec | A | −29 | 14 | −38 | −16 | −10 | −16 | −95 | 0 |
| 1 | Rec | BB | −84 | 12 | −33 | −25 | −18 | −38 | −186 | 0 |
| 1 | Rec | CCC | −177 | 9 | −24 | −42 | −21 | −151 | −405 | 0 |

## 13.6  CONCLUSION: KVA

This chapter has derived a comprehensive model for XVA including a new term to include capital in derivative pricing, KVA. Approaches to the calculation of KVA have also been developed. Practical examples of KVA on an interest rate swap have demonstrated that KVA is broadly similar in magnitude to CVA, DVA and FVA. It is also clear that while KVA has been developed in the context of a single portfolio, some elements of the capital framework apply at portfolio level. Hence a full portfolio level model for KVA is required and this is the subject of Chapter 15. Note also that the model assumes that the credit risk has been perfectly hedged and that this assumption is relaxed in section 14.4.

# CHAPTER 14

# CVA Risk Warehousing and Tax Valuation Adjustment (TVA)

*Estragon: He should be here.*
*Vladimir: He didn't say for sure he'd come.*
*Estragon: And if he doesn't come?*
*Vladimir: We'll come back tomorrow.*
*Estragon: And then the day after tomorrow.*

—Samuel Becket
*Waiting for Godot (1953)*

## 14.1 RISK WAREHOUSING XVA

Whether by choice or not risk warehousing is an element of all XVA management. This chapter explores the consequence of risk warehousing, focusing on the warehousing of credit risk and to do so follows the approach of Kenyon and Green (2015c). As is described, one consequence of risk warehousing is the presence of profits and losses, which are subject to taxation. This leads directly to the introduction of *Tax Valuation Adjustment (TVA)*.

## 14.2 TAXATION

Taxation has rarely been tackled within quantitative finance save for the papers by Kenyon and Kenyon (2013) and Kenyon and Green (2015c), with discussions on taxation largely limited to corporate finance. It is in fact easy to see why this is the case as quantitative finance is built on replication in which a derivative is fully hedged and hence there are no profits or losses. However, once profits and losses can occur taxation will follow and hence should be included in the model. If a bank warehouses counterparty risk then profits and losses will follow and so in this case taxation must be considered. It is important to note that while profits will be taxed, in many jurisdictions losses give rise to future tax benefits. The details of any taxation will of course depend on the tax law operating within the geographic regions in which the bank operates. The effect of including tax is to give rise to a further XVA, *Tax Valuation Adjustment (TVA)*.

In the case of risk warehousing tax will come into play in two different situations. Firstly, any cash flow stream that is paid to shareholders as a return on capital will, in general, be treated as a profit and therefore be subject to tax. Secondly, when a default occurs and the portfolio is not fully hedged against the risk of default and the loss on default, a loss will occur. This loss will create a deferred tax asset that may be used to offset tax that might otherwise be due in the future.

## 14.3  CVA HEDGING AND REGULATORY CAPITAL

Given that under risk warehousing not all of the CVA VaR will be hedged, a CVA VaR capital requirement will appear under Basel III. To establish the link between CVA, KVA and TVA it is therefore important to explicitly include the impact that choosing to hedge or not hedge CVA has on capital requirements. Hence the impact of CVA hedging on regulatory capital is made explicit. To simpify matters a counterparty bond will be used as the credit hedging instrument and assumed to be eligible for capital relief under Basel III.

## 14.4  WAREHOUSING CVA RISK AND DOUBLE SEMI-REPLICATION

This section follows the approach of Kenyon and Green (2015c) closely, which itself follows and extends Burgard and Kjaer (2013) and Green, Kenyon and Dennis (2014) as discussed in Chapters 9 and 13 respectively. The semi-replication approach is extended to double semi-replication where now the counterparty default is only partially hedged. As in earlier chapters the aim is to find the economic value of the portfolio, $\hat{V}$. The additional notation is given in Table 14.1.

**TABLE 14.1**  Notation used in the CVA risk warehousing model (in addition to that listed in Tables 9.1 and 13.1).

| Parameter | Description |
|---|---|
| $E$ | Cash flow liable to tax as a function of time |
| $d\bar{\beta}_E$ | Growth in the cash account associated with tax (prior to rebalancing) |
| $\lambda_C^{\mathbb{P}}$ | Physical measure hazard rate for counterparty C |
| $\tilde{\lambda}_C$ | Effective hazard rate under semi-replication |
| $\gamma_E$ | Effective tax rate |
| $\Delta_E$ | Tax effect on counterparty default |
| $\bar{\Delta}_E$ | Tax effect on counterparty default when $\psi = 0$ |
| $\epsilon_C$ | Hedging error on counterparty default |
| $\psi$ | Fraction of counterparty bond $P_C$ used in the hedge portfolio relative to full hedge |
| $K_U; K_R$ | Capital requirement with no CVA hedging; Capital relief from 100% hedging |
| $\Gamma_C$ | Compensator of the counterparty jump-to-default |
| $m_{\lambda_C}$ | Market price of default risk for C |

The dynamics of the underlying assets remain unchanged from Chapter 9:

$$dS = \mu S dt + \sigma S dW \tag{14.1}$$
$$dP_C = r_C P_C dt - P_C dJ_C \tag{14.2}$$
$$dP_i = r_i P_i dt - (1 - R_i) P_i dJ_B \quad \text{for} \quad i \in \{1, 2\}, \tag{14.3}$$

as do the close-out conditions,

$$\hat{V}(t, S, 1, 0) = g_B(M_B, X) \tag{14.4}$$
$$\hat{V}(t, S, 0, 1) = g_C(M_C, X), \tag{14.5}$$

where the usual assumption is that

$$g_B = (V - X)^+ + R_B(V - X)^- + X \tag{14.6}$$
$$g_C = R_C(V - X)^+ + (V - X)^- + X. \tag{14.7}$$

The derivative funding equation takes the form in Chapter 13,

$$\hat{V} - X + \alpha_1 P_1 + \alpha_2 P_2 - \phi K = 0. \tag{14.8}$$

The growth in the cash accounts associated with the stock and collateral are unchanged:

$$d\bar{\beta}_S(t) = \delta(t)(\gamma - q)S dt \tag{14.9}$$
$$d\bar{\beta}_X(t) = -r_X X dt. \tag{14.10}$$

The growth in the cash account associated with the counterparty bond is modified with two changes:

$$d\bar{\beta}_C = \psi \alpha_C q_C P_C dt - \Gamma_C dt \quad \text{where} \quad \psi \in [0, 1]. \tag{14.11}$$

Firstly the bond holding is now given by $\psi \alpha_C$ to reflect the partial hedging of the counterparty risk, with $\alpha_C$ being the bond holding of a full hedge, and $\psi$ representing the fraction of the full hedge that is used. Secondly, a compensator, $\Gamma_C$ has been added for the losses that will occur should the counterparty default and only partial hedging has been performed. The growth in the cash account associated with the capital requirement is also modified to explicitly represent the capital relief associated with CVA hedging:

$$d\bar{\beta}_K = -\gamma_K(K^U - \psi K^R)dt. \tag{14.12}$$

$K^U$ is the capital requirement with no hedging and $K^R$ is the capital relief associated with 100% hedging. As noted earlier, the assumption is that the risk bond is eligible as a hedging instrument under Basel III. Note also that for hedging with CDS the amount of relief is determined by the creditworthiness of the CDS issuer. Finally a further cash account is added to the model to account for tax,

$$d\bar{\beta}_E = -\gamma_E(t)E(t)dt + \Delta_E dJ_C. \tag{14.13}$$

The first term in this expression reflects the tax liability (credit) due to tax prior to default, while the second is the tax liability (credit) on counterparty default. Tax effects on issuer default are assumed to be included in the issuer recovery $R_i$.

The application of Itô's lemma gives the same expression for $\hat{V}$ as before:

$$d\hat{V} = \frac{\partial \hat{V}}{\partial t}dt + \frac{1}{2}\sigma^2 S^2 \frac{\partial^2 \hat{V}}{\partial S^2}dt + \frac{\partial \hat{V}}{\partial S}dS + \Delta\hat{V}_B dJ_B + \Delta\hat{V}_C dJ_C. \tag{14.14}$$

The change in the replicating portfolio now has extra terms:

$$d\Pi = \delta dS + \delta(\gamma - q)Sdt + \alpha_1 dP_1 + \alpha_2 dP_2 + \psi\alpha_C dP_C - \psi\alpha_C q_C P_C dt \tag{14.15}$$
$$- r_X X dt - \gamma_K(K^U - \psi K^R)dt - \Gamma_C dt - \gamma_E E dt + \Delta_E dJ_C.$$

Combining the change in the derivative and replicating portfolio gives

$$d\hat{V} + d\Pi = \left[\frac{\partial \hat{V}}{\partial t} + \frac{1}{2}\sigma^2 S^2 \frac{\partial^2 \hat{V}}{\partial S^2} + \delta(\gamma_S - q_S) + \alpha_1 r_1 P_1 + \alpha_2 r_2 P_2 - r_X X \right. \tag{14.16}$$

$$\left. + \psi\alpha_C r_C P_C - \psi\alpha_C q_C P_C - \gamma_K(K^U - \psi K^R) - \Gamma_C - \gamma_E E \right]dt$$

$$+ \epsilon_B dJ_B + \epsilon_C dJ_C$$

$$\left[\delta + \frac{\partial \hat{V}}{\partial S}\right]dS.$$

The hedging error on own default takes the same form as earlier,

$$\epsilon_B = \left[\Delta V_B - (P - P_D)\right] \tag{14.17}$$
$$= g_B - X + P_D - \phi K$$
$$= \epsilon_{B_0} + \epsilon_{B_K},$$

where the second term on the last line contains all of the capital-related terms (see Chapter 13). There is now a hedging error on the default of the counterparty given by

$$\epsilon_C = \Delta V_C - \psi\alpha_C P_C + \Delta_E \tag{14.18}$$
$$= g_C - \hat{V} - \psi\alpha_C P_C$$
$$= (1 - \psi)(g_C - \hat{V} + \bar{\Delta}_E),$$

where $\alpha_C P_C = g_V - \hat{V}$ and the tax effect is assumed to scale linearly with the hedge amount so that $\Delta_E = (1 - \psi)\bar{\Delta}_E$.

The compensator process must now be defined and here it is chosen to price in the expected cost under the physical measure so that

$$\Gamma_C = -\mathbb{E}_t^{\mathbb{P}}[\epsilon_C dJ_C] \tag{14.19}$$
$$= -(1 - \psi)(g_C - \hat{V})\lambda_C^{\mathbb{P}},$$

where $\lambda_C^{\mathbb{P}}$ is the physical measure hazard rate. The hazard rate is the risk-neutral measure that takes the form used in Chapters 9 and 13, $\lambda_C = r_C - q_C$. The physical measure and risk-neutral measure hazard rates are related through the market price of risk,

$$
\begin{aligned}
\lambda_C^{\mathbb{P}} &= \lambda_C - m_{\lambda_C} \\
&= \lambda_C(1 - \xi).
\end{aligned}
\tag{14.20}
$$

It is useful to define an effective hazard rate, $\tilde{\lambda}_C$, as the hedge weighted sum of the risk-neutral and physical measure hazard rates,

$$
\begin{aligned}
\tilde{\lambda}_C &= \psi \lambda_C + (1 - \psi)\lambda_C^{\mathbb{P}} \\
&= \psi \lambda_C + (1 - \psi)(1 - \xi)\lambda_C.
\end{aligned}
\tag{14.21}
$$

In the limits of full and no hedging the effective hazard rate ranges between the risk-neutral hazard rate and physical measure hazard rates,

$$
\begin{aligned}
\psi &= 1 \quad \tilde{\lambda}_C = \lambda_C \\
\psi &= 0 \quad \tilde{\lambda}_C = \lambda_C^{\mathbb{P}}.
\end{aligned}
\tag{14.22}
$$

Using these results leads to the following PDE under double semi-replication:

$$
\begin{aligned}
0 = {} & \frac{\partial \hat{V}}{\partial t} + \mathcal{A}_t \hat{V} - (r + \lambda_B + \tilde{\lambda}_C)\hat{V} + \tilde{\lambda}_C g_C + \lambda_B g_B - \epsilon_B \lambda_B \\
& - s_X X - (\gamma_K - r\phi)(K^U - \psi K^R) - \gamma_E E - \lambda_C(1 - \xi)(1 - \psi)\bar{\Delta}_E
\end{aligned}
\tag{14.23}
$$
$$
\hat{V}(T, S) = H(S),
$$

where the operator $\mathcal{A}_t$ defined by

$$
\mathcal{A}_t := \frac{1}{2}\sigma^2 S^2 \frac{\partial^2}{\partial S^2} - (\gamma - q)S\frac{\partial}{\partial S}.
$$

has been used, and the following expression has been derived from the derivative funding equation (14.8), with the issuer bond yield $r_i = r + (1 - R_i)\lambda_B$ and the issuer hedging error from equation (14.17),

$$
\alpha_1 r_1 P_1 + \alpha_2 r_2 P_2 = rX - (r + \lambda_B)U - \lambda_B(\epsilon_h - g_B) - r\phi(K^U - \psi K^R).
\tag{14.24}
$$

Using the same approach as in Chapters 9 and 13 yields the following PDE for $U$:

$$
\begin{aligned}
& \frac{\partial U}{\partial t} + \mathcal{A}_t U - (r + \lambda_B + \tilde{\lambda}_C)U = V\tilde{\lambda}_C - \tilde{\lambda}_C g_C + V\lambda_B - \lambda_B g_B + \epsilon_B \lambda_B \\
& + s_X X + (\gamma_K - r\phi)(K^U - \psi K^R) + \gamma_E E + \lambda_C(1 - \xi)(1 - \psi)\bar{\Delta}_E \\
& U(T, S) = 0.
\end{aligned}
\tag{14.25}
$$

Applying the Feynman-Kac theorem gives the integral form

$$U = \text{CVA} + \text{DVA} + \text{FCA} + \text{COLVA} + \text{KVA} + \text{TVA} \tag{14.26}$$

where

$$\text{CVA} = -\int_t^T \tilde{\lambda}_C(s) e^{-\int_t^s r(u)+\lambda_B(u)+\tilde{\lambda}_C(u)du} \mathbb{E}\left[V(s) - g_C(V(s), X(s))\right] ds \tag{14.27}$$

$$\text{DVA} = -\int_t^T \lambda_B(s) e^{-\int_t^s r(u)+\lambda_B(u)+\tilde{\lambda}_C(u)du} \mathbb{E}\left[V(s) - g_B(V(s), X(s))\right] ds \tag{14.28}$$

$$\text{FCA} = -\int_t^T \lambda_B(s) e^{-\int_t^s r(u)+\lambda_B(u)+\tilde{\lambda}_C(u)du} \mathbb{E}\left[\epsilon_{B_0}(s)\right] ds \tag{14.29}$$

$$\text{COLVA} = -\int_t^T s_X(s) e^{-\int_t^s r(u)+\lambda_B(u)+\tilde{\lambda}_C(u)du} \mathbb{E}\left[X(s)\right] ds \tag{14.30}$$

$$\text{KVA} = -\int_t^T e^{-\int_t^s r(u)+\lambda_B(u)+\tilde{\lambda}_C(u)du} \tag{14.31}$$

$$\times \mathbb{E}\left[(\gamma_K(s) - \phi r(s))(K^U(s) - \psi K^R(u)) + \lambda_B \epsilon_{B_K}(u)\right] ds$$

$$\text{TVA} = -\int_t^T e^{-\int_t^s r(u)+\lambda_B(u)+\tilde{\lambda}_C(u)du} \mathbb{E}\left[\gamma_E E(u) + \lambda_C(1 - \xi)(1 - \psi)\bar{\Delta}_E\right] ds. \tag{14.32}$$

The tax terms occur because of profits and losses so that

$$E(t) = \gamma_K(t)(K^U(t) - K^R(t)) + \mathbb{1}_{\text{Tax}} \lambda_B(t)\epsilon_B(t) \tag{14.33}$$

$$\bar{\Delta}_E = -\gamma_E(t)(V(t) - g_C(V(t), X(y))), \tag{14.34}$$

where $\mathbb{1}_{\text{Tax}}$ is an indicator function indicating the behaviour of the local tax authority.

The set of equations (14.27) through (14.34) can now be examined in detail.

- The first observation is that aside from the addition of TVA, the equations have the same basic form as found in Chapter 13, although in the case of KVA itself the effect of CVA is now explicit.
- The introduction of double semi-replication has, however, seen the risk-neutral hazard rate $\lambda_C$ replaced by the effective hazard rate $\tilde{\lambda}_C$.
- The market price of risk can be either positive or negative, although typically the market price of risk will be positive and the physical measure probability of default will be lower than the risk-neutral one. When this is the case $\tilde{\lambda}_C < \lambda_C$. The size and sign of market price of risk will be a function of the business cycle. This would lead to a lower CVA value from this model, although the conditioning effect through $e^{-\int_t^u \tilde{\lambda}_C(s)ds}$ would increase the size of the remaining terms. As discussed in Kenyon and Green (2013a), the CDS price contains an element that can be associated with CVA capital hedging activity and this can be considered part of the market price of risk.
- TVA describes the cost associated with taxation.
- The running taxation described in equation (14.33) applies to the total capital, whether it is used for funding purposes or not so that the term in $\phi r$ does not appear.

- The indicator function $\mathbb{1}_{\text{Tax}}$ describes the choice of the taxation authority to recognise cash flows accrued relative to own default. If the tax authority follows accounting treatments described in FASB (2006) or IASB (2012) then $\mathbb{1}_{\text{Tax}} = 1$.
- Equation (14.34) describes the tax impact of counterparty default.

Overall it should be apparent that the introduction of double semi-replication has led to a set of equation where there is a potential optimisation. Reducing the hedge amount can lower the CVA, however this leads to additional capital requirements and gains/losses which in turn are taxed. If the CVA desk has a choice of whether or not to hedge it is precisely this risk-reward assessment that will determine the hedging strategy.

## CHAPTER 15

# Portfolio KVA and the Leverage Ratio

*When you combine ignorance and leverage, you get some pretty interesting results.*
—Warren Buffett
*American business magnate, investor, and philanthropist (1930–)*

## 15.1 THE NEED FOR A PORTFOLIO LEVEL MODEL

Up to this point in the book, all calculations have been formulated at netting set or counterparty level.[1] This reflects the fact that in the models presented to date there have only been terms relating directly to the two counterparties involved in the portfolio of transactions. As a result it is common for XVA calculation platforms to be aligned to netting set level (see Chapter 20). However, the regulatory capital framework includes items that are calculated at bank-wide level, in particular the *leverage ratio*. To deal with these the model must be expanded to portfolio level.

KVA or Capital Valuation Adjustment was introduced by Chapter 13 and Green, Kenyon and Dennis (2014). The KVA model extended the Burgard-Kjaer semi-replication model of CVA and FVA to include capital at netting set level and in doing so explicitly assumed that regulatory capital can be allocated down to netting sets. However, it is clear that some elements of the regulatory capital framework are calculated at entity level rather than per counterparty (BCBS, 2006b; BCBS, 2011b) and hence the corresponding KVA term includes elements that are calculated across all counterparties. The *leverage ratio* for example, is clearly a function of all bank positions, while market risk is calculated per asset class whether on a standardised basis or through IMM.

In Chapter 13, shareholders' capital was also assumed to be readily available in any quantity at treasury level to be allocated down to individual businesses in return for the payment of a return $\gamma_K$. In practice, however, shareholder capital cannot be increased or decreased on demand. Additional equity capital is normally obtained through a block share sale either as a placement or through a rights issue, a relatively rare and expensive operation for a company. Equity capital can be returned to shareholders through stock buy backs and

---

[1] This chapter is based on Green and Kenyon (2014b).

dividend payments, although these operations are highly regulated and certainly do not occur on demand when capital becomes surplus. It is therefore arguable that the cost of capital at portfolio level should depend on the overall capital requirement in some way and not be the constant $\gamma_K$ assumed in Chapter 13.

As was made clear in the examples of Chapter 13, a trade and hedge as a pair will imply two counterparties and capital charges due to both transactions. The hedge attracts capital and hence to hedge the overall portfolio will require an iterative process to neutralise the risk of the whole portfolio including KVA across all counterparty positions. It is not possible, therefore, to consider counterparty level positions independently. Capital links the positions of the bank and hence demands a portfolio level treatment.

This chapter provides a portfolio level calculation of KVA, with particular emphasis on the *leverage ratio*. It also proposes an algorithm that allows the netting set to remain the primary unit of calculation with the addition of one Monte Carlo simulation that spans all asset classes but that does not require all trades to be valued within it. To achieve this the algorithm makes extensive use of Longstaff-Schwartz regression, introduced in Chapter 10.

## 15.2 PORTFOLIO LEVEL SEMI-REPLICATION

To proceed the semi-replication PDE model, as discussed in Chapters 3, 9 and 13, is further extended to the case with M counterparties and N assets. A summary of the notation can be found in Table 15.1. The sign convention is that the value of a cash amount is positive if received by the issuer. The dynamics of the underlying assets are

$$dS_i = \mu_{S_i} S_i dt + \sigma_{S_i} S_i dW_i \tag{15.1}$$

$$dP_{C_j} = r_{C_j} P_{C_j} dt - P_{C_j} dJ_{C_j} \tag{15.2}$$

$$dP_k = r_k P_k dt - (1 - R_k) P_k dJ_B. \tag{15.3}$$

On the default of the issuer, $B$, and counterparty $C_j$, the value of the derivatives book takes the following values:

$$\hat{V}(t, S, 1, 0) = g_B(M_B(V_1, \ldots, V_M), X_1, \ldots, X_M) \tag{15.4}$$

$$\hat{V}(t, S, 0, J) = g_{C_j}(M_{C_j}, X_J) + \hat{V}^{-J}(t, S). \tag{15.5}$$

where $\hat{V}^{-J}(t, S)$ is the value of the derivative portfolio after the default of counterparty $J$, excluding the positions with counterparty $J$, and $S$ is the state vector of the stocks.

Again, the $g$ functions allow different close-out conditions to be considered with the usual close-out assumption that

$$g_B = \sum_{j=1}^{M}(V_j - X_j)^+ + R_B \sum_{j=1}^{M}(V_j - X_j)^- + \sum_{j=1}^{M} X_j \tag{15.6}$$

$$g_{C_j} = R_{C_j}(V_j - X_j)^+ + (V_j - X_j)^- + X_j. \tag{15.7}$$

**TABLE 15.1** A summary of the notation used in the portfolio KVA model, which is an extension of that used in Chapters 3, 9 and 13.

| Parameter | Description |
|---|---|
| $\hat{V}(t, S)$ | The value of the derivative or derivative portfolio |
| $V$ | The risk-free value of all the derivatives with all counterparties |
| $U$ | The valuation adjustment for all counterparties |
| $V_j$ | The risk-free value of derivatives with counterparty $j$, so $\sum_{j=l}^{M} V_j = V$ |
| $U_j$ | The valuation adjustment for counterparty $j$ |
| $X_j$ | Collateral associated with counterparty $j$ portfolio |
| $K$ | Capital requirement |
| $K_j$ | Capital requirement attributed to counterparty $j$ |
| $\Pi$ | Replicating portfolio |
| $S_i$ | Underlying stock $i$ |
| $\mu_{S_i}$ | Stock drift |
| $\sigma_{S_i}$ | Stock volatility |
| $P_{C_j}$ | Counterparty bond (zero recovery) |
| $P_1$ | Issuer bond with recovery $R_1$ |
| $P_2$ | Issuer bond with recovery $R_2$ |
| $d\bar{\beta}_{S_i}$ | Growth in the cash account associated with stock $i$ (prior to rebalancing) |
| $d\bar{\beta}_{C_j}$ | Growth in the cash account associated with counterparty bond (prior to rebalancing) |
| $d\bar{\beta}_{X_j}$ | Growth in the cash account associated with collateral (prior to rebalancing) |
| $d\bar{\beta}_K$ | Growth in the cash account associated with capital (prior to rebalancing) |
| $r$ | Risk-free rate |
| $r_{C_j}$ | Yield on counterparty $j$ bond |
| $r_k$ | Yield on issuer bonds for $k \in \{1, 2\}$ |
| $r_{X_j}$ | Yield on the collateral position |
| $r_F$ | Yield on issuer bond (one-bond case) |
| $M_B$ | Close-out value on issuer default |
| $M_{C_j}$ | Close-out value on counterparty $j$ default |
| $\alpha_{C_j}$ | Holding of counterparty $j$ bonds |
| $\alpha_k$ | Holding of issuer bond $k$ |
| $\delta_i$ | The stock position |
| $\gamma_{S_i}$ | Stock $i$ dividend yield |
| $q_{S_i}$ | Stock $i$ repo rate |
| $q_{C_j}$ | Counterparty $j$ bond repo rate |
| $J_{C_j}$ | Default indicator for counterparty $j$ |
| $J_B$ | Default indicator for issuer |
| $g_B$ | Value of the derivative portfolio after issuer default |
| $g_{C_j}$ | Value of the derivative portfolio after counterparty $j$ default |
| $\lambda_{C_j}$ | Effective financing rate of counterparty $j$ bond $\lambda_{C_j} = r_{C_j} - r$ |
| $\lambda_B$ | Spread of a zero-recovery zero-coupon issuer bond $(1 - R_k)\lambda_B = r_k - r$ |
| $s_F$ | Funding spread in one bond case $s_F = r_F - r$ |
| $s_{X_j}$ | Spread on collateral account $j$ |
| $\gamma_K(t)$ | The cost of capital (the assets comprising the capital may themselves have a dividend yield and this can be incorporated into $\gamma_K(t)$) |
| $\Delta\hat{V}_B$ | Change in value of derivative on issuer default |
| $\Delta\hat{V}_{C_j}$ | Change in value of derivative on counterparty $j$ default |
| $\epsilon_h$ | Hedging error on default of issuer |
| $\epsilon_{hj}$ | Hedging error on default of issuer associated with counterparty $j$, Note that this can be separated into non-capital dependent and capital-dependent terms $\epsilon_{hj} = \epsilon_{k_0 j} + \epsilon_{k_K j}$ |
| $P$ | $P = \alpha_1 P_l + \alpha_2 P_2$ is the value of the own bond portfolio prior to default |
| $P_D$ | $P_D = R_1 \alpha_1 P_1 + R_2 \alpha_2 P_2$ is value of the own bond portfolio after default |
| $\phi$ | Fraction of capital available for derivative funding |

The funding condition now spans the whole derivatives portfolio and all counterparties,

$$\hat{V} - \sum_{i=1}^{M} X_j + \alpha_1 P_1 + \alpha_2 P_2 - \phi K = 0, \tag{15.8}$$

where as in Chapter 13, $\phi K$ represents the use of capital to offset derivative funding. The cash accounts grow at the following rates, prior to rebalancing, with one cash account per counterparty bond, one per stock and one per collateral account:

$$d\bar{\beta}_{S_i} = \delta_i(\gamma_{S_i} - q_{S_i})S_i dt \tag{15.9}$$

$$d\bar{\beta}_{C_j} = -\alpha_{C_j} q_{C_j} P_{C_j} dt \tag{15.10}$$

$$d\bar{X}_j = -r_{X_j} X_j dt. \tag{15.11}$$

As above, $K$ is the capital requirement for the replicating portfolio and the derivative portfolio, although now this is the total capital associated with the entire portfolio. The change in the cash account associated with the capital position is

$$d\bar{\beta}_K = -\gamma_K(t)K dt. \tag{15.12}$$

As in Chapter 13 there are no terms in $dJ_B$ as any recovery value associated with capital is assumed to form part of the recovery rate, $R_B$.

Using multi-dimensional Itô's lemma, the change in the value of the derivative portfolio is given by

$$d\hat{V} = \frac{\partial \hat{V} \partial t}{d} t + \frac{1}{2} \sum_{a=1}^{N} \sum_{b=1}^{N} \sigma_a \sigma_b S_a S_b \frac{\partial^2 \hat{V}}{\partial S_a \partial S_b} \tag{15.13}$$

$$+ \sum_{a=1}^{N} \frac{\partial \hat{V}}{\partial S_a} dS_a + \Delta \hat{V}_B dJ_B + \sum_{j=1}^{M} \Delta \hat{V}_{C_j} dJ_{C_j},$$

assuming that default does not impact any of the stocks. The usual self-financing assumption leads to the change in value of $\Pi$ being given by

$$d\Pi = \sum_{a=1}^{N} \delta_a dS_a + \sum_{a=1}^{N} \delta_a (\gamma_{S_a} - q_{S_a}) S_a dt + \alpha_1 dP_1 + \alpha_2 dP_2 + \sum_{j=1}^{M} \alpha_{C_j} dP_{C_j} \tag{15.14}$$

$$- \sum_{j=1}^{M} \alpha_{C_j} q_{C_j} P_{C_j} dt - \sum_{j=1}^{M} r_{X_j} X_j dt - \gamma_K K dt.$$

The combined portfolio of derivative positions and replicating portfolio is therefore given by

$$d\hat{V} + d\Pi = \left[ \frac{\partial \hat{V}}{\partial t} + \frac{1}{2} \sum_{a=1}^{N} \sum_{b=1}^{N} \sigma_a \sigma_b S_a S_b \frac{\partial^2 \hat{V}}{\partial S_a \partial S_b} + \sum_{a=1}^{N} \delta_a (\gamma_{S_a} - q_{S_a}) S_a \right. \tag{15.15}$$

$$+ \alpha_1 r_1 P_1 + \alpha_2 r_2 P_2 - \sum_{j=1}^{M} \alpha_{C_j} q_{C_j} P_{C_j} + \sum_{j=1}^{M} \alpha_{C_j} r_{C_j} P_{C_j}$$

$$- \sum_{j=1}^{M} r_{X_j} X_j - \gamma_K K \Bigg] dt$$

$$+ \left[ \Delta \hat{V}_B - \alpha_1 (1 - R_1) P_1 - \alpha_2 (1 - R_2) P_2 \right] dJ_B \tag{15.16}$$

$$+ \sum_{j=1}^{M} \left[ \Delta \hat{V}_{C_j} - \alpha_{C_j} P_{C_j} \right] dJ_{C_j} \tag{15.17}$$

$$+ \sum_{a=1}^{N} \left( \delta_a + \frac{\partial \hat{V}}{\partial S_a} \right) dS_a. \tag{15.18}$$

Assuming replication of the derivative by the hedging portfolio, except at the default of the issuer, gives

$$d\hat{V} + d\Pi = 0. \tag{15.19}$$

Semi-replication means that the sources of risk, apart from the default of the issuer, are hedged so the parameters $\delta_a$ and $\alpha_{C_j}$, are set by

$$\delta_a = -\frac{\partial \hat{V}}{\partial S_a} \tag{15.20}$$

and

$$\alpha_{C_j} P_{C_j} = \Delta \hat{V}_{C_j}$$
$$= g_{C_j} + \hat{V}^{-j} - \hat{V}, \tag{15.21}$$

that is the $\alpha_{C_j}$'s hedge the jump on the default of counterparty $j$. Applying these expressions gives the PDE for $\hat{V}$,

$$\frac{\partial \hat{V}}{\partial t} + \frac{1}{2} \sum_{a=1}^{N} \sum_{b=1}^{N} \sigma_a \sigma_b S_a S_b \frac{\partial^2 \hat{V}}{\partial S_a \partial S_b} - \sum_{a=1}^{N} \frac{\partial \hat{V}}{\partial S_a} (\gamma_{S_a} - q_{S_a}) S_a \tag{15.22}$$

$$+ \alpha_1 r_1 P_1 + \alpha_2 r_2 P_2 + \sum_{j=1}^{M} [g_{C_j} + \hat{V}^{-j} - \hat{V}](r_{c_j} - q_{C_j})$$

$$- \sum_{j=1}^{M} r_{X_j} X_j - \gamma_K K = 0$$

$$\hat{V}(T, S) = H(S). \tag{15.23}$$

The bond funding equation (15.8) has been used in this expression, along with the yield of the issued bond, $r_i = r + (1 - R_i)\lambda_B$ to derive the result

$$\alpha_1 r_1 P_1 + \alpha_2 r_2 P_2 = r \sum_{i=1}^{M} X_j - r\hat{V} + \epsilon_h \lambda_B + \lambda_B[g_B - \hat{V}] + r\phi K, \tag{15.24}$$

where

$$\epsilon_h = \Delta\hat{V}_B - \alpha_1(1 - R_1)P_1 - \alpha_2(1 - R_2)P_2 \tag{15.25}$$

is the hedging error on issuer default. This gives the PDE for $\hat{V}$,

$$\frac{\partial\hat{V}}{\partial t} + \frac{1}{2}\sum_{a=1}^{N}\sum_{b=1}^{N}\sigma_a\sigma_b S_a S_b \frac{\partial^2\hat{V}}{\partial S_a\partial S_b} - \sum_{a=1}^{N}\frac{\partial\hat{V}}{\partial S_a}(\gamma_{S_a} - q_{S_a})S_a \tag{15.26}$$

$$- r\hat{V} + \epsilon_h\lambda_B + \lambda_B[g_B - \hat{V}] + \sum_{j=1}^{M}[g_{C_j} + \hat{V}^j - \hat{V}]\lambda_{C_j}$$

$$- \sum_{j=1}^{M} s_{X_j}X_j - \gamma_K K + r\phi K = 0$$

$$\hat{V}(T, S) = H(S), \tag{15.27}$$

where $\lambda_{C_j} = r_{c_j} - q_{C_j}$.

As above, the next step is to find a PDE for $U$, the valuation adjustment. Hence a multi-counterparty version of the earlier ansatz

$$\hat{V} = V + U = \sum_{j=1}^{M} V_j + U \tag{15.28}$$

where all the $V_j$'s satisfy the multi-asset Black-Scholes PDE with no credit risk,

$$\frac{\partial V_j}{\partial t} + \frac{1}{2}\sum_{a=1}^{N}\sum_{b=1}^{N}\sigma_a\sigma_b S_a S_b \frac{\partial^2 V_j}{\partial S_a\partial S_b} - \sum_{a=1}^{N}\frac{\partial V_j}{\partial S_a}(\gamma_{S_a} - q_{S_a})S_a - rV_j = 0. \tag{15.29}$$

Eliminating the terms in $V_j$ gives the PDE for $U$,

$$\frac{\partial U}{\partial t} + \frac{1}{2}\sum_{a=1}^{N}\sum_{b=1}^{N}\sigma_a\sigma_b S_a S_b \frac{\partial^2 U}{\partial S_a\partial S_b} - \sum_{a=1}^{N}\frac{\partial U}{\partial S_a}(\gamma_{S_a} - q_{S_a})S_a - (r + \lambda_B)U \tag{15.30}$$

$$= -\epsilon_h\lambda_B - \lambda_B[g_B - V] - \sum_{j=1}^{M}[g_{C_j} + \hat{V}^{-j} - V - U]\lambda_{C_j}$$

$$+ \sum_{j=1}^{M} s_{X_j} X_j + \gamma_K K - r\phi K$$

$$U(T, S) = 0. \tag{15.31}$$

The PDE for $U$ spans all counterparties $j$ so to solve it we would like to be able to separate $U$ into individual contributions from counterparties for ease of computation. Hence we would like to be in a position to write

$$U = \sum_{j=1}^{M} U_j, \tag{15.32}$$

where each of the $U_j$'s satisfies a PDE of the form

$$\frac{\partial U_j}{\partial t} + \frac{1}{2} \sum_{a=1}^{N} \sum_{b=1}^{N} \sigma_a \sigma_b S_a S_b \frac{\partial^2 U_j}{\partial S_a \partial S_b} - \sum_{a=1}^{N} \frac{\partial U_j}{\partial S_a} (\gamma_{S_a} - q_{S_a}) S_a - (r + \lambda_B + \lambda_{C_j}) U_j \tag{15.33}$$
$$= -\epsilon_{hj} \lambda_B - \lambda_B [g_{Bj} - V_j] - [g_{C_j} - V_j] \lambda_{C_j}$$
$$+ s_{X_j} X_j + \gamma_K K_j - r\phi K_j$$
$$U_j(T, S) = 0.$$

The condition for this separation to be allowable is that all the terms on the right-hand side of equation (15.30) must also be able to be expressed at counterparty level.

The first step is to separate the hedging error per counterparty, that is we define $\epsilon_{hj}$, that satisfies

$$\epsilon_h = \sum_{j=1}^{M} \epsilon_{hj}. \tag{15.34}$$

For this to hold,

$$\epsilon_{hj} = \Delta \hat{V}_{Bj} - \alpha_{1j}(1 - R_1)P_1 - \alpha_{2j}(1 - R_2)P_2 \tag{15.35}$$
$$= g_{Bj} - V_j - U_j - \alpha_{1j}(1 - R_1)P_1 - \alpha_{2j}(1 - R_2)P_2.$$

The issuer bond positions can easily be attributed to counterparty level so that

$$\alpha_1 = \sum_{j=1}^{M} \alpha_{1j} \tag{15.36}$$

$$\alpha_2 = \sum_{j=1}^{M} \alpha_{2j} \tag{15.37}$$

and from equation (15.6) that under standard close-out conditions

$$g_B = \sum_{j=1}^{M} g_{Bj}.$$

(15.38)

In general this must be true as $g_B$ is simply the total close-out claim made against the issuer on their default. The relationship between $\epsilon_h$ and the counterparty level $\epsilon_{hj}$ is now clear:

$$\epsilon_h = g_B - \hat{V} - \alpha_1(1 - R_1)P_1 - \alpha_2(1 - R_2)P_2$$

(15.39)

$$= \sum_{j=1}^{M} g_{Bj} - \sum_{j=1}^{M} V_j - \sum_{j=1}^{M} U_j - \sum_{j=1}^{M}(\alpha_{1j}(1 - R_1)P_1 + \alpha_{2j}(1 - R_2)P_2)$$

$$= \sum_{j=1}^{M} \epsilon_{bj}.$$

Hence $\epsilon_h$ can be separated if $U$ itself can be separated and this therefore relies on the capital $K$ being separable at counterparty level.[2] Writing

$$\nu \equiv (\gamma_K - r\phi)K,$$

(15.40)

we see that $\gamma_K$ and $K$ will determine if this separation is possible. Unfortunately, in general, $K$ cannot be directly expressed at counterparty level and so a scheme of *capital allocation* is required.

## 15.3   CAPITAL ALLOCATION

Capital needs to be allocated to counterparty level such that

$$K = \sum_{j=1}^{M} K_j.$$

(15.41)

In fact capital allocation approaches are widely represented in the literature with considerable emphasis on *Euler allocation*, as was used in the context of CVA allocation in section 3.6.2. Tasche (2008), for example, makes extensive use of Euler allocation in his work on capital allocation to business units, although a number of other approaches have also been proposed (see for example Balog, 2010). In general a capital allocation will always be possible, although as will be demonstrated, Euler allocation does not work for all elements of the regulatory capital framework.

---

[2]This relies on the assumption that equation (15.32) holds and hence the argument appears circular. This is not in fact the case as the hedging error term is actually a grouping of terms relating to issuer default. Equation (15.30) could be rearranged to remove any dependence on $U$ on the right-hand side.

### 15.3.1 Market Risk

As was discussed in section 12.2, market risk capital can be calculated in one of two ways under the Basel II framework (BCBS, 2006b), *Standardized Method* and *Internal Models Method* for those institutions with the required regulatory approval. The forthcoming *Fundamental Review of the Trading Book* (BCBS, 2013c) will introduce changes to both methods but does not radically change the modelling approach. Market risk capital is calculated at portfolio level and not at trade or counterparty level so some form of allocation is required.

The standardised method is a formula-based approach as discussed in the examples in Chapter 13. It is clear that the interest rate methodology involves linear operations on netted position information. Hence, given that the operations are linear functions then they are homogeneous of order one by the definition of linearity and hence Euler allocation can be applied. The same is true for the remaining risk categories with a small number of exceptions such as approach two for general market risk under the standard equity method (Financial Conduct Authority, 2014, BIPRU 7.3.42), although even though this particular operation is nonlinear it is still a homogeneous function of order one. Hence in general Euler allocation can be used with the standardised method.

The internal model method uses a Value-at-Risk (VaR) approach to estimate the regulatory capital requirement and under the fundamental review of the trading book, expected shortfall (ES) will be used. Euler allocation can be used with both methods (Tasche, 2008). In practice, VaR, SVaR and ES can be attributed to trade level using Euler allocation applied during the aggregation phase where vectors of P&Ls from each trade and scenario are combined. Trade level results can then aggregated back to portfolio level.

### 15.3.2 Counterparty Credit Risk (CCR)

Counterparty credit risk capital is already calculated at netting set level under the current regulatory framework (BCBS, 2006b; BCBS, 2011b). Institutions with IMM approval calculate netting set level exposures over a one-year time horizon to generate the regulatory expected exposure. For those institutions using the non-IMM methods, current exposure method and standardised method, the calculations remain at netting set level and under the proposed revised standardised approach (BCBS, 2014b) this remains the case. Hence it is clear that capital as calculated under CCR is already defined on a per counterparty basis irrespective of regulatory approval status.

### 15.3.3 CVA Capital

As with IMM CCR, CVA capital calculations for banks with IMM approval are performed at counterparty level with the internal exposure engine providing either full revaluation scenarios for VaR using equation (12.15) or, more likely, regulatory CS01 values for use in the bank's VaR/SVaR model using equation (12.16).

The standardised CVA formula is calculated across all counterparties and is not a simple sum of counterparty level terms as can be seen from equation (12.13). With no CVA hedging and for large numbers of counterparties this formula is well approximated by a sum over counterparty level terms (see section 12.4.1),

$$K_{\text{CVA}}^i \approx \frac{2.33}{2} \sqrt{h} \omega_i M_i \text{EAD}_i^{\text{total}}. \tag{15.42}$$

However, the general case with hedging $K_{CVA}$ cannot be easily expressed as a sum of counterparty level terms. Unfortunately Euler allocation is of no help either as equation (12.13) is not a homogenous function and hence it does not satisfy the requirements for Euler allocation to be applied. However, it is possible to define a suitable allocation which satisfies equation (15.41):[3]

$$
K_{CVAj} = \frac{\left( M_i EAD_i^{total} - M_i^{hedge} B_i \right)}{\sum_{j=1}^{M} \left( M_i EAD_i^{total} - M_i^{hedge} B_i \right)} K_{CVA}.
\tag{15.43}
$$

### 15.3.4 Leverage Ratio

The Basel III leverage ratio was described in section 12.5.2 with the measure defined by equation (12.17). For derivatives the exposure measure is given by calculation under the *current exposure method* and hence

$$
ExposureMeasure = \sum_{j=1}^{M} \max(RC_{Net}^{j}, 0) + (0.4 \times A_{Gross}^{j}) + (0.6 \times NGR \times A_{Gross}^{j}),
\tag{15.44}
$$

where $RC_{Net}^{j}$ is the net replacement cost for counterparty $j$ and

$$
A_{Gross}^{j} = \sum_{l=1}^{n_j^{trades}} A_l^{j}
\tag{15.45}
$$

is the sum of add-ons for each trade $l$ in the portfolio of counterparty $j$ and $NGR$ is the net-to-gross ratio given by

$$
NGR = \frac{NetMTM}{GrossMTM}.
\tag{15.46}
$$

The leverage ratio is constrained to be greater than 3% under Basel III or restrictions are placed on the distributions of dividends and bonuses.[4]

The leverage ratio for derivatives is given by

$$
LR = \frac{\sum_{j}^{M} K_j + K'}{\sum_{j=1}^{M} E_j}
\tag{15.47}
$$

---

[3]There are many possible methods of allocation, however, to be useful as a means of allocating capital the allocation should be related to the parameters of the problem domain and appear sensible.

[4]The actual implementation of the leverage ratio does not follow directly the Basel formula with differences under CRD IV (European Parliament and the Council of the European Union, 2013b; European Parliament and the Council of the European Union, 2013a) and the US leverage ratio implementation (Office of the Comptroller of the Currency, Treasury; the Board of Governors of the Federal Reserve System; and the Federal Deposit Insurance Corporation, 2014b).

where $K'$ is any additional capital required to satisfy the leverage ratio and $E_j$ is the exposure calculated for counterparty $j$. Rearranging and imposing the Basel III constraint shows that

$$K^{LR} = \max\left(0.03 \times \sum_j^M E_j - \sum_j^M K_j, 0\right)$$

$$= \max\left(\sum_j^M a_j h_j\right). \tag{15.48}$$

where $h_j = (0.03E_j - K_j)/a_j$ and all the $a_j$'s are equal to one. Given that this is a max function, it is possible to attribute any leverage ratio capital using Euler allocation, leading to,

$$K_j^{LR} = \mathbb{1}_{\{\sum_j^M a_j h_j \geq 0\}} h_j. \tag{15.49}$$

### 15.3.5 Capital Allocation and Uniqueness

It should be immediately clear that the attribution scheme proposed above is not unique and there are other methods. The implication of this is that the PDEs for the terms $U_j$ are also not unique, and this is certainly true. Different allocation schemes will give different counterparty level adjustments. However, the overall solution for $U$ will remain the same.

## 15.4 COST OF CAPITAL TO THE BUSINESS

Capital is a finite resource at any point in time. If more capital is required then this will typically involve the bank going to market to place newly issued shares, either through a block placement or through a rights issue, both of which are time-consuming and potentially expensive operations. Reducing capital can be achieved through share buy backs and profit distribution as dividends but the ability to do this is still restricted. For small incremental changes to a trading book it can be argued that a constant cost of capital is justifiable. However, at portfolio level this is hard to sustain.

If the cost of capital where a function of the total capital requirement,

$$\gamma_K \equiv \gamma_K(K), \tag{15.50}$$

then the behaviour of the capital cost can be made more realistic. A bank with a leverage ratio well below the threshold might be very intolerant of any increase in capital. Making the cost of capital a function of the capital requirement naturally reflects the treatment of capital as a scarce resource.

## 15.5   PORTFOLIO KVA

It has been possible to split the single PDE for $U$, equation (15.30), as a sum over PDEs that satisfy equation (15.33). Hence to solve for the $U_j$ we apply the Feynman-Kac theorem in the usual way to obtain

$$U_j = CVA_j + DVA_j + FCA_j + COLVA_j + KVA_j, \tag{15.51}$$

where

$$\begin{aligned}
\text{CVA}_j &= -\int_t^T \lambda_{C_j}(u) e^{-\int_t^u (r(s) + \lambda_B(s) + \lambda_{C_j}(s)) ds} \\
&\quad \times \mathbb{E}_t \left[ V_j(u) - g_{C_j}(V_j(u)) X_j(u)), \frac{\partial V_j}{\partial S}(u), X_j(u)) \right] du \tag{15.52} \\[2mm]
\text{DVA}_j &= -\int_t^T \lambda_B(u) e^{-\int_t^u (r(s) + \lambda_B(s) + \lambda_{C_j}(s)) ds} \\
&\quad \times \mathbb{E}_t \left[ V_j(u) - g_{B_j}(V_j(u), X_j(u)) \right] du \tag{15.53} \\[2mm]
COLVA_j &= -\int_t^T \lambda_B(u) e^{-\int_t^u (r(s) + \lambda_B(s) + \lambda_{C_j}(s)) ds} \mathbb{E}_t \left[ \epsilon_{h_j}(u) \right] du \tag{15.54} \\[2mm]
COLVA_j &= -\int_t^s X_j(u) e^{-\int_t^u (r(s) + \lambda_B(s) + \lambda_{C_j}(s)) ds} \mathbb{E}_t \left[ X_j(u) \right] du \tag{15.55} \\[2mm]
\text{KVA}_j &= -\int_t^T (\gamma_K(K, u) - r(u)\phi_j) e^{-\int_t^u (r(s) + \lambda_B(s) + \lambda_{C_j}(s)) ds} \mathbb{E}_t \left[ K_j(u) \right] du. \tag{15.56}
\end{aligned}$$

These expressions are identical with those derived in the single counterparty case as described in Chapter 13.

## 15.6   CALCULATING PORTFOLIO KVA BY REGRESSION

Capital allocation has allowed portfolio KVA to be broken down into a series of counterparty level calculations. However, while the valuation adjustment can be calculated at counterparty level there is still a need to estimate the full bank capital requirement as the cost of capital is a function of the total capital requirement. Furthermore the attribution process that is required for market risk, CVA (standardised) and leverage ratio capital also requires the total capital requirement in each category before it can be allocated to counterparty level. To proceed with a counterparty level calculation then we need to have the total capital $K$ and the portfolio level constituents in every Monte Carlo state. This could be done with a single Monte Carlo simulation across all counterparties, which is feasible, although computationally demanding and memory intensive.

The following algorithm offers an alternative based on the use of regression approximation. Two counterparty level simulations are required alongside one "global" simulation. The first counterparty level simulation is used to obtain regression approximations for trade valuations, portfolio exposures under CEM, CCR and CVA capital. A global simulation, spanning all asset classes in the portfolio, is then used to find a regression approximation for market risk capital and any additional capital from the leverage ratio. The total capital is fully attributed to counterparty level and then the second counterparty level simulation is used to estimate the counterparty level XVA. The algorithm is presented is full in algorithm 3.

---

**Algorithm 3** Estimate total capital K as a function of state and the attributed capital $K_i$ as a function of state for market risk, CVA (standardised) and leverage ratio.

---

1: **for all** Counterparties j **do**
2:     Run MC simulation for Counterparty j, simulating only required assets
3:     Calculate portfolio value $V_j$ at each state and time step
4:     Regress against appropriate basis to find $V_j(S_i, t)$ (see *LSAC* technique described in Chapter 10)
5:     Calculate $K_j^{CVA}$ and $K_j^{CCR}$ at each state and time step
6:     Regress against appropriate basis to find $K_j^{CVA}(S_i, t)$ and $K_j^{CCR}(S_i, t)$
7:     Calculate CEM exposures for the leverage ratio, $E_j$ at each state and time step
8:     Regress against appropriate basis to find $E_j(S_i, t)$
9: **end for**
10: $\sum_j^M V_j(S_i, t) = V(S_i, t)$ (portfolio valuation)
11: Run a MC simulation across all assets
12: Calculate $K^{MarketRisk}$ at each state and time step (using VaR/SVaR – see Green, Kenyon and Dennis, 2014))
13: Regress against appropriate basis to find $K^{MarketRisk}(S_i, t)$
14: $\sum_j^M K_j^{CVA}(S_i, t) = K^{CVA}(S_i, t)$
15: $\sum_j^M K_j^{CCR}(S_i, t) = K^{CCR}(S_i, t)$
16: $\sum_j^M E_j(S_i, t) = E(S_i, t)$
17: Use $K^{MarketRisk}(S_i, t)$, $K^{CCR}(S_i, t)$, $K^{CVA}(S_i, t)$ and $E(S_i, t)$ to estimate $K^{LR}$ at each state and time step
18: Regress against appropriate basis to find $K^{LR}(S_i, t)$
19: $K(S_i, t) = K^{MarketRisk}(S_i, t) + K^{CCR}(S_i, t) + K^{CVA}(S_i, t) + K^{LR}(S_i, t)$
20: Use $K(S_i, t)$ to give $\gamma_K(S_i, t)$
21: Attribute $K^{MarketRisk}$ to counterparties j
22: Attribute $K^{LR}$ to counterparties j
23: **for all** counterparties j **do**
24:     Run MC simulation for counterparty j, simulating only required assets
25:     Use $K_j(S_i, t) = K_j^{MarketRisk}(S_i, t) + K_j^{CCR}(S_i, t) + K_j^{CVA}(S_i, t) + K_j^{LR}(S_i, t)$ to give $KVA_j$
26:     $KVA = KVA + KVA_j$
27: **end for**

# XVA Implementation

## CHAPTER 16

# Hybrid Monte Carlo Models for XVA: Building a Model for the Expected-Exposure Engine

*One should never mistake pattern for meaning.*

—Iain M. Banks
*The Hydrogen Sonata (2012)*

## 16.1 INTRODUCTION

### 16.1.1 Implementing XVA

Part IV is about the implementation of XVA models. Implementation involves a large number of modelling *and* computational decisions; the two cannot be readily separated because of the computational requirements of a typical XVA calculation. It it simply not feasible to build a model and then try to implement it on a hardware platform as this could lead to much higher computational requirements than desired.

XVA implementation is largely about hybrid models using Monte Carlo techniques and hence this chapter describes how to construct a set of model dynamics to generate the *states of the world* that will be used in the valuation phase of the exposure calculation. Monte Carlo techniques are clearly critical and hence Chapter 17 discusses practical Monte Carlo implementation issues, while Chapter 18 discusses variance reduction techniques. The trade valuation phase generates trade and hence netting set valuations from each state of the world and are these discussed in Chapter 19. Finally the technological infrastructure to support XVA is explored in Chapter 20.

### 16.1.2 XVA and Monte Carlo

XVA and related calculations are, in general, performed using Monte Carlo models for dynamics, with a variety of models used to value trades in each Monte Carlo state.

In the context of instrument valuation where there is a choice of approaches available, Monte Carlo is often seen as the least favoured numerical approach in quantitative finance as it is slow relative to analytic formulae and numerical approaches such as trees, PDE solvers and grid-based numeric integration. Monte Carlo is used when these alternative methods are unavailable, because analytic models cannot be derived or because the dimensionality of the model precludes the use of tree, PDE or grid-based numeric integration. Monte Carlo is also used in low dimensional contexts because of its flexibility; so, for example, a new derivative payout can be quickly coded when a Monte Carlo engine with the appropriate dynamics for the underlying assets is available. Often *payout languages* are defined that allow new payouts to be scripted by end users and used with an existing Monte Carlo engine application, see Chapter 20.

Monte Carlo is used for XVA calculation for a number of reasons. The first is driven by the dimensionality of the calculation. *Close-out netting*, as discussed in section 2.4.1, is a major credit mitigant that allows both counterparties to net all bilateral transaction mark-to-markets together before closing out in the event of default. However, the direct consequence of netting is that the portfolio that falls into each *netting set* must be valued together inside the Monte Carlo engine. Given the fact that netting sets can contain practically any derivative transaction on any underlying asset the dimensionality of XVA calculations can be very high and Monte Carlo methods are the only practical solution technique. A second driver is the lack of a realistic alternative to Monte Carlo. While PDE models have been developed in Chapters 3, 9, 13 and 14, these do not represent practical calculation techniques but rather a convenient mathematical framework to work within before moving to an integral solution via the Feynman-Kac theorem, and ultimately evaluation by Monte Carlo. The PDE would not be viable because of the high dimensionality. Analytic formulae for CVA were developed in Chapter 5 but only exist for a small number of edge cases.

It should also be noted that the XVA calculation is in fact mildly path-dependent, although this is not immediately obvious from equations (3.13) and (3.47). Valuation at future dates will often require knowledge of rate fixings and option exercise decisions between today and the forward valuation date. Hence, the expected exposure simulation is path-dependent and a *multi-step* Monte Carlo simulation is needed. This does not actually change the fact that XVA, where credit/funding/cost of capital is independent of exposure, is still an integral over a series of *European options*. We could therefore argue that a series of multi-step Monte Carlo simulations is needed, one for each expected exposure value. In practice it makes sense to combine these simulations in one multi-step Monte Carlo. Some institutions have used multiple *single-step* Monte Carlo simulations which take a single time step from the start of the simulation to the exposure date and apply approximations for trade events, although the utility of this approach must be questioned as there is no gain in performance and a full path-dependent simulation is typically no more difficult to implement.

### 16.1.3 XVA and Models

This chapter is about the variety of Monte Carlo models that can be applied to XVA calculations. The models presented here cover all asset classes as XVA applies across all derivatives. The chapter covers a wide spectrum of models from the simple to the complex. Many of the models presented here do not include smile and skew and could, therefore, be considered out of date by the standards of single asset-class modelling. Is this OK or does XVA modelling deserve a reputation for "bad models"?

The decision to include a wide variety of models in based on a number of factors:

- This book is deliberately intended to be accessible and readable by those who want an introduction to the subject.
- Simpler models are commonly found in XVA systems today and even if these are considered legacy systems, they will remain in use for many years.
- Simpler Monte Carlo models are often used in XVA systems in combination with valuation models that are more complex and do include skew/smile dynamics (see Chapter 19). This involves the use of inconsistent dynamics but is a common approach. It is logically similar to multi-curve modelling approaches that use a simple Gaussian discount model in combination with skew/smile dynamics in the spread (see for example Moreni and Pallavicini, 2013).
- Simpler models still have a place in XVA calculations on the basis of materiality considerations, breadth of modelling requirements and computational costs.

When and why are simple models acceptable? There are three factors to consider: materiality, hybrid modelling requirements and computational performance.

**Materiality** A key consideration is materiality and all aspects of the model choice should reflect the relative importance of accuracy. So, for example, if the model is to be used purely for reserving purposes there may be limited need to invest in sophisticated modelling approaches. If the derivative portfolio mainly consists of vanilla trades there may be no need to implement sophisticated dynamics to gain accurate exposure profiles for a small number of exotic trades.

The accuracy of some inputs to the XVA calculation is limited. As was discussed in section 4.6, in many cases the input CDS curve is based on a proxy rather than on a directly linked CDS contract. In such circumstances it is hard to argue that the survival probability is well known. Hence the use of models that give exposure profiles with sub-basis point accuracy in trade valuation seems excessive if they are then only to be used in an integral with poorly known parameters. If the difference between a sophisticated model and an unsophisticated one is not material at portfolio level then why expend scarce resources on unneeded sophistication?

**Hybrid Modelling Requirements** XVA is a hybrid modelling problem cutting across all asset classes and as a result is far more challenging than single asset-class modelling. A sophisticated single asset-class model can be difficult enough to develop. A sophisticated hybrid Monte Carlo model would require "glueing" multiple such models together and this is far more difficult than is often assumed. For example, local-stochastic volatility models are now prevalent in the literature, particularly for modelling FX exotic products such as barrier options. However, there are very few such models in the literature that consider stochastic interest rates and those that do tend to be limited to simpler models such as Hull-White.

Complex hybrid models are also inherently difficult to calibrate. Furthermore there is a strong argument that XVA should be robust in the face of a wide variety of market conditions. While it may not be a disaster if a single trade experiences a model calibration failure, if the XVA model calibration fails then it potentially means no XVA results for the entire portfolio, a much more significant issue. Complex model calibrations do break down under extreme market conditions. This was a noted feature of the crisis period of 2007–2009 where complex models repeatedly failed to calibrate, while simpler models continued through the period untroubled.

Hybrid models are high dimensional with a correspondingly large set of correlations. Complex multi-factor models including stochastic volatility will also require the co-dependence between different stochastic factors to be specified. Simply combining multiple complex models together will lead to a complex covariance structure that will be difficult to understand.

To see how the number of stochastic factors can quickly mount up in a hybrid model consider the following formula:

$$
\begin{aligned}
\text{No. Factors} = &\ N_{CCYs} \times (N_{IR} + N_{SV-IR} + N_{TBasis} \times N_{SB_jR}) \\
&+ (N_{CCYs} - 1) \times (N_{FX} + N_{SV-FX}) \\
&+ \sum_{j}^{N_{CCYs}} (\mathbb{1}_{jInflation} \times (N_{IR} + N_{SV-IR} + N_{FX} + N_{SV-FX})) \\
&+ (N_{Equities}) \times (N_E + N_{SV-E}) \\
&+ (N_{PMetals}) \times (N_E + N_{SV-E}) \\
&+ (N_{FwdCommod}) \times (N_{Comm} + N_{SV-Comm}) \\
&+ (N_{Credit}) \times (N_C)
\end{aligned}
$$

where

- $N_{CCYs}$ is the number of currencies
- $N_{IR}$ is the number of stochastic factors used for the discount curve model
- $N_{SV-IR}$ is the number of stochastic factor used for the stochastic volatility of the discount curve model
- $N_{TBasis}$ is the number of tenor basis curves
- $N_{SB_jR}$ is the number of stochastic factors used in the basis curve model
- $N_{FX}$ is the number of stochastic factors driving the FX rate
- $N_{SV-FX}$ is the number of stochastic factors driving the FX stochastic volatility
- $\mathbb{1}_{jInflation}$ is an indicator function which is 1 if currency j has inflation products
- The Jarrow-Yildirim (FX analogy) is assumed for inflation
- $N_{Equities}$ is the number of equities
- $N_E$ is the number of stochastic factors used in the equity model
- $N_{SV-E}$ is the number of stochastic factors used in the equity stochastic volatility
- $N_{PMetals}$ is the number of precious metals
- Precious metals are modelled in the same way as equities
- $N_{FwdCommod}$ is the number of forward-based commodity assets
- $N_{Comm}$ is the number of stochastic factors used in the forward-based commodity asset model
- $N_{SV-Comm}$ is the number of stochastic factors used in the forward-based commodity stochastic volatility model
- $N_{Credit}$ is the number of hazard rates to be simulated
- $N_C$ is the number of stochastic factors used in the credit model.

Consider a three-currency case with GBP, EUR and USD. The netting set contains GBP inflation products but no equities, precious metals, commodities or credit products. The counterparty and issuer spreads are treated deterministically. The netting set requires three basis curves in each currency.

In the first example, a simple one-factor Hull-White interest rate model with no stochastic volatility and no stochastic basis is used. The FX rate is modelling using a simple one-factor Black-Scholes approach. In this case the number of stochastic factors is given by

$$
\begin{aligned}
\text{No. Factors} &= 3 \times (1) \\
&\quad + 2 \times (1) \\
&\quad + 1 \times (1 + 1) \\
&= 7.
\end{aligned}
$$

Now consider the use of an interest rate model with two curve factors and one stochastic volatility factor. Basis is assumed to be stochastic with one factor per basis curve. The FX rate model now becomes a local-stochastic volatility model with one factor driving the FX rate and one stochastic volatility factor. Now the number of factors is given by

$$
\begin{aligned}
\text{No. Factors} &= 3 \times (2 + 1 + 3 \times 1) \\
&\quad + 2 \times (1 + 1) \\
&\quad + 1 \times (2 + 1 + 1 + 1) \\
&= 27.
\end{aligned}
$$

The complexity rapidly increases as the number of assets in the netting set increases and as the sophistication of the model used for each one increases. While 27 factors may not present a computational problem with modern computational resources, it certainly will make the management of the overall covariance structure of the model far more difficult.

**Computational Performance**  Computational performance remains a major consideration for XVA models, notwithstanding major advances in techniques such as AAD (see Chapter 21) and hardware acceleration using platforms such as those provided by GPU (see Chapter 20). Complex multi-factor models require more computation and hence are slower than simpler ones. This applies equally to the Monte Carlo simulation path construction and to the model calibration phase. Furthermore the next generation models of XVA will inevitably be more complex than today's and require more computational power. Hence there is a balance to be struck between the complexity of the overall XVA model and the selected dynamics for the Monte Carlo simulation.

## 16.1.4  A Roadmap to XVA Hybrid Monte Carlo

The remainder of the chapter is split into two sections. A decision about the type of calibration has to be made, whether to use historical or implied model calibrations for the exposure generation, and this is covered in section 16.2. The construction of a hybrid risk-neutral model for XVA is the subject of sections 16.3 through 16.8, covering the modelling of interest rates, FX, inflation, equities, commodities and credit.

## 16.2   CHOOSING THE CALIBRATION: HISTORICAL VERSUS IMPLIED

The first question to pose in the context of implementing a Monte Carlo model for XVA is the choice of calibration. Section 4.2 presented the case for the use of historical and implied default probabilities for CVA calculations. Here the critical question is whether a historical or implied calibration is appropriate for the Monte Carlo simulation used for expected exposure.

### 16.2.1   The Case for Historical Calibration

Historical calibrations can take a variety of different forms. Given the typical diffusive processes used to model assets within the Monte Carlo simulation we can divide the calibration into volatility and drift components. A historical volatility calibration is generally used in all historical calibrations and involves calibrating the process volatility to the historical volatility obtained from time series data. A historical drift calculation can sometimes also be used where the drift is calibrated to the drift from time series data over some specified horizon.

Why might we want to use some form of historical calibration for CVA and FVA models? In the early days of CVA management desks in banks, a historical calibration was often used as the Monte Carlo model applied to CVA was often the same one that was also used for potential future exposure calculations used in credit limit management. A fully implied cross-asset Monte Carlo model is also relatively complex when compared to some of the simpler models used in PFE such as one-factor Vasicek.

For banks that seek to warehouse all the risk associated with XVA then there is an argument for the use of a historical calibration. If no hedging takes place then there is no need to match the prices of hedging instruments. The CVA would then give an estimate of the expected loss on a portfolio due to defaults over the lifetime of the portfolio. FVA would become a measure of the expected cost of funding the portfolio to maturity. However such a choice is clearly inconsistent with no-arbitrage arguments. In standard derivative pricing theory it does not matter if the risk is actually hedged or not because the market sets the price.

While some banks have been able to maintain the use of historical calibrations for a period, standard market practice today is to use a risk-neutral calibration for the underlying Monte Carlo dynamics. In fact the CVA capital term introduced in Basel III (BCBS, 2011b) specifies that banks with IMM approval should use risk-neutral default probabilities in an approximate unilateral CVA formula. The exposures, however, should come from the approved exposure model that would also be used to compute the EAD for the CCR term under IMM. The only specification for the exposure model is that is should satisfy backtesting requirements and there is no stated preference for risk-neutral or historical calibration. Given the nature of the approvals process many banks, therefore, will continue to use historically calibrated Monte Carlo models to compute capital requirements for the Basel framework CCR and CVA terms. At the same time XVA trading desks and bank finance arms are likely to use internal risk-neutral Monte Carlo models to price, risk manage and account for CVA.

In theory a different choice could be made for calibration of a Monte Carlo model applied to different XVA terms, for example where an exposure-driven approach to calculating FVA has been adopted. However, this would not make sense where an integrated XVA model had been selected as the exposures would need to be consistent between different XVA terms irrespective of what form that model took (for example BCVA + UFVA versus

**TABLE 16.1** A summary of the case for historical calibration for the XVA Monte Carlo simulation.

| Issue | Status |
|---|---|
| Consistent with credit risk/PFE | ✓ |
| Matches historical expected loss | ✓ |
| Arbitrage free | ✗ |
| Consistent with hedge instrument | ✗ |
| Market standard (for accounting) | ✗ |

UCVA + BFVA). Of course the discounting approaches to FVA calculation are naturally risk neutral.[1]

The case for historical calibration is summarised in Table 16.1.

**Historical Interest Rate Calibration**  A typical choice of interest rate model for use in credit exposure models with historical calibration is the *Hull-White* model (Hull and White, 1990; Hull and White, 1994) with dynamics given by the mean reverting process

$$dr(t) = (\theta(t) - \alpha(t)r(t))dt + \sigma(t)dW(t). \tag{16.1}$$

The Hull-White model was originally developed for applications in pricing interest rate derivatives and as such is widely discussed in many texts such as Brigo and Mercurio (2006) and Pelsser (2000). In the context of historical calibration for applications in credit risk the key question is whether to calibrate all the parameters to historical data or whether to retain the risk-neutral drift by calibrating the mean-reversion level, $\theta(t)$, to the initial term structure. In the historical case it makes sense to reduce the two volatility parameters $\alpha$ and $\sigma$ to constants and this is the case analysed here. For pricing applications, however, the term structure of the volatility $\sigma(t)$ is normally retained to allow calibration to a term structure of volatilities such as the coterminal European swaptions with exercises matching those of a Bermudan swaption when building a model to value these derivatives.

If the risk-neutral drift is retained then it can be shown that $\theta(t)$ should take the form

$$\theta(t) = \frac{\partial f(0,t)}{\partial t} + \alpha(t)f(0,t) + \frac{\sigma^2}{2\alpha}(1 - e^{-2\alpha t}), \tag{16.2}$$

which ensures that the model matches the initial term structure of interest rates.[2] It is important to note that this fitting process does require the instantaneous forward rate, $f(0,t)$, to be continuous as it involves its first derivative. Yield curve models do not always have this property so some care should be taken.

Once $\theta(t)$ has been calibrated the volatility parameters much be selected to historical time series data. One approach to this is to use the general method of moments (GMM) as

---

[1]See Chapter 9 for an extended discussion on the choice of funding curve and whether or not different choices can be considered risk neutral.
[2]Note that in a multi-currency model with multiple interest rates an additional drift correction will appear in the dynamics of all currencies other that that of the numeraire asset. This is discussed in more detail in the context of implied volatility calibration in section 16.3.

is analysed in detail by James and Webber (2000). Before performing the calibration it is necessary to develop the model further. The standard approach to the Hull-White model is to introduce a change of variable,

$$x(t) = r(t) - \phi(t), \tag{16.3}$$

where $\phi(t)$ is chosen to make $dx(t)$ take the form of an *Ornstein-Uhlenbeck* process,

$$dx(t) = -\alpha(t)x(t) + \sigma(t)dW(t). \tag{16.4}$$

The transformation for the Hull-White model has the form

$$\phi(t) = r(0)e^{-\alpha t} + \int_0^t e^{-\alpha s}\theta(s)ds, \tag{16.5}$$

and hence

$$r(t) = x(t) + r(0)e^{-\alpha t} + \int_0^t e^{-\alpha s}\theta(s)ds. \tag{16.6}$$

The solution to equation (16.4) is given by (see for example Karatzas and Shreve, 1991)

$$x(t) = e^{-\alpha t}x(0) + \sigma \int_0^t e^{\alpha(s-t)}dW(s), \tag{16.7}$$

where we can assume that $x(0) = 0$. Hence $r(t)$ can be expressed as

$$r(t) = x(t) + f(0, t) + \frac{\sigma^2}{2\alpha^2}(1 - e^{-\alpha t})^2, \tag{16.8}$$

where equation (16.2) has been used.

To calibrate the volatility using the GMM approach equations (16.7) and (16.8) need to be expressed in discrete form using a Euler approximation scheme:

$$x_{i+1} = e^{-\Delta t}x_i + \sigma\sqrt{\frac{1 - e^{-2\alpha\Delta t}}{2\alpha}}\epsilon_{i+1} \tag{16.9}$$

$$r_{i+1} = x_{i+1} + f(0, t_{i+1}) + \frac{\sigma^2}{2\alpha^2}(1 - e^{-\alpha t_{i+1}})^2, \tag{16.10}$$

where the $\epsilon_i$ are $N(0, 1)$ random variates. Once a time series of values for the short rate $r_i$ have been obtained, equation (16.10) can be used to obtain the corresponding sequence for $x_i$ in terms of the unknown parameters $\sigma$ and $\alpha$. Furthermore the discrete variable $y_i$ defined by

$$y_{i+1} = x_{i+1} - e^{-\Delta t}x_i \tag{16.11}$$

is normally distributed with mean zero and variance

$$Var(y_i) = \hat{\sigma}^2 = \frac{\sigma^2}{2\alpha}(1 - e^{-2\alpha\Delta t}),$$ (16.12)

and this allows the first two moments to be used for calibration. It is also true that

$$\mathbb{E}(y_{i+1}x_i) = 0$$ (16.13)
$$\mathbb{E}(y_{i+1}^2 x_i) = \hat{\sigma}^2 x_i,$$ (16.14)

and hence forming the four moments

$$f_i^1 = y_{i+1}$$ (16.15)
$$f_i^2 = y_{i+1}^2 - \hat{\sigma}^2$$ (16.16)
$$f_i^3 = y_{i+1}x_i$$ (16.17)
$$f_i^4 = (y_{i+1}^2 - \hat{\sigma}^2)$$ (16.18)

allows an objective function to be formed,

$$F = \sum_{i=1}^{N}\sum_{j=1}^{4}(f_i^j)^2,$$ (16.19)

and this can be minimised to calibrate $\sigma$ and $\alpha$.

If the initial term structure is not matched then the mean reversion level would be set to a constant, $\theta$. This then becomes a third parameter to be fitted during the GMM method from the time series data for the short rate. The choice to not fit the model to the initial term structure does have a significant implication in that the model would not reprice linear instruments should the Monte Carlo model be used in this way. Furthermore the mean reversion level would also be sensitive to the choice of window selected for the calibration and it is questionable whether this is desirable. Of course under a historical calibration the two volatility parameters are also sensitive to the choice of the window and its length but this is less directional in behaviour if the initial term structure is matched. The choice of window itself is an important decision. A long window would damp local changes in volatility while a short window would emphasise them.

**Historical FX Calibration**    A standard model for historically calibrated FX rates is a log-normal process,

$$dX(t) = \mu(t)X(t)dt + \sigma_X(t)X(t)dW(t).$$ (16.20)

The first question to address is how to calibrate the volatility $\sigma_X(t)$. The easiest assumption to make is that the volatility is constant and then it can be calibrated directly from a time series of spot FX values, $X_i$, through the variance of the log-returns over the calibration horizon. Suppose there are $N$ dates in the time series, then the volatility is simply given by

$$\sigma_X = \sqrt{Var\left(\log \frac{X_{i+1}}{X_i}\right) \times N_{trading}},$$

(16.21)

where $N_{trading}$ is the number of trading days per year and this is simply to annualise the volatility. The choice of calibration horizon again clearly affects how much near-term realised volatility will affect the calibration with longer horizons smoothing out short-term changes in volatility. Of course this is itself a reflection that in practice the market displays stochastic behaviour in realised volatility but in general this volatility of volatility is not included in historically calibrated models for credit risk on grounds of complexity.

Variants of this are possible and sometimes implemented. Some banks may choose to have a volatility term structure with multiple segments of historically calibrated volatility. For example, one possibility is to build the volatility term structure forward using a reversed historical calibration so that the first segment $\sigma_0$ applying over the period $t_0 < t < t_1$ is calibrated to the time series of FX rates occurring over the past period, $t_1$, and the second segment $\sigma_1$ applying over the period $t_1 < t < t_2$ is calibrated to the time series of FX rates from the past period $t_2$ to $t_1$ and so on. This introduces some dynamics into the volatility so that the short-term volatility reflects near-term historical conditions, while longer-term volatility reflects longer-term behaviour.

The choice of drift $\mu(t)$ is critical as it drives the behaviour of the FX rate in the long term. If the decision is made to fit the constant drift, $\mu$, to the historical drift then it can simply be chosen to match the average log return. The problem with this approach is that it can lead to quite extreme FX rate behaviour over the long horizons seen in a credit risk simulation, which can extend to fifty years or more. The calibration horizons in such models are often in the range one to three years so it is not impossible to see strong drifting behaviour over such time horizons as a result of central bank action to devalue the currency. However, it is also often the case that this will not persist for long periods. So, for example, the GBP USD exchange rate fell from \$1.98 in July 2008 to \$1.37 in January 2009, which if used as the historical drift would imply an exchange rate of \$0.0001 in 30 years' time which is not remotely realistic on an economic basis (at the time of writing GBP USD is now \$1.57). Worse still this is the *central prediction of the model* not an outlying extreme case so all the Monte Carlo paths will centre around this point. Introducing a historical term structure in the manner described above would help to control such behaviour if long time series are available.

An alternative with a log-normal model is to match the drift to the current FX forward rate. Clearly the FX forward rate just reflects the impact of the interest rate differential in both economies rather than the market view of where the FX rate will be in the future, that is,

$$F(t) = X(0) \exp \int_0^t (r_d(s) - r_f(s))ds,$$

(16.22)

where $r_d$ and $r_f$ are the domestic and foreign short rates respectively. In the context of the historical volatility calibration the FX can either be modelled independently of the two interest rates or with them. In the former case the drift is treated as deterministic but is set by the current FX forward rate so that

$$\mu(t) = \log\left(\frac{F(t)}{X(0)}\right). \tag{16.23}$$

If the FX rates are to be modelled in an integrated fashion with the interest rates then the drift is given by

$$\mu(t) = r_d(t) - r_f(t), \tag{16.24}$$

where both short rates are stochastic. Here the model is effectively risk neutral apart from the FX volatility which remains historic. A full treatment of the risk-neutral case is given in section 16.4.

If the risk-neutral drift is not viewed as desirable then it is of course possible to set the drift to zero and then the current spot value would remain the centre of the distribution of future FX rates.

One further possibility is to use a mean-reverting process for the FX rate as this would allow both a directional historically calibrated drift but retaining control of the long-term behaviour of the FX rate. Of course such a process requires the mean reversion level and mean reversion speed to be specified or calibrated using historical data.

**Historical Equity Calibration**   Historical equity processes are often modelling in a similar way to FX process so much of the discussion from section 16.2.1 also applies here. Historical volatility calibration would proceed in the same manner using equation (16.21) or the term structure variant. Again the choice of drift is important and the same criticisms apply in the case of a historically determined drift in that it can lead to extreme behaviour over long periods. Alternatively the drift may be determined deterministically from the equity forward or treated as a full part of a risk-neutral simulation with historical volatility. The slight difference here is that in the stochastic case the drift is given by

$$\mu(t) = r_d(t) - q(t), \tag{16.25}$$

where $q(t)$ contains a continuous dividend yield and adjustments from the equity repo rate for the stock in question. In generally the repo rate will not be treated as stochastic in a risk-neutral model as there is no source of implied volatility information and in any case it would add little to the sophistication of the model as the sensitivity to the repo rate is not generally considered important enough to warrant a stochastic treatment. In a historically calibrated context historical repo rate volatilities are available so it could be treated stochastically, although whether this is beneficial is questionable. The dividend is treated as a continuous yield in this case, although other choices are possible (see section 16.6.2).

Of course single stocks are not the only traded equity instrument and derivatives based on equity indices will often form a large part of an equity derivatives portfolio. The question then is how to model both the index and single stocks. This will be addressed in section 16.6 but essentially there are three choices: model the index directly, model the constituents and create the index as a basket or model index and stocks using common factors. In practice modelling large numbers of single stocks may be prohibitive computationally so the index

**TABLE 16.2**   Categories of commodities.

| Spot | Forward (storable) | Forward (limited storage) | Special (non-storable) |
|---|---|---|---|
| Gold | Base Metals e.g. Aluminium | Agricultural e.g. Wheat | Electricity |
| Silver | Oil | Natural Gas | $CO_2$ Emissions |
| Platinum | Oil Fractions e.g. Jet Fuel | | |
| Palladium | | | |

will be modelled directly in the same way as a single stock including the historical volatility calibration.

**Historical Commodity Calibration**   Commodities broadly fit into three categories: spot commodities, forward commodities and "special" commodities that do not readily fall into the other categories. These special commodities cannot be readily stored unlike other types of commodities. Table 16.2 gives examples of each type.

**Spot commodities**   Spot commodities are those which trade like a spot asset and behave in a similar manner to equities and FX. These are not considered to have strong mean reversion and so are frequently modelled using log-normal processes in the same manner as the equity and FX models described above and as such they can be modelled and calibrated in the same way.

**Forward commodities**   Forward commodities trade through markets consisting of forward and/or futures contracts. These commodities often have strong mean reversion or seasonal behaviour. Seasonal behaviour manifests itself when commodities cannot be stored indefinitely. Agricultural commodities are clearly seasonal in nature, while energy commodities like natural gas have a seasonal term structure based on the naturally higher demand in the northern hemisphere winter.[3]

There are a number of models used to describe forward-based commodity markets and in general these are derived from models used in the context of interest rate derivatives. Common examples then are models involving the use if a mean-reverting Ornstein-Uhlenbeck process and models that focus on the forward rates themselves by analogy with short rate and LIBOR market models respectively. The Clewlow-Strickland model (Clewlow and Strickland, 1999) is a commonly used model for commodities that specifies log-normal evolution of the forward curve:

$$dF(t, T) = F(t, T) \sum_{i=1}^{n} \sigma_F^i(t, T) dW_F^i(t). \tag{16.26}$$

---

[3]Mitigated in some respect by gas storage facilities.

Hence the forward curve evolves according to

$$F(t,T) = F(0,T) \exp\left[\sum_{i=1}^{n}\left\{-\frac{1}{2}\int_{s=0}^{t}\sigma_F^i(s,T)^2 ds + \int_{s=0}^{t}\sigma_F^i(s,T)dW^i(s)\right\}\right], \quad (16.27)$$

and the spot rate is given by setting $T = t$,

$$S(t) = S(0) \exp\left[\sum_{i=1}^{n}\left\{-\frac{1}{2}\int_{s=0}^{t}\sigma_F^i(s,T)^2 ds + \int_{s=0}^{t}\sigma_F^i(s,T)dW^i(s)\right\}\right]. \quad (16.28)$$

The critical question is what should be chosen as the volatility function. As an example consider reducing the model to one factor and choosing the volatility to be

$$\sigma(t,T) = \sigma \exp\left[-\alpha(T-t)\right]. \quad (16.29)$$

With this choice the dynamics of the spot rate become

$$\frac{dS(t)}{S(t)} = \left[\frac{\partial F(0,t)}{\partial t} + \alpha\left(\log F(0,t) - \log S(t)\right) + \frac{\sigma^2}{4}\left(1 - \exp(-2\alpha t)\right)\right]dt + \sigma dW_F(t), \quad (16.30)$$

and a Euler approximation to this SDE can be used to regress the volatility parameters, $\sigma$ and $\alpha$. A two-factor variant can be calibrated in a similar way.

The convenience yield approach is also relatively common in commodity markets (see for example Brigo and Bakkar, 2009; Carmona and Ludkovski, 2004; Schwartz and Smith, 2000). The model developed by Schwartz and Smith (2000) drives the commodity spot price, $S(t)$ with two stochastic factors, a short-term deviation $\chi(t)$ and an equilibrium level $\xi(t)$, where

$$\log S(t) = \chi(t) + \xi(t) \quad (16.31)$$
$$d\chi(t) = -\kappa\chi(t)dt + \sigma_\chi dW_\chi(t) \quad (16.32)$$
$$d\xi(t) = \mu_\xi dt + \sigma_\xi dW_\xi(t) \quad (16.33)$$
$$dW_\chi(t)dW_\xi(t) = \rho_{\chi,\xi}dt. \quad (16.34)$$

This model was later applied by Brigo and Bakkar (2009) in the context of counterparty credit risk. The two stochastic factors are jointly normally distributed with mean

$$\mathbb{E}[(\chi(t),\xi(t)] = [e^{-\kappa t}\chi(0),\xi(0) + \mu_\xi t], \quad (16.35)$$

and covariance

$$\text{Cov}[(\chi(t),\xi(t)] = \begin{bmatrix} (1-e^{-2\kappa t})\frac{\sigma_\chi^2}{2\kappa} & (1-e^{-\kappa t})\frac{\rho_{\chi,\xi}\sigma_\chi\sigma_\xi}{\kappa} \\ (1-e^{-\kappa t})\frac{\rho_{\chi,\xi}\sigma_\chi\sigma_\xi}{\kappa} & \sigma_\xi^2 t \end{bmatrix}. \quad (16.36)$$

With the initial values of the two factors the spot price is log-normally distributed with

$$\mathbb{E}[\log S(t)] = \mu_S(t) = e^{-\kappa t}\chi(0) + \xi(0) + \mu_\xi t \tag{16.37}$$

$$\text{Var}[\log S(t)] = \sigma_S(t) = (1 - e^{-2\kappa t})\frac{\sigma_\chi^2}{2\kappa} + \sigma_\xi^2 t + 2(1 - e^{-\kappa t})\frac{\rho_{\chi,\xi}\sigma_\chi\sigma_\xi}{\kappa}. \tag{16.38}$$

The model can be calibrated using a Kalman filter (Schwartz and Smith, 2000).

The Schwartz and Smith (2000) model does not explicitly define the convenience yield but it is in fact completely equivalent to the stochastic convenience yield model of Gibson and Schwartz (1990) that was also used by Gabillon (1991) in the context of Oil futures. If $X(t) = \log S(t)$ the dynamics of the Gibson and Schwartz (1990) model are:

$$dX(t) = \left(\mu - \delta(t) - \frac{1}{2}\sigma_1^2\right)dt + \sigma_1 dW_1(t) \tag{16.39}$$

$$d\delta(t) = \kappa(\alpha - \delta(t))dt + \sigma_2 dW_2(t), \tag{16.40}$$

where $\delta(t)$ is the convenience yield. The parameters of the Schwartz and Smith (2000) model are related to that of Gibson and Schwartz (1990) by

$$\chi(t) = \frac{1}{\kappa}(\delta(t) - \alpha) \tag{16.41}$$

$$\xi(t) = X(t) - \chi(t). \tag{16.42}$$

**Special commodities: electricity**    Electricity markets are principally traded through forward contracts for continuous delivery of electricity for a specified period, which can span a range lasting a few minutes through to continuous delivery of power (known as *baseload*). Unlike other commodities, electricity cannot be readily stored,[4] and hence the usual *cash and carry* argument linking spot and forward contracts does not apply (Geman, 2005). The forward contract markets depend strongly on the organisation of the national market in question. Exchange-traded futures markets are available but options are rarely traded. One critical feature of electricity markets is seasonality with demand in Northern Europe, for example, cyclical around the northern hemisphere winter (see for example Borovkova and Geman, 2007; Geman and Roncoroni, 2006). The second feature of electricity prices is small random movements due to short-term imbalances between supply and demand. The last main feature is the existence of sharp demand spikes where the cost of electricity spikes sharply upward for short periods of time and then moves down rapidly. The spikes are related to natural demand driving events such as a heat wave or may be related to falls in supply due to power plant outage.

One example of a historically calibrated power model is given by Geman and Roncoroni (2006) who propose a model of the form

$$dE(t) = \frac{d\mu}{dt}dt + \theta_1[\mu(t) - E(t^-)]dt + \sigma dW(t) + h(t^-)dJ(t), \tag{16.43}$$

---

[4]Aside from storage facilities such as the pumped-storage hydroelectric power station at Dinorwig in North Wales. The availability of such storage facilities depends on the region in question.

where E is the spot price of electricity, $f(t^-)$ is the left limit of the function $f$ at time $t$ and $\mu(t)$ is the seasonal trend of price dynamics. The process is of mean-reverting type ensuring that over time the price will diffuse back to the seasonal curve. The diffusive random behaviour is provided by the Brownian motion, while the spikes are driven by the jump process, $dJ(t)$. To obtain the desired behaviour of the jumps the sign of the jump is level-dependent so that after a large upward jump the subsequent jumps will be down. The number of jumps up to time $t$ is given by a counting process $N(t)$. The frequency of jumps is given by the intensity process,

$$\iota(t) = \theta_2 \times s(t) \tag{16.44}$$

where $s(t)$ is the normalised jump intensity shape and $\theta_2$ is the maximum number of expected jumps per unit time. The jumps are increments of a compound jump process,

$$J(t) = \sum_{i=1}^{N(t)} J_i, \tag{16.45}$$

where the $J_i$'s are independent and identically distributed with density

$$p(x; \theta_3, \psi) = c(\theta_3) \times \exp(\theta_3 f(x)), \quad 0 \leq x \leq \psi, \tag{16.46}$$

with $c(\theta_3)$ scaling the density and $\psi$ is the maximum jump size. The jump direction is given by the function

$$h(E(t)) = \begin{cases} +1 & \text{if} \quad E(t) < \mathcal{T}(t) \\ -1 & \text{if} \quad E(t) \geq \mathcal{T}(t) \end{cases}, \tag{16.47}$$

that is the jumps are upward if the price $E(t)$ is below the threshold $\mathcal{T}(t)$ and downward if above. This is done to achieve the characteristic price "spikes" which are difficult to achieve through other forms of jump process. To calibrate the model, four structural elements, $\mu(t), s(t), \mathcal{T}(t), p(x)$, and four parameters, $\theta_1, \theta_2, \theta_3$ and $\sigma$, must be fitted to the time series data. Geman and Roncoroni specify functional forms for the structural elements and then use a maximum likelihood method to fit the parameters to time series data of electricity prices.

A range of different models have been proposed for electricity prices. It is important to note that while all electricity markets share the same fundamental properties, the contracts traded and the details of each market are quite different. The range of available power generation facilities and the fuel sources that they use will make a difference to the behaviour of the price in each individual market. A good introduction to electricity markets can be found in Geman (2005).

**Special commodities: emissions**  Carbon emissions trading frameworks are designed to enforce a cap on overall emissions of $CO_2$ with the aim of reducing emissions over time. The *EU ETS* scheme (European Commission, 2013) covers power stations, manufacturing plants and airlines in the 28 EU member states along with Iceland, Liechtenstein and Norway. All companies that fall under the scheme must have allowances for every ton of $CO_2$ they emit or the equivalent in $N_2O$ or PFCs, otherwise they face steep fines. Emission allowances were primarily distributed by governments for free prior to 2013 but are now subject to an auction

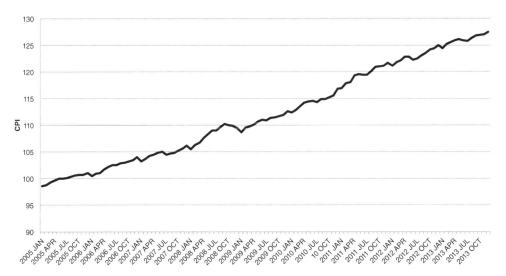

**FIGURE 16.1** UK CPI between January 2005 and December 2013 (Adapted from data from the Office for National Statistics licensed under the Open Government Licence v.2.0).

process. Once obtained, companies are then free to buy and sell emission allowances between themselves.

Carbon emissions permits can be very volatile in price. The price is also bounded rather than unbound and this adds complexity to modelling frameworks. For a review of emissions derivatives and suitable modelling techniques see Bloch (2010) and references therein.

**Historical Inflation Calibration** Inflation is defined in terms of the movement of the price of a basket of products. The price of the basket is indexed and normalised to a specific date. This index, commonly known as the Consumer Price Index (CPI), is published on a monthly schedule. UK CPI between 2005 and 2013 is illustrated in Figure 16.1. The composition of the basket of goods and services used to calculate CPI does vary between different countries and each index definition is periodically updated to ensure that the index remains relevant.

Inflation derivatives generally either reference the value of the CPI index directly or reference *year-on-year* inflation, which is defined as

$$Y(t_s, t_e) = \frac{I(t_e) - I(t_s)}{I(t_s)}. \tag{16.48}$$

For XVA calculations we need to value the inflation derivatives in the portfolio at all time steps and this will require not just the inflation index value but the full forward inflation curve. Option products will of course require implied volatilities.[5] Hence the model that is selected must model either the full inflation curve or decompose inflation into the spot CPI value and *real rate* using the Jarrow-Yildirim approach (Jarrow and Yildirim, 2003).

---

[5]Embedded options are relatively common in structured inflation products as caps and floors on inflation. Zero strike floors that prevent negative inflation are also common.

Full details of inflation modelling approaches are describe in section 16.5 below. In the context of historical calibration, one approach would be to use the Jarrow-Yildirim approach with a simple interest rate model. A time series of inflation curves would be used as input and decomposed into the spot CPI and real rates, with nominal rates provided by the regular discount curve in the relevant currency. The spot CPI would then be calibrated in the same way as that proposed for FX in section 16.2.1 while the real rate process would be calibrated as an interest rate in section 16.2.1. Correlations between the spot CPI, real short rate and nominal short rate would also be needed and would again be provided using historical time series.

**Historical Credit Spread Calibration**   The context here is specific to the modelling of CDS spreads inside an XVA (or PFE) calculation to allow the exposure to CDS and other credit derivative products to be estimated. A full discussion of modelling credit spreads is deferred until section 16.8. Here it is sufficient to note the critical properties of CDS spreads in the context of the $\mathbb{P}$-measure. CDS spreads will typically be modelled in terms of the hazard rate, $\lambda$, which is analogous to the short rate in the interest rate context. The probability of survival behaves like a discount bound price and is bounded on the interval between zero and one and is given by

$$P(\tau > t) = \exp\left(-\int_{s=0}^{t} \lambda(s)ds\right). \tag{16.49}$$

This suggests that the machinery of interest rates can be applied directly and indeed it can, although with important caveats. The first suggestion would be to apply a short rate model such as the Hull-White model described in section 16.2.1 with a similar historical calibration process. Such a model would suffer from the same defect, that is the hazard rate could become negative and imply a negative probability of default. This is perhaps even less desirable than negative interest rates but still may be acceptable because of the analytic tractability it would provide. However, the bigger problem will be that the volatility of the input CDS spreads is much higher than the volatility of interest rates, even historically. The model can be calibrated to higher volatilities but at a cost of higher probability of negative hazard rates. A CIR-type model would not offer much improvement, as while the hazard rate would be constrained to be positive, the volatility could not match the observed behaviour. A further alternative is to add jump processes and this is discussed in section 16.8. In practice the historical and implied modelling challenges are similar and dictated largely by the observed high volatility of both. If a high volatility is not required then a simple short rate model can be applied directly.

**Historical Correlations**   Historical and risk-neutral models need correlations as an input and typically these are used as the correlations between the Brownian motions driving the asset processes in the model. In the context of a Monte Carlo model the correlation matrix is constructed and then an appropriate method of inducing correlation on a set of independent normal samples is chosen such as *Cholesky decomposition*.[6] The key point to make is that these Brownian correlations are model-dependent and must be related to observable quantities in the market.

---

[6]See section 17.4.2.

Consider the simplest case of two single-factor geometric Brownian motions driving two asset prices, $S_1$ and $S_2$,

$$dS_1 = \mu S_1 dt + \sigma_1 dW_1 \tag{16.50}$$
$$dS_2 = \mu S_2 dt + \sigma_2 dW_2, \tag{16.51}$$

where $dW_1 dW_2 = \rho dt$. Using a Euler discretisation these equations become

$$\log S_1(t_{i+1}) = \log S_1(t_i) + (\mu - \frac{1}{2}\sigma_1^2)\Delta t + \sigma_1 \sqrt{\Delta t}\epsilon_1(t_i) \tag{16.52}$$

$$\log S_2(t_{i+1}) = \log S_2(t_i) + (\mu - \frac{1}{2}\sigma_2^2)\Delta t + \sigma_2 \sqrt{\Delta t}\epsilon_2(t_i), \tag{16.53}$$

where the random samples, $\epsilon_j(t_i)$ are drawn from the bivariate normal distribution with correlation $\rho$ and $\Delta t = t_{i+1} - t_i$. From the definition of covariance,

$$Covar(A, B) = \mathbb{E}\left[(A - \mathbb{E}(A))(B - \mathbb{E}(B))\right]$$

it is easy to show that the covariance of the log returns of the two assets gives the required input correlation,

$$\rho = \frac{Covar(\log(S_1(t_{i+1})/S_1(t_i)), \log(S_2(t_{i+1})/S_2(t_i)))}{\sigma_1 \sigma_2 \Delta t}. \tag{16.54}$$

For a short rate interest rate model we can adopt the same approach and consider the correlation between a interest rate following a Hull-White model and a separate spot process that follows a geometrical Brownian motion. The discrete form of the Hull-White model is given by equation (16.10) and this can be used to form the covariance. The model correlation is given by

$$\rho = \frac{Covar(\log(S(t_{i+1})/S(t_i)), r_{i+1} - r_i)}{\sigma_S \sigma \left(\frac{1-e^{-2\alpha\Delta t}}{2\alpha}\right)^{-\frac{1}{2}}\Delta t}. \tag{16.55}$$

As was the case with the historical volatility calibration this focuses attention on what is chosen as a proxy for the unobservable short rate, although clearly the same rate should be chosen for both historical volatility and historical correlation estimation. For the risk-neutral case, where historical correlations are used, the choice of proxy falls to a representative rate.

Care does need to be exercised when using historical correlations. While a single number with no term structure is often the only practical choice, there is no reason to believe that the correlation observed from time series will remain fixed. Indeed for risk-neutral models, imposing a term structure on the correlation or indeed more complex models of the covariance may be appropriate. Furthermore the degree to which the correlation changes depends on the length of time series window chosen to measure the correlation. In general the longer the window, the more damped short-term correlation changes will be. In the context of credit risk models that are intended to measure the "worst-case" credit exposure and manage credit risk through credit limits and diversification then a stable correlation is appropriate. Credit limits are a passive method of managing credit risk and there is little to be gained if historical correlations or volatilities change rapidly and cause limit breaches as a result. Figure 16.2 illustrates the effect of the choice of window size on the measured historical correlation between the log returns of EURUSD and EURGBP over the period from 1999 to 2009. The longer correlation windows show considerably less volatility.

For CVA, even if risk-neutral models are chosen, in all likelihood some correlation inputs will be historical. There are few instruments that can be used to infer market implied correlation and even where they exist market liquidity is often too limited to be able to draw meaningful conclusions about correlations from observed market prices. The choice of window for correlation estimation is then driven by two competing factors, a shorter window will have a more implied character, changing in response to changing market conditions while a longer window will be more stable but may miss real changes in market conditions. Of course if historical calibrations are used they cannot be hedged in any meaningful sense.

The choice of approach to correlation depends also on how critical it is to the modelling of the exposure. For correlation products correlation is a major contributor to the value and hence to the resultant exposure, while for more benign instruments, the correlation behaviour is less critical, although still important for accurate pricing.

Correlation also appears in the co-dependence between the exposure and the integration density in XVA integrals, that is in right-way/wrong-way risk. In some circumstances a historical correlation might be appropriate to use. However, marking the correlation to a conservative level is just as valid in many circumstances.

## 16.2.2　The Case for Market Implied Calibration

The use of a market implied risk-neutral model and calibration for XVA is driven by two main factors; the fact that the XVAs are elements of derivative valuation and by the desire or need to hedge the risk associated with them. Viewed this way the true value of the derivative portfolio includes the impact of credit, funding and capital and hence the XVAs are simply a convenient way of separating the risk factors for optimal internal risk management purposes. It is therefore clear that XVA must be valued risk-neutrally using a model calibrated to market implied data to be consistent with standard valuation practice for derivatives. Furthermore, it could be argued that a single self-consistent model that includes all the risk factors to which a derivative portfolio is sensitive could, and perhaps should, be used to value all derivative portfolios in a bank including counterparty credit risk, funding costs and capital.

Related to the valuation argument are market and accounting standards. CVA is also an accounting requirement so the accountancy firms performing account audits must be satisfied that the calculation used to estimate CVA is appropriate and to a degree consistent across the market. This will also be an element for FVA calculation as banks increasingly take FVA reserves. As noted in Chapter 12, regulators are also increasingly engaged in the debate around valuation methodology and valuation adjustments including CVA and FVA. The introduction of *prudent valuation* includes significant impact on the way banks are required to value derivative portfolios which in turn impacts on CVA and FVA calculation. Market standard accounting practice is to use a risk-neutral approach for CVA and FVA.

The second main driver of risk neutrality is the requirement to hedge XVA. Just as with exotic derivative products, it is important for hedging purposes that the model correctly revalues the desired hedging instruments. If this is not done there is no guarantee that the hedge portfolio will correctly eliminate the desired risks. In practice, however, the need for

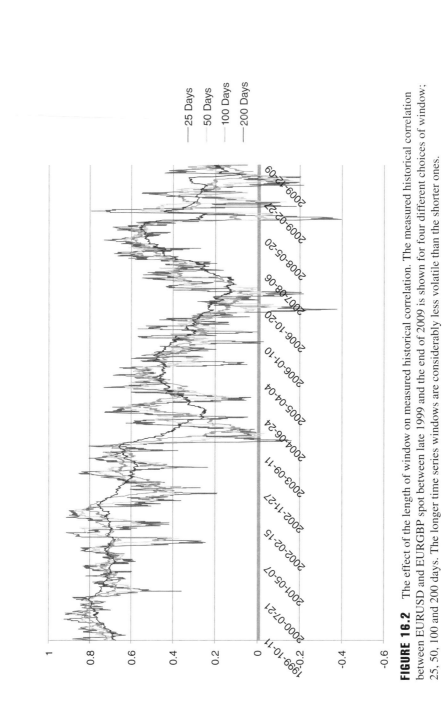

**FIGURE 16.2** The effect of the length of window on measured historical correlation. The measured historical correlation between EURUSD and EURGBP spot between late 1999 and the end of 2009 is shown for four different choices of window; 25, 50, 100 and 200 days. The longer time series windows are considerably less volatile than the shorter ones.

**TABLE 16.3**  A summary of the case for market implied calibration for the XVA Monte Carlo simulation.

| Issue | Status |
| --- | --- |
| Consistent with credit risk/PFE | ✗ |
| Matches historical expected loss | ✗ |
| Arbitrage free | ✓ |
| Consistent with hedge instrument | ✓ |
| Market standard (for accounting) | ✓ |

a fully risk-neutral model is more nuanced. A model which matched all forward curves and was properly adjusted for the choice of numeraire asset would correctly re-price all linear instruments even if a historical volatility calibration was used.

For the most part, CVA hedging consists of delta hedging rather than using option hedges, so such an approach could be justified on these grounds. Options are sometimes used to hedge the volatility sensitivity of the CVA, which can be a significant risk factor. The CVA is in effect a compound option on the portfolio value that arises through the max function that is applied on close-out. Despite this, historically volatility hedging is often limited by the practicality of estimating the vega risk. For example, calculating the interest rate vega using finite difference would require a potentially huge number of CVA calculations to cover the full interest rate swaption volatility surface. Vega is expensive to compute by finite difference and is often not calculated because of limitations on computational capacity, although the introduction of algorithmic differentiation and related techniques is now making sensitivities far less expensive to calculate (see Chapter 21). Out-of-the-money options can also be used as a low-cost "catastrophe" hedge to limit losses in extreme market moves. The problem is that the most common types of models used in CVA such as the Hull-White interest rate model do not calibrate or match to the volatility skew in any way and so the price of the out-of-the-money option calculated in the CVA model will still not match the market price, even if the model is calibrated risk-neutrally using the at-the-money volatilities.

The case for market implied calibration is summarised in Table 16.3.

**Hybrid Approaches and Risk-Neutral Calibration in Practice**  XVA calculations typically demand huge amounts of market data and it is frequently the case that not all of that demand can be met within a given organisation. A typical example of this would be a bank calculating XVA on portfolios containing emerging market currency FX forwards (often non-deliverable forwards). The CVA/FVA model would frequently assume that all interest rates are stochastic and so under a risk-neutral calibration interest rate option volatilities are required for all the emerging market currencies in the portfolio. Unfortunately some of these markets will not have developed interest rate options markets and so no volatility information may be available or it may be limited to very short maturities. Even if option volatilities are available some institutions will not trade these markets so volatilities may not be readily available. This leaves a question about how to generate the appropriate calibration data for all assets in the portfolio. Where market data has to be generated, the sophistication of the approach adopted should reflect the materiality of the contribution to XVA of the affected trades.

One option would be to use a historical calibration where volatility information is not available. This would give a risk-neutral/historical hybrid approach. Given that if the implied volatility data is not available it is very likely that there are no options that can be purchased and hence from a hedging perspective there is no need to make up implied volatilities. The alternative is to use proxy data sources. It could be appropriate, for example, to proxy some emerging market interest rate volatilities by a regional representative where interest rate volatility is available. A proxy process could also involve the use of spreads above or below known market data so for example a proxy implied volatility surface may be $x\%$ above an underlying volatility surface. While such an approach may appear to lack rigour, there is evidence that some option markets trade in this fashion.

Where alternatives to market implied data have been used there are implications for risk management. Where a proxy has been used the instruments associated with the proxy can be used for hedging purposes. Of course should the proxy change in the future or indeed be replaced by actual market data then the hedge trades will not match the new risk position. Where historical volatility data is used then delta hedging is the only risk management option.

**Standard Market Practice and the Basel Committee**    As has already been noted, standard market practice for the calculation of CVA and FVA uses a risk-neutral approach, while the most common approach for Monte Carlo models used for potential future exposure and credit limit management is historical (see for example Thompson and Dahinden, 2013). As noted earlier in Chapter 12, under the *internal model method* approach to the CVA capital calculation for those banks with appropriate regulatory approvals, the CVA formula is given by (BCBS, 2011b)

$$
\begin{aligned}
CVA = (LGD_{MKT}) \sum_{i=t}^{T} \max \left( 0; \exp \left( \frac{-s_{i-1} t_{i-1}}{LGD_{MKT}} \right) - \exp \left( \frac{-s_i t_i}{LGD_{MKT}} \right) \right) \\
\times \left( \frac{EE_{i-1} + EE_i}{2} \right).
\end{aligned}
\tag{16.56}
$$

The formula is a simplification of the standard unilateral CVA formula, equation (3.13), where the survival probability is implicitly calculated from the CDS spreads using

$$
\Phi(\tau > t_i) \approx \exp \left( \frac{-s_i t_i}{LGD_{MKT}} \right).
$$

The use of market loss-given-default values, $LGD_{MKT}$, and market CDS spreads, $s$, is consistent with standard market practice for unilateral CVA, although the formula is simplified by removing the intermediate step of generating the survival probabilities using a credit curve model.

Neither the Basel framework nor the implementation in CRD IV (European Parliament and the Council of the European Union, 2013a; European Parliament and the Council of the European Union, 2013b) specifies what approach should be taken to calculate the expected exposure values. The only requirements are those needed to obtain authorisation to use internal models. Most of the models will in fact be calibrated historically because of the usual requirement that the engine used for IMM is already in use for credit risk measurement. This leads to a potential discrepancy between between the manner in which CVA capital and accounting CVA are calculated. This is even more of a potential problem when CVA hedging is considered as the optimal hedge to minimise CVA capital requirements may be different from that needed to eliminate CDS spread risk from accounting CVA. Of course this assumes the use of a unilateral CVA model; if bilateral is used then the differences between CVA capital and accounting CVA will be magnified.

## 16.3 THE CHOICE OF INTEREST RATE MODELLING FRAMEWORK

Ultimately CVA and FVA models are hybrid derivative valuation models and as such they can be viewed as complex extensions of models previously used in the pricing of hybrid derivatives such as *Power-Reverse Dual Callables* (PRDCs) and *long-dated FX barrier options* with both long-dated interest rate risk and FX risk. Given that the key risk in the modelling of credit exposures is interest rate risk the foundation of any XVA model is the choice of interest rate model. Interest rates are inevitably treated as stochastic and this brings in the full spectrum of interest rate derivative modelling. Once the interest rate model has been chosen, the models for all other asset classes can be chosen and modelled alongside it. Because interest rates are stochastic the choice of measure/numeraire influences the form of all other stochastic processes. The full machinery of stochastic calculus is therefore applied and familiarity with it is essential.[7]

The earliest attempt to model interest rate derivatives was the extension of the Black-Scholes model by Fisher Black (Black, 1976) to price interest rate caps and floors. The first term structure model was a model of the so-called short rate or instantaneous interest rate by Vasicek (1977). The short rate term structure framework was enhanced and expanded by a number of different authors including Hull and White (1990) whose model built on that of Vasicek but allowed term structure calibration to a series of option prices. Ultimately this led to the continuous time Heath-Jarrow-Morton (HJM) framework (Heath, Jarrow and Morton, 1992). In the early to mid-1990s, a second framework was developed by a number of market practitioners and academic researchers. This model was based on a set of discrete interest rate forwards that make up the yield curve. The forward rates were most often those that underlay the product being valued such as a Bermudan swaption. This type of model is known as BGM (Brace-Gatarek-Musiela) (Brace, Gatarek and Musiela, 1997) or LMM (LIBOR Market Model). Both short rate and LMM model frameworks have been further developed with focus centred on matching of the observed volatility skew in the market. All term structure models were initially targeted at the pricing of structured interest rate derivatives and this continues to be the primary area of application. While both HJM and LMM frameworks can be used to price all interest rate derivatives, there is a slight bias towards more exotic products under LMM and less exotic products under HJM models.

The drivers behind interest rate models applied in the context of expected exposure modelling differ from those in the interest rate derivatives market. CVA and FVA models are almost always required to be multi-currency and multi-asset so the framework imposed by the

---

[7]For mathematical preliminaries there are many good textbooks of which Brigo and Mercurio (2006) and Shreve (2004) are two popular examples.

interest rate model has to be amenable to this, although the main exposures will be to interest rates, FX and inflation. In practice this means that the joining between the different asset-class models needs to be well controlled. The need for a multi-asset framework may also mean that simpler models that are well understood may be more appropriate than highly complex models where the overall model structure and joining between different elements of the model is difficult to appreciate. The key issue though with the implementation of CVA and FVA models is the requirement for high performance Monte Carlo. In general the bulk of the time in the simulation should be spent in trade valuations and Monte Carlo path building should be a relatively low computational cost. For interest rate models this requirement immediately favours Markovian models over non-Markovian, as with the former much of the calculation can be done at the initialisation stage and then cached for each path to use as it is generated. Non-Markovian models have path-dependent drift calculations that can be expensive to perform. Another related consideration is the speed at which the discount function can be generated at each time step for each path. For any portfolio it is highly likely that the most frequently called function during the valuation is `getDiscountFactor`. Models which give a discount function that can either be evaluated using a simple fast analytic formula or simple numerical procedure will win over more complex numerical approaches. Of course data caching strategies inside the Monte Carlo simulation also play a role.

### 16.3.1 Interest Rate Models (for XVA)

The number and variety of models for interest rates that have been developed since the 1970s is huge but some of the most significant and the relationships between them are illustrated in Figure 16.3. Broadly there are four categories of model: *short-rate* models, *Heath-Jarrow-Morton (HJM)* models, *Market Models* and *Markov Functional Models*. HJM models are constructed around the instantaneous forward rate, although in most cases this is equivalent to a representation constructed around the dynamics of the instantaneous short rate. Hence most short rate models are also HJM models and hence early models of this type were later found to fit within the HJM modelling framework. HJM models are, in general, constructed to be Markovian. Market models are constructed around the dynamics of discrete forward rates or more infrequently swap rates. Market models became popular in the 1990s as the structured interest rate derivative market grew in size and complexity since market models generally allow a much greater variety of yield curve shapes than HJM models. Market models are non-Markovian. Markov functional models are a class of model that aims to recover the benefits of market models but remain Markovian. The remainder of this section discusses HJM models and market models. Markov functional models will not be discussed explicitly, although some Cheyette and Quadratic Gaussian model variants can be considered Markov functional models.

### 16.3.2 The Heath-Jarrow-Morton (HJM) Framework and Models of the Short Rate

The HJM framework (Heath, Jarrow and Morton, 1992) specifies the dynamics of the instantaneous forward rate, $f(t, T)$,

$$df(t, T) = \alpha(t, T)dt + \sigma(t, T) \cdot dW(t), \tag{16.57}$$

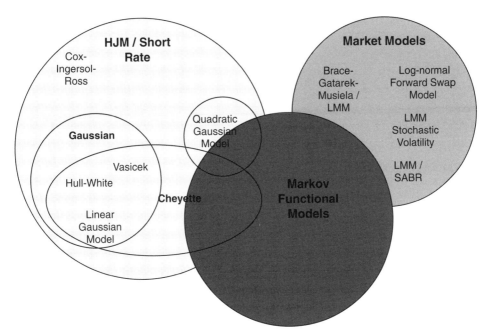

**FIGURE 16.3**   Popular interest rate models and modelling frameworks and the relationships between them. Of course the number of different types of interest rate model is vast and only a subset is shown.

where $W$ is an N-dimensional Brownian motion and $\sigma$ is the N-dimensional volatility vector. The relationship between the forward rate and the discount bond price is given by

$$f(t, T) = -\frac{\partial \log P(t, T)}{\partial T}, \tag{16.58}$$

which can be used to set the initial term structure by specifying $f(0, T)$. In order to be arbitrage free Heath, Jarrow and Morton proved that there are constraints on the drift process, $\alpha(t, T)$,[8]

$$\alpha(t, T) = \sigma(t, T) \int_t^T \sigma(t, s)ds. \tag{16.59}$$

Hence the dynamics of the forward rates are given by

$$\boxed{f(t, T) = f(0, T) + \int_0^t \sigma(u, T) \cdot \int_u^T \sigma(t, s)dsdu + \int_0^t \sigma(t, T) \cdot dW(s).} \tag{16.60}$$

---

[8]See for example Pelsser (2000); Shreve (2004).

The short rate $r(t)$ is just the instantaneous forward rate at maturity, $f(t, t)$, so the dynamics of the short rate are given by

$$r(t) = r(0) + \int_0^t \sigma(u, t) \cdot \int_u^t \sigma(t, s) ds du + \int_0^t \sigma(t, t) \cdot dW(s). \qquad (16.61)$$

In general the models in the section specify the dynamics in terms of the behaviour of the short rate; nevertheless they are also HJM models.

## Hull-White (Generalised)

**The model**   The Hull-White model (Hull and White, 1990) is probably the most popular model for interest rate evolution in the context of XVA calculations. The model offers a combination of properties that make it a pragmatic choice for XVA, although one that is subject to criticism:

- It is Markovian allowing a high degree of caching and hence high computational performance (although this is much less important on GPUs than on CPUs).
- Analytically tractable, particularly the bond price formula which again leads to high computational performance.
- Simple to calibrate to European swaption or interest rate caplet/floorlet prices.

There are some shortcomings in an XVA context:

- The model displays a volatility skew with respect to log-normal models but there is no control over its behaviour. Interest rate markets often display strong volatility skews where options on different strikes but the same maturity and tenor show different option implied volatilities (from the Black model). As will be illustrated below, in the Hull-White model, discrete forwards have a shifted-log-normal distribution which naturally displays a skew relative to a log-normal model. The key issue is that this skew does not match market behaviour.
- The model does not generate a rich set of yield curve shapes even if more than one stochastic factor is used (see for example Rebonato and Cooper, 1994).
- The model is not a multi-curve model, however, it is straightforward to extend the model using deterministic spread curves (see section 16.3.5).

In addition the short rate is Gaussian and so negative rates will be produced in a Monte Carlo simulation. Negative rates are now a real feature of interest rate markets, although historically this was not always the case. Hence, negative rates should now be regarded as a desirable property of an interest rate model, even if once this was regarded as undesirable.

The model in its original form was a simple extension of the Vasicek model and it is often referred to as the *Extended Vasicek* model as a result:

$$dr(t) = (\theta(t) - \alpha r(t)) dt + \sigma dW(t),$$

where the mean reversion level, $\theta(t)$ has been made a function of time and, as will be demonstrated later, this allows the model to be fitted to the initial term structure of rates. In general the volatility is also allowed to be a function of time, often a piecewise constant function, to allow calibration to a set of interest rate options such as a strip of coterminal European swaptions,

$$dr(t) = (\theta(t) - \alpha r(t))dt + \sigma(t)dW(t), \tag{16.62}$$

where the measure is taken to be that associated with the continuous rolling money-market account. To obtain a solution note that

$$d(e^{\alpha t}r(t)) = \alpha e^{\alpha t}r(t)dt + e^{\alpha t}dr(t),$$

and hence that

$$d(e^{\alpha t}r(t)) = e^{\alpha t}\theta(t)dt + e^{\alpha t}\sigma(t)dW(t).$$

This can be integrated to give r(t),

$$r(t) = r(0)e^{-\alpha t} + \int_0^t \theta(s)e^{\alpha(s-t)}ds + \int_0^t e^{\alpha(s-t)}\sigma(s)dW(s). \tag{16.63}$$

To obtain a formula for the bond price first note that under the Feynman-Kac theorem (see for example Karatzas and Shreve, 1991) the value of derivatives, $V(t, r)$, must satisfy the following PDE,

$$\frac{\partial V}{\partial t} + (\theta(t) - \alpha r(t))\frac{\partial V}{\partial r} + \frac{1}{2}\sigma(t)^2\frac{\partial^2 V}{\partial r^2} - r(t)V = 0. \tag{16.64}$$

Applying this in the context of the bond price and noting that the bond price will be affine we use the form

$$\boxed{V(t, r) = P(t, T) = A(t, T)e^{-B(t,T)r(t)},} \tag{16.65}$$

as a trial solution. Substituting this into equation (16.64) gives

$$V\left(\frac{1}{A}\frac{\partial A}{\partial t} - r\frac{\partial B}{\partial t}\right) - BV(\theta(t) - \alpha r) + \frac{1}{2}\sigma(t)^2B^2V - rV = 0$$

$$\left(\frac{1}{A}\frac{\partial A}{\partial t} - B\theta(t) + \frac{1}{2}\sigma(t)^2B^2\right) - r\left(\frac{\partial B}{\partial t} - \alpha + 1\right) = 0.$$

The only way this expression can be zero for all $t$ is if both expressions in brackets are zero so this gives PDEs that $A$ and $B$ must satisfy the following simple Riccati equations,

$$\frac{1}{A}\frac{\partial A}{\partial t} - B\theta(t) + \frac{1}{2}\sigma(t)^2B^2 = 0 \tag{16.66}$$

$$\frac{\partial B}{\partial t} - \alpha + 1 = 0. \tag{16.67}$$

Equation (16.67) can be solved to give B, noting that $B(T, T) = 0$,

$$
B(t, T) = \frac{1}{\alpha}\left(1 - e^{-\alpha(T-t)}\right). \tag{16.68}
$$

Equation (16.66) can then be solved for A, given that $A(T, T) = 1$,

$$
\begin{aligned}
A(t, T) &= \exp\left[-\int_t^T \theta(s)B(s, T) - \frac{1}{2}\sigma(s)^2 B(s, T)^2 ds\right] \\
&= \exp\left[-\int_t^T \theta(s)\frac{1}{\alpha}\left(1 - e^{-\alpha(T-s)}\right) - \frac{\sigma(s)^2}{2\alpha^2}\left(1 - e^{-\alpha(T-s)}\right)^2 ds\right].
\end{aligned} \tag{16.69}
$$

Hence the bond price can be obtained from the short rate $r$ using these expressions. Note that the bond price only depends on the short rate.

**Calibration to bond prices**    To calibrate the model two steps need to be taken; the mean reversion level, $\theta(t)$, needs to be fitted to the initial term structure, while the volatility function, $\sigma(t)$, needs to be fitted to interest rate option prices. To fit the initial term structure the bond price formula can be used for $t = 0$,

$$
P(0, T) = A(0, T)e^{-r(0)B(0,T)}. \tag{16.70}
$$

Note that the instantaneous forward rate is given by

$$
f(t, T) = -\frac{\partial \log P(t, T)}{\partial T},
$$

and so by differentiating the log of equation (16.70) gives

$$
-\frac{\partial \log P(0, T)}{\partial T} = f(0, T) = \int_0^T \left(\theta(s) + \sigma^2(s)B(s, T)\right)\frac{\partial B(s, T)}{\partial T} ds + r(0)\frac{\partial B(0, T)}{\partial T}. \tag{16.71}
$$

Differentiating this expression again gives

$$
\begin{aligned}
\frac{\partial f(0, T)}{\partial T} &= \theta(T) + \int_0^T \theta(s)\frac{\partial^2 B(s, T)}{\partial T^2} ds + \int_0^T \sigma^2(s)B(s, T)\left(\frac{\partial B(s, T)}{\partial T}\right)^2 ds \\
&\quad + \int_0^T \sigma^2(s)B(s, T)\frac{\partial^2 B(s, T)}{\partial T^2} ds + r(0)\frac{\partial^2 B(s, T)}{\partial T^2}.
\end{aligned} \tag{16.72}
$$

Combining equations (16.71) and (16.72) gives an expression for $\theta(T)$ in terms of the initial instantaneous forward curve and its first derivative,

$$
\theta(T) = \alpha f(0, T) + \frac{\partial f(0, T)}{\partial T}
$$

$$- \int_0^T \sigma^2(s) \left[ \left( \frac{\partial B(s,T)}{\partial T} \right)^2 + B(s,T) \frac{\partial^2 B(s,T)}{\partial T^2} + \alpha B(s,T) \frac{\partial B(s,T)}{\partial T} \right] ds. \quad (16.73)$$

Note that the expression contains the derivative of the initial instantaneous forward rate $\frac{\partial f(0,T)}{\partial T}$ which could be problematic. However, in general only discrete integrals are used so in practice this derivative is unlikely ever to be needed. In the case that the volatility is constant, this expression can be simplified. The derivatives of $B(t,T)$ are

$$\frac{\partial B(t,T)}{\partial T} = -e^{-\alpha(T-t)} \quad (16.74)$$

$$\frac{\partial^2 B(t,T)}{\partial T^2} = \alpha e^{-\alpha(T-t)}. \quad (16.75)$$

Hence

$$\boxed{\begin{aligned} \theta(T) &= \alpha f(0,T) + \frac{\partial f(0,T)}{\partial T} - \sigma^2 \int_0^T \left[ e^{-2\alpha(T-t)} \right] ds \\ &= \alpha f(0,T) + \frac{\partial f(0,T)}{\partial T} + \frac{\sigma^2}{2\alpha} [1 - e^{-2\alpha T}]. \end{aligned}} \quad (16.76)$$

The mean reversion speed is often specified as a constant parameter under the Hull-White model, although it is possible to allow it to be time-dependent and this is the case in the *Linear Gaussian model* variant of Hull-White discussed in section 16.3.2. When the mean reversion speed is fixed it is often calibrated historically or directly specified to give acceptable physical behaviour of the short rate. That is the mean reversion speed controls how fast the short rate reverts to its long-term mean and hence should be specified so that the speed is consistent with observed market behaviour.

**Calibration to option prices** To calibrate the volatility parameter term structure, formulae for the prices of vanilla interest rate options are required. To derive an analytic formula for the prices of caplets and European swaptions the dynamics of the bond price in the T-forward measure, the measure associated with the discount bond maturing at time $T$ as numeraire asset, are required. The dynamics of the bond price in the money market account numeraire are given by an application of Itô's lemma to equation (16.70). This gives the bond price dynamics as:

$$\begin{aligned} \frac{dP(t,T)}{P(t,T)} &= \left[ \frac{1}{A(t,T)} \frac{\partial A(t,T)}{\partial t} - r(t) \frac{\partial B(t,T)}{\partial t} - B(t,T)\{\theta(t) - r(t)\alpha\} \right. \\ &\left. + \frac{1}{2}\sigma^2(t)B^2(t,T) \right] dt - B(t,T)\sigma(t)dW(t) \end{aligned} \quad (16.77)$$

Recalling that $A$ and $B$ satisfy equations (16.66) and (16.67) allows this to be simplified:

$$\frac{dP(t,T)}{P(t,T)} = r(t)dt - B(t,T)\sigma(t)dW(t). \quad (16.78)$$

The money market account is given by

$$M(t) = e^{\int_0^t r(s)ds} \tag{16.79}$$

and obeys

$$dM(t) = M(t)dt. \tag{16.80}$$

Hence the change of measure to the T-forward measure is given by (see Brigo and Mercurio, 2006)

$$dW(t) = dW^T(t) - B(t, T)\sigma(t)dt. \tag{16.81}$$

The bond price dynamics may now be written in the T-forward measure

$$\frac{dP(t, T)}{P(t, T)} = \left[ r(t) - \frac{1}{2}\sigma^2(t)B^2(t, T) \right] dt - B(t, T)\sigma(t)dW^T(t). \tag{16.82}$$

The price of a caplet with strike $K$ on the forward rate beginning at time $T_B$ and ending at $T_E$ is given by

$$C(0, T_B, T_E) = P(0, T_E)\mathbb{E}^{T_E}[(L(T_B, T_E) - K)^+], \tag{16.83}$$

where $L(T_B, T_E)$ is the forward rate defined by

$$L(t, T_B, T_E) = \frac{1}{a(T_B, T_E)} \left( \frac{P(t, T_B)}{P(t, T_E)} - 1 \right), \tag{16.84}$$

and $a(T_B, T_E)$ is the day count fraction and the trade notional has been set equal to 1. Writing

$$Y(t) = \frac{P(t, T_B)}{P(t, T_E)} \tag{16.85}$$

allows the caplet price to be re-written as an option on $Y(T_B)$ with a modified strike $K' = 1 + aK$,

$$C(0, T_B, T_E) = P(0, T_E)\frac{1}{a}\mathbb{E}^{T_E}[(Y(T_B) - K')^+]. \tag{16.86}$$

To proceed further the dynamics of the bond price ratio are needed. Applying the Itô product rule,

$$dXY = XdY + YdX + dXdY, \tag{16.87}$$

and noting that $Y(t)$ is a martingale in the $T_E$-forward measure it is easy to show that these are given by

$$dY(t) = Y(t)[B(t, T_E) - B(t, T_B)]\sigma(t)dW^{T_E}(t). \tag{16.88}$$

$Y(t)$ is a log-normal variable and hence we can directly solve the equation with a Black-type formula

$$\boxed{C(0, T_B, T_E) = P(0, T_E)Y(0)N(d_1) - P(0, T_E)K'N(d_2),} \tag{16.89}$$

where

$$d_1 = \frac{\log(Y(0)/K')}{\Sigma} + \frac{1}{2}\Sigma$$
$$d_2 = \quad d_1 - \Sigma$$

and

$$\Sigma = \int_0^{T_B} \left[B(t, T_B) - B(t, T_E)\right]^2 \sigma^2(t)dt.$$

A similar formula can be derived for the price of a physically settled European swaption. The value of a European swaption maturing at time $T_F$ under the $T_F$-forward measure is given by

$$S(0) = P(0, T_F)\mathbb{E}^{T_F}\left[\left(K\sum_{i=1}^N a_iP(t, T_i) + P(t, T_N) - P(t, T_0)\right)^+ \frac{1}{P(t, T_F)}\right], \tag{16.90}$$

where $K$ is the strike, the $T_i$ are the coupon dates of the underlying swap, $T_0$ is the start date of the swap and $a_i$ are the day count fractions of each coupon. The variable $t$ has been left in place so that the origin of the discount bond ratios is clear, while in fact $t = T_F$ and $P(T_F, T_F) = 1$. The notional has been set equal to 1. Defining $b_i$ by the following:

$$b_i = \quad Ka_i$$
$$b_N = 1 + Ka_N$$
$$b_0 = \quad 1$$

equation (16.90) becomes

$$S(0) = P(0, T_F)\mathbb{E}^{T_F}\left[(H_{T_F} - b_0)^+\right], \tag{16.91}$$

where

$$H(t) = \sum_{i=1}^N b_i \frac{P(t, T_i)}{P(t, T_F)}.$$

The approach outlined here is not the only possibility and other schemes are possible. In particular the *Jamshidian Decomposition* (1989)) allows European swaptions to be valued exactly as portfolios of put options on zero-coupon bonds for models that satisfy the constraint that

$$\frac{\partial P(t, T, r)}{\partial r} < 0 \qquad \text{for} \qquad 0 < t < T,$$

which is true of the one-factor Hull-White model (Brigo and Mercurio, 2006). However, the Jamshidian decomposition does not work in more than one factor, while the approach adopted here, although approximate, can be readily extended to the multi-factor case.

To proceed the dynamics of $H(t)$ are needed but given this is just a sum of discount bond ratios the results of the caplet calculation can also be applied directly. The dynamics of the discount bond ratios, $Y_i(t) = P(t, T_i)/P(t, T_F)$ are given by

$$dY_i(t) = Y_i(t)[B(t, T_i) - B(t, T_F)]\sigma(t)dW^{T_F}(t). \tag{16.92}$$

Hence the dynamics of $H(t)$ are given by

$$\frac{dH(t)}{H(t)} = \left( \frac{\sum_{i=1}^{N} b_i(B(t, T_i) - B(t, T_F))P(t, T_i)}{\sum_{i=1}^{N} b_i P(t, T_i)} \right) \sigma(t)dW^{T_F}(t). \tag{16.93}$$

Unfortunately this expression cannot be handled analytically so the diffusion coefficient is replaced by its $t = 0$ value so that

$$\frac{dH(t)}{H(t)} \approx \bar{\Sigma}dW^{T_F}(t), \tag{16.94}$$

where

$$\bar{\Sigma}(t) = \sigma(t) \left( \frac{\sum_{i=1}^{N} b_i(B(t, T_i) - B(t, T_F))P(0, T_i)}{\sum_{i=1}^{N} b_i P(0, T_i)} \right). \tag{16.95}$$

This approximation is commonly known as *freezing* the forward rates. In this case $H(t)$ is log-normal and so the price of a European swaption is a simple Black function

$$\boxed{S(t) = P(0, T_F)[H(0)N(d_1) - b_0 N(d_2)],} \tag{16.96}$$

where

$$d_1 = \frac{\log H(0)/b_0}{V(T_F)} + \frac{1}{2}V(T_F)$$

$$d_2 = d_1 - V(T_F)$$

$$V(T_F) = \sqrt{\int_0^{T_F} \bar{\Sigma}^2(s)ds}.$$

Having obtained formulae for the price of caplets and European swaptions in terms of the volatility function $\sigma(t)$ the model can be calibrated to the market prices of those options. The simplest way to proceed is to assume that the volatility function is piecewise constant. Then each step in the volatility function can be bootstrapped, either to caplet prices or to swaption prices. For *caplet calibration* the volatility function can be fitted to a strip of at-the-money caplets out to some specified maximum maturity. So, for example, the function could be specified in segments of six months and the volatility function calibrated to the value of six-month caplets out to say 30 years. For *swaption calibration* the most appropriate choice would be to calibrate to a set of at-the-money coterminal swaptions with a specified final maturity. Each segment of the volatility function can then be bootstrapped using successive swaption prices, each covering one less segment of volatility.

In general such bootstrap approaches are fast and stable. The actual numerical solution can be done using a root-finding algorithm such as *Brent's Method* (Brent, 1973). In practice the available liquid option data may be shorter than the time period over which expected exposure calculations will run and so extrapolation behaviour for the volatility function may need to be specified. Suitable choices could be to extrapolate flat from the last calibrated point or to use an average volatility over segments.

**Monte Carlo implementation**  The implementation of the Monte Carlo is exact and will be done using the short rate as the key stochastic state variable. The equation for the short rate, (16.63), can be written as

$$
r(t_i) = r(t_{i-1})e^{-\alpha t_i} + \int_{t_{i-1}}^{t_i} \theta(s)e^{\alpha(s-t_i)}ds + \int_{t_{i-1}}^{t_i} e^{\alpha(s-t_i)}\sigma(s)dW(s) \qquad (16.97)
$$

and hence the short rate at each simulation time step $t_i$ can be obtained by evaluating the deterministic integral segments

$$
\int_{t_{i-1}}^{t_i} \theta(s)e^{\alpha(s-t_i)}ds
$$

and evaluating the increments in the stochastic integral

$$
\int_{t_{i-1}}^{t_i} e^{\alpha(s-t_i)}\sigma(s)dW(s),
$$

along each path. The deterministic elements of the integrals can be cached if necessary. Each segment is independent, has mean zero and volatility,

$$
\bar{\sigma}(t_{i-1}, t_i) = \sqrt{\int_{t_{i-1}}^{t_i} e^{2\alpha(s-t_i)}\sigma^2(s)ds}. \qquad (16.98)
$$

Hence these can be readily simulated from a sequence of i.i.d. normal variates $z_i$ using

$$
\bar{\sigma}(t_{i-1}, t_i)z_i.
$$

Once $r(t_i)$ has been obtained then the bond price equation can be used to give discount bond prices for any maturity on path $j$,

$$P_j(t_i, T) = A(t_i, T)e^{-r_j(t_i)B(t_i, T)}. \tag{16.99}$$

The functions $A(t, T)$ and $B(t, T)$ involve integrals that cannot be fully evaluated in advance unless $T$ is known. There are several different computational strategies available at this point. If at the start of the simulation all the required maturities $T_k$ are known, as will in general be the case, then it is possible to simply calculate all the values of $A(t_i, T_k)$ and $B(t_i, T_k)$ up front and store them if necessary. A lookup process could then be used inside the Monte Carlo simulation whenever a bond price is called for. For very large portfolios where large numbers of discount bond prices will be called for by trade valuation routines, the tables of $A$ and $B$ may become large. The alternative therefore would be to compute the integrals numerically on the fly whenever the bond price function is called. Of course examination of the two functions shows that the terms dependent on maturity $T$ can be factored somewhat, offering opportunities for partial caching of the calculation.

**Multi-factor**    All of this section has discussed the single factor Hull-White model and of course it is entirely possible to generalise this to a multi-factor model. In the multi-factor case the volatility function becomes a vector as does the Brownian motion,

$$dr(t) = (\theta(t) - \alpha r(t))dt + \sigma(t) \cdot dW(t). \tag{16.100}$$

### Linear Gaussian Model (LGM)

**The model**    The Linear Gaussian model is a variant of the Hull-White model (Hull and White, 2001; Karoui, Myneni and Viswanathan, 1992a; Karoui, Myneni and Viswanathan, 1992b) with the mean reversion speed set to be a function of time. However, it can be specified directly in terms of the discount bond price and this gives a higher degree of efficiency in the context of a Monte Carlo simulation. The dynamics of the bond price are given by

$$\frac{dP_d(t, T)}{P_d(t, T)} = r_d(t)dt + \sigma_d(t, T)dW^d(t). \tag{16.101}$$

The discount bond prices are log-normal and hence the solution is given by

$$P_d(t, T) = \frac{P_d(0, T)}{P_d(0, t)} \exp\left\{ -\frac{1}{2}\int_0^t (\sigma_d^2(s, T) - \sigma^2(s, t))ds + \int_0^t (\sigma_d(s, T) - \sigma_d(s, t))dW^d(s) \right\} \tag{16.102}$$

where the short rate has been eliminated using the result that $P(t, t) = 1$. The key point here is that the model fits the initial term structure of interest rates by construction. The short rate has also been eliminated from the bond price expression and if a bond price is chosen as numeraire there is no need to keep track of the short rate at all.

To ensure the model is Markovian the volatility function is made separable (see Cheyette, 1992, and discussion below in section 16.3.2), that is a product of two functions that depend separately on $t$ and $T$,

$$\sigma(t, T) = \phi(t)(\Psi(T) - \Psi(t)) \tag{16.103}$$

$$\Psi(t) = \int_0^t \psi(s)ds. \tag{16.104}$$

The two functions $\phi(t)$ and $\psi(t)$ are then assumed to be piecewise constant.

**Caplets and swaption pricing**   Analytic formulae for the prices of caplets and European swaptions can be derived in the same way as discussed above in the context of the Hull-White model. Hence the price of a caplet is given by

$$\boxed{C(0, T_B, T_E) = P_d(0, T_E)Y(0)N(d_1) - P_d(0, T_E)K'N(d_2),} \tag{16.105}$$

where

$$K' = 1 + aK$$
$$d_1 = \frac{\log(Y(0)/K')}{\Sigma} + \frac{1}{2}\Sigma$$
$$d_2 = d_1 - \Sigma$$
$$\Sigma = \Phi(T_B)(\Psi(T_B) - \Psi(T_E))$$
$$\Phi(T_B) = \int_0^{T_B} \phi^2(t)dt.$$

The price of a European swaption is given by

$$\boxed{S(t) = P_d(0, T_F)[H(0)N(d_1) - b_0N(d_2),} \tag{16.106}$$

where

$$\bar{\Sigma}(t) = \phi(t)\left(\frac{\sum_{i=1}^N b_i(\Psi(t, T_i) - \Psi(t, T_F))P_d(0, T_i)}{\sum_{i=1}^N b_iP_d(0, T_i)}\right)$$
$$d_1 = \frac{\log H(0)/b_0}{V(T_F)} + \frac{1}{2}V(T_F)$$
$$d_2 = d_1 - V(T_F)$$
$$V(T_F) = \sqrt{\int_0^{T_F} \bar{\Sigma}^2(s)ds,}$$

and the forward freezing approximation has been used again.

**Calibration**   The pricing formulae for caplets and European swaptions allows the two volatility functions, $\phi(t)$ and $\psi(t)$, to be calibrated. These are assumed to be piecewise constant. It is notable that in this model there is no explicit mean reversion speed parameter and the mean reversion speed is implicitly set by the volatility functions. A number of different types of calibration are available:

- *Caplet* Set $\phi = 1$ for all $t$ and calibrate $\psi(t)$ to a strip of caplets out to the desired maturity. This can be done using a bootstrap approach in maturity.
- *Swaption* Set $\psi = 1$ for all $t$ and calibrate $\phi(t)$ to a set of coterminal swaptions with the desired maturity using a bootstrap approach.
- *Swaption and Caplet* Calibrate both $\phi$ and $\psi$ to a set of 2N caplets and swaptions where the parameters have been split into N segments. In practice the most obvious choice is the set of caplets and coterminal swaptions that "meet" at the desired maturity date. This forms a "V" on the at-the-money implied volatility surface. Other choices are possible and an arbitrary set of 2N options could be selected. Close examination of the caplet and swaption price formulae will demonstrate that both are dependent on $\phi$ and $\psi$. Hence this will require a global fitting procedure and calibration will take significantly longer than either caplet or swaption only modes.
- Other calibration types are possible for this model such as co-expiry swaption calibration.

**Calibration choices**  This model with its multiple calibration options presents a useful case study for XVA calculations as it raises the question of what choice is most suitable in this context. The key demands on an interest rate model calibration for XVA calculations are:

1. Calibration of interest rate volatility for many different currencies, often including emerging market currencies
2. Fast calibration time
3. Calibration to as much of the implied volatility surface as possible including skew/smile
4. Stable calibration that produces stable vega sensitivities.

Clearly very few if any models have calibration procedures that satisfy all of these requirements. The models discussed so far clearly do not fit to skew/smile and so could only ever partially satisfy [3]. The desire to have fast calibration times is likely to conflict heavily with the desire to fit to as much of the volatility surface as possible. For currencies with liquid interest rate option markets then the use of a *swaption and caplet* calibration is likely to be appropriate as this provides a reasonable compromise between the four requirements listed above.

**Monte Carlo implementation**  As was discussed earlier it makes sense to use a bond price as numeraire.[9] With this in mind a long-dated bond maturing beyond the end of the simulation period is a suitable choice for the T-forward measure. If we label the maturity of this bond $T^h$ then the change of measure from the domestic spot measure to the $T_d^h$-forward measure is given by

$$dW^{T_d^h}(t) = dW^d(t) - \sigma_d(t, T^h)dt. \tag{16.107}$$

---

[9]See also section 16.3.4.

Hence the discount bond under the $T_d^h$-forward measure is given by

$$
P_d(t, T) = \frac{P_d(0, T)}{P_d(0, t)} \exp \left\{ -\frac{1}{2} \int_0^t [\sigma_d(s, T) - \sigma(s, t)](\sigma_d(s, T) - 2\sigma_d(s, T^h) + \sigma(s, t)) ds \right.
$$
$$
\left. + \int_0^t (\sigma_d(s, T) - \sigma_d(s, t)) dW^{T_d^h}(s) \right\}. \tag{16.108}
$$

Substituting the separable volatility function (16.103) into the bond price formula, (16.102), gives

$$
\boxed{
\begin{aligned}
P(t, T) = \frac{P(0, T)}{P(0, t)} \exp \left\{ -\frac{1}{2}(\Psi(T) - \Psi(t))(\Psi(T) - 2\Psi(T^h) + \Psi(t)) \int_0^t \phi^2(s) ds \right. \\
\left. + (\Psi(T) - \Psi(t)) \int_0^t \phi(s) dW^{T_d^h} \right\}.
\end{aligned}
} \tag{16.109}
$$

This is an exact formula and so the Monte Carlo is stable irrespective of the size of the time step. The stochastic integral is simulated to each time step $t_i$ and then the formula can be used to generate the bond price for any maturity.

**Multi-factor** A multi-factor extension is possible by making the volatility function and Brownian motion into vectors,

$$
\frac{dP_d(t, T)}{P_d(t, T)} = r_d(t) dt + \sigma_d(t, T) \cdot dW^d(t), \tag{16.110}
$$

where

$$
\sigma_d(t, T) = \phi(t)[\Psi(T) - \Psi(t)] \tag{16.111}
$$

$$
\Psi(t) = \left( \begin{matrix} \int_0^t \psi^1(s) ds \\ \int_0^t \psi^2(s) ds \end{matrix} \right), \tag{16.112}
$$

and

$$
dW^d(t) \equiv \left( \begin{matrix} dW_1^d(t) \\ dW_2^d(t) \end{matrix} \right) \tag{16.113}
$$

$$
\langle dW_1^d, dW_2^d \rangle = 0. \tag{16.114}
$$

The bond price under the domestic spot risk-neutral measure is given by

$$
P_d(t, T) = \frac{P_d(0, T)}{P_d(0, t)} \exp \left\{ -\frac{1}{2} \int_0^t (\|\sigma_d(s, T)\|^2 - \|\sigma(s, t)\|^2) ds \right.
$$
$$
\left. + \int_0^t (\sigma_d(s, T) - \sigma_d(s, t)) \cdot dW^d(s) \right\}. \tag{16.115}
$$

**Gaussian Models and Negative Interest Rates** The above models all have Gaussian short rates and hence have a finite probability of the short rate becoming negative. This behaviour is not limited to the short rate and other derived interest rates such as forward rates can become negative. Historically this behaviour is one of major sources of criticism of Gaussian models as this is sometimes seen as unphysical behaviour. However, in the post-crisis period with very low interest rates, interest rate behaviour has become more Gaussian and negative interest rates have now been seen on a fairly regular basis (see for example Anderson and Liu, 2013).

In the context of XVA calculations negative interest rates present a particular practical difficulty. Setting aside any discussion of whether the rates distribution is acceptable negative rates when they occur need to be used to value portfolios of products. The outcome of this depends on the strategy chosen to value netting sets at each time step and on each path, which is the subject of Chapter 19. Should trade valuation be done by standard derivative pricing models, then whatever model is chosen must be able to handle negative rates as an input. An example of where this would potentially be problematic would be the use of a Black's model for interest rate caps and floors. Of course the underlying assumptions of Black's model are inconsistent with those of Gaussian interest rate models.[10] Black's model assumes log-normal forward rates, which can therefore never be negative. Inputting a negative forward rate is likely to cause the valuation routine to throw an error condition unless the case of negative rates is handled specifically. It is important to note that paths with negative rates cannot simply be ignored or replaced as this would seriously bias the distribution and results.

**Cox-Ingersoll-Ross (CIR)** The Cox-Ingersoll-Ross model or CIR model (Cox, Ingersoll and Ross, 1985) is a short rate model that can ensure that rates remain positive under certain constraints. The short rate follows a square root process and in its most basic form the dynamics are given by

$$dr(t) = (\theta - \alpha r(t))dt + \sigma \sqrt{r(t)}dW(t), \tag{16.116}$$

where $\theta$, $\alpha$ and $\sigma$ are constant parameters. To ensure that the short rate remains positive $2\theta > \sigma^2$. Following the procedure used above the bond price can be assumed to be affine with the usual form

$$P(t, T) = A(t, T)e^{-r(t)B(t,T)},$$

and this must satisfy the PDE derived from the dynamics using the Feynman-Kac theorem,

$$\frac{\partial P}{\partial t} + (\theta - \alpha r(t))\frac{\partial P}{\partial r} + \frac{1}{2}\sigma^2 r(t)\frac{\partial^2 P}{\partial r^2} - r(t)P = 0. \tag{16.117}$$

---

[10]Further discussion on combining valuation models with Monte Carlo dynamics can be found in Chapter 19.

By substituting the affine form into the above PDE it is possible to show that the affine coefficients are given by

$$A(t,T) = \left[ \frac{ae^{b(T-t)}}{b(e^{a(T-t)} - 1) + a} \right]^{\frac{2\theta}{\sigma^2}} \tag{16.118}$$

$$B(t,T) = \frac{e^{a}(T-t) - 1}{b(e^{a(T-t)} - 1) + a} \tag{16.119}$$

$$a = \sqrt{\alpha^2 + 2\sigma^2} \tag{16.120}$$

$$b = \frac{\alpha + a}{2}. \tag{16.121}$$

The solution provides a means of obtaining bond prices at different time steps in a Monte Carlo simulation, where the short rate is simulated. However, in its basic form the model cannot be calibrated to the initial discount function or to the prices of interest rate options. Hence in this form it is not suitable for use in XVA calculations in a risk-neutral measure. However it could be used with a full historical calibration of the three parameters, $\theta$, $\alpha$ and $\sigma$. To deal with the calibration to the initial term structure, Brigo and Mercurio (2006) propose a model with a deterministic shift. The CIR model then becomes

$$dx(t) = (\theta - \alpha x(t))dt + \sigma \sqrt{x(t)}dW(t) \tag{16.122}$$
$$r(t) = x(t) + \psi(t).$$

The parameter $\psi(t)$ can be used to calibrate to the initial term structure. However, there are only three parameters that can be used to calibrate to interest rate volatilities. This is insufficient for accurate calibration to at least at-the-money options.

To extend the model to allow term structure correlation requires allowing the parameters to become functions of time (Hull and White 1990),

$$dr(t) = (\theta(t) - \alpha(t)r(t))dt + \sigma(t)\sqrt{r(t)}dW(t). \tag{16.123}$$

The discount bond price is still given by the affine form and adopting the usual procedure gives equations for $A(t,T)$ and $B(t,T)$:

$$\frac{1}{A(t,T)} \frac{\partial A(t,T)}{\partial t} = \theta(t)B(t,T) \tag{16.124}$$

$$\frac{\partial B(t,T)}{\partial t} = \frac{1}{2}\sigma^2(t)B^2(t,T) + \alpha(t)B(t,T) - 1. \tag{16.125}$$

The equation for $B(t,T)$ is a Riccati equation and cannot be solved in the general case with non-constant coefficients. Hence a numerical PDE solver must be used to obtain $B(t,T)$ which can in turn then be used to obtain $A(t,T)$.

In the context of a CVA model with a Monte Carlo simulation this is not ideal. However, the numerical solution of the PDEs for the two functions only has to be done once for each simulation so the computational demands are not that excessive. There is, as Brigo and Mercurio (2006) point out, no reason to believe that a numerical procedure would ensure positive values of the short rate. The Jamshidian (1995) proposal can be used to ensure that short rate remains positive by choosing

$$\frac{\theta(t)}{\sigma^2(t)} = \delta, \tag{16.126}$$

where $\delta > 1/2$. A deterministic shift can then be used to fit to the initial term structure.

**Cheyette or Quasi-Gaussian Models**   *Cheyette* or *Quasi-Gaussian* models are a broad subclass of models that sit within the HJM framework (Beyna, 2010). Cheyette (1992), Babbs (1993), Jamshidian (1991) and Ritchken and Sankarasubramaniam (1992) independently demonstrated how to specify the volatility structure in HJM models in such a way as to guarantee a Markovian model. The N-factor HJM model can be written

$$df(t, T) = \sigma^T(t, T, \omega) \left( \int_t^T \sigma(t, s, \omega) ds \right) dt + \sigma^T(t, T) dW(t), \tag{16.127}$$

where the superscript $T$ indicates a transpose, $\sigma(t, T, \omega)$ is a d-dimensional stochastic process and $W(t)$ is a d-dimensional Brownian motion.

If the volatility structure is separable in time and maturity so that

$$\boxed{\sigma^T(t, T, \omega) = g^T(t, \omega) h(T),} \tag{16.128}$$

where $g$ is a $d \times d$ stochastic matrix process and $h(T)$ is a $d$-dimensional deterministic vector function of time, then the resulting model is Markovian. It should be immediately apparent that the extended Hull-White and LGM models described above satisfy the criterion and hence fall with the Cheyette class of models (although $g$ is reduced to a deterministic process in these cases). However, Hull-White and LGM models are not really what is intended with the description Cheyette model.

Andreasen (2001) describes a CEV-Cheyette model which allows fitting to the interest rate volatility skew through a *constant-elasticity-of-variance* form for the volatility. A second paper (Andreasen, 2005) describes the development of a multi-factor stochastic volatility Cheyette model where the calibration approach is motivated by Piterbarg (2003b). Chibane and Law (2013) adopt a different approach with a parametric local volatility Cheyette model. A detailed description of Cheyette models in the single and multi-dimensional cases is provided by Andersen and Piterbarg (2010b).

Andreasen (2014) has recently indicated that he has applied a multi-factor Cheyette model with local and stochastic volatility to XVA. The advantage of Cheyette models for XVA is that these models are Markovian and provide an analytic bond price formula, while allowing volatility smiles to be fitted.

Cheyette models have great potential for application to XVA. Following the approach of Andersen and Piterbarg (2010b), define the matrix

$$H(t) = \text{diag}(h(t)) = \begin{pmatrix} h_1(t) & 0 & \cdots & 0 \\ 0 & h_2(t) & \cdots & 0 \\ \vdots & \vdots & \vdots & \vdots \\ 0 & \cdots & 0 & h_d(t) \end{pmatrix}, \tag{16.129}$$

and assume that the $h_i$ are non-zero for all $t$ so that the inverse matrix exists. Define the diagonal matrix

$$\kappa(t) = -\frac{dH(t)}{dt} H(t)^{-1}. \tag{16.130}$$

Next define the two volatility functions,

$$G(t, T) = \int_t^T H(u)H(u)^{-1} 1 du \tag{16.131}$$

$$\sigma_r(t, \omega) = g(t, \omega)H(t) \tag{16.132}$$

where 1 is a column vector of 1's. With this setup and two stochastic processes defined by

$$dx(t) = (y(t)1 - \kappa(t)x(t))dt + \sigma_r(t, \omega)^T dW(t) \tag{16.133}$$

$$dy(t) = (\sigma_r(t, \omega)^T \sigma_r(t, T) - \kappa(t)y(t) - y(t)\kappa(t))dt, \tag{16.134}$$

with $x(t)$ a d-dimensional process and $y(t)$ a $d \times d$-dimensional process. The discount bond price is then given by an analytic formula,

$$P(t, T) = P(t, T, x(t), y(t)) \tag{16.135}$$

$$= \frac{P(0, T)}{P(0, t)} \exp\left(-G(t, T)^T x(t) - \frac{1}{2}G(t, T)^T y G(t, T)\right). \tag{16.136}$$

Hence with the values of the vector $x$ and matrix $y$ at a given time step, equation (16.135) can be used to give the zero-coupon bond price for all maturities. It is immediately apparent that this is a generalisation of the Linear Gaussian model, discussed in section 16.3.2. A Monte Carlo implementation is therefore straightforward.

To actually implement a multi-factor Cheyette model requires the volatility structure to be specified. Andersen and Piterbarg (2010b) use a parametrisation which has the form of a local-stochastic volatility model and allows calibration to $d$ strips of at-the-money European swaptions, the slopes of the volatility for these $d$ strips of swaptions and the smile curvature of one swaption strip. This allows a fairly comprehensive calibration to the at-the-money swaption surface for multiple tenors and expiries along with the general slope of the smile.

**Other HJM Models** Many short rate models have been developed over the years with a variety of different dynamics. Of the single-factor models that I have not discussed so far the *Black-Karasinski* model and its extensions (Black and Karasinski, 1991; Brigo and Mercurio,

2006), is perhaps the best known. This model assumes that the log of the short rate follows an Ornstein-Uhlenbeck process,

$$d \log r(t) = [\theta(t) - \alpha(t) \log r(t)]dt + \sigma(t)dW(t). \tag{16.137}$$

By adopting this form the short rate is guaranteed to be positive. However, no analytic formula for the bond price exists and hence it must be computed numerically. This makes a Monte Carlo implementation of Black-Karasinski cumbersome and in practice this model was commonly used with trees. The numerical nature of the model means that it is not really suitable for use in XVA calculations. Furthermore the Black-Karasinski model is known to suffer from *explosions* in the continuously compounded money market account, which can become infinite (see Brigo and Mercurio, 2006: 64).

Two-factor short rate models are also common and, as was described earlier, a straightforward extension in the context of the Gaussian models. A two-factor extension of the LGM model in section 16.3.2 can be achieved by using a multi-dimensional Brownian model. Brigo and Mercurio (2006) adopt a slightly different approach in their *G2++* or *two additive-factor Gaussian model* by using two Gaussian processes, coupled with a deterministic shift to ensure the model fits the initial term structure:

$$r(t) = x(t) + y(t) + \psi(t) \tag{16.138}$$
$$x(t) = -a(t)x(t)dt + \sigma_1 dW_1(t)$$
$$y(t) = -b(t)y(t)dt + \sigma_2 dW_2(t).$$

Multi-factor Gaussian models retain the analytic tractability of the one-factor models and have analytic functional forms for the bond price. This makes Monte Carlo implementation fast and convenient and hence these models are very suited to use in XVA. Calibration is also very tractable and a simple extension of the one-factor Gaussian models. The addition of more stochastic factors allows for more varied yield curve shapes and the use of more calibrating instruments, however yield curve shapes are still limited when compared to those obtainable from LMM models.

In recent years *Quadratic Gaussian models* have become popular in some interest rate modelling contexts (Piterbarg, 2009; Andersen and Piterbarg, 2010b; Pelsser, 2000; Ahn, Dittmar and Gallant, 2002; Assefa, 2007; McCloud, 2008; McCloud, 2010; Bloch and Assefa, 2009a; Bloch and Assefa, 2009b). These models have a quadratic form for the short rate,

$$r(t) = z(t)^T \gamma(t) z(t) + \beta(t)^T z(t) + \alpha(t), \tag{16.139}$$

where $z(t)$ is a N-dimensional Gaussian factor defined by

$$dz(t) = \sigma(t) \cdot dW(t). \tag{16.140}$$

This model has an affine-like analytic formula for the bond price

$$P(t, T) = \frac{P(0, T)}{P(0, t)} \exp \left[ -z(t)^T \gamma(t, T) z(t) - \beta(t, T)^T z - \alpha(t, T) \right]. \tag{16.141}$$

Following the PDE approach used above through the Feynman-Kac theorem will demonstrate that the matrices $\gamma(t, T)$ and $\beta(t, T)$ satisfy Riccati equations. Hence the Quadratic Gaussian model offers the type of properties that are suitable for use in XVA calculations as it is very amenable to Monte Carlo simulation. The Gaussian factor can be simulated directly and is stable over any size of time step. The bond price is analytic and hence fast to calculate although relatively complex in functional form.

The advantage that a Quadratic Gaussian model has over Linear Gaussian models is that it can generate controllable volatility smiles (see Andersen and Piterbarg, 2010b, for details of model calibration to volatility smiles) and the model can be written in a form of a Linear Gaussian model with stochastic volatility. To see this consider a two-factor model where the volatility matrix is diagonal (Piterbarg, 2009),

$$\sigma(t) = \begin{pmatrix} \sigma_{11}(t) & 0 \\ 0 & \sigma_{22}(t) \end{pmatrix}, \tag{16.142}$$

the $\beta$ vector has the form

$$\beta(t) = \begin{pmatrix} e^{-\kappa t} \\ 0 \end{pmatrix}, \tag{16.143}$$

and the $\gamma$ matrux is given by

$$\gamma(t) = \begin{pmatrix} \epsilon\rho e^{-\kappa t} & \frac{\epsilon}{2}\sqrt{1 - \rho^2}e^{-\kappa t} \\ \frac{\epsilon}{2}\sqrt{1 - \rho^2}e^{-\kappa t} & 0 \end{pmatrix}. \tag{16.144}$$

With this model specification the short rate is given by

$$r(t) = z_1(t)e^{-\kappa t}[z_1(t)\epsilon\rho e^{-\kappa t} + \epsilon\sqrt{1 - \rho^2}z_2(t) + 1] + \alpha(t) \tag{16.145}$$

$$= z_1(t)e^{-\kappa t}[\epsilon v(t) + 1] + \alpha(t) \tag{16.146}$$

and so the term $\epsilon v(t)$ behaves as a stochastic volatility term.

Overall the Quadratic Gaussian model provides a means of introducing volatility smiles into XVA calculations at relatively low computational cost.

A summary of the properties of the HJM models discussed in the section is presented in Table 16.4.

### 16.3.3 The Brace-Gaterak-Musiela (BGM) or Market Model Framework

Market models have been popular in the world of exotic interest rate derivatives since the mid-1990s. Brace, Gatarek and Musiela (1997) were the first to define the model rigorously with other significant early contributions from Jamshidian (1997) and Miltersen, Sandmann and Sondermann (1997). The fundamental driver behind market models is the desire to model observable market rates directly. Short rate models, and HJM models, either explicitly or implicitly model the instantaneous short rate, which is not a market observable quantity.

**TABLE 16.4** A summary of the properties of interest rate models discussed in sections 16.3.2 and 16.3.3. The three types of volatility calibration listed refer to which elements of the input swaption volatility surface may be used to calibrate the model. *Lines* refers to the ability to calibrate to one or more row, column or diagonal in the surface, *Surface* refers to the ability to calibrate to the whole at-the-money swaption volatility surface and *Smile* refers to the ability to to calibrate to smiles/skews. A tick indicates that the model can display the feature, a cross that it cannot and a star indicates that the model partially allows the feature.

| | | | | Vol Calibration | | |
|---|---|---|---|---|---|---|
| **Model** | **N-factor** | **Negative Rates** | **Analytic DF** | **Lines** | **Surface** | **Smile** |
| Hull-White | ✓ | ✓ | ✓ | ✓ | ✗ | ✗ |
| LGM | ✓ | ✓ | ✓ | ✓ | ✗ | ✗ |
| CIR | ✓ | ✗ | ✗ | ✓ | ✗ | ✗ |
| Cheyette | ✓ | ✓ | ✓ | ✓ | ✓ | ✓ |
| Black-Karasinski | ✓ | ✗ | ✗ | ✓ | ✗ | ✗ |
| G2++ | ✓ | ✓ | ✓ | ✓ | ✗ | ✗ |
| QGM | ✓ | ✓ | ✓ | ✓ | ✓ | ✓ |
| LFM | ✓ | ✗ | ✗ | ✓ | ✓ | ✗ |
| LSM | ✓ | ✗ | ✗ | ✓ | ✓ | ✗ |
| LFM-shifted | ✓ | ✓ | ✗ | ✓ | ✓ | ✶ |
| LFM-CEV | ✓ | ✗ | ✗ | ✓ | ✓ | ✶ |
| LFM-MM | ✓ | ✗ | ✗ | ✓ | ✓ | ✶ |
| LFM-SV | ✓ | ✗ | ✗ | ✓ | ✓ | ✓ |

Market models in contrast model discrete forward rates or swap rates which can be readily observed in the market and indeed form part of the product the market model is being used to value. Market models can be identified as natural successors of the Black model (Black, 1976) for pricing European-style interest rate options. This approach makes calibration to market instruments more transparent and the initial term structure is fitted by construction. However, calibration to the implied volatility surface can still be complex and numerically intensive, depending on how the volatility structure is specified. Market models typically have a much richer volatility and correlation structure than short rate models as a set of individual discrete rates is modelled. Hence they naturally have high dimensionality, although sometimes this is reduced by making assumptions about the dependence between rates.[11] In general, market models can generate much more realistic yield curve shapes than short rate models. The richness comes at the cost of additional complexity and the fact that the model is not Markovian. Drift terms are state-dependent and this means that market models are typically much more computationally intensive than short rate models. In addition the construction of hybrid models covering interest rates and other asset classes as required for XVA calculations is more difficult than with short rate and HJM models.

Market models are described in a large number of texts such as Brigo and Mercurio (2006), Rebonato (1999), Pelsser (2000) and Andersen and Piterbarg (2010b). In the remainder

---

[11]While in principle HJM models are infinite dimensional, practical HJM models in general use a driving Brownian vector with a dimension in the range 1–4.

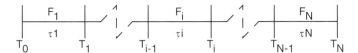

**FIGURE 16.4**   Forward rates in the log-normal forward rate market model. Forward rates are denoted by F, times by T and day-count fractions by $\tau$.

of this section I provide an outline of the use of market models in the context of XVA calculation.

### Log-Normal Forward Rate Model

**The Model**   The *Log-Normal Forward Rate Model (LFM)* uses a set of discrete forward rates, $F_i$, spanning the time periods $T_{i-1} - T_i$, as its primary state variables. The forward rates form a contiguous block and hence the yield curve is modelled over the time period $T_0$ to $T_N$.

$$F_i(t) \equiv F(t, T_{i-1}, T_i). \tag{16.147}$$

Each forward rate has an associated day-count fraction $\tau_i$ used to project the rate. Each forward rate, $F_i$, is modelled until it fixes as time $T_{i-1}$. The model setup is illustrated in Figure 16.4.

The forward rate is expressed in terms of the prices of discount bonds maturing at time $T_{i-1}$ and $T_i$,

$$F_i(t) = \frac{1}{\tau_i} \left[ \frac{P(t, T_{i-1})}{P(t, T_i)} - 1 \right]. \tag{16.148}$$

In the measure with the discount bond maturing at the payment date of the forward, $T_i$, the forward rate $F_i$ is a martingale. The forward is assumed to be log-normal and so the dynamics in this measure are given by

$$dF_i(t) = F_i(t)\sigma_i(t)dW_i^{Q_i}, \tag{16.149}$$

where $\sigma_i(t)$ is a volatility matrix and $dW_i^{Q_i}$ is a vector Brownian motion in the $Q_i$ measure. In general the model is assumed to have a single Brownian motion driving each forward rate so that the vector quantities can be reduced to scalars,

$$dF_i(t) = F_i(t)\sigma_i(t)dW_i^{Q_i}. \tag{16.150}$$

The model's correlation structure is then defined by the correlation between the Brownians associated with each forward,

$$dW_j^{Q_i}dW_k^{Q_i} = \rho_{jk}(t)dt. \tag{16.151}$$

The log-normal form of the forward rates ensures that negative interest rates do not occur.

**Change of measure**  To change measure between that associated with a bond maturity at time $T_i$ and that maturity at time $T_{i+1}$ is given by (Brigo and Mercurio, 2006)

$$dW_j^{Q_{i+1}} = dW_j^{Q_i} + \frac{\tau_{i+1}F_{i+1}(t)}{1 + \tau_{i+1}F_{i+1}(t)}\rho_{i,i+1}\sigma_{i+1}(t)dt. \qquad (16.152)$$

Hence the dynamics of forward rates in measures other than their native one are given by

$$i < j : dF_j(t) = \sigma_j(t)F_j(t)\sum_{k=i+1}^{j}\frac{\rho_{k,j}\tau_k\sigma_k(t)F_k(t)}{1 + \tau_kF_k(t)}dt + \sigma_j(t)F_j(t)dW_j^{Q_i}(t) \qquad (16.153)$$

$$i > j : dF_j(t) = -\sigma_j(t)F_j(t)\sum_{k=j+1}^{i}\frac{\rho_{k,j}\tau_k\sigma_k(t)F_k(t)}{1 + \tau_kF_k(t)}dt + \sigma_j(t)F_j(t)dW_j^{Q_i}(t). \qquad (16.154)$$

It should be immediately clear from the form of the drift terms that the model is non-Markovian. To simulate a set of forward rates in a given numeraire will require these drifts to be calculated along each path and at each time step. Hence the LFM is considerably more computationally expensive than a Markovian short rate model.

**Calibration, Volatility and Correlation Structure**  The instantaneous volatility function for each forward rate, $\sigma_i(t)$, needs to be calibrated to interest rate option prices. There are a wide variety of different ways that the volatility functions can be parameterised and a good summary is provided by Brigo and Mercurio (2006). The simplest method of all is to choose a "flat" volatility with

$$\sigma_i(t) = \sigma_i, \qquad (16.155)$$

a constant. In this case the volatility is immediately given by the implied volatility of the caplet corresponding to the period of the forward.

In practice, however, for XVA calibration to European swaptions is important. There are a number of drivers behind this:

- European swaptions tend to be more liquid at medium and long maturities.
- Portfolio exposures can be long-dated.
- Amongst the largest contributors to XVA are long-dated interest rate swaps and it is important to calibrate to options that are similar to the underlying exposures.
- Any hedging of the implicit sensitivity to interest rate volatility in XVA will be done with at-the-money European swaptions.

To calibrate to European swaptions two things are needed, the parametrisation of the forward rate volatilities needs to be chosen and a means of calculating the prices of European swaptions found.

A simple parametrisation can be obtained by choosing a set of discrete time steps equal to the time periods of the forwards themselves. The forwards then evolve through a set of discrete time steps until the forward matures and this arrangement is illustrated in Figure 16.5. Over each time step the volatility of each forward is assumed to be constant, meaning that the

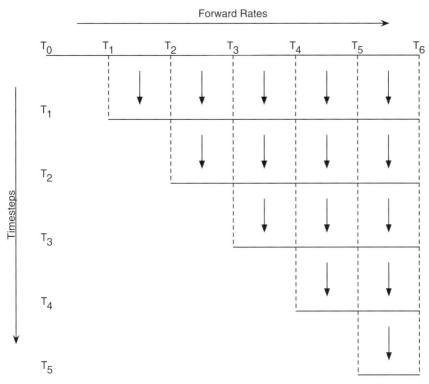

**FIGURE 16.5** The standard approach to a LFM model is to choose time steps equal to the durations of each of the forward rates. Then each forward evolves through a series of time steps until it fixes, giving the upper triangle arrangement illustrated here.

volatility of each forward over its life is piecewise constant. Hence for forward $F_i$ the volatility is given by

$$\sigma_i(t) = \sigma_{ij} \qquad t_{j-1} < t \le t_j. \tag{16.156}$$

Hence the volatility structure becomes

$$\begin{array}{ccccc} F_2 & F_3 & F_4 & F_5 & F_6 \\ \hline \sigma_{21} & \sigma_{31} & \sigma_{41} & \sigma_{51} & \sigma_{61} \\ & \sigma_{32} & \sigma_{42} & \sigma_{52} & \sigma_{62} \\ & & \sigma_{43} & \sigma_{53} & \sigma_{63} \\ & & & \sigma_{54} & \sigma_{64} \\ & & & & \sigma_{64}. \end{array}$$

Clearly this structure can be simplified further (see Brigo and Mercurio, 2006).

The correlation structure must also be specified. The instantaneous correlation is given by equation (16.151). Generally two properties are expected for the correlation matrix (Brigo and Mercurio, 2006): that forward rates widely separated in maturity have much lower correlations than forwards that are close to each other or neighbouring and that for larger yield curve tenors neighbouring forwards become more correlated. In general all the forward rates should be positively correlated. Rather than empirically determine the full correlation structure, in general it is parameterised. As might be expected there are several different approaches to the parametrisation of which one example is provided by Rebonato's *long correlation* (Rebonato, 1998),

$$\rho_{ij} = \rho_{\text{long}} + (1 - \rho_{\text{long}}) \exp\left[\beta |t_i - t_j|\right] \qquad (16.157)$$
$$\beta = d_1 - d_2 \max(t_i, t_i)$$

where $t_i$ is the maturity of forward $i$ and $\rho_{\text{long}}$, $d_1$ and $d_2$ are all model parameters. For more detailed information on setting the correlation structure the reader is referred to more extended treatments of LIBOR market models such as Brigo and Mercurio (2006), Rebonato (2004) or Andersen and Piterbarg (2010b).

The final issue to consider is the analytic pricing of European swaptions to allow calibration of the forward rate volatilities. Again there are a number of different approximate pricing formulas available. One of the simplest is Rebonato's formula (Rebonato, 1998; Brigo and Mercurio, 2006), which provides an approximation for the Black implied European swaption volatility for the option of the interest rate swap spanning $(t_\alpha, t_\beta)$,

$$(v_{\alpha,\beta}^{\text{LFM}})^2 = \sum_{i,j=\alpha+1}^{\beta} \frac{w_i(0)w_j(0)F_i(0)F_j(0)\rho_{i,j}}{S_{\alpha,\beta}(0)^2} \int_0^{T_\alpha} \sigma_i(t)\sigma_j(t)dt, \qquad (16.158)$$

where

$$S_{\alpha,\beta}(t) = \sum_{i=\alpha+1}^{\beta} w_i(t)F_i(t)$$

$$w_i(t) = \frac{\tau_i \prod_{j=\alpha+1}^{i} \frac{1}{1+\tau_i F_j(t)}}{\sum_{k=\alpha+1}^{\beta} \tau_k \prod_{j=\alpha+1}^{k} \frac{1}{1+\tau_i F_j(t)}}.$$

Hence this formula can be used to calibrate the forward volatilities to implied European swaption volatilities. This inevitably involves a numerical calibration process which will depend on the chosen volatility parametrisation. Examples of numerical procedures can be found in Brigo and Mercurio (2006).

**Monte Carlo implementation**    A Monte Carlo implementation evolves the full yield curve forward by evolving the initial set of consecutive forward rates through each time step. The forward rates are log-normal but the state-dependent drift forces the use of a discrete approximation. Choosing to simulate in the measure that corresponds with the payment date of the last forward rate, $t_N$, gives the dynamics of earlier maturing rates as

$$dF_j(t) = \sigma_j(t)F_j(t) \sum_{k=i+1}^{j} \frac{\rho_{k,j}\tau_k\sigma_k(t)F_k(t)}{1 + \tau_k F_k(t)} dt + \sigma_j(t)F_j(t)dW_j^{Q_N}(t). \qquad (16.159)$$

Hence the logarithm of the forward has the dynamics

$$d \log F_j(t) = \sigma_j(t) \sum_{k=i+1}^{j} \frac{\rho_{k,j} \tau_k \sigma_k(t) F_k(t)}{1 + \tau_k F_k(t)} dt - \frac{1}{2} \sigma_j(t)^2 dt + \sigma_j(t) dW_j^{Q_N}(t). \quad (16.160)$$

This allows the use of a Euler discretisation scheme to simulate the process,

$$\log F_j(t + \Delta t) = \log F_j(t) + \sigma_j(t) \sum_{k=i+1}^{j} \frac{\rho_{k,j} \tau_k \sigma_k(t) F_k(t)}{1 + \tau_k F_k(t)} \Delta t - \frac{1}{2} \sigma_j(t)^2 \Delta t + \sigma_j(t) \sqrt{\Delta t} z_t,$$

$$(16.161)$$

where $\Delta t$ is the time step and $z_t$ is drawn from the multi-variate normal distribution $N(0, \rho)$. As with all Monte Carlo schemes without exact solutions to the SDE, numerical errors will accumulate in the simulation and depend on the size of time step. To combat these errors alternative Monte Carlo schemes have been proposed such as the no-arbitrage discretisation scheme of Glasserman and Zhao (2000), predictor-corrector stepping of Hunter, Jäckel, and Joshi (2001) and Bruti-Liberati and Platen (2008) and the robust drift approximations of Joshi and Stacey (2008).

**Use in XVA calculations**    The question remains as to how suitable market models and the LFM models in particular are for use in an XVA simulation model. One advantage of using the LFM is that complex yield curve shapes are generated. However, the LFM model in its basic form is also log-normal and so cannot generate negative interest rates (see section 16.3.2) or volatility smiles/skews. Hence, there are a number of major disadvantages to the use of market models in XVA:

- The dynamics are complex and non-Markovian. This means that the drift has to be calculated separately for each forward on each Monte Carlo path. This adds significant computational overheads when compared to Markovian models where the drift is calculated once and cached for every path. The use of more advanced discretisation schemes only adds to the computational cost. Markovian dynamics often mean that path generation is not a significant component of the overall computation time for XVA, non-Markovian dynamics may mean this is not the case.
- Not multi-curve: the basic model assumes there is no tenor basis, although this can be added (see for example Mercurio, 2010b).
- There is no analytic bond-price formula in this model. The prices of discount bonds must be generated from the forward rates at each time step by inverting equation (16.148). This process gives the discount bond prices at the start and end of each forward rate at each time step on each path. To obtain discount bond prices between these discrete observation points requires interpolation, preferably using a log-linear interpolation scheme. This adds further computation expense to the Monte Carlo simulation.
- The complexity of the model means that extending it to a multi-currency, multi-asset context is very difficult. Short rate and HJM models offer a simpler basis upon which to develop hybrid models.

▪ The standard LFM has no volatility smile or skew and while this is often the case with interest rate models applied to XVA, adding this behaviour to the model adds further complexity.

Overall then, market models are not that suitable for use in general XVA calculations. They may be applied in more restricted contexts such as single currency portfolios or two-currency portfolios but beyond that the model becomes unwieldy. The remaining sections of this chapter discuss the extension of interest rate models to include other asset classes in a full hybrid model. To facilitate this and in keeping with the difficulties introduced by LIBOR market models, only the short rate modelling framework will be used.

**Market Model Variants**    There are a number of ways in which market models have been modified beyond the simplest types. The first such extension was to model swap rates in the *Log-normal Forward-Swap Model (LSM)* (Jamshidian, 1997; Brigo and Mercurio, 2006), although this suffers from the same set of issues as the LFM model, described above. This model models a set of coterminal swaps to maturity rather than forward rates. In the annuity measure the swap rates have the following dynamics:

$$dS_{\alpha,\beta}(t) = \sigma^{\alpha,\beta}(t)S_{\alpha,\beta}(t)dW_t^{\alpha,\beta}. \tag{16.162}$$

LSM was popular initially because it modelled swap rates, allowing models for Bermudan swaptions and callable swaps to be constructed with a straightforward calibration to European swaption implied volatilities. However, with the advent of more sophisticated calibration routines for LFM, swap market models have become less favoured.

There have been a number of attempts to incorporate volatility skews and smiles into market models. The three simplest, deterministic, approaches are to use a *shifted log-normal* process (Brigo and Mercurio, 2003), a *Constant Elasticity of Variance (CEV)* process (Andersen and Andreasen, 2000) or a mixture of log-normal models (Brigo and Mercurio, 2006). Under a shifted log-normal process the forward $F_i$ evolves according to

$$dF_i(t) = (F_i(t) - \alpha)\sigma_i(t)dW_i^{Q_i}, \tag{16.163}$$

while under CEV the forward evolves according to a power-law process rather than a log-normal one,

$$dF_i(t) = (F_i(t))^\gamma \sigma_i(t)dW_i^{Q_i}, \tag{16.164}$$

where the power, $\gamma$ lies between 0 (normal) and 1 (log-normal).

There have also been numerous stochastic volatility extensions of the LFN model including those proposed by Andersen and Brotherton-Ratcliffe (2001), Piterbarg (2003a), and Joshi and Rebonato (2003). The SABR model (Hagan et al., 2002; Obłój, 2008) has become the market standard model for vanilla interest rate options. The model has also been subject to a number of revisions, including some to allow the model to cater for negative interest rates (Hagan et al., 2014; Doust, 2012; Andreasen and Huge, 2011; Antonov, Konikov and Spector, 2015). As a consequence of this popularity, there have also been a variety of attempts to unify SABR and market models (Mercurio and Morini, 2009; Rebonato, McKay and White 2009) in a different form of stochastic volatility market model. All of these stochastic volatility models add considerable complexity to the basic market model.

A summary of the properties of all market models discussed in this section can be found in Table 16.4.

## 16.3.4  Choice of Numeraire

To construct the hybrid model an appropriate choice of numeraire asset must be made in order to allow valuation to proceed as all other assets will be valued with respect to the numeraire. To see why this is the case requires a brief technical interlude.

Harrison and Pliska (1983) first defined the *fundamental theorem of asset pricing*, which was subsequently extended by Geman, Karoui and Rochet (1995). The theorem states that if there are no arbitrage opportunities and that the market is complete, then the value of any traded asset $X$ relative to the numeraire asset $N$ is a martingale

$$\frac{X_t}{N_t} = \mathbb{E}^N \left[ \frac{X_T}{N_T} \middle| F_T \right].$$ 

(16.165)

Hence a numeraire asset must be chosen. Given that rates are stochastic an interest-rate related asset is the obvious choice, although in principle any asset could be chosen. A standard choice of numeraire, particularly with short rate models, is the continuously rolled-up money market account,

$$M(t) = \exp \left( \int_{s=0}^{t} r(s)ds \right).$$ 

(16.166)

This works well for models where the short rate is actively modelled and tracked; however, for many models the primary instrument of modelling is the discount bond (LGM) or the discrete forward rate (LFM). In these cases a discount bond is a more appropriate choice of numeraire. In the case of the Linear Gaussian model a discount bond that matures after all the cash flows in the portfolio is the best choice. In this case equation (16.165) becomes

$$\frac{X_0}{B(0, T_H)} = \mathbb{E}^H \left[ \frac{X_T}{B(T, T_H)} \right].$$ 

(16.167)

The choice of numeraire asset then must be made between different currencies. There are a number of considerations:

- If the simulation spans all assets for all counterparties then a single numeraire is selected for the whole calculation. However, if the simulation is organised on a counterparty-by-counterparty basis then a different numeraire could be chosen for each simulation.
- If a multi-curve environment is being used then the reference curve for discounting and against which currency basis is measured can be an appropriate choice.
- The reporting currency can also be an appropriate choice.

■ A further alternative is the currency in which the majority of single currency trades are denominated. Often this will be the same as the reporting currency. This choice reduces the number of interest rates that need to be simulated.

Once the choice of numeraire has been made then the dynamics must be written and implemented in this measure.

## 16.3.5   Multi-curve: Tenor and Cross-currency Basis

Chapter 8 gave a description of the approaches to the construction of the discount curve, including tenor and cross-currency basis. The basis must of course be included in the interest rate model within the Monte Carlo simulation. There are two cases to consider, deterministic basis and stochastic basis.

**Deterministic Basis**   Deterministic basis can be readily accommodated into both short rate and LMM model frameworks. As an example consider the Linear Gaussian model described in section 16.3.2. The single discount bond dynamics are replaced by dynamics for a projection curve and a discount curve, both driven by the same Brownian motion,

$$\frac{dP^{\text{proj}}(t, T)}{P^{\text{proj}}(t, T)} = r^{\text{proj}}(t)dt + \sigma(t, T) \cdot dW(t). \tag{16.168}$$

$$\frac{dP^{\text{disc}}(t, T)}{P^{\text{disc}}(t, T)} = r^{\text{disc}}(t)dt + \sigma(t, T) \cdot dW(t). \tag{16.169}$$

The solutions to these dynamics are

$$P^{\text{proj}}(t, T) = \frac{P^{\text{proj}}(0, T)}{P^{\text{proj}}(0, t)} \exp \left\{ \int_0^t (\sigma(s, T) - \sigma(s, t)) \cdot dW(s) \right. \tag{16.170}$$

$$\left. - \frac{1}{2} \int_0^t (||\sigma(s, T)||^2 - ||\sigma(s, t)||^2) ds \right\}.$$

$$P^{\text{disc}}(t, T) = \frac{P^{\text{disc}}(0, T)}{P^{\text{disc}}(0, t)} \exp \left\{ \int_0^t (\sigma(s, T) - \sigma(s, t)) \cdot dW(s) \right. \tag{16.171}$$

$$\left. - \frac{1}{2} \int_0^t (||\sigma(s, T)||^2 - ||\sigma(s, t)||^2) ds \right\}.$$

The ratio of the projection and discount bonds is deterministic:

$$\frac{P^{\text{proj}}(t, T)}{P^{\text{disc}}(t, T)} = \frac{P^{\text{proj}}(0, T)P^{\text{disc}}(0, t)}{P^{\text{disc}}(t, T)P^{\text{proj}}(0, t)} \tag{16.172}$$

$$= \exp \left( -\int_t^T \left[ r^{\text{proj}}(s) - r^{\text{disc}}(s) \right] ds \right),$$

and hence is equivalent to a deterministic spread for the projection curve over the discount curve. A similar approach can be adopted for other models. For market models the deterministic spread can be introduced through a series of projection forward rates.

Figure 8.1 clearly shows that basis is not constant and during the crisis period tenor basis increased sharply before later falling back. A deterministic basis allows the model to match the basis on any given date and to correctly re-price basis swaps. However, a deterministic approach will ignore the inherent volatility of the basis. Hence, a deterministic treatment of basis will miss some of the embedded optionality in the XVA model that comes from the max function. The importance of this will depend on the fraction of basis swaps and other products that are sensitive to the basis in the portfolio and overall sensitivity to basis in the XVA.

**Stochastic Basis**   A stochastic treatment of basis is possible but there are a number of challenges that need to be overcome:

- Cross-currency basis can clearly have either a positive or negative sign.
- Tenor basis should be expected to have a positive sign with respect to the OIS curve. That is the expected behaviour is that curves of increasing tenor will have an increasing spread and that a curve of a longer tenor will not cross inside that of a short tenor. Hence one might expect a series of curves with increasing spread over OIS:

$$OIS \rightarrow 1M \rightarrow 3M \rightarrow 6M \rightarrow 12M.$$

   In practice of course this is not guaranteed to be the case.
- Options on basis swaps are very illiquid and the prices are not readily observable so there are no instruments available to directly calibrate the volatility of the tenor basis.
- Options on cross-currency swaps are also only rarely traded.
- European swaptions will typically only be quoted for one underlying tenor in any given currency. Caps and floors might be quoted on the same or a different tenor to the swaptions, depending on local market conventions. Even if the caps and floors are quoted on a different tenor to swaptions, the options will only relate to a short underlying trade tenor. Hence, for some tenors there will be limited or no volatility information available.
- Stochastic basis will add a potentially large number of additional stochastic factors to the Monte Carlo simulation with consequences for computational performance.

The major benefit of a stochastic basis is to allow the vega derived from basis swaps to be included in XVA.

A number of authors have attempted to model the discount curve and the forward rates directly. Mercurio (2010a) proposed the extension of the market model to model OIS forwards and tenor forward curves simultaneously with the OIS curve providing discounting. In the context of short rate models the obvious choice would be to adopt an approach similar to that described below in the context of FX and inflation, that is to use Gaussian short rate models for each of the projection curves and set an "FX" rate between each. Kenyon (2010) set up a model of this type using the G1++ model of Brigo and Mercurio (2006) as a basis. Kenyon notes, however, that such a model will give rise to negative basis. Kenyon (2013) later extended the approach to overcome this problem. Moreni and Pallavicini (2013); Moreni and Pallavicini (2014) model the discount curve using instantaneous forward rates and the forward floating rates directly. Kienitz (2013) models the forward floating rates using a market model approach while allowing a variety of short rate and market model-style specifications for the discount curve. Crépey and Rahal (2013) propose a comprehensive multi-curve framework based on Levy processes.

The second alternative approach is to model the discount curve and then the projection curves as spreads over the discount curve driven by stochastic processes. Three different types of specification have been investigated by different groups of researchers. The first type of specification is additive spreads where the LIBOR curve is defined as a spread over the discounting curve forwards (OIS),

$$S^{\text{tenor}}(t) = L^{\text{tenor}}(t) - F^{\text{disc}}(t), \tag{16.173}$$

where $S$ is the spread, $L$ is the floating rate and $F$ is the discount curve forward. This type of model has been explored by Fujii, Shimada and Takahashi (2009), Amin (2010) and Mercurio (2010a). An alternative specification is to use spreads that are defined as a multiplier of the discount curve,

$$1 + \alpha S^{\text{tenor}}(t) = \frac{1 + \alpha L^{\text{tenor}}(t)}{1 + \alpha F^{\text{tenor}}(t)}, \tag{16.174}$$

where $\alpha$ is the day-count fraction. Henrard (2009); Henrard (2013) explore models with multiplicative spreads. The last specification used by Andersen and Piterbarg (2010a); Andersen and Piterbarg (2010b); Andersen and Piterbarg (2010c) is instantaneous spreads,

$$P^{\text{proj}}(t, T) = P^{\text{disc}}(t, T) \exp \left( \int_t^T s(u) du \right) \tag{16.175}$$

where $s(t)$ is the instantaneous spread over the discount curve.

**Adjusting Model Calibration**    The use of tenor basis curves also implies that the model calibration also has to be modified. Consider the impact on the Hull-White model calibration discussed in section 16.3.2:

**Caplet**    The forward rate is now given by the projection curve so $L(T_B, T_E)$ is the now defined by

$$L(t, T_B, T_E) = \frac{1}{a(T_B, T_E)} \left( \frac{P^{\text{proj}}(t, T_B)}{P^{\text{proj}}(t, T_E)} - 1 \right). \tag{16.176}$$

Hence the bond ratio becomes

$$Y^{\text{proj}}(t) = \frac{P^{\text{proj}}(t, T_B)}{P^{\text{proj}}(t, T_E)}. \tag{16.177}$$

The price of a caplet is then given by

$$C(0, T_B, T_E) = P^{\text{disc}}(0, T_E) Y^{\text{proj}}(0) N(d_1) - P^{\text{disc}}(0, T_E) K' N(d_2), \tag{16.178}$$

where

$$d_1 = \frac{\log(Y^{\text{proj}}(0)/K')}{\Sigma} + \frac{1}{2}\Sigma$$

$$d_2 = d_1 - \Sigma.$$

**Swaption**  With a discount and projection curve, the value of a European swaption maturing at time $T_F$ under the $T_F$-forward measure is given by

$$S(0) = P^{\text{disc}}(0, T_F)\mathbb{E}^{T_F}\left[\left(K\sum_{i=1}^{N} a_i P^{\text{disc}}(t, T_i) - \sum_{j=1}^{M} L(T_{j-1}, T_j)\beta_j P^{\text{disc}}(t, T_j)\right)^+ \frac{1}{P^{\text{disc}}(t, T_F)}\right],$$

(16.179)

where $\beta_j$ is the day count fraction for the floating leg. Again the time variable $t$ has been left in place for clarity of expression with $t = T_F$. Assuming that the fixed and floating legs have the same payment frequency simplifies the indexing, giving

$$S(0) = P^{\text{disc}}(0, T_F)\mathbb{E}^{T_F}\left[\left(\sum_{i=1}^{N} Ka_i P^{\text{disc}}(t, T_i) - L(T_{i-1}, T_i)\beta_i P^{\text{disc}}(t, T_i)\right)^+ \frac{1}{P^{\text{disc}}(t, T_F)}\right].$$

(16.180)

In this expression the forward rate is given by

$$L(T_{i-1}, T_i) = \frac{1}{\beta_i}\left(\frac{P^{\text{proj}}(t, T_{i-1})}{P^{\text{proj}}(t, T_i)} - 1\right)$$

(16.181)

$$= \frac{1}{\beta_i}\left(\frac{P^{\text{disc}}(t, T_{i-1})}{P^{\text{disc}}(t, T_i)}\exp\left(\int_{T_{i-1}}^{T_i}\mu(s)ds\right) - 1\right),$$

where $\mu(t)$ is the basis spread. Using this expression equation (16.180) can be written as

$$S(0) = P^{\text{disc}}(0, T_F)\mathbb{E}^{T_F}\left[(\hat{H}_{T_F} - \hat{b}_0)^+\right],$$

(16.182)

where

$$\hat{H}(t) = \sum_{i=1}^{N} \hat{b}_i \frac{P^{\text{disc}}(t, T_i)}{P^{\text{disc}}(t, T_F)},$$

and

$$\hat{b}_0 = \frac{P^{\text{disc}}(t, T_0)}{P^{\text{disc}}(t, T_F)}\exp\left(\int_{T_0}^{T_1}\mu(s)ds\right)$$

$$\hat{b}_i = 1 + a_i K - \exp\left(\int_{T_i}^{T_{i+1}} \mu(s)ds\right)$$

$$\hat{b}_N = 1 + a_i K.$$

$\hat{H}(t)$ is again log-normal and so the price of a European swaption is a simple Black function

$$S(t) = P^{\text{disc}}(0, T_F)[\hat{H}(0)N(d_1) - \hat{b}_0 N(d_2)], \tag{16.183}$$

where

$$d_1 = \frac{\log \hat{H}(0)/\hat{b}_0}{V(T_F)} + \frac{1}{2}V(T_F)$$

$$d_2 = d_1 - V(T_F)$$

$$V(T_F) = \sqrt{\int_0^{T_F} \bar{\Sigma}^2(s)ds}.$$

## 16.3.6    Close-out and the Choice of Discount Curve

Recall the close-out valuations, $M_B$ and $M_C$, in the Burgard-Kjaer semi-replication model discussed in Chapter 9 and the extension to KVA in Chapter 13. The use of these terms allows the valuation in default to be varied within the model. In the context of a multi-curve and OIS discounting framework this raises a question of what discount curve should be used to value trades inside the Monte Carlo engine.

From the perspective of CVA and DVA this valuation represents the value that would be used in close-out should default occur at a particular time step. For funding this could be seen as the reference valuation for a trade with no funding costs. For KVA and capital this valuation is the value that would be used in a regulatory context as input to the capital requirement calculation. The value that should be used, however, is not clear.

For purely unsecured trade portfolios with no supporting CSA there is still considerable debate around the close-out value:

- ▪ *Three-month floating rate discounted* Before the crisis and the advent of OIS discounting three-month floating rate curves were generally used for derivative valuation. Secured derivatives have been moved to OIS but in many institutions primary trade valuation for accounting purposes remains on three-month discounting for unsecured trades. Hence there is an argument that the reference XVA valuation should be based on three-month floating rate discounting. This prompts the further question of which currency should be used as the primary discount curve? In general in multi-curve environments USD is regarded as the primary currency against which currency basis is measured. However, for banks which do not fund themselves in USD it may be more appropriate to use the reporting currency as the primary curve and adjust any currency basis accordingly. A more complex scenario is presented by a mixture of single-currency and multi-currency discounting, similar to that which prevailed prior to the advent of multi-curve models. In such an environment single-currency three-month floating rate curves were used to discount single currency derivatives and USD three-month floating rate was used to discount USD and cross-currency derivatives. Such a framework is, of course, inconsistent but still may be what is used in practice. If a mixed model like this is used within an XVA calculation, spread curves will be required to adjust the trade valuations appropriately.

- *OIS discounted* The OIS discounted value has been argued to be the risk-free value as was discussed in Chapter 8. Hence, the OIS discounted value is an obvious choice for the reference valuation. Furthermore, if the close-out were to take place using reference values provided by third parties, there is an argument that a typical valuation would in fact be based on the most common CSA discount curve.
- *Funding included* The wording of the ISDA close-out protocol (ISDA, 2009c) suggests that the non-defaulted counterparty can take into account funding costs in their close-out. This suggests the reference value should be funding adjusted as discussed in Chapter 9.

For partially secured and secured portfolios then the choice of reference value is more clear cut. The value that would be obtained using the discount curve appropriate to the CSA is the most appropriate.

## 16.4 FX AND CROSS-CURRENCY MODELS

In general an XVA Monte Carlo simulation will be multi-currency and will require $N$ currencies and $N − 1$ FX rates between the currencies and the numeraire currency to be simulated. Once the FX pairs against the numeraire have been generated, these can be used to give any cross-rates that may be required. The dynamics of the FX rate can be selected independently of the rates model, with log-normal being the simplest choice.

A log-normal model may seem overly simplistic, particularly as the standard approach to FX modelling is the local-stochastic volatility model. However, this underestimates the complexity added to the model from the use of stochastic interest rates and the need to model multiple currencies. With two currencies in the portfolio then only two interest rates will be modelled with the FX rate between them. Add a third currency and a third interest rate and a second FX rate will be modelled. However, in this case there is also implicitly a third FX cross-rate generated from the two modelled FX rates. There will be FX options on this cross FX rate and ideally the model should be consistent with them. In practice this means the model must have term structure of correlation to have any hope of full calibration. Add sophisticated FX rate models to this context and the picture rapidly becomes very complex. The third FX rate would have implied volatility smiles to consider, for example. This section discusses the implementation of log-normal models for FX before moving on to outline the possible extension to local-stochastic volatility. Purely local volatility is considered in the context of equities in section 16.6.

The exact form of the model will depend on the choice of dynamics for rates. The model can either be formulated in terms of the dynamics of the FX spot rate or an FX forward rate and the choice depends on what is most convenient for the chosen model dynamics and numeraire. Models formulated in terms of the FX forward can often be simpler to implement, particularly as the volatility of the FX forward rate maturing at time $T$ is the same as the implied volatility of the FX option maturing on the same date. However, the correlation structure of the model is more likely to be expressed in terms of the correlation against the spot FX, particularly if historical correlations are used. This would therefore require the correlations to be transformed to those associated with the forward FX. The alternative would be to measure the historical correlation of the FX forward rate directly.

### 16.4.1  A Multi-currency Generalised Hull-White Model

As an example multi-currency model consider the extension of the generalised Hull-White model. In this model the interest rates are driven by Hull-White processes and the FX spot is log-normal. Denoting the numeraire currency by $d$ for *domestic* and $f$ for *foreign* the dynamics of the model are given by

$$\frac{dX(t)}{X(t)} = \left(r_d(t) - r_f(t)\right) dt + \sigma_X(t) dW_X^d(t) \tag{16.184}$$

$$dr_d(t) = \left(\theta_d(t) - \alpha_d r_d(t)\right) dt + \sigma_d(t) dW_d^d(t) \tag{16.185}$$

$$dr_f(t) = \left(\theta_f(t) - \alpha_f r_f(t)\right) dt + \sigma_f(t) dW_f^f(t). \tag{16.186}$$

Here the FX rate $X$ represents the price of one unit of foreign currency in the domestic currency. Several changes of measure will be required in what follows so to keep track of the measure and asset the notation for the Brownian motions is as follows. The *subscript* defines the asset which the Brownian motion is driving. The *superscript* defines the measure in which the Brownian is a martingale. A Brownian motion of the form $dW_{\text{asset}}^d(t)$ is the spot risk-neutral measure of the domestic currency, while a Brownian of the form $dW_{\text{asset}}^{T_d}(t)$ is in the measure associated with the domestic discount bond maturing at time $T$.

The foreign rates are defined in the foreign risk-neutral measure in equation (16.186) and the first step is to change the measure so that the foreign rate is expressed in the domestic risk-neutral measure. The Radon-Nikodym derivative for this change of measure is given by (see Brigo and Mercurio, 2006):

$$\frac{d\mathbb{Q}^f}{d\mathbb{Q}^d} = \frac{X(t) \exp\left(\int_0^t r_f(s)ds\right)}{X(0) \exp\left(\int_0^t r_d(s)ds\right)}, \tag{16.187}$$

and hence from the form of equation (16.184) it is easy to see that the change of measure is given by

$$dW_f^f(t) = dW_f^d(t) - \rho_{X,f}(t)\sigma_X(t)dt, \tag{16.188}$$

and hence the foreign dynamic becomes,

$$dr_f(t) = \left(\theta_f(t) - \alpha_f r_f(t) - \rho_{X,f}(t)\sigma_X(t)\sigma_f(t)\right) dt + \sigma_f(t) dW_f^d(t). \tag{16.189}$$

If the model is simulated in the domestic risk-neutral measure then the same approach described above in the single currency case can be adopted for the foreign rate, although with the additional drift correction.

**Calibration**   The foreign rates are calibrated in exactly the same way as that described for the single currency case. Hence in practice all interest rates can be calibrated independently in parallel prior to the simulation. To calibrate the FX spot volatility an expression for the spot volatility in terms of the FX forward volatility is needed as this will allow the FX spot volatility to be bootstrapped from at-the-money forward FX options of increasing maturity.

To proceed all the processes need to be expressed in the domestic T-forward measure. The change of measure for the domestic Brownian was given earlier. The change of measure for the FX and foreign rate is given by

$$dW_f^{T_d}(t) = dW_f^d(t) - \rho_{f,d}(t)B_d(t,T)\sigma_d(t)dt \tag{16.190}$$

$$dW_X^{T_d}(t) = dW_X^d(t) - \rho_{X,d}(t)B_d(t,T)\sigma_d(t)dt. \tag{16.191}$$

The dynamics of the domestic discount bond in the domestic spot risk-neutral measure are given by equation (16.77) and it is therefore straightforward to derive the dynamics of the foreign discount bond in the domestic T-forward measure by using equations (16.188) and (16.190). Hence the foreign bond price has the dynamics

$$\frac{dP_f(t,T)}{P_f(t,T)} = \left[ r_f(t) - \rho_{X,f}(t)B_f(t,T)\sigma_f(t)\sigma_X(t) - \rho_{f,d}(t)B_f(t,T)\sigma_f(t)B_d(t,T)\sigma_d(t) \right]dt$$

$$\tag{16.192}$$

$$- B_f(t,T)\sigma_f(t)dW_f^{T_d}(t).$$

The FX forward rate maturing at time $T$ has the following value at time $t$,

$$F(t,T) = \frac{X(t)P_f(t,T)}{P_d(t,T)}. \tag{16.193}$$

To determine the volatility of the forward rate in terms of the volatility of the spot the dynamics of the forward need to be determined. To do this two applications of the chain rule for stochastic processes are made to give

$$dF(t,T) = \frac{P_f dX}{P_d} + \frac{X dP_f}{P_d} + XP_f d\left(\frac{1}{P_d}\right) + \frac{dX dP_f}{P_d} + P_f dX d\left(\frac{1}{P_d}\right) + X dP_f d\left(\frac{1}{P_d}\right). \tag{16.194}$$

Given that the forward FX rate is clearly a tradable asset in the T-forward measure, it must be a martingale with zero drift,

$$dF(t,T) = F\Sigma(t,T)dW_F^{T_d}(t). \tag{16.195}$$

Using equation (16.194) is therefore clear that

$$dF(t,T) = F\left[ \sigma_X dW_X^{T_d}(t) + \sigma_f(t)B_f(t,T)dW_f^{T_d} - \sigma_d(t)B_d(t,T)dW_d^{T_d}(t) \right]. \tag{16.196}$$

Hence the instantaneous variance of the FX forward is given by

$$
\begin{aligned}
\Sigma^2(t, T) &= \mathrm{Var}\left(\sigma_X dW_X^{T_d}(t) + \sigma_f(t)B_f(t, T)dW_f^{T_d} - \sigma_d(t)B_d(t, T)dW_d^{T_d}(t)\right) \\
&= \sigma_X^2(t) + \sigma_f^2(t)B_f^2(t, T) + \sigma_d^2(t)B_d^2(t, T) + 2\rho_{X,f}(t)\sigma_X(t)\sigma_f(t)B_f(t, T) \\
&\quad - 2\rho_{X,d}(t)\sigma_X(t)\sigma_d(t)B_d(t, T) - 2\rho_{f,d}(t)\sigma_f(t)B_f(t, T)\sigma_d(t)B_d(t, T).
\end{aligned}
\tag{16.197}
$$

The FX option implied variance is simply the integral over the instantaneous variance so

$$
\sigma_{\mathrm{imp}}^2(T)T = \int_0^T \Sigma^2(s, T)ds.
\tag{16.198}
$$

Assuming a functional form for the spot FX volatility such as piecewise constant allows equations (16.197) and (16.198) to be used to bootstrap the FX spot volatility if the correlations are known.

One potential problem with this calibration is that the FX spot volatility can become negative at longer maturities. Examination of equation (16.197) shows that is possible for certain combinations of interest rate volatility and correlations. One possible solution to this is to allow the correlations to be time-dependent.

**Spot or Forward Evolution**   Equations (16.195) and (16.196) also suggest that it is equally possible to model the FX forward maturing at time $T$ instead of the FX spot process. This has the advantage that the volatility of the process is the same as that derived directly from implied option volatilities. The disadvantage is that the correlations will likely be expressed in terms of correlations with the FX spot. To convert these correlations will involve the FX spot volatility meaning that the calibration cannot be avoided.

## 16.4.2   The Triangle Rule and Options on the FX Cross

One deficiency of the modelling approach outlined above is that FX calibration is only performed for FX pairs against the numeraire currency. Hence the prices of at-the-money options on these FX pairs will be correctly reproduced by the model. However, the options on the FX crosses will not be calibrated and the model is not guaranteed to correctly value such options. In XVA terms this means that exposures on products that are sensitive to the cross FX rate will not be correct. As an example consider the calculation of expected exposures on a EURGBP cross-currency swap with exchange of notional at the start and end of the transaction. The expected positive exposure of the last exchange of notional is identical to a long-dated FX option. If the model has a USD numeraire and is calibrated to options on USD-GBP and USD-EUR there is a good chance that the model will not correctly price long-dated options on EURGBP and hence the expected exposure will be incorrect.

Consider the three-currency extension of the Hull-White model. The three interest rates, domestic d, foreign currency 1, f, and foreign currency 2, g, have the dynamics

$$
dr_d(t) = \left(\theta_d(t) - \alpha_d r_d(t)\right)dt + \sigma_d(t)dW_d^d(t)
\tag{16.199}
$$

$$
dr_f(t) = \left(\theta_f(t) - \alpha_f r_f(t) - \rho_{df,f}(t)\sigma_{df}(t)\sigma_f(t)\right)dt + \sigma_f(t)dW_f^d(t)
\tag{16.200}
$$

$$
dr_g(t) = \left(\theta_g(t) - \alpha_g r_g(t) - \rho_{dg,g}(t)\sigma_{dg}(t)\sigma_g(t)\right)dt + \sigma_f(t)dW_g^d(t),
\tag{16.201}
$$

and the two FX rates that will be modelled against the numeraire currency, $X_{df}$ and $X_{dg}$, follow the dynamics

$$\frac{dX_{df}(t)}{X_{df}(t)} = \left( r_d(t) - r_f(t) \right) dt + \sigma_{df}(t) dW_{df}^d(t) \tag{16.202}$$

$$\frac{dX_{dg}(t)}{X_{dg}(t)} = \left( r_d(t) - r_g(t) \right) dt + \sigma_{dg}(t) dW_{dg}^d(t). \tag{16.203}$$

The correlation structure is given by the matrix

$$\begin{pmatrix} 1 & \rho_{d,f}(t) & \rho_{d,g}(t) & \rho_{d,df}(t) & \rho_{d,dg}(t) \\ \rho_{d,f}(t) & 1 & \rho_{f,g}(t) & \rho_{f,df}(t) & \rho_{f,dg}(t) \\ \rho_{d,g}(t) & \rho_{f,g}(t) & 1 & \rho_{g,df}(t) & \rho_{g,dg}(t) \\ \rho_{d,df}(t) & \rho_{f,df}(t) & \rho_{g,df}(t) & 1 & \rho_{df,dg}(t) \\ \rho_{d,dg}(t) & \rho_{f,dg}(t) & \rho_{g,dg}(t) & \rho_{df,dg}(t) & 1 \end{pmatrix} \tag{16.204}$$

The FX cross in this system is $X_{gf}$ and this is related to $X_{df}$ and $X_{dg}$ by the relation

$$X_{gf}(t) = X_{gd}(t) X_{df}(t) \tag{16.205}$$

$$= \frac{X_{df}(t)}{X_{dg}(t)}. \tag{16.206}$$

Application of the Itô product rule to this expression and the use of equations (16.202) and (16.203) give a log-normal dynamic for $X_{gf}$,

$$\frac{dX_{gf}(t)}{X_{gf}(t)} = \left( r_g(t) - r_f(t)\sigma_{dg}^2(t) - \rho_{df,dg}(t)\sigma_{df}(t)\sigma_{dg}(t) \right) dt \tag{16.207}$$

$$+ \sigma_{df}(t)dW_{df}^d(t) - \sigma_{dg}(t)dW_{dg}^d(t).$$

From this it is clear that $X_{gf}(t)$ can be written in the form

$$\frac{dX_{gf}(t)}{X_{gf}(t)} = \mu_{gf}(t)dt + \sigma_{gf}(t)dW_{gf}^d(t), \tag{16.208}$$

where the usual *triangle* relationship holds,

$$\sigma_{gf}^2(t) = \sigma_{df}^2(t) + \sigma_{dg}^2(t) - 2\rho_{df,dg}(t)\sigma_{df}(t)\sigma_{dg}(t). \tag{16.209}$$

The volatility of the options on the FX cross is the volatility of the FX cross forward, $F_{gf}(t)$. Hence to obtain a relationship between the implied volatility of the options on the FX cross and the other correlations and volatilities in the system requires an expression for the dynamics of $F_{gf}(t)$. The forward is related to the other quantities in the system by

$$F_{gf}(t) = X_{gf}(t)\frac{P_f(t,T)}{P_g(t,T)} \qquad (16.210)$$
$$= \frac{X_{df}(t)P_f(t,T)}{X_{dg}(t)P_g(t,T)}.$$

Application of the Itô product rule to this expression and a derivation similar to that performed in equation (16.197) gives the following:

$$\Sigma_{gf}^2(t,T) = \sigma_{df}^2(t) + \sigma_{dg}^2(t) + \bar{\sigma}_g^2(t,T) + \bar{\sigma}_f^2(t,T) \qquad (16.211)$$
$$-2\rho_{df,dg}(t)\sigma_{df}(t)\sigma_{dg}(t) - 2\rho_{g,f}(t)\bar{\sigma}_g(t,T)\bar{\sigma}_f(t,T) + 2\rho_{df,f}(t)\sigma_{df}(t)\bar{\sigma}_f(t,T)$$
$$-2\rho_{dg,f}(t)\sigma_{dg}(t)\bar{\sigma}_f(t,T) - 2\rho_{df,g}(t)\sigma_{df}(t)\bar{\sigma}_g(t,T) + 2\rho_{dg,g}(t)\sigma_{dg}(t)\bar{\sigma}_g(t,T),$$

where

$$\bar{\sigma}_f(t,T) = \sigma_f(t)B_f(t,T) \qquad (16.212)$$
$$\bar{\sigma}_g(t,T) = \sigma_g(t)B_g(t,T) \qquad (16.213)$$

and

$$\sigma_{imp\text{-}gf}^2(T)T = \int_0^T \Sigma_{gf}^2(s,T)ds. \qquad (16.214)$$

Using these relationships and allowing the correlation structure to become time dependent will allow the model to fit the options on the FX cross as well as the options on the two FX rates that are modelled explicitly. The disadvantage of this is that the FX calibration process is now global across all FX rates, rather than on a per FX pair basis. In the three-currency case the model is already relatively complex; in the $N$ currency case it will be far more complex with many options on FX crosses to consider. Furthermore there may well be data issues as some FX pairs may not have active options markets. Hence in practice a combination of FX cross calibrations and FX pair calibrations may be optimal.

### 16.4.3 Models with FX Volatility Smiles

Implied volatility skews and smiles are a feature of the FX options market and hence it may be seen as desirable to be able to match this behaviour in the XVA model. For short-dated options this may not in fact be that important as it is likely that their short maturity will mean they have only a small impact on the overall XVA figure. However, long-dated products with FX sensitivities such as *Power Reverse Dual Currency Notes (PRDC)* and indeed cross-currency swaps will have sensitivity to the FX smile/skew.

There are a number of options to extend the FX dynamics to match market implied FX volatility smiles with stochastic interest rates. The simplest approach is to use a local volatility type model where the dynamics of the FX spot are generalised,

$$\frac{dX_{df}(t)}{X_{df}(t)} = \left(r_d(t) - r_f(t)\right)dt + \sigma_{df}(t, X_{df})dW_{df}^d(t). \tag{16.215}$$

Piterbarg (2006) and Deelstra and Rayée (2012) have explored models of this type in the context of pricing long-dated FX products. A second alternative is to use a stochastic volatility model for the FX process and Gnoatto and Grasselli (2014) present a model of this type. A local volatility model with this form is presented in the context of equities below in section 16.6.

**Local-Stochastic Volatility Models**   In the FX options market the most popular type of model for pricing exotic products is the *Local-Stochastic Volatility* model or *LSV*. This class of models combines both local and stochastic volatility, sometimes combined with jump processes. The earliest such examples were those developed by Jex, Henderson and Wang (1999), Lipton (2001), Lipton (2002) and Lipton and McGhee (2014). However, very few formulations have included stochastic interest rates although Deelstra and Rayée (2012) and Bloch (2009) are two examples. LSV models tend to be used in PDE or PIDE[12] frameworks as the focus is on the pricing of FX products like FX barrier options. The literature for LSV models is now large and surveys are provided by Homescu (2014) and Lipton, Gal and Lasis (2014).

There are a wide variety of different forms for the FX process under local-stochastic volatility, although perhaps most popular are those with *Heston*-like dynamics. The Heston-type models use a mean reverting square root process for the stochastic volatility and combine this with a local volatility multplier,

$$\frac{dX(t)}{X(t)} = (r_d(t) - r_f(t))dt + \sigma_X(t, X(t))\sqrt{v(t)}dW_X^d(t) \tag{16.216}$$

$$dv(t) = \kappa(t)(\theta(t) - v(t))dt + \gamma \xi(t)\sqrt{v(t)}dW_v^d(t) \tag{16.217}$$

$$< dW_X^d, dW_v^d > = \rho_{X,v}(t)dt, \tag{16.218}$$

where the parameters $\kappa$, $\theta$ and $\xi(t)$ have a term structure and $\gamma$ is a mixing parameter that controls the degree of stochasticity. If $\gamma = 0$ then the model reduces to a local volatility model. The model defined by Lipton (2002), Lipton and McGhee (2014) and Lipton, Gal and Lasis (2002) is of this form,

$$\frac{dX(t)}{X(t)} = (r_d(t) - r_f(t) - \Gamma_X)dt + \sigma_X(t, X(t))\sqrt{v(t)}dW_X^d(t)$$

$$+ (\exp[J] - 1)dN(t) \tag{16.219}$$

$$dv(t) = \kappa(\theta - v(t))dt + \gamma\sqrt{v(t)}dW_v^d(t) \tag{16.220}$$

$$< dW_X^d, dW_v^d > = \rho_{X,v}dt, \tag{16.221}$$

which includes a jump process and compensator $\Gamma_X$.

---

[12]Partial Integro-Differential Equation.

The calibration of the model is, in general, a two-stage process (Homescu, 2014):

1. Calibrate the stochastic volatility model (by setting the local volatility $\sigma_X(t, X(t))$ and the mixing parameter $\gamma$ equal to 1)
2. Calibrate the local volatility correction and the mixing parameter

and an outline of one possible approach is given below in the context of a Heston-style model with no jumps,

$$\frac{dX(t)}{X(t)} = (r_d(t) - r_f(t))dt + \sigma_X(t, X(t))\sqrt{v(t)}dW_X^d(t)$$

$$dv(t) = \kappa(\theta - v(t))dt + \gamma\sqrt{v(t)}dW_v^d(t) \tag{16.222}$$

$$< dW_X^d, dW_v^d > = \rho_{X,v}dt. \tag{16.223}$$

The stochastic volatility calibration needs to take account of the fact that interest rates are stochastic, which increases the dimensionality of the problem significantly. To counter this it is much more convenient to work with the FX forward in the domestic T-forward measure associated with its maturity (see Grzelak and Oosterlee, 2012). The FX forward is given by

$$F(t, T) = \frac{X(t)P_f(t, T)}{P_d(t, T)}. \tag{16.224}$$

The dynamics of the bond prices could take any desired form, although for simplicity here the Hull-White form is adopted,

$$\frac{dP_d(t, T)}{P_d(t, T)} = \left[r(t) - \frac{1}{2}\sigma_d^2(t)B_d^2(t, T)\right]dt - B_d(t, T)\sigma_d(t)dW^T(t) \tag{16.225}$$

$$\frac{dP_f(t, T)}{P_f(t, T)} = \left[r_f(t) - \rho_{X,f}(t)B_f(t, T)\sigma_f(t)\sigma_X(t) - \rho_{f,d}(t)B_f(t, T)\sigma_f(t)B_d(t, T)\sigma_d(t)\right]dt$$

$$\tag{16.226}$$

$$-B_f(t, T)\sigma_f(t)dW_f^{T_d}(t).$$

Applying the Itô product rule to the forward FX rate in the same manner as described in equation (16.194) gives a very similar result for the dynamics of the FX forward,

$$\frac{dF(t, T)}{F(t, T)} = \left[\sigma_X(t, X(t))\sqrt{v(t)}dW_X^{T_d}(t) + \sigma_f(t)B_f(t, T)dW_f^{T_d} - \sigma_d(t)B_d(t, T)dW_d^{T_d}(t)\right]. \tag{16.227}$$

Setting $\sigma_X(t, X(t)) = 1$ gives the purely stochastic volatility form,

$$\frac{dF(t, T)}{F(t, T)} = \left[\sqrt{v(t)}dW_X^{T_d}(t) + \sigma_f(t)B_f(t, T)dW_f^{T_d} - \sigma_d(t)B_d(t, T)dW_d^{T_d}(t)\right]. \tag{16.228}$$

Furthermore since the sum of the three Gaussian variables on the right-hand side of this expression is also Gaussian it is possible to write

$$dF(t, T) = F\Sigma_{SV}(t, T)dW_F^{T_d}(t), \tag{16.229}$$

where

$$\Sigma_{SV}^2(t, T) = v(t) + \sigma_f^2(t)B_f^2(t, T) + \sigma_d^2(t)B_d^2(t, T) + 2\rho_{X,f}(t)\sqrt{v(t)}\sigma_f(t)B_f(t, T)$$
$$- 2\rho_{X,d}(t)\sqrt{v(t)}\sigma_d(t)B_d(t, T) - 2\rho_{f,d}(t)\sigma_f(t)B_f(t, T)\sigma_d(t)B_d(t, T). \tag{16.230}$$

These simplifications allow a PDE to be formed that can be used to calibrate the stochastic volatility model parameters (see Grzelak and Oosterlee, 2012).

Having obtained the stochastic volatility model parameters the second step is to combine this with the local volatility. Given a pure local volatility model $\sigma_{LV}(t, X)$ it is possible to combine it with the stochastic volatility using a *mimicking* theorem (Combes, 2011; Clark, 2011). The local volatility is related to the stochastic volatility through

$$\sigma_{LV}^2(t, x) = \mathbb{E}\left[\sigma_X^2(t, X(t))v(t)|X(t) = x\right] = \sigma_X^2(t, x)\mathbb{E}\left[v(t)|X(t) = x\right] \tag{16.231}$$

$$p_{LV}(t, x) = \int_0^\infty p_{LSV}(t, x, y)dy, \tag{16.232}$$

where $p_{LV}$ and $p_{LSV}$ are the transition probability densities of the local volatility and local-stochastic volatility model respectively. The local volatility could be obtained using the approach outlined below in section 16.6, while the transition probability density could be obtained from the Fokker-Planck PDE (Clark, 2011). The mixing parameter will also need to be specified either through calibration or exogenous specification.

Other calibration approaches will be possible including more direct methods such as the Markovian projection approach of Piterbarg (2007).

## 16.5 INFLATION

There are a number of approaches to the modelling of inflation in a risk-neutral context. The *foreign-currency analogy* or *Jarrow-Yildirim* approach (Barone and Castagna, 1998; Jarrow and Yildirim, 2003) is one of the most popular and, given the multi-currency framework in use for XVA, one of most convenient as it allows direct re-use of the interest rate and FX models.

### 16.5.1 The Jarrow-Yildirim Model (using Hull-White Dynamics)

The Jarrow-Yildirim approach uses a foreign-currency analogy and hence is a general approach that can be applied using any cross-currency model. Jarrow and Yildirim (2003) initially used an HJM model but alternatives such as market models are also perfectly viable (Mercurio, 2005). A normal market model has also been developed by Kenyon (2008). The Jarrow-Yildirim approach using the multi-currency Hull-White model described above in section 16.4 is given as an example.

In the Jarrow-Yildirim approach two interest rates, nominal and real rates, and the inflation index are modelled. In the general multi-asset framework the nominal interest rate is the domestic interest rate, assuming that the inflation rate relates to the domestic economy. Hence in the following expressions the subscript $d$ should be equated with the $n$ frequently used in pure inflation models. The real rates will follow a process equivalent to that of a foreign currency and be indicated by the subscript $r$ while the inflation index is represented by $I$ and is equivalent to the FX process. Inflation displays pronounced seasonal behaviour, however, this is directly incorporated into the model through the real rates as they are fitted to the inflation forward curve through a series of zero-coupon inflation-index swaps:

$$\frac{dI(t)}{I(t)} = \left(r_d(t) - r_r(t)\right) dt + \sigma_I(t)dW_I^d(t) \tag{16.233}$$

$$dr_d(t) = \left(\theta_d(t) - \alpha_d r_d(t)\right) dt + \sigma_d(t)dW_d^d(t) \tag{16.234}$$

$$dr_r(t) = \left(\theta_r(t) - \alpha_r r_r(t) - \rho_{I,r}(t)\sigma_I(t)\sigma_r(t)\right) dt + \sigma_r(t)dW_r^d(t). \tag{16.235}$$

As with the earlier results we can write the domestic and real bond prices in affine form,

$$P_d(t, T) = A_d(t, T)e^{-r_d(t)B_d(t,T)} \tag{16.236}$$

$$P_r(t, T) = A_r(t, T)e^{-r_r(t)B_r(t,T)}. \tag{16.237}$$

The functions $A(t, T)$ and $B(t, T)$ are given by

$$B_d(t, T) = \frac{1}{\alpha_d}\left(1 - e^{-\alpha_d(T-t)}\right) \tag{16.238}$$

$$B_r(t, T) = \frac{1}{\alpha_r}\left(1 - e^{-\alpha_r(T-t)}\right), \tag{16.239}$$

and

$$A_d(t, T) = \exp\left[-\int_t^T \left(\theta_d(s)B_d(s, T) - \frac{\sigma_d(s)^2}{2}B_d(s, T)^2\right) ds\right] \tag{16.240}$$

$$A_r(t, T) = \exp\left[-\int_t^T \left(\theta_r(s)B_r(s, T) - \frac{\sigma_r(s)^2}{2}B_r(s, T)^2\right) ds\right]. \tag{16.241}$$

**Calibration of the Real Bond Price**    The first step to calibrate the model is to fit the real zero-coupon bond price to the prices of Zero-Coupon Inflation-Indexed Swaps (ZCIIS). Following the approach of Mercurio (2005), we can express the real zero-coupon bond prices in terms of the ZCIIS prices price and the domestic nominal bond in a model independent way. The ZCIIS has two cash flows occurring at the maturity of the trade, $T_M$, a fixed flow based on a compounded fixed rate $K$,

$$N[(1 + a_i K)^m - 1],$$

and an inflation index flow,

$$N\left[\frac{I(T_M)}{I(T_{ref})} - 1\right],$$

where $N$ is the trade notional, $I(T_{ref})$ is the value of the inflation index on the reference date for the start of the trade, $a_i$ is the day-count fraction and $m$ is the number of compounding periods. The value of the inflation index leg of the ZCIIS is given by

$$V_{\text{ZCIIS-inf}}(t, T_M, I_0, N) = N\mathbb{E}^d\left[e^{-\int_t^{T_M} r_d(s)ds}\left\{\frac{I(T_M)}{I(T_{ref})} - 1\right\}|\mathcal{F}_t\right]. \qquad (16.242)$$

We know the following equality holds between two currencies (see Brigo and Mercurio, 2006),

$$X(t)B_d(t)\mathbb{E}^f\left[\frac{Y_f(T)}{B_F(T)}|\mathcal{F}_t\right] = B_d(t)\mathbb{E}^d\left[\frac{Y_f(T)X(T)}{B_d(T)}|\mathcal{F}_t\right] \qquad (16.243)$$

where $B_d(t)$ and $B_f(t)$ are the domestic and foreign money market accounts as defined by equation (16.79) and $Y_f(t)$ is a derivative that pays $Y_f(T)$ at time $T$ in foreign currency. It is also true that

$$P_f(t, T) = \mathbb{E}^f\left[e^{-\int_t^T r_f(s)ds}|\mathcal{F}_t\right] \qquad (16.244)$$

$$P_d(t, T) = \mathbb{E}^d\left[e^{-\int_t^T r_d(s)ds}|\mathcal{F}_t\right]. \qquad (16.245)$$

Hence it is possible to write the following equality,

$$I(t)P_r(t, T) = I(t)\mathbb{E}^f\left[e^{-\int_t^T r_f(s)ds}|\mathcal{F}_t\right] \qquad (16.246)$$

$$= \mathbb{E}^d\left[I(T)e^{-\int_t^T r_d(s)ds}|\mathcal{F}_t\right]. \qquad (16.247)$$

Substituting these results into equation (16.242) gives the value of the ZCIIS at time $t = 0$ in terms of real and domestic zero-coupon bond prices,

$$V_{\text{ZCIIS-inf}}(0, T_M, I_0, N) = N[P_r(0, T_M) - P_d(0, T_M)], \qquad (16.248)$$

thus allowing the initial real discount curve to be stripped from ZCIIS prices.

**Volatility Calibration**   The second step in the calibration process is to calibrate the model volatility parameters to prices of year-on-year inflation-indexed options. Before proceeding to look at the option price it is necessary to derive a formula for the price of a year-on-year inflation-indexed swap, YYIIS. The YYIIS pays an inflation-linked floating leg which represents the growth of inflation over a year,

$$Na_i\left[\frac{I(T_i)}{I(T_{i-1})} - 1\right].$$

The value of this YYIIS coupon is given by

$$V_{\text{YYIIS-inf}}(t, T_{i-1}, T_i, a_i, N) = Na_i \mathbb{E}^d \left[ e^{-\int_t^T r_d(s)ds} \left\{ \frac{I(T_i)}{I(T_{i-1})} - 1 \right\} |\mathcal{F}_t \right]. \quad (16.249)$$

The tower property of expectations allows this to be written as

$$Na_i \mathbb{E}^d \left[ e^{-\int_t^{T_{i-1}} r_d(s)ds} \mathbb{E}^d \left[ e^{-\int_{T_{i-1}}^{T_i} r_d(s)ds} \left( \frac{I(T_i)}{I(T_{i-1})} - 1 \right) |\mathcal{F}_{T_{i-1}} \right] |\mathcal{F}_t \right] \quad (16.250)$$

$$= Na_i \mathbb{E}^d \left[ e^{-\int_t^{T_{i-1}} r_d(s)ds} (P_r(T_{i-1}, T_i) - P_d(T_{i-1}, T_i)) |\mathcal{F}_t \right]$$

$$= Na_i \mathbb{E}^d \left[ e^{-\int_t^{T_{i-1}} r_d(s)ds} P_r(T_{i-1}, T_i) |\mathcal{F}_t \right] - Na_i P_d(t, T_i),$$

where the result from the ZCIIS swap has been used to replace the inner expectation. To calculate the expectation in the first term of the remaining expression change to the $T_{i-1}$ domestic measure,

$$Na_i \mathbb{E}^d \left[ e^{-\int_t^{T_{i-1}} r_d(s)ds} P_r(T_{i-1}, T_i) |\mathcal{F}_t \right] = Na_i P_d(t, T_{i-1}) \mathbb{E}^{d, T_{i-1}} \left[ P_r(T_{i-1}, T_i) |\mathcal{F}_t \right]. \quad (16.251)$$

The dynamics of the real bond in the $T_{i-1}$-forward domestic measure are given by

$$\frac{dP_r(t, T)}{P_r(t, T)} = [r_r(t) + \rho_{I,r}(t)\sigma_I(t)B_r(t, T)\sigma_r(t) - \rho_{r,d}(t)B_d(t, T_{i-1})\sigma_d(t)B_r(t, T)\sigma_r(t)]dt \quad (16.252)$$

$$- B_r(t, T)\sigma_r(t)dW_r^{T_{i-1}, d}(t).$$

Integrating this expression and using the fact that $P(T_{i-1}, T_{i-1}) = 1$ allows the real bond in the expectation to be written as

$$P_r(T_{i-1}, T_i) = \frac{P_r(t, T_i)}{P_r(t, T_{i-1})} \exp \left[ \int_t^{T_{i-1}} \rho_{I,r}(s)\sigma_I(s)\sigma_r(s)(B_r(s, T_i) - B_r(s, T_{i-1}))ds \right. \quad (16.253)$$

$$- \frac{1}{2} \int_t^{T_{i-1}} \sigma_r(s)^2 (B_r(s, T_i)^2 - B_r(s, T_{i-1})^2)ds$$

$$- \int_t^{T_{i-1}} \rho_{r,d}(s)B_d(s, T_{i-1})\sigma_d(s)\sigma_r(t)(B_r(s, T_i) - B_r(s, T_{i-1}))ds$$

$$\left. - \int_t^{T_{i-1}} (B_r(s, T_i) - B_r(s, T_{i-1}))\sigma_r(s)dW_r^{T_{i-1}, d}(t). \right]$$

The bond is of course log-normal and hence the expected value of this real bond takes the form

$$\mathbb{E}^{T_{i-1}, d}[P(T_{i-1}, T_i) |\mathcal{F}_t] = \frac{P_r(t, T_i)}{P_r(t, T_{i-1})} e^{C(t, T_{i-1}, T_i)}, \quad (16.254)$$

where

$$C(t, T_{i-1}, T_i) = \int_t^{T_{i-1}} \sigma_r(s)[B_r(s, T_i) - B_r(s, T_{i-1})] \tag{16.255}$$
$$\times \left\{ \rho_{I,r}(s)\sigma_I(s) - \sigma_r(s)B_r(s, T_{i-1}) - \rho_{r,d}(s)\sigma_d(s)B_d(s, T_{i-1}) \right\} ds.$$

Finally the value of the inflation index coupon on the year-on-year inflation swap is given by

$$V_{\text{YYIIS-inf}}(t, T_{i-1}, T_i, a_i, N) = Na_i \frac{P_r(t, T_i)}{P_r(t, T_{i-1})} e^{C(t, T_{i-1}, T_i)} - Na_i P_d(t, T_i). \tag{16.256}$$

The final step is to derive a formula for the price of a year-on-year inflation-indexed caplet (YYIIC) with payout

$$Na_i \left[ \frac{I(T_i)}{I(T_{i-1})} - 1 - K \right]^+ ,$$

where $K$ is the strike. Writing $K + 1 = K-$ allows this to take the standard option form. The dynamics of $I$ in equation (16.233) show that the ratio $I(T_i)/I(T_{i-1})$ is a log-normal quantity so that in the $T_i$-forward domestic measure,

$$\frac{I(T_i)}{I(T_{i-1})} = \exp \left\{ \int_{T_{i-1}}^{T_i} \left( r_d(s) - r_r(s) - \frac{1}{2}\sigma_I(s)^2 - \rho_{d,I}(s)\sigma_I(s)\sigma_d(s)B_d(s, T_i) \right) ds \right. \tag{16.257}$$
$$\left. + \int_{T_{i-1}}^{T_i} \sigma_I(s)dW_I^{T_i,d}(s) \right\}.$$

Hence writing

$$Z = \log \frac{I(T_i)}{I(T_{i-1})}, \tag{16.258}$$

if we know the mean, $\mu$, and variance, $v^2$ of Z, then

$$m = \mathbb{E}\left[ e^Z \right] = e^{\mu + \frac{v^2}{2}}$$

and the price of a YYIIC can be written as a Black-Scholes equation,

$$V_{\text{YYIIC}}(t, T_{i-1}, T_i, a_i, N) = m\Phi\left( \frac{\log \frac{m}{\bar{K}} + \frac{1}{2}v^2}{v} \right) - \bar{K}\Phi\left( \frac{\log \frac{m}{\bar{K}} - \frac{1}{2}v^2}{v} \right), \tag{16.259}$$

where $\Phi$ is the cumulative normal.

The value of the the YYIIS can be written in terms of the $T_i$-forward domestic measure,

$$V_{\text{YYIIS-inf}}(t, T_{i-1}, T_i, a_i, N) = Na_i P_d(t, T_i) \mathbb{E}^{T_i,d} \left[ \left\{ \frac{I(T_i)}{I(T_{i-1})} - 1 \right\} \Big| \mathcal{F}_t \right] \quad (16.260)$$

$$= Na_i P_d(t, T) \mathbb{E}^{T_i,d} \left[ \frac{I(T_i)}{I(T_{i-1})} \Big| \mathcal{F}_t \right] - Na_i P_d(t, T).$$

Using equation (16.256) it is straightforward to show that

$$\mu = \left[ \frac{I(T_i)}{I(T_{i-1})} \Big| \mathcal{F}_t \right] = \frac{P_d(t, T_{i-1})}{P_d(t, T_i)} \frac{P_r(t, T_i)}{P_r(t, T_{i-1})} e^{C(t, T_i, T_{i-1})}. \quad (16.261)$$

The only part remaining to be calculated is the variance of $Z$, $v^2$, which is given by

$$v^2 = \text{Var}^{T_i,d} \left[ \log \frac{I(T_i)}{I(T_{i-1})} \Big| \mathcal{F}_t \right]. \quad (16.262)$$

It is more convenient to work in the spot domestic measure as the variance is unaffected by the change of measure and hence

$$v^2 = \text{Var}^d \left[ \int_{T_{i-1}}^{T_i} (r_d(s) - r_r(s)) ds + \int_{T_{i-1}}^{T_i} \sigma_I(s) dW_I^d(s) \Big| \mathcal{F}_t \right] \quad (16.263)$$

This expression contains three stochastic integrals,

$$A = \int_{T_{i-1}}^{T_i} r_d(s) ds \quad (16.264)$$

$$B = - \int_{T_{i-1}}^{T_i} r_r(s) ds \quad (16.265)$$

$$C = \int_{T_{i-1}}^{T_i} \sigma_I(s) dW_I^d(s). \quad (16.266)$$

To calculate the variance requires the following expansion:

$$\text{Var}[A + B + C] = \text{Var}[A] + \text{Var}[B] + \text{Var}[C] + 2\text{Cov}[A, B] + 2\text{Cov}[B, C] + 2\text{Cov}[A, C], \quad (16.267)$$

and the next step is to derive each of these quantities.

The variance of A is given by

$$\text{Var}[A] = \text{Var}^d \left[ \int_{T_{i-1}}^{T_i} r_d(s) ds \Big| \mathcal{F}_t \right] \quad (16.268)$$

$$= \text{Var}^d \left[ \int_{T_{i-1}}^{T_i} \sigma_d(s) \int_t^s e^{-\alpha_d(s-u)} dW_d^d(u) ds \Big| \mathcal{F}_t \right].$$

To solve this expression, the order of integration must be changed and the integral split into two segments covering the intervals $[t, T_{i-1}]$ and $[T_{i-1}, T_i]$,

$$\text{Var}[A] = \text{Var}[A_1] + \text{Var}[A_2] \tag{16.269}$$

$$= \text{Var}^d \left[ \int_t^{T_{i-1}} \left( \int_{T_{i-1}}^{T_i} \sigma_d(s) e^{-\alpha_d(s-u)} ds \right) dW_d^d(u) \Big| \mathcal{F}_t \right]$$

$$+ \text{Var}^d \left[ \int_{T_{i-1}}^{T_i} \left( \int_u^{T_i} \sigma_d(s) e^{-\alpha_d(s-u)} ds \right) dW_d^d(u) \Big| \mathcal{F}_t \right].$$

$A_1$ and $A_2$ are independent as they cover different time segments and hence there is no cross-term. The variances are given by

$$\text{Var}[A_1] = \int_t^{T_{i-1}} \left( \int_{T_{i-1}}^{T_i} \sigma_d(s) e^{-\alpha_d(s-u)} ds \right)^2 du \tag{16.270}$$

$$\text{Var}[A_2] = \int_{T_{i-1}}^{T_i} \left( \int_u^{T_i} \sigma_d(s) e^{-\alpha_d(s-u)} ds \right)^2 du. \tag{16.271}$$

Given that $B$ has the same form as $A$, it is immediately clear that

$$\text{Var}[B] = \text{Var}[B_1] + \text{Var}[B_2], \tag{16.272}$$

where

$$\text{Var}[B_1] = \int_t^{T_{i-1}} \left( \int_{T_{i-1}}^{T_i} \sigma_r(s) e^{-\alpha_r(s-u)} ds \right)^2 du \tag{16.273}$$

$$\text{Var}[B_2] = \int_{T_{i-1}}^{T_i} \left( \int_u^{T_i} \sigma_r(s) e^{-\alpha_r(s-u)} ds \right)^2 du. \tag{16.274}$$

The variance of $C$ is straightforward to obtain:

$$\text{Var}[C] = \text{Var} \left[ \int_{T_{i-1}}^{T_i} \sigma_I(s) dW_I^d(s) \Big| \mathcal{F}_t \right] \tag{16.275}$$

$$= \int_{T_{i-1}}^{T_i} \sigma_I(s)^2 ds.$$

The covariance terms are given by similar approaches. The covariance of the two rates terms is given by

$$\text{Cov}[A, B] = \text{Cov}^d \left[ \int_{T_{i-1}}^{T_i} r_d(s) ds, \int_{T_{i-1}}^{T_i} r_d rs) ds \right] \tag{16.276}$$

$$
= \mathbb{E}^d \left[ \left( \int_{T_{i-1}}^{T_i} \sigma_d(s) \int_t^s e^{-\alpha_d(s-u)} dW_d^d(u) ds \right) \right.
$$
$$
\left. \times \left( \int_{T_{i-1}}^{T_i} \sigma_r(s) \int_t^s e^{-\alpha_r(s-u)} dW_r^d(u) ds \right) \right].
$$

The same approach adopted above for the variance of the rates terms can also be used here. Hence,

$$
\text{Cov}[A, B] = \mathbb{E}^d[AB_1] + \mathbb{E}^d[AB_2] \tag{16.277}
$$

where

$$
\mathbb{E}^d[AB_1] = \int_t^{T_{i-1}} \rho_{d,r}(u) \left( \int_{T_{i-1}}^{T_i} \sigma_d(s) e^{-\alpha_d(s-u)} ds \right) \left( \int_{T_{i-1}}^{T_i} \sigma_r(s) e^{-\alpha_r(s-u)} ds \right) du \tag{16.278}
$$
$$
\mathbb{E}^d[AB_2] = \int_{T_{i-1}}^{T_i} \rho_{d,r}(u) \left( \int_u^{T_i} \sigma_d(s) e^{-\alpha_d(s-u)} ds \right) \left( \int_u^{T_i} \sigma_r(s) e^{-\alpha_r(s-u)} ds \right) du,
$$

and as before there is no cross-term as $AB_1$ and $AB_2$ are independent. The covariance of $A$ with $C$ is given by

$$
\text{Cov}[A, C] = \text{Cov}^d \left[ \int_{T_{i-1}}^{T_i} r_d(s) ds, \int_{T_{i-1}}^{T_i} \sigma_I(s) dW_I^d(s) \right] \tag{16.279}
$$
$$
= \mathbb{E}^d \left[ \left( \int_{T_{i-1}}^{T_i} \sigma_d(s) \int_t^s e^{-\alpha_d(s-u)} dW_d^d(u) ds \right) \left( \int_{T_{i-1}}^{T_i} \sigma_I(s) dW_I^d(s) \right) | \mathcal{F}_t \right].
$$

Changing the order of integration in the rates integral and splitting the first integral into two segments over the intervals $[t, T_{i-1}]$ and $[T_{i-1}, T_i]$ gives

$$
\text{Cov}[A, C] = \mathbb{E}^d \left[ \left( \int_{T_{i-1}}^{T_i} \left( \int_u^{T_i} \sigma_d(s) e^{-\alpha_d(s-u)} ds \right) dW_d^d(u) \right) \left( \int_{T_{i-1}}^{T_i} \sigma_I(s) dW_I^d(s) \right) \right] \tag{16.280}
$$
$$
= \int_{T_{i-1}}^{T_i} \rho_{d,I}(u) \sigma_I(u) \left( \int_u^{T_i} \sigma_d(s) e^{-\alpha_d(s-u)} ds \right) du,
$$

where the term corresponding to the rate over the interval $[t, T_{i-1}]$ is zero. Again it is now possible to write down the final covariance term which takes the same form

$$
\text{Cov}[B, C] = \int_{T_{i-1}}^{T_i} \rho_{r,I}(u) \sigma_I(u) \left( \int_u^{T_i} \sigma_r(s) e^{-\alpha_r(s-u)} ds \right) du. \tag{16.281}
$$

Finally the variance is given by

$$
v^2 = \text{Var}[A_1] + \text{Var}[A_2] + \text{Var}[B_1] + \text{Var}[B_2] + \text{Var}[C] \tag{16.282}
$$
$$
+ 2\mathbb{E}^d[AB_1] + 2\mathbb{E}^d[AB_2] + 2\text{Cov}[A, C] + 2\text{Cov}[B, C]
$$

$$
= \int_t^{T_{i-1}} \left( \int_{T_{i-1}}^{T_i} \sigma_d(s) e^{-\alpha_d(s-u)} ds \right)^2 du + \int_{T_{i-1}}^{T_i} \left( \int_u^{T_i} \sigma_d(s) e^{-\alpha_d(s-u)} ds \right)^2 du
$$

$$
+ \int_t^{T_{i-1}} \left( \int_{T_{i-1}}^{T_i} \sigma_r(s) e^{-\alpha_r(s-u)} ds \right)^2 du + \int_{T_{i-1}}^{T_i} \left( \int_u^{T_i} \sigma_r(s) e^{-\alpha_r(s-u)} ds \right)^2 du
$$

$$
+ \int_{T_{i-1}}^{T_i} \sigma_I(s)^2 ds
$$

$$
+ 2 \int_t^{T_{i-1}} \rho_{d,r}(u) \left( \int_{T_{i-1}}^{T_i} \sigma_d(s) e^{-\alpha_d(s-u)} ds \right) \left( \int_{T_{i-1}}^{T_i} \sigma_r(s) e^{-\alpha_r(s-u)} ds \right) du
$$

$$
+ 2 \int_{T_{i-1}}^{T_i} \rho_{d,r}(u) \left( \int_u^{T_i} \sigma_d(s) e^{-\alpha_d(s-u)} ds \right) \left( \int_u^{T_i} \sigma_r(s) e^{-\alpha_r(s-u)} ds \right) du
$$

$$
+ 2 \int_{T_{i-1}}^{T_i} \rho_{d,I}(u)\sigma_I(u) \left( \int_u^{T_i} \sigma_d(s) e^{-\alpha_d(s-u)} ds \right) du
$$

$$
+ 2 \int_{T_{i-1}}^{T_i} \rho_{r,I}(u)\sigma_I(u) \left( \int_u^{T_i} \sigma_r(s) e^{-\alpha_r(s-u)} ds \right) du. \tag{16.283}
$$

This complex expression will reduce to the simpler form found in Brigo and Mercurio (2006), Mercurio (2005) and Scardovi (2011) if the volatility parameters are constants. In the context of this model, the volatility parameters will be piecewise constant and hence the more complex integral form must be retained. Once the variance has been obtained the Black-Scholes formula in equation (16.259) gives the price of the YYIIC.

To calibrate the volatility, a strip of year-on-year caplets or floorlets will be used to find the volatility of the inflation spot process, in a similar way to the approach taken to the FX spot calibration. Here, however, there are a number of other parameters that must be specified first, the real rate volatility parameters, $\sigma_r(s)$ and $\alpha_r$ and the model correlations, $\rho_{d,r}$, $\rho_{d,I}$ and $\rho_{r,I}$. The real and nominal (domestic) rates are closely related to each other and hence often the correlation, $\rho_{d,r}$ is specified at a high positive value and the real volatility is set as a multiplier on the domestic volatility $\sigma_r(t) = \lambda \sigma_d(t)$ where $\lambda$ is a number close to 1.0. The correlation between the index and domestic short rate, $\rho_{d,I}$, can be obtained from historical data or specified, typically at a small value. The final correlation, $\rho_{r,I}$, will similarly be specified at a low value that allows good calibration results for the index volatility.

When the inflation model is used alongside other assets in a Monte Carlo model, then a series of other correlations with the two additional stochastic factors in the inflation model, real rates and spot inflation, will need to be specified. The inflation index/asset correlations can be taken from historical data. The correlation between interest rates and other assets may be set equal to the domestic rate/asset correlation.

**Inflation in a Foreign Currency**  Inflation need not only be specified in the numeraire currency and it may be the case that several inflation processes defined in different currencies must be modelled in the same netting set. In the measure associated with the foreign currency the inflation index and real rates have the expected form

$$\frac{dI_f(t)}{I_f(t)} = \left(r_f(t) - r_{rf}(t)\right) dt + \sigma_{If}(t)dW^f_{If}(t) \tag{16.284}$$

$$dr_f(t) = \left(\theta_f(t) - \alpha_f r_f(t)\right) dt + \sigma_f(t)dW^f_f(t) \tag{16.285}$$

$$dr_{rf}(t) = \left(\theta_{rf}(t) - \alpha_{rf} r_{rf}(t) - \rho_{If,rf}(t)\sigma_{If}(t)\sigma_{rf}(t)\right) dt + \sigma_{rf}(t)dW^f_{rf}(t). \tag{16.286}$$

The inflation parameters can be calibrated using the same approach as above. However, to simulate the processes the measure must be changed to a domestic one. In the spot domestic measure the processes are given by

$$\frac{dI_f(t)}{I_f(t)} = \left(r_f(t) - r_{rf}(t) - \rho_{X,If}(t)\sigma_X(t)\sigma_{If}(t)\right) dt + \sigma_{If}(t)dW^d_{If}(t) \tag{16.287}$$

$$dr_f(t) = \left(\theta_f(t) - \alpha_f r_f(t) - \rho_{X,f}(t)\sigma_X(t)\sigma_f(t)\right) dt + \sigma_f(t)dW^d_f(t) \tag{16.288}$$

$$dr_{rf}(t) = \left(\theta_{rf}(t) - \alpha_{rf} r_{rf}(t) - \rho_{If,rf}(t)\sigma_{If}(t)\sigma_{rf}(t) - \rho_{X,rf}(t)\sigma_X(t)\sigma_{rf}(t)\right) dt \tag{16.289}$$
$$+ \sigma_{rf}(t)dW^d_{rf}(t).$$

### 16.5.2 Other Approaches

Other approaches to modelling inflation have been used, although Jarrow-Yildirim is probably the most popular approach. A simpler model is provided by the two-process Hull-White model (Dodgson and Kainth, 2006). There the nominal rate is again assumed to follow an extended Hull-White process. However, the inflation rate is modelled as a second Hull-White process, rather than the real rate in the Jarrow-Yildirim approach. Hence the inflation index is given by

$$I(T) = I(t)\exp\left(\int_t^T i(s)ds\right), \tag{16.290}$$

where

$$di(t) = \left(\theta_i(t) - \alpha_i i(t)\right) dt + \sigma_i(t)dW^d_i(t). \tag{16.291}$$

A number of different market models of inflation have also been developed (Kazziha, 1999; Belgrade, Benhamou and Koehler, 2004; Mercurio, 2005). Market model approaches are suitable where a market model has been adopted for the modelling of interest rates. As an example consider a model where a series of discrete inflation forwards maturing at times $T_j$ are modelled as log-normal processes:

$$\frac{dI(t, T_j)}{I(t, T_j)} = \mu_{Ij}(t)dt + \sigma_{Ij}(t)dW_{Ij}(t). \tag{16.292}$$

In the $T_j$-forward measure $I(t, T_j)$ will be a martingale. A number of different variants of the model are possible.

A normal market model with smile has been developed by Kenyon (2008). Kenyon uses mixtures of normal distributions and a normal-gamma model to fit the observed smile in YYIIC prices.

A Quadratic Gaussian model with the ability to at least partially fit the observed volatility smile has been proposed by Gretarsson (2013). This model proposes a multi-factor Quadratic Gaussian process for year-on-year inflation. Other smile models have focussed on modelling the inflation index, including with the SABR model (Mercurio and Moreni, 2006; Mercurio and Moreni, 2009).

Smiles can also be included by using more sophisticated dynamics in the Jarrow-Yildirim approach. A model of this type using the Quadratic Gaussian model has been proposed by McCloud (2008).

## 16.6  EQUITIES

Equities can be modelled in an XVA simulation in a very similar way to FX and many of the models discussed in section 16.4 can be applied here. The key differences are:

- Equities are driven by one interest rate not two.
- Equities normally pay dividends.
- Equity options tend to show a volatility skew rather than a smile, reflecting the buying of options to protect against falls in value. This is often more pronounced in equity indices rather than single stocks.

In practice equity derivatives make a much lower contribution to XVA than either interest rates or FX and there are a number of reasons for this. Equity derivatives tend to be shorter in maturity and hence contribute less. There are also considerably fewer equity derivatives with corporates. Many OTC equity derivatives will be traded with equity funds. Equity derivative structures such as CPPI are also distributed to retail clients; however, they are transacted in the form of a note sold to the investor so there is no XVA applied to the transaction. The associated hedge will lead to XVA but will also probably be done through a CSA. There will, of course, be KVA associated with equity derivatives, although again the shorter maturity of such transactions will mitigate compared to other asset classes.

### 16.6.1  A Simple Log-normal Model

The simplest approach to modelling equities is to use a log-normal model with

$$\frac{dS(t)}{S(t)} = (r_d(t) - \mu(t))dt + \sigma_S(t)dW_S^d(t) \tag{16.293}$$

in the domestic risk-neutral measure, where the stock price is measured in units of the domestic currency and $\mu(t)$ contains the continuous dividend yield for the stock and any adjustments from the stock repo rate.[13] In the T-forward measure with Hull-White interest rates, the dynamics become

$$\frac{dS(t)}{S(t)} = (r_d(t) - \mu(t) - \rho_{S,d}(t)\sigma_S(t)\sigma_d(t)B_d(t,T))dt + \sigma_S(t)dW_S^{T_d}(t). \tag{16.294}$$

Of course not all of the equities will have prices in the domestic currency so there is a need to cater for stocks in foreign currencies. In the foreign measure the stock price follows

$$\frac{dS_f(t)}{S_f(t)} = (r_f(t) - \mu_f(t))dt + \sigma_{S_f}(t)dW_{S_f}^f(t). \tag{16.295}$$

Changing to the spot domestic measure gives the expected *quanto* correction,

$$\frac{dS_f(t)}{S_f(t)} = (r_f(t) - \mu_f(t) - \rho_{X,S_f}(t)\sigma_X(t)\sigma_{S_f}(t))dt + \sigma_{S_f}(t)dW_{S_f}^d(t). \tag{16.296}$$

Finally transformation to the T-forward measure is given by

$$\frac{dS_f(t)}{S_f(t)} = (r_f(t) - \mu_f(t) - \rho_{X,S_f}(t)\sigma_X(t)\sigma_{S_f}(t) - \rho_{S_f,d}(t)\sigma_{S_f}(t)\sigma_d(t)B_d(t,T))dt \tag{16.297}$$
$$+ \sigma_{S_f}(t)dW_{S_f}^d(t).$$

These are all log-normal processes and so can be simulated directly using the standard exponential solution,

$$S_d(t) = S_d(0)\exp\left\{ \int_0^t \left( r_d(t) - \mu(t) - \rho_{S,d}(t)\sigma_S(t)\sigma_d(t)B_d(t,T) - \frac{1}{2}\sigma_{S_d}(t)^2 \right) dt \right. \tag{16.298}$$
$$\left. + \int_0^t \sigma_S(t)dW_S^{T_d}(t) \right\}.$$

**Calibration**   As was the case with the modelling of FX described above, the implied volatility of equity options observed in the market is the volatility of the equity forward. The domestic equity forward rate is given by

$$F(t,T) = S(t)\frac{e^{-\int_t^T \mu(t)dt}}{P_d(t,T)}, \tag{16.299}$$

which is of course virtually identical to the expression for the FX forward given in equation (16.193) except that there are now only two stochastic factors here, one driving the spot process

---

[13]That is we choose $\mu(t)$ to match the equity forward and assume that dividends are paid on a continuous basis.

and one driving domestic interest rates. Using the Itô product rule the dynamics of the equity forward are given by

$$dF(t,T) = dS(t)\frac{e^{-\int_t^T \mu(t)dt}}{P_d(t,T)} + S(t)e^{-\int_t^T \mu(t)dt} d\left(\frac{1}{P_d(t,T)}\right) \quad (16.300)$$

$$+ e^{-\int_t^T \mu(t)dt} dS(t) d\left(\frac{1}{P_d(t,T)}\right).$$

In the T-forward domestic measure $F(t,T)$ is a martingale and hence the dynamics must take the form

$$dF(t,T) = F(t,T)\Sigma(t,T)dW_F^{T_d}(t). \quad (16.301)$$

Using the dynamics for $S_d(t)$ in equation (16.294) and those for the domestic bond in equation (16.82) allows the volatility $\Sigma(t,T)$ to be related to the volatility of the stock and the bond:

$$\Sigma(t,T)^2 = \text{Var}\left(\sigma_S(t)dW_S^{T_d}(t) - \sigma_d(t)B_d(t,T)dW_d^{T_d}(t)\right) \quad (16.302)$$

$$= \sigma_S(t)^2 + \sigma_d(t)^2 B_d(t,T)^2 - 2\rho_{S,d}(t)\sigma_d(s)B_d(t,T).$$

The implied volatility of an option maturing at time $T$ is given by

$$\sigma_{\text{imp}}(T)^2 = \int_0^T \Sigma(s,T)^2 ds. \quad (16.303)$$

## 16.6.2   Dividends

Dividends paid on stocks are paid as discrete amounts on an annual or semi-annual basis, they are not paid as a continuous yield. When the dividend is paid the stock price drops to reflect the size of the cash flow. Models for equity derivatives do pay considerable attention to the modelling of dividends and often provide sensitivity calculations for the size of the dividend. In general equity derivative models prefer to model the discrete nature of the dividend directly and then either include fixed discrete dividends or discrete dividends that scale with the stock price or some combination of the two. The near-term dividends are known with more certainty than the longer term and hence some models assume fixed dividends for the next few payments and then blend this with a scaling approach for longer time scales. Models of this type can be found in Shreve (2004), Hull (2011) and other entry level texts on quantitative finance.

In the context of XVA the merit of modelling discrete dividends is questionable unless the underlying equity portfolio is material. This adds a fair degree of complexity to the model and will have little impact on the exposure profiles. Other issues such as volatility skew will have a larger impact and hence will be of higher priority.

## 16.6.3   Indices and Baskets

As was noted earlier in section 16.2.1, equity basket products and equity indices will frequently need to be modelled as the underlying for an equity derivative trade. The index or basket can be modelled independently or reconstructed from individual stocks. If there is no overlap between the basket and single stock underlyings in the same netting set then it is clear that the basket can be modelled directly with a single process. If there is an overlap, then there is a question as to whether or not the basket should be reconstructed. There is a heavy incentive to avoid reconstructing the basket, particularly if it contains many individual stocks. The computational cost of modelling hundreds of stocks is considerable, even if a simple log-normal approach is used for the stock dynamics. In some cases it will be possible to model the index and the single stock position separately. So, for example, if there are trades on a large traded index and a small number of equity options on constituent stocks in the same netting set it would be perfectly acceptable to model index and stocks separately with the appropriate correlation between them. If, however, the netting set contained a structured position involving a considerable number of the stocks in the index, perhaps offsetting an index option position against positions in the major index contributors, then it would be necessary to reconstruct the index.

A further complexity is found with the introduction of skew. As is well known, indices display much more skew that what would be implied by the individual stock components (Fengler, Herwartz and Werner, 2012). Dealing with this issue is beyond the scope of this volume but a number of approaches have been tried including local correlation models (Guyon, 2013), stochastic correlation (Fonseca, Grasselli and Tebaldi, 2007; Marabel Romo, 2012), and dynamic copula techniques (Fengler, Herwartz and Werner, 2012).

### 16.6.4 Managing Correlations

An equity derivative portfolio can have sensitivity to many stocks in the same netting set. If hundreds of equities are required this can lead to difficulties with the construction of a large correlation matrix and associated operations such as regularisation. The size of the main correlation matrix can be reduced by adopting an approach similar to the one-factor Gaussian copula approach popular in CDO models. Instead of entering all equities in the main correlation matrix, enter only an equity systemic factor per currency, $E_S$. This systemic factor might represent the behaviour of all stocks denominated in that currency as an abstract or actually represent the dynamics of an index. So, for example, in the US market the S&P 500 index might be selected and then the behaviour of all stocks in USD correlated with the index. Each individual stock is then correlated with the systemic factor so that

$$\frac{dS_d(t)}{S_d(t)} = (r_d(t) - \mu(t))dt + \sigma_S(t)\{\rho_{S,E_S}(t)dW^d_{E_S}(t) + \sqrt{(1 - \rho_{S,E_S}(t)^2)}dW^d_S(t)\}. \quad (16.304)$$

### 16.6.5 Skew: Local Volatility and Other Models

Including volatility skew in the equity model is an important consideration for XVA on equity derivative portfolios. The simplest extension is to use a local volatility model so that

$$\frac{dS_d(t)}{S_d(t)} = (r_d(t) - \mu(t))dt + \sigma_S(t, S(t))dW^d_S(t). \quad (16.305)$$

The volatility $\sigma_S(t, S(t))$ is now a function of the stock price. This is the extension of the Dupire model (Dupire 1994) to the case of stochastic interest rates.

The Dupire approach can be adopted in the case of stochastic interest rates (see Benhamou, Rivoira and Gruz, 2008; Andersen and Andreasen, 2000). The call option payout is given by

$$\mathbb{E}\left[e^{-\int_0^t r(s)ds}(S(t) - K)^+ | \mathcal{F}_t\right]. \tag{16.306}$$

As with Dupire this expression is differentiated, with the order of the derivative and expectation exchanged. The derivative of the call payout is given by

$$d\left[e^{-\int_0^t r(s)ds}(S_t - K)^+\right] = -\mu(t)e^{-\int_0^t r(s)ds}\left[(S_d(t) - K)^+ K\mathbb{1}_{\{S(t)>K\}}\right]dt \tag{16.307}$$
$$+ e^{-\int_0^t r(s)ds}r_d(t)K\mathbb{1}_{\{S(t)>K\}}dt$$
$$+ \frac{1}{2}e^{-\int_0^t r(s)ds}\sigma_S(t, S)^2 S^2 \delta(S(t) - K)dt$$
$$+ e^{-\int_0^t r(s)ds}\sigma_S(t, S)dW_S^d(t)[(S(t) - K)^+ + K\mathbb{1}_{\{S(t)>K\}}],$$

where $\mathbb{1}$ is an indicator function and $\delta(S(t) - K)$ is a Dirac delta function. Hence the derivative of the call value is given by

$$d\mathbb{E}\left[e^{-\int_0^t r(s)ds}(S_t - K)^+\right] = \mathbb{E}\left[(r_d(t) - \mu(t))K\mathbb{1}_{\{S(t)>K\}}\right]dt \tag{16.308}$$
$$- \mu\mathbb{E}\left[e^{-\int_0^t r(s)ds}(S_t - K)^+\right]dt$$
$$- \frac{1}{2}\sigma_S(t, K)^2 K^2 \mathbb{E}\left[e^{-\int_0^t r(s)ds}\delta(S(t) - K)\right]dt.$$

Writing

$$C(t, K) = \mathbb{E}\left[e^{-\int_0^t r(s)ds}(S(t) - K)^+\right] \tag{16.309}$$

and noting that

$$\frac{\partial C}{\partial K} = -\mathbb{E}[e^{-\int_0^t r(s)ds}\mathbb{1}_{\{S(t)>K\}}] \tag{16.310}$$

$$\frac{\partial^2 C}{\partial K^2} = \mathbb{E}[e^{-\int_0^t r(s)ds}\delta(S(t) - K)] \tag{16.311}$$

allows an expression for the local volatility to be found,

$$\sigma_S(t, K)^2 = \frac{\frac{\partial C}{\partial t} + \mu(t)\left(C - K\frac{\partial C}{\partial K}\right) - K\mathbb{E}[r_d(t)e^{-\int_0^t r(s)ds}\mathbb{1}_{\{S(t)>K\}}]}{\frac{1}{2}K^2\frac{\partial^2 C}{\partial K^2}}. \tag{16.312}$$

Comparing this with the Dupire formula for deterministic interest rates,

$$\sigma_S^{\text{det}}(t, K)^2 = \frac{\frac{\partial C}{\partial t} + \mu(t)C + (r_d(t) - \mu(t))K\frac{\partial C}{\partial K}}{\frac{1}{2}K^2\frac{\partial^2 C}{\partial K^2}} \qquad (16.313)$$

shows that

$$\sigma_S(t, K)^2 = \sigma_S^{\text{det}}(t, K)^2 - \frac{\left(r_d^0(t)K\frac{\partial C}{\partial K} + K\mathbb{E}[r_d(t)e^{-\int_0^t r(s)ds}\mathbb{1}_{\{S(t)>K\}}]\right)}{\frac{1}{2}K^2\frac{\partial^2 C}{\partial K^2}}, \qquad (16.314)$$

where $r_d^0(t)$ is given by the initial yield curve. Hence the local volatility is adjusted from the deterministic value by a correction term in the case of stochastic interest rates.

Local volatility is a model that has been popular in the equity market and allows a relatively straightforward way of matching the initial volatility skew in the presence of stochastic interest rates. Of course more sophisticated models are perfectly possible and those described in the context of FX smiles can be readily adapted here.

## 16.7  COMMODITIES

### 16.7.1  Precious Metals

As noted earlier in section 16.2.1 precious metals can be modelled in the same way as FX or equities, depending on whether or not there is a desire to see the lease rate modelled stochastically. Precious metals have a *lease* rate which is the cost of borrowing the precious metal. The lease rate plays exactly the same role as repo in equities.

### 16.7.2  Forward-based Commodities

For general forward-based commodities such as those described in Table 16.2 on page 274 the full forward curve must be modelled for XVA calculations as the commodity derivatives themselves rely on the full forward curve. The Clewlow-Strickland model (Clewlow and Strickland, 1999) described in the context of historical calibration in section 16.2.1 can also be calibrated risk-neutrally and applied to forward-based commodities, both seasonal and non-seasonal. Here, however, I show how we can arrive at a similar result through an approach similar to the Jarrow-Yildirim Inflation model.

As an example, consider another use of the *FX analogy* in this context where two additional stochastic processes are used to describe the behaviour of the commodity asset. A model of this type was originally proposed by Miltersen and Schwartz (1998) and modified by Larsson (2011). As above the domestic interest rate follows an extended Hull-White dynamic,

$$dr_d(t) = (\theta_d(t) - \alpha_d r_d(t))dt + \sigma_d(t)dW_d(t). \qquad (16.315)$$

The commodity spot process follows a log-normal dynamic,

$$dC(t) = (r_d(t) - \gamma_C(t))dt + \sigma_C(t)dW_C^d(t), \tag{16.316}$$

where $\gamma_C(t)$ is the *convenience yield* and has the dynamics

$$d\gamma_C(t) = \left(\theta_{\gamma_C}(t) - \alpha_{\gamma_C}\gamma_C(t) - \rho_{C,\gamma_C}(t)\sigma_C(t)\sigma_{\gamma_C}(t)\right)dt + \sigma_{\gamma_C}(t)dW_{\gamma_C}^d(t). \tag{16.317}$$

Hence by direct analogy with FX, the commodity forward is given by

$$F_C(t, T) = C(t)\frac{P_{\gamma_C}(t, T)}{P_d(t, T)}, \tag{16.318}$$

where $P_{\gamma_C}(t, T)$ is the convenience yield "bond". The commodity forward has the following dynamics:

$$dF_C(t, T) = F_C\Sigma_C(t, T)dW_{F_C}^{T_d}(t) \tag{16.319}$$

in the domestic T-forward measure and hence in a general T-forward domestic measure, $T_h$,

$$\frac{dF_C(t, T)}{F_C(t, T)} = -\rho_{F_C,d}(t)\Sigma_C(t, T)\sigma_d(t)[B_d(t, T_h) - B(t, T)]dt + \Sigma_C(t, T)dW_{F_C}^{T_h}(t). \tag{16.320}$$

In practice it will be easier to model the forward curve directly inside the Monte Carlo as the forward curve is what will be required for trade valuation at each time step. The spot commodity value will then be given by

$$C(t) = F_C(t, t). \tag{16.321}$$

The consequence of this is that correlations must be specified against the commodity forward and not the spot. If correlations are only available against the commodity spot then these must be converted to forward correlations and this will also require the correlation versus the convenience yield to be specified and the volatility of the convenience yield, which is otherwise implicit.

**Calibration**    The instruments available for calibration depend on the details of each commodity market and trade conventions do vary. The most common products available for calibration are commodity swaps and swaptions (see Geman, 2005; Larsson, 2011, for more details).

**Swaps**    The commodity swap is specified in the same way as an interest rate swap where the commodity buyer pays a fixed price $K$ and receives a fixed amount of commodity $q$ on a series of regular dates $T_i$ where the frequency can vary. Note that in some markets there can be a payment delay, where payment takes place after commodity delivery in a specific window and in some cases delivery of the commodity is continuous rather than discrete.[14] For the purpose of this derivation these effects will be ignored.

The value of the commodity swap is given by

$$V_C(t) = \sum_{i=1}^{N} \mathbb{E}^d \left[ e^{-\int_t^{T_i} r_d(s)ds} \left( C(T_i) - K \right) |\mathcal{F}_t \right] \tag{16.322}$$

$$= \sum_{i=1}^{N} P_d(t, T) \left( F(t, T_i) - K \right).$$

Hence a strip of commodity swaps can be used to determine the initial forward curve $F(0, T)$.

**Swaptions**   The value of a non-averaged commodity swaption is given by

$$C(t; K, T) = \mathbb{E}^d \left[ e^{-\int_t^T r_d(s)ds} \max(V_C(T), 0) |\mathcal{F}_t \right] \tag{16.323}$$

$$= \mathbb{E}^d \left[ e^{-\int_t^T r_d(s)ds} \left( \sum_{i=1}^{N} P_d(T, T_i) \left( F(T, T_i) - K \right) \right)^+ |\mathcal{F}_t \right].$$

Writing the annuity as

$$A(t) = \sum_{i=1}^{N} P_d(t, T_i) \tag{16.324}$$

and defining

$$y(t) = \frac{\sum_{i=1}^{N} P_d(t, T_i) F_C(t, T_i)}{A(t)}, \tag{16.325}$$

allows the value of the commodity swaption to be written as

$$C(t; K, T) = \mathbb{E}^d \left[ e^{-\int_t^T r_d(s)ds} A(T) (y(T) - K)^+ \right] \tag{16.326}$$

$$= A(t) \mathbb{E}^{A_d} \left[ (y(t) - K)^+ \right],$$

where the last expectation has been taken with respect to the annuity measure. It is therefore apparent that a Black-Scholes-type formula will result if $y(t)$ is log-normal. To proceed the dynamics of $y(t)$ in the annuity measure are needed. In the annuity measure $y(t)$ is a martingale and so takes the form

$$dy(t) = y(t)\Sigma_y(t)dW_y^{A_d}(t). \tag{16.327}$$

---

[14]Natural gas through a pipeline for example or power, although power has a different market structure.

In the annuity measure the dynamics of the bond and commodity forward have the form

$$\frac{dP_d(t, T_i)}{P_d(t, T_i)} = (\ldots)dt + \sigma_d(t)B_d(t, T_i)dW_d^{A_d}(t) \tag{16.328}$$

$$\frac{dF_C(t, T_i)}{F_C(t, T_i)} = (\ldots)dt + \Sigma_C(t, T)dW_{F_C}^{A_d}(t), \tag{16.329}$$

where the drift is unimportant for this calculation, given $y(t)$ is a martingale. The dynamics of the annuity follow from equations (16.324) and (16.328),

$$dA(t) = (\ldots)dt + \sigma_A(t)A(t)dW_d^{A_d}(t) \tag{16.330}$$

$$\sigma_A(t) = \sigma_d(t)\frac{\sum_{i=1}^{N} B_d(t, T_i)P_d(t, T_i)}{A(t)}. \tag{16.331}$$

The dynamics of $y(t)$ can be obtained by applying the Itô product rule to equation (16.325),

$$dy(t) = \sum_{i=1}^{N} \left[ \frac{F_C(t, T_i)dP_d(t, T_i)}{A(t)} + \frac{P_d(t, T_i)dF_C(t, T_i)}{A(t)} + F_C(t, T_i)P_d(t, T_i)d\left(\frac{1}{A(t)}\right) \right] \tag{16.332}$$

$$+ \ldots$$

$$= \sum_{i=1}^{N} \left[ \frac{F_C(t, T_i)P_d(t, T_i)}{A(t)} \right]$$

$$\times \left\{ \sigma_d(t)B_d(t, T_i)dW_d^{A_d}(t) + \Sigma_C(t, T_i)dW_{F_C}^{A_d}(t) - \sigma_A(t)dW_d^{A_d}(t) \right\} + \ldots$$

$$= y(t) \left[ (\sigma_d(t)\phi(t) - \sigma_A(t))dW_d^{A_d}(t) + \psi(t)dW_{F_C}^{A_d}(t) \right],$$

where

$$\phi(t) = \sum_{i=1}^{N} \frac{F_C(t, T_i)P_d(t, T_i)B_d(t, T_i)}{A(t)y(t)} \tag{16.333}$$

$$\psi(t) = \sum_{i=1}^{N} \frac{F_C(t, T_i)P_d(t, T_i)\Sigma_C(t, T_i)}{A(t)y(t)}. \tag{16.334}$$

The two volatility functions $\phi(t)$ and $\psi(t)$ can be written as weighted sums over the bond and commodity forwards respectively:

$$\phi(t) = \frac{\sum_{i=1}^{N} F_C(t, T_i)P_d(t, T_i)B_d(t, T_i)}{\sum_{i=1}^{N} F_C(t, T_i)P_d(t, T_i)} \tag{16.335}$$

$$= \sum_{i=1}^{N} w_d(t, T_i)B_d(t, T_i)$$

$$\psi(t) = \frac{\sum_{i=1}^{N} F_C(t, T_i) P_d(t, T_i) \Sigma_C(t, T_i)}{\sum_{i=1}^{N} F_C(t, T_i) P_d(t, T_i)} \tag{16.336}$$

$$= \sum_{i=1}^{N} w_C(t, T_i) \Sigma_C(t, T_i).$$

These two functions involve sums over the forward and bond value but can be approximated by freezing the weights at their initial values,

$$\phi(t) = \sum_{i=1}^{N} w_d(0, T_i) B_d(t, T_i) \tag{16.337}$$

$$\psi(t) = \sum_{i=1}^{N} w_C(0, T_i) \Sigma_C(t, T_i). \tag{16.338}$$

With this approximation in place the volatility of $y(t)$ can now be calculated:

$$\sigma_y(t)^2 = \text{Var} \left[ (\sigma_d(t)\phi(t) - \sigma_A(t)) dW_d^{A_d}(t) + \psi(t) dW_{F_C}^{A_d}(t) \right] \tag{16.339}$$

$$= \sigma_d(t)^2 \phi(t)^2 - 2\sigma_A(t)\sigma_d(t)\phi(t) + \sigma_A(t)^2 + \psi(t)^2$$

$$+ 2\rho_{F_C,d}(t)\psi(t)(\sigma_d(t)\phi(t) - \sigma_A(t)).$$

Finally the commodity swaption price is given by a Black-Scholes type formula,

$$C(t; K, T) = A(t)[y(t)N(d_1) - KN(d_2)], \tag{16.340}$$

where

$$d_1 = \frac{\log\left(\frac{y(t)}{K}\right) + \frac{1}{2}\Phi(t, T)}{\sqrt{\Phi(t, T)}} \tag{16.341}$$

$$d_2 = d_1 - \sqrt{\Phi(t, T)} \tag{16.342}$$

and

$$\Phi(t, T) = \int_t^T \sigma_y(s)^2 ds. \tag{16.343}$$

Hence a strip of swaptions will allow the commodity forward volatility, $\Sigma_C(t, T)$, to be determined. If the commodity swaption is of the averaging type then the above formula will need to be modified accordingly.

**Spreads and Crack Spreads**    Spreads are very important in the commodities market, both in the manner in which contracts are priced and behave and in the interest in derivatives that are based on spreads. There are numerous places where it may be appropriate to model commodity curves as a spread over another commodity curve, rather than as an outright asset.

One example of this can be found in the US gas market where a large number of gas forward curves are quoted based on different locations for delivery from the gas pipeline network. The prices are driven by a number of factors including the cost of transportation from one location to another; however, the curves are closely related to each other. Hence it may be more appropriate to model these curves as spreads over a base curve.

Crack spreads are the spreads between crude oil and refined oil products that are produced from it through the *cracking process*. Key refined oil products derived through cracking include gasoline (petroleum), kerosine (jet fuel/paraffin), diesel, heating oil, naphtha and liquid petroleum gas (LPG/propane/butane). The crack spread ratio X:Y:Z is defined as the quantity of the base X, crude oil, that is exchanged for two derived products X and Y such that X = Y + Z (CME Group, 2013). The spread ratio can be used by refiners to hedge the differential between their input costs and the price obtained by selling refined product. The two main types of (diversified) crack spreads are 3:2:1 and 5:3:2. A typical refinery will produce twice as much petroleum as distillate fuel oil, which contains diesel and kerosene. Hence the 3:2:1 ratio is the most common benchmark.

Crack spread options are options on the spread between crude oil and a derived product. Exchange-traded crack spread options exercise into two futures positions on the underlying spread, one long and one short.

From an XVA perspective with risk-neutral calibration crack spreads are an important consideration when calculating XVA on crude oil and refined products. For example if a netting set contains a long position in a refined product and a short position on crude oil then the exposure is a synthetic crack spread option. Ideally, therefore, the underlying XVA model and calibration should reflect the prices of crack spread options in the market. This does add considerable complexity and so any decision will ultimately rest on the relative importance of any exposures.

### 16.7.3 Electricity and Spark Spreads

Power models were introduced in the context of historical calibration in section 16.2.1 with the Geman and Roncoroni (2006) model. The major issue for risk-neutral modelling of power, noted earlier, is the lack of storability in most markets. For securities the standard condition

$$F(t, T) = S(t)e^{\int_t^T r(s)ds} \tag{16.344}$$

holds between spot and forward. This condition relies upon the assumption that securities can be stored at zero cost (Aïd et al., 2009). For storable commodities this can be extended through the introduction of storage costs through the *convenience yield*. Unfortunately this condition does not hold for electricity markets as electricity cannot in general be stored, although hydro-electric storage facilities do exist in some markets. In principle this means that the spot-forward relationship does not hold directly.

The second issue to be considered in electricity modelling is *spark spreads*, that is the spread between electricity prices and commodities that provide fuel for power stations. So if gas is used as a fuel then the spark spread is defined by

$$S_S(t) = S_e(t) - q_g S_g(t), \tag{16.345}$$

where $S_e$ is the electricity price, $S_g$ is the gas price and $q_g$ is the gas *heat rate*. While electricity cannot be stored, the fuels that provide the energy for power stations can and this leads to a relationship between the forward curve of electricity and those of the underlying fuels (Aïd et al., 2009). If we assume that only one fuel, $f$, can be used for power stations and that there is a single efficiency rate for conversion of fuel to electricity then the following relationship should hold,

$$F_e(t, T) = q_f F_f(t, T), \tag{16.346}$$

where $q_f$ is the heat rate for fuel $f$. This relationship will only hold in a situation with no generation capacity constraints. In practice there are multiple fuels available and multiple power plants with different efficiencies. There are also physical constraints on the heat rate from the maximum theoretical efficiency of the power plant so that there is a maximum possible heat rate. Options are also traded on the spark spread and these are known as *spark spread options* or *heat rate options*.

These issues combined to create a difficult modelling environment for power in a risk-neutral context. Ideally any model should:

- Match the electricity forward curve observed in the market
- Reproduce the demand spikes that are observed periodically
- Match the prices of power options
- Reproduce behaviour consistent with spark spreads
- Match the prices of heat rate options
- Allow negative prices (where supply exceeds demand which can occur for short periods).

From the perspective of XVA this is a considerable challenge and one that needs careful consideration. The modeller needs to decide if any electricity model should match all of these points or whether some aspects can be ignored. Any decision will be governed by materiality and practical considerations.

One possible solution to this is provided by the structural risk-neutral model of Aïd et al. (2009). This approach models each of the underlying fuels, $S_i(t)$, and then ranks the fuels according to the cheapest for electricity generation purposes, that is

$$q_1 S_1(t) \leq \ldots \leq q_i S_i(t) \leq \ldots \leq q_n S_n(t).$$

The demand for electricity $D(t)$ is stochastic and then the spot price of electricity is the price of the last fuel used to meet demand. Spikes can be introduced when demand exceeds the supply from all available fuels.

An overview of the electricity market can be found in Deng and Oren (2006). Alternative models for electricity can be found in Deng, Johnson and Sogomonian (2001), Benth, Kholodnyi and Laurence (2013), Aïd (2015) and references therein.

## 16.8 CREDIT

Credit as discussed to date is already stochastic in the sense that for CVA, as discussed in Chapter 3, default is the first jump of a Poisson process with intensity $\lambda(t)$. In most of the text so far, aside from a brief discussion in Chapter 7, the hazard rate $\lambda(t)$ has been deterministic. Here, however, $\lambda$ becomes stochastic and default modelled as a doubly stochastic process.

### 16.8.1 A Simple Gaussian Model

In the spirit of reusing the generalised Hull-White model as much as possible, it is of course possible to use it again to model the stochastic intensity. The analogy with interest rates is very strong as the survival probability is similar to a zero-coupon bond,

$$P(\tau > t) = \mathbb{E}[\mathbb{1}_{\tau > t}] = \mathbb{E}[e^{-\int_0^t \lambda(s)ds}] = P_{cr}(0, t) \tag{16.347}$$

with the expected properties,

$$P_{cr}(t, t) = 1$$
$$\lim_{t \to \infty} P_{cr}(0, t) = 0.$$

Hence the intensity is given by

$$d\lambda(t) = (\theta_{cr}(t) - \alpha_{cr}\lambda_{cr}(t))dt + \sigma_{cr}(t)dW_{cr}^d(t). \tag{16.348}$$

As might be expected this gives an affine "bond-link" formula for the survival probability,

$$P_{cr}(t, T) = A_{cr}(t, T)e^{-\lambda(t)B_{cr}(t, T)}. \tag{16.349}$$

Hence the initial survival probability can be calibrated by setting

$$P_{cr}(0, T) = A_{cr}(0, T)e^{-\lambda(0)B_{cr}(0, T)}, \tag{16.350}$$

as with the interest rate case.

The survival probability can be obtained from the usual credit curve model where a deterministic hazard rate is assumed. In reality the calibration should be done using a model for the CDS that incorporates stochastic interest rates and hazard rates with the correlation between the two and using the deterministic survival probability will introduce some error. However, this will be small as Brigo and Mercurio point out (Brigo and Mercurio, 2006). The hazard rate can then be simulated alongside other assets in the portfolio, with the driving Brownian motion correlated with those driving other assets.

As noted earlier in the historical context, there are two key problems with such a model:

- The hazard rate is Gaussian and hence can go negative, implying negative instantaneous default probabilities.
- The volatility cannot match the high volatilities observed from both historical CDS spread volatilities or implied volatilities from CDS swaptions.

The lack of volatility such a model gives naturally is a significant problem and to get a high enough observed volatility is likely to also lead to an unacceptably large probability of negative hazard rates. No volatility calibration is provided here for this reason as there is little point in attempting to calibrate to CDS swaptions. The Gaussian model may still prove useful in a limited context. It does allow a correlation between the hazard rate and other assets and so could be used as the basis of a basic approach to wrong-way risk.

### 16.8.2   JCIR++

To deal with the problem of negative rates a model that does not allow a negative short rate can be used. The CIR model discussed in section 16.3.2 can be used as the square root process means that hazard rates would not go negative as long as the Feller condition, $2\theta_{cr} > \sigma_{cr}^2$, was satisfied, where the hazard rate follows a mean reverting square root process,

$$d\lambda(t) = (\theta_{cr} - \alpha_{cr} r(t))dt + \sigma_{cr}\sqrt{\lambda(t)}dW_{cr}^d(t). \tag{16.351}$$

Unfortunately the Feller condition restricts the volatility significantly and effectively prevents the model achieving the level of volatility needed. To obtain a higher volatility jumps must be added to the process.

Brigo and Pallavicini (2008) developed a model, *JCIR++*, with a correlated stochastic interest rate and stochastic hazard rate processes. The interest rate component of this model is a two-factor Gaussian interest rate model, *G2++*, which was discussed above in section 16.3.2. This model is a two-factor Gaussian model that is broadly similar to the two-factor Hull-White model. The credit component is a shifted CIR model with jumps:

$$\lambda(t) = y(t) + \psi(t; \beta) \tag{16.352}$$

$$dy(t) = \kappa(\mu - y(t))dt + v\sqrt{y(t)}dW_3^d + dJ(t, \xi_1, \xi_2),$$

where the jump component is the sum of jumps driven by a Poisson process with intensity $\xi_1$,

$$J(t, \xi_1, \xi_2) = \sum_{i=1}^{M(t,\xi_1)} X_i(\xi_2) \tag{16.353}$$

with individual jump sizes $X_i(\xi_2)$ independent of each other and drawn from the exponential distribution with mean $\xi_2$. The initial hazard rate curve is set through the shift $\psi(t; \beta)$. The jump process allows a higher volatility to be achieved while still satisfying $2\kappa\mu > v^2$, however this may still not be high enough to match observed spread volatilities.

**Calibration**   CDS calibration of the model can be performed by assuming zero correlation between interest rates and credit. This allows a closed form formula for the model to match the market (Brigo and Pallavicini, 2008; Brigo and Mercurio, 2006; Brigo and El-Bachir, 2010). Calibration of the credit process volatility is not straightforward. To date no closed form has been developed for the stochastic interest rate case, although for the credit only version of the model, *SSRJD*, Brigo and El-Bachir (2010) did produce an analytic formula for the CDS swaption. Calibration could of course proceed via a numerical procedure and Monte Carlo could be used for this purpose, although at considerable computational cost.

### 16.8.3 Other Credit Models, Wrong-way Risk Models and Credit Correlation

If the underlying interest rate model is a market model, then it makes sense to use a market model approach to stochastically model the credit risk. Credit risky market models have been developed by Lotz and Schlögl (2000), Schönbucher (2000), Brigo (2004) and Eberlein, Kluge and Schönbucher (2006). An alternative approach is the conditional survival model of Peng and Kou (2008), where the integrated intensities are allowed to have jumps. An alternative approach is provided by the Dirac process (Kenyon and Green, 2015a), which adds Dirac delta functions to the hazard rate leading to jumps in the integrated hazard rate. This allows a much higher volatility to be obtained for the hazard rate.

Stochastic hazard rate dynamics can be used as part of a right-way/wrong-way risk model in the context of XVA. More detail on such models can be found in Chapter 7.

XVA on credit correlation products is a particularly difficult problem to solve. If the correlation product can be treated separately then the best approach to estimating the CVA on such correlation products is to use existing modelling techniques for correlation products and avoid simulating multiple hazard rates. The CVA on CDOs, for example, can be shown to be equivalent to CDO-squared products and Elouerkhaoui (2011) and Crépey and Rahal (2013) provide descriptions of appropriate modelling techniques.

If multiple hazard rates must be simulated together, say for a portfolio of CDS trades, then hazard rate models of the types described in this section combined with correlation of the driving Brownian motions will only give a weak dependence between spreads. If purely idiosyncratic jumps are included in the process as in JCIR++ this will weaken the impact of the diffusive correlation. To obtain a stronger dependence then a systemic jump must be included. The Dirac process could also potentially be used in the same way as a systemic jump.

## CHAPTER 17

# Monte Carlo Implementation

*Chance doesn't mean meaningless randomness, but historical contingency. This happens rather than that, and that's the way that novelty, new things, come about.*
—Rev Dr John Polkinghorne KBE FRS
*Theoretical Physicist and Theologian (1930–)*

## 17.1 INTRODUCTION

Most XVA calculation engines are based on Monte Carlo methods and this chapter explores a number of technical issues related to implementation of a large scale Monte Carlo simulation. Core implementation issues are discussed here while Chapter 18 examines variance reduction techniques that can be applied to XVA.

Monte Carlo methods are extensively used in many different fields and hence the literature on the subject is vast. For a general theoretical introduction to the Monte Carlo method see Fishman (1996). Monte Carlo is, of course, widely used to implement models across finance and Glasserman's *Monte Carlo Methods in Financial Engineering* (Glasserman, 2004) provides a comprehensive guide to the subject.

## 17.2 ERRORS IN MONTE CARLO

Monte Carlo like all numerical techniques is subject to errors. There are broadly two types of error in a Monte Carlo simulation, *discretisation errors* and *random errors*. To see where these errors occur it is useful to return to the XVA integral representation.

Monte Carlo simulation as applied to XVA is a numerical integration technique designed to estimate the integral formulae presented for the XVA terms as shown in Chapters 3, 9 and 13. These expressions typically involve two integration steps, the calculation of the expected positive and expected negative exposure profiles and then integration of the final formula over the time partition. So, for example, the classical unilateral CVA formula,

$$\text{CVA} = -(1 - R_C) \int_t^T \lambda_C(s) e^{-\int_t^s \lambda_C(u)du} \mathbb{E}\left[ e^{-\int_t^s r(u)du} (V(s))^+ \right] ds, \qquad (17.1)$$

is partitioned,

$$\text{CVA} \approx -(1 - R_C) \sum_{i=0}^{N} P(t_i < \tau < t_{i+1}) \mathbb{E}\left[e^{-\int_0^{t_{i+1}} r(u)du}(V(t_{i+1}))^+\right], \qquad (17.2)$$

where the time partition is chosen such that $0 = t_0 < \ldots < t_i < \ldots < t_N = T$, and $T$ is the maturity date of the portfolio. This partitioning is performed under the assumption that the probability of default and market state variable are independent of each other. As noted earlier, if this is not the case then the integral cannot be solved by partitioning in this way and a Monte Carlo with stochastic credit will be used. The expected positive exposure will itself be solved by integration, that is

$$\mathbb{E}\left[e^{-\int_0^{t_{i+1}} r(u)du}(V(t_{i+1}))^+\right] = \int e^{-\int_0^{t_{i+1}} r(u)du} \max(V(t_{i+1}, Z), 0)\phi(Z)dZ, \qquad (17.3)$$

where the $Z$ is a vector of market state variables, and $\phi(Z)$ is its probability density. It is this inner integral that is normally solved by Monte Carlo in XVA calculations.

The discretisation errors come from two sources, the time-partitioning if the credit-market independence assumption is maintained and the Monte Carlo discretisation. It is important to note that these two schedules, that used to generate the Monte Carlo paths and that used to partition the XVA time integral, can be different. It may be necessary, for example, for some Monte Carlo models to use very short time steps to gain accuracy of path generation, while the exposure partition points remain more widely spaced.

The random error component comes from the Monte Carlo simulation itself and so is present whenever an expectation is taken.

### 17.2.1 Discretisation Errors

The first type of discretisation error comes from the Monte Carlo simulation and relates to the manner in which the state variables are evolved through each time step. Given a stochastic differential equation,

$$dS(t) = \mu(S, t)dt + \sigma(S, t)dW(t), \qquad (17.4)$$

then the SDE will either have an exact solution or the SDE will have to be integrated numerically using a discretisation scheme. Geometric Brownian motion is an example of a stochastic process with an exact solution,

$$dS(t) = \mu S(t)dt + \sigma S(t)dW(t) \qquad (17.5)$$

$$S(t) = S(0) \exp\left[\left(\mu - \frac{1}{2}\sigma^2\right)t + \sigma \int_0^t dW(s)\right]. \qquad (17.6)$$

This exact solution can be used in the Monte Carlo simulation as

$$\int_0^t dW(s) \sim N(\sqrt{t}, 0), \qquad (17.7)$$

and hence the simulation uses the form

$$S(t) = S(0) \exp \left[ \left( \mu - \frac{1}{2}\sigma^2 \right) t + \sigma \sqrt{t} Z_i \right] \tag{17.8}$$

$$Z_i \sim N(0, 1), \tag{17.9}$$

and the $Z_i$ are a sequence of random numbers. An exact solution means that there is no discretisation error for taking large time steps.

If no exact solution exists then the only possible solution is to discretise the SDE. The simplest approach is the *Euler* scheme which is given by

$$S(t_i) = S(t_{i-1}) + \mu(S(t_{i-1}), t_{i-1})\Delta t + \sigma(S(t_{i-1}), t_{i-1})\sqrt{\Delta t} Z_{ji}, \tag{17.10}$$

where the drift and diffusion coefficient are evaluated at the previous time step and $\Delta t = (t_i - t_{i-1})$. The $Z_{ij}$ are the sequence of normal random samples for the $i$th time step and $j$th Monte Carlo path. If an SDE discretisation is used then in general small time steps are required to control errors in the Monte Carlo path building process. There are in fact many possible approaches to building discrete Monte Carlo paths. One alternative is the higher order *Milstein* scheme,

$$S(t_i) = S(t_{i-1}) + \mu(S(t_{i-1}), t_{i-1})\Delta t + \sigma(S(t_{i-1}), t_{i-1})\sqrt{\Delta t} Z_{ji} \tag{17.11}$$

$$+ \frac{1}{2}\mu(S(t_{i-1}), t_{i-1})\frac{\partial \mu}{\partial S}\bigg|_{S(t_{i-1}), t_{i-1}} \Delta t(Z_{ij}^2 - 1). \tag{17.12}$$

The Milstein scheme takes the derivative of the drift term into consideration and so partially factors in the impact on the change of $S$ over a time step.

There are in fact many possible alternative schemes available and this coupled with the control of discretisation errors is a large topic in itself. Glasserman (2004) provides a review of the topic, while a comprehensive treatments can be found in Kloeden and Platen (1992) and Platen and Bruti-Liberati (2010). However, it should be clear that there is a distinct advantage for XVA Monte Carlo simulation from models that admit analytic solutions to the SDE as this can lead to a considerably faster simulation than those that require discrete approximation schemes. In general the generation of Monte Carlo paths should not be the largest contributor to the overall computational time of the XVA model.

The accuracy of the numerical integration scheme used on the discrete approximation to the XVA integrals, such as the unilateral integral in equation (17.1), is governed by two things, the choice of *numeric integration scheme* and the choice of *time partition*.

**Choice of Numeric Integration**   The scheme shown in equation (17.2) is the simplest possible scheme and effectively replaces the expected exposure with a piecewise constant function with the value of the exposure at the end of each section of the time partition. Other numeric integration schemes are possible and the next step up is the use of the trapezium rule. Setting

$$\text{EPE}(t_i) = \mathbb{E}\left[ e^{-\int_0^{t_i} r(u)du}(V(t_i))^+ \right] \tag{17.13}$$

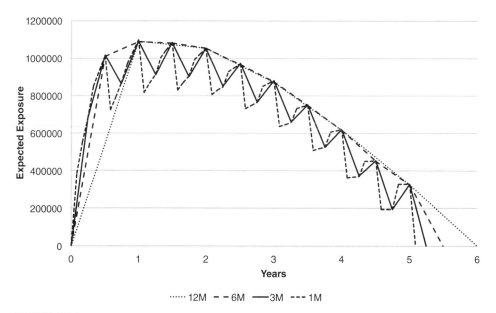

**FIGURE 17.1** The expected positive exposure profile for an interest rate swap with a semi-annual fixed leg and a quarterly floating leg. The expected positive exposure was calculated using four different Monte Carlo time step frequencies of 12, 6, 3 and 1 month. Only the quarterly and monthly simulation schedules resolve the features of the swap exposure profile.

gives the trapezium rule scheme,

$$\text{CVA} \approx -(1 - R_C) \sum_{i=0}^{N} P(t_i < \tau < t_{i+1}) \frac{1}{2} (EPE(t_i) + EPE(t_{i+1})). \tag{17.14}$$

Clearly highly order numerical schemes such as Simpson's rule are also possible.

**Choice of Time Partition** The accuracy of the integration also depends on the choice of time partition upon which the discrete approximation to the EPE or ENE is defined. Expected exposures are typically not smooth for a portfolio of trades. Trade events such as cash flows, option exercises and trade maturity lead to jumps in the exposure profile. Differing coupon frequencies between fixed and floating legs on an interest rate swap lead to a characteristic saw-tooth pattern in the exposure profile. These features are illustrated in Figure 17.1.

We can define two types of date that enter the time partition, ones that are based on *tenor points* and ones that are based on *fixed dates*.

**Tenor point** Tenor point-based time partitions use dates that are generated using today's date as the start and then offsetting from today by a fixed tenor set such as

$$1D, 1W, 2W, 1M, 2M, 3M, 6M, 9M, 1Y, 2Y, 3Y, 4Y, 5Y, 7Y, 10Y, 15Y, 20Y, 30Y, \dots$$

where the date is rolled to a suitable business day using a date rolling convention. The advantage of such a scheme is that it provides the expected exposure on dates that are easy to visualise and at points which correspond to the maturity dates of likely market risk hedging instruments, although not CDS as the maturity convention places the end points of these on a fixed date on the 20th on the IMM months.[1] Tenor-based partitions are also often found in the context of PFE calculations. The major disadvantage of a purely tenor-based partition is its impact on the carry behaviour of XVA. Given that the true exposure can change significantly on cash flow dates, carry will flow into the book in jumps. This is a particular problem for portfolios with instruments with regular tenor-based cash flows. Typically all of these will "roll" through the tenor-based schedule points on the same date leading to a jump in XVA on this date. This can make it difficult to explain the XVA P&L.

**Fixed dates**    A fixed date schedule allows the time partition to accurately capture changes in the exposure profile on event dates, so for example the partition might include a cash flow date and the day after the cash flow to capture the change in exposure on this date. The advantage of this comes through the carry calculation as carry behaviour will now be smooth day-on-day. However, the exposure profile is no longer readily visualised on tenor dates or points that are relevant for either market risk or credit risk hedging.

**Mixed partition**    The final option is to combine both tenor-based and fixed dates in one time partition as this gives the benefits of both approaches. However, there are still some disadvantages in the behaviour of the Brownian motion generated by this technique. The random number sequence used will still change when the number of times in the partition changes such and with a mixed partition this will occur whenever a tenor point and a fixed date coincide.

The impact of partition choice on carry behaviour is discussed in more detail in Chapter 21, while path construction is discussed in section 17.5 below.

### 17.2.2  Random Errors

Equation (17.3) is to be solved by Monte Carlo simulation. If we consider a general multi-dimensional integral of the form

$$I = \int_{\Omega} f(x)dx, \tag{17.15}$$

which is an integral over $\Omega \in \mathbb{R}^M$, then assume with loss of generality that the volume of $\Omega$ is 1,[2]

$$V = \int_{\Omega} dx = 1. \tag{17.16}$$

---

[1] See Chapter 4.

[2] This is easy to achieve in practice if the random samples are drawn from the uniform distribution on the interval $(0,1)$ and hence the random vectors $x_i$ are points with the unit hypercube.

The Monte Carlo method selects a series of $N$ random vectors $x_i$ that are points within $\Omega$ and then approximates the integral by

$$I \approx \bar{I}_N = \frac{1}{N} \sum_{i=1}^{N} f(x_i). \tag{17.17}$$

The *strong law of large numbers* (see for example Glasserman, 2004) ensures that

$$\lim_{N \to \infty} \bar{I}_N \to I, \tag{17.18}$$

with probability 1.

To estimate the error from a finite sample of size $N$ we need the variance of the estimator $\bar{I}_N$,

$$Var(\bar{I}_N) = Var\left(\frac{1}{N} \sum_{i=1}^{N} f(x_i)\right) \tag{17.19}$$

$$= \frac{1}{N^2} \sum_{i=1}^{N} Var(f(x_i))$$

$$= \frac{1}{N} Var(f(x)).$$

$Var(f(X))$ is unknown but it can be approximated by the sample variance, which is an unbiased estimator,

$$s_N^2 = \frac{1}{N-1} \sum_{i=1}^{N} (f(x_i) - \bar{I}_N)^2. \tag{17.20}$$

Hence the random error in the Monte Carlo simulation is given by the *standard error*,

$$\epsilon_N = \frac{s_N}{\sqrt{N}}. \tag{17.21}$$

This is a well-known derivation and it shows two key features of the Monte Carlo method:

- Monte Carlo random errors scale independently of the dimension of the vector's $x$.
- The Monte Carlo random errors only fall as the square root of the number of samples so that to reduce the error by a factor of 2 requires 4 times as many samples.

To see how an expected exposure calculation converges, consider an example where the expected positive exposure is calculated for a single ten-year interest rate swap with zero value at trade inception, where the expected exposure is calculated five years into the future.

There are only two ways to reduce the random error in a Monte Carlo simulation. The obvious choice is to use more sample paths but this is computationally expensive because of the square root scaling behaviour, as illustrated in Figure 17.2. Hence two further options are

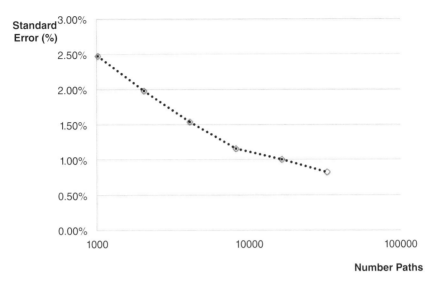

**FIGURE 17.2** Convergence of a CVA calculation using pseudo-random numbers from the Mersenne Twister. The test case was a GBP 10-year interest rate swap at par.

available, the use of *quasi-random sequences*, as described in section 17.3.2, and the use of *variance reduction techniques* as described in Chapter 18. However, the benefit gained from these techniques depends on the details of the simulation model in question.

## 17.3  RANDOM NUMBERS

### 17.3.1  Pseudo-random Number Generators

All Monte Carlo simulations require "random" numbers to generate the state of the Brownian motions that drive the dynamics of each asset. A genuine random sequence of numbers can only be generated from a natural physical process that is random, such as the arrival times of radioactive decay or white noise. In fact Monte Carlo methods themselves pre-date the large scale use of computers. Scientists would draw number balls from an urn roll dice to generate random integers (Knuth, 1997).

The statistical sampling technique that would later be called Monte Carlo was first used by Enrico Fermi when studying neutron diffusion problems in Rome as early as 1934 (Anderson, 1986). Stanislaw Ulam came up with the same idea when working at Los Alamos on nuclear weapons research in 1946 and described the approach to John Von Neumann who then set about trying to use computers to perform the calculations (Eckhardt, 1987). The *Monte Carlo method* was first published in 1949 by Metropolis and Ulam (1949) and it is Nicholas Metropolis who named the method "Monte Carlo" after an uncle of Stanislaw Ulam who borrowed money from relatives to gamble at the casinos in the city (Metropolis, 1987).

Generating true random numbers on a computer could be done by using special purpose hardware. The Feranti Mark I computer built in 1951 has a special instruction to generate 20 random bits using a resistance noise generator (Knuth, 1997). Yet such approaches were limited and algorithmic approaches to generating random numbers rapidly became more popular. Algorithmic methods though generate *pseudo-random* numbers rather than truly random numbers. These are sequences of numbers that give the appearance of being random but are not, and are in fact periodic but with very long periods. One early algorithm of this type suggested by John Von Neumann was called the *middle-square* method, where a number with the required number of digits is squared and the middle digits of this squared number form the next random number in the sequence (Knuth, 1997).

**Generators and Good Generators**    Clearly it is not sufficient to have sequences that simply *look* random, a pseudo-random sequence must be defined mathematically. To this a generator must be defined and then the question about what makes a good generator can be properly posed. L'Ecuyer (1994) defines a generator as:

**Definition 17.1.** *A generator is defined as a structure $G = (S, s_0, T, U, G)$, where S is a finite set of states containing an initial state or* seed $s_0 \in S$, $T : S \rightarrow S$ *is the* transition function, $U$ *is a finite set of* output *symbols and* $G : S \rightarrow U$ *is the* output function. *The generator operates:*

- *Start with the seed value $s_0$ and generate $u_0 = G(s_0)$.*
- *For $i = 1, 2, \ldots$, let $s_i = T(s_{i-1})$ and $u_i = G(s_i)$.*
- *The sequence $u_i$ is the output from the generator.*

*A pseudo-rdandom generator will produce a sequence $u_i$ that is indistinguishable from a set of i.i.d. uniformly distributed random variables. The output could be integers or numbers on the interval (0, 1).*

The problem is then how to identify a good generator? As L'Ecuyer points out (L'Ecuyer, 1994) we could use statistical tests to determine if the sequence is sufficiently random, however ultimately this will not work as we know the sequence is *not* random and hence it is always possible to find a statistical test that will fail if sufficient samples are drawn from the sequence. One possible criterion, derived from cryptographic applications, is the idea of *PT-perfect* generators. Such a generator would have the property that no polynomial-time[3] algorithm will be able to predict the next element in the sequence, $u_{i+1}$, given the previous set of outputs $u_0, \ldots, u_i$ with a probability larger than $1/|U| + \epsilon_k$ or larger than doing so randomly. The problem is that no generators have been found that satisfy the PT-perfect criterion. Hence the only realistic alternative is to define a set of desirable properties that a generator should satisfy and then use theoretical properties to identify suitable candidate generators before testing those using statistical tests (L'Ecuyer, 1994).[4]

**Practical Pseudo-random Number Generators**    L'Ecuyer (1994), Glasserman (2004) and many others have articulated the desirable properties of random number generators:

- *Period length* – All random number generators produce deterministic sequences of numbers that by their very nature must repeat at some point. Pseudo-random number generators

---

[3] A polynomial-time algorithm is one for which the run time has an upper bound that is a polynomial function of the number of inputs $n$, that is $T(n) \leq O(n^k)$ for finite $k$.

[4] Of course such an approach only tests the properties of the random number generator in the abstract, that is the properties of the random sequence prior to input into the simulation. This does not mean that tests of the final output, here the XVA metrics, can be eliminated if the input generator satisfies the desired properties. Testing of the behaviour of the output is also required.

should have long period lengths as then more random numbers can be drawn from the sequence before its non-random nature is revealed.

▪ *Repeatability* – The random number generator must be repeatable, that is, given the same initialisation the same sequence should be produced. This may sound completely counterintuitive as *surely the whole point of a random sequence is that it is random!* In fact no, for most applications and certainly for XVA we do not actually want a random sequence. A repeatable sequence allows the same calculation to be reliably be re-run. Accurate sensitivity calculations, the subject of Chapter 21, require repeatable sequences. Repeatable sequences allow conditions for stable models and hence better risk management and pricing of XVA. It is still, however, important to be able to change the sequence of random numbers that is used and to allow the random component of the error in any Monte Carlo simulation to be measured.[5]

▪ *Computational performance* – The generator algorithm should be fast enough so that random number generation itself is not a significant contributor to the overall run-time of the simulation. The other elements of an XVA Monte Carlo simulation, particularly trade valuation, can be unavoidably computationally intensive so it is important not add computational cost unnecessarily.

▪ *Portability* – The algorithm must be portable and produce the same sequence of random numbers on different computers.[6]

▪ *Ease of implementation* – The random number generator should be straightforward to implement.

▪ *Fast skipping* – Ideally the random number generator should have a *fast skip* algorithm that allows the state of the generator to be advanced through $n$ steps quickly without actually generating all the intermediate random numbers. This is a very useful property and is one way a *parallel* random number generator can be implemented.

▪ *Distribution* – The generator should provide a good approximation to the uniform distribution and vectors of random numbers from the generator should be equidistributed in the unit hypercube with the same dimension. Good distributional properties are important for high dimensional scenarios such as those found in XVA calculations.

Testing of the random number generator using statistical tests is very important. There are several suits of such tests and those discussed by Knuth (1997) are amongst the best known as are the *Diehard* tests proposed by Marsaglia (1995). In general, however, any recommended random number generators will have satisfied these tests and others prior to publication and all readers are strongly recommended to choose a generator from the existing literature.

**A Simple Example: The Linear Congruential Generator**   Consider the *linear congruential generator* with recurrence relation given by

$$x_{i+1} = (ax_i + c) \mod m \tag{17.22}$$
$$u_{i+1} = x_{i+1}/m.$$

---

[5]I have sometimes heard calls for a sequence to be seeded with the current time so that the sequence is always random. This is almost always inappropriate.

[6]Note that even portable random number generators can give different results once the random integer has been converted to floating point.

**TABLE 17.1** An example sequence from the Park-Millar linear congruential generator.

| $x_i$ | $u_i$ |
| --- | --- |
| 1014231875 | 0.472288521 |
| 1617416886 | 0.75316843 |
| 1077599276 | 0.501796266 |
| 1481436581 | 0.689847666 |
| 579213549 | 0.269717327 |

If the parameters are chosen as follows:

$$m = 2^{31} - 1 = 2147483647$$
$$a = 16807$$
$$c = 0$$

then the Park-Millar (Park and Millar, 1988) random number generator is obtained. To see how it works set the *seed* value $x_0 = 84262864$ and iterate through some steps in the sequence as illustrated in Table 17.1.

The Park-Millar random number generator was very popular in the late 1980s and early 1990s, although as Glasserman (2004) points out, even at the time better generators were available. The Park-Millar algorithm has the advantage that it is a very simple algorithm and is fast but its sequence length is small. It has now been superseded by vastly superior generators but it remains a useful tool for illustration purposes.

**The Mersenne Twister** The most popular psuedo-random number generator used in quantitative finance today is almost certainly the *Mersenne Twister* developed by Matsumoto and Nishimura (1998). This generator has an enormous sequence length at $2^{19937} - 1$ and equidistribution properties in 623 dimensions. The Mersenne Twister is also fast because of its implementation in terms of bitwise operators such as shifts, XOR and AND. The benefits come at the cost of the generator having a much larger state that more primitive generators. The Mersenne Twister has been implemented in many programming languages including C/C++, Java and CUDA and is also available in some third-party software libraries. A faster implementation of the Mersenne Twister using the SIMD instruction set has been developed (Saito and Matsumoto, 2006). When initially developed, there was no way to fast skip the state of the Mersenne Twister forward; however, this has subsequently been developed (Haramoto et al., 2008a; Haramoto et al., 2008b).

**Parallel Random Number Generation** Monte Carlo models are inherently highly parallel operations as each Monte Carlo is independent of all other Monte Carlo paths. Technically this is not always the case as some variance reduction techniques induce dependence between paths and the Longstaff-Schwartz technique requires a full set of Monte Carlo paths to be available for the regression phase. Nevertheless the path generation and path-wise calculation phase of the Monte Carlo can always be run in parallel. Chapter 20 discusses strategies for implementing the XVA calculation of which parallelisation is a critical part. To run the Monte Carlo simulation in parallel requires a mechanism that ensures each part of the simulation that is distributed has access to an independent set of random numbers.

To achieve Monte Carlo parallelism there are several different possible approaches:

- Run the random number generator and generate all the random numbers in a single process, then distribute them to each parallel calculation block. The path generation and subsequent path-wise operations will then run in parallel.
- Initialise the generator for the first parallel segment and then use fast skip to set the state of the generator at the start of every other parallel segment. The random numbers are then generated in parallel. Note, if fast skip is not available on the random number generator then running through the whole block of random numbers to get to the start of the required block for each parallel segment may still be viable computationally. In general the generation of random samples from the uniform distribution from a pseudo-random number generator is very fast when compared to other operations in the Monte Carlo such as generating normally distributed samples from uniform ones, path construction and trade valuation. Hence it is possible that iterating through a large block of random numbers may still not present a high computational overheads. Nevertheless, it should be avoided if possible.
- Use a pseudo-random number generator where the state has been captured at regular intervals. This allows the generator to mimic a true parallel random number generator by using separate blocks of the sequence in different parallel blocks of the Monte Carlo simulation. Typically the number of available seed values is heavily restricted as the state will only be captured for a small set of initialisations of the generator (or maybe just one).
- Use an inherently parallel pseudo-random number generator which is initialised with both a *seed value* and an *index*. Each indexed generator produces a completely separate sequence. Parallel random number generators tend to have weaker properties than non-parallel ones.

Note that a common approach to "parallel" random number generation is to simply use different seeds for each parallel stream from the same random number generator. This just uses different parts of the same random number sequence for the parallel segments. However, there is no guarantee that the sub-sequences generated in this way do not overlap and hence this approach should not be used.

A number of inherently parallel pseudo-random number generators have been developed. Notable examples include the SPRNG library developed by Mascagni and Srinivasan (2006), the streaming version of the *combined multiple-recursive generator* by L'Ecuyer et al. (2002) and a parallel version of the Mersenne Twister (Matsumoto and Nishimura, 2000). However, in general the use of a standard generator with fast skip is preferred because of the better distributional properties. With the advances in GPU technology and application to Monte Carlo there has been increasing interest in the production of pseudo-random number generators for use on GPU cards. For example, the CUDA environment includes an implementation of the Mersenne Twister (NVIDIA, 2014). Further discussion of parallel pseudo-random for GPUs can be found in L'Ecuyer, Oreshkin and Simard (2014) and Bradley et al. (2011).

### 17.3.2  Quasi-random Number Generators

**Low-discrepancy Point Sets**   Quasi-random sequences which are perhaps better described as *low discrepancy sequences* are special sets of points that have the property of low discrepancy. *Discrepancy* is a measure of the deviation from uniformity and hence low-discrepancy sequences have the property of low deviation from uniformity while not suffering from the dimensionality problems associated with integration grids. Discrepancy can be defined as (Glasserman, 2004):

**Definition 17.2.**  *If $A$ is a collection of Lebesque measurable subsets of $[0, 1)^d$, the discrepancy of a set of points $\{x_1, \dots, x_n\}$ with respect to $A$ is given by*

$$D(x_1, \dots, x_n; A) = \sup_{A \in \mathcal{A}} \left| \frac{N(x_i \in A)}{n} - vol(A) \right|, \qquad (17.23)$$

*where $N(x_i \in A)$ is the number of points $x_i$ contained within A and vol(A) is the volume of A.*

*The ordinary discrepancy is given by taking $A$ to be the collection of all rectangles in $[0, 1)^d$ of the form*

$$\prod_{j=1}^{d} [u_j, v_j), \quad 0 \le u_j < v_j \le 1. \qquad (17.24)$$

*The star discrepancy $D^*$ is given by restricting $A$ to rectangles of the form*

$$\prod_{j=1}^{d} [0, u_j). \qquad (17.25)$$

Low discrepancy sequences then are points sets that have low values for these discrepancy measures.

Unlike pseudo-random numbers, quasi-random numbers are not designed to resemble actual random sequences. Quasi-random sequences have a *space filling* property in which successive points in the sequence slowly fill in the space to give something like an irregular integration grid and this is illustrated in Figure 17.3. To some degree quasi-random points can be thought of as a hybrid between a lattice and random numbers.

It is well known that in low dimension grid-based integration techniques such as quadrature or PDE solvers perform much better than Monte Carlo methods. However, unlike such grid-based techniques, Monte Carlo is independent of the problem dimension and so for higher dimensional problems, Monte Carlo performs much better than any other technique. Quasi-random sequences can be thought of as a halfway proposition with some of the properties of both approaches.

A key difference between pseudo-random and quasi-random numbers is the dimensional dependence of quasi-random sequences (Glasserman, 2004). Originally it was thought that quasi-random sequences only gave a benefit over pseudo-random sequences for low dimensions, 40 or less according to some reports or maybe as low as 10 according to others (Glasserman, 2004). Nevertheless, authors have reported that in financial applications quasi-random

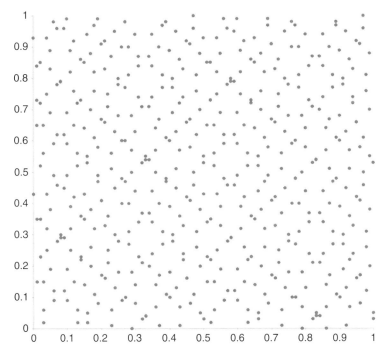

**FIGURE 17.3** Two dimension projection of points from the Sobol sequence.

numbers continue to outperform Monte Carlo even in high dimension (see for example Paskov and Traub, 1995).

There are many different types of low discrepancy sequence with perhaps the best-known examples being Sobol (1967) and Faure (1982). Both these approaches derive from the earlier work of der Corput (1935). An alternative is provided by *Lattice Rules* which are in effect derived from the full sequence of a small pseudo-random generator and a comprehensive guide can be found in Sloan and Joe (1994).

The most widely used type of sequence in quantitative finance is the Sobol sequence. The generation of the Sobol sequence is described in a number of textbooks and articles such as those by Bratley and Fox (1988), Glasserman (2004), Joe and Kuo (2008b) and Press *et al.* (2007). The original approach of Sobol was improved through the use of Gray codes by Antonov and Saleev (1979). The best currently available *direction numbers* used by the algorithm to generate the point set have been published by Joe and Kuo (2008a). A two-dimensional projection of the Sobol sequence is shown in Figure 17.3 alongside a pseudo-random sequence in Figure 17.4.

In summary, to generate the sequence a series of direction numbers, $v_{k,j}$, are generated and then used to construct the points in the Sobol sequence. The points $x_{i,j}$, that is the $i$th component of the $j$th point, in the sequence are generated by XORing (bitwise exclusive OR operation) together all the direction numbers $k$ for which the corresponding bit in the binary representation of $i$ is 1. This can be written

$$x_{i,j} = i_1 v_{1,j} \oplus i_2 v_{2,j} \oplus \dots, \tag{17.26}$$

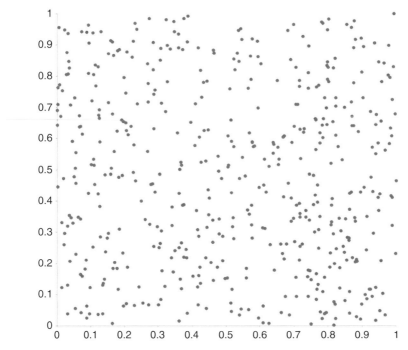

**FIGURE 17.4**   Two dimension projection of pseudo-random numbers.

where $\oplus$ represents the XOR operation and $i = (i_1 i_2 \ldots)$ in binary. The direction numbers are derived from the relationship,

$$v_{k,j} = \frac{m_{j,k}}{2^k} \tag{17.27}$$

$$m_{j,k} = 2a_{i,j}m_{k-1,j} \oplus 2^2 a_{2,j}m_{k-2,j} \oplus \ldots \tag{17.28}$$
$$\oplus 2^{s_j-1}a_{s_j-1,j}m_{k-s_j+1,j} \oplus 2^{s_j}m_{k-s_j,j} \oplus m_{k-s_j,j}.$$

The recurrence relation for the integers $m_{k,j}$ is initialised with a set of values
$m_{1,j}, m_{2,j}, \ldots$ that must be odd and less than $2^k$. The coefficients are derived from primitive polynomials which take the form

$$x^{s_j} + a_{1,j}x^{s_j-1} + a_{2,j}x^{s_j-2} + \ldots + a_{s_j-1,j}x + 1 \tag{17.29}$$

and the coefficients $a_{k,j}$ are either zero or one.

**Randomisation and Parallelism**   The Sobol sequence and indeed all low-discrepancy point sets have fixed positions in the unit hypercube once the main parameters such as direction numbers have been chosen. This means that given a selected sequence length only one set of points can ever be used. This is a potential problem in two areas; the estimation of errors and the division of the simulation into parts that can be parallelised.

The standard error defined in equation (17.21) cannot be applied to a low-discrepancy sequence as the points are not random nor designed to appear random. The derivation of the standard error assumes that the estimates of the function $f(x)$ are independent of each other so this formula cannot be applied in this case.

The second issue is the use of parallel processing, as a low discrepancy sequence is not guaranteed to have a *fast skip* method that would allow the sequence to be broken into segments. In fact the Sobol sequence does have this property (Bradley et al., 2011) and hence the sequence can be divided for parallel processing.

Randomised quasi-Monte Carlo can also actually improve the performance of a quasi-random sequence. Owen (1997b) shows that for the case of randomised nets used to integrate smooth functions, the rms error is lower for the randomised nets than for the un-randomised nets. However, it is not clear just how widely this reduction in error occurs and whether it applies to all types of randomisation. Randomisation processes do change the discrepancy of the point set, although these approaches do not destroy their low discrepancy properties.

**Cranley-Patterson rotation** Cranley and Patterson (1976) proposed a simple rotation of the point set using a random M-dimensional vector drawn from the uniform distribution, $u$, modulo 1,

$$y = x + u \bmod 1. \tag{17.30}$$

A series of random vectors, $u$, can be used to generate a series of point sets $y$ that are independent of each other but retain the structure of the quasi-random point set. An example is shown in Figure 17.6 alongside the original Sobol points $i$ Figure 17.5. Each random shifted point set is then independent and can be used to estimate the error in the result formed by combining all randomly shifted point sets.

**Random permutation of digits** Consider expressing the coordinates of each quasi-random vector, $x_k$, in base $b$,

$$x_k = 0.a_1(k)a_2(k)\dots. \tag{17.31}$$

The random permutation operates by taking random permutations of this representation of the point in base $b$, that is drawing random permutations of $0, 1, \dots, b\text{-}1$ from the $b!$ possible such permutations and using the resultant permutation to map $x_k$ to the new point,

$$y_k = 0.\pi_1(a_1(k))\pi_2(a_2(k))\dots. \tag{17.32}$$

Each point is randomised using the same permutation and different dimensions of the quasi-random vector use independent permutations. The randomised points remain in $[0, 1)^d$ and the random vectors $y$ are uniformly distributed over $[0, 1)^d$ and hence can be applied in the same way as the base point set. For more details the reader is referred to Glasserman (2004), Matoušek (1998) and L'Ecuyer and Lemieux (2002).

**Scrambling** Art Owen proposed the *scrambling* approach to randomisation of quasi-random sequences in a series of papers (Owen, 1995; Owen, 1997b; Owen, 1997a; Owen, 1998). The procedure performs a hierarchical permutation process on each dimension of a quasi-random

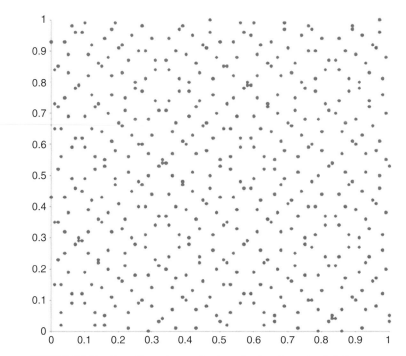

**FIGURE 17.5**   Two dimension projection of points from the Sobol sequence.

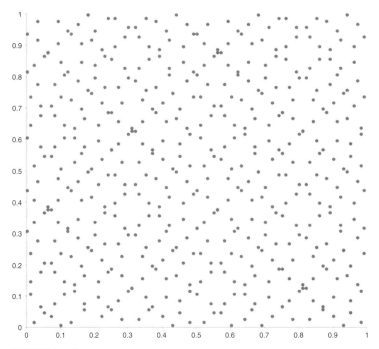

**FIGURE 17.6**   Sobol points with Cranley-Patterson rotation.

point set. For each dimension the unit interval is divided into $b$ parts and then each part is randomly permuted. With each of these $b$ parts, the interval is further subdivided into $b$ parts and again each one is randomly permuted. This process continues for $j$ steps. The process is relatively time consuming because of the number of permutations.

**Linear scrambling**  Linear scrambling is a simplified version of the full scrambling algorithm, described by Matoušek (1998). Here a base $b$ expansion of the point set as described by equation (17.31) is mapped to another point $y_k = 0.\bar{a}_1.\bar{a}_2. \ldots$ using the transformation,

$$\bar{a}_j = \sum_{i=1}^{j} h_{ij} a_i + g_j \mod b. \tag{17.33}$$

The lower triangle elements of matrix $h_{ij}$ and the elements of the vector $g_i$ are chosen randomly and independently from $0, 1, \ldots, b-1$. The diagonal elements of the matrix, $h_{ii}$, must be positive to ensure that the matrix is non-singular so these are drawn from $1, 2, \ldots, b$ -1.

**Padding with pseudo-random points**  Because of limitations in quasi-random point sets in high dimensions, prior to the development of randomisation, some authors (Ötken, 1996; Spanier, 1995) suggested *padding* a quasi-random sequence with pseudo-random numbers. The suggestion was to make use of the high quality first few dimensions of the quasi-random sequence but then revert to pseudo-random numbers for the lower dimensions. For financial applications of Monte Carlo simulations this would have inevitably meant using the *Brownian Bridge* construction of the Brownian motion, as described in section 17.5 below. In practice this is no longer needed as good high-dimensional randomised quasi-random sequences are now readily available in numerical libraries.

## 17.3.3  Generating Normal Samples

Once a pseudo-random or quasi-random point set has been obtained the next step is to convert these from a set of points that are uniformly distributed on the interval $[0, 1)$ to points that are distributed normally $N(0, 1)$. There are a number of methods to do this, but it is important to note that for quasi-random sequences a one-to-one mapping must be maintained between the input uniform random number and the output normal sample as if this is not the case, the low discrepancy properties of the quasi-random sequence will be destroyed, potentially leading to biased results. This effectively means that only an approximation of the inverse cumulative normal can be used with quasi-random points.

**Box-Muller and Modified Box-Muller**  The simplest approach to the generation of normally distributed random samples is the Box-Muller technique. However, this does not preserve a one-to-one mapping with the underlying random sequence and so should not be used for quasi-random sequences.

To generate samples from the standard normal distribution,

$$\phi(x) = \frac{1}{\sqrt{2\pi}} e^{-x^2/2}, \tag{17.34}$$

the original *Box-Muller* method (Box and Muller, 1958) relied upon the Jacobian transformation,

$$p(x_1, x_2, \ldots)dx_1 dx_2 \ldots = p(y_1, y_2, \ldots) \left| \frac{\partial(y_1, y_2, \ldots)}{\partial(x_1, x_2, \ldots)} \right| dy_1 dy_2 \ldots, \tag{17.35}$$

where $\partial(y_1, y_2, \ldots)/\partial(x_1, x_2, \ldots)$ is the Jacobian. Writing two transformation equations,

$$x_1 = \sqrt{-2 \log y_1} \cos 2\pi y_2 \tag{17.36}$$
$$x_2 = \sqrt{-2 \log y_1} \sin 2\pi y_2, \tag{17.37}$$

inverting these equations gives

$$y_1 = e^{-\frac{1}{2}\left(x_1^2 + x_2^2\right)} \tag{17.38}$$
$$y_2 = \frac{1}{2\pi} tan^{-1}\left(\frac{x_2}{x_1}\right),$$

and it is easy to show that the Jacobian matrix is given by

$$\begin{pmatrix} \dfrac{\partial y_1}{\partial x_1} & \dfrac{\partial y_1}{\partial x_2} \\ \dfrac{\partial y_2}{\partial x_1} & \dfrac{\partial y_2}{\partial x_2} \end{pmatrix} = \begin{pmatrix} -x_1 y_1 & -x_2 y_1 \\ -\dfrac{1}{2\pi}\dfrac{x_2}{x_1^2 + x_2^2} & \dfrac{1}{2\pi}\dfrac{x_1}{x_1^2 + x_2^2} \end{pmatrix} \tag{17.39}$$

Hence the determinant of the Jacobian is

$$\begin{vmatrix} \dfrac{\partial y_1}{\partial x_1} & \dfrac{\partial y_1}{\partial x_2} \\ \dfrac{\partial y_2}{\partial x_1} & \dfrac{\partial y_2}{\partial x_2} \end{vmatrix} = -\left[ \frac{1}{\sqrt{2\pi}} e^{-\frac{1}{2}\left(x_1^2\right)} \right] \left[ \frac{1}{\sqrt{2\pi}} e^{-\frac{1}{2}\left(x_2^2\right)} \right] \tag{17.40}$$

Hence it is clear that by using two input uniformly distributed random numbers the output of the transformation will be two independently normally distributed numbers. The problem with this algorithm is that the sine and cosine functions are computationally expensive operations. A modification was therefore proposed by Marsaglia and Bray (1964) which eliminated the use of the sine and cosine functions but introduced *rejection*.

The *Modified Box-Muller* method chooses pairs of uniform samples $(y_1, y_2)$ in the square defined by the range $(-1, 1), (-1, 1)$ until a pair is found with

$$s = y_1^2 + y_2^2 < 1, \tag{17.41}$$

and when this condition is satisfied then

$$x_1 = y_1 \sqrt{\frac{-2 \log s}{s}} \tag{17.42}$$
$$x_2 = y_2 \sqrt{\frac{-2 \log s}{s}},$$

are normally distributed. In general random number generation is much faster that sine and cosine computationally and so the method is more computationally efficient.

**Inverse Cumulative Normal**   The *cumulative normal distribution function* is given by

$$\Phi(x) = \frac{1}{\sqrt{2\pi}} \int_{-\infty}^{x} e^{-\frac{1}{2}(t^2)} dt, \tag{17.43}$$

and takes values on the interval $[0, 1)$. The *inverse cumulative normal* is the inverse of this function,

$$\Phi^{-1}(u) = z \quad \text{where} \quad z \sim N(0, 1). \tag{17.44}$$

Unfortunately there is no analytic expression for the inverse CDF of the normal distribution and so a numerical approximation is required. A number of such algorithms exist in various library implementations and perhaps the best known is that developed by Beasley and Springer (1977).

The algorithm of Beasley and Springer (1977), later modified by Moro (1995), provides the following approximation for the normal distribution (Glasserman, 2004):

$$\Phi^{-1}(u) \approx \frac{\sum_{n=0}^{3} a_n (u - \frac{1}{2})^{2n+1}}{1 + \sum_{n=0}^{3} b_n (u - \frac{1}{2})^{2n}} \quad \text{for} \quad 0.5 \leq u \leq 0.92 \tag{17.45}$$

$$\approx \sum_{n=0}^{8} c_n \left[ \log(-\log(1-u)) \right]^n \quad \text{for} \quad 0.92 < u < 1 \tag{17.46}$$

$$= \Phi^{-1}(1-u) \quad \text{for} \quad 0 < u < 0.5, \tag{17.47}$$

where

$$
\begin{aligned}
a_0 &= 2.50662823884 & c_0 &= 0.3374754822726147 \\
a_1 &= -18.61500062529 & c_1 &= 0.9761690190917186 \\
a_2 &= 41.39119773534 & c_2 &= 0.1607979714918209 \\
a_3 &= -25.44106049637 & c_3 &= 0.0276438810333863 \\
b_0 &= -8.47351093090 & c_4 &= 0.0038405729373609 \\
b_1 &= 23.08336743743 & c_5 &= 0.0003951896511919 \\
b_2 &= -21.06224101826 & c_6 &= 0.0000321767881768 \\
b_3 &= 3.13082909833 & c_7 &= 0.0000002888167364 \\
& & c_8 &= 0.0000003960315187
\end{aligned}
$$

The analysis by Moro shows that the algorithm is accurate to an absolute value of $3 \times 10^{-9}$ out to seven standard deviations from the mean.

A number of other approximation schemes are available including those by Wichura (1988) and Aklam (2003).

## 17.4  CORRELATION

XVA calculations are frequently multi-asset and hence require multi-dimensional random number sequences that have been correlated. Hence there are two key elements required for XVA implementation, *correlation matrix regularisation* and *correlation induction*.

### 17.4.1  Correlation Matrix Regularisation

For a correlation matrix to be valid it must be square, real, positive semi-definite and Hermitian, that is it must satisfy

$$\sum_{i=1}^{N}\sum_{j=1}^{N} a^i a^j C_{ij} \geq 0 \quad \text{for all} \quad a^i, a^j \in \mathbb{R}, \tag{17.48}$$

and

$$C = C^T. \tag{17.49}$$

If a correlation matrix is estimated from historical time series then in theory it is guaranteed to satisfy the above conditions as long as all elements are estimated from time series defined on exactly the same tenor points. However, in practice this is frequently not the case. For some correlations used in XVA, implied correlations may be used, or time series data may not be available for some elements of the matrix. Even with a correlation matrix fully estimated from time series data, the matrix may fail the above conditions due to purely numerical effects. This is exacerbated by the high dimensionality of XVA calculations. If correlation matrices are formed for individual counterparties, large interbank positions could easily see dimensionality of 30 or higher, while if a matrix is estimated for a full XVA portfolio the number of factors could rise to be 300 or more. It is relatively common, therefore, to have invalid correlation matrices as an input to an XVA Monte Carlo simulation.

It is also essential to have a valid correlation matrix for Monte Carlo simulation as both the common methods of inducing correlation, *Cholesky* and *eigenvalue decomposition*, rely on the input being positive semi-definite. The Cholesky approach will simply fail if this is the case while the eigenvalue decomposition will have negative eigenvalues. Hence some way must be found of *regularizing* correlation matrices, that is turning an invalid correlation matrix into a valid one.

The problem can be defined as follows. Given an input matrix with elements $C_{ij}$ the regularisation process aims to find a matrix $\bar{C}_{ij}$ that is positive semi-definite and Hermitian and that minimises the sum,

$$r = \sum_{i=1}^{N}\sum_{j>1}^{N}(C_{ij} - w_{ij}\bar{C}_{ij})^2, \tag{17.50}$$

where $w_{ij}$ is a matrix of weights. The weights allow certain elements within the matrix to be favoured over others. The problem can be solved directly using constrained optimisation or with a special purpose algorithm (Borsdorf and Higham, 2010; Jiang et al., 2012; Qi and Sun, 2006).

## 17.4.2  Inducing Correlation

If $x$ is a random vector drawn from the multivariate normal distribution,

$$x \sim N(\mu, C),$$  (17.51)

then

$$Ax \sim N(A\mu, ACA^T).$$  (17.52)

Hence if

$$z \sim N(0, 1)$$  (17.53)

then

$$x = Az$$  (17.54)
$$x \sim N(0, AA^T).$$

Hence if the correlation matrix can be factorised,

$$C = AA^T,$$  (17.55)

then the matrix $A$ can be used to induce correlation on uncorrelated normally distributed samples.

There are two possible factorisations, *Cholesky* and *eigenvalue*.

**Cholesky**  The Cholesky factorization seeks to find the lower triangle matrix $L$ such that

$$C = LL^T.$$  (17.56)

Cholesky is the favoured factorisation for correlation induction because it produces a lower triangle matrix. This means that when correlation is induced via the matrix multiplication with the uncorrelated random vector $z$ there will be around half the multiplication operations that would be required were the factorisation matrix to have all non-zero elements.

The Cholesky factorisation (see Press et al., 2007) follows by using the two equations

$$L_{ii} = \sqrt{\left( C_{ii} - \sum_{k=1}^{i-1} L_{ik}^2 \right)}$$  (17.57)

$$L_{ji} = \frac{1}{L_{ii}} \left( C_{ij} - \sum_{k=1}^{i-1} L_{ik} L_{jk} \right) \qquad j = i+1, i+2, \ldots, N,$$  (17.58)

successively for $i = 1, \ldots, N$. These fill in the elements of the lower triangle matrix as index $i$ is stepped over.

**Eigenvalue**    The alternative factorisation is provided by the eigenvalue approach (see Glasserman, 2004). The matrix $C$ must have $N$ real non-negative eigenvalues, $\lambda_1, \ldots, \lambda_N$ and a set of $N$ orthogonal eigenvectors, $v_1, \ldots, v_N$ such that

$$v_i^T v_i = 1 \tag{17.59}$$

$$v_i^T v_j = 0 \quad j \neq i \tag{17.60}$$

$$C v_i = \lambda_i v_i. \tag{17.61}$$

Hence it is possible to write

$$C = V \Lambda V^T, \tag{17.62}$$

where $V$ is the matrix whose columns are the eigenvectors of $C$,

$$V = \begin{pmatrix} v_{11} & \cdots & v_{N1} \\ \vdots & \ddots & \vdots \\ v_{1N} & \cdots & v_{NN} \end{pmatrix} \tag{17.63}$$

and $\Lambda$ is a diagonal matrix of the eigenvalues,

$$\Lambda = \begin{pmatrix} \lambda_1 & & 0 \\ & \ddots & \\ 0 & & \lambda_N \end{pmatrix} \tag{17.64}$$

Hence it is clear that the transformation matrix is given by

$$A = V \sqrt{\Lambda}. \tag{17.65}$$

For a real symmetric matrix the eigenvalues and eigenvectors can be found by transforming the correlation matrix to tridiagonal form using Householder reduction and then applying the *QR* algorithm (Press et al., 2007; Golub and Van Loan, 1996). An implementation of these numerical routines can be found in *LAPACK* (Anderson et al., 1999). The potential advantage this approach has over Cholesky is that the numerical routine itself is less likely to fail if the input matrix is not positive semi-definite, but negative eigenvalues will result. It is possible to correct this by replacing negative eigenvalues with small positive ones and rescaling the remainder. However, this will only work if the negative eigenvalues are small and is no substitute for regularisation.

## 17.5  PATH GENERATION

The final step in the implementation of the Monte Carlo simulation is to turn the correlated normal samples into increments of a Brownian motion, that is we set

$$W(t_i) - W(t_{i-1}) = \sqrt{(t_i - t_{i-1})}z_i. \qquad (17.66)$$

In fact there are two possible approaches to building the Brownian motion path, *forward induction* and *backward induction* or *Brownian Bridge*.

### 17.5.1  Forward Induction

Forward induction is the classical step-wise construction where the sequence of random numbers is used to generate steps in the Brownian motion incrementing forward in time so that

$$W(t_1) = W(t_0) + \sqrt{(t_1 - t_0)}z_1$$
$$W(t_2) = W(t_0) + \sqrt{(t_1 - t_0)}z_1 + \sqrt{(t_1 - t_0)}z_2$$
$$\vdots$$

### 17.5.2  Backward Induction

Backward induction orders the time steps hierarchically with the first step used to generate the last simulated point on the Brownian motion and then intermediate points generated using the conditional distribution or *Brownian Bridge*. The organisation of time steps is illustrated in Figure 17.7. The conditional distribution of a Brownian motion is normal. If the Brownian takes the value $W(t_1)$ at the start and $W(t_2)$ at the end then the distribution of the value at $t_s$,

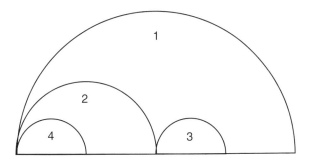

**FIGURE 17.7**  Generating paths of Brownian motion by backward induction. The order in which the steps are taken is labelled by the numbers in the figure. The pattern aligns the lowest dimensions in the sequence with the largest steps in the Brownian motion and hence this approach is frequently used with quasi-random sequences to maximise the benefit that can be gained from the better properties of the lower dimensions.

$W(t_s)$ has mean and variance given by

$$\mu = \frac{(t_2 - t_s)W(t_1) + (t_s - t_1)W(t_2)}{(t_2 - t_1)} \tag{17.67}$$

$$\sigma = \frac{(t_s - t_1)(t_2 - t_s)}{(t_2 - t_1)}. \tag{17.68}$$

These can readily be used with normal samples from $N(0, 1)$ to generate the intermediate points on the Brownian motion.

The advantage of the Brownian bridge construction is that it uses the lowest dimensions of the sequence to create the largest steps in the Brownian motion. This is useful when used in conduction with quasi-random sequences as the lowest dimensions generally have the best properties. This has been found to be effective in finance (Glasserman, 2004; Moskowitz and Caflisch, 1996).

## CHAPTER 18

# Monte Carlo Variance Reduction and Performance Enhancements

*Uhura: Entering planet's outer atmosphere, sir. Ship's outer skin is beginning to heat, Captain. Orbit plot shows we have about 8 minutes left.*
*Captain Kirk: Scotty!*
*Scotty: I canna change the laws of physics! I've got to have 30 minutes!*

—John D.F. Black, Gene Roddenberry
*The Naked Time, Star Trek (1966)*

## 18.1  INTRODUCTION

Monte Carlo methods are fundamentally slow to converge, cursed by the fact that the error scales as the square root of the number of paths. In this chapter I review variance reduction techniques and other performance enhancements designed to allow faster convergence. One technique, quasi-random numbers, is sometimes classed as variance reduction but this is discussed in Chapter 17. Variance reduction of some sort is essential to XVA Monte Carlo as it allows the overall number of paths to be reduced while still obtaining good convergence.

## 18.2  CLASSIC METHODS

There are a number of basic methods of variance reduction that are common to the literature of Monte Carlo and I review these here for completeness. In practice, however, the classic methods of variance reduction are not that useful in the context of XVA.

### 18.2.1  Antithetics

The classical approach of antithetics is given a vector of random normally distributed variates $z_i$ to be used in the simulation, to also use the vector $-z_i$. It is clear that by doing this the first moment of the distribution is matched as

$$\mathbb{E}\left[\frac{z_i - z_i}{2}\right] = 0, \tag{18.1}$$

by construction.

Suppose we have two variates $z_1$ and $z_2$ and that we seek to find an unbiased estimator of $V = \mathbb{E}[f(z)]$. An unbiased estimator is given by

$$\hat{V} = \mathbb{E}\left[\frac{f(z_1) + f(z_2)}{2}\right], \tag{18.2}$$

with variance

$$Var(\hat{V}) = \frac{Var(f(z_1)) + Var(f(z_2)) + 2Cov(f(z_1), f(z_2))}{4}. \tag{18.3}$$

If $z_1 = -z_2$ then $Var(f(z_1)) = Var(f(z_2))$ hence it is clear that variance reduction will be achieved if

$$Cov(f(z_1), f(-z_1)) < 0. \tag{18.4}$$

If the function $f(z)$ is monotonic then it can be shown that the covariance is indeed always negative. Even if the function is not always monotonic then some variance reduction may still be achieved.

In practice antithetic variates do not offer any real advantage over methods which match the first two moments such as *orthogonalisation* described below. Hence in general there is limited use for antithetics in XVA simulation.

### 18.2.2 Control Variates

Suppose we have a derivative whose value can only be estimated by Monte Carlo simulation so that the value estimator is

$$V = \mathbb{E}[V(\omega, T)] = \frac{1}{n}\sum_{i=1}^{n} V_i(T). \tag{18.5}$$

Now suppose we have a second derivative, $V^C$, whose value is known analytically. This derivative can also be valued inside the simulation $V_i^C$. A second unbiased estimator of the value of the original derivative is given by

$$\mu = V_i + c(V_i^C - V^C), \tag{18.6}$$

as the last term has expectation equal to zero, $\mathbb{E}[c(V_i^C - V^C)] = 0$. The variance of $\mu$ is given by

$$Var(\mu) = Var(V_i) + c^2 Var(V_i^C) + 2cCov(V_i, V_i^C). \tag{18.7}$$

To minimise the variance of $\mu$ the coefficient $c$ should be chosen,

$$c = -\frac{Cov(V_i, V_i^C)}{Var(V_i^C)} \tag{18.8}$$

and then

$$Var(\mu) = Var(V_i) - \frac{Cov(V_i, V_i^C)^2}{Var(V_i^C)}. \tag{18.9}$$

Equation (18.9) shows that variance reduction is obtained if the values of the derivative $V_i$ and the *control variate* $V_i^C$ are positively correlated. The classic example of this and described in all basic literature on Monte Carlo methods in finance is that of the geometric average rate option as a control variate to the arithmetic average rate option. For trade valuation good control variates can sometimes be found. For XVA this is in general not the case unless the portfolio is particularly simple. Complex portfolios with many diverse derivative products will not lend themselves to the use of control variates. Hence, in general control variates are used infrequently in the context of XVA Monte Carlo simulations.

## 18.3 ORTHOGONALISATION

In the limit of an infinite number of random variates input into the Monte Carlo simulation, all will be independent and identically distributed normal samples with mean zero and a variance-covariance matrix equal to the identity matrix. In practice, however, because of the finite number of samples this will not be true. The orthogonalisation technique (Curran, 1999) can be thought of as either a moment matching scheme where the first two moments are matched in the multi-dimensional case or as a method where the samples are cleaned up to match their theoretical properties in the limit of an infinite number of paths for a finite sample.

Consider a sample set with $n$ sample paths and $m$ stochastic factors and $z_{ij}$ is the sample for the $i$th sample path and $j$th stochastic factor. The method only works if the samples have mean zero so the first step is to subtract the mean of each sample across all paths,

$$\bar{z}_{ij} = z_{ij} - \frac{1}{n} \sum_{i=1}^{n} z_{ij}. \tag{18.10}$$

The next step is to measure the variance-covariance matrix of the sample vectors $\bar{z}_i = (z_{i1}, \ldots, z_{im})$ which gives a $m \times m$ matrix $\bar{\Sigma}$. The linearity property of multivariate normal distributions means that given a vector

$$\bar{z} \sim N(0, \bar{\Sigma}), \tag{18.11}$$

then it is possible to find a transformation matrix $A$ such that

$$A\bar{z} \sim N(0, A\bar{\Sigma}A^T) = N(0, I), \tag{18.12}$$

that is the matrix $A$ serves to remove any correlation from the sample vectors. Hence we must have the relation

$$A\bar{\Sigma}A^T = I, \tag{18.13}$$

and so

$$\bar{\Sigma} = A^{-1}(A^{-1})^T. \tag{18.14}$$

The transformation matrix is formed by the inverse of the decomposition of the sample covariance matrix. As might be expected this is very similar to the approach to inducing correlation described in section 17.4.2. A Cholesky decomposition of the sample covariance matrix will generate the inverse of the desired matrix.

The Cholesky decomposition is potentially an expensive process computationally as it scales like $O(m^3/3)$. For large dimension simulations the cost of the Cholesky will outweigh the benefit of using fewer paths. It is important to note that here $m$ is the full dimension of the Monte Carlo simulation, that is

$$m = \text{factors} \times \text{time steps}. \tag{18.15}$$

This means that the method serves to remove all correlation from the samples, including serial correlation between time steps. Unfortunately, in the context of XVA it is very easy

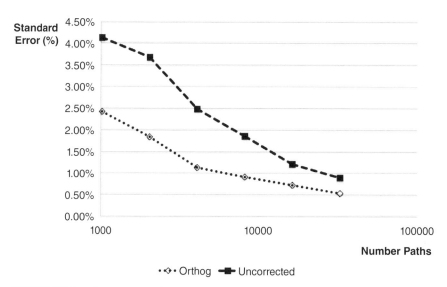

**FIGURE 18.1**   Convergence of the orthogonalisation scheme compared to plain pseudo-random numbers. The test case was a swap portfolio consisting of three 10-year interest rate swaps in GBP, EUR and USD, with all swaps at par. Five stochastic factors were used in the simulation for three interest rate processes and two FX processes. The unilateral CVA was then calculated and the standard error computed from 16 independent batches that when combined gave the listed path count.

to have $m$ large enough for orthogonalisation to be prohibitively expensive computationally because of the Cholesky decomposition. The solution of this is to only orthogonalise across the sample vectors used for each time step rather than all the samples. This reduces the dimensionality significantly making orthogonalisation viable for XVA calculations. This is technically acceptable as the XVA Monte Carlo simulation is ultimately estimating a series of European options and hence the residual serial correlation down the paths that this approach implies is not important.

It is important to note that orthogonalisation removes the independence of the sample paths. This means that the usual approach to estimating the standard error does not work. Hence the situation is similar to that of quasi-random sequences. To introduce the required independence batches of samples must be orthogonalised separately and then the ensemble of batches used to estimate the standard error across the whole simulation. This can readily be achieved by dividing the unadjusted sample paths into groups.

The orthogonalisation in general gives good results in the multi-factor case. An example is given in figure 18.1 and shows that orthogalisation approximately halves the standard error compared to unadjusted pseudo-random numbers. Hence in this case orthogonalisation gives approximately the same benefit as using four times as many sample paths.

## 18.4 PORTFOLIO COMPRESSION

The final consideration on performance enhancement is whether the portfolio itself can be *compressed*, that is represented with a small number of representative trades or with a valuation approach that reduces the overall execution time of the valuation. This approach is acceptable when only the netted portfolio value is needed for XVA such as for CVA. However, some elements of the regulatory capital framework require trade valuations and so portfolio compression is not suitable for KVA.

In general it is possible to construct a representative portfolio of trades that is much simpler than the actual portfolio through manual analysis of the portfolio sensitivities and scenario behaviour. However, the Longstaff-Schwartz methodology again offers a simple way to do this and this has been applied already in the calculation of MVA in Chapter 10. Longstaff-Schwartz regression can be applied perfectly well at portfolio level just as at trade level. The regression approach will yield a function that can be used to value the portfolio inside the XVA simulation. This simple function will be very fast to evaluate and hence offers potentially a significant speed up.

Of course this method suffers from the limitations of the Longstaff-Schwartz approach. In addition the choice of regression function is made more difficult by the complexity of the portfolio. However, the choice of state variables that would be made if the regression were to be performed at trade level will of course inform the choice at portfolio level.

The final alternative is to use trade level regression but a common set of basis functions and state variables across all trades in the portfolio, as described in Kenyon and Green (2014a). If this approach is used, portfolio compression is simply a case of summing the regression coefficients generated by individual trades. Hence trade level regression allows portfolio compression where it can be used but retains trade level information when needed.

## 18.5  CONCLUSION: MAKING IT GO FASTER!

In reality there are limited means by which the complexity of XVA models can be made more performant by variance reduction or related techniques. Hence to obtain truly significant performance enhancements then there are four remaining possibilities:

- Parallelism and distributed computing
- Special purpose hardware
- Fast sensitivity calculations
- Trade level regression.

The first two of these are discussed in Chapter 20 while the last two points are explored in Chapter 21.

## CHAPTER 19

# Valuation Models for Use with Monte Carlo Exposure Engines

*Admiral Adama: Captain Adama and Colonel Tigh are working on the plan now
and I need some serious "out-of-the-box" thinking.
Starbuck: "Out-of-the-box" is where I live.*

—Ronald D. Moore
*Hand of God, Battlestar Galactica (2004)*

## 19.1 VALUATION MODELS

If the usual assumption of independence between credit/funding/cost of capital and market
state is made then all XVA metrics resolve to integrals of the form

$$\text{XVA}(t) = \int_t^T a(s)e^{-\int_t^s b(u)du} \mathbb{E}\left[(V(s) - X(s))^{\pm}\right]ds. \tag{19.1}$$

In discrete form this always results to a weighted sum of European options,

$$\text{XVA} \approx \sum_{i=1}^{N} w(t_i)\mathbb{E}\left[(V(s) - X(s))^{\pm}\right]. \tag{19.2}$$

The inner expectations are calculated using the Monte Carlo simulation described in Chapters
16 and 17. While this simulation is normally arranged as a full path-dependent simulation, in
reality expressions of the form found in equations (19.1) and (19.2) are *not path-dependent*,
save for any fixings and option exercise information. That is XVA is an integral over a strip of
path-dependent European-style options.

To evaluate the expected exposure at a given time index $t_i$ the Monte Carlo simulation is
evolved to the exposure date and then the portfolio value calculated on every path. To calculate
the value of the derivatives in the portfolio valuation models must be used and the choices
available for this are the subject of this chapter.

### 19.1.1 Consistent or Inconsistent Valuation?

The first question to be asked is whether or not the valuation model should be consistent with the choice of Monte Carlo dynamics. The models used to value the underlying products for the unadjusted books and records valuations are widely varied. Different asset classes use very different model approaches and within asset classes the model dynamics and implementation techniques vary from product to product. Even if a class of products share a set of model dynamics, individual trades can have independent calibrations. Bermudan swaptions, for example, are frequently calibrated to the underlying coterminal European swaptions which differ for each trade. It is highly unlikely, therefore, that a single set of model dynamics will be used across all derivative products traded by a bank.

The XVA Monte Carlo simulation imposes a set of dynamics on all assets within the portfolio and enforces a single calibration for each simulation. At a minimum all the products within a single netting set must use the same simulation model and calibration. It is still possible to use separate calibrations and calibration instruments for each netting set and this is entirely equivalent to the use of multiple models for different products in the unadjusted trade level valuations. Nevertheless, some institutions may prefer to use a single global calibration for all netting sets and counterparties.

Overall it is almost certain to be the case that the model dynamics used in the XVA model are inconsistent with some or all of the models used to provided unadjusted trade level valuations for accounting and risk management purposes. Valuation models must be used within the XVA simulation to obtain portfolio values in each Monte Carlo state. This forces a choice between three options on the model developer:

1. The XVA valuation models are consistent with the XVA Monte Carlo dynamics.
2. The XVA valuation models are the same as those used for product valuation, but potentially inconsistent with the XVA Monte Carlo dynamics.
3. The XVA valuation models are distinct from both XVA Monte Carlo dynamics and product valuation models.

It is important to note that only the first choice will lead to a self-consistent and arbitrage free model for XVA. While this may suggest that this is in fact the only correct approach, practical considerations must also be made and a fully consistent model may not be the optimal choice. Materiality should be the guide to determining how important different elements of the model are.

### 19.1.2 Performance Constraints

The critical constraint on the choice of XVA valuation models is performance. Some complex valuation models can take several minutes to provide a valuation for a product, perhaps because they themselves rely on Monte Carlo simulation with a complex choice of model. Monte Carlo within Monte Carlo is clearly something that should be avoided from a performance perspective. Furthermore one of the key drivers of valuation time is trade maturity with longer trades consuming more processing time and certainly with some models' processing time increasing as some power of the maturity. Longer trades will also require a longer XVA simulation to calculate the expected exposure and hence many more trade valuations, compounding the valuation time problem.

Consider an example with a trade valuation that runs for 5 minutes on a trade with maturity 30 years and assume for simplicity that the trade valuation time does not change with maturity.[1] Assume that the XVA simulation uses 5000 paths and has an exposure calculation time step every three months. The XVA calculations will take (ignore the simulation time itself):

$$5 \min \times 30 \times 4 \times 5000 = 50,000 \, \text{hours}.$$

Clearly vast computational resources would be required to complete such a calculation. The calculation could be parallelised down to path level readily but this would still leave 50 hours of compute on 5000 cores. Parallelising further down to individual valuations could reduce the execution time to 5 minutes but would require 600,000 cores.

In practice not all valuation models can be used directly with an XVA simulation model. The limitation on time is driven by the availability of computational resources and the size of the portfolio so it is very difficult to provide guidance on what is acceptable for trade level valuation models and what is not. The nature of the trade portfolio is also critical and in particular the number of exotic trades. Nevertheless the above example suggests that trade valuation should not be more that 100ms and substantially less for the bulk of the portfolio.

### 19.1.3 The Case for XVA Valuation Consistent with Trade Level Valuations

The key driver behind a desire for XVA valuation to be consistent with underlying valuations comes from the requirement to match the actual exposure to a counterparty today, which would inevitably be calculated using the sum of trade valuations. If there is a discrepancy between the model used for valuation and those for XVA, the exposure calculated in a given Monte Carlo state would be different from what would actually occur if that market state were to occur in practice. Hence the close-out value, funding and capital measures calculated from the exposures could be inaccurate. Furthermore, sales and trading staff in general prefer to see the same spot exposure coming out of the XVA model as seen in the underlying valuation as it provides a degree of reassurance on the accuracy of the XVA model and any differences between the two are a frequent source of questions.

The nature of XVA models is such that the major source of valuation differences will be for option rather than linear products, assuming that a risk-neutral calibration has been used or that a historical volatility calibration rather than a historical calibration is used (see Chapter 16). The linear products will be unaffected by the choice of dynamics for the Monte Carlo model and hence should have the same value as the linear pricing model used for the unadjusted valuation. Nevertheless, there are still likely to be small numerical differences.

Trade valuations dominate the overall XVA risk and so the use of a model consistent with the valuation model will lead to XVA market risk hedges that are more consistent with the market risk hedges used on the primary trading book. As an example consider a valuation model that is sensitive to volatility smiles and assume that the valuation model used in the XVA calculation for the same product always uses the at-the-money volatility and the XVA Monte Carlo model is itself calibrated to at-the-money volatility. In this case the XVA model

---

[1]In practice inside the XVA simulation the later expected exposure calculations will be on a shorter trade and so trade valuation should take less time on later time steps.

will never show any volatility smile sensitivity from either the Monte Carlo model or the trade valuation model, while the unadjusted trade valuation certainly will. If the valuation model at least were sensitive to the smile, the XVA calculation would acquire smile sensitivity and imply smile sensitivity in the same part of the volatility surface as the valuation model.

A further advantage of this approach is that the valuation models may also be available in a form that can be called from within the Monte Carlo engine. If the valuation library can be called directly this can prove to be a significant cost saving as valuation models would not need to be redeveloped inside the XVA Monte Carlo model. Nevertheless, there are technical challenges and it is important to ensure that the calling mechanism itself is performant as well as the underlying model. Many valuation models are written with the intention of being instantiated for the purpose of a single valuation, and while for a valuation system this may convenient for implementation purposes, in an XVA Monte Carlo engine the continual requirement to instantiate and destroy the trade representation may itself add significant computational costs. The use of external library calls for valuation purposes also requires more careful management as the valuation library and XVA library are often run separately within an organisation and have different development and release cycles.

However, as has already been noted, it is simply not always possible to use the same valuation model for XVA as is used for the underlying valuation on performance grounds. Hence in practice it is unlikely that all the main valuation models can be used for XVA and so differences are inevitable. Furthermore there are often areas of the XVA calculation which are highly uncertain. As was noted in Chapter 4, often the bulk of counterparties are illiquid and rely on a curve mapping process to identify the implied default probability function. Given that this is the case, it can be argued that a high degree of accuracy in the expected exposure calculation is unnecessary.

## 19.1.4   The Case for Consistent XVA Dynamics

From a modelling perspective the use of different dynamics for valuation models within the XVA Monte Carlo from those governing the Monte Carlo model itself is difficult to justify. Such a combination is effectively a hotchpotch mix of models and is clearly inconsistent. The behaviour of the combined XVA model is difficult to understand with P&L movements that are potentially hard to explain.

The use of a set of consistent dynamics for all valuations is desirable for hedging purposes and mathematically justifiable. Such a model is inherently simpler as everything is consistent. The model is more readily explainable as it is clear that all market risk sensitivity comes from a single model calibration.

The valuation models used inside the XVA Monte Carlo can still use a variety of approaches such as analytic formulae or PDE models, depending on the choice of dynamics. However, the most obvious choice here is to use the Longstaff-Schwartz approach (see section 19.3.2 and Cesari et al., 2009) at least for all products with optionality as this will always give a valuation that is consistent with the XVA Monte Carlo, assuming that the Longstaff-Schwartz regression phase uses the same XVA model and calibration. In general the Longstaff-Schwartz approach gives very fast valuations so there is little risk that such a model would prove too slow. It is possible to use the Longstaff-Schwartz approach for all products, perhaps combined with the use of a payout language so that in effect there is only a single valuation model in use throughout the XVA simulation.

One disadvantage of the use of a consistent set of dynamics is that in order to deal with the high dimensionality and complexity of a cross-asset model, the dynamics of XVA models are frequently simpler than those that would be used for the valuation of a single product with its own asset class (see Chapter 16). For example, the model used for valuing single currency complex callable interest rate structures could be a multi-factor LMM with stochastic volatility which would be tractable in the single currency context but intractable with multiple currencies and other assets. This simplicity means that some elements of market behaviour may not be captured by the combined XVA valuation framework.

The second disadvantage of the consistent dynamics approach is that the valuation implied by the XVA valuation model will differ, potentially significantly, from the valuation derived from the unadjusted valuation model. Linear products should, at least in theory, remain consistent but option products could have very different valuations. The degree of difference will depend on the choice of dynamics in the XVA model and in the underlying valuation model. More sophisticated XVA models with more calibration points are likely to show smaller differences to the underlying valuation models than simpler ones.

## 19.1.5 Simulated Market Data and Valuation Model Compatibility

When valuation models are called inside the XVA Monte Carlo the simulated path at the time step in question is treated as simulated market data. This data is packaged up in the manner in which the valuation model expects it and then the model is called to produce a valuation. This means that the input market data must be compatible with the modelling assumptions used by the valuation model. If the dynamics used by the Monte Carlo and valuation model are different then it is possible that the market data may take a state from which the valuation model simply cannot give a value. For example, if a Gaussian short rate model is used for the Monte Carlo interest rate dynamics then negative interest rates will occur in the simulation at some point. Were these rates to be used directly with the Black model valuing caps and floors inside the simulation, then the model would likely fail and throw an exception if the input forward rate is negative. Hence steps need to be taken to ensure that valuation failure does not occur in such circumstances, either by modifying the simulated market data or by adjusting the model so that a valuation can still be produced.

## 19.1.6 Valuation Differences as a KPI

One approach to tackling the issue of valuation differences between the XVA model and the unadjusted trade valuation model is to monitor it and use it as a *key performance indicator*. It is a metric that can be easily monitored on a daily basis and investigated if the difference as a whole becomes too large or if individual trade models show significant differences.

## 19.1.7 Scaling

The alternative approach to dealing with differences between XVA valuation and the unadjusted trade valuation models is to scale the valuation in the XVA model to match the trade valuation. This gives a relative shift to the trade valuation that would then be applied to all the trade valuation inside the XVA Monte Carlo model on every path and time step. This ensures that irrespective of the choice of model the XVA Monte Carlo will always give the same value as the trade valuation at $t = 0$.

The problem with this is that the relative shift implied by the spot difference in valuation is not guaranteed to apply in all Monte Carlo states nor at every time step. The actual difference between the underlying model and XVA valuation could be larger or smaller than that implied by the relative shift. A second issue is that it tends to hide the valuation differences unless the actual valuation difference remains monitored as a KPI. A large discrepancy between trade valuation and XVA model during pricing, indicating a problem with either model, could simply be missed. Scaling provides potential benefits but it should be carefully monitored.

## 19.2  IMPLIED VOLATILITY MODELLING

If the XVA valuation models are inconsistent with the XVA Monte Carlo dynamics then in most cases some modelling of the input implied volatility will be required. So for example, were the Black model (Black, 1976) to be used to value European swaptions within an XVA Monte Carlo where rates are driven by Hull-White dynamics the implied volatility input to the Black function must be specified at each simulation time step. At $t = 0$ the input should be that volatility that is used in the underlying trade valuation but at later time steps a number of choices present themselves.

### 19.2.1  Deterministic Models

To explore the choices of deterministic implied volatility modelling it is useful to choose an example. Consider the valuation of a European swaption using the Black model (Black, 1976) with an implied volatility surface, $\sigma_{imp}(T_o, T_s)$, with volatility specified by option maturity $T_o$ and swap maturity $T_s$ where $T_s > T_o$. For simplicity I ignore any strike dependence in the volatility. At $t = 0$ the Black function takes the initial implied volatility $\sigma_{imp}(T_o, T_s)$, interpolated from the volatility surface so that the variance is given by

$$\text{var}(0) = \int_{s=0}^{T_o} \sigma_{imp}(T_o, T_s)^2 sds = \sigma_{imp}(T_o, T_s)^2 T_o. \tag{19.3}$$

At time step $t = t_1$ two options are available. Firstly the option could be assumed to have a variance that is time scaled to reflect the fact that there is now less time to the maturity of the option so that

$$\text{var}(t_1) = \text{var}(0)\frac{(T_o - t_1)}{T_o} = \sigma_{imp}(T_o, T_s)^2 (T_o - t_1), \tag{19.4}$$

that is the implied volatility is assumed to be *constant*. The second option is to re-interpolate the volatility from the surface using the reduced option tenor, so that the variance is given by

$$\text{var}(t_1) = \int_{s=t_1}^{T_o} \sigma_{imp}((T_o - t_1), T_s)^2 sds = \sigma_{imp}((T_o - t_1), T_s)^2 (T_o - t_1). \tag{19.5}$$

In this case the implied volatility *rolls down* the implied volatility surface as it approaches expiry. In terms of volatility sensitivity the constant implied volatility approach will give sensitivity only to the volatility defined by the option expiry. This is consistent with the assumptions made by the underlying valuation model which uses a single implied volatility interpolated from the volatility surface to derive the rate variance between now and option expiry. The roll down approach will give a volatility sensitivity to a set of implied volatilities for constant swap maturity but varying option tenor out to the maturity of the option. This is inconsistent with the assumptions made by the valuation model but is consistent with the behaviour *implied* by the structure of the volatility surface itself. The degree of difference between the two approaches depends entirely on the degree of volatility heterogeneity in the volatility surface. For more complex volatility structures the above methods may need to be extended to include strike dependence, which itself may vary if the volatility surface is defined in terms of relative strikes.

### 19.2.2 Stochastic Models

In reality the implied volatility itself is stochastic and changes day-on-day due to moves in the option markets. This of course makes clear that *XVA is dependent on forward volatility* through the valuation of options. When the counterparty defaults the value of the close-out depends on the option valuation at the time of close-out and hence on the state of the implied volatility surface at that time.

Building models that are consistent with the behaviour of forward implied volatilities has proved very difficult. A small number of option products that have uncertain strikes such a *cliquets* found in the equity derivatives market have similar sensitivity to forward implied volatilities. Numerous models exist for the pricing of such products but there has been little work on the kind of general model that would be required for XVA. If the behaviour of the implied volatility was assumed to be independent of all other stochastic factors and indeed of the model dynamics then it may be possible to construct a model based on the *principal components analysis* of the historical behaviour of the volatility surface. However, whether such a model would present a viable basis for risk managing XVA is not clear.

## 19.3 STATE VARIABLE-BASED VALUATION TECHNIQUES

For more exotic derivatives state variable-based valuation techniques are likely to be the only viable option available for valuation inside an XVA Monte Carlo simulation. The approaches are based on the principle that at each Monte Carlo time step $t_i$ a function can be identified that provides the value of the derivative depending on the value of $N$ state variables, $S_j$, evaluated inside the Monte Carlo at that time step and path so the value of derivative $k$ is given by

$$V_k(t_i) = f(S_1, \ldots, S_N). \tag{19.6}$$

Of course if the trade is path-dependent then it is always possible that it will depend on earlier state, that is,

$$V_k(t_i) = f(S_{11}, \ldots, S_N 1, \ldots, S_{Ni}). \tag{19.7}$$

The key questions for state variable-based techniques are how to determine the function $f$ and how to choose the state variables. There are two techniques of this type available, *grid interpolation* and *Longstaff-Schwartz regression*.

### 19.3.1  Grid Interpolation

Many valuation models are implemented either using trees or as PDEs with a finite difference approximation. A PDE model will by virtue of its construction have a grid of values with one time axis and one or more "space" dimensions. The "space" dimensions will be indexed by some state variable $x$ with relevance to the model dynamics and the option payout being valued. The grid is commonly of fixed dimension, although sometimes with steps and other features to deal with discrete dividends or other features of the problem domain. The PDE must maintain a value for the derivative at each node in the tree in order to solve the PDE and calculate the value of the derivative at the current time and current market state. Tree models behave in a similar fashion, although they expand from a single node today to a large number of nodes at the maturity of the option.

These "grids" of option values can be used to provide valuation information at times between the valuation and maturity dates. Grid interpolation techniques rely on running a valuation model in parallel to the Monte Carlo model. On each Monte Carlo path a *linking state variable* is calculated at each time step and used to interpolate the grid at that time point to obtain a value for the derivative. Hence using this technique allows a single invocation of the pricing model to be used to estimate all the trade valuations used in the XVA Monte Carlo simulation, rather than running the tree or PDE model at every time step on every path, a considerable saving of computational cost. Note, however, that many PDE and tree models will not actually store the full grid or tree but only the grid points relevant to the current time step as this reduced storage requirements. For the grid interpolation valuation method the full grid or tree must be maintained during the life of the Monte Carlo simulation. This is illustrated in Figure 19.1.

The state variables used in the grid or tree will be optimised for the choice of model and payout. If the underlying stochastic dynamics of the valuation model differ from those used in the Monte Carlo simulation then these state variables may not be an optimal choice of linking variable. Hence the model should allow for the Monte Carlo state variables to be a function of the grid variables,

$$S = f(x) \qquad (19.8)$$

This immediately requires that the inverse function exists,

$$x = f^{-1}(S). \qquad (19.9)$$

If the underlying dynamics of the valuation model differ from the XVA Monte Carlo this relationship is not guaranteed to exist and care must be taken to ensure that any transformations of this type preserve the inverse relationship, at least numerically.

The obvious question with this type of approach is what happens if the Monte Carlo path lands out of bounds, that is outside the state space defined by the finite the tree or grid. In general tree and PDE models will use relatively wide grids and most of the Monte Carlo points will land within the grid; nevertheless it is inevitable that a small number will fall outside.

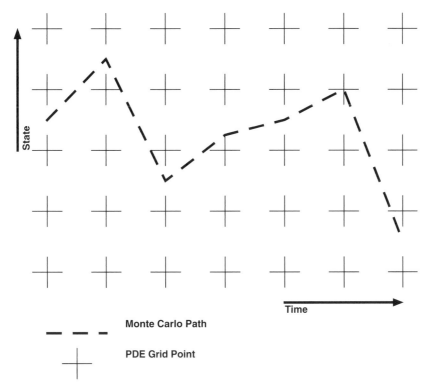

**FIGURE 19.1** The grid interpolation valuation technique; the PDE grid is interpolated at the time steps of the Monte Carlo.

For these points a suitable extrapolation technique must be used that respects the boundary conditions of the underlying derivative, that is the extrapolation must match the asymptotic behaviour of the derivative.

Trade events such as rate fixings, option exercises and barriers must be handled by the XVA Monte Carlo. So for example, if the PDE model is valuing an up-and-out barrier Option then should the Monte Carlo path imply that the asset value that triggers the barrier has indeed done so then the option will remain exercised at later states along the Monte Carlo path and grid interpolation will not be used to generate the product value at subsequent Monte Carlo time steps.

Ultimately the technique relies upon interpolation of the grid at least in the spatial direction. For the temporal direction there is no guarantee that the tree or grid with time steps chosen for best performance in trade valuation will include the observation dates of the XVA Monte Carlo simulation. While interpolation in the time direction is possible it is preferable to modify the tree or grid to place additional points on the observations date of the simulation. In this way an accurate valuation can be obtained on the dates of interest for the XVA calculation.

### 19.3.2 Longstaff-Schwartz

The Longstaff-Schwartz algorithm as applied to the valuation of derivatives inside an XVA Monte Carlo simulation has already been discussed in detail in Chapter 10 so there is no need to present it again here. Longstaff-Schwartz is widely used by practitioners as a valuation technique in XVA (Cesari et al., 2009). The Longstaff-Schwartz algorithm produces a function,

$$\bar{F}(\alpha_m, O_i(\omega, t_k), t_k) = \sum_{m=1}^{n^f} \alpha_m f_m(O_i(\omega, t_k)), \qquad (19.10)$$

that provides a valuation in terms of the basis functions $f_m(O_i(\omega, t_k))$. The state variables are carefully chosen to suit the derivative being valued so there are no variable transformation issues of the type noted in the context of grid interpolation techniques. It is, however, important to ensure that the regression approximation is available on the time steps of the XVA Monte Carlo. Should Longstaff-Schwartz be used to value a derivative the natural choice of time steps is likely to reflect the structure of the trade and any associated events. For XVA purposes, additional time steps will need to be added to ensure accuracy on the dates of importance for the XVA calculation.

The implications of using Longstaff-Schwartz to value trades inside an XVA simulation is that the valuation dynamics are inherently those of the XVA Monte Carlo. Typically XVA models use simpler models because of the hybrid nature of the calculation so the valuation could be quite different from that of the valuation model even if Longstaff-Schwartz is used for valuation but with a more sophisticated model (for example LMM with stochastic volatility).

One possible alternative strategy is to calibrate the regression function approximation using either a different calibration or different set of dynamics. In this way the price distribution implied by the regression function in the XVA simulation will more closely resemble that of the valuation model. However, the impact this would have on sensitivities is not clear. Furthermore if finite difference approximations were used for risk then the model is limited to holding the regression functions constant across a market data shift. More details on the calculation of XVA sensitivities can be found in Chapter 21.

# Building the Technological Infrastructure

*Any sufficiently advanced technology is indistinguishable from magic.*
> —Sir Arthur C. Clarke
> *Science Fiction Writer (1917-2008)*

## 20.1  INTRODUCTION

The XVA model must ultimately be implemented in an IT system. For institutions that do not manage XVA actively a finance system to calculate XVA for accounting purposes will be needed. Such a finance system will require a P&L explain capability. Where XVA is managed a similar P&L process to other trading desks will be needed. This means daily P&L alongside a range of sensitivities and scenarios to allow the XVA management function to understand and risk manage the position. XVA must also be priced correctly when new deals are priced for clients. This implies the need for an incremental pricing capability for new transactions, restructures and novations. This chapter describes how a system capable of batch processing for accounting and risk management and intraday trade pricing can be constructed.

## 20.2  SYSTEM COMPONENTS

An XVA system, like any trading system, has three basic operational stages,

1. Gather input data
2. Perform calculations
3. Report results

and the system components are designed around this basic workflow. A schematic of the workflow is given in Figure 20.1. Pricing follows the same workflow but typically involves a single counterparty rather than the whole portfolio.

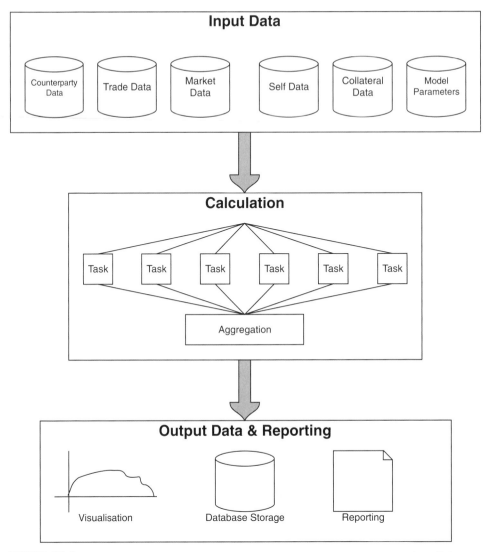

**FIGURE 20.1** XVA logical system workflow. The workflow for an XVA system can be split into three separate phases, input data preparation, calculation and reporting.

## 20.2.1 Input Data

XVA calculations are some of the most data intensive in financial markets. We can identify six different types of data required by every XVA calculation: counterparty data, self data, trade data, market data, collateral data and model parameters.

Any XVA calculation is only as good as the quality of the input data and as such it should be considered a *zero order risk*.[1] The correctness of input data should therefore be of primary

---

[1] The term zero order risk was coined by Simon O'Callaghan.

**TABLE 20.1**  Typical counterpart data requirements for XVA.

Full Legal Name
Name in Linked Systems
External Credit Ratings
Internal Credit Ratings
Geographical Location
Sector or Sectors
Netting Sets
Group-Subsidiary-Branch Hierarchy

importance to the development and operation of an XVA system. There is little use in building a sophisticated XVA platform only to run it using incorrect data.

**Counterparty Data**    Counterparty data is of course perhaps the most obvious data requirement for CVA calculations, although as is clear from the earlier discussion it is a key input for all XVA metrics. Typical counterpart data requirements are listed in Table 20.1. In many cases there will be a central counterparty database that holds this information, most likely associated with existing credit limit management systems. However, not all the required information may be co-located and if not a "join" across multiple systems may be required.

**Full legal name**    Each counterparty will have a full legal name associated with it that the counterparty is incorporated under. In many counterparts the legal structure is quite complex, consisting of numerous subsidiaries and branches located in different geographical regions. These names will often be similar and it is important to ensure that the correct one is referenced. The legal name is obviously used as a primary index against which reporting of XVA will take place. If the counterparty has liquid CDS then the counterparty name will form part of the mapping process. Of course it may well be the case that the CDS does not exactly represent the counterparty to the portfolio of derivatives. The CDS will reference securities issues by that counterparty and these can sometimes be issued by a different entity to the derivatives counterparty. In such circumstances the user will have to decide whether the mapping is appropriate or not. In all cases the full legal name is critical to identifying and maintaining a link to the liquid CDS market.

**Name in linked systems**    Even if the counterparty information is co-located in one system, it will be necessary to link that counterparty information with trade and collateral data in other systems. It is very unlikely that the same reference will be used in all systems in a modern bank with multiple trading systems. Hence it will be important to have a full record of what the counterparty name is in all systems to which a link is required. Typically this will be trading and collateral management systems. In certain circumstances it may be necessary to review all legal documentation associated with a counterparty. There may be a central electronic repository for this information and if so a link to this system will also be required. It may also be the case that some legal information remains on paper documents and hence will require archive retrieval.

**External credit ratings**   If a counterparty is externally rated then all external ratings will be required for XVA. These can be used in a variety of ways. One primary use will be as part of the credit curve mapping process described in section 4.6, although internal ratings are sometimes used for the mapping process. One potential advantage that the external rating has is that it is very clearly public information. The second use for external ratings will be to determine the current status of any rating triggers in CSAs or embedded in ISDAs. External ratings may also contribute to capital calculations and hence to KVA.

**Internal credit ratings**   Internal ratings will also be used in the XVA process, particularly if no external rating exists. In general, only a fraction of the counterparties faced will have an external rating. However, as a function of being able to do business with the counterparty it is highly likely to have an internal rating. Internal ratings will typically be used as part of the credit curve mapping process (see section 4.6). The internal credit rating will be based on the bank's internal credit rating models and these may also be used as part of the regulatory capital framework under FIRB or AIRB (see Chapter 12). Hence internal ratings may also contribute to KVA.

Internal ratings could in theory be partly based on private side information, that is, the bank's view on the credit worthiness of a counterparty could be influenced by information such as a pending bond issue that would fall under the category of material non-public information that would be protected by a Chinese wall until the bond issue took place. The CVA trading desk, however, will normally sit within the financial markets area and hence on the public side of the bank. The CVA desk, therefore, cannot be made party to private side information without wall crossing. In such circumstances it may become necessary to ensure that credit ratings seen and used by the CVA desk are based on public information only. The alternative would be to place the CVA desk within the private side of the firm but this may present operational difficulties.

**Geographical location**   The geographical location of a counterparty can be used in a number of different contexts in XVA calculations. The main usage will be to form part of the CDS mapping process (section 4.6). It may also be used as part of the broader counterparty credit risk management process to identify concentrations and country/regional exposures. For counterparties which as quasi-governmental bodies it will clearly be used to identify the associated national or regional government which is particularly important if explicit or implicit governmental support is provided.

The geographical location may not be that straightforward to identify and potentially may not be single-valued even at the subsidiary level. A company may be legally incorporated in one geographical location but operate outside that location. Larger counterparties can be multi-nationals and have a complex legal structure with subsidiaries in multiple locations and branches below that in the legal hierarchy.

**Sectors**   Sector information will also form part of the CDS mapping process (section 4.6) for illiquid counterparties. The sector will provide information about the trade or trades that the counterparty operates in and hence allow similar counterparties to be identified. The sector can also be used to identify concentrations and sector exposures.

The sector information itself may come in a variety of different forms. The sectors may be very broad or very granular, although if the latter is the case then there is usually some form of hierarchy that allows a broader categorisation to be constructed from the more granular sector information. Sector information may be held using a purely bank internal categorisation or through a separate standard such as *UK Standard Industrial Classification (SIC) 2007* codes (Prosser, 2007).

Sector information evolves relatively quickly so it is important to keep it up to date. The sectors within which a company operates may change over time as their business mix evolves. The sector standard itself evolves as new types of business are created so that, for example, UK SIC codes have been revised several times since the first set were created in 1948 (Prosser, 2007).

**Netting sets**   The netting sets for a counterparty define how the trades net together at close-out when a counterparty defaults (see section 6.2). The netting information itself will be based on trade and counterparty documentation as well as national laws. The XVA system may be able to source the trade membership of each netting set. However, it may also simply receive a set of netting rules which must be applied to the counterparty portfolio. In this latter case the XVA system will need to implement the business logic to determine the netting sets. This may involve an element of mapping between the netting set rules which may be specified in terms of asset classes and eligible trades.

**Hierarchy**   Many counterparties actually consist of groups of related legal entities and hence the CVA system is likely to need the counterparty hierarchy that allows the different entities to be related to each other. Company hierarchies can be quite complex but we can identify three key levels:

- **Group** – A group lies at the top of the corporate structure and is the parent of all entities within the group.
- **Subsidiary** – A subsidiary is a separately incorporated legal entity in which a group has a shareholder of greater than 50%.
- **Branch** – A branch is a subdivision of a group or subsidiary that does not have separate legal status from its parent.

CVA will normally be calculated at subsidiary level or sometimes at group level, particularly if that group has no subsidiaries.

**Self Data**   The institution will also need a set of "self data" for XVA calculations. In particular it will need information about its own corporate structure and the entities within that structure. The institution will need regulatory information about itself including regulatory status and the approved methodology to be used to calculate the regulatory capital requirements for all transactions for the various different legal entities within the institution's hierarchy.

**Trade Data**   XVA needs to value all of the relevant trades inside a Monte Carlo simulation and so normally needs access to full trade representations for all trades in scope for XVA. Even in smaller institutions, trades will frequently be held in multiple different trading systems, often a mixture of proprietary and third-party systems, each with different data formats and databases. The XVA system will require access to all of the trades and so some of the trades will need to be converted to a format that the XVA system can understand. Ideally this will be achieved by building a common trade data access platform or "bus", across which all trades from all systems can be accessed. An alternative would be to build separate access mechanisms

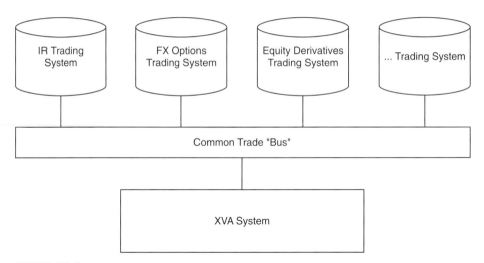

**FIGURE 20.2**   Typically individual trade records will be stored in the repositories of multiple different trading systems, each with their own proprietary data formats and databases. XVA needs to have access to all of the relevant trades. This will typically involve a common trade format and ideally a common trade access layer or "bus".

to each trading system individually but this gives less benefit than a common platform would provide. Figure 20.2 illustrates this.

A common trade platform may exist within an organisation, perhaps if it was associated with a single multi-asset quant group responsible for providing valuation models. If not then one of the major implementation challenges faced by XVA system implementors is to build the trade feed.

**Batch and intraday access**   It is important to note that XVA requires two types of trade feed, *batch* and *intraday*. Batch access is required for overnight XVA P&L and sensitivity calculations, typically after the close of business. Of course if there are multiple trading locations, there may in fact be different batches occurring at each regional close of business. The batch requires access to all of the relevant trades, which can be a very data intensive process.

Intraday trade access is required for the pricing of new trades, tear-ups and amendments. In this mode, typically only the trades of the specific counterparty are needed. However, it will also be necessary to track any portfolio changes as they occur during the trading day.

**Market Data**   XVA is the single most demanding calculation for market data in a bank. The XVA calculation will normally require all of the data required to value all of the trades within a given portfolio, with additional market data requirements on top. The market data is required for three separate elements within the calculation: trade valuation models inside the Monte Carlo, the Monte Carlo model itself and the XVA integrals that apply after the Monte Carlo model has generated exposure profiles. Typical market data requirements per asset class are given in Table 20.2. Each element has its own data requirements:

**TABLE 20.2** Typical market data requirements per asset class for XVA calculations. Not all of these may be needed and some provide alternatives to each such as equity forward curves and equity repo rate curves.

| Interest Rates | Inflation | FX | Equities | Spot Commod. | Forward Commod. | Credit |
|---|---|---|---|---|---|---|
| OIS Curve | Inflation Index | FX Spot | Equity Prices | Spot Price | Spot Price | Bond Price |
| Tenor Curves | Inflation Forward Curve | FX Forwards | Equity Forward | Forward Curve | Forward Curve | CDS & CDX Curves |
| Caplet Volatilities | Year-on-Year Option Volatilities | Currency Basis | Repo Curve | Lease Rate Conv. Yield | Seasonality Curve | Tranche Prices |
| Swaption Volatilities | ZCIIS Option Volatility | FX Option Volatility | Equity Option Volatility | Option Volatility | Option Volatility | Option Volatility |

- **Trade valuation** – If individual valuation models are executed within the Monte Carlo then each valuation model will have its own data requirements. Some of this data will be simulated by the Monte Carlo but some, typically implied volatilities, may not be. Hence this market data must be supplied to the model. If the Longstaff-Schwartz regression approach is used, however, the only data requirements are those of the Monte Carlo and XVA calculation phases.
- **Monte Carlo** – The Monte Carlo model will typically require forward curves and implied volatilities for every market data element that will be modelled in the simulation. This may lead to a requirement for proxy market data as discussed in section 16.2.2 and below.
- **XVA integrals** – The XVA integrals will require credit curves and funding curves to be provided.

As with trade data the market data may be spread across a number of different systems, particularly if the data set is associated directly with trading systems. A common data format for market data while not absolutely essential is certainly very useful and this may lead to the development of a common market data platform or "bus" if one is not already available.

Market data is not always just a series of instrument prices and in many cases the data is associated with a pricing model for linear products or vanilla options. So, for example, the yield curve data may be closely associated with the discounting model used within the bank, say OIS. For vanilla options in interest rates this will almost certainly be the case if the SABR or ZABR model is used for valuation purposes and the volatility surface will consist of at-the-money volatilities and a series of other parameters that are interpolated to give the option price. The XVA system is likely to need access to the quant models that underlie the data format in this case so that the data is interpreted correctly and the market data needed for the XVA calculation obtained.

**Proxy data**    As was noted earlier in section 16.2.2 proxy data will sometimes be required by an XVA model. In general for the trade valuation phase, market data will be available as this will be needed for the primary valuation. However, if the trade is valued using a third-party valuation system then market data may not be available as this would be controlled by the third-party vendor. For the Monte Carlo model there may also be market data requirements that arise from modelling decisions. Typically all the interest rates in the model will be treated stochastically; however, in some cases market data for those interest rate markets may not be available internally. The bank in question may only trade those currencies through FX products and have no interest rate trading business or for some emerging markets there may simply be no interest rate options available. In such cases proxy market data may be needed, where the required market data is mapped to a suitable proxy. So for example, interest rate option volatility may be mapped to a neighbouring country where options are available. The XVA system would, in these cases, need to maintain a mapping table. There may also be additional demands on Finance teams responsible for *Independent Price Verification (IPV)* as they will be required to test the appropriateness of the proxy.

**Batch and intraday requirements**    For an XVA overnight batch, all market data for the calculation of XVA for all counterparties will be needed. This means sourcing the appropriate *close-of-business* market data that has been approved for P&L purposes by IPV teams. The main issue is that a lot of market data will be required at batch initiation. For resilience purposes it may be necessary to prepare fallback processes if data is missing so that the batch can proceed. This may involve falling back to an earlier data set. Materiality will be a consideration in whatever strategy is adopted so while a delay to the batch may be the consequence if the market data from a primary currency is missing, falling back to the previous day may be appropriate if a minor currency with little XVA contribution is missing.

Intraday, XVA will ideally need access to the current snapshot of market data. If the simulation is organised on a per counterparty basis, then this will only involve the market data required to calculate incremental XVA for that counterparty.

**Time series data**    For historical correlations at least, time series of market data will be required. If a form of historical calibration is selected for some or all of the XVA Monte Carlo then, potentially, a much larger set of time series data will be needed. The length of time series and choice of instrument will depend on modelling choices.

**Identifying data requirements**    Given the complexity of market data required by an XVA model, the best approach to identifying market data requirements is to make the model self-describing. This means making a query available on the model that, given a portfolio of trades, returns a list of market data requirements. This makes it much easier for technology teams to manage the input data gathering processes.

**Collateral Data**    By *collateral data* I refer to both CSA parameters and the current collateral position with a counterparty and its composition. In section 6.4 I described how financial collateral under a CSA agreement can be included in the XVA model. If collateralised names are included in XVA then the CSA parameters will be needed by the model and must be sourced. Typically the collateral management system will maintain this information, although it may be held separately in a legal database. Table 2.1 lists the CSA parameters that are likely to be required.

For CVA and FVA, depending on which approach to modelling the CSA is adopted, the current collateral amount and its composition as a series of eligible currencies and securities may be needed and these will need to be sourced from the collateral management system.

Capital calculations including KVA will also need this information in order to correctly model the capital requirement.

**Security**   As discussed in section 6.5, it may be appropriate to model the loss directly through the default waterfall in some circumstances such as when non-financial security is held against the position. The value of the security and potentially modelling parameters associated with it will need to be provided to the XVA system.

**Model Parameters and Static Data**   The XVA model itself will require a number of parameters to be supplied prior to calculation. The different elements of the model, trade valuation, Monte Carlo and XVA integrals will typically require separate sets of model parameters. If full trade valuation routines are called within the Monte Carlo model, these models may have their own model parameters, meaning that each trade will have parameters associated with it. The model will also require access to static data such as market conventions.

## 20.2.2   Calculation

Once the input data has been marshalled and prepared the calculation phase can proceed.

**Calibration**   The Monte Carlo model will require some form of calibration, although the precise details will be model-dependent. Each asset class in the simulation will require calibration and there are clear dependencies between calibrations. The interest rate calibrations will need to be performed first as these parameters will be needed for subsequent calibrations. FX calibrations will be dependent on interest rate calibrations and can be performed next. Other asset classes such as equities and commodities will be dependent on interest rates and may depend on FX and so these will be performed last. Some commodities such as oil fractions may need to be calibrated together as a group. This is illustrated in Figure 20.3.

The actual performance of the calibration will be model-dependent. Bootstrap type calibrations will often be much faster than those that involve some kind of optimisation. Optimisation calibrations may also show considerable variance in the time taken to achieve convergence. The calibration phase can be parallelised to some degree as is clear from Figure 20.3. In the case illustrated, the interest rate calibrations are independent of each other and can be run in parallel.

**Ticking calibration**   For intraday XVA calculations it may be necessary to have a ticking calibration process running, which runs the calibration on a periodic basis or in response to changes in market data. If the model calibration is relatively slow, then a ticking calibration process will provide a recent calibration without the cost of running the calibration ahead of the Monte Carlo simulation.

**Simulation and Valuation**   The central part of the XVA calculation and the most computationally demanding is the Monte Carlo simulation with its trade valuation loop. Fortunately, each path in the Monte Carlo simulation is independent of all other paths and at each stopping date on each path the trade valuations are also independent of one another. This implies that the calculation would benefit from a high degree of parallelism.

The exception to this independence between paths in the XVA Monte Carlo simulation are the regression techniques such as Longstaff-Schwartz and LSAC. In these cases there are

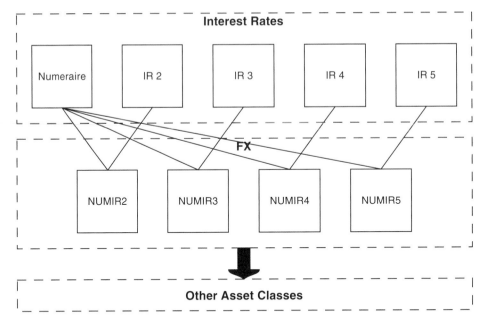

**FIGURE 20.3** A typical calibration hierarchy for an XVA Monte Carlo model.

at least two simulations, one to "calibrate" the regression function and one to perform the XVA calculation. The first simulation is used for regression so all the information required for the regression must be extracted from the full set of Monte Carlo paths. So while the paths which are independent of each other can be run in parallel, the regression process cannot. Even so multiple regressions can be run in parallel and some of the numerical routines used in the regression can themselves benefit from parallel processing.

XVA typically requires the expected exposure values at a series of exposure dates and that these individual exposure calculations have no dependency on each other. In theory then a series of "single step" Monte Carlo simulations could be used. However, in practice trade life-cycling breaks this seeming time independence. Fixings and option exercises must occur so that calculation becomes path-dependent and a "multi-step" Monte Carlo must be used. For vanilla products though this time independence can be used to advantage and a further axis of parallelism exploited, although this will require careful engineering.

Parallelism is therefore the central element of the calculation that can be exploited to boost performance and how this can be done in practice is discussed in section 20.4.7.

The Monte Carlo simulation can be organised in two different ways, with *counterparty orientation*, where each counterparty or potentially each individual netting set is simulated separately, or with a *global simulation* where all counterparties are simulated with the same Monte Carlo paths. Both approaches have strengths and weaknesses.

**Counterparty (or netting set) orientated simulation** In counterparty (netting set) ori-entated simulations, each counterparty is treated separately. A set of Monte Carlo paths is constructed just for the counterparty and only the assets that are relevant to the counterparty

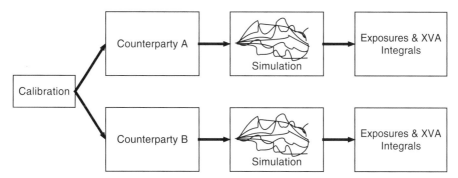

**FIGURE 20.4**   Workflow for the counterparty or netting set orientated simulation.

are simulated. The simulation results are then reduced and exposures calculated. The exposures are then fed into the XVA integral calculation. This workflow is illustrated in Figure 20.4.

The advantage of this approach is that the simulations are each relatively small in general as only the relevant assets are simulated, although there are likely to be large portfolios with CCPs or major interbank market counterparties. This also places less stress on the construction of the correlation matrix as this too will be much smaller and hence processes such as regularisation (see section 17.4.1) and correlation induction (see section 17.4.2) will be less computationally intensive. Furthermore, variance reduction techniques such as orthogonalisation (see section 18.3) will also be more efficient. The counterparty orientation also lends itself more readily to intraday pricing activity. For counterparty orientated simulations, the paths will typically be generated at the time the simulation is run, rather than separately. This can make the model more flexible and maintainable.

In general, however, the random numbers used in each case will be different so that the physical Monte Carlo paths generated for asset X for counterparty A will be different from the paths for asset X for counterparty Y. This means that global analysis involving trade valuations on a per path basis and in-memory reduction processes are not available. Nevertheless, as Chapter 15 showed, a counterparty level simulation does not prevent global quantities being calculated.

**Global simulation**   The alternative to counterparty level simulation is a global simulation of all assets required to value all of the trades subject to XVA being simulated simultaneously. This is illustrated in Figure 20.5. The advantage of this approach is that the same paths for each asset are used for all counterparties and this allows global elements such as the leverage ratio to be taken into consideration within a single simulation. It also enables the use of in-memory analysis and reduction techniques.

The disadvantage of a global simulation is that the simulation itself becomes very large and this can present problems. The correlation matrix could easily contain many thousands of correlations and this would make regularisation (see section 17.4.1) and correlation induction (see section 17.4.2) problematic and computationally intensive, although a block-structured correlation matrix may mitigate this somewhat. Furthermore the large simulation is not readily amenable to intraday use for pricing purposes, even though it will not be necessary to generate all of the paths for all assets when conducting a single counterparty simulation for incremental

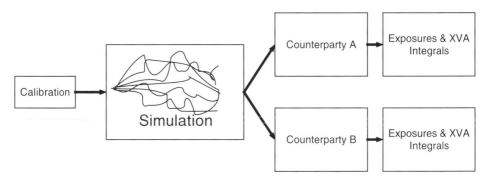

**FIGURE 20.5**    Workflow for a global XVA simulation.

pricing as the only requirement is that the correct random numbers are fed to the relevant assets.

**Longstaff-Schwartz**    The use of Longstaff-Schwartz regression (see section 19.3.2) for some or all trade valuations adds a requirement for a second simulation. This simulation is used as an input to the regression process and hence can be thought of as a "calibration" simulation used to find the coefficients of the regression functions. This simulation must be independent of the second simulation where the exposures are calculated to ensure there is no bias. Hence a different set of random numbers should be used. In fact this simulation need only simulate the assets relevant to the trade that will be valued using Longstaff-Schwartz. The workflow for the Longstaff-Schwartz case is illustrated in Figure 20.6.

**XVA Integrals**    After the simulation is complete and reductions have taken place to obtain exposure profiles the XVA integrals must be calculated. This means implementing a numerical integral of the form

$$\text{XVA}(t) = \int_t^T L(s)\xi(s)e^{-\int_0^s \xi(u)du}e^{-\int_0^s C(u)du}\mathbb{E}[D(s)E(s)]ds. \tag{20.1}$$

Clearly this is only true in the case where the "density" $\xi(t)$ is independent of the state variables in the expectation, otherwise conditioning is required (see Chapter 7). Obviously there are a number of suitable discretisations and integration schemes for this integral and these have been discussed earlier. The key point from an implementation point of view is that the integral occurs after the simulation and that it is a relatively inexpensive operation.

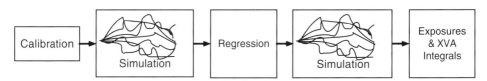

**FIGURE 20.6**    Workflow for Longstaff-Schwartz regression.

### 20.2.3 Reporting

Ultimately XVA values and sensitivities will be reported after the calculation is complete. In general, results will be returned at counterparty level, potentially with risk aggregated across the portfolio. Trade level results for XVA using Euler allocation were discussed in section 3.6.2 and this can also be exported. Trade level results are particularly useful if CVA must be reported to business areas within the firm. Individual counterparties will transact business in multiple asset classes and hence across several different business lines so CVA allocation provides a means of accurately reporting the XVA to those businesses. Trade level risk allocation is also possible (see Kenyon and Green, 2014a) and would prove useful for tracking the behaviour of larger trades within a portfolio. In the case that the XVA business itself is divided between divisions within an institution, so that individual business lines manage their own XVA, risk allocation will be necessary to correctly report XVA risk to the individual XVA management functions. Risk allocation would then allow the XVA sub-businesses to hedge the XVA risk associated with their business lines.

Feeds of results will be necessary to the XVA trading function, finance and risk at a minimum. In general, however, XVA will be reported quite widely and, for example, may need to be fed to sales and relationship manager systems to provide XVA information to those dealing directly with the client.

**Reduction versus in-memory analysis**   Some third-party vendors offer *Online Analytical Processing (OLAP)* platforms in the area of XVA and of course these can be built internally. These facilities typically consist of in-memory databases that store results from the XVA calculation and provide analysis and query tools. As all of the data is in memory, queries can be performant, even across large data sets. One typical model of operation is to store the individual pathwise valuations from the Monte Carlo simulation and then provide the reduction/XVA integrals as an online operation that is calculated on the fly. Given that OLAP is typically optimised for such reduction processes, these do not present a computational obstacle. The advantage of this approach is that it allows the user to perform what-if analysis and drill down using an interactive facility. The disadvantage of such systems is that to ensure coherence across the whole data set between Monte Carlo paths requires a global simulation as discussed in section 20.2.2. A second disadvantage is that these systems primarily lend themselves to the case where the XVA integral is independent of the simulation phase, which will not be the case if say hazard or funding rates are correlated within the Monte Carlo simulation.

A final point about OLAP is that it provides a benefit when the Monte Carlo simulation phase is slow as it allows analysis to be performed without the need to run the Monte Carlo simulation again in full and this has often been the case in the past. However, the development of GPU-based systems and the growth of fast XVA calculations based on Longstaff-Schwartz techniques and algorithmic risk can have a significant effect on the overall performance of the Monte Carlo simulation (see for example Kenyon and Green, 2014a; Andreasen, 2014). At some point the performance gain from such approaches may make OLAP unnecessary.

## 20.3 HARDWARE

The heavy computational workload imposed by XVA means that hardware selection is an important consideration. Parallelism is a prerequisite for the calculation platform and is therefore assumed in this section. Here I explore the advantages and disadvantages of different hardware types as applied to XVA.

### 20.3.1  CPU

The *Central Processing Unit (CPU)* is synonymous with the development of the PC from the early 1980s onwards. In the context of high performance computing the most common CPUs are high end multicore processors. At the time of writing the two most commonly encountered examples are the Intel®Xeon®processor and the AMD Opteron™.[2,3] However, other servers based on the ARM® processor are also starting to appear on the market (Sverdlik, 2014).[4] The processors will be encountered in desktop PCs, rack servers and blade servers.

Although these processors are already multi-core a typical XVA platform in a medium-sized bank will require on the order of thousands of CPU cores to complete the required XVA valuation and sensitivity calculations. Hence even with 10 physical cores on a single CPU and perhaps two CPUs on a blade server, at least 50 blade servers will be needed. For larger institutions the hardware requirement could be considerably greater than this with hundreds or thousands of blade servers.

CPU farms offer perhaps the most straightforward platform on which to develop an XVA calculation. The server would typically use either a Microsoft®Windows Server®or a Linux®operating system.[5,6] Analytics libraries will often be written in C++, perhaps the most commonly used language by quantitative analysts and developers. Alternatives such as C# are also viable options. A full discussion on language use can be found in section 20.4.3.

The calculation must still be distributed across multiple cores and servers and a distribution mechanism is also required. A number of third-party vendors offer suitable platforms, or an in-house solution can be developed.

The disadvantage of CPUs is that compared to other more specialised alternatives they offer less performance per unit hardware cost or lower energy efficiency (MIPS per Watt).

### 20.3.2  GPU and GPGPU

*Graphic Processing Units (GPUs)* are literally the specialised processors for displaying graphics output from PCs. Specialist graphics cards became popular from the mid to late 1990s as computer gaming on the PC platform became popular. The display of graphics for gaming purposes is a highly parallel operation as it is based on ray-tracing. As a result the graphics cards used for gaming became specialised for high parallel operations. In the early post-millenium

---

[2]Celeron, Centrino, Intel, the Intel logo, Intel Atom, Intel Core, Intel Inside, the Intel Inside logo, Intel vPro, Intel Xeon Phi, Itanium, Pentium, and Xeon are trademarks of Intel Corporation in the US and/or other countries.

[3]AMD Opteron™is a trademark of AMD.

[4]ARM is a registered trademark of ARM Limited (or its subsidiaries) in the EU and/or elsewhere. All rights reserved. This publication is independent and it is not affiliated with, or endorsed, sponsored or authorised by ARM Limited.

[5]Microsoft and Windows Server are either registered trademarks or trademarks of Microsoft Corporation in the United States and/or other countries.

[6]Linux®is the registered trademark of Linus Torvalds in the US and other countries.

period it was realised that this parallelism could be exploited in other areas of computation and this led to so-called GPGPU, *general purpose computing on GPU.*

GPUs applied to computing problems typically sit on special purpose cards designed to fit expansion slots in servers. Special purpose cards have been designed for numerical processing and these do not have graphics outputs. The GPU card has its own dedicated memory on the card. The GPU itself is a highly parallel processor, typically including thousands of physical cores but with simpler instruction sets than those of CPUs and running at clock speeds of less than 1 GHz. The high number of cores allows highly efficient parallel execution for problems which involve multiple calls to the same *kernel* but with different inputs. Monte Carlo simulation is a prime example of such an algorithm. To access the GPU special code, known as a *kernel*, must be written for the device. Data must be copied to the card in advance of executing the kernel and then the results copied back to main memory. A CPU is still required to drive the GPU and the server chassis within which it sits.

For parallel computing problems such as Monte Carlo simulations, GPUs are highly performant. Scaling factors of ×50 are reported (Giles, 2014) for a single GPU versus a single CPU core.[7] Correspondingly they offer better energy efficiency than CPUs.

GPUs still sit in rack servers, although a typical server would contain between four and eight GPU cards. Distribution of the calculation across multiple GPUs and servers will still be a requirement and hence software will still be needed for this purpose.

The disadvantage of GPUs is that specialist code must be written in NVIDIA®CUDA™or OpenCL™and this requires development experience and training.[8,9] As CUDA and OpenCL develop, however, the barrier to the use of GPU computing is reducing. The supporting tools available for GPU development such as compilers and debuggers are now mature. There are benefits as well as costs to re-writing code for GPU. Such a re-write inevitably involves a degree of re-architecting which can give performance benefits independently of the hardware acceleration.

### 20.3.3  Intel® Xeon Phi™

The Intel Xeon Phi co-processor was formally introduced in November 2012. It acts as a numerical co-processor to the Xeon CPU but has a higher degree of parallel processing capability. The current generation of Xeon Phi processors have up to 61 physical cores (Intel, 2013) and run at clock speeds of just over 1 GHz. The aim of the Phi processor is to exploit the existing x86 processor architecture while obtaining a higher number of cores than current CPUs. The use of the x86 architecture is targeted at reducing the amount of code that would need to be redeveloped to take advantage of the parallelism when compared to that required to make use of GPUs. Like Intel Xeon CPUs, the Xeon Phi offers hyperthreading, that is the ability to execute multiple threads on the same physical core thereby giving the appearance of a higher number of cores than are actually present on the processor. Intel Xeon processors have two times hyperthreading so there are twice as many hyperthreaded cores available than actual cores, while Intel Xeon Phi processors have four times hyperthreading so an Intel Xeon Phi

---

[7]My own personal experience has shown factors of between 40–100 fold performance improvement for a single GPU over a CPU core.

[8]NVIDIA®CUDA™ is a trademark of the NVIDIA Corporation in the US and/or other countries.

[9]OpenCL and the OpenCL logo are trademarks of Apple Inc. used by permission by Khronos.

7120P has 61 physical cores and 244 logical cores. The Intel Xeon Phi is currently supplied as a PCIe-16x expansion card that runs its own Linux operating system.

### 20.3.4  FPGA

*Field Programmable Gate Arrays (FPGA)* are chips that contain arrays of logic gates that can be programmed directly by the end user. As such they allow an algorithm to be represented directly "in hardware" rather than relying on the execution of a low-level instruction set as on CPUs and GPUs. As the algorithm is effectively coded directly into the ship, very high performance is possible. Multiple copies of the same algorithm can be encoded onto the processor allowing parallel operation. Algorithms are encoded using a *hardware description language*, although higher level languages have been developed for FPGA (see for example Celoxica, 2005). The chip can be reconfigured dynamically, although there is a latency associated with this process while the hardware is reconfigured with a new algorithm.

FPGAs are best suited to solving single complex numerical problems. They have been applied in Finance to CDO models by J.P. Morgan (Feldman, 2011) where reported performance improvements were in the range of 130 times. FPGAs have also been applied in high frequency trading. However, FPGAs do not seem that well suited to XVA models because of the wide range of products across many different asset classes that make up a typical portfolio. Whether any institutions have applied FPGAs to XVA is unknown.

### 20.3.5  Supercomputers

Supercomputers represent the largest computing platforms available on the market today. Given the complexity of XVA models, a supercomputing platform would present the ultimate in computing resource and perhaps the most suitable solution.

In practice modern supercomputers consist of large arrays of industry standard processors coupled with a high performance network. For example, the Tianhe-2 cluster uses Intel Xeon and Intel Xeon Phi processors to give a total of 3,120,000 cores and a performance of 33.86 petaflop/s (Top500, 2014), while *Titan*, a Cray®XK7™uses AMD Opteron processors and NVIDIA®Tesla®K20X GPUs to give 560,640 cores and a performance of 17.59 petaflops/s (Top500, 2014).[10,11] Both use variants of Linux as the operating system.

Such large computing resources are probably well beyond the needs of XVA models for even the very largest institutions. It is clear, however, that the line between compute grids and supercomputing facilities has become blurred. A typical XVA grid computing solution is likely to have performance capabilities of the order of 1 petaflop/s.

## 20.4  SOFTWARE

Developing software is central to the production of an XVA system and is the most complex element of the technological infrastructure. This section discusses the key aspects of the development process. An XVA system can either be developed entirely in-house or may

---

[10]Cray®XK7™is a trademark of Cray Inc. and is registered in the United States and other countries.
[11]NVIDIA®Tesla®is a trademark of the NVIDIA Corporation in the US and/or other countries.

involve the implementation of a third-party vendor system. Even in the latter case software development will be required to some degree to integrate the vendor solution alongside other internal systems.

## 20.4.1  Roles and Responsibilities

The implementation of an XVA system is a considerable undertaking and will necessarily be at least a moderately sized project. As such it will certainly involve project and programme management and managers. Implementation timescales will typically be 1–2 years for a full system. In a typical project the following groups will be involved and it is useful to identify the roles and responsibilities of each group.

**Accountable Executive and Steering Committee**  There will almost certainly be an accountable executive responsible for the delivery of the XVA system and this is most likely to be a senior business leader with responsibility for XVA management. There will also be a steering committee that is responsible for providing project steering and governance. Membership of the steering committee will likely include the major stakeholders in the development process. There may be additional working groups that report into the steering committee to manage aspects of the project at a lower level.

**Project/Programme Management**  The project manager will have responsibility for planning the project and then tracking the project against that plan. The project manager will also be responsible for reporting project status to the steering committee. Overall the project may be managed using different models including *waterfall* and *agile* methodologies of which more is said below in section 20.4.2.

**Business Analysis**  Business analysis will certainly be required for numerous aspects of the project from overall requirements capture to detailed analysis of data feeds and the like. This may involve business analysts if the technology model has a separate business analysis function or alternatively analysts-developers may fulfil this role. Some aspects of the project will inevitably be highly technical in nature and in these cases quantitative analysts may perform some elements of business analysis.

**Quantitative Analysts and Developers**  For an in-house system or a third-party system that accesses models developed in-house, quantitative analysts and developers will be responsible for model development. This will involve all aspects of model development from model specification through to implementation. In my own view the best results are obtained by quantitative analysts and developers implementing their own models rather than by quants specifying models for technologists to separately implement. Given the need for parallelism this may involve bringing appropriate expertise into the quant team to support them. The quants are also best placed to design the calculation workflow, given their familiarity with the models and the relative computational costs of the different elements of the calculation.

**Technology Development**  IT development staff will develop the non-model aspects of the XVA system, principally data management. This means calculation preparation, execution of tasks on the compute grid and reporting of results. The IT development team will have to work very closely with the quant team so good working relationships are a key aspect in a successful project.

**Other IT Staff**    A number of other teams of IT staff will also be involved in the project. IT Support staff will be required to provide support to the final application and will also be responsible for actual software release (in order to be compliant with Sarbanes-Oxley: Sarbanes and Oxley, 2002). IT architecture teams may be responsible for architectural design or review of design. Testing teams may be responsible for application testing. Hardware and network specialists will be involved in the commissioning of new hardware.

**Model Validation and Governance**    The model developed by the quant team will need to validated in accordance with the model governance policy of the institution. This will involve an independent review of the model and its implementation. Given that the XVA model is likely to be very material and much more material than any single pricing model, model governance may be more rigorous than for other models. Model validation may involve testing the model or indeed a full implementation of a parallel model.

## 20.4.2    Development and Project Management Practice

How should the project proceed and which project management approach should be adopted? Here I consider two approaches, *waterfall* and *Agile*, and the strengths and weaknesses of each in the context of XVA implementation. In reality there are a wide variety of software development models of which which waterfall and Agile are examples representing two ends of a spectrum.

**Waterfall**    The classic waterfall model of software development images a sequential development process where each phase of development follows linearly from the previous one. The project plan for such a model resembles a waterfall. The waterfall approach was introduced from engineering industries where similar sequential processes were used (Benington, 1983). One of the first papers to discuss such models was given by Herbert Benington at a symposium in 1956. The waterfall model was described in detail in a paper by Winston Royce (1970). In Royce's waterfall model there are seven steps: system requirements, software requirements, analysis, program design, coding, testing and operations and this is illustrated in Figure 20.7.

The waterfall model envisages a rigorous software development process which proceeds step by step and where a new step is not commenced until the previous one is complete. It lends itself well to a highly documented process, with each stage being separately documented and approved. The step-wise approach with approvals is attractive in a highly regulated environment. As the software design is done up front, it can prove beneficial when working with inexperienced development teams who code to specification.

However, there is a major problem with the waterfall model in its pure form as you cannot go back to earlier steps in the process after they have been completed and as such it assumes that the development will proceed in a single pass. This means there is substantial risk inherent in the waterfall approach as if mistakes are made in any single step then they will result in the failure of the project. This is a particular problem as it assumes that all requirements of the system are known in advance and that the software design and implementation will be optimal at the first attempt. In reality many requirements will not be known in advance and will only be discovered during the development cycle. As design and implementation proceed

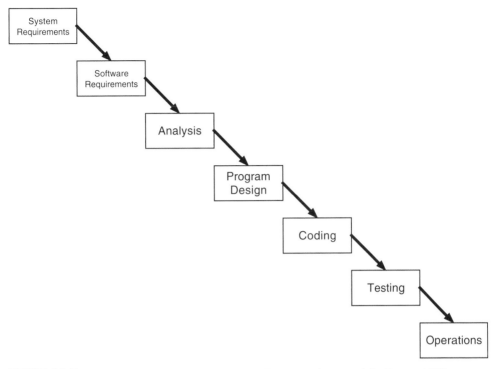

**FIGURE 20.7**   The steps in the waterfall model of software development (after Royce, 1970).

developers learn from mistakes and can improve the solution, but the waterfall model does not allow lessons learned to influence the final software solution. In a banking environment where change is ever present an inflexible approach to development can be a disaster. Long waterfall development processes will likely lead to software that does not fit the requirements of the business when it is delivered. At worst the software may never be delivered as business needs have changed during the development process leading to the project being scrapped.

The flaws in the waterfall model are well known and were clearly recognised as early as 1970 by Royce in his article, which was critical of the waterfall model. Royce advocated updating the model with iterative processes. Nevertheless, the waterfall approach or variants of it are still widely used in software engineering.

**Agile**   *Agile* refers to a group of software development practices that are iterative and incremental in nature and provide the ability to adapt to changing circumstances. The name Agile derives from the *Manifesto for Agile Software Development* which was introduced by a group of software developers in 2001. The Agile Manifesto is given in Figure 20.8.

Agile development is based on twelve principles (Beck et al., 2001):

1. Our highest priority is to satisfy the customer through early and continuous delivery of valuable software.
2. Welcome changing requirements, even late in development. Agile processes harness change for the customer's competitive advantage.

Manifesto for Agile Software Development

We are uncovering better ways of developing
software by doing it and helping others do it.
Through this work we have come to value:

Individuals and interactions over processes and tools
Working software over comprehensive documentation
Customer collaboration over contract negotiation
Responding to change over following a plan

That is, while there is value in the items on
the right, we value the items on the left more.

| | | |
|---|---|---|
| Kent Beck | James Grenning | Robert C. Martin |
| Mike Beedle | Jim Highsmith | Steve Mellor |
| Arie van Bennekum | Andrew Hunt | Ken Schwaber |
| Alistair Cockburn | Ron Jeffries | Jeff Sutherland |
| Ward Cunningham | Jon Kern | Dave Thomas |
| Martin Fowler | Brian Marick | |

© 2001,the above authors
this declaration may be freely copied in any form,
but only in its entirety through this notice.

**FIGURE 20.8** The Agile Manifesto.

3. Deliver working software frequently, from a couple of weeks to a couple of months, with a preference to the shorter timescale.
4. Business people and developers must work together daily throughout the project.
5. Build projects around motivated individuals. Give them the environment and support they need, and trust them to get the job done.
6. The most efficient and effective method of conveying information to and within a development team is face-to-face conversation.
7. Working software is the primary measure of progress.
8. Agile processes promote sustainable development. The sponsors, developers and users should be able to maintain a constant pace indefinitely.
9. Continuous attention to technical excellence and good design enhances agility.
10. Simplicity – the art of maximising the amount of work not done – is essential.
11. The best architectures, requirements and designs emerge from self-organising teams.
12. At regular intervals, the team reflects on how to become more effective, then tunes and adjusts its behaviour accordingly.

Central to Agile is the concept of iterative and incremental development. The software evolves as development proceeds. Requirements are discovered during the software development process through direct interaction between the business and the developers. The aim of Agile processes is to deliver working software to the business early and then update it frequently.

In a banking environment, Agile-style software development works well in my experience. It fits well with the rapidly changing business environment. The business can see the software quickly and have a direct influence on development. This tends to reassure the business and builds bridges with the development team. Smaller frequent releases reduce the risk of each single release as development is done in small incremental steps. However, it is important to note that the business does not actually manage the project directly. A project manager will still be responsible for the overall project. Agile is, however, less transparent as a process than waterfall, although the nature of Agile means that in practice there is often something for the business to see far earlier than would be the case under waterfall development. The iterative nature makes it difficult to produce traditional project plans and the rapid evolution of the project makes it sometimes difficult to track overall progress and present this in a meaningful way to the business. It is more difficult to design an approval and sign-off process for Agile as there are no "gate-steps" as there are in the waterfall development process. This makes Agile less compatible with a highly regulated environment.

Iterative and incremental development practices predate Agile as Larman and Basili (2003) point out. Walter Shewhart of Bell Labs proposed a cyclic approach to improve quality in the 1930s (Shewhart, 1939). This approach later became known as the *plan-do-study-act (PDSA)* or *plan-do-check-act (PDCA)* cycle (Deming, 1982). Iterative and incremental project management was used on a number of major engineering projects in the 1950s including the X-15 hypersonic aircraft (Larman and Basili, 2003). Iterative and incremental development practice was also applied in software development from the 1950s onwards, being used on a variety of aerospace and defence-related projects including the software for NASA's Project Mercury and for the Space Shuttle (Larman and Basili, 2003). With the advent of personal computers and widespread development of applications for them, iterative and incremental development were used in a wide variety of contexts. For example, Booch (1983); Jacobson, Booch and Rumbaugh (1999) advocated the use of iterative development as part of object orientated analysis and design. Today, Agile and variants of it are widely used across software development.

**Development Best Practice**   The following items will seem very natural to most quants working in roles that involve the implementation of models. Nevertheless I believe they are worth raising here. XVA is very demanding of models and systems and this alone requires a disciplined approach to development. A model framework for XVA can be complex and involves calling pricing models inside a Monte Carlo simulation. The Monte Carlo simulation will naturally produce "stressed" states of the world, and then call valuation routines in those states. The valuation models must therefore be robust as a single failure on a single path at a single time step will lead to the failure of the XVA calculation for that counterparty. XVA models then have a multiplicity of potential points of failure and the only defence against production errors is a solid approach to model development. Agile project management aims to deliver quickly and often and this is not incompatible with disciplined development, rather it requires the strong quality control that best practice development will bring.

**Coding standard**   All software development projects should have a documented coding standard that developers are required to adhere to. A coding standard ensures that the C++ used on the project is appropriate to the environment in which the code will be developed and used. The standard will also ensure sufficient stylistic coherence between developers to allow effective team work. Code written to a coding standard will certainly be easier to maintain and extend in the future.

**Test-driven development**   Test-driven development is often associated with *Extreme Programming (XP)* (Beck, 1999), itself a set of development practices that are closely associated with Agile. As a development practice it stands on its own whether or not XP and/or Agile are employed. The basic idea of test-driven development is that the tests are written first before any actual code. In its pure form test-driven development follows the following steps (see for example Beck, 1999):

- **Write tests** – write a set of tests that the new feature must pass based on the set of requirements. An interface will need to be written for the new feature, although at this stage there will be no functional code behind it.
- **Run tests** – run all the tests and the new tests should fail.
- **Implement code** – implement the new feature behind the interface.
- **Run tests** – run all the tests and the new tests should now pass. Given that the tests match the requirements the developer can be confident that the new code matches the requirements.
- **Refactor** – if the tests do not pass then the developer must refactor the code until they do.

A less stringent form of test-driven development is to ensure that the test plan rather than the actual tests themselves are is complete prior to the new feature being implemented. For numerical code this should include numerical tolerances. The test plan should be subject to *peer review*. Once the development is complete and the tests implemented the results of the tests should be reviewed during a *code review*.

There are three types of test that need to be written:

- **Unit tests** – tests that confirm that the unit of code performs as expected in isolation and meets the requirements.
- **Integration tests** – tests that confirm that the unit of code has been integrated correctly with the wider code base.
- **Regression tests** – tests that confirm that a change has not caused issues elsewhere in the system.

**Peer review**    As noted above, test plans should be subject to peer review prior to the start of development. My personal belief is that all code should be peer reviewed prior to integration and that the results of any testing should form part of that review. The peer review should cover, as a minimum:

- Code design
- Compliance with *coding standard*
- Comments in the code base
- Test results and adequacy of testing
- Documentation.

**Source code management**    All source code should be managed using a source code repository that maintains versioned copies of the source code. The source code repository should maintain a "trunk" version that is the current version of the source with all integrated changes. Typically developers will "branch" off trunk to work on a task before merging back to the trunk version.

The repository should also allow the source code in any release of the software to be identified along with the ability to identify which changes contributed to it. The source code repository should be linked either directly or through external process to a development workflow management tool. There are a number of different source code management systems and popular open source source code control systems include Subversion (Pilato et al., 2008) and Git (Chacon and Straub, 2014).

**Development workflow management**    All development workflow should be managed using an appropriate set of tools, typically a software issue tracking database. The tools should allow the test and peer review process to be managed and provide evidence of it. The tracking tool should be linked to the source code management tool.

**Continuous integration**    Continuous integration (Fowler, 2006) is a process where all developers integrate their changes back to trunk on a frequent basis, perhaps as often as several times a day. Once code is submitted this initiates an automatic build of the trunk version and an automated testing process. This allows errors to be identified quickly and prevents difficulties in integration, particularly with a number of developers working on the same code base. A number of tools are available to support the automated build and testing process.

Continuous integration is often linked to Extreme Programming and Agile development practice. It provides support for tactics such as *time boxing*[12] and allows the library to be maintained as *ready to ship*. Releases become a snapshot of the current tested trunk at the designated release time.

**Performance and optimisation**    XVA as a large Monte Carlo simulation is, as discussed, highly demanding on computational resources. Hence performance of the code is crucial to minimising the physical hardware requirement. Performance of the model should, therefore, be a key consideration during the system design phase and the during implementation. Performance testing should be an element of the test plan and testing process. It is also essential that performance forms part of regression testing. Any performance degradation of a model should be identified long before it reaches production.

Optimisation of code is also something that will be common in an XVA code base. It is, of course, important to get a new model element operational first but once this is complete, one or more iterations of optimisation should be expected. Optimisation should be targeted on the bottlenecks in the calculation which means that performance information needs to be captured. This can be done using external tools but even if these are available it is best practice to capture performance information as a matter of course from the calculation.

### 20.4.3  Language Choice

The choice of programming language is an important decision when developing a system in-house and will impact the overall performance of the system. This section reviews some of the possible choices.

---

[12]Time boxing limits the development time to a specific period.

### 20.4.4 CPU Languages

**C++**   C++ was originally developed by Stroustrup (1985) as an object-orientated extension of the C language (Kernighan and Ritchie, 1988). C++ is a full objected orientated language with a rich syntax that allows a variety of different programming paradigms to be adopted including *high level assembly*, *structured programming*, *data abstraction*, *object-orientation*, *generic programming* (Downey, 2013) and *functional programming*. At the time of writing the current standard for C++ is version 11 (ANSI, 2011), although version 14, a minor release, has been agreed and is awaiting publication with a major revision due in 2017.

C++ is probably the most commonly used language for quantitative analytics libraries in finance and hence is also the language known by most quants. C++, with its origins in C, is very suitable for the development of computationally intensive algorithms. The object-orientated nature of C++ also makes it very suitable to support the structure of an analytics library that evolves through time. Written well C++ is highly performant but it is a complex language and it is relatively easy to write code that gives poor computational performance or uses large amounts of memory unnecessarily. Some libraries written in C++ will be designed for flexibility or for use from tools such as Microsoft Excel. Such libraries may give suitable performance in the context for which they were written but may not be adequate if applied to XVA.

Multi-threading is not that straightforward in C++ and is complex to support. In fact prior to the C++ 11 standard (ANSI, 2011), multithreading was not a core feature of C++. Thread safety is not easy in C++ because it requires a detailed understanding of how memory will be accessed by different threads. Some elements of the C++ language such as `static` variables are inimical to multithreading. Nevertheless, it is relatively straightforward to implement parallel processing through the use of multiple processes rather than multiple threads.

Overall C++ is the most appropriate language for the development of the model elements of an XVA system if it is to be used on a CPU-based platform, irrespective of whether the operating system is Windows or Linux.

**C#**   C# is an object-orientated language for the Microsoft®Windows®platform that was developed as part of the Microsoft®.Net®framework.[13] The language was developed from the C family of languages under the leadership of Anders Hejlsberg at Microsoft from 2000 onwards (Hejlsberg et al., 2010). C# shares much of its syntax with C++ and so is familiar to developers used to C, C++ and Java[TM].[14] It supports the following key features (Hejlsberg et al., 2010):

- Object orientation
- Component orientation – providing support for software components with interfaces that self-describe themselves
- Garbage collection – automated memory management and reclamation of memory
- Exception handling
- Type safety

---

[13]Microsoft®Windows®and Microsoft®.Net®are either registered trademarks or trademarks of Microsoft Corporation in the United States and/or other countries.

[14]Oracle and Java are registered trademarks of Oracle and/or its affiliates. Other names may be trademarks of their respective owners.

- Unified type system – where all types derive from a single type
- Versioning.

C# could be used as the basis for a quantitative analytics library and hence XVA model components on a Microsoft Windows platform. Even if the analytics are written in C++ it is highly likely than other software components within the application will use C# if the operating system used is Microsoft Windows.

**Java™**   The Java programming language is an object-orientated language with syntax drawn from C and C++. It was developed by Patrick Naughton, Mike Sheridan and James Gosling at Sun Microsystems from December 1990 onwards (Gosling, 2001). The aims of Java were to provide a language that enables applications to be written that are (Oracle, 1997)

- secure
- high performance
- highly robust
- run on multiple platforms in heterogeneous, distributed networks.

As such it was targeted specifically at Internet applications which were beginning to develop around the time the language was being written.

The key facility of Java is that source code is compiled to *bytecode* that can then be executed by the Java interpreter on multiple platforms. The language also provides garbage collection and support for multithreading natively.

Java is now widely used in client-server applications and distributed computing. Some elements of a distributed computing system will almost certainly be written in Java. However, Java is not commonly used for numerically intensive code.

**Others**   There are a wide variety of other languages than can be and have been used to write quantitative models and have found favour with quants at one time or another. The procedural languages Fortran and C are perhaps the most prominent. However, while these languages are performant they do not have the structure to maintain the large code-base associated with an XVA model.

*Functional Programming* has gained support within the quantitative finance community using languages such as Haskell and F#. XVA calculations clearly can be expressed in functional terms and this potentially offers an alternative approach to the calculation and one that allows parallelism to be embedded naturally. F# in offers cross-platform support and could be used on CPU and GPU (F# Software Foundation, 2014).

### 20.4.5   GPU Languages

**OpenCL**   Software development environments to support GPGPU (See section 20.3.2) have been developed since the late 2000s. A generic multi-platform environment called *Open Computing Language (OpenCL)* was released in 2008 and is available on a wide variety of platforms (Khronos Group, 2014). OpenCL initially provided a C-like language that allowed specialist code, *kernels*, to be written for GPUs and other specialised hardware. OpenCL 2.0 has added a number of elements of C++ 11. APIs exist for a variety of other languages.

**CUDA C** In 2006 NVIDIA®introduced the proprietary language CUDA (Wilt, 2013) for its own graphics cards and specialised GPGPU cards designed specifically for computation rather than graphics processing. CUDA provides two languages, CUDA C and CUDA Fortran, with CUDA C now containing elements of the C++ language. CUDA is, however, tied to GPUs produced by NVIDIA. As with OpenCL it is possible to integrate CUDA with other languages.

CUDA is widely used across a number of different industries that require high performance parallel processing. Quantitative finance is now beginning to use GPUs and CUDA, although usage has been limited when compared to other disciplines such as computational chemistry and biology, fluid dynamics, and the media and defence sectors.

In my own experience CUDA C has proved straightforward to use and to apply to XVA. The support for multithreading on the GPU card is natural within CUDA and hence parallel applications are relatively easy to craft. Integrated development environment (IDE) solutions are also available for CUDA.

## 20.4.6 Scripting and Payout Languages

In an XVA system there is also a place for scripting and payout languages. Payout languages are reasonably common in quantitative finance, providing the capability to quickly value new products on suitable models through the use of a script rather than waiting for a specific payout to be developed in compiled code. A payout language in the context of XVA would allow new products to also have their XVA values and sensitivities calculated. Payout languages work well with the Longstaff-Schwartz technique in the context of valuation and this carries straight across to XVA. A solution of this type has been developed by Cesari et al. (2009).

Payout languages are by their very nature interpreted and this can impose a significant penalty on performance. Nevertheless the ability to generate XVA for a new product in a matter of minutes or hours is a significant benefit. A particular payout can of course be later replaced by compiled code. Even if a payout can be created quickly, appropriate control and validation processes are still needed as the script will be released into a production environment and generate official P&L.

## 20.4.7 Distributed Computing and Parallelism

**The Importance of Parallelism to XVA** As is already abundantly clear, XVA metrics are computationally expensive to calculate. The only advantage the calculation has is that being based on Monte Carlo techniques it can be parallelised as was discussed in section 20.2.2. Hence it is essential that any XVA system can take advantage of the parallelism. This means breaking up the elements of the calculation that can be operated in parallel and distributing them across a grid. We can clearly identify a number of different ways that the calculation can be parallelised (these can be thought of as *axes* of parallelism):

- **Counterparties/Netting sets** – all counterparties are independent of each other and each netting set a given counterparty has is independent of all others. Hence the netting sets can be calculated in parallel.
- **Monte Carlo paths** – each Monte Carlo path is independent of all others and hence can be calculated in parallel. Some variance reduction techniques such as orthogonalisation described in section 18.3 introduce a dependence between the random samples used on

each path. Even in such circumstances only the pseudo-random samples have a dependence and the path itself and subsequent valuations can still be executed in parallel. In the context of the Longstaff-Schwartz approach all the results from the first simulation used to "calibrate" the regression function approximation are required. However, again the paths themselves may be run in parallel and only the regression phase cannot be executed in parallel. The smallest unit of parallel execution will be the single Monte Carlo path, however, it is likely to be more optimal to group more than one path together. The optimal choice of grouping will be determined in large part by the performance of the valuation models used for trades in a given netting set.

- **Trades** – each trade on a given path and at a given time step can be valued independently, once the Monte Carlo simulation has generated the required "state-of-the-world". This is a more difficult step to parallelise as it can only be separated after the Monte Carlo simulation has generated the required state variables. The Monte Carlo paths will almost certainly also be parallelised.
- **Time steps** – as was noted in section 20.2.2 the expected exposures at each time step are in fact independent of each other. The only dependence between time steps comes through trade events such as rate fixings, barrier observations and option exercises. If these are not present then the trade valuation at each time step can be parallelised. If trade events do create a dependence across time steps then the execution can still be parallelised if provision is made for the event processing. This may mean, for example, generating all the Monte Carlo states for all time steps prior to executing the trade valuation loop.

The choice of how to parallelise the calculation will depend on a number of factors:

- The choice of hardware
- The choice of model components (Monte Carlo and valuation models)
- The counterparty and trade population.

XVA has a very high dynamic range in the calculation. A small number of counterparties such as CCPs will have very large and diverse portfolios while typically there will also be a large number of small counterparties with very few or indeed just one trade. Whatever parallelism strategy is chosen it must be sufficiently flexible to cope with this range. Given the need for parallelism, any XVA system should be designed for parallel processing from the outset as it is difficult to add parallelism to a system at a later stage.

**Managing the Workflow** An XVA calculation consists of a series of sub-tasks some of which may be executed in parallel and some which must be operated sequentially as they rely on the results of an earlier step in the calculation. The *workflow* of the calculation can be described by a *flow graph*,[15] a diagram of all of the sub-tasks required to complete the calculation. The flow graph also shows the dependency relationships between tasks and hence which tasks must be operated sequentially. Tasks that can be operated in parallel are represented by the diagram spreading out to several parallel tasks, while reduction operations

---

[15]I would like to acknowledge the work of Dr Chris Dennis who alerted me to the use of flow graphs as both a design tool for parallel operation and as the basis for actual workflow management of XVA calculations.

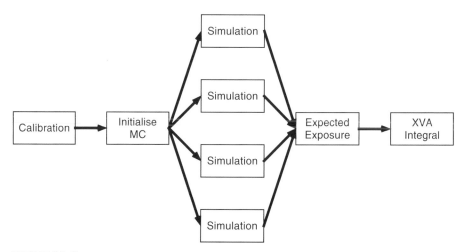

**FIGURE 20.9** A simplified flow graph describing the sub-tasks in an XVA calculation. The simulation has been divided up into four separate parallel tasks.

are represented by the reverse. An example of a flow graph for an XVA calculation is given in Figure 20.9.

Flow graphs provide a ready description of the work flow which is extremely useful as a design tool. However, flow graphs can be used directly as an operational tool to manage workflow. Each sub-task in the tree of tasks represents by the flow graph represents an atomic unit of calculation. These sub-tasks can be distributed across the compute grid. The dependencies between tasks determine the order of execution and which tasks can be executed in parallel. The flow graph also provides a useful means of debugging failing calculations as the problematic task can quickly be identified and executed in isolation.

**Tuning the Calculation** The high dynamic range of the XVA calculations typically leads to a wide range of execution times for tasks in the workflow. For a typical overnight batch there will be large numbers of small tasks with little computational requirement through to a small number of very computationally demanding tasks, with a range of intermediate tasks. Large tasks will lead to a long tail in the calculation, with the overall run-time dominated by the small number of long running tasks. Distributing tasks across a grid is not cost free and will lead to latency in the calculation. Hence the size of tasks should be large enough, that the latency introduced by distribution is not significant.

A parallel system will work better if the size of each execution block is relatively uniform and the size of each calculation is large relative to the size of the latency introduced by distribution. The four axes of parallelism described above give a number of mechanisms that can be used to divide large tasks up into smaller ones, while small tasks can always be combined to produce bigger ones. It is very unlikely that all of the parameters of a calculation will be known in advance and hence it will be necessary to tune the calculation when in operation to obtain the best overall execution time on the compute grid. Time must be allowed during the development phase to perform initial tuning of the calculation and the system must be sufficiently flexible that it can be tuned via the use of parameters to divide or combine tasks at run-time. Once the system is in operation, continual tuning will be required to retain an optimal execution profile.

## 20.5 CONCLUSION

This chapter has presented an overview of the implementation of the steps involved in the implementation of XVA systems and the key issues that arise in the implementation process. As such it concludes the discussion on models for XVA. However, the implications brought by XVA management and in particular the calculation of XVA sensitivities have not been discussed and so this is presented in the next part of the book on *Managing XVA*.

# Managing XVA

## CHAPTER 21

# Calculating XVA Sensitivities

*Audentis Fortuna iuuat*
Fortune favours the bold!

—Virgil
*The Aeneid*

## 21.1 XVA SENSITIVITIES

If XVA is managed actively then sensitivity calculations are essential. Even if XVA metrics just provide reserve numbers of accounting purposes it is highly likely that sensitivities will be required to allow daily P&L changes to be explained. This chapter presents two different approaches to calculating XVA sensitivities, *finite difference approximation* and *pathwise derivatives*. Finite difference approximation is of course the classical approach of shifting the input market data and revaluing, in this case recalculating the XVA metric in the shifted state. Pathwise derivatives calculate the sensitivities directly using Monte Carlo simulation and they are often implemented using *algorithmic differentiation (AD)*[1] in either *forward* or *backward* mode. The backward mode of algorithmic differentiation is also known as the *adjoint* mode and leads to the name *adjoint algorithmic differentiation*. The chapter concludes with a look at scenarios and stress testing with the latter becoming increasingly important for both internal book management and regulatory risk oversight.

### 21.1.1 Defining the Sensitivities

When we refer to sensitivities or "Greeks" we mean first or second order partial derivatives of the XVA metric in question with respect to an input, most often a piece of input market data but it could also be to a model parameter. Typically market data inputs will also be

---

[1] Sometimes known as *automatic differentiation*.

hedging instruments. For completeness and consistency of terminology it is useful to define the sensitivities. Hence for first order sensitivities we have

$$\text{first order} = \left. \frac{\partial \text{XVA}}{\partial a_i} \right|_{a_{j \neq i}} \tag{21.1}$$

where $a_i$ is the input for which we require the sensitivity and all the other market data inputs are held constant. Where $a_i$ is a piece of *linear* input market data such as a yield curve instrument or an FX rate then the first order sensitivity is commonly known as a *delta*. Where $a_i$ is a volatility input such as a European swaption implied volatility then the sensitivity is known as a *vega*. Normally individual sensitivities are packaged together to reflect any grouping of input market data so that, for example, an interest rate delta is usually the vector of partial derivatives with respect to all of the yield curve instruments. Given the hybrid nature of XVA the number of sensitivities in inevitably large even to first order.

We define second order sensitivities as the partial derivative with respect to two market data inputs, $a_i$ and $a_j$:

$$\text{second order} = \left. \frac{\partial^2 \text{XVA}}{\partial a_i \partial a_j} \right|_{a_{k \neq i,j}}. \tag{21.2}$$

When the market data inputs $a_i$ and $a_j$ are of the same type and are linear input market data the sensitivity is normally referred to as a *gamma*. So the interest rate gamma matrix is the set of partial derivatives where $a_i$ and $a_j$ correspond to all the input yield curve instruments. Sometimes only the *diagonal gamma* is calculated which is just the subset of partial derivatives for which $i = j$. Where $a_i$ and $a_j$ are different types of linear input market data, for example yield curve instruments and credit curve instruments, the resultant matrix of partial derivatives is known as *cross-gamma*. When one of the $a$'s is a volatility and the other is a linear market data input the second order sensitivity is known as *vanna* and when both of the $a$'s are volatility inputs are volatilities then the sensitivity is known as *volga*.

If we were to consider all the market data inputs as a vector $a_i$ then we could in theory calculate the full matrix of second order partial derivatives implied by that vector according to equation (21.2). In practice this is not done as many of the entries would be close to zero and of little use. Hence in most cases only a subset of recognised second order sensitivities is calculated. However, the hybrid nature of XVA means that there are still a large number of second order sensitivities that are important.

## 21.1.2 Jacobians and Hessians

In some circumstances it will be appropriate to calculate the sensitivities of XVA with respect to derived data rather than the input market data. As an example of this consider calculating vega for the Hull-White model described in section 16.3.2. The calibrated model will have a piecewise constant volatility,

$$\sigma(t) = \sigma_i \quad \text{for} \quad t_i < t < t_{i+1}, \tag{21.3}$$

and potentially derivatives could be calculated with respect to these parameters so that the following partial derivatives are obtained:

$$\frac{\partial \text{XVA}}{\partial \sigma_j}. \tag{21.4}$$

However, we would like to express this sensitivity in terms of the at-the-money European swaption implied volatilities used as the market data input, $\bar{\sigma}_i$. These will be the most liquid instruments for hedging purposes and the points that will most often be used in a P&L explain. To do this we apply the chain rule to obtain

$$\frac{\partial \text{XVA}}{\partial \bar{\sigma}_i} = \sum_j \frac{\partial \text{XVA}}{\partial \sigma_j} \frac{\partial \sigma_j}{\partial \bar{\sigma}_i} \tag{21.5}$$

and we recognise the (calibration) *Jacobian* matrix

$$J_{ij} = \frac{\partial \sigma_j}{\partial \bar{\sigma}_i}. \tag{21.6}$$

For the second order derivatives where market data inputs are labelled $\bar{a}_i$ and the derived parameters $a_l$ we have

$$\frac{\partial^2 \text{XVA}}{\partial \bar{a}_i \partial \bar{a}_j} = \sum_k \frac{\partial \text{XVA}}{\partial a_k} \frac{\partial^2 a_k}{\partial \bar{a}_i \partial \bar{a}_j} + \sum_{k,l} \frac{\partial^2 \text{XVA}}{\partial a_k \partial a_l} \frac{\partial a_k}{\partial \bar{a}_i} \frac{\partial a_l}{\partial \bar{a}_j} \tag{21.7}$$

$$= \sum_k \frac{\partial \text{XVA}}{\partial a_k} H_{ij}^k + \sum_{k,l} \frac{\partial^2 \text{XVA}}{\partial a_k \partial a_l} J_{ki} J_{lj}$$

where

$$H_{ij}^k = \frac{\partial^2 a_k}{\partial \bar{a}_i \bar{a}_j} \tag{21.8}$$

is the *Hessian* matrix.

## 21.1.3 Theta, Time Decay and Carry

XVA is time sensitive:

- If the counterparty does not default between today and tomorrow, then UCVA and the counterparty term in BCVA will reduce assuming all other elements remain constant and assuming no cash flows occur. This is because the cumulative probability of counterparty default during the lifetime of the derivative will have reduced.
- If the issuer does not default between today and tomorrow then under bilateral CVA models the DVA term will be reduced and hence the overall CVA number will increase.
- All the XVA metrics involve a max function and hence are types of (compound) option. The effective option is one day closer to expiry and hence the optionality is subject to time decay.

- If a day passes less funding will be required overall so FVA cost will fall but so will FVA benefit.
- One day's capital cost will have been paid to shareholders and hence KVA will fall.

Mathematically we express this sensitivity as *theta*

$$\theta = \frac{\partial \text{XVA}}{\partial t}. \tag{21.9}$$

In practice the time effect is known by a number of names including *theta*, *time decay* and *carry*.[2] Any explain process must account for theta as it can be a large effect, particularly for distressed counterparties with a high probability of default. In such cases the fact that the distressed counterparty did not default can have a significant positive impact on the CVA.

Theta is often calculated directly by finite difference approximation over a period of one business day. This gives the actual theta impact to feed into the P&L explain. In some cases the effect of theta may be split into several pieces, and in particular we may wish to separate out model effects that come from the partitioning of the XVA integral.

### Model Effects on Theta

**Coupon carry**    In section 17.2.1 I noted the impact of the choice of time steps for the time partitioning of the XVA integral on theta. If a tenor-based date schedule is used then the dates on which the time steps fall will change from one day to the next. Such a schedule interacts with the cash flow and event dates of the instruments in the portfolio. The impact of the cash flow will be included in a given exposure tenor until the tenor falls on the same date as the cash flow and then the cash flow will fall out of one expected exposure point and into the previous one. We can see this illustrated in Figure 21.1.

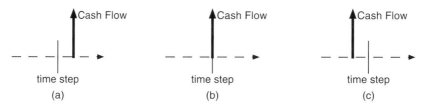

**FIGURE 21.1**    The interaction between a tenor-based time partition and cash flows when calculating expected exposures is illustrated in the three diagrams, (a), (b) and (c). In case (a) the cash flow occurs one business day after the exposure date so that the expected exposure at *time step* includes the effect of the cash flow. In case (b) the cash flow occurs on the same business date as the time step and so will be included if the model includes *cash-on-the-day* in the trade valuation. Finally in case (c), one day further on, the tenor-based time step has rolled across the cash flow meaning it is no longer included and the exposure will drop.

---

[2]The different names for the time effect come from different sub-disciplines within derivatives so *theta* and *time decay* are closely associated with option trading, while carry is associated with linear products such as interest rate swaps and CDS.

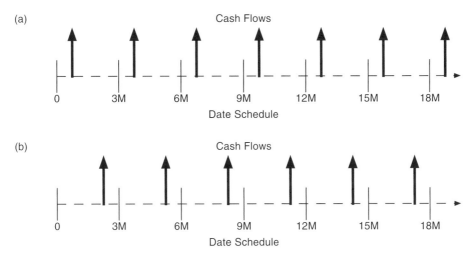

**FIGURE 21.2**   The interaction between a tenor-based time partition and regular cash flows is illustrated in (a) and (b). Case (b) shows that the tenor-based schedule rolls across all the regular cash flows on the same date.

For a single cash flow this effect is not that pronounced. However, if a regular tenor-based schedule is used for portfolios of instruments with regular cash flows then this effect can occur for all cash flows of a given trade at the same time. Consider an interest rate swap with quarterly cash flows being used with a tenor-based date schedule that is also quarterly. Every three months all the tenor points in the schedule will roll across the corresponding cash flow dates leading to a drop in expected exposure across the whole profile. This effect is illustrated in Figure 21.2.

The effect of the behaviour is to give a large drop in expected exposure on all tenor points on the day after the tenor dates have rolled across the cash flow dates. On subsequent dates the effect will slowly unwind as the tenor dates get closer to the cash flows again. This gives a significant theta effect where there is a large positive carry on the day after the roll over and then a slow negative carry as it unwinds. The size of this effect can be large and will likely dwarf the real day-on-day carry on the book. Furthermore, many counterparties seek to align the cash flow dates of multiple trades within a portfolio and to align these cash flows with year end, quarter end or month end. This means that the biggest *coupon carry* impact will be seen at year end, with smaller effects at quarter and month ends.

To counteract this issue there are two possible solutions. One is to adopt a date-based schedule rather than a tenor-based one as was discussed in section 17.2.1. The second is to introduce a specific theta scenario to isolate the tenor effect. This can be done by calculating the XVA on two schedules, based on the dates that would be generated on either the previous or next business date, but holding everything else constant. The XVA difference between the two scenarios allows the size of the tenor effect to be estimated.

**Changing random numbers**   In order to obtain stable sensitivities by finite difference approximation, the recommendation is to use common random numbers in the base and shifted states. When the valuation date used to calculate XVA is changed, as is inevitable from one day to the next, the random numbers used by each path may change. For example consider the use of a fixed date schedule where all the cash flow dates in a portfolio have a simulation date associated with them. If a cash flow or event date rolls off the front of the schedule as a time moves forward then the number of remaining dates in the time partition will fall by one. This means that to generate each path in the simulation, fewer random numbers will be needed. If the random numbers for each path are drawn sequentially from the random number generator this means that the sequence of random numbers will be used in a different order, leading to changes in each Monte Carlo path. Hence the paths used from one day to the next will be quite different and this can lead to a change in the XVA on the order of the calculation standard error. Other changes such as the addition of a new trade of longer maturity or the cancellation of the longest maturity trade in the portfolio give rise to the same effect.

The only way to fully counteract this effect would be to use a fixed alignment between dates in the time partition and the random numbers used. When a date rolled off the random numbers associated with generating path information for that date would be generated but remain unused in the Monte Carlo. However, this would be complex to implement. The impact of the change of random number order is fully captured by the two schedule scenarios discussed above, which serves to measure the Monte Carlo "noise" associated with it.

**The CDS Roll Date**    A CDS curve will change as market quotes for the curve constituents change. However, because the end dates of the CDS contracts are fixed between roll dates the knot points in the underlying hazard rate curve only change on the CDS market roll date. As was noted in Chapter 4 the market convention for the CDS market is for each CDS to end on the 20th of the IMM month. Hence on the 20th of the IMM month the end date of each new contract rolls forward to the new end date. The hazard rate knot points change on this date and this can lead to discontinuities in the implied probabilities of default on this date because:

▪ The spreads are rolled forward and not the underlying survival probability curve.
▪ The standard credit curve model uses piecewise constant hazard rates with node points on the CDS contract end dates. On the CDS roll date the hazard rate segments all change length. Of course other credit curve models will behave differently but the piecewise constant hazard rate curve is the most common.

It may be useful for XVA trading desks to separate the effect of the CDS roll from changes in the CDS spread on the roll date. This can be done using two credit curves on this date during the explain process. XVA would be calculated using each curve in succession to explain the move in terms of date change and spread move. If the XVA models assume independence of credit and market, then there is no need to re-simulate as the exposure profiles can be re-used.

Here are two alternative approaches:

1. Roll date, hold spreads:
   ▪ Curve 1: Hold the CDS spreads constant and roll the contract end dates forward to the new IMM month.
   ▪ Curve 2: Shift CDS spreads to new values (using the new contract end date).
2. Hold hazard rates constant, imply new spreads:
   ▪ Curve 1: Hold the hazard rates constant and imply CDS spreads for contracts with the new dates. Construct a new credit curve with the new end dates from these spreads.
   ▪ Curve 2: Shift CDS spreads to new values (using the new contract end date).

Of the two approaches the second is more technically correct as it implies the first set of CDS spreads by assuming the hazard rates remain constant. This allows the isolation of the change due to change of knot points from that due to change of spreads.

**Carry, Warehousing and Rebates**   The credit element of CVA theta is often of particular interest in XVA management, that is the positive (and negative) carry associated with the fact that the counterparty (and the bank) did not default from one day to the next. This can be separated from other sources of theta such as pure interest rate discounting or a pure funding curve. Considering first unilateral CVA models, if the CVA is full hedged with CDS then the positive carry on the CVA will be offset by the negative carry on the CDS hedge. In the case of bilateral CVA models the same would be true if both CVA and DVA were hedged, that is the positive CVA term carry would be offset by the negative carry on the counterparty CDS hedge, while the negative carry on the DVA term would be offset by positive carry on the hedge. As discussed, however, it is impossible to directly hedge the DVA and so it is inevitable that there will be net carry arising from the DVA term. If the DVA is included in accounts and remains unhedged then this will lead to a constant negative carry and P&L "bleed" from the CVA book. If the DVA is hedged with proxies then there will be a mismatch between the DVA carry and hedge carry that reflects the basis risk associated with the hedge. Consider the basis risk that would have arisen from hedging DVA with a basket of names including Lehman brothers during the run up to their eventual default.

Clearly in many cases the CVA itself is not fully hedged with the risk being either warehoused or hedged with proxies. As has already been seen, the market for available CDS is limited and the bulk of any bank portfolio will not have single name CDS available for hedging. Some institutions may choose to warehouse the CVA credit risk and in this case the CVA book will see a net positive carry as long as a counterparty does not default. KVA is also an element in decisions around risk warehousing as the choice to warehouse CVA credit risk implies a higher capital requirement through CVA capital.[3]

It is still likely that the XVA desk will hedge the non-credit risks associated with the CVA. In such circumstances the sales teams that originated a particular transaction may still be charged for CVA as an up-front fee by the XVA desk. However, this CVA may be returned to the sales desk over time as a *rebate* if the counterparty does not default. Internal pricing and fee structures are discussed in more detail in section 22.6.

### 21.1.4   The Explain

A P&L explain is required by XVA just as it is for every other trading function. Even if XVA is not actively managed it is still likely that some form of P&L explain will be needed to allow management to understand why changes in an XVA reserve have occurred. The explain will need to provide information on what caused the movement in P&L and it is important to note that could be any input to the XVA calculation, including:

- Market data including CDS spreads, yield curves, FX rates, etc.
- Counterparty data including credit ratings
- Collateral information
- Trade data – new trades/amendments/cancellations.

Changes in the non-market data inputs can have just as significant an impact on XVA as market data changes. For example, if a CSA were signed with the counterparty, it would be desirable to confirm that the expected reduction in XVA had occurred. The explain process

---

[3]A full discussion of the impact of risk warehousing can be found in section 14.4.

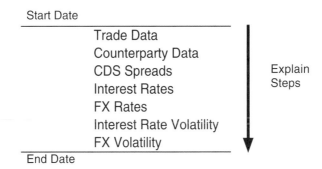

**FIGURE 21.3**   An example step-wise explain for a
counterparty portfolio with interest rate and FX products.

could, in theory, apply across any time period, although in practice from one business day to
the next is the most likely period.

**Step-wise Explain**   The simplest form of explain is one that is based on a series of steps in
which the inputs are steadily changed from the start date of the explain to the end date of the
explain. The advantage of this approach is that a complete explain is guaranteed so there is
no *unexplained* P&L. On the start date all the start date input data is used and on the final step
all the end date data is used with the steps in between steadily accumulating the difference in
P&L. A full revaluation is required at each step, although only steps that change inputs to the
Monte Carlo actually require re-simulation. While a number of revaluations are needed this
is generally small compared to those that are used by finite-difference approximations to risk
sensitivities.

   This disadvantage of this approach is that while it assigns P&L changes to the various
factors it does not give much information on cross-risks. So, for example, if in the explain
process the credit spreads were moved before the interest rates, the cross credit-interest rate
risk would appear in both steps and could not be separated. The process does not actually
use any traditional sensitivities and so the XVA trading desk will still need to calculate these
separately. An example ordering of such a step-wise explain is given in Figure 21.3; however,
the choice of step ordering is entirely up to the choice of the organisation and in theory any
permutation could be used.

**Risk-based Explain**   The classic risk-based explain is based on the Taylor expansion. So if
the XVA metric has a series of market data inputs, $x_i$, then the difference between the XVA at
times $t_1$ and $t_2$ is explained using

$$\text{XVA}(t_2) = \text{XVA}(t_1) + \frac{\partial \text{XVA}}{\partial t}\bigg|_{t_1} \Delta t + \sum_i \frac{\partial \text{XVA}}{\partial x_i}\bigg|_{t_1} \Delta x_i + \frac{1}{2} \sum_i \sum_j \frac{\partial^2 \text{XVA}}{\partial x_i \partial x_j}\bigg|_{t_1} \Delta x_i \Delta x_j + \epsilon,$$

(21.10)

where the series includes terms to second order and $\epsilon$ is the *unexplained*.[4]

---

[4]Equation (21.10) could equally be defined with sensitivities calculated at time $t_2$ and project backwards
to time $t_1$.

The risk-based explain is accurate to the limit that Taylor's expansion is accurate. In P&L explains the Taylor expansion is typically truncated at second order and even then not all of the partial derivatives in the second order matrix will normally be included (as was noted earlier in section 21.1.1). Taylor's approximation is always better closer to the initial state, $t_1, x_i$, and so the explain will perform better over small market data shifts that large ones. The residual error term, $\epsilon$, represents the change that cannot be explained through the sensitivities.

The risk-based explain has the major advantage that it is much more granular than a step-wise explain. Each risk sensitivity provides an element of the explain. The sensitivities themselves will also be used by the XVA trading desk to risk manage the book and as a means to determine the required notional of any hedge trades. In general the sensitivities will be taken with respect to hedging instruments. A risk-based explain does require a considerable number of sensitivities to be calculated and this can be computationally expensive, particularly if finite difference approximation is used (see section 21.2). It also does not explain changes to inputs that have no sensitivities associated with them such as discrete counterparty credit ratings which change in steps. Hence in practice some element of step-wise explain will be required to assess the impact of such changes.

As was discussed above, theta is often subject to special considerations in XVA explains. Theta is also most often estimated through finite difference approximation and it can also be quite difficult to separate out the components. With this in mind a specific hybrid of step-wise and risk-based explains can be useful, the *orthogonal explain*.

**Orthogonal Explain**   In the orthogonal explain theta and non-market data inputs are split from the market data inputs, with the former subject to a step-wise explain and the latter subject to an intraday risk-based explain. This has the advantage that theta/carry effects are cleanly separated from the risk explain. The explain proceeds initially using a step-wise approach, with a full revaluation at each step,

1. Model effects (i.e. shift the simulation schedule – see section 21.1.3)
2. Counterparty data including credit ratings
3. Collateral information
4. Trade data – new trades/amendments/cancellations
5. Roll value date to start of next business day. Roll market data start date but hold input rates at existing values.

The last step in this sequence involves rolling the market data inputs to the start of the next business day but holding all the previous close of day values constant. This process is essentially creating a start-of-business-day data set assuming that all inputs initially take their values from the previous market close. Combined together the steps give a breakdown of the components of the theta. In fact the last step could be broken down into more segments if desired.

With the input data and value date rolled to the start of the business day, market movements between the start and close are explained using a risk-based explain, using

$$\text{XVA}(t_2^{\text{end}}) = \text{XVA}(t_2^{\text{start}}) + \sum_i \frac{\partial \text{XVA}}{\partial x_i}\bigg|_{t_2^{\text{start}}} \Delta x_i + \frac{1}{2}\sum_i \sum_j \frac{\partial^2 \text{XVA}}{\partial x_i \partial x_j}\bigg|_{t_2^{\text{start}}} \Delta x_i \Delta x_j + \epsilon. \quad (21.11)$$

There is no partial derivative with respect to time as in effect the model assumes that all the market data changes between start and end of day occur instantaneously.

## 21.2  FINITE DIFFERENCE APPROXIMATION

The standard approach to estimating sensitivities in finance has been finite difference approximation. While simple models such as Black-Scholes have analytic derivatives available, in general this has not been the case for more complex models, particularly those that involve numerical techniques such as PDEs or Monte Carlo. Prior to the introduction of techniques such as algorithmic differentiation finite difference approximation was often the only viable approach.

### 21.2.1  Estimating Sensitivities

There are three ways of approximating a first order derivative, *forward*, *backward* and *central* differences. If the market data input in question is $x$ and the shift size is $h$, these are given by

$$
\text{forward} \quad \frac{\partial \text{XVA}}{\partial x} \approx \frac{\text{XVA}(x + h) - \text{XVA}(x)}{h} \tag{21.12}
$$

$$
\text{backward} \quad \frac{\partial \text{XVA}}{\partial x} \approx \frac{\text{XVA}(x) - \text{XVA}(x - h)}{h} \tag{21.13}
$$

$$
\text{central} \quad \frac{\partial \text{XVA}}{\partial x} \approx \frac{\text{XVA}(x + h) - \text{XVA}(x - h)}{2h}. \tag{21.14}
$$

The obvious advantage of the *forward* and *backward* approximations is that they only require one additional XVA calculation over the baseline, while the central difference requires two. However, the accuracy of the estimated derivative is an important consideration. Given that XVA is calculated by Monte Carlo simulation the convergence of the estimator to the actual derivative as a function of the number of simulation paths is a significant element in the overall consideration of performance. Furthermore, care must be taken when choosing the size of the shift, $h$. Elementary considerations from calculus suggest that $h$ should be relatively small, while considerations of machine precision place limits on how small $h$ can be while retaining sufficient precision in floating point calculations. Glasserman (2004) demonstrates that the convergence rate of forward and backward differences is $O(n^{-1/4})$, where $n$ is the number of simulation paths, when the two simulations are independent, while the central difference converges faster as $O(n^{-1/3})$. Furthermore, Glasserman (2004) also shows that the bias and variance of the finite difference estimator is affected by the choice of $h$. The bias increases as $h$ increases but the variance decreases as $h$ increases, pointing to an optimal choice of $h$. In practice the choice of $h$ will usually be fixed after appropriate testing of the finite difference approximation as a function of $h$ and the number of paths. $h$ could be specified on a relative or absolute basis, with a relative shift adapting to different market data regimes but meaning that the actual size used each day changes.

The second order derivatives can be approximated as follows:

$$\frac{\partial^2 \text{XVA}(x, y)}{\partial x^2} \approx \frac{\text{XVA}(x + h, y) - 2\text{XVA}(x, y) + \text{XVA}(x - h, y)}{h^2} \tag{21.15}$$

$$\frac{\partial^2 \text{XVA}(x, y)}{\partial x \partial y} \approx \frac{1}{4hk} \Big( \text{XVA}(x + h, y + k) - \text{XVA}(x + h, y - k) \tag{21.16}$$

$$- \text{XVA}(x - h, y + k) + \text{XVA}(x - h, y - k) \Big)$$

These are central difference schemes and the most commonly used to calculate second order sensitivities. Other second order schemes are possible including forward and backward schemes and higher order schemes that use additional shifts for greater accuracy. Given the number of shifts required second order sensitivities are expensive to calculate. In the context of XVA this can often mean that the second order sensitivities are too expensive to calculate, at least at a fully granular level.

**Common Random Numbers**  Intuitively, the use of common random numbers between the Monte Carlo simulations used in a finite difference approximation will lead to lower variance than if different sets of random numbers were to be used. If common random numbers are used then each individual path with a shifted input will be very similar to the unshifted path leading to smooth and accurate sensitivities. The intuitive understanding is also confirmed in theory as Glasserman (2004) demonstrates. Common random numbers increase the rate of convergence to $O(n^{-1/3})$ for the forward and backward difference approximations and to $O(n^{-2/5})$ for the central difference approximation.

### 21.2.2   Recalibration?

A further question to ask in the context of finite difference approximation is whether or not to recalibrate the model with the shifted market data. So for example, if the yield curve instruments were shifted to calculate the Interest Rate Delta, the model calibration to interest rate implied option volatility, would either be held constant or a recalibration would be triggered. Of course if the shift is unrelated to the calibration in question, re-calibrating or not re-calibrating will have no impact. If recalibration is performed then there is often a choice to be made as to which calibration inputs are changed. In the interest rate case, the recalibration when the yield curve was shift could involve either keeping the at-the-money option volatilities constant and recalibrating in response to the yield curve or using new implied volatilities consistent with a new at-the-money point given by the shifted yield curve.

From a technical perspective, the sensitivities are partial derivatives and so the variables that are not being shifted should be held constant. This argues in favour of holding the volatility calibration constant across a market data shift. However, in practice a better explain may result from risk with re-calibration, although this would result in sensitivities that are not pure partial derivatives.

## 21.2.3    Exercise Boundaries and Sensitivities

**Longstaff-Schwartz**    Recall the Longstaff-Schwartz regression approach that has been applied both in the context of MVA (Chapter 10) and trade valuation (Chapter 19). The algorithm consists of two Monte Carlo simulations, with the first being used to generate a regression approximation and the second to apply the regression approximation to give trade and portfolio values. In the original context of trade valuation, Longstaff and Schwartz (2001) applied regression to obtain the exercise boundary of Bermudan and American callable trades. Piterbarg (2003a) argues in favour of the re-use of the exercise boundary obtained in the first half of the algorithm when calculating sensitivities by finite difference approximation. That is, Piterbarg argues that the exercise boundary should be estimated once and then used in the multiple subsequent simulations used to estimate sensitivities, leading to much smoother results.

In XVA, the Longstaff-Schwartz regression function is used to give a full value, not just to determine the exercise boundary. Nevertheless, there remains a decision to be made whether the coefficients of the regression functions should be held constant across a finite difference "bump". In practice which is the best approach seems to depend on the details of the payout and the dynamics. Recalibrating the Longstaff-Schwartz approximation in the "bumped" state will increase accuracy as the revised regression function will give a more accurate price. However, the regression process introduces numerical noise. Hence it is appropriate to test the behaviour of each product and decide whether or not the regression should be held across the shift or not.

**Differential Exercise**    In XVA, uniquely, we also need to choose whether or not an *exercise decision* is held constant across a market data shift applied to estimate sensitivities by finite difference. As each Monte Carlo path is walked down during the simulation, trade events are processed, including option exercises. If a shift is applied to the market data this can affect the locations where exercises occur along individual Monte Carlo paths. Technically this is absolutely the correct and expected behaviour. However, this *differential exercise* can lead path level results to vary considerably between the simulations that are used to estimate the sensitivity. This variation in path level results can be thought of as destroying the smoothness introduced by the use of common random numbers in section 21.2.1. This is illustrated in Figure 21.4.

This effect can add considerable noise to the simulation and is a particular problem with Bermudan swaptions, given the number of exercises and the typical length of the trades. There are essentially two ways to deal with the numerical noise:

- Increase the number of paths. This will overcome the noise through better statistics, although a significant number of paths may be needed to obtain the desired convergence for the sensitivities.
- Hold the exercise decisions constant across the bump. This is of course technically incorrect and will introduce a small bias into the results. However, the bias is typically small compared with the noise that would otherwise be introduced.

The second approach is more computationally efficient. In practice it means that during the baseline XVA simulation the location where each trade exercises must be recorded and

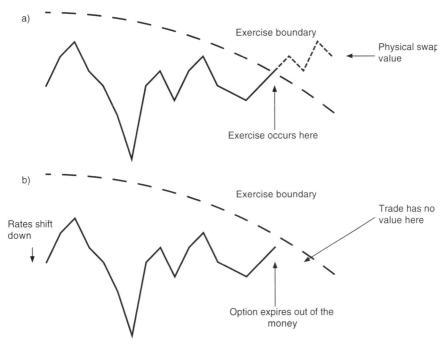

**FIGURE 21.4** An example of *differential exercise* occurring in an XVA Monte Carlo simulation. In case (a) the option exercises at the time step indicated into an interest swap giving value on this path at subsequent time steps. In case (b) interest rates have been shifted down, although as common random numbers have been used, the path retains the original shape. However, exercise no longer occurs and the option expires out of the money. Hence the later steps have no value. The results for the two paths are considerably different adding significant noise to the simulation.

then when a bumped simulation is run, the options will exercise in the recorded locations, irrespective of whether or not this remains optimal.

## 21.3 PATHWISE DERIVATIVES AND ALGORITHMIC DIFFERENTIATION

Both pathwise derivatives and algorithmic differentiation provide sensitivities by direct simulation rather than by finite difference approximation. A simple way to explain the difference between the two is that the pathwise derivatives are generated by differentiating the equations while algorithmic differentiation differentiates the computer code.

Broadie and Glasserman (1996) described two approaches to estimate sensitivities directly by Monte Carlo simulation techniques, the *pathwise method* and the *likelihood method*. The use of simulation rather than finite difference approximation has the obvious advantage that repeated Monte Carlo simulation is not required and hence presents the potential for massive performance improvement versus finite difference approximation. Prior to the paper by Broadie and Glasserman (1996) the use of such techniques was almost unknown in finance, except for earlier works by and Fu and Hu (1995). However, sensitivity analysis by perturbative techniques were well known in other disciplines such as queuing theory (Glasserman, 1991) and stochastic optimisation (Rubinstein, 1993).

The problem with such techniques is that they are not generic and require a degree of analytic development for each new model and/or payoff. As such they require careful mathematics, which is time consuming, and then specific code to be implemented. In some cases the analytic work can prove intractable. However, the introduction of *algorithmic differentiation* has changed this significantly, as it provides a generic technique that can be applied to practically all models and payouts. Algorithmic differentiation still requires a significant investment, and in particular is difficult to "retrofit" onto an existing analytics library. Nevertheless, there is significant take up of this approach and this had led to articles suggesting that advanced hardware such as GPUs is not required by derivative models (Sheriff, 2015). Hence section 21.3.3 presents an overview of algorithmic differentiation. However, algorithmic differentiation does have some deficiencies, and in particular can be memory intensive. *Hybrid approaches* provide an alternative and are described in section 21.3.4.

### 21.3.1   Preliminaries: The Pathwise Method

Given a vector-valued stochastic process,

$$dX(t) = a(t, X(t))dt + b(t, X(t))dW(t), \tag{21.17}$$

where $X$ is $m$-dimensional, $a$ is an $m$-dimensional vector, $W(t)$ is a $d$-dimensional Brownian motion and $b$ is an $m \times d$-dimensional matrix, the value of a derivative is given by the expected value of a function of this stochastic process,

$$V = \mathbb{E}\left[g(X(t))\right]. \tag{21.18}$$

The first order sensitivities of this derivative value with respect to the inputs to this process are given by

$$\frac{\partial V}{\partial X_j(t_0)} = \frac{\partial}{\partial X_j(t_0)}\left(\mathbb{E}\left[g(X(t))\right]\right). \tag{21.19}$$

The *pathwise method* (Broadie and Glasserman, 1996; Glasserman, 2004; Giles and Glasserman, 2006) estimates this sensitivity using

$$\mathbb{E}\left[\frac{\partial g(X(t))}{\partial X_j(t_0)}\right], \tag{21.20}$$

which is an unbiased estimator if certain conditions, described below, are met. Hence the pathwise method can estimate the sensitivities using Monte Carlo simulation by evaluating $\frac{\partial g(X(t))}{\partial X_j(t_0)}$ on each path, alongside the original payout function $g(X(t))$.

The conditions under which equation (21.20) is an unbiased estimator of equation (21.19) are as follows (Broadie and Glasserman, 1996; Glasserman, 2004). These are mild conditions on the smoothness of the payout function and on the behaviour of the evolution of the stochastic process. Suppose that the state vector $X$ is a function of a scalar parameter $\theta$ which ranges over an open interval $\Theta$ such that each component of $X$ is a random function on $\Theta$. The four conditions are:

1. At each $\theta \in \Theta$,

$$X'_i \equiv \lim_{h \to 0} \frac{X_i(\theta + h) - X_i(\theta)}{h}$$

exists with probability 1.

2. If $D_g$ is the set of points at which $g$ is differentiable, then

$$P(X(\theta) \in D_g) = 1, \quad \text{for all} \quad \theta \in \Theta.$$

This ensures the existence of the pathways derivative.

3. The function $g$ must satisfy the Lipschitz smoothness condition, that is there exists a constant $k$ such that for all $x, y \in \mathbb{R}^m$

$$|g(x) - g(y)| \le k\|x - y\|.$$

4. There exist random variables $K_i$ for $i = 1, 2, \ldots$, such that

$$\|X_i(\theta_2) - X_i(\theta_1)\| \le K_i|\theta_2 - \theta_1|,$$

for all $i$ and for all $\theta_1, \theta_2 \in \Theta$, where for each $i$, $\mathbb{E}[K_i] < \infty$.

Not all payouts satisfy these conditions, and in particular while the standard call does, despite the discontinuity at $X(T) = K$, the digital payout does not. Nevertheless, even in such cases payout smoothing can be applied (see for example Chen and Glasserman, 2008; Joshi and Kainth, 2004).

The partial derivative of the payout function is given by application of the chain rule,

$$\frac{\partial g(X(T))}{\partial X_j(t_0)} = \sum_{i=1}^{m} \frac{\partial g(X(T))}{\partial X_i(T)} \frac{\partial X_i(T)}{\partial X_j(t_0)}. \tag{21.21}$$

As an example, consider a simple European call option on a stock that follows geometric Brownian motion,

$$g(S(T)) = \max(S(T) - K, 0) \tag{21.22}$$

$$S(T) = S(0) \exp\left(rT - \frac{\sigma^2}{2}T + \sigma\sqrt{T}z_i\right) \tag{21.23}$$

where $z_i \sim N(0, 1)$. The delta of the payout is given by

$$\frac{\partial g(S(T))}{\partial S(0)} = \frac{\partial g(S(T))}{\partial S(T)} \frac{\partial S(T)}{\partial S(0)} \tag{21.24}$$

$$= \mathbb{1}_{\{S(T)>K\}} \times \exp\left(rT - \frac{\sigma^2}{2}T + \sigma\sqrt{T}z_i\right),$$

which is then calculated in the Monte Carlo simulation.

## 21.3.2  Adjoints

As Giles and Glasserman (2006) make clear, the pathways method described above can be represented in terms of *adjoints*. Consider first the discrete Monte Carlo implementation of the stochastic process in equation (21.17) using the Euler discretisation scheme,

$$X(t_{n+1}) = X(t_n) + a(X(t_n))\Delta t_n + b(X(t_n))\sqrt{\Delta t_n}z(t_{n+1}), \tag{21.25}$$

where $X(t_0)$ are the initial asset values, $\Delta t_n = t_{n+1} - t_n$ and $z(t_{n+1})$ is a vector of standard normal samples. To generate the samples at the payout maturity $T = t_N$ requires $N$ iterations of equation (21.25).

Writing the Jacobian matrix in equation (21.21) as

$$J_{ij}(t_N) = \frac{\partial X_i(t_N)}{\partial X_j(t_0)} \tag{21.26}$$

allows the pathwise estimator to be written as

$$\frac{\partial g(X(t_N))}{\partial X_j(t_0)} = \sum_{i=1}^{m} \frac{\partial g(X(t_N))}{\partial X_i(t_N)} J_{ij}(t_N). \tag{21.27}$$

To make the next steps clearer it is easier to consider a single component of the vector process,

$$X_i(t_{n+1}) = X_i(t_n) + a_i(X_1(t_n), \dots, X_m(t_n))\Delta t_n \tag{21.28}$$

$$+ \sum_{l=1}^{d} b_{li}(X_1(t_n), \dots, X_m(t_n))\sqrt{\Delta t_n}z_{li}(t_{n+1}).$$

Differentiating this expression gives a recursion for the Jacobian matrix, $J_{ij}(t_n)$,

$$J_{ij}(t_{n+1}) = J_{ij}(t_n) + \sum_{k=1}^{m} \frac{\partial a_i}{\partial X_k(t_n)} J_{kj}(t_n)\Delta t_n \tag{21.29}$$

$$+ \sum_{l=1}^{d} \sum_{k=1}^{m} \frac{\partial b_{li}}{\partial X_k(t_n)} J_{kj}(t_n)\sqrt{\Delta t_n}z_{li}(t_{n+1}).$$

Defining the matrix $D(t_n)$ by

$$D_{ik}(t_n) = \delta_{ik} + \frac{\partial a_i}{\partial X_k(t_n)} \Delta t_n + \sum_{l=1}^{d} \frac{\partial b_{li}}{\partial X_k(t_n)} \sqrt{\Delta t_n} z_{li}(t_{n+1}), \tag{21.30}$$

where $\delta_{ik}$ equals 1 for $i = k$ and is zero otherwise, allows the recursion to be written as a matrix

$$J(t_{n+1}) = D(t_n)J(t_n). \tag{21.31}$$

It is now clear that the pathwise delta estimate in equation (21.21) can be written as

$$\begin{aligned}
\frac{\partial g(X(t_N))}{\partial X(t_0)} &= \frac{\partial g(X(t_N))}{\partial X(t_N)} J(t_N) \\
&= \frac{\partial g(X(t_N))}{\partial X(t_N)} D(t_{N-1})D(t_{N-2}) \dots D(t_0)J(t_0).
\end{aligned} \tag{21.32}$$

The advantage of this representation is that the payout $g$ is separate from the Jacobian recursion, so that the same matrices $D$ can be applied to multiple payouts, once they have been derived. However, this approach is relatively expensive computationally as this is a matrix relation and requires $m^2$ variables to be updated every time step. This is known as the *forward* calculation.

The matrix recursion can be re-written as

$$\frac{\partial g(X(t_N))}{\partial X(t_0)} = V(t_0)^T J(t_0), \tag{21.33}$$

where the vector $V$ is defined by

$$V(t_n) = D(t_n)^T V(t_{n+1}), \tag{21.34}$$

and

$$V(t_N) = \left( \frac{\partial g(X(t_n))}{\partial X(t_N)} \right)^T. \tag{21.35}$$

This recursion operates backwards and requires the payout sensitivities as an input. The Monte Carlo simulation will be run forward to generate the payout and payout derivative before the backward recursion will be run to estimate the sensitivities. Hence this approach is known as the *backward* or *adjoint* approach. Because the relation (21.34) involves the $m$-dimensional adjoint vectors $V$, only $m$ variables need be updated at each step, which can involve considerably less effort than the forward mode. However, this can only be done for each payout in turn and so the adjoint mode is best suited to obtaining large number of sensitivities for a single payout. In addition the elements of the matrices $D$ need to be stored during the forward Monte Carlo sweep for later use in the backward adjoint sweep. This can lead to considerable storage requirements. If the Monte Carlo simulation is being run sequentially, one path at a time, then this is less of an issue as only the adjoint variables for the current path need be stored. However, if the Monte Carlo is being run in parallel using a GPU, for example, then all the adjoints for all paths will need to be stored, potentially leading to memory limitations. One potential solution to this problem would be to store only those elements that are computationally expensive during the forward sweep and then recalculate anything straightforward during the backward sweep. A further alternative, hybrid approaches, is discussed below.

Each XVA is a single "payout" function and a large number of potential sensitivities are required so the adjoint approach is the most appropriate and could, potentially, lead to massive computational savings. The adjoint approach has been successfully applied in the context of CVA by Capriotti and Lee (2014) and Andreasen (2014).

### 21.3.3  Adjoint Algorithmic Differentiation

The adjoint method is in fact an example of a broader class of techniques known as *algorithmic differentiation* or sometimes as *automatic differentiation*. These methods were developed to calculate the derivatives of functions defined as computer programs. The adjoint method is therefore known as *adjoint algorithmic differentiation (AAD)*. The application of these methods is therefore far wider than just Monte Carlo simulation.

Following the approach of Capriotti and Giles (2012) it is easy to see how the adjoint method can be defined generally. Consider a computer program that implements the mapping of an $n$-dimensional input vector $X$ to an $m$-dimensional output vector $Y$,

$$Y = f(X), \tag{21.36}$$

where the function $f$ is a computer program. The computer program implements this function as a series of steps and these could be considered anything from high-level functions down to individual instructions on the processor, so that

$$X \rightarrow \ldots \rightarrow U \rightarrow V \rightarrow \ldots \rightarrow Y,$$

where $U$ and $V$ are intermediate variables. To calculate the sensitivities of the vector $Y$ with respect to $X$ the adjoint of $X$ is formed:

$$\bar{X}_i = \sum_{j=1}^{m} \bar{Y}_j \frac{\partial Y_j}{\partial X_i}. \tag{21.37}$$

It is immediately clear that to obtain the full Jacobian matrix $J_{ij} = \frac{\partial Y_j}{\partial X_i}$ requires that the adjoint vector $\bar{V}$ be set equal to the $\mathbb{R}^m$ basis vectors in turn. Application of the chain rule gives

$$\begin{aligned}
\bar{X}_i &= \sum_{j=1}^{m} \bar{Y}_j \frac{\partial Y_j}{\partial X_i} \\
&= \sum_{j=1}^{m} \bar{Y}_j \sum_k \frac{\partial Y_j}{\partial U_k} \frac{\partial U_k}{\partial X_i} \\
&= \sum_{j=1}^{m} \bar{Y}_j \sum_k \sum_l \frac{\partial Y_j}{\partial V_l} \frac{\partial V_l}{\partial U_k} \frac{\partial U_k}{\partial X_i}.
\end{aligned} \tag{21.38}$$

The adjoints of the intermediate variables are given by

$$\bar{V}_l = \sum_{j=1}^{m} \bar{Y}_j \frac{\partial Y_j}{\partial V_l} \tag{21.39}$$

$$\bar{U}_k = \sum_{l} \bar{V}_l \frac{\partial V_l}{\partial U_i}, \tag{21.40}$$

and hence the adjoint of $X$ can be written,

$$\bar{X}_i = \sum_{k} \sum_{l} \bar{V}_l \frac{\partial V_l}{\partial U_k} \frac{\partial U_k}{\partial X_i} \tag{21.41}$$

$$= \sum_{k} \bar{U}_k \frac{\partial U_k}{\partial X_i}.$$

So by forming the adjoints of the intermediate variables it is possible to obtain the desired sensitivities by working backwards from $\bar{Y}$ to $\bar{X}$,

$$\bar{X} \leftarrow \dots \leftarrow \bar{U} \leftarrow \bar{V} \leftarrow \dots \leftarrow \bar{Y}.$$

The key theoretical result is that the cost of computing the adjoints is around 3–4 times the cost of computing the original function. Hence in financial applications the sensitivities can be calculated at a cost only a few times greater than that of the original valuation using AAD, which in general is considerably better than could be obtained using finite difference approximation.

AAD lends itself to automation and the adjoints can be implemented semi-automatically using software tools. A number of such tools have been developed and a good introduction to what is available can be found at www.autodiff.org. Tools are available for multiple languages. In C++ the tools work either using *operator overloading* or through *source code transformation*.

For more information on the financial application of AAD, the reader is referred to the paper by Capriotti and Giles (2012). For a comprehensive technical treatment of algorithmic differentiation see the textbooks by Griewank and Walther (2008) and Naumann (2012).

### 21.3.4  Hybrid Approaches and Longstaff-Schwartz

Recall the pathwise estimator in equation (21.20) and consider the typical application of this to XVA. Consider a unilateral CVA model with the assumption of independence between credit and market and the usual discrete approximation scheme,

$$V_{\text{CVA}}(t_0) = (1 - R) \sum_{i=1}^{n} \left[ \Phi(\tau > t_{i-1}) - \Phi(\tau > t_i) \right] B_d(0, t_i) \mathbb{E}^{Q_{t_i}} \left[ (P(t_i))^+ \right]. \tag{21.42}$$

Hence, it is clear that the CVA delta sensitivity with respect to interest rate input instruments, $S_j(t_0)$, will involve the calculation of pathwise sensitivities of the form

$$\mathbb{E}^{Q_{t_i}} \left[ \frac{\partial (P(t_i))^+}{\partial S_j(t_0)} \right]. \tag{21.43}$$

where the conditions for this to be an unbiased estimator of $\frac{\partial}{\partial S_j(t_0)} \mathbb{E}^{Q_{t_i}} \left[ (P(t_i)^+ \right]$ were described in section 21.3.1.

Applying the chain rule gives

$$\frac{\partial (P(t_i))^+}{\partial S_j(t_0)} = \mathbb{1}_{P(t_i)>0} \sum_k \sum_m \sum_l \frac{\partial P(t_i)}{\partial \bar{S}_k(t_i)} \frac{\partial \bar{S}_k(t_i)}{\partial B(t_i, t_m)} \frac{\partial B(t_i, t_m)}{\partial B(t_0, t_l)} \frac{\partial B(t_0, t_l)}{\partial S_j(t_0)}, \tag{21.44}$$

where

| | |
|---|---|
| $\dfrac{\partial P(t_i)}{\partial \bar{S}_k(t_i)}$ | Sensitivity of the portfolio value to state variables as defined at $t_i$ in the simulation |
| $\dfrac{\partial \bar{S}_k(t_i)}{\partial B(t_i, t_m)}$ | Sensitivity of state variables at $t_i$ to simulation variables at $t_i$ generated by the Monte Carlo evolution equations (i.e. bond prices in this case) |
| $\dfrac{\partial B(t_i, t_m)}{\partial B(t_0, t_l)}$ | Sensitivity of the simulation variables at $t_i$ to the initial values of the simulation variables at $t_0$ |
| $\dfrac{\partial B(t_0, t_l)}{\partial S_j(t_0)}$ | Sensitivity of the initial values of the simulation variables to the input state variables of interest (typically hedging instruments). |

It is clear from the above discussion that AAD could be applied in full to the problem and hence generate the sensitivity directly using adjoints. However, the separation of terms shows that AAD could in theory be applied only to a portion of the calculation with other techniques used to estimate the other partial derivatives. Indeed the whole pathwise simulation weight could be generated by differentiating the terms analytically and implementing the partial derivatives.

Now consider a more concrete example. Suppose that the portfolio consists of interest rate swaps of various maturities. To value these trades within the simulation adopt the Longstaff-Schwartz technique but with a common set of basis functions for all trades as was used in Chapter 10 and is discussed in Kenyon and Green (2014a). It is clear that the first partial derivative is therefore the derivative of the portfolio value with respect to the Longstaff-Schwartz regression variables. As Kenyon and Green (2014a) point out, this derivative is easy to compute analytically as the portfolio value is simply a summation over a set of basis functions and the basis functions that are normally used can be easily differentiated.[5] Furthermore, given that the Longstaff-Schwartz approach will be generic, this step will also be generic once the regression variables have been selected and will not need to be implemented for each new trade type.

---

[5]The basis functions are quite commonly polynomials.

The second partial derivative in the chain is the derivative of the regression variables with respect to the primary simulation variables. In a typical interest rate simulation these will be discount bond prices. Again this derivative may be straightforward to compute analytically. In the case here with interest rate swaps, the regression variables would be swap rates and annuities and obtaining the partial derivatives with respect to the simulated bond prices straightforward.

The third partial derivative represents the derivative of the simulation variables with respect to the input values of the simulation variables. In the case of a short rate model like the Linear Gaussian model this will be easy to compute analytically. For a more complex model such as a market model, this may need to be computed using AD.

The final derivative represents the derivative of the Monte Carlo input variables with respect to the input state variables. In the example this would be the sensitivities of the initial discount bond prices with respect to the yield curve instruments. The complexity of this step in the example would depend on the choice of yield curve model.

Why adopt such a strategy when full automation is available by AAD? As noted earlier, AAD can lead to significant memory overheads as the intermediate variables are stored during the forward sweep. This is a particular problem with GPU implementations as all the paths are executed in parallel and hence the intermediate state variables would be stored for the backward step. GPU cards currently have fixed memory amounts, and although the available memory is steadily increasing it remains below the main memory normally available on workstations and servers. Hybrid approaches offer a viable alternative, where the structure of the problem is utilised to generate analytic partial derivatives when they are easy to compute but uses AD techniques when they are not.

## 21.4 SCENARIOS AND STRESS TESTS

Scenario analysis has long been an element in trading desk management and has allowed desks to examine the behaviour of trading books under moderate to large market data shifts. Stress testing, that is large market data shifts often implied by economic scenarios, is becoming an increasingly common element of business practice. Stress tests are now a major part of the regulatory framework with regulators devising a series of economic scenarios and testing bank capital under adverse conditions. Stress testing is therefore something that should be considered in any XVA system.

The key issue is actually getting the stress tests to work successfully. The multi-asset nature of XVA means that there are significantly more market data inputs and associated calibration steps that any single trade valuation model, and hence there are correspondingly larger opportunities for failures to occur. In a typical XVA model there are three main areas to consider:

1. **Calibration** In stress scenarios the model should almost certainly be fully re-calibrated in the stressed market state. The purpose of the stress scenario is to replicate XVA in the market scenario so the model should be re-calibrated, even if, for example, only interest rates were shifted and no change was made to the input volatility surface. However, the market stress test can make the input data set inconsistent. So, for example, a volatility surface itself may require a calibration step and become invalid over large input yield curve shifts. For the calibration to succeed the model needs to be able to successfully extract the prices of calibration instruments from underlying market data objects. Even

if the XVA calibration step can obtain instrument prices, the calibration could still fail if the input prices are inconsistent with the assumptions of the model dynamics. A classic example of this would be negative interest rates. If the scenario implies negative rates but the interest rate model assumes that interest rates are always positive, the calibration is likely to fail or produce meaningless results. Of course negative rates have been observed on a number of occasions since the credit crisis and are now a feature of interest rate markets.

2. **Valuation models** If the Longstaff-Schwartz approach is adopted universally then the model dynamics will determine all valuation. However, if full valuation models are used inside the Monte Carlo these can fail in stress scenarios. This can occur if the model uses some input market data directly, perhaps implied volatilities, and the state of the input data is inconsistent with the assumptions underlying the model.

3. **Credit curves and yield curves** If the usual independence assumption is made then yield curves and credit curves will also be used outside the Monte Carlo simulation. Hence these elements need to operate well under stress. Problems can sometimes occur with yield curves in negative rate scenarios. Credit curves can fail when the shift of spreads implies a negative hazard rate. Clearly such issues are not just a feature of XVA calculations and apply to other areas of the bank. Hence it is preferable if these are addressed centrally through the stress testing framework.

Model choice and implementation design can mitigate these issues to a greater or lesser extent.

# CHAPTER 22

# Managing XVA

*Morpheus: Unfortunately, no one can be told what the Matrix is. You have to see it for yourself. This is your last chance. After this, there is no turning back. You take the blue pill, the story ends, you wake up in your bed and believe whatever you want to believe. You take the red pill, you stay in Wonderland, and I show you how deep the rabbit hole goes.*

—Andy & Lana Wachowski
*The Matrix (1999)*

## 22.1  INTRODUCTION

CVA has been part of accounting practice since the the introduction of *FASB 157* (2006). At the time of writing the majority of major global banks now include a reserve for FVA. Capital and margin are central concerns of banks and many are now directly managing their balance sheet usage, while collateral is increasingly moving from an operational to a business function. XVA management is therefore inevitable, even where the risk is not actively hedged.

This chapter explores XVA management in detail. Sections 22.2 and 22.3 examine different organisational designs for XVA and the relationships between the XVA desk and bank treasury and between the XVA desk and loan portfolio management. In sections 22.4 and 22.5 two XVA management styles are explored, *active* where XVA is hedged through CDS and market risk hedges and *passive* where the risk is warehoused to some degree. Charging for XVA is an important consideration and the internal charging structure for new transactions often a major source of debate between sales functions and the XVA desk. Section 22.6 explores several different options for how XVA can be charged internally. Finally, the organisational implications of the management of default and distress alongside XVA management are considered in section 22.7.

## 22.2   ORGANISATIONAL DESIGN

There are a multitude of possible organisational designs for XVA management functions so to simplify the discussion this section considers the merits and feasibility of having separate XVA functions versus having a centralised XVA desk.

### 22.2.1   Separate XVA Functions

In many institutions XVA functions have been separated during the evolution of these functions. In some cases this is a function of "organic" development, while in others it is by design. There are two cases to examine, the first where the XVA functions themselves are separate, and the second where the XVA functions are unified across metrics but split by business/asset class.

**XVA Management as Discrete Business Functions**   Historically some CVA and FVA desks developed independently, while capital management has only recently become a front office financial markets concern, as has collateral management. With the first generation discounting models for FVA, this is perfectly natural as these had no overlap with CVA. However, with the advent of Burgard and Kjaer (2011a); Burgard and Kjaer (2011b); Burgard and Kjaer (2013) and similar models this is no longer the case and FVA cannot be cleanly separated from CVA.

Consider Tables 22.1 and 22.2: these provide a guide to the sensitivity of each of the XVA metrics with respect to input data, with Table 22.1 referring to the use of semi-replication with no shortfall on default and Table 22.2 to semi-replication with one bond.

The choice of model does influence the separability of CVA and FVA. In the case of semi-replication with one bond a single FVA term is given and this can be unambiguously associated with the bank funding spread. In this case a small dependence on the counterparty spread is retained but FVA is perhaps more amenable to separate management.

However, under semi-replication with no shortfall on default it would be difficult to clearly separate CVA and FVA. DVA is retained within the model with the funding cost term, FCA, added to it. Both would refer to $\lambda_B$, the issuer hazard rate, and hence be difficult to separate.

**TABLE 22.1**   Sensitivity of XVA metrics to input data under semi-replication with no shortfall at own default (see Chapter 9). ++ = high sensitivity, + = low sensitivity, - = no sensitivity. Most XVA metrics are very sensitive to market data through the expected exposure profile, giving the high sensitivity across almost all metrics. All the XVA integrals contain $\lambda_B$ and $\lambda_C$ and hence have some degree of sensitivity to credit spreads.

| XVA | Ctpy Credit Spread | Own Credit Spread | Coll. Spread | Initial Margin Spread | Market Data | Cost of Capital | Tax Rate |
|---|---|---|---|---|---|---|---|
| CVA | ++ | + | - | - | ++ | - | - |
| DVA | + | ++ | - | - | ++ | - | - |
| FCA | + | ++ | - | - | ++ | - | - |
| COLVA | + | + | ++ | - | + | - | - |
| KVA | + | + | - | - | ++ | ++ | - |
| MVA | + | + | - | ++ | + | - | - |
| TVA | + | + | - | - | + | + | ++ |

**TABLE 22.2** Sensitivity of XVA metrics to input data under semi-replication with one bond (see Chapter 9). ++ = high sensitivity, + = low sensitivity, - = no sensitivity. Most XVA metrics are very sensitive to market data through the expected exposure profile, giving the high sensitivity across almost all metrics. All the XVA integrals contain $\lambda_C$ and hence have some degree of sensitivity to counterparty credit spreads and similarly with the issuer funding spread, $s_F$.

| XVA | Ctpy Credit Spread | Funding Spread | Coll. Spread | Initial Margin Spread | Market Data | Cost of Capital | Tax Rate |
|---|---|---|---|---|---|---|---|
| CVA | ++ | + | - | - | ++ | - | - |
| FVA | + | ++ | - | - | ++ | - | - |
| COLVA | + | + | ++ | - | + | - | - |
| KVA | + | + | - | - | ++ | ++ | - |
| MVA | + | + | - | ++ | + | - | - |
| TVA | + | + | - | - | + | + | ++ |

In practice, however, even if this model is used, then the effective spread applied to the DVA and FCA terms may differ, with DVA containing the full bank CDS spread and FCA containing the funding element of that spread. This approach is not strictly what the model implies but is used for accounting purposes by some institutions. If this approach is adopted then the FCA term would retain some dependence on the counterparty CDS curve but this would be limited and otherwise be dependent on the pure funding spread, allowing it to be managed separately.

The other XVA metrics that have been discussed, KVA and MVA, are relatively new. Capital management has increasingly been a concern of banks in the aftermath of the 2007–2009 credit crisis but has only recently acquired the moniker "KVA", while MVA is only now appearing as part of pricing methodology. The capital management desk may be independent of XVA, depending on where it sits within the organisation. The capital management function may be responsible only for management of balance sheet usage rather than the KVA metric and so could be separated from CVA and FVA management, although there is clear overlap with counterparty credit risk management through the CCR and CVA capital terms.

Although COLVA could be considered a funding cost/benefit, it is most closely associated with collateral. The management of COLVA could therefore be associated with the collateral management function. It could also be contained within a CSA modelling framework and thus be associated with a "CSA" management function that also manages the basis risks associated with different collateral eligibility in CSA agreements.

MVA, as is clear from Chapter 10, is a funding cost and therefore is most closely associated with FVA. However, given that it is associated with the posting of initial margin it could also be managed by the collateral management function. MVA is a critical metric when considering backloading and compression trades so the function responsible for these activities may manage MVA. When bilateral margin (BCBS, 2013d) comes into force between 2015 and 2019, MVA will be a greater concern that it is at present.

TVA is *Tax Valuation Adjustment* and was introduced in Chapter 14. It reflects the taxation associated with profits and losses associated with warehousing some or all of XVA and with the profits associated with the dividend payment to shareholders, $\gamma_K$. This term does have market risk sensitivities as the gain or loss will be driven by market rates as well as the degree of hedging that takes place. TVA is a new concept and at present is unlikely to be managed

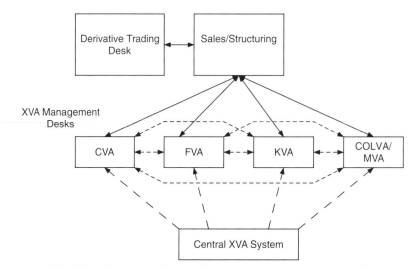

**FIGURE 22.1** The organisational design with multiple independent XVA desks. When a new client trade is structured the sales team would potentially have to engage multiple XVA desks in addition to the appropriate derivative trading desk. The XVA functions may need to engage with each other to optimise the trade structure for XVA. A central XVA system would mitigate the complexity of interaction.

directly by an XVA desk. However, consideration of taxation is closely related to balance sheet management.

From an operational perspective multiple XVA desks will lead to a requirement for multiple trading books as each desk manages its own risks. It is clear from Tables 22.1 and 22.2 that CVA, FVA and KVA have a strong dependence on market risk. DVA and the component of FVA relating to the expected negative exposure will have market risk sensitivities opposite to those of CVA and FCA. Hence it is quite likely that separate XVA trading functions will have offsetting risks to some degree. Operationally, separating the XVA management functions will certainly lead to more internal hedging trades and potentially more external trades unless the risk positions are carefully managed. Hence the separation of the individual XVA functions inevitably comes with additional costs through extra finance and operational requirements and potentially extra hedging costs.

Pricing client trades is more complex with separate XVA management functions as each sales team would potentially need to interface with multiple XVA management functions in addition to the appropriate product aligned trading desk. This could make pricing complex and slow. Furthermore, each individual XVA desk many need to interact with the other XVA desks to fully optimise the trade structure. However, even with multiple XVA functions this could be improved potentially through central XVA pricing tools and by making one of the XVA functions responsible for the support of pricing. An organisational sign with multiple XVA desks is illustrated in Figure 22.1.

**Business/Asset-Class Aligned XVA** Larger banks tend to have derivatives managed across multiple business lines and these business lines tend to be grouped by asset class. As was noted earlier, this is a function of historical development of the derivatives market. Hence in some

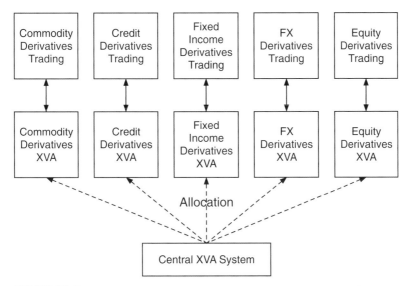

**FIGURE 22.2**  The organisational design with asset-class aligned XVA desks. This design can work as long as XVA calculation is centralised and allocated to the individual businesses.

cases XVA management functions have developed in tandem with the business organisation and have therefore been split across the bank in multiple desks. This is of course potentially problematic as netting sets can span multiple asset classes. In practice though clients may only interact with a limited number of asset classes, so for example a corporate client may only trade interest rate derivatives to manage balance sheet risks. Such a client would only therefore face the fixed income division of the bank. A counterparty netting set may only "overlap" the multiple XVA desks in a limited number of cases, therefore.

Having multiple XVA desks is certainly feasible if a single XVA system is used for all desks and XVA allocation is performed as described in section 3.6.2. XVA would be allocated to trades and then re-aggregated back to the groups of trades managed by each desk. Risk allocation is feasible using the same approach; however, if Longstaff-Schwartz is adopted universally as the approach to trade valuation then as Kenyon and Green (2013a) show XVA and XVA sensitivities can be readily allocated to trade level. This organisational design is illustrated in Figure 22.2.

## 22.2.2  Central XVA

It should be clear from the above discussion that the optimal arrangement for XVA management is to have a central XVA desk that is responsible for all XVA management across CVA (DVA), FVA, KVA, COLVA, MVA and TVA but particularly across CVA, FVA and KVA. The terms are not readily separable and all have cross-dependence on the counterparty spread and on the bank's own CDS spread and/or funding costs. A central XVA desk also eliminates any hedge duplication and centralises associated finance, risk and operations functions. Pricing is also centralised and hence only two trading desks need be involved in a typical pricing request, the product trading desk and the XVA desk. The central XVA desk organisational design is illustrated in Figure 22.3.

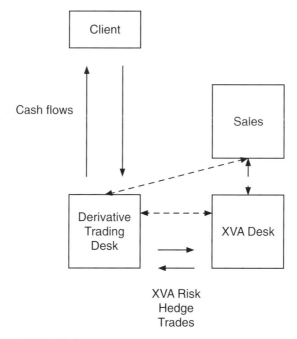

**FIGURE 22.3**  The organisational design with a central XVA desk. This design means that new trades typically only involve a single derivative trading desk and the central XVA function. Note that here the client trade will appear in the trading book of the derivative trading business and only the XVA will appear in the trading book of the XVA desk.

A central XVA trading desk does raise one further question: should the XVA desk face the (corporate) client directly, as illustrated in Figure 22.4? In this case the XVA trading desk would actually manage the total value of the derivative rather than just the XVA. The unadjusted value would come from the normal valuation system and then the allocated XVA added on top. Of course a universal valuation model could be used to value all of the derivatives in a consistent fashion and then the sensitivities of the whole book could then be allocated to individual trading desks to manage. The XVA desk would then hedge out the various market risks with other risk management desks through internal trades. So, for example, suppose a corporate trades an interest rate swap with the bank on an unsecured basis. The XVA desk would face the client directly and place the client interest rate swap and XVA adjustment in their trading book. The XVA desk would then hedge out the various market risks internally, hedging the total interest rate risk with the interest rate swap desk and the counterparty credit risk with the CDS trading desk. The interest rate swap and CDS trading desks would still trade with market counterparties, that is the interbank market including cleared trades through CCPs. These trades would be collateralised and hence have limited CVA and FVA, although MVA would still need to be considered. Hence the XVA desk could certainly face the client directly and there are no operational reasons why this could not happen.

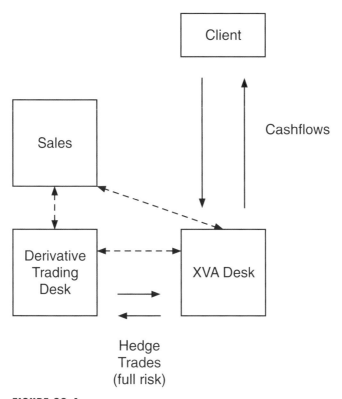

**FIGURE 22.4** In this design the central XVA desk faces the client directly so the full client trade is placed in the trading book of the XVA desk. The derivative trading desks then hedge out the risks on the trade including those of the XVA position.

## 22.3 XVA, TREASURY AND PORTFOLIO MANAGEMENT

### 22.3.1 Treasury

What should be the appropriate relationship between the XVA desk and the bank's treasury function? The XVA desk will charge for derivative funding costs and manage the associated FVA reserve. The bank treasury is responsible for actually raising funding for the bank's derivative portfolio, alongside other bank products such as loan origination. There is an argument for combining the treasury function with the XVA desk because of the overlap between raising and charging for funding costs. The treasury function will also be responsible for managing compliance with liquidity regulation in the form of the NSFR and LCR (see section 12.1.2). There are also other overlaps as treasury operations are also where the bank's balance sheet is managed, at least for the banking book, if not the trading book. As has already been considered some aspects of the regulatory capital framework such as the leverage ratio apply across the bank. Hence bank *asset liability management (ALM)* frequently resides with the treasury. ALM modelling often uses exactly the same techniques as XVA modelling, although the former are defined in the physical measure. At least one major bank has adopted this approach, and even where the XVA management function remains separate, treasury will have a high degree of interaction with the XVA desk.

### 22.3.2  Loan Portfolio Management

The loan portfolio management function within a bank will manage the loan portfolio after origination. Funding of the loan will be done at inception by the treasury function and then any subsequent funding will form part of the overall bank financing activity again managed by the treasury. Loan portfolio management's main concern is the credit risk on the loans within the portfolio. Secondary concerns will be managing the balance of the portfolio across credit ratings and sectors to avoid undesirable concentrations. Loan portfolio management may not actively manage the credit risk through the CDS market and the accounting approach to the loan book will be accrual rather than mark-to-market. Nevertheless there are considerable similarities between the activities of CDS trading and loan portfolio management and in some cases direct links between their activities.

Loan portfolio management may in fact need to value loans on a mark-to-market basis for internal risk management purposes. In this case a map will be needed between loan counterparties and the CDS market, which of course mirrors the CVA valuation process.

There are also links between the CVA desk and Loan Portfolio Management as is clear from the discussion in section 6.5. In many cases loan issuance accompanies derivative issuance in trades with corporate clients. As such the total exposure will include both loan and derivative, even if from the perspective of accounting CVA applies only to the derivative. In the case when non-financial security is pledged against the position, then the recovery on loan and derivative will be determined by the ranking in the waterfall of loan and derivative as well as the value of the derivative and loan principal. Where the situation exists there is a strong incentive to manage both loan and derivative together. Even where the loan and derivative are not linked in this way there is still an argument to manage the overall credit risk of the bank in a holistic fashion. Although the loan, as a banking book transaction, will not face the same P&L volatility as the derivative from credit risk, it still faces the same ultimate default risk. Hence an overall management strategy for both loan and derivative will be beneficial for at least some counterparts.

## 22.4  ACTIVE XVA MANAGEMENT

Active XVA management, in general, means hedging the XVA risk with traded instruments through the interbank market. The XVA management function is therefore a trading desk in the same way as any other derivative trading desk. As such the XVA desk requires the same support functions as other trading desks: product control, independent price verification and market risk. The XVA desk will have XVA positions and trading books of offsetting hedge instruments. These are likely to be valued through different systems and require risk aggregation. The P&L of the trading desk will need to be explained including the movement in XVA position and hedges. If the trading desk is involved in marking positions, most likely in marking the CDS curves associated with certain names, then IPV will be required. Market risk will be measured and trading risk limits applied. This may be done through a VaR/SVaR model, although this is distinct from the VaR model that would be applied to estimate CVA capital under Basel III. Trading mandates will be needed to describe which activities XVA trading can undertake and which markets they are allowed to trade. The hybrid nature of the risk will by necessity mean that these are likely to be amongst the widest trading mandates in the bank.

In this section I examine what active XVA management means in practice and what approaches to hedging can be used by the trading desk.

## 22.4.1  Market Risks

By market risks I refer to the sensitivity of XVA with respect to market traded instruments, excluding CDS which will be treated separately. Chapter 21 provided a detailed description of how these sensitivities can be estimated for XVA metrics. Market risk is the easiest element of XVA risk that can be hedged. In general the overall risk position of the book, including all relevant XVA metrics, can be hedged together.

**Delta**  XVA has a number of first order sensitivities to market inputs and the sensitivity of any XVA desk will depend on the types of derivatives that the associated derivatives business is involved with. Given the nature of the derivatives business and the fact that longer-dated derivatives are more common in fixed income means that the largest delta position is likely to be in interest rate delta. If the business is involved in trading inflation derivatives then the long-dated nature of such trades also means that inflation delta is likely to be signifiant. All banks will have some element of FX risk but for regional banks the bulk of any derivatives business is likely to be done in the domestic currency of the bank, while for an international bank the derivatives business will be done in a variety of currencies and will also include multi-currency derivatives. The XVA desk will, therefore, have at least some FX risk. If there are derivatives on commodities or equities then the XVA desk will inevitably have this risk as well. If there are credit derivatives in the portfolio then these will also give a CS01 risk on the exposure element of the XVA but given that this is indistinguishable from the CS01 arising from counterparty risk this can be hedged in the same way (see section 22.4.2).

The delta risk can be readily hedged through linear instruments. So, for example, interest rate risk will primarily be hedged through interest rate swaps. The XVA desk may face the market directly, or may trade internally with the appropriate derivative trading desk for the asset class in question.

**Vega**  As was noted earlier, XVA is also sensitive to implied volatility. Some of this sensitivity arises from the volatility sensitivity of underlying option products, but the majority arises from the max function present in the expected positive and negative exposure calculations. Large volatility surfaces with multiple maturities, strikes and, in the case of interest rates, tenors mean the vega is often expensive to calculate by finite difference approximation. In some cases a vega may not be calculated at all, or be performed on a less granular basis that the underlying data. Simulation risk (see section 21.3) obviously reduces the computational problem but is still not that common in XVA systems. Hence an XVA desk may only have limited information available about their vega risk. This, as well as the complexity associated with managing a hybrid book, makes vega hedging less common for XVA desks, at least at the very granular level, than might be undertaken by an option trading desk. If vega hedging is performed then this will be done by trading the vanilla options associated with the asset class in question.

**Gammas, Cross-gammas and Correlations**   The XVA "payout" is option-like as it includes the max function and as an option it is inevitably nonlinear with gamma and cross-gamma risk sensitivities. The multi-asset nature of the model also means that a considerable number of correlations are required. As was noted earlier in section 21.2, the calculation of the large number of second order sensitivities associated with XVA may prove prohibitively expensive using finite difference. The use of algorithmic differentiation and related techniques may, however, allow these to be calculated.

Even if gamma and cross-gamma sensitivities are available, they may prove to be of limited use for hedging purposes, although they will certainly be used in the P&L explain process. The construction of appropriate gamma hedges may prove too complex to practically implement and the XVA desk may choose to rebalance the delta hedging on a regular basis rather than rely on gamma hedging.

The sensitivity of XVA to correlation will depend to some extent on the choice of model dynamics and on the nature of the derivative portfolio. For a regional bank with the bulk of its derivative portfolio in a single currency, sensitivity to correlations may be relatively limited. A more diverse portfolio will have a greater sensitivity to correlation. Whether or not correlation sensitivity is an issue for the trading desk, there is very little that can be done to hedge any exposure. Spread options are the only real means to hedge correlation risk and are only available in a limited number of cases. In general it is unlikely than an XVA desk will choose to hedge correlations.

**Credit-rates cross-gamma**   The most important cross-gamma to an XVA desk is almost certainly credit-interest rates. If the independence assumption between market rates and credit has been adopted then credit-rates cross-gamma is no more expensive to calculate than interest rate delta by finite difference approximation. Hence the XVA desk will probably have access to this sensitivity. The importance stems from the size and typical position of the XVA desk. If the bank is a net receiver of unsecured fixed rates then expected positive exposures will rise if interest rates fall. This position is very common as many corporate clients will trade interest rate swaps with banks to hedge balance sheet exposures arising through fixed rate loans or bond issuance. The corporate client will pay fixed rates to the bank and receive floating in return. If interest rates fall the mark-to-market on these interest rate swaps will increase and so will the exposure the bank has to the client. Typically long-term interest rates fall in recessionary scenarios at the same time that credit spreads widen. In these circumstances the exposure rises at the same time the exposure becomes more expensive per unit as the probability of counterparty default has increased. Credit-rates cross-gamma is important as it is a measure of how sensitive the XVA desk is to this adverse scenario.

Hedging the credit-rates cross-gamma effect is very difficult, although buying out of the money swaptions as described below may provide one option.

**Tail-risk Hedges**   XVA has inherent elements of tail risk. Furthermore even if XVA is routinely risk warehoused the bank may seek to take out some "insurance" to avoid very adverse outcomes and hence seek to hedge the tail risk. The credit-rates cross-gamma as described above is a measure of the sensitivity to an adverse low interest-rates, high credit spreads recessionary scenario and could be considered one example of a tail risk. To hedge this scenario the XVA desk could buy out-of-the-money European swaptions in which they receive fixed. If rates decline the value of the option would increase. This does not directly hedge the credit element, which could, at least in theory, be hedged by buying out-of-the-money

CDSwaptions in which the XVA desk buy an option to buy CDS at a strike above the current level. In practice, however, CDSwaptions are very illiquid and expensive. An alternative could be to over hedge with the swaptions to account for the expected credit move and cross-gamma effect.

### 22.4.2  Counterparty Credit Risk Hedging

**Single Name CDS**    Where the counterparty has a single name CDS available and the derivative exposure ranks *pari passu* with the debt that is deliverable into the CDS, the CDS contract can be used to hedge the spread and exposure sensitivity of the XVA metrics. The CS01s from the XVA model provide the basis for the strip of CDS to be bought as a hedge. In practice, however, the CDS market is relatively illiquid and the point of maximum liquidity is typically the five-year CDS. Furthermore the XVA desk may have counterparty exposures that are longer in maturity than any CDS contract that is available in the market. Hence the XVA desk may by choice or by necessity be required to hedge the position with single name CDS of different maturities to those the XVA model would suggest.

If the derivative exposure does not rank *pari passu* with the debt that is deliverable into the CDS contract then the XVA desk will need to decide if the single name CDS hedge remains appropriate. If the desk decides to use the CDS then the hedge notional may need to be adjusted up or down to reflect the difference in relative seniority and expected recovery.

The market in USD denominated CDS contracts amounts to around 1600 names, with even fewer liquid single name contracts available in other currencies (Kenyon and Green, 2015c). The single name CDS market is therefore much smaller than the number of counterparties with whom banks trade derivatives and this leads directly to the requirement to map counterparties to CDS curves as described in Chapter 4. Even when CDS contracts are available, CDS market depth is limited (Carver, 2013). Alternative approaches to single name hedging are therefore inevitable and this leads directly to the use of alternatives or to risk warehousing.

**Index CDS and Baskets**    Index CDS and bespoke baskets of CDS provide a reasonably generic mechanism for hedging credit spread sensitivity. They do not provide any means of hedging exposure at default unless the counterparty in question is part of the index or basket. In the cases where no single name CDS exists then an index or basket may provide the only means to hedge the spread sensitivity.

In some cases the CDS mapping model may be written directly in terms of the index, in which case the CS01s versus the index may be directly available from the XVA model. If not then the trading desk will need to estimate the amount of index hedge required from the individual counterparty level CS01s and the correlation of the counterparty spreads with the index.

There will inevitably be some basis risk associated with index/basket hedging. Nevertheless, index CDS is more liquid than single name CDS and so even if a single name CDS is available, the XVA trading desk may choose to hedge the risk with the index rather than the single name CDS.

**Proxy Hedging**    Where a counterparty spread is proxied to another single name CDS then it is appropriate to hedge the position using the proxy CDS. However, it should always be noted that this will hedge the spread risk of the XVA and not the actual exposure at default. Furthermore, the proxy will need to be monitored carefully over time to see if it remains appropriate. For example, should the credit rating of either counterparty or proxy change then the suitability of the proxy will need to be reviewed. If the proxy changes or if the proxy is removed and the counterparty spread remapped then this will necessitate re-hedging.

**CLNs**   A further option to hedge XVA CS01s is to sell the risk on to a third party through a *Credit Linked Note (CLN)*. A CLN will pay a fixed coupon to the security buyer and then will be redeemed at par unless the reference credit defaults, in which case the recovery value is paid. The CLN therefore has similar sensitivities to a CDS and the XVA desk is in effect buying protection from the buyer of the note.

The difficulty for the trading desk is that the CLN will normally have a fixed notional, while the XVA CS01s will vary with the expected exposure. Hence the CLN may provide an under or over hedge of the XVA position as time evolves.

Nevertheless, if a private buyer of the risk can be identified, a CLN may provide a means of hedging larger exposures in a cost effective manner. CLNs could also be issued for counterparties where there is no CDS available, the CLN therefore providing a single name hedge where it would not otherwise be available.

**Capital Relief on Hedging**   As was discussed in Chapter 12, hedge trades can be used to offset CVA capital under certain circumstances. Under Basel III (BCBS, 2011b, 2012b), single name CDS where the reference name is the same as the counterparty exposure and index CDS are eligible for CVA capital relief. These trades must be documented and controlled as CVA hedges in order to be eligible. Other possible types of credit risk hedging, including proxies, CLNs and CDO tranches, do not produce capital relief. Eligible CDS hedges are also explicitly removed from the market risk capital regime so no market risk capital is due on these hedges.

Market risk hedges are also not eligible for capital relief under Basel III. This could lead to these hedge trades appearing as open market risk positions and hence subject to market risk capital requirements. As was clear from the discussion in Chapter 13 market risk capital is expensive and hence an open risk position from a capital perspective should be avoided. However, under the US implementation of Basel III market risk hedges of CVA are exempt from market risk capital (Office of the Comptroller of the Currency, Treasury; the Board of Governors of the Federal Reserve System; and the Federal Deposit Insurance Corporation, 2013).

**CVA Securitisation**   CVA securitisation has often been seen as the ultimate way of dealing with CVA risk. The bank securitises the CVA in the manner of a CDO and then sells off the individual trenches of the risk to investors. In practice this is very complex to achieve as the underlying CVA risk is itself variable and highly complex. To make such a securitisation successful the bank needs to identify an appropriate structure that will both satisfy regulators and be attractive to investors. In reality this has proved very difficult to achieve (Whittall, 2013) and few securitisations of CVA have been done.

### 22.4.3   Hedging DVA?

Many banks, even after the introduction of Funding Costs and FVA, still retain at least an element of DVA reserve. As has already been discussed, the sensitivity to the bank's own credit spread cannot be hedged directly and hence the only option that is available is to hedge the risk through a proxy.

The proxies that are available include:

- An appropriate single name CDS
- A bespoke basket containing CDS for appropriate peer banks
- An appropriate index CDS.

In all cases there will be considerable basis risk between the proxy and the bank's own credit spread. Furthermore this risk is not just a basis on the spread as any hedging with proxies will also expose the hedger to gains and losses on the defaults of the proxies. Some banks have certainly attempted to hedge the DVA, while others have chosen to warehouse this risk and leave it unhedged. If banks move to an accounting framework where DVA is replaced by funding benefit then DVA hedging may disappear as an issue.

### 22.4.4   Hedging FVA

FVA is an emerging element of bank accounting practice and as more and more banks take an FVA reserve there will be increasing incentives to hedge the associated risks. The market risk of FVA can be hedged directly in the same way as any other XVA metric. If the funding curve used (see Chapter 11) to mark the FVA is the bank's own internal funding curve then the sensitivity to the funding cost could be hedged internally with the bank Treasury who would then manage the funding requirement as part of their overall funding requirement. If, however, the accounting FVA is marked using an external funding curve then the accounting FVA would be sensitive to a curve that is not associated with any readily traded instrument. An external funding curve could not be hedged directly and would need some kind of proxy to be used instead.

### 22.4.5   Managing and Hedging Capital

KVA has exactly the same kind of sensitivities as the other XVA metrics so there is no reason why the market risk cannot be hedged. The problem, as discussed earlier, was that any KVA hedges would themselves acquire a capital requirement. Hence KVA hedging would take the form of an optimisation of hedge positions versus the net capital requirement.

The management of regulatory capital extends far wider than hedging activity and includes:

- Managing market risk capital by assessing open risk positions with individual trading desks to make the capital costs clear alongside any VaR trading limits
- Backloading of transactions to clear through CCPs
- Renegotiation of CSA agreements to, for example, reduce thresholds and hence exposures
- Agreeing netting agreements, checking and amending coverage as required
- Portfolio compression to reduce the number of trades in bilateral portfolios
- Structuring new and old transactions to make them more capital efficient
- Managing the bank balance sheet and leverage ratio impact
- Data cleaning.

### 22.4.6   Managing Collateral and MVA

MVA has limited direct sensitivity to market rates as its value is typically driven by a VaR model (see Tables 22.1 and 22.2). The level of the underlying "exposure" is driven by the VaR and not an absolute level. Intuitively future VaR levels will be affected by realised volatility in the $\mathbb{P}$ measure, although to fully model this effect would require a model specified jointly in the $\mathbb{P}$ and $\mathbb{Q}$ measures.

The funding cost of the initial margin will be driven primarily by the bank funding spread as in FVA and so the comments in section 22.4.4 apply directly to MVA.

The COLVA adjustment will be determined by the difference between the spread paid by the margin recipient and the risk-free rate. This will be determined to some extent by the collateral mix, with some CCPs paying different rates on different types of collateral.

Hedging and managing MVA will therefore consist of a mixture of hedging of the funding requirements, collateral management and the hedging of any residual market risk. MVA will also incentivise banks to reduce the overall risk associated with each margin recipient be that a CCP or a counterparty to whom the bilateral margin rules apply.

## 22.5   PASSIVE XVA MANAGEMENT

As was discussed earlier in Chapter 14, not all banks hedge their XVA and in practice as described above in section 22.4 it is not possible to fully hedge all of the risks associated with XVA. Hence to a greater or lesser extent the risk associated with XVA is warehoused. Some banks will hedge the market risk component/exposure component but leave the "integral" component, particularly counterparty credit risk, unhedged. Some banks may leave the entirety of XVA unhedged.

In the past, if CVA could be marked on a historical basis with market inputs derived from historical data and default probabilities marked at historic values, this was certainly a feasible option. There would be limited P&L volatility deriving from a historical XVA model. However, current market practice is to use implied market information and CDS spreads so a fully unhedged position will attract a great deal of P&L volatility, while the regulatory capital framework encourages active management of CVA.

Passive XVA management may be discouraged, but it may be a choice that an institution makes. Smaller institutions may find that setting up an active XVA management function or functions expensive for a small portfolio. In economic terms the model presented in Chapter 14 can be used in such circumstances but the book would almost certainly be marked at the risk-neutral level for accounting purposes. The choice of passive versus active management of XVA may then resolve to a measurement of how much P&L volatility is acceptable to senior management.

## 22.6   INTERNAL CHARGING FOR XVA

When a new transaction is added to a derivative portfolio then the XVA desk will see an incremental change in XVA. In the majority of cases this will be an increase in XVA and the XVA desk will need to be compensated for taking on the additional XVA or a loss will be recorded by the desk. Some trades may be risk reducing or a trade may be amended or terminated early resulting in a gain for the XVA desk. In such cases the XVA desk may be required to pay a cash flow to compensate the counterparty. Given that in general the XVA desk does not face the client directly trade changes will result in internal cash flows between the transacting desk and the XVA desk. In some cases the full trade P&L will be booked directly into the asset-class trading book and then the XVA desk will receive a cash flow from the trading desk. In some cases the transaction profit is retained by the sales team in which case the XVA desk will receive a cash flow from sales.

### 22.6.1   Payment Structures

The internal XVA charge can take a number of different forms.

**Upfront Fee**   The most common form is for the XVA desk to receive an upfront cash flow equal to the incremental XVA charge. This means that the XVA desk has no change at inception in their P&L. If the XVA charge is negative then the cash flow will simply be reversed with the XVA desk paying back the incremental gain in XVA.

There are considerable variations on the flat fee. Some XVA desks may choose to offer a discount on the full incremental charge, meaning they would face an accounting loss on the new trade, but this might be one that they would expect to gain back through carry, for example. The XVA desk may also not pay back the full benefit of any risk reducing trades.

The upfront fee is not the only possible billing structure, however.

**Running Cost**   The sales desk may prefer to pay a running premium to the XVA desk, rather than an upfront fee. The premium could run to maturity of the deal irrespective of whether the counterparty defaults, in which case it would take the form of a simple annuity. The premium could also be paid only until the counterparty defaults, in the manner of a CDS, in which case the XVA fee would be spread across a risky annuity.

**Fee and Premium Return**   Some sales desks may like to receive the CVA premium back if the counterparty does not default during the lifetime of the deal. This is similar to some insurance contract structures. In this case the fee will be increased at inception by an amount equal to the CVA charge paid at the end of the new trade conditioned on the survival of the counterparty.

### 22.6.2   The Charging Process

In general an XVA desk will only be involved in pricing the XVA on particularly complex deals or where there is a significant risk associated with the transaction. The XVA desk will simply not have enough staff to manually price the XVA on every transaction. Hence it is common practice for automated pricing systems to be provided to sales teams to allow them to price the XVA into new transactions.

To complete the XVA charging process an automated process will be needed to create a cash flow for the correct amount between the sales team and XVA desk. This process could be triggered directly by the pricing process or may be part of a later batch process that picks up new transactions or amendments to existing transactions and creates the appropriate cash flows. Note that if multiple trades and multiple desks are involved it may be necessary to create multiple bills for different trade components. In this case XVA allocation (see section 3.6.2) can be used.

## 22.7  MANAGING DEFAULT AND DISTRESS

When counterparty default actually occurs or in some cases when the counterparty becomes distressed then the process of resolution will need to be managed. A key question is where this resolution process is managed within the institution. For pure derivative counterparties a credit event would only involve the derivatives business and be the result of a missed payment, etc. In such cases the XVA desk may be the appropriate place to manage the resolution process. However, in many cases the derivative may be only part of a package provided the counterparty that includes loans or bonds. In such cases the counterparty may trigger covenants before any actual credit event takes place. The bank may therefore seek to manage such counterparties separately, particularly if an impairment needs to be taken on a loan. Where there are multiple products the XVA desk may handle the resolution of the derivative elements or in fact hand over distressed counterparties to a specialist unit.

If the XVA desk is responsible, even in part, for the management of defaulted or distressed counterparties then it is likely that specialists will be needed to support this activity. Commercial lawyers will certainly be needed as well as potentially other specialists with knowledge of the workout process. If the XVA desk does not manage the resolution process at all then the bank will need to define the process through which the counterparty and associated XVA reserves are handed over by the XVA desk to the "distressed counterparty management unit".

# Six

# The Future

# 23

# The Future of Derivatives?

*I never think of the future – it comes soon enough.*

—Albert Einstein
*Theoretical Physicist and Nobel Laureate (1879–1955)*

## 23.1 REFLECTING ON THE YEARS OF CHANGE...

In the years since the start of the credit crisis in 2007 there have clearly been wholesale changes in the banking industry and financial markets. This period certainly bears comparison with the tumultuous years of the great depression because of the impact of the crisis on national economies, and major changes in the banking industry and associated regulation. The development of "XVA" has certainly been part of this story and as far as derivatives are concerned one of the major elements of market change.

In 2003, CVA was clearly a backwater as far as the quant research function was concerned. By the end of 2008, CVA had become one of the most important issues facing the banking industry; FVA and "XVA" followed quickly thereafter. In 2005, building models for fixed income exotics was often considered to be the most prestigious area of quantitative finance. It certainly involved some of the most advanced mathematics and numerical techniques and attracted some of the best minds in the industry. Today the fixed income exotics business is largely moribund and quant research activity is now heavily focused on XVA and related areas. A glance at any major derivatives conference, even those targeted at interest rates or fixed income, shows that these are focused on XVA or issues such as collateralisation, clearing and regulation.

## 23.2 THE MARKET IN THE FUTURE

What will the derivatives market look like in the future? It is of course impossible to know but this section presents some "educated guesswork" to project major trends in derivatives and the financial markets in general.

### 23.2.1  Products

In the aftermath of the crisis, "exotic" derivatives largely disappeared from the market. Some exotic products such as PRDCs have made a limited comeback (Woolner, 2014) although on nothing like the scale found pre-crisis. Some markets such as short-dated FX derivatives have seen less impact than other markets such as exotic interest rate derivatives, reflecting the lower capital requirements associated with such products. "Vanilla" products form the bulk of derivatives traded now and this seems unlikely to change in the future as the capital requirements and risks associated with "exotics" make them uneconomic.

The structured credit market in fact made a return of sorts soon after the crisis as banks structured notes eligible for the various liquidity facilities provided by central banks. Even synthetic CDOs have now reappeared (Abramowicz, 2015). This reflects market conditions and a "search for yield" in a low interest rate environment. In such market conditions it should be expected that products that offer yield enhancement will be traded. CLO structures clearly also fit into this category (Haunss, 2015). Exotic equity structures may also return on the same basis, although these will likely remain relatively short-dated.

Nevertheless, very high leverage products such as the $CDO^2$ have, thankfully, not come back and given the enhanced regulatory framework it seems unlikely they ever will.

### 23.2.2  CCPs, Clearing and MVA

At the G20 meeting in Pittsburg in 2009 (G20, 2009) the leaders made a statement committing to the introduction of mandatory clearing for standardised derivatives. Since then CCPs have developed to provide this clearing facility and an increasing number of derivatives can be cleared, although the timescales have perhaps been slower than originally anticipated by the G20. Given the move towards clearing of standardised derivatives and the fact that few non-standardised products now trade does this mean that eventually all derivatives will be cleared? Furthermore does the high collateralisation associated with clearing mean the end of CVA?

The answer to both these questions is no. Many corporates will still not be in a position to clear as they will not have ready access to eligible collateral nor will they have the operational capability to clear. In practice then clearing is replacing existing bilateral relationships collateralised under CSAs. The impact on CVA then depends on whether or not collateralised counterparties form a large portion of the CVA. For a commercial bank for whom the bulk of CVA is derived from small to medium-sized regional corporates, clearing may have little or no impact on CVA. However, for a major international bank, with large CVA reserves associated with interbank counterparties and major corporates, CVA would decline substantially under clearing. So although CVA will not disappear under clearing it will probably decline in importance.

Of course CCPs demand initial margin, as was discussed in Chapter 10, leading directly to MVA. Bilateral relationships between financials will also require initial margin under BCBS-261 (2013e) and hence have MVA associated with them. Collateral, margin and the cost associated with them will increasingly be a major issue in the future. CVA may decline, therefore, only to be replaced by MVA.

As CCPs become increasingly important, questions are being raised about what happens to CCPs in extreme circumstances such as the default of one or more clearing members (Sourbes, 2015). Regulators are also focussed on improving risk management standards at CCPs and on recovery and resolution arrangements (Bailey, 2014). Practitioners and academics have highlighted potential problems with CCPs such as the impact of competitive pressures on margin arrangements (Kenyon and Green, 2013c) and questioned whether in fact CCPs actually reduce counterparty risk (Duffie and Zhu, 2011; Amini et al., 2014). Nevertheless CCPs are clearly here to stay and will form a central part of derivatives markets in the future.

### 23.2.3  Regulation, Capital and KVA

Chapter 12 noted a series of regulatory changes that were already under discussion. These changes, particularly the *fundamental review of the trading book*, will be a central element of regulatory change over the next few years. There will be further regulatory changes in the future and it is impossible to predict what they will be or the capital implications of them.

It is clear that regulatory capital and the management of capital as a scare resource is now a central business concern of banks. This does not mean that banks are engaged in a process to reduce overall capital and increase bank risks as a result, rather it is an attempt by banks to better understand the risk-return profile. There is an opportunity to both de-risk the balance sheet and improve the returns to shareholders through careful management of resources.

KVA and similar *return-on-capital* models provide the means for banks to correctly assess the return they make for shareholders both at point of sale and throughout the lifetime of a transaction. KVA will incentivise banks to use transactions that perform over the lifetime of the trade, not trades that look good over the first year and then produce poor returns for the remainder of the deal. Trades that attract lower capital are, in general, trades that have lower risks associated with them. One development that has started to appear is discussion around whether or not an accounting adjustment needs to be made for KVA, on the basis that it forms part of the *exit price*, although there are no firm conclusions either way at present.

### 23.2.4  Computation, Automation and eTrading

The discussion in Chapters 20 and 21 shows that high performance computing platforms such as GPUs and new techniques such as AAD are revolutionising XVA model implementation and indeed the infrastructure of trading and risk management platforms as a whole. Faster performance means more sophisticated model treatments can be applied and better risk sensitivities available on a fast and frequent basis. While the introduction of AAD and associated sensitivity calculations provides a step change in capability, ongoing computational development shows no sign of slowing down. The future is one of ever increasing computational performance; however, it should also be clear that this computational performance will be absolutely necessary. While products are getting simpler, the models used to value them are getting more sophisticated because the complexity of the market is also increasing. More computational power will therefore be required.

There is also a general trend of automation appearing in parallel with computational developments. eTrading platforms will increasingly provide the interface between banks and their clients, reducing the need for sales staff but relationship managers will still remain. Algorithmic and automatic trading will revolutionise the management of trading books where algorithms will risk manage trades rather than human trading staff, although traders will still be needed to oversee the algorithms and define the boundaries that the algorithms operate within. This trend towards automation will leverage off higher computational performance of valuation models. Quants and technologists will likely be the beneficiaries of these changes as they will be needed to create the computational infrastructure.

### 23.2.5 Future Models and Future XVA

The *valuation paradigm shift* is now in full swing. Derivative valuation is moving away from the Black-Scholes-Merton framework and its assumptions to include more realism and currently this is being expressed through XVA. XVA itself is growing, with more adjustments being added to the framework. In a sense XVA is about elucidating the costs of doing derivatives business. In some cases these costs have always been present but ignored, while in others the costs are new and associated with changes in the market. Will the current focus on XVA continue indefinitely? Probably not, but what XVA has done is broaden the horizons of quant researchers beyond the Black-Scholes framework. The focus on XVA may decline but the changes in financial markets that have come with that focus are unlikely to change. Models now need to match market realities, however mathematically or technically unpleasant this may be to deal with. This means that quants now and in the future have to deal with complexity on a huge scale. The sophisticated risk-neutral models of the pre-crisis period will look simplistic compared to the modelling frameworks that will be needed in the future.

However, the division between XVA and model is artificial and an artefact of bank organisational design rather than anything fundamental. XVA adjusts a price from a model that is not realistic to one that is. XVA therefore simply corrects the deficiencies of the underlying model. Why not simply build a model that values the derivatives correctly in the first instance and generates the correct overall sensitivities? Why not build a universal valuation model? Increasingly there seems no reason not to and at some point in the future the artificial distinction between model and XVA will be removed.

What would such a universal valuation model look like? It would certainly have to value all the financial contracts that a bank has collectively. It should be clear that there are effects such as the leverage ratio that span the entire bank and hence trade "valuation" is actually an exercise in allocating an overall value function down to trade level. Such a model would inevitably be complex and capture the key elements of the behaviour of each asset class and the dependencies between them. While this would be difficult, it is not far from the sophistication of existing XVA models. The advantage of such a model is that it would bring consistency and transparency to the valuation of the bank balance sheet. It would also allow a much greater sophistication in risk management and risk assessment. Bank management would truly be able to understand and control the behaviour of the balance sheet in different market conditions and plan accordingly.

★ ★ ★

*Even if there is only one possible unified theory, it is just a set of rules and equations. What is it that breathes fire into the equations and makes a universe for them to describe?*

Stephen Hawking CBE CH FRS FRSA<br>
*Emeritus Lucasian Professor for Cambridge and*<br>
*author of A Brief History of Time (1942–)*

# Bibliography

Abramowicz, Lisa (2015). "Goldman Sachs Hawks CDOs Tainted by Credit Crisis Under New Name". *Bloomberg*. url: http://www.bloomberg.com/news/articles/2015-02-04/goldman-sachs-hawks-cdos-tainted-by-credit-crisis-under-new-name.

Adams, Ken (2001). "Smooth Interpolation of Zero Curves". 4.1, *Algo Research Quarterly*, pp. 11–22.

Ahn, D-H, R. Dittmar, and A. Gallant (2002). "Quadratic Term Structure Models: Theory and evidence". 15, *Review of Financial Studies*, pp. 243–280.

Aïd, René (2015). *Electricity Derivatives (SpringerBriefs in Quantitative Finance)*. Springer.

Aïd, René et al. (2009). "A Structural Risk-Neutral Model of Electricity Prices". 12.07, *International Journal of Theoretical and Applied Finance*, pp. 925–947.

Aklam, Peter J. (2003). "An algorithm for computing the inverse normal cumulative distribution function". *Peter's Page*. url: http://home.online.no/~pjacklam/notes/invnorm/index.html.

Ambac (2010). "*Ambac Files for Bankruptcy Under Chapter 11 of the United States Bankruptcy Code*". url: http://www.ambac.com/press/110810.html.

Ameritrano, Ferdinando and Marco Bianchetti (2009). "Bootstrapping the Illiquidity: Multiple Yield Curve Construction for Market Coherent Forward Rates Estimation". *Modelling Interest Rates*, Ed. by Fabio Mercurio. Risk Books.

Amin, Ahsan (2010). "Calibration, Simulation and Hedging in a Heston Libor Market Model with Stochastic Basis". *SSRN*. url: http://ssrn.com/abstract=1704415.

Amini, Hamed, Damir Filipovic, and Andreea Minca (2014). "Systemic Risk with Central Counterparty Clearing". *SSRN*. url: http://ssrn.com/abstract=2275376.

Andersen, Leif B. G. (2007). "Discount Curve Construction with Tension Splines". 10.3, *Review of Derivatives Research*, pp. 227–267.

Andersen, Leif B. G. and Jesper Andreasen (2000). "Jump-Diffusion Processes: Volatility Smile Fitting and Numerical Methods for Option Pricing". 4.3, *Review of Derivatives Research*, pp. 231–262.

Andersen, Leif B. G. and R. Brotherton-Ratcliffe (2001). "Extended Libor Market Models with Stochastic Volatility". *SSRN*. url: http://ssrn.com/abstract=294853.

Andersen, Leif B. G. and Vladimir V. Piterbarg (2010a). *Interest Rate Modeling. Volume 1: Foundations and Vanilla Models*. Atlantic Financial Press.

Andersen, Leif B. G. and Vladimir V. Piterbarg (2010b). *Interest Rate Modeling. Volume 2: Term Structure Models*. Atlantic Financial Press.

Andersen, Leif B. G. and Vladimir V. Piterbarg (2010c). *Interest Rate Modeling. Volume 3: Products and Risk Management*. Atlantic Financial Press.

Anderson, E. et al. (1999). *LAPACK Users' Guide*. 3rd ed., Society for Industrial and Applied Mathematics. url: http://www.netlib.org/lapack/lug/.

Anderson, Herbert L. (1986). "Metropolis, Monte Carlo, and the MANIAC". *Los Alamos Science*, pp. 96–108. url: http://library.lanl.gov/cgi-bin/getfile?00326886.pdf.

Anderson, Richard G. and Yang Liu (2013). "How Low Can You Go? Negative Interest Rates and Investors' Flight to Safety". *The Regional Economist*, January.

Andreasen, Jesper (2001). "Turbo Charging the Cheyette Model". *SSRN*. url: http://ssrn.com/abstract=1719142.

Andreasen, Jesper (2005). "Back to the Future". 18.9, *Risk*, pp. 104–109.

Andreasen, Jesper (2014). "CVA on an iPad Mini". *Global Derivatives 2014*, ICBI, Amsterdam.

Andreasen, Jesper and Brian Norsk Huge (2011). "ZABR – Expansions for the Masses". *SSRN*. url: http://ssrn.com/abstract=1980726.

ANSI (2011). "ISO/IEC 14882:2011 Standard C++ 11".

Antonov, Alexandre, Marco Bianchetti, and Ion Mihai (2013). "Funding Value Adjustment for General Financial Instruments: Theory and Practice". *SSRN*. url: http://ssrn.com/abstract=2290987.

Antonov, Alexandre, Michael Konikov, and Michael Spector (2015). "The Free Boundary SABR: Natural Extension to Negative Rates". *SSRN*. url: http://ssrn.com/abstract=2557046.

Antonov, Alexandre and Vladimir Piterbarg (2014). "Options for Collateral Options". *Risk*, 27.3.

Antonov, I. A. and V. M. Saleev (1979). "An Economic Method of Computing $LP_\tau$ – Sequences". *U.S.S.R. Comput. Maths. Math. Phys.*, pp. 252–256.

Artaud, Gilles and Veronique Berger (2011). "Trading versus banking approach of CVA". *2nd Annual CVA and Counterparty Risk Conference*, Marcus Evans.

ASB (2000). "Financial Reporting Standard 18". *Accounting Standards Board*. url: http://www.frc.org.uk/Our-Work/Publications/ASB/FRS-18-Accounting-Policies/FRS-18-Accounting-Policies.aspx.

Assefa, Samson (2007). "Calibration and Pricing in a multi-factor quadratic Gaussian model". *Quantitative Finance Research Centre, University of Technology, Sydney*. url: http://www.qfrc.uts.edu.au/research/research_papers/rp197.pdf.

Avanitis, Angelo and Jon Gregory (2001). *Credit: The Complete Guide to Pricing, Hedging and Risk Management*. Risk Books.

Babbs, Simon (1993). "Generalised Vasicek Models of the Term Structure". 9, *Applied Stochastic Models and Data Analysis*, pp. 49–62.

Bailey, David (2014). "The Bank of England's perspective on CCP risk management, recovery and resolution arrangements". *Bank of England*. url: http://www.bankofengland.co.uk/publications/Documents/speeches/2014/speech781.pdf.

Balog, Dóra (2010). "Risk Based Capital Allocation". *Proceedings of FIKUSZ '10*, Óbuda University, Keleti Faculty of Business and Management.

Barone, Emilio and Antonio Castagna (1998). "The Information Content of Tips". *SSRN*. url: http://ssrn.com/abstract=2170675.

Barr, Alistair (2008). "Lehman CDS auction prices bonds at 8.625 cents on the dollar". *Market Watch*. url: http://www.marketwatch.com/story/lehman-cds-auction-prices-bonds-at-8625-cents-on-the-dollar.

Bases, Daniel and William James (2012). "ISDA declares Greek credit event, CDS Payments triggered". *Reuters*. url: http://www.reuters.com/article/2012/03/09/us-greece-cds-isda-trigger-idUSBRE82817B20120309.

BBC (2002). "*ENRON: Timeline*". url: http://news.bbc.co.uk/1/hi/business/1759599.stm.

BCBS (1975). "Report to the governors on the supervision of banks' foreign establishments". *Bank for International Settlements*. url: http://www.bis.org/publ/bcbs00a.pdf.

BCBS (1983). "Principles for the Supervision of Banks' Foreign Establishments". *Bank for International Settlements*. url: http://www.bis.org/publ/bcbsc312.pdf.

BCBS (1987). "Proposals for International Convergence of Capital Measurement and Standards – consultative document". *Bank for International Settlements*. url: http://www.bis.org/publ/bcbs03a.pdf.

BCBS (1988). "The Basel Accord". *Bank for International Settlements*. url: http://www.bis.org/publ/bcbs04a.pdf.

BCBS (1990). "Information Flows Between Banking Supervisory Authorities". *Bank for International Settlements*. url: http://www.bis.org/publ/bcbsc313.pdf.

BCBS (1991). "Amendment of the Basle Capital Accord in respect of the Inclusion of General Provisions/General Loan-Loss Reserves in Capital". *Bank for International Settlements*. url: http://www.bis.org/publ/bcbs09.pdf.

BCBS (1992). "Minimum Standards for the Supervision of International Banking Groups and their Cross-Border Establishments". *Bank for International Settlements*. url: http://www.bis.org/publ/bcbsc314.pdf.

BCBS (1995). "Basle Capital Accord: Treatment of Potential Exposure for Off-Balance-Sheet Items". *Bank for International Settlements*. url: http://www.bis.org/publ/bcbs18.pdf.

BCBS (1996a). "Amendment to the Capital Accord to Incorporate Market Risks Amendment to the Capital Accord to Incorporate Market Risks". *Bank for International Settlements*. url: http://www.bis.org/publ/bcbs24.pdf.

BCBS (1996b). "Interpretation of the Capital Accord for the Multilateral Netting of Forward Value Foreign Exchange Transactions". *Bank for International Settlements*. url: http://www.bis.org/publ/bcbs25.pdf.

BCBS (1996c). "The Supervision of Cross-Border Banking". *Bank for International Settlements*. url: http://www.bis.org/publ/bcbs27.pdf.

BCBS (1997). "Core Principles for Effective Banking Supervision". *Bank for International Settlements*. url: http://www.bis.org/publ/bcbs30a.pdf.

BCBS (1999). "A New Capital Adequacy Framework". *Bank for International Settlements*. url: http://www.bis.org/publ/bcbs50.pdf.

BCBS (2004). "International Convergence of Capital Measurement and Capital Standards". *Bank for International Settlements*. url: http://www.bis.org/publ/bcbs107.htm.

BCBS (2006a). "Core Principles for Effective Banking Supervision". *Bank for International Settlements*. url: http://www.bis.org/publ/bcbs129.pdf.

BCBS (2006b). "International Convergence of Capital Measurement and Capital Standards". *Bank for International Settlements*. url: http://www.bis.org/publ/bcbs128.htm.

BCBS (2008). "Principles for Sound Liquidity Risk Management and Supervision". *Bank for International Settlements*. url: http://www.bis.org/publ/bcbs144.pdf.

BCBS (2009a). "Enhancements to the Basel II Framework". *Bank for International Settlements*. url: http://www.bis.org/publ/bcbs157.pdf.

BCBS (2009b). "Guidelines for Computing Capital for Incremental Risk in the Trading Book". *Bank for International Settlements*. url: http://www.bis.org/publ/bcbs159.pdf.

BCBS (2009c). "Range of Practices and Issues in Economic Capital Frameworks". *Bank for International Settlements*. url: http://www.bis.org/publ/bcbs152.pdf.

BCBS (2011a). "Application of Own Credit Risk Adjustments to Derivatives – Consultative Document". *Bank for International Settlements*. url: http://www.bis.org/publ/bcbs214.pdf.

BCBS (2011b). "Basel III: A global regulatory framework for more resilient banks and banking systems". *Bank for International Settlements*. url: http://www.bis.org/bcbs/basel3.htm.

BCBS (2011c). "Operational Risk – Supervisory Guidelines for the Advanced Measurement Approaches". *Bank for International Settlements*. url: http://www.bis.org/publ/bcbs196.pdf.

BCBS (2011d). "Principles for the Sound Management of Operational Risk". *Bank for International Settlements*. url: http://www.bis.org/publ/bcbs195.pdf.

BCBS (2012a). "About the Basel Committee". *Bank for International Settlements*. url: http://www.bis.org/bcbs/about.htm.

BCBS (2012b). "Basel III Counterparty Credit Risk and Exposures to Central Counterparties – Frequently asked questions". *Bank for International Settlements*. url: http://www.bis.org/publ/bcbs284.htm.

BCBS (2012c). "Capital Requirements for Bank Exposures to Central Counterparties". *Bank for International Settlements*. url: http://www.bis.org/publ/bcbs227.pdf.

BCBS (2012d). "Compilation of Documents that Form the Global Regulatory Framework for Capital and Liquidity". *Bank for International Settlements*. url: http://www.bis.org/bcbs/basel3/compilation.htm.

BCBS (2012e). "Consultative Document – Margin requirements for non-centrally-cleared derivatives". *Bank for International Settlements*. url: http://www.bis.org/publ/bcbs226.pdf.

BCBS (2012f). "Core Principles for Effective Banking Supervision". *Bank for International Settlements*. url: http://www.bis.org/publ/bcbs230.pdf.

BCBS (2012g). "Fundamental Review of the Trading Book". *Bank for International Settlements*. url: http://www.bis.org/publ/bcbs219.pdf.

BCBS (2012h). "Margin Requirements for Non-centrally-cleared Derivatives". *Bank for International Settlements*. url: http://www.bis.org/publ/bcbs226.htm.

BCBS (2013a). "A Brief History of the Basel Committee". *Bank for International Settlements*. url: http://www.bis.org/bcbs/history.pdf.

BCBS (2013b). "Basel III: The Liquidity Coverage Ratio and liquidity risk monitoring tools". *Bank for International Settlements*. url: http://www.bis.org/publ/bcbs238.pdf.

BCBS (2013c). "Fundamental Review of the Trading Book – second consultative document". *Bank for International Settlements*. url: http://www.bis.org/publ/bcbs265.htm.

BCBS (2013d). "Margin Requirements for Non-centrally-cleared Derivatives". *Bank for International Settlements*. url: http://www.bis.org/publ/bcbs261.htm.

BCBS (2013e). "Second Consultative Document Margin Requirements for Non-centrally Cleared Derivatives". *Bank for International Settlements*. url: http://www.bis.org/publ/bcbs242.pdf.

BCBS (2013f). "The Non-internal Model Method for Capitalising Counterparty Credit Risk Exposures". *Bank for International Settlements*. url: http://www.bis.org/publ/bcbs254.pdf.

BCBS (2014a). "Fundamental Review of the Trading Book: Outstanding issues – consultative document". *Bank for International Settlements*. url: http://www.bis.org/bcbs/publ/d305.htm.

BCBS (2014b). "The Standardised Approach for Measuring Counterparty Credit Risk Exposures". *Bank for International Settlements*. url: http://www.bis.org/publ/bcbs279.pdf.

BCBS (2015). "Margin Requirements for Non-centrally Cleared Derivatives". *Bank for International Settlements*. url: http://www.bis.org/bcbs/publ/d317.htm.

Beasley, J. D. and S. G. Springer (1977). "Percentage Points of the Normal Distribution". 26, *Applied Statistics*, pp. 118–121.

Beck, Kent (1999). *Extreme Programming Explained: Embrace Change*. Addison-Wesley Professional.

Beck, Kent, et al. (2001). *Manifesto for Agile Software Development*. url: http://agilemanifesto.org/.

Belgrade, N., E. Benhamou, and E. Koehler (2004). "A Market Model for Inflation". *SSRN*. url: http://ssrn.com/abstract=576081.

Benhamou, Eric, Arnaud Rivoira, and Anne Gruz (2008). "Stochastic Interest Rates for Local Volatility Hybrids Models". *SSRN*. url: http://ssrn.com/abstract=1107711.

Benington, Herbert D. (1956). "Production of Large Computer Programs". *Symposium on advanced programming methods for digital computers: Washington, D.C., June 28, 29, 1956*, Office of Naval Research, Dept. of the Navy.

Benington, Herbert D. (1983). "Production of Large Computer Programs". 5.4, *Annals of the History of Computing*, pp. 350–361.

Benth, Fred, Valery Kholodnyi, and Peter Laurence eds. (2013). *Quantitative Energy Finance: Modeling, Pricing, and Hedging in Energy and Commodity Markets*. Springer.

Beyna, I. (2010). *Interest Rate Derivatives*. Springer-Verlag.

Bianchetti, Marco (2010). "Two Curves, One Price". 23.8, *Risk*, pp. 74–80.

Black, Fischer (1976). "The Pricing of Commodity Contracts". 3, *Journal of Financial Economics*, pp. 167–179.

Black, Fischer and Piotr Karasinski (1991). "Bond and Option Pricing when Short Rates are Lognormal". 47, *Financial Analysts Journal*, pp. 52–59.

Black, Fischer and Myron Scholes (1973). "The Pricing of Options and Corporate Liabilities". 81.3, *Journal of Political Economy*, pp. 637–654.

Bloch, Daniel (2009). "Multi-Currency Fast Stochastic Local Volatility Model". *SSRN*. url: http://ssrn.com/abstract=1492086.

Bloch, Daniel (2010). "A Note on Emissions Trading: The Pricing of Carbon Derivatives". *SSRN*. url: http://ssrn.com/abstract=1701619.

Bloch, Daniel and Samson Assefa (2009a). "Fast Calibration of Interest Rate Claims in the Quadratic Gaussian Model: 1 The Caplets". *SSRN*. url: http://ssrn.com/abstract=1361609.

Bloch, Daniel and Samson Assefa (2009b). "Fast Calibration of Interest Rate Claims in the Quadratic Gaussian Model: 2 The Swaptions". *SSRN*. url: http://ssrn.com/abstract=1441187.

Booch, Grady (1983). *Software Engineering with Ada*. Benjamin/Cummings Pub. Co.

Borovkova, Svetlana and Helyette Geman (2007). "Seasonal and Stochastic Effects in Commodity Forward Curves". 9, *Review of Derivatives Research*, pp. 167–186.

Borsdorf, Rüdiger and Nicholas J. Higham (2010). "A Preconditioned Newton Algorithm for the Nearest Correlation Matrix". 30.1, *IMA Journal of Numerical Analysis*, pp. 94–107.

Box, G. E. P. and M. E. Muller (1958). "A Note on the Generation of Random Normal Deviates". 29, *Annals of Mathematical Statistics*, pp. 610–611.

Boyle, Phelim, Mark Broadie, and Paul Glasserman (1997). "Monte Carlo Methods for Security Pricing". 21, *Journal of Economic Dynamics and Control*, pp. 1267–1321.

Brace, Alan, Dariusz Gatarek and Marek Musiela (1997). "The Market Model of Interest Rate Dynamics". 7.2, *Mathematical Finance*, pp. 127–155.

Bradley, Thomas, Jaques du Toit, Mike Giles, Robert Tong, and Paul Woodhams (2011). "Parallelisation Techniques for Random Number Generators". *GPU Computing Gems*, Ed. by Wen mei W. Hwu, pp. 231–246.

Bratley, Paul and Bennett L. Fox (1988). "Algorithm 659: Implementing Sobol's Quasirandom Sequence Generator". 14.1, *ACM Trans. Math. Softw.*, pp. 88–100.

Brent, Richard (1973). *Algorithms for Minimization without Derivatives*. Prentice-Hall.

Brigo, Damiano (2004). "Market Models for CDS Options and Callable Floaters". *Risk*, 17.11.

Brigo, Damiano and Aurelien Alfonsi (2005). "Credit Default Swaps Calibration and Interest-Rate Model". 9, *Finance and Stochastics*, pp. 29–42.

Brigo, Damiano and Imane Bakkar (2009). "Accurate counterparty risk valuation for energy-commodities swaps". *Energy Risk*, March.

Brigo, Damiano and Naoufel El-Bachir (2010). "An Exact Formula for Default Swaptions' Pricing in the SSRJD Stochastic Intensity Model". 20.3, *Mathematical Finance*, pp. 365–382.

Brigo, Damiano and Fabio Mercurio (2003). "Analytical Pricing of the Smile in a Forward LIBOR Market Model". 3.1, *Quantitative Finance*, pp. 15–27.

Brigo, Damiano and Fabio Mercurio (2006). *Interest Rate Models – Theory and Practice*. 2nd ed., Springer.

Brigo, Damiano and Massimo Morini (2011). "Close Out Convention Tensions". *Risk*, 24.12.

Brigo, Damiano and Andrea Pallavicini (2008). "Counterparty Risk and CCDSs under Correlation". 21.2, *Risk*, pp. 84–88.

Brigo, Damiano, Cristin Buescu, Andrea Pallavicini, and Qing Lui (2012). "Illustrating a Problem in the Self-Financing Condition in Two 2010-2011 Papers on Funding, Collateral and Discounting". *SSRN*. url: http://ssrn.com/abstract=2103121.

Broadie, Mark and Paul Glasserman (1996). "Estimating Security Price Derivatives Using Simulation". 42.2, *Management Science*, pp. 269–285.

Bruti-Liberati, Nicola and Eckhard Platen (2008). "Strong Predictor–Corrector Euler Methods for Stochastic Differential Equations". 08.03, *Stochastics and Dynamics*, pp. 561–581.

Burgard, Christoph and Mats Kjaer (2011a). "In the Balance". *Risk*, 24.10.

Burgard, Christoph and Mats Kjaer (2011b). "Partial Differential Equation Representations of Derivatives with Bilateral Counterparty Risk and Funding Costs". 7, *Journal of Credit Risk*, pp. 75–93.

Burgard, Christoph and Mats Kjaer (2012a). "A Generalised CVA with Funding and Collateral via Semi-Replication". *SSRN*. url: http://ssrn.com/abstract=2027195.

Burgard, Christoph and Mats Kjaer (2012b). "Addendum to: 'PDE Representations of Derivatives with Bilateral Counterparty Risk and Funding Costs'". *SSRN*. url: http://ssrn.com/abstract=2109723.

Burgard, Christoph and Mats Kjaer (2012c). "CVA and FVA with Funding Aware Close Outs". *SSRN*. url: http://ssrn.com/abstract=2157631.

Burgard, Christoph and Mats Kjaer (2013). "Funding Strategies, Funding Costs". 26.12, *Risk*, pp. 82–87.

Cameron, Matt (2011). "Margin Models Converge as CCPs Battle for Dealer Support". *Risk*, 24.10.

Cameron, Matt (2012). "Breaking with Tradition". *Risk*, 25.3.

Cameron, Matt (2014a). "Isda Forced to Rework Year-old Standard CSA". *Risk*, 27.2.

Cameron, Matt (2014b). "The Black Art of FVA, Part II: Conditioning chaos". *Risk*, 27.4.

Capriotti, Luca and Mike Giles (2012). "Algorithmic Differentiation: Adjoint Greeks Made Easy". *Risk*, 25.9.

Capriotti, Luca and Jacky Lee (2014). "Adjoint Credit Risk Management". *Risk*, 27.8.

Carmiel, Oshrat (2012). "Lehman Lives to Pay 18 Cents on Dollar With New Sales: Mortgages". *Bloomberg*. url: http://www.bloomberg.com/news/2012-08-13/lehman-lives-to-pay-18-cents-on-dollar-with-new-sales-mortgages.html.

Carmona, René and Michael Ludkovski (2004). "Spot Convenience Yield Models for the Energy Markets". 351, *Contemporary Mathematics*, pp. 65–80.

Carver, Laurie (2010). "Quant Congress USA: Ban DVA, Counterparty Risk Quant Says". *Risk*, 23.7.

Carver, Laurie (2011). "Quants Call for Isda to Clarify Close-out Values". *Risk*, 24.12.

Carver, Laurie (2012a). "DVA is a Shameful Scam". *Risk*, 25.11.

Carver, Laurie (2012b). "Traders Close Ranks against FVA Critics". *Risk*, 25.9.

Carver, Laurie (2013). "Proxy War: Shrinking CDS market leaves CVA and DVA on shaky ground". *Risk*, 26.3.

Castagna, Antonio (2012). "Yes, FVA is a Cost for Derivatives Desks – A Note on 'Is FVA a Cost for Derivatives Desks?' by Prof. Hull and Prof. White". *SSRN*. url: http://ssrn.com/abstract=2141663.

Celoxica (2005). "Handel-C Language Reference Manual". *Celoxica*.

Cesari, Giovanni, John Aquilina, Niels Charpillon, Zlatko Filipović, Gordon Lee, and Ion Manda (2009). *Modelling, Pricing and Hedging Counterparty Credit Exposure*. Springer.

Chacon, Scott and Ben Straub (2014). *Pro Git*. Apress.

Chen, Zhiyong and Paul Glasserman (2008). "Sensitivity Estimates for Portfolio Credit Derivatives using Monte Carlo". 12.4, *Finance and Stochastics*, pp. 507–540.

Cheyette, Oren (1992). "Markov Representation of the Heath-Jarrow-Morton Model". *SSRN*. url: http://ssrn.com/abstract=6073.

Chibane, Messaoud and Dikman Law (2013). "A Quadratic Volatility Cheyette Model". *Risk*, 26.6.

Chibane, Messaoud and Guy Sheldon (2009). "Building Curves on a Good Basis". *SSRN*. url: http://ssrn.com/abstract=1394267.

Chourdakis, Kyriakos, Eduardo Epperlein, Marc Jeannin, and James McEwen (2013). "A Cross-section across CVA". *Nomura*.

Cifuentes, Arturo and Georgios Katsaros (2007). "The One-Factor Gaussian Copula Applied to CDOs: Just Say NO (Or, If You See a Correlation Smile, She Is Laughing at Your "Results")". *R.W. Pressprich & Co.*

Clark, Iain J. (2011). *Foreign Exchange Option Pricing: A Practitioners Guide*. John Wiley & Sons.

Clewlow, Les and Chris Strickland (1999). "Valuing Energy Options in a One Factor Model Fitted to Forward Prices". *SSRN*. url: http://ssrn.com/abstract=160608.

CME Group (2013). "Introduction to Crack Spreads". *CME Group*. url: http://www.cmegroup.com/trading/energy/files/EN-211\_CrackSpreadHandbook\_SR.PDF.

Combes, Rémi Tachet Des (2011). "Calibration non paramétriques de modèles en finance". Ph.D. thesis, Ecole Centrale Paris. url: https://tel.archives-ouvertes.fr/file/index/docid/658766/filename/tachet.pdf.

Cox, J. C., J. E. Ingersoll, and S. Ross (1985). "A Theory of the Term Structure of Interest Rates". 53, *Econometrica*, pp. 385–407.

Cox, John Carrington and Stephen Ross (1976). "The Valuation of Options for Alternative Stochastic Processes". *Journal of Financial Economics*, pp. 145–166.

Cranley, R. and T. N. L. Patterson (1976). "Randomization of Number Theoretic Methods for Multiple Integration". 13, *SIAM Journal of Numerical Analysis*, pp. 904–914.

Crépey, Stéphane (2015a). "Bilateral Counterparty Risk Under Funding Constraints Part I: Pricing". 25.1, *Mathematical Finance*, pp. 1–22.

Crépey, Stéphane (2015b). "Bilateral Counterparty Risk Under Funding Constraints Part II: CVA". *Mathematical Finance*, pp. 23–50.

Crépey, Stéphane and Abdallah Rahal (2013). "Simulation/Regression Pricing Schemes for CVA Computations on CDO Tranches". *SSRN*.

Curran, Michael (1999). "Recovering Identity". *Monte Carlo: Methodologies and Applications for Pricing and Risk Management*, Ed. by Bruno Dupire. Risk Books.

Deelstra, Griselda and Grégory Rayée (2012). "Local Volatility Pricing Models for Long-dated FX Derivatives". *Arxiv*. url: http://arxiv.org/pdf/1204.0633v1.pdf.

Deming, W. Edwards (1982). *Out of the Crisis*. MIT.

Deng, S.J., Blake Johnson, and Aram Sogomonian (2001). "Exotic Electricity Options and the Valuation of Electricity Generation and Transmission Assets". 30, *Decision Support Systems*, pp. 383–392.

Deng, S.J. and S.S. Oren (2006). "Electricity Derivatives and Risk Management". 31, *Energy*, pp. 940—953.

Deutsche Bundesbank (2007). "Basel II – the New Capital Accord". *Bundesbank*. url: http://www.bundesbank.de/Navigation/EN/Tasks/Banking_supervision/Basel2/basel2.html.

D'Hulster, Katia (2001). "Re: Calculation of Regulatory Capital for Counterparty Risk". *ISDA*.

Dodgson, Matthew and Dherminder Kainth (2006). "Inflation-Linked Derivatives". *RBS*. url: http://www.quarchome.org/inflation/inflationlinkedderivatives20060908.pdf.

Doust, Paul (2012). "No-abritrage SABR". 15.3, *Journal of Computational Finance*, pp. 3–31.

Downey, Steve (2013). "The Paradigms of C++". *Embarcadero Developer Network*.

Duffie, Darrell and Haoxiang Zhu (2011). "Does a Central Clearing Counterparty Reduce Counterparty Risk?" *SSRN*. url: http://ssrn.com/abstract=1348343.

Dupire, Bruno (1994). "Pricing with a Smile". 7.1, *Risk*, pp. 18–20.

EBA (2012). "Discussion Paper: Relating to Draft Regulatory Technical Standards on prudent valuation under Article 100 of the draft Capital Requirements Regulation (CRR)". *European Banking Authority*. url: http://www.eba.europa.eu/documents/10180/41517/EBA-DP-2012-03--RTS-on-Prudent-Valuation---Final.pdf.

EBA (2013a). "Consulation Paper: Draft Regulatory Technical Standards (RTS) on prudent valuation under Article 105(14) of Regulation (EU) 575/2013 (Capital Requirements Regulation – CRR)". *European Banking Authority*.

EBA (2013b). "EBA Final draft Regulatory Technical Standards on credit valuation adjustment risk for the determination of a proxy spread and the specification of a limited number of smaller portfolios under Article 383 (7) of Regulation (EU) No 575/2013 (Capital Requirements Regulation – CRR)". *European Banking Authority*. url: http://www.eba.europa.eu/documents/10180/535344/EBA-RTS-2013-17+%28Final+draft+RTS+on+CVA%29.pdf.

EBA (2014a). "Commission Implementing Regulation (EU) No 680/2014 of 16 April 2014 laying down implementing technical standards with regard to supervisory reporting of institutions according to Regulation (EU) No 575/2013 of the European Parliament and of the Council". *European Banking Authority*.

EBA (2014b). "EBA Final draft implementing technical standards on disclosure of the leverage ratio under Article 451(2) of Regulation (EU) No 575/2013 (Capital Requirements Regulation – CRR)". *European Banking Authority*.

EBA (2014c). "EBA Final draft Regulatory Technical Standards on prudent valuation under Article 105(14) of Regulation (EU) No 575/2013 (Capital Requirements Regulation – CRR)". *European Banking Authority*. url: https://www.eba.europa.eu/documents/10180/642449/EBA-RTS-2014-06+RTS+on+Prudent+Valuation.pdf.

Eberlein, Ernst, Wolfgang Kluge, and Philipp Schönbucher (2006). "The Lévy Libor model with default risk". *Journal of Credit Risk*, 2.2.

Ebrahimi, Helia (2009). "Lehman Collapse: PwC's Tony Lomas sees 20-year slog to unravel biggest bankruptcy". *The Telegraph*. url: http://www.telegraph.co.uk/finance/financialcrisis/6195059/Lehman-collapse-PwCs-Tony-Lomas-sees-20-year-slog-to-unravel-biggest-bankruptcy.html.

Eckhardt, Roger (1987). "Stan Ulam, John Von Neumann, and the Monte Carlo Method". *Los Alamos Science*, pp. 131–143.

Elliott, Larry and Jill Treanor (2009). "UK was hours from bank shutdown". *The Observer*, 6 September.

Elouerkhaoui, Youssef (2011). "Trading CVA: A New Development in Correlation Modelling". *Kings College London Financial Mathematics and Applied Probability Seminars*.

Elouerkhaoui, Youssef (2014). "From FVA To RWA: Should The Cost Of Equity Be Included In The Pricing Of Deals?" In *ICBI Global Derivatives*.

Emmer, Susanne, Marie Kratz, and Dirk Tasche (2013). "What is the best risk measure in practice? A comparison of standard measures". *arXiv.org*. url: http://ideas.repec.org/p/arx/papers/1312.1645.html.

ESMA (2014). "Public Register for the Clearing Obligation under EMIR". *European Securities and Markets Authority*. url: http://www.esma.europa.eu/system/files/public_register_for_the_clearing_obligation_under_emir.pdf.

European Commission (2013). "The EU Emissions Trading System (EU ETS)". *European Commission*. url: http://ec.europa.eu/clima/policies/ets/index_en.pdf.

European Parliament and the Council of the European Union (2012a). "Regulation (EU) No 236/2012 of the European Parliament and of the Council of 14 March 2012 on short selling and certain aspects of credit default swaps". *Official Journal of the European Unions*. url: http://eur-lex.europa.eu/legal-content/EN/TXT/?qid=1434529997342&uri=CELEX:32012R0236.

European Parliament and the Council of the European Union (2012b). "Regulation (EU) No 648/2012 of the European Parliament and of the Council of 4 July 2012 on OTC derivatives, central counterparties and trade repositories Text with EEA relevance". *Official Journal of the European Union*. url: http://eur-lex.europa.eu/legal-content/EN/TXT/PDF/&uri=CELEX:32012R0648&from=EN.

European Parliament and the Council of the European Union (2013a). "Directive 2013/36/EU of the European Parliament and of the Council". *Official Journal of the European Union*, L176.

European Parliament and the Council of the European Union (2013b). "Regulation (EU) No 575/2013 of the European Parliament and of the Council". *Official Journal of the European Union*, L176.

F# Software Foundation (2014). "About F#". *F# Software Foundation*. url: http://fsharp.org/about/index.html.

FASB (2006). "Fair Value Measurements". *Financial Accounting Standards Board*, 157.

Faure, H. (1982). "Discrépence de suites associées à un systeme de numération (en dimension s)". 41, *Acta Arithmetica*, pp. 337–351.

FCIC (2010). "AIG-Goldman Collateral Call Timeline & Supporting Docs". *Federal Crisis Inquiry Commission*. url: http://fcic-static.law.stanford.edu/cdn_media/fcic-testimony/2010-0701-AIG-Goldman-supporting-docs.pdf.

Feldman, Michael (2011). "JP Morgan Buys Into FPGA Supercomputing". *HPC Wire*.

Fengler, Matthias R., Helmut Herwartz, and Christian Werner (2012). "A Dynamic Copula Approach to Recovering the Index Implied Volatility Skew". 10.3, *Journal of Financial Econometrics*, pp. 457–493. url: http://jfec.oxfordjournals.org/content/10/3/457.abstract.

Financial Conduct Authority (2014). "Prudential Sourcebook for Banks, Building Societies and Investment Firms". *Financial Conduct Authority*. url: http://fshandbook.info/FS/html/handbook/BIPRU.

Financial Stability Board (2010). "Implementing OTC Derivatives Market Reforms". *Financial Stability Board*. url: http://www.financialstabilityboard.org/publications/r_101025.pdf.

Fishman, George S. (1996). *Monte Carlo: Concepts, Algorithms and Applications*. Springer.

Fonseca, Joséda, Martino Grasselli, and Claudio Tebaldi (2007). "Option Pricing when Correlations are Stochastic: An analytical framework". 10.2, *Review of Derivatives Research*, pp. 151–180.

Fowler, Martin (2006). "Continuous Integration". url: http://martinfowler.com/articles/continuousIntegration.html.

Friedman, Milton (1992). *Capitalism and Freedom*. University of Chicago Press.

Fu, Michael C. and Jian-Qlang Hu (1995). "Sensitivity Analysis for Monte Carlo Simulation of Option Pricing". 9, *Probability in the Engineering and Informational Sciences*, pp. 417–446.

Fujii, Masaaki, Yasufumi Shimada, and Akihiko Takahashi (2009). "A Market Model of Interest Rates with Dynamic Basis Spreads in the Presence of Collateral and Multiple Currencies". *SSRN*. url: http://ssrn.com/abstract=1520618.

Fujii, Masaaki, Yasufumi Shimada, and Akihiko Takahashi (2010a). "A Note on Construction of Multiple Swap Curves with and without Collateral". *FSA Research Review*, 6.

Fujii, Masaaki, Yasufumi Shimada, and Akihiko Takahashi (2010b). "On the Term Structure of Interest Rates with Basis Spreads, Collateral and Multiple Currencies". *SSRN*. url: http://ssrn.com/abstract=1556487.

G20 (2009). "Leaders' Statement The Pittsburgh Summit". url: https://g20.org/wp-content/uploads/2014/12/Pittsburgh_Declaration_0.pdf.

Gabillon, Jacques (1991). "The Term Structures of Oil Futures". *Oxford Institute for Energy Studies*. url: http://www.oxfordenergy.org/wpcms/wp-content/uploads/2010/11/WPM17-TheTermStructureof OilFuturesPrices-JGabillon-1991.pdf.

Geman, Helyette (2005). *Commodities and Commodity Derivatives*. John Wiley & Sons.

Geman, H., N. El Karoui, and J. C. Rochet (1995). "Changes of Numeraire, Changes of Probability Measures and Pricing of Options". 32, *Journal of Applied Probability*, pp. 443–458.

Geman, Helyette and Andrea Roncoroni (2006). "Understanding the Fine Structure of Electricity Prices". 79.6, *Journal of Business*, pp. 1225–1261.

Giada, Lorenzo and Claudio Nordio (2013). "Bilateral CVA of optional early termination clauses". *Asia Risk*, 2 May, pp. 44–48.

Gibson, Rajna and Eduardo S. Schwartz (1990). "Stochastic Convenience Yield and the Pricing of Oil Contingent Claims". 45.3, *The Journal of Finance*, pp. 959–976.

Giles, Mike (2014). "Lecture 0: CPUs and GPUs". *Oxford University Mathematical Institute and Oxford e-Research Centre*. url: http://people.maths.ox.ac.uk/gilesm/cuda/lecs/lec0.pdf.

Giles, Mike and Paul Glasserman (2006). "Smoking Adjoints: Fast Monte Carlo Greeks". 19, *Risk*, pp. 92–96.

Glasserman, Paul (1991). *Gradient Estimation via Perturbation Analysis*. Kluwer Academic Publishers.

Glasserman, Paul (2004). *Monte Carlo Methods in Financial Engineering*. Springer.

Glasserman, Paul and Linan Yang (2013). "Bounding Wrong Way Risk in CVA". *ICBI Global Derivatives*.

Glasserman, Paul and Bin Yu (2004). "Number of Paths versus Number of Basis Functions in American Option Pricing". 14.4, *The Annals of Applied Probability*, pp. 2090–2119.

Glasserman, Paul and Xiaoliang Zhao (2000). "Arbitrage-Free Discretization Of Lognormal Forward Libor And Swap Rate Models". 4, *Finance and Stochastics*, pp. 35–68.

Gnoatto, A. and M. Grasselli (2014). "An Affine Multicurrency Model with Stochastic Volatility and Stochastic Interest Rates". 5.1, *SIAM Journal on Financial Mathematics*, pp. 493–531.

Golub, G. H. and C. F. Van Loan (1996). *Matrix Computations*. 3rd ed., Johns Hopkins University Press.

Gosling, James (2001). "A Brief History of the Green Project". url: http://web.archive.org/web/20050609085739/http://today.java.net/jag/old/green/.

Green, Andrew and Chris Kenyon (2014a ). "MVA: Initial Margin Valuation Adjustment by Replication and Regression". *SSRN*. url: http://ssrn.com/abstract=2432281.

Green, Andrew and Chris Kenyon (2014b). "Portfolio KVA: I Theory". *SSRN*. url: http://ssrn.com/abstract=2519475.

Green, Andrew, Chris Kenyon, and Chris R. Dennis (2014). "KVA: Capital Valuation Adjustment". *Risk*, 27.12.

Gregory, Jon (2012). *Counterparty Credit Risk: The new challenge for global financial markets*. 2nd ed., John Wiley & Sons.

Gregory, Jon and Ilya German (2012). "Closing out DVA?" *Solum Financial Partners*.

Gretarsson, Hringur (2013). "A Quadratic Gaussian Year-on-Year Inflation Model". PhD thesis. Imperial College London. url: http://ssrn.com/abstract=2274034.

Griewank, Andreas and Andrea Walther (2008). *Evaluating Derivatives: Principles and Techniques of Algorithmic Differentiation*. 2nd ed., Society for Industrial and Applied Mathematics.

Grzelak, Lech A. and Cornelis W. Oosterlee (2012). "On Cross-Currency Models with Stochastic Volatility and Correlated Interest Rates". 19.1, *Applied Mathematical Finance*, pp. 1–35.

Guyon, Julien (2013). "A New Class of Local Correlation Models". *SSRN*. url: http://ssrn.com/abstract=2283419.

Hagan, P. S. and G. West (2006). "Interpolation Methods for Curve Construction". 13.2, *Applied Mathematical Finance*, pp. 89–129.

Hagan, P. S. and G. West (2008). "Methods for Constructing a Yield Curve". *Wilmott Magazine*, pp. 70–81.

Hagan, P. S., Deep Kumar, Andrew S. Lesniewski, and Diana E. Woodward (2002). "Managing Smile Risk". *Wilmott Magazine*, pp. 84–108.

Hagan, P. S., Deep Kumar, Andrew S. Lesniewski, and Diana E. Woodward (2014). "Arbitrage-free SABR". *Wilmott Magazine*, pp. 60–75.

Haramoto, Hiroshi, Makoto Matsumoto, and Pierre L'Ecuyer (2008a). "A Fast Jump Ahead Algorithm for Linear Recurrences in a Polynomial Space". *Sequences and their Applications – SETA 2008*. Springer, pp. 290–298.

Haramoto, Hiroshi, Makoto Matsumoto, Takuji Nishimura, and Franois Panneton (2008b). "Efficient Jump Ahead for F2-Linear Random Number Generators". 20.3, *INFORMS Journal on Computing*, pp. 385–390.

Harrison, J. M. and S. R. Pliska (1983). "A Stochastic Calculus Model of Continuous Trading: Complete Markets". 15, *Stochastic Processes and their Applications*, pp. 313–316.

Harrison, J. Michael and David M. Kreps (1979). "Martingales and Arbitrage in Multiperiod Securities Markets". 20, *Journal of Economic Theory*, pp. 381–408.

Haunss, Kristen (2015). "European Investors Offer U.S. CLOs Opportunity as Slump Looms". *Bloomberg*. url: http://www.bloomberg.com/news/articles/2015-03-09/european-investors-offer-u-s-clos-opportunity-as-slump-looms.

Hays, Kristen (2004). "Enron gets OK on bankruptcy emergence". *Washington Post*. url: http://www.washingtonpost.com/wp-dyn/articles/A51504-2004Jul15.html.

Heath, David, Robert Jarrow, and Andrew Morton (1992). "Bond Pricing and the Term Structure of Interest Rates: A New Methodology for Contingent Claims Valuation". 60.1, *Econometrica*, pp. 77–105.

Hejlsberg, Anders, Mads Torgersen, Scott Wiltamuth, and Peter Golde (2010). *The C# Programming Language (Covering C# 4.0) (4th Edition) (Microsoft Windows Development Series)*. Addison-Wesley Professional.

Henrard, Marc (2007). "The Irony in the Derivatives Discounting". *SSRN*. url: http://ssrn.com/abstract=970509.

Henrard, Marc (2009). "The Irony in the Derivatives Discounting Part II: The Crisis". *SSRN*. url: http://ssrn.com/abstract=1433022.

Henrard, Marc (2013). "Multi-curves Framework with Stochastic Spread: A Coherent Approach to STIR Futures and Their Options". *OpenGamma Quantitative Research*.

Hirshleifer, J. (1958). "On the Theory of Optimal Investment Decision". 66.4, *Journal of Political Economy*, pp. 329–352.

Homescu, Christian (2014). "Local Stochastic Volatility Models: Calibration and Pricing". *SSRN*. url: http://ssrn.com/abstract=2448098.

Hull, John C. (1997). *Options, Futures, and Other Derivatives*. 3rd ed., Prentice Hall.

Hull, John C. (2011). *Options, Futures, and Other Derivatives*. 8th ed., Pearson.

Hull, John C. and Alan White (1990). "Pricing Interest Rate Derivative Securities". 3, *The Review of Financial Studies*, pp. 573–592.

Hull, John C. and Alan White (1994). "Branching Out". 7, *Risk*, pp. 34–37.

Hull, John C. and Alan White (2000). "Valuing Credit Default Swaps I: No Counterparty Default Risk". 8, *Journal of Derivatives*, pp. 29–40.

Hull, John C. and Alan White (2001). "One Factor Term Structure Models and Super Calibration". 57.6, *Financial Analysts Journal*, pp. 34–43.

Hull, John C. and Alan White (2004). "Valuation of a CDO and nth to Default CDS Without Monte Carlo Simulation". 12, *Journal of Derivatives*, pp. 8–23.

Hull, John C. and Alan White (2012a). "CVA and Wrong Way Risk". 68.5, *Financial Analysts Journal*, pp. 58–69.

Hull, John C. and Alan White (2012b). "The FVA debate". 25.7, *Risk*, 25th Anniversary ed., pp. 83–85.

Hull, John C. and Alan White (2012c). "The FVA Debate Continued". 25.10, *Risk*, 10, p. 52.

Hull, John C. and Alan White (2013). "LIBOR vs. OIS: The Derivatives Discounting Dilemma". 11.3, *Journal of Investment Management*, pp. 14–27.

Hull, John C. and Alan White (2014a). "Collateral and Credit Issues in Derivatives Pricing". 10.3, *Journal of Credit Risk*, pp. 3–28.

Hull, John C. and Alan White (2014b). "Valuing Derivatives: Funding Value Adjustments and Fair Value". 70.3, *Financial Analysts Journal*, pp. 46–56.

Hull, John C. and Alan White (2014c). "Risk Neutrality Remains". *Risk*, 27, p. 10.

Hume, Neil (2010). "Of CVA and sovereign CDS". *FT Alphaville*. url: http://ftalphaville.ft.com/2010/06/15/261671/of-cva-and-sovereign-cds/?

Hunter, Christopher, Peter Jäckel, and Mark Joshi (2001). "Getting the Drift". 14.7, *Risk*, pp. 81–81.

IASB (2004). "IAS 39 Financial Instruments: Recognition and Measurement". *International Accounting Standards Board.*

IASB (2012). "IFRS 13 Fair Value Measurement". *International Accounting Standards Board.*

IASB (2014). "IFRS 9 Financial Instruments". *International Accounting Standards Board.*

Ingersoll, Jonathan E. (1976). "Using the Black Scholes Option Model in Investment Decision Making: Designing a Convertible Preferred Issue". In *Proceedings: Seminar on the Analysis of Security Prices*, CSRP.

Intel (2013). "The Intel Xeon Phi Product Family". *Intel.* url: http://www.intel.com/content/www/us/en/processors/xeon/xeon-phi-detail.html.

ISDA (1992). "1992 ISDA Master Agreement". *International Swaps and Derivatives Association.*

ISDA (2002). "2002 ISDA Master Agreement". *International Swaps and Derivatives Association.*

ISDA (2003). "2003 ISDA Credit Derivative Definitions". *International Swaps and Derivatives Association.*

ISDA (2009a). "2009 ISDA Credit Derivatives Determinations Committees and Auction Settlement Supplement to the 2003 ISDA Credit Derivatives Definitions". *International Swaps and Derivatives Association.* url: http://www.isda.org/companies/auctionhardwiring/docs/Supplement-CLEAN.doc.

ISDA (2009b). "2009 ISDA Credit Derivatives Determinations Committees, Auction Settlement and Restructuring CDS Protocol". *International Swaps and Derivatives Association.* url: http://www.isda.org/smallbang/docs/Small-Bang-Protocol-Text.pdf.

ISDA (2009c). "ISDA Close-out Amount Protocol". *International Swaps and Derivatives Association.*

ISDA (2011). "Overview of ISDA Standard Credit Support Annex (SCSA)". *International Swaps and Derivatives Association.*

ISDA (2012). "EBA Consultation Paper On Draft Regulatory Technical Standards for credit valuation adjustment risk on the determination of a proxy spread and the specification of a limited number of smaller portfolios (EBA/CP/2012/09), Response of the International Swaps and Derivatives Association, Inc. (ISDA), and the Association for Financial Markets in Europe (AFME)". *International Swaps and Derivatives Association.* url: http://www2.isda.org/attachment/NDc4OQ==/Industry%20Response%20-%20EBA%20CVA%20RTS.pdf.

ISDA (2013). "Standard Initial Margin Model for Non-Cleared Derivatives". *International Swaps and Derivatives Association*.

ISDA (2014a). "2014 ISDA Credit Derivatives Definitions". *International Swaps and Derivatives Association*.

ISDA (2014b). "The euro swaps surprise". *derivatiViews*.

Jacobson, Ivar, Grady Booch and James Rumbaugh (1999). *The Unified Software Development Process*. Addison-Wesley.

James, Jessica and Nick Webber (2000). *Interest Rate Modelling*. John Wiley & Sons.

Jamshidian, F. (1989). "An Exact Bond Option Pricing Formula". 44, *The Journal of Finance*, pp. 205–209.

Jamshidian, F. (1991). "Bond and Option Evaluation in the Gaussian Interest Rate Model". 9, *Research in Finance*, pp. 131–170.

Jamshidian, F. (1995). "A Simple Class of Square-Root Interest Rate Models". 2, *Applied Mathematical Finance*, pp. 61–72.

Jamshidian, F. (1997). "LIBOR and Swap Market Models and Measures". 1, *Finance and Stochastics*, pp. 293–330.

Jarrow, RA, D. Lando, and S.M. Turnbull (1997). "A Markov Model for the Term Structure of Credit Risk Spreads". 10.2, *Review of Financial Studies*, pp. 481–523.

Jarrow, Robert and Yildiray Yildirim (2003). "Pricing Treasury Inflation Protected Securities and Related Derivative Securities using a HJM Model". 38, *Journal of Financial and Quantitative Analysis*, pp. 337–358.

Jex, Mark, Robert Henderson, and David Wang (1999). "Pricing Exotics under the Smile". 12, *Risk*, p. 75.

Jiang, K., D. Sun and K. Toh (2012). "An Inexact Accelerated Proximal Gradient Method for Large Scale Linearly Constrained Convex SDP". 22.3, *SIAM Journal on Optimization*, pp. 1042–1064.

Joe, Stephen and Frances Y. Kuo (2008a). "Constructing Sobol Sequences with Better Two-Dimensional Projections". 30.5, *SIAM Journal on Scientific and Statistical Computing*, pp. 2635–2654.

Joe, Stephen and Frances Y. Kuo (2008b). "Notes on generating Sobol 0 sequences". *University of New South Wales*. url: http://web.maths.unsw.edu.au/~fkuo/sobol/joe-kuo-notes.pdf.

Jorion, Philippe (2000). *Value at Risk*. McGraw Hill.

Joshi, Mark and Riccardo Rebonato (2003). "A Stochastic Volatility, Displaced-diffusion Extension of the LIBOR Market Model". 3, *Quantitative Finance*, pp. 458–469.

Joshi, Mark and Alan Stacey (2008). "New and Robust Drift Approximations for the LIBOR Market Model". 11, *Quantitative Finance*, pp. 547–558.

Joshi, Mark S and Dherminder Kainth (2004). "Rapid and Accurate Development of Prices and Greeks for nth to Default Credit Swaps in the Li Model". 4.3, *Quantitative Finance*, pp. 266–275.

Kaminska, Izabella (2012). "Ronia to the rescue". *FT Alphaville*. url: http://ftalphaville.ft.com/2012/03/08/914291/ronia-to-the-rescue/.

Karatzas, Ioannis and Steven E. Shreve (1991). *Brownian Motion and Stochastic Calculus*. 2nd ed., Springer.

Karoui, N. El, R. Myneni, and R. Viswanathan (1992a). "Arbitrage Pricing and Hedging of Interest Rate Claims with State Variables I". *Working Paper Paris VI and Stanford University*.

Karoui, N. El, R. Myneni, and R. Viswanathan (1992b). "Arbitrage Pricing and Hedging of Interest Rate Claims with State Variables II". *Working Paper Paris VI and Stanford University*.

Kazziha, Soraya (1999). *Interest Rate Models, Inflation-based Derivatives, Trigger Notes and Cross-currency Swaptions*. Ph.D. thesis, Imperial College of Science, Technology and Medicine.

Kenyon, C. and R. D. Kenyon (2013). "DVA for Assets". *Risk*, 26.10.

Kenyon, Chris (2008). "Inflation is Normal". *Risk*, 21.7.

Kenyon, Chris (2010). "Short-Rate Pricing after the Liquidity and Credit Shocks: Including the Basis". *Risk*, 23.11.

Kenyon, Chris (2013). "Short Rate Models with Stochastic Basis and Smile". In *Interest Rate Modelling after the Financial Crisis*, edited by Massimo Morini and Marco Bianchetti. Risk Books.

Kenyon, Chris and Andrew Green (2013a). "Collateral-Enhanced Default Risk". *SSRN*. url: http://ssrn.com/abstract=2208755.

Kenyon, Chris and Andrew Green (2013b). "Pricing CDSs' Capital Relief". 26.10, *Risk*, pp. 62–66.

Kenyon, Chris and Andrew Green (2013c). "Why CCPs are the New Rating Agencies". *Risk*, 26.8.

Kenyon, Chris and Andrew Green (2014a). "Efficient XVA Management: Computation, Hedging, and Attribution Using Trade-Level Regression and Global Conditioning". *SSRN*. url: http://ssrn.com/abstract=2539532.

Kenyon, Chris and Andrew Green (2014b). "Exit Prices as Quantum States". *Risk*, 27.10.

Kenyon, Chris and Andrew Green (2014c). "Regulatory Costs Break Risk Neutrality". *Risk*, 27.9.

Kenyon, Chris and Andrew Green (2014d). "Regulatory-optimal Funding". *Risk*, 27.4.

Kenyon, Chris and Andrew Green (2014e). "VAR and ES/CVAR Dependence on Data Cleaning and Data Models: Analysis and Resolution". *SSRN*. url: http://ssrn.com/abstract=2443445.

Kenyon, Chris and Andrew Green (2015a). "Default Modelling with Dirac Processes". *Forthcoming*.

Kenyon, Chris and Andrew Green (2015b). "Self-Financing Trading and the Ito-Doeblin Lemma". *SSRN*. url: http://ssrn.com/abstract=2548676.

Kenyon, Chris and Andrew Green (2015c). "Warehousing Credit Risk: Pricing, capital and tax". *Risk*, 28.2.

Kenyon, Chris and Roland Stamm (2012). *Discounting, LIBOR, CVA and Funding*. Palgrave MacMillan.

Kernighan, Brian W. and Dennis M. Ritchie (1988). *The C Programming Language*. Prentice Hall.

Kienitz, Joerg (2013). "Libor Market Model with Stochastic Basis – Calibration Using OIS Yield and Money Market Basis Spreads". *SSRN*. url: http://ssrn.com/abstract=2211175.

King, Barry (2013). "Introduction to the EMIR technical standards". *Financial Conduct Authority*. url: http://www.fca.org.uk/static/fca/documents/emir-implementation-presentation.ppt.

Kloeden, Peter A. and Ekhardt Platen (1992). *Numerical Solution of Stochastic Differential Equations*. Springer.

Khronos Group (2014). "The open standard for parallel programming of heterogeneous systems". *Kronos Group*. url: https://www.khronos.org/opencl/.

Knuth, Donald E. (1997). *The Art of Computer Programming, Volume 2: Seminumerical Algorithms*. Addison-Wesley Professional.

Kou, Jianming and Simone Varotto (2005). "Predicting Agency Rating Migrations with Spread Implied Ratings". *ISMA Centre Discussion Papers in Finance*. url: http://www.icmacentre.ac.uk/pdf/discussion/DP2005-06.pdf.

Lanman, Scott and Jeff Black (2011). "Central Banks Cut Cost of Borrowing Dollars to Ease Crisis". *Bloomberg*. url: http://www.bloomberg.com/news/2011-11-30/fed-five-central-banks-lower-interest-rate-on-dollar-swaps.html.

Larman, Craig and Victor R. Basili (2003). "Iterative and Incremental Development: A Brief History". 36.6, *Computer*, pp. 47–56.

Larsson, Karl (2011). "Pricing Commodity Swaptions in Multifactor Models". 19.2, *The Journal of Derivatives*, pp. 32–44.

Laughton, Stephen and Aura Vaisbrot (2012). "In Defense of FVA – a Response to Hull and White". *Risk*, 25.9.

LCH (2010a). "OIS discounting valuation adjustment". *LCH.Clearnet*, LCH.Clearnet Ltd Circular No 2638. url: http://www.lchclearnet.com/member_notices/circulars/2010-06-15.asp.

LCH (2010b). "SwapClear: Revised initial Margin Multipliers". *LCH.Clearnet*. url: http://www.lchclearnet.com/member_notices/circulars/2010-08-13.asp.

LCH (2012a). "Default Fund Rules". *LCH.Clearnet*. url: http://www.lchclearnet.com/Images/default%20fund%20rules_tcm6-43735.pdf.

LCH (2012b). "How it works". *LCH.Clearnet*. url: http://www.lchclearnet.com/swaps/swapclear_for_clearing_members/how_it_works.asp.

LCH (2012c). "LCH.Clearnet Group History". *LCH.Clearnet*. url: http://www.lchclearnet.com/about_us/history.asp.

LCH (2012d). "Managing the Lehman Brothers' Default". *LCH.Clearnet*. url: http://www.lchclearnet.com/swaps/swapclear_for_clearing_members/managing_the_lehman_brothers_default.asp.

LCH (2012e). "SwapClear Margin Methodology". *LCH.Clearnet*. url: http://www.lchclearnet.com/risk_management/ltd/margining/swapclear.asp.

LCH (2013). "Clearing House Procedures Section 2C". *LCH.Clearnet*.

L'Ecuyer, Pierre (1994). "Uniform Random Number Generation". 53, *Annals of Operations Research*, pp. 77–120.

L'Ecuyer, Pierre and Christiane Lemieux (2002). "Recent Advances in Randomized Quasi-Monte Carlo Methods". In *Modeling Uncertainty: An Examination of Stochastic Theory, Methods, and Application*, edited by M. Dror, P. L'Ecuyer and F. Szidarovszki, pp. 419–474. Kluwer Academic Publishers.

L'Ecuyer, Pierre, Boris Oreshkin, and Richard Simard (2014). "Random Numbers for Parallel Computers: Requirements and Methods". *Université de Montréal*. url: http://www.iro.umontreal.ca/~lecuyer/myftp/papers/parallel-rng-imacs.pdf.

L'Ecuyer, Pierre, Richard Simard, E. Jack Chen, and W. David Kelton (2002). "An Object-Orientated Random-Number Package with Many Long Streams and Substreams". 50.6, *Operations Research*, pp. 1073–1075.

Levine, Matt (2014). "It Cost JPMorgan $1.5 Billion to Value Its Derivatives Right". *Bloomberg*. url: http://www.bloombergview.com/articles/2014-01-15/it-cost-jpmorgan-1-5-billion-to-value-its-derivatives-right.

Li, David X. (2000). "On Default Correlation: A Copula Function Approach". 9, *Journal of Fixed Income*, pp. 43–54.

Lipton, A. (2001). *Mathematical Models for Foreign Exchange*. World Scientific.

Lipton, A. (2002). "The Vol Smile Problem". 15.2, *Risk*, pp. 61–65.

Lipton, A. and W. McGhee (2002). "Universal Barriers". 15.5, *Risk*, pp. 81–85.

Lipton, Alexander, Andrey Gal and Andris Lasis (2014). "Pricing of Vanilla and First-generation Exotic Options in the Local Stochastic Volatility Framework: Survey and new results". 14.11, *Quantitative Finance*, pp. 1899–1922.

Longstaff, Francis (2000). "The Term Structure of Very Short-term Rates: New Evidence for the Expectations Hypothesis". 58, *Journal of Financial Economics*, pp. 397–415.

Longstaff, Francis and Eduardo Schwartz (2001). "Valuing American Options by simulation: A simple least-squares approach". 14.1, *The Review of Financial Studies*, pp. 113–147.

Lotz, Christopher and Lutz Schlögl (2000). "Default Risk in a Market Model". 24.1–2, *Journal of Banking & Finance*, pp. 301–327.

Marabel Romo, Jacinto (2012). "Worst-Of Options and Correlation Skew Under a Stochastic Correlation Framework". *International Journal of Theoretical and Applied Finance*, 15.7.

Markit (2009a). "CDS Small Bang: Understanding the Global Contract & European Convention Changes". *Markit*. url: http://www.markit.com/cds/announcements/resource/cds_small_bang_07202009_upd.pdf.

Markit (2009b). "The CDS Big Bang: Understanding the Changes to the Global CDS Contract and North American Conventions". *Markit*. url: http://www.markit.com/cds/announcements/resource/cds_big_bang.pdf.

Marsaglia, G. and T. A. Bray (1964). "A Convenient Method for Generating Normal Variables". 6, *SIAM Review*, pp. 260–264.

Marsaglia, George (1995). "The Marsaglia Random Number CDROM including the Diehard Battery of Tests of Randomness". *Florida State University*. url: http://www.stat.fsu.edu/pub/diehard/.

Marshall, A. W. and I. Olkin (1967). "A Multivariate Exponential Distribution". 62, *Journal of the American Statistical Association*, pp. 30–44.

Mascagni, M. and A. Srinivasan (2006). "Algorithm 806: SPRNG: A Scalable Library for Pseudorandom Number Generation". 26, *ACM Transactions on Mathematical Software*, pp. 436–461.

Matoušek, Jiří (1998). "On the L2-discrepancy for Anchored Boxes. 14.4, *J. Complex"*. pp. 527–556.

Matsumoto, M. and T. Nishimura (1998). "Mersenne Twister: A 623-dimensionally equidistributed uniform pseudorandom number generator". 8, *ACM Trans. on Modeling and Computer Simulation*, pp. 3–30.

Matsumoto, Makoto and Takuji Nishimura (2000). "Dynamic Creation of Pseudorandom Number Generators". In *Monte Carlo and Quasi-Monte Carlo Methods 1998*, pp. 56–69. Springer.

McCarroll, John and Goind Ram Khatri (2011). "Credit Risk In Fair Value Measurement". 43.6, *Accountancy Ireland*, pp. 52–53.

McCloud, Paul (2008). "Exponential-Quadratic Semimartingale Models of Interest Rate and Asset Volatility". *SSRN*. url: http://ssrn.com/abstract=1269577.

McCloud, Paul (2010). "Putting the Smile Back on the Face of Derivatives". *Risk*, 23.1.

McCulloch, J. Huston and Levis A. Kochin (2000). "The inflation premium implicit in the US real and nominal term structures of interest rates". *Ohio State University Economic Department*. url: http://economics.sbs.ohio-state.edu/pdf/mcculloch/qnspline.pdf.

McEwen, J., C. Kyriakos, and M. Jeannin (2012). "Cross-section methodology for proxy spreads and recovery rates". *Nomura*.

Mengle, David (2010). "The Importance of Close-Out Netting". *ISDA Research Notes*, 1. url: www2.isda.org/attachment/MTY4MQ==/Netting-ISDAResearchNotes-1-2010.pdf.

Mercurio, F. (2005). "Pricing Inflation-Indexed Derivatives". 5.3, *Quantitative Finance*, pp. 289–302.

Mercurio, F. (2010a). "LIBOR Market Models with Stochastic Basis". *SSRN*. url: http://ssrn.com/abstract=1563685.

Mercurio, F. (2010b). "Interest Rates and The Credit Crunch: New Formulas and Market Models". *SSRN*. url: http://ssrn.com/abstract=1332205.

Mercurio, F. and N. Moreni (2006). "Inflation with a Smile". 19.3, *Risk*, pp. 70–75.

Mercurio, F. and N. Moreni (2009). "Inflation Modelling with SABR Dynamics". 22.6, *Risk*, pp. 106–111.

Mercurio, F. and M. Morini (2009). "No-Arbitrage Dynamics for a Tractable SABR Term Structure Libor Model". In *Modelling Interest Rates: Advances in Derivatives Pricing*, edited by Fabio Mercurio. RISK Books.

Merton, Robert C. (1973). "Theory of Rational Option Pricing". 4.1, *Bell Journal of Economics and Management Science*, pp. 141–183.

Merton, Robert C. (1976). "Option Pricing When Underlying Stock Returns are Discontinuous". *Journal of Financial Economics*, 3.125–144.

Metropolis, Nicholas (1987). "The Beginning of the Monte Carlo Method". *Los Alamos Science*, pp. 125–130.

Metropolis, Nicholas and S. Ulam (1949). "The Monte Carlo Method". 44.247, *Journal of the American Statistical Association*, pp. 335–341.

Miltersen, K. R., K. Sandmann, and D. Sondermann (1997). "Closed Form Solutions for Term Structure Derivatives with Log-Normal Interest Rates". 52, *The Journal of Finance*, pp. 409–430.

Miltersen, Kristian R. and Eduardo S. Schwartz (Mar. 1998). "Pricing of Options on Commodity Futures with Stochastic Term Structures of Convenience Yields and Interest Rates". 33, *Journal of Financial and Quantitative Analysis*, pp. 33–59.

Milwaukee Sentinel (1971). "Magic Forms Municipal Bond Insurance Company". *Milwaukee Sentinel*.

Miron, Paul and Philip Swannell (1991). *Pricing and Hedging Swaps*. Euromoney Books.

Modigliani, Franco and Merton H. Miller (1958). "The Cost of Capital, Corporation Finance and the Theory of Investment". 48.3, *The American Economic Review*, pp. 261–297.

Moreni, N. and A. Pallavicini (2013). "Parsimonious HJM Modelling for Multiple Yield Curve Dynamics". *Interest Rate Modelling after the Financial Crisis*, Ed. by Massimo Morini and Marco Bianchetti. Risk Books.

Moreni, N. and A. Pallavicini (2014). "Parsimonious HJM Modelling for Multiple Yield Curve Dynamics". 14.2, *Quantitative Finance*, pp. 199–210.

Moreno, Manuel and Javier F. Navas (2003). "On the Robustness of Least-Squares Monte Carlo (LSM) for Pricing American Derivatives". *Review of Derivatives Research*, 6.2.

Morini, Massimo (2012). "Model Risk in Today's Approaches to Funding and Collateral". *8th Fixed Income Conference*, Vienna.

Morini, Massimo and Andrea Prampolini (2011). "Risky Funding: A unified framework for counterparty and liquidity charges". *Risk*, 24.3.

Moro, B. (1995). "The Full Monte". 8.2, *Risk*, pp. 57–58.

Moskowitz, B. and R. E. Caflisch (1996). "Smoothness and Dimension Reduction in quasi-Monte Carlo Methods". 23, *Mathematical and Computer Modelling*, pp. 37–54.

Murphy, David (2012). "The doom loop in sovereign exposures". *FT Alphaville*. url: http://ftalphaville.ft.com/2012/04/12/946181/the-doom-loop-in-sovereign-exposures/?.

Naumann, Uwe (2012). *The Art of Differentiating Computer Programs: An Introduction to Algorithmic Differentiation (Software, Environments and Tools)*. SIAM-Society for Industrial and Applied Mathematics.

Neftci, Salih N. (2008). *Principles of Financial Engineering*. Elsevier.

Nelson, Roger B. (2006). *An Introduction to Copulas*. 2nd ed., Springer.

NVIDIA (2014). *cuRAND User Guide*. NVIDIA. url: http://docs.nvidia.com/cuda/curand/index.html#axzz3A07AZsou.

Oakley, David (2012). "Greek CDS drama holds lessons for investors". *The Financial Times*. url: http://www.ft.com/cms/s/0/0997e7f4-71c4-11e1-b853-00144feab49a.html\}axzz2B2yiDKvT.

Obłój, Jan (2008). "Fine-tune your smile: Correction to Hagan et al". *Wilmott Magazine*.

Office of the Comptroller of the Currency, Treasury; the Board of Governors of the Federal Reserve System; and the Federal Deposit Insurance Corporation (2013). "Regulatory Capital Rules: Regulatory Capital, Implementation of Basel III, Capital Adequacy, Transition Provisions, Prompt Corrective Action, Standardized Approach for Risk-weighted Assets, Market Discipline and Disclosure Requirements, Advanced Approaches Risk-Based Capital Rule, and Market Risk Capital Rule". 78.198, *Federal Register*, pp. 62018–62291.

Office of the Comptroller of the Currency, Treasury; the Board of Governors of the Federal Reserve System; and the Federal Deposit Insurance Corporation (2014a). "Regulatory Capital Rules: Regulatory Capital, Enhanced Supplementary Leverage Ratio Standards for Certain Bank Holding Companies and Their Subsidiary Insured Depository Institutions". *Federal Register* 7984, pp. 24528–24541.

Office of the Comptroller of the Currency, Treasury; the Board of Governors of the Federal Reserve System; and the Federal Deposit Insurance Corporation (2014b). "Regulatory Capital Rules: Regulatory Capital, Revisions to the Supplementary Leverage Ratio". 79.187, *Federal Register*, pp. 57725–57751.

O'Kane, Dominic (2008). *Modelling Single-name and Multi-name Credit Derivatives*. John Wiley & Sons.

O'Kane, Dominic and Matthew Livesey (2004). "Base Correlation Explained". *Lehman Brothers*.

Onaran, Yalman (2008). "Lehman Shares Fall After Talks With Korean Bank End". *Bloomberg*. url: http://www.bloomberg.com/apps/news?pid=newsarchive&sid=aXucA2p.fqmg.

Oracle (1997). "The Java Language Environment". *Oracle*.

Ötken, Giray (1996). "A Probabilistic Result on the Discrepancy of a Hybrid-Monte Carlo Sequence and Applications". 2, *Monte Carlo Methods and Applications*, pp. 255–270.

Owen, A. B. (1995). "Randomly Permuted (t, m, s)-nets and (t,s)-sequences". *Monte Carlo and Quasi-Monte Carlo Methods in Scientific Computing*, Ed. by H. Niederreiter and J.-S. Shiue. Springer.

Owen, A. B. (1997a). "Monte Carlo Variance of Scrambled Net Quadrature". 34, *SIAM Journal of Numerical Analysis*, pp. 1884–1910.

Owen, A. B. (1997b). "Scrambled Net Variance for Integrals of Smooth Functions". 25.4, *The Annals of Statistics*, pp. 1541–1562.

Owen, A. B. (1998). "Scrambling Sobol' and Niederreiter-Xing Points". 14, *Journal of Complexity*, pp. 466–489.

Pallavicini, Andrea, Daniele Perini, and Damiano Brigo (2012). "Funding, Collateral and Hedging: Uncovering the Mechanics and the Subtleties of Funding Valuation Adjustments". *SSRN*. url: http://ssrn.com/abstract=2161528.

Park, S. K. and K. W. Millar (1988). "Random Number Generators: Good ones are hard to find". 31, *Communications of the ACM*, pp. 1192–1201.

Parker, Edmund and Mayer Brown (2003). "The 2003 ISDA Credit Derivatives Definitions". *PLC Finance*.

Paskov, S. and J. Traub (1995). "Faster Valuation of Financial Derivatives". 22, *Journal of Portfolio Management*, pp. 113–120.

Pelsser, Antoon (2000). *Efficient Methods for Valuing Interest Rate Derivatives*. Springer.

Peng, Xianhua and Steven Kou (2008). "Default Clustering and Valuation of Collateralized Debt Obligations". *Winter Simulation Conference*.

Pilato, C. Michael, Ben Collins-Sussman, and Brian W. Fitzpatrick (2008). *Version Control with Subversion*. O'Reilly Media.

Piterbarg, Vladimir (2003a). "A Practitioner's Guide to Pricing and Hedging Callable Libor Exotics in Forward Libor Models". *SSRN*. url: http://ssrn.com/abstract=427084.

Piterbarg, Vladimir (2003b). "A Stochastic Volatility Forward Libor Model with a Term Structure of Volatility Smiles". *SSRN*. url: http://ssrn.com/abstract=472061.

Piterbarg, Vladimir (2006). "Smiling Hybrids". 19.5, *Risk*, pp. 66–71.

Piterbarg, Vladimir (2007). "Markovian Projection for Volatility Calibration". 20.4, *Risk*, pp. 84–89.

Piterbarg, Vladimir (2009). "Rates Squared". *Risk*, 1 March.

Piterbarg, Vladimir (2010). "Funding beyond Discounting: Collateral agreements and derivatives pricing". 23.2, *Risk*, pp. 97–102.

Piterbarg, Vladimir (2012). "Cooking with Collateral". *Risk*, 25.8.

Piterbarg, Vladimir (2013). "Stuck with Collateral". *Risk*, 26.11.

Platen, Eckhard and Nicola Bruti-Liberati (2010). *Numerical Solution of Stochastic Differential Equations with Jumps in Finance (Stochastic Modelling and Applied Probability)*. Springer.

Pollack, Lisa (2011). "The naked derivative exposures of banks to sovereigns". *FT Alphaville*. url: http://ftalphaville.ft.com/2011/11/16/750201/the-naked-derivative-exposures-of-banks-to-sovereigns/.

Press, William H. et al. (2007). *Numerical Recipes: The Art of Scientific Computing*. 3rd ed., Cambridge University Press.

Prosser, Lindsay (ed.) (2007). *UK Standard Industrial Classification 2007*. Palgrave MacMillan.

Prudential Regulation Authority (2006). "External Credit Assessment Institutions (ECAIs) recognised under the Capital Requirements Regulations 2006 (SI 2006/3221) for the purposes of BIPRU 3 The Standardised Approach: mapping of the ECAIs' credit assessments to credit quality steps". *Bank of England*. url: http://www.bankofengland.co.uk/publications/Documents/other/pra/policy/2013/ecaisstandardised.pdf.

PWC (2011). "Lehman Brothers' Administration – Frequently Asked Questions". *Pricewaterhouse-Coopers*. url: http://www.pwc.co.uk/business-recovery/administrations/lehman/lehman-faq.jhtml.

Pykhtin, Michael and Dan Rosen (2010). "Pricing Counterparty Risk at the Trade Level and CVA Allocations". 6.4, *Journal of Credit Risk*, pp. 3–38.

Qi, Houduo and Defeng Sun (June 2006). "A Quadratically Convergent Newton Method for Computing the Nearest Correlation Matrix". 28.2, *SIAM J. Matrix Anal. Appl.*, pp. 360–385.

Quinn, James (2008a). "Lehman Brothers files for bankruptcy as credit crisis bites". *The Telegraph*. url: http://www.telegraph.co.uk/finance/newsbysector/banksandfinance/4676621/Lehman-Brothers-files-for-bankruptcy-as-credit-crisis-bites.html.

Quinn, James (2008b). "Lehman Brothers holds sale talks with rivals as shares plunge". *The Telegraph*. url: http://www.telegraph.co.uk/finance/newsbysector/banksandfinance/2953134/Lehman-Brothers-holds-sale-talks-with-rivals-as-shares-plunge.html.

Quinn, James (2008c). "Lehman Brothers teeters on verge of collapse as Barclays pulls out". *The Telegraph*. url: http://www.telegraph.co.uk/finance/newsbysector/banksandfinance/4676589/Lehman-Brothers-teeters-on-verge-of-collapse-as-Barclays-pulls-out.html.

Quinn, James (2008d). "Lehman unveils first lost since going public". *The Telegraph*. url: http://www.telegraph.co.uk/finance/newsbysector/banksandfinance/2791390/Lehman-unveils-first-loss-since-going-public.html.

Rebonato, Riccardo (1998). *Interest-Rate Option Models*. 2nd ed., John Wiley & Sons.

Rebonato, Riccardo (1999). "On the Simultaneous Calibration of Multifactor Lognormal Interest Rate Models to Black Volatilities and to the Correlation Matrix". 2, *Journal of Computational Finance*, pp. 57–76.

Rebonato, Riccardo (2004). *Volatility and Correlation: The Perfect Hedger and the Fox*. 2nd ed., John Wiley & Sons.

Rebonato, Riccardo and Ian Cooper (1994). "The Limitations of Simple Two-Factor Interest Rate Models". 5.1, *The Journal of Financial Engineering*, pp. 1–16.

Rebonato, Riccardo, Kenneth McKay, and Richard White (2009). *The SABR/LIBOR Market Model*. John Wiley & Sons.

Reboul, P. et al. (2014). "Corporate and investment banking outlook". *Roland Berger and Nomura*.

Rennison, J. (2013). "CMS vs. LCH.Clearnet: Clients may face CCP-specific pricing, warn FCMs". *Risk*, 26.7.

Ritchken, P. and L. Sankarasubramaniam (1992). "On Markovian Representations Of The Term Structure". *Cleveland Federal Reserve Bank*.

Rosen, Dan (2011). "CVA, Basel III and Wrong-Way Risk". *R2 Financial Technologies*.

Rosen, Dan and David Saunders (2012). "CVA the Wrong Way". 5.3, *Journal of Risk Management in Financial Institutions*, pp. 252–272.

Royce, Winston W. (1970). "Managing the Development of Large Software System". In *Proceedings of IEEE WESTCON 26*, pp. 1–9.

Rubinstein, Reuven (1993). *Discrete Event Systems: Sensitivity analysis and stochastic optimization by the score function method*. John Wiley & Sons.

Rushton, Katherine (2014). "Lehman Brothers' creditors finally in line for payout". *The Telegraph*. url: http://www.telegraph.co.uk/finance/newsbysector/banksandfinance/11038039/Lehman-Brothers-creditors-finally-in-line-for-payout.html.

Saito, Mutsuo and Makoto Matsumoto (2006). "SIMD-oriented Fast Mersenne Twister: a 128-bit Pseudorandom Number Generator". *Monte Carlo and Quasi-Monte Carlo Methods 2006*, pp. 607–622. Springer.

Salmon, Felix (2009). "Recipe for disaster: The formula that killed Wall Street". *Wired Magazine*, 23 February.

Sarbanes, Paul and Michael G. Oxley (2002). "Sarbanes-Oxley Act of 2002". *Public and Private Laws – 107th Congress*.

Scardovi, Elena (2011). Jarrow-Yildirim Model for Inflation: Theory and applications. MA thesis, Università di Bologna.

Schönbucher, Philipp (2000). "A Libor Market Model with Default Risk". *SSRN*. url: http://ssrn.com/abstract=261051.

Schönbucher, Philipp (2003). *Credit Derivative Pricing Models*. John Wiley & Sons.

Schwartz, Eduardo and James E. Smith (2000). "Short-Term Variations and Long-Term Dynamics in Commodity Prices". 46.7, *Management Science*, pp. 893–911.

Sengupta, Rajdeep and Yu Man Tam (2008). "The LIBOR-OIS Spread as a Summary Indicator". *Economic SYNOPSES*, 25.

Sheriff, Nazneen (2015). "AAD vs GPUs: Banks turn to maths trick as chips lose appeal". *Risk*, 28.1.

Shewhart, Walter Andrew (1939). *Statistical Methods of Quality Control*. Washington, D.C.: The Graduate School, the Department of Agriculture.

Shreve, Steven E. (2004). *Stochastic Calculus for Finance II: Continuous-Time Models*. Springer.

Sims, Jocelyn and Jessie Romero (2013). "The Latin American Debt Crisis of the 1980s". *The Federal Reserve*. url: http://www.federalreservehistory.org/Events/DetailView/46.

Sloan, I. H. and S. Joe (1994). *Lattice Methods for Multiple Integration*. Oxford University Press.

Sobol, I. M. (1967). "On the Distribution of Points in a Cube and the Approximate Evaluation of Integrals". 7.4, *USSR Computational Mathematics and Mathematical Physics*, pp. 86—112.

Solum Financial Partners (2014). "Funding Valuation Adjustment Solum Survey December 2014". *Solum Financial Partners*. url: http://www.solum-financial.com/wp-content/uploads/2015/01/SolumFVASurveyDec2014.pdf.

Sommer, Daniel et al. (2013). "FVA – Putting Funding into the Equation". *KPMG*.

Sourbes, Cecile (2015). "CCPs Confront the Difficult Maths of Default Management". *Risk*, 28.1.

Spanier, Jerome (1995). "Quasi-Monte Carlo Methods for Particle Transport Problems". *Monte Carlo and Quasi-Monte Carlo Methods in Scientific Computing*, Ed, by Harald Niederreiter and Peter Jau-Shyong Shiue. vol. 106. Lecture Notes in Statistics. Springer New York, pp. 121–148.

Standard and Poor's (2012). "Counterparty Risk Framework Methodology and Assumptions". *Standard and Poor's Ratings Direct*. url: http://www.standardandpoors.com/spf/upload/Ratings_EMEA/2012-11-29_CounterpartyRiskFrameworkMethodology.pdf.

Stroustrup, Bjarne (1985). *The C++ Programming Language (Addison-Wesley series in computer science)*. 1st ed., Addison-Wesley Publishing Company, Inc.

Sverdlik, Yevgeniy (2014). "HP Starts Shipping 64-bit ARM Servers". *Data Centre Knowledge*. url: http://www.datacenterknowledge.com/archives/2014/09/29/hp-starts-shipping-64-bit-arm-servers/.

Tasche, Dirk (2008). "Capital Allocation to Business Units and Sub-portfolios: The Euler principle". In *Pillar II in the New Basel Accord: The Challenge of Economic Capital*, Ed. by Andrea Resti. Risk Books, pp. 423–453.

Teather, David, Andrew Clark, and Jill Treanor (2008). "Barclays agrees $1.75bn deal for core Lehman Brothers business". *The Guardian*. url: http://www.guardian.co.uk/business/2008/sep/17/barclay.lehmanbrothers1.

Telegraph Staff (2008). "Nomura buys Lehman's European and Middle East business". *The Telegraph*. url: http://www.telegraph.co.uk/finance/3067912/Nomura-buys-Lehmans-European-and-Middle-East-business.html.

Thompson, Tim and Vincent Dahinden (2013). "Counterparty Risk and CVA Survey". *Deloitte and Solum Financial Partners*. url: http://www.solum-financial.com/wp-content/uploads/2014/11/Deloitte-Solum-CVA-Survey.pdf.

Top500 (2014). "November 2014". *Top500*. url: http://www.top500.org/lists/2014/11/.

Vaillant, Noel (1995). "Convexity Adjustment between Futures and Forward Rates Using a Martingale Approach". *BZW*. url: http://www.probability.net/convex.pdf.

Van der Corput, J. G. (1935). "Verteilungsfunktionen. I. Mitt". 38, *Proc. Akad. Wet. Amsterdam*, pp. 813–821.

Vasicek, Oldrich (1977). "An Equilibrium Characterization of the Term Structure". 5.2, *Journal of Financial Economics*, pp. 177–188.

Wang, Yang and Russell Caflisch (2010). "Pricing and Hedging American-style Options: A simple simulation-based approach". 13.4, *Journal of Computational Finance*, pp. 95–125.

Wei, Wei (2011). "Counterparty Credit Risk on a Standard Swap in 'Risky Closeout'". 2, *International Journal of Financial Research*, pp. 40–51.

Whittall, Christopher (2013). "Banks struggle to securitise CVA". *Reuters*, 26.3. url: http://www.reuters.com/article/2013/03/11/bank-cva-abs-idUSL6NOC36FS20130311.

Whittall, Christopher (2014). "Derivatives: JP Morgan books US$1.5bn FVA loss". *Reuters*. url: http://www.reuters.com/article/2014/01/14/banks-jpmorgan-fva-ifr-idUSL6NOKO3BZ20140114.

Wichura, Michael J. (1988). "The Percentage Points of the Normal Distribution". 37, *Journal of the Royal Statistics Society, Series C (Applied Statistics)*, pp. 477–484.

Wilt, Nicholas (2013). *The CUDA Handbook: A Comprehensive Guide to GPU Programming*. Addison-Wesley.

Winnett, Robert and John Arlidge (2008). "Bear Stearns latest victim of financial panic". *The Telegraph*. url: http://www.telegraph.co.uk/news/uknews/1581740/Bear-Stearns-latest-victim-of-financial-panic.html.

Woolner, Aaron (2014). "PRDC notes back in fashion". *Asia Risk*, 12 May.

Ziegel, Johanna F. (2014). "Coherence and Elicitability". *Mathematical Finance*.

# Index

*Index compiled by Indexing Specialists (UK) Ltd*